Practical Programming in Tcl & Tk

Second Edition

Brent B. Welch

To join a Prentice Hall PTR Internet mailing list,
point to http://www.prenhall.com/mail_lists/

Prentice Hall PTR
Upper Saddle River, NJ 07458
http://www.prenhall.com

```
Library of Congress Cataloging-in-Publication Data

Welch, Brent B.
  Practical programming in Tcl & Tk / by Brent B. Welch -- 2nd ed.
     p.  cm.
  ISBN 0-13-616830-2
  1. Tcl (Computer program language) 2. Tk toolkit. I. Title.
 QA76.73.T44W45 1997
 005.13'3--dc21                    97-16392
                                      CIP
```

Acquisitions editor: *Mark Taub*
Editorial assistant: *Tara Ruggiero*
Editorial/production supervision: *Eileen Clark*
Cover design director: *Jerry Votta*
Cover design: *Design Source*
Manufacturing manager: *Alexis Heydt*
Marketing Manager: *Dan Rush*

Prentice Hall books are widely used by corporations and government agencies for training, marketing, and resale. The publisher offers discounts on this book when ordered in bulk quantities.

For more information, contact:

Corporate Sales Department
Phone: 800-382-3419 Fax: 201-236-7141
E-mail: corpsales@prenhall.com

or write: Prentice Hall PTR
Corp. Sales Dept.
One Lake Street
Upper Saddle River, NJ 07458

Printed in the United States of America
10 9 8 7 6

ISBN 0-13-616830-2

PRENTICE-HALL INTERNATIONAL (UK) LIMITED, *LONDON*
PRENTICE-HALL OF AUSTRALIA PTY. LIMITED, *SYDNEY*
PRENTICE-HALL CANADA INC., *TORONTO*
PRENTICE-HALL HISPANOAMERICANA, S.A., *MEXICO*
PRENTICE-HALL OF INDIA PRIVATE LIMITED, *NEW DELHI*
PRENTICE-HALL OF JAPAN, INC., *TOKYO*
PEARSON EDUCATION ASIA PTE. LTD., *SINGAPORE*
EDITORA PRENTICE-HALL DO BRASIL, LTDA., *RIO DE JANEIRO*

to

Jody,
Christopher, and Daniel

Contents

List of Examples

List of Tables

Preface

Tcl stands for *Tool Command Language*. Tcl is really two things: a scripting language, and an interpreter for that language that is designed to be easy to embed into your application. Tcl and its associated graphical user interface toolkit, Tk, were designed and crafted by Professor John Ousterhout of the University of California, Berkeley. You can find these packages on the Internet (as explained later) and use them freely in your application, even if it is commercial. The Tcl interpreter has been ported from UNIX to DOS, Windows, OS/2, NT, and Macintosh environments. The Tk toolkit has been ported from the X window system to Windows and Macintosh.

I first heard about Tcl in 1988 while I was Ousterhout's Ph.D. student at Berkeley. We were designing a network operating system, Sprite. While the students hacked on a new kernel, John wrote a new editor and terminal emulator. He used Tcl as the command language for both tools so users could define menus and otherwise customize those programs. This was in the days of X10, and he had plans for an X toolkit based on Tcl that would help programs cooperate with each other by communicating with Tcl commands. To me, this cooperation among tools was the essence of Tcl.

This early vision imagined that applications would be large bodies of compiled code and a small amount of Tcl used for configuration and high-level commands. John's editor, *mx*, and the terminal emulator, *tx*, followed this model. While this model remains valid, it has also turned out to be possible to write entire applications in Tcl. This is because the Tcl/Tk shell, *wish*, provides access to other programs, the file system, network sockets, plus the ability to create a graphical user interface. For better or worse, it is now common to find applications that contain thousands of lines of Tcl script.

This book was written because, while I found it enjoyable and productive to use Tcl and Tk, there were times when I was frustrated. In addition, working at Xerox PARC, with many experts in languages and systems, I was compelled to understand both the strengths and weaknesses of Tcl and Tk. While many of my colleagues adopted Tcl and Tk for their projects, they were also just as quick to point out its flaws. In response, I have built up a set of programming techniques that exploit the power of Tcl and Tk while avoiding troublesome areas. This book is meant as a practical guide to help you get the most out of Tcl and Tk and avoid some of the frustrations I experienced.

Why Tcl?

As a scripting language, Tcl is similar to other UNIX shell languages such as the Bourne Shell (sh), the C Shell (csh), the Korn Shell (ksh), and Perl. Shell programs let you execute other programs. They provide enough programmability (variables, control flow, and procedures) to let you build complex scripts that assemble existing programs into a new tool tailored for your needs. Shells are wonderful for automating routine chores.

It is the ability to easily add a Tcl interpreter to your application that sets it apart from other shells. Tcl fills the role of an extension language that is used to configure and customize applications. There is no need to invent a command language for your new application, or struggle to provide some sort of user-programmability for your tool. Instead, by adding a Tcl interpreter, you structure your application as a set of primitive operations that can be composed by a script to best suit the needs of your users. It also allows other programs to have programmatic control over your application, leading to suites of applications that work well together.

The Tcl C library has clean interfaces and is simple to use. The library implements the basic interpreter and a set of core scripting commands that implement variables, flow control, and procedures (see page 20). There is also a set of commands that access operating system services to run other programs, access the file system, and use network sockets. Tk adds commands to create graphical user interfaces. Tcl and Tk provide a "virtual machine" that is portable across UNIX, Windows, and Macintosh environments.

The Tcl virtual machine is extensible because your application can define new Tcl commands. These commands are associated with a C or C++ procedure that your application provides. The result is applications that are split into a set of primitives written in a compiled language and exported as Tcl commands. A Tcl script is used to compose the primitives into the overall application. The script layer has access to shell-like capability to run other programs and access the file system, as well as call directly into the compiled part of the application through the application-specific Tcl commands you define. In addition, from the C programming level, you can call Tcl scripts, set and query Tcl variables, and even trace the execution of the Tcl interpreter.

There are many Tcl extensions freely available on the Internet. Most extensions include a C library that provides some new functionality, and a Tcl interface to the library. Examples include database access, telephone control, MIDI controller access, and *expect*, which adds Tcl commands to control interactive programs.

The most notable extension is Tk, a toolkit for graphical user interfaces. Tk defines Tcl commands that let you create and manipulate user interface widgets. The script-based approach to user interface programming has three benefits:

- Development is fast because of the rapid turnaround; there is no waiting for long compilations.
- The Tcl commands provide a higher-level interface than most standard C library toolkits. Simple user interfaces require just a handful of commands to define them. At the same time, it is possible to refine the user interface in order to get every detail just so. The fast turnaround aids the refinement process.
- The user interface is clearly factored out from the rest of your application. The developer can concentrate on the implementation of the application core and then fairly painlessly work up a user interface. The core set of Tk widgets is often sufficient for all your user interface needs. However, it is also possible to write custom Tk widgets in C, and again there are many contributed Tk widgets available on the network.

There are other choices for extension languages that include Visual Basic, Scheme, Elisp, Perl, Python, and Javascript. Your choice between them is partly a matter of taste. Tcl has simple constructs and looks somewhat like C. It is easy to add new Tcl primitives by writing C procedures. In addition, the Tcl community has contributed many Tcl commands that you can access as-is. To me, the strength of the Tcl community is more important than the details of the language.

Java has exploded onto the computer scene since this book was first published. Java is a great systems programming language that in the long run could displace C and C++. This is fine for Tcl, which is designed to glue together building blocks written in any system programming language. Tcl was designed to work with C, but has been adapted to work with the Java Virtual Machine. Where I say "C or C++", you can now say "C, C++, or Java", but the details are a bit different with Java. This book does not describe the Tcl/Java interface, but you can find the `TclInterp` and `TkApplication` Java classes on the CD-ROM.

Javascript is a language from Netscape that is designed to script interactions with Web pages. Javascript is important because Netscape is widely deployed. However, Tcl provides a more general purpose scripting solution that can be used in a wide variety of applications.

Tcl and Tk Versions

Tcl and Tk continue to evolve. See `http://www.beedub.com/book` for updates and news about the latest Tcl releases. Tcl and Tk have separate version numbers for historical reasons, but they are released in pairs that work together. The original edition of this book was based on Tcl 7.4 and Tk 4.0, and there were a few references to features in Tk 3.6. This second edition has been updated to reflect new features added in later versions:

- Tcl 7.5 and Tk 4.1 had their final release in May 1996. These releases feature the port of Tk to the Windows and Macintosh environments. The Safe-Tcl security mechanism was introduced to support safe execution of network applets. There is also network socket support and a new Input/Output (I/O) subsystem to support high-performance event-driven I/O.
- Tcl 7.6 and Tk 4.2 had their final release in October 1996. These releases include improvements in Safe-Tcl, and improvements to the `grid` geometry manager introduced in Tk 4.1. Cross-platform support includes virtual events (e.g., `<<Copy>>` as opposed to `<Control-c>`), standard dialogs, and more file manipulation commands.
- Tcl 7.7 and Tk 4.3 were internal releases used for the development of the Tcl/Tk plug-in for the Netscape Navigator and Microsoft Internet Explorer Web browsers. Their development actually proceeded in parallel to Tcl 7.6 and Tk 4.2. The plug-in has been released for a wide variety of platforms, including Solaris/SPARC, Solaris/INTEL, SunOS, Linux, Digital UNIX, IRIX, HP/UX, Windows 95, Windows NT, and the Macintosh. The browser plug-in supports Tcl applets in Web pages and uses the sophisticated security mechanism of Safe-Tcl to provide safety.
- Tcl 8.0 features an on-the-fly compiler for Tcl that provides many times faster Tcl scripts. The compiler is transparent to Tcl scripts, but extension writers need to learn some new C APIs to take advantage of its potential.
- Tk changed its version to match Tcl at 8.0. Tk 8.0 includes a new platform-independent font mechanism, native menus and menu bars, and more native widgets for better native look and feel on Windows and Macintosh. Internationalization of Tk is in progress as of this writing, but it may not appear until Tk 8.1. Tcl/Tk 8.0 had its first alpha release in December 1996.

Who Should Read This Book

This book is meant to be useful to the beginner in Tcl as well as the expert. For the beginner and expert alike I recommend careful study of Chapter 1, *Tcl Fundamentals*. The programming model of Tcl is designed to be simple, but it is different from many programming languages. The model is based on string substitutions, and it is important that you understand it properly to avoid trouble in complex cases. The remainder of the book consists of examples that demonstrate how to use Tcl and Tk productively. For your reference, each chapter has tables that summarize the Tcl commands and Tk widgets they describe.

This book assumes that you have some programming experience, although you should be able to get by even if you are a complete novice. Knowledge of UNIX shell programming will help, but it is not required. Where aspects of window systems are relevant, I provide some background information. Chapter 2 describes the details of using Tcl and Tk on UNIX, Windows, and Macintosh.

How to Read This Book

This book is best used in a hands-on manner, at the computer, trying the examples. The book tries to fill the gap between the terse Tcl and Tk manual pages, which are complete but lack context and examples, and existing Tcl programs that may or may not be documented or well written.

I recommend the on-line manual pages for the Tcl and Tk commands. They provide a detailed reference guide to each command. This book summarizes much of the information from the manual pages, but it does not provide the complete details, which can vary from release to release. HTML versions of the on-line manual pages can be found on the CD-ROM that comes with this book.

Other Tcl Books

I recommend the book by John Ousterhout, *Tcl and the Tk Toolkit* (Addison-Wesley, 1994), which provides a broad overview of all aspects of Tcl and Tk, even though it only covers Tcl 7.3 and Tk 3.6. The book provides a more detailed treatment of C programming for Tcl extensions.

Exploring Expect (O'Reilly & Associates, Inc., 1995) by Don Libes is a great book about an extremely useful Tcl extension. *Expect* lets you automate the use of interactive programs like *ftp* and *telnet* that expect to interact with a user. By combining *expect* and Tk, you can create graphical user interfaces for old applications that you cannot modify directly.

Graphical Applications with Tcl & Tk (M&T Press, 1996) by Eric Johnson is oriented toward Windows users. It is based on Tcl 7.5 and Tk 4.1 and gives a lighter treatment of the Tcl and Tk fundamentals.

Tcl/Tk Tools (O'Reilly & Associates, Inc., 1997) by Mark Harrison describes many useful Tcl extensions. These include Oracle and Sybase interfaces, object-oriented language enhancements, additional Tk widgets, and much more. The chapters were contributed by the authors of the extensions, so they provide authoritative information on some excellent additions to the Tcl toolbox.

CGI Developers Resource, Web Programming with Tcl and Perl (Prentice Hall, 1997) by John Ivler presents Tcl-based solutions to programming Web sites.

Effective Tcl/Tk Programming (Addison Wesley, 1997) by Michael Mclennan and Mark Harrison illustrate Tcl and Tk with examples and application design guidelines.

On-line Examples

The book comes with a CD-ROM that has source for all of the examples, plus a selection of Tcl freeware found on the Internet. The CD-ROM has dual formats: the ISO 9660 partition is readable on UNIX and Windows, and the HFS partition is readable on Macintosh. There you will also find the versions of Tcl and Tk that were available as the book went to press. You can also retrieve the sources shown in the book from Prentice Hall:

```
ftp://ftp.prenhall.com/pub/software/welch/
```

Ftp Archives

The primary site for the Tcl and Tk distributions is given below as a Universal Resource Location (URL):

```
ftp://ftp.sunlabs.com/pub/tcl
```

You can use FTP and log in to the host (e.g., `ftp.sunlabs.com`) under the `anonymous` user name. Give your email address as the password. The directory is in the URL after the host name (e.g., `/pub/tcl`). There are many sites that mirror this distribution. At the mirror sites you may see directories named `ftp.smli.com`, which is the old name for `ftp.sunlabs.com`. The mirror sites provide an archive site for contributed Tcl commands, Tk widgets, and applications. There is also a set of Frequently Asked Questions files. These sites maintain Tcl archives:

```
ftp://ftp.neosoft.com/pub/tcl          (primary archive site)
ftp://ftp.syd.dit.csiro.au/pub/tk
ftp://ftp.ibp.fr/pub/tcl
ftp://src.doc.ic.ac.uk/packages/tcl/
ftp://ftp.luth.se/pub/unix/tcl/
ftp://sunsite.cnlab-switch.ch/mirror/tcl
ftp://ftp.sterling.com/programming/languages/tcl
ftp://ftp.sunet.se/pub/lang/tcl
ftp://ftp.cs.columbia.edu/archives/tcl
ftp://ftp.uni-paderborn.de/pub/unix/tcl
ftp://sunsite.unc.edu/pub/languages/tcl
ftp://ftp.funet.fi/pub/languages/tcl
```

You can use a World Wide Web browser like *Mosaic*, *Netscape*, or *Lynx* to access these sites. Enter the URL as specified above and you are presented with a directory listing of that location. From there you can change directories and fetch files.

If you do not have direct FTP access, you can use an email server for FTP. Send email to `ftpmail@decwrl.dec.com` with the message `Help` to get directions. If you are on BITNET, send email to `bitftp@pucc.princeton.edu`.

You can search for FTP sites that have Tcl by using the *Archie* service that indexes the contents of anonymous FTP servers. Information about using *Archie* can be obtained by sending mail to `archie@archie.sura.net` that contains the message `Help`.

World Wide Web

Start with these World Wide Web pages about Tcl:

```
http://www.scriptics.com/
http://www.sco.com/Technology/tcl/Tcl.html
http://www.teraform.com/~lvirden/tcl-faq/
```

The home page for this book contains errata for all editions. This is the only URL I control personally, and I plan to keep it up-to-date indefinitely:

```
http://www.beedub.com/book/
```

The Prentice Hall page for this edition of this book is:

```
http://www.prenhall.com/books/ptr_0136168302.html
```

The page for the first edition of this book is:

```
http://www.prenhall.com/books/ptr_0131820079.html
```

Newsgroups

The `comp.lang.tcl` newsgroup is very active. It provides a forum for questions and answers about Tcl. Announcements about Tcl extensions and applications are posted to the `comp.lang.tcl.announce` newsgroup.

Typographic Conventions

The more important examples are set apart with a title and horizontal rules, while others appear in-line. The examples use `courier` for Tcl and C code. When interesting results are returned by a Tcl command, those are presented below in *`oblique courier`*. The => is not part of the return value in the following example.

```
expr 5 + 8
=> 13
```

The `courier` font is also used when naming Tcl commands and C procedures within sentences.

The usage of a Tcl command is presented in the following example. The command name and constant keywords appear in `courier`. Variable values appear in *`courier oblique`*. Optional arguments are surrounded with question marks.

```
set varname ?value?
```

The name of a program is in italics:

xterm

Hot Tips

The icon in the margin marks a "hot tip" as judged by the reviewers of the book. The visual markers help you locate the more useful sections in the book. These are also listed in the index under Hot Tip.

Book Organization

The chapters of the book are divided into 7 parts. The first part describes basic Tcl features. The first chapter describes the fundamental mechanisms that characterize the Tcl language. This is an important chapter that provides the basic grounding you will need to use Tcl effectively. Even if you have programmed in Tcl already, you should review Chapter 1. Chapter 2 goes over the details of using Tcl and Tk on UNIX, Windows, and Macintosh. Chapter 3 presents a sample application, a CGI script, that illustrates typical Tcl programming. The rest of Part I covers the basic Tcl commands in more detail, including string handling, data types, control flow, procedures, and scoping issues. Part I finishes with a description of the facilities for file I/O and running other programs.

Part II describes advanced Tcl programming. It starts with `eval`, which lets you generate Tcl programs on the fly. Regular expressions provide powerful string processing. If your data processing application runs slowly, you can probably boost its performance significantly with the regular expression facilities. Namespaces, which are new in Tcl 8.0, let you partition the global scope of procedures and variables. Libraries and packages provide a way to organize your code for sharing among projects. The introspection facilities of Tcl can tell you about all the internal state of Tcl. Event driven I/O helps server applications manage several clients simultaneously. Network sockets are used to implement the HTTP protocol used to fetch pages on the World Wide Web. Safe-Tcl is used to provide a secure environment to execute applets downloaded over the network.

Part III introduces Tk. It gives an overview of the toolkit facilities. A few complete examples are examined in detail to illustrate the features of Tk. Event bindings associate Tcl commands with events like keystrokes and button clicks. Part III ends with three chapters on the Tk geometry managers that provide powerful facilities for organizing your user interface.

Part IV describes the Tk widgets. These include buttons, menus, scrollbars, labels, text entries, multiline and multifont text areas, drawing canvases, listboxes, and scales. The Tk widgets are highly configurable and very programmable, but their default behaviors make them easy to use as well. The resource database that can configure widgets provides an easy way to control the overall look of your application.

Part V describes the rest of the Tk facilities. These include selections, keyboard focus, and standard dialogs. Fonts, colors, images, and other attributes that are common to the Tk widgets are described in detail. This part ends with a few larger Tk examples.

Part VI is an introduction to C programming and Tcl. The goal of this part is to get you started in the right direction when you need to integrate Tcl into a custom application.

Part VII has a chapter on each of the Tcl/Tk releases covered by the book. They provide details about what features were changed and added. These chapters provide a quick reference if you need to update a program or start to use a new version.

First Edition Thanks

I would like to thank my managers and colleagues at Xerox PARC for their patience with me as I worked on this book. The tips and tricks in this book came partly from my own work as I helped lab members use Tcl, and partly from them as they taught me. Dave Nichols' probing questions forced me to understand the basic mechanisms of the Tcl interpreter. Dan Swinehart and Lawrence Butcher kept me sharp with their own critiques. Ron Frederick and Berry Kerchival adopted Tk for their graphical interfaces and amazed me with their rapid results. Becky Burwell, Rich Gold, Carl Hauser, John Maxwell, Ken Pier, Marvin Theimer, and Mohan Vishwanath made use of my early drafts, and their questions pointed out large holes in the text. Karin Petersen, Bill Schilit, and Terri Watson kept life interesting by using Tcl in very non-standard ways. I especially thank my managers, Mark Weiser and Doug Terry, for their understanding and support.

I thank John Ousterhout for Tcl and Tk, which are wonderful systems built with excellent craftsmanship. John was kind enough to provide me with an advance version of Tk 4.0 so I could learn about its new features well before its first beta release.

Thanks to the Tcl programmers out on the Net, from whom I learned many tricks. John LoVerso and Stephen Uhler are the hottest Tcl programmers I know.

Many thanks to the patient reviewers of early drafts: Pierre David, Clif Flynt, Simon Kenyon, Eugene Lee, Don Libes, Lee Moore, Joe Moss, Hador Shemtov, Frank Stajano, Charles Thayer, and Jim Thornton.

Many folks contributed suggestions by email: Miguel Angel, Stephen Bensen, Jeff Blaine, Tom Charnock, Brian Cooper, Patrick D'Cruze, Benoit Desrosiers, Ted Dunning, Mark Eichin, Paul Friberg, Carl Gauthier, David Gerdes, Klaus Hackenberg, Torkle Hasle, Marti Hearst, Jean-Pierre Herbert, Jamie Honan, Norman Klein, Joe Konstan, Susan Larson, Håkan Liljegren, Lionel Mallet, Dejan Milojicic, Greg Minshall, Bernd Mohr, Will Morse, Heiko Nardmann, Gerd Neugebauer, TV Raman, Cary Renzema, Rob Riepel, Dan Schenk, Jean-Guy Schneider, Elizabeth Scholl, Karl Schwamb, Rony Shapiro, Peter Simanyi, Vince Skahan, Bill Stumbo, Glen Vanderburg, Larry Virden, Reed Wade, and Jim Wight. Unfortunately I could not respond to every suggestion, even some that were excellent. I am always open to comments about this book. My email address is `welch@acm.org`.

Thanks to the editors and staff at Prentice Hall. Mark Taub has been very helpful as I progressed through my first book. Lynn Schneider and Kerry Reardon were excellent copy and production editors, respectively.

Second Edition Thanks

I get to thank John Ousterhout again, this time for supporting me as I worked in the Tcl/Tk group at Sun Microsystems. The rest of the group deserve a lot of credit for turning Tcl and Tk into a dynamite cross-platform solution. Scott Stanton led the Tk port to the PC. Ray Johnson led the Tk port to the Macintosh.

Jacob Levy implemented the event-driven I/O system, Safe-Tcl, and the browser plug-in. Brian Lewis built the Tcl compiler. Ken Corey worked on Java integration and helped with the SpecTcl user interface builder. Syd Polk generalized the menu system to work with native widgets on the Macintosh and Windows. Colin Stevens generalized the font mechanism and worked on internationalization for Tk.

Stephen Uhler deserves special thanks for inspiring many of the cool examples I use in this book. He was the lead on the SpecTcl user interface builder. He built the core HTML display library on which I based an editor. We worked closely together on an HTTP server. He taught me how to write compact, efficient Tcl code and to use regular expression substitutions in amazing ways. I hope he has learned at least a little from me.

Thanks again to Mark Taub, Eileen Clark, and Martha Williams at Prentice Hall. George Williams helped me assemble the files for the CD-ROM.

Finally, I thank my wonderful wife Jody for her love, kindness, patience, wit, and understanding as I worked long hours. Happily, many of those hours were spent working from home. I now have two sons, Christopher and Daniel, who get the credit for keeping me from degenerating into a complete nerd.

PART I

Tcl Basics

Part I introduces the basics of Tcl. Everyone should read Chapter 1 that describes the fundamental properties of the language. Tcl is really quite simple, so beginners can pick it up quickly. The experienced programmer should review Chapter 1 to eliminate any misconceptions that come from using other languages.

Tcl can be used in a variety of places, everywhere from the firmware of a robot to the control system for an oil drilling platform. Chapter 2 is a short introduction to running Tcl and Tk on UNIX, Windows, and Macintosh systems. You may want to see that chapter first so you can try out the examples as you read Chapter 1.

Chapter 3 presents a sample application, a CGI script, that implements a guestbook for a Web site. The example uses several facilities that are described in detail in later chapters. The goal is to provide a working example that illustrates the power of Tcl.

The rest of Part I covers basic programming with Tcl. Simple string processing is covered in Chapter 4. Tcl lists, which share the syntax rules of Tcl commands, are explained in Chapter 5. Control structure like loops and if statements are described in Chapter 6. Chapter 7 describes Tcl procedures, which are new commands that you write in Tcl. Chapter 8 is about Tcl arrays. Arrays are the most flexible and useful data structure in Tcl. Chapter 9 describes file I/O and running other programs. These facilities let you build Tcl scripts that glue together other programs and process data in files.

After reading Part I you will know enough Tcl to read and understand other Tcl programs, and to write simple programs yourself.

CHAPTER 1

Tcl Fundamentals

This chapter describes the basic syntax rules for the Tcl scripting language. It describes the basic mechanisms used by the Tcl interpreter: substitution and grouping. It touches lightly on the following Tcl commands: `puts`, `format`, `set`, `expr`, `string`, `while`, `incr`, and `proc`.

Tcl is a string-based command language. The language has only a few fundamental constructs and relatively little syntax, which makes it easy to learn. The Tcl syntax is meant to be simple. Tcl is designed to be a glue that assembles software building blocks into applications. A simpler glue makes the job easier. In addition, Tcl is interpreted when the application runs. The interpreter makes it easy to build and refine your application in an interactive manner. A great way to learn Tcl is to try out commands interactively. If you are not sure how to run Tcl on your system, see Chapter 2 for instructions for starting Tcl on UNIX, Windows, and Macintosh systems.

This chapter takes you through the basics of the Tcl language syntax. Even if you are an expert programmer, it is worth taking the time to read these few pages to make sure you understand the fundamentals of Tcl. The basic mechanisms are all related to strings and string substitutions, so it is fairly easy to visualize what is going on in the interpreter. The model is a little different than some other programming languages you may already be familiar with, so it is worth making sure you understand the basic concepts.

Tcl Commands

The basic syntax for a Tcl command is:

```
command arg1 arg2 arg3 ...
```

The *command* is either the name of a built-in command or a Tcl procedure.

White space (i.e., space or tab) is used to separate the command name and its arguments, and a newline or semicolon is used to terminate a command. The arguments to a command are just strings.

Tcl has syntax for *grouping*, which allows multiple words in one argument, and *substitution*, which is used with programming variables and nested command calls. The Tcl interpreter does grouping first, then substitutions, and finally it calls the command. It is up to the command to interpret its arguments. This model is described in detail in this Chapter.

Hello, World!

Example 1–1 The "Hello, World!" example.

```
puts stdout {Hello, World!}
=> Hello, World!
```

In this example, the command is `puts`, which takes two arguments: an I/O stream identifier and a string. `puts` writes the string to the I/O stream along with a trailing newline character. There are two points to emphasize:

- Arguments are interpreted by the command. In the example, `stdout` is used to identify the standard output stream. The use of `stdout` as a name is a convention employed by `puts` and the other I/O commands. Also, `stderr` is used to identify the standard error output, and `stdin` is used to identify the standard input. Chapter 9 describes how to open other files for I/O.
- Curly braces are used to group words together into a single argument. The `puts` command receives `Hello, World!` as its second argument.

The braces are not part of the value.

The braces are syntax for the interpreter, and they get stripped off before the value is passed to the command. Braces group all characters, including newlines and nested braces, until a matching brace is found. Tcl also uses double quotes for grouping. Grouping arguments will be described in more detail later.

Variables

The `set` command is used to assign a value to a variable. It takes two arguments: the first is the name of the variable and the second is the value. Variable names can be any length, and case *is* significant. In fact, you can use any character in a variable name.

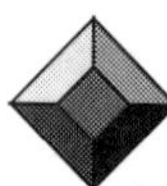

It is not necessary to declare Tcl variables before you use them.

The interpreter will create the variable when it is first assigned a value. The value of a variable is obtained later with the dollar-sign syntax illustrated in Example 1–2:

Example 1–2 Tcl variables.

```
set var 5
=> 5
set b $var
=> 5
```

The second `set` command assigns to variable `b` the value of variable `var`. The use of the dollar sign is our first example of substitution. You can imagine that the second `set` command gets rewritten by substituting the value of `var` for `$var` to obtain a new command.

```
set b 5
```

The actual implementation is a little different, but not much.

Command Substitution

The second form of substitution is *command substitution*. A nested command is delimited by square brackets, `[ ]`. The Tcl interpreter takes everything between the brackets and evaluates it as a command. It rewrites the outer command by replacing the square brackets and everything between them with the result of the nested command. This is similar to the use of backquotes in other shells, except that it has the additional advantage of supporting arbitrary nesting of commands.

Example 1–3 Command substitution.

```
set len [string length foobar]
=> 6
```

In the example, the nested command is:

```
string length foobar
```

This command returns the length of the string `foobar`. The `string` command is described in detail starting on page 43. The nested command runs first. Then command substitution causes the outer command to be rewritten as if it were:

```
set len 6
```

If there are several cases of command substitution within a single command, the interpreter processes them from left to right. As each right bracket is encountered, the command it delimits is evaluated. This results in a sensible ordering in which nested commands are evaluated first so their result can be used in arguments to the outer command.

Math Expressions

The Tcl interpreter itself does not evaluate math expressions. Instead, the expr command is used to evaluate math expressions. The interpreter treats expr just like any other command, and it leaves the expression parsing up to the expr implementation. The math syntax supported by expr is the same as the C expression syntax. The expr command deals with integer, floating point, and boolean values. Logical operations return either 0 (false) or 1 (true). Integer values are promoted to floating point values as needed. Octal values are indicated by a leading zero (e.g., 033 is 27 decimal). Hexadecimal values are indicated by a leading 0x. Scientific notation for floating point numbers is supported. A summary of the operator precedence is given on page 18.

The implementation of expr takes all its arguments, concatenates them into a single string, and then parses the string as a math expression. After expr computes the answer, the answer is formatted into a string and returned:

Example 1–4 Simple arithmetic.

```
expr 7.2 / 4
=> 1.8
```

You can include variable references and nested commands in math expressions. The following example uses expr to add 7 to the length of the string foobar. As a result of the innermost command substitution, the expr command sees 6 + 7, and len gets the value 13:

Example 1–5 Nested commands.

```
set len [expr [string length foobar] + 7]
=> 13
```

The expression evaluator supports a number of built-in math functions. For a complete listing, see page 19. The following example computes the value of *pi*:

Example 1–6 Built-in math functions.

```
set pi [expr 2*asin(1.0)]
=> 3.1415926535897931
```

Backslash Substitution

The final type of substitution done by the Tcl interpreter is *backslash substitution*. This is used to quote characters that have special meaning to the interpreter. For example, you can specify a literal dollar sign, brace, or bracket by quoting it with a backslash. As a rule, however, if you find yourself using lots of backslashes, there is probably a simpler way to achieve the effect you are striving for. In particular, the `list` command described on page 55 will do quoting for you automatically. In Example 1–7 backslash is used to get a literal `$`:

Example 1–7 Quoting special characters with backslash.

```
set dollar \$foo
=> $foo
set x $dollar
=> $foo
```

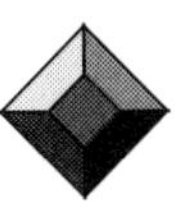

Only a single round of interpretation is done.

The second `set` command in the example illustrates an important property of Tcl. The value of `dollar` does not affect the substitution done in the assignment to `x`. In other words, the Tcl parser does not care about the value of a variable when it does the substitution. After the example, the value of `x` and `dollar` is the string `$foo`. In general, you do not have to worry about the value of variables until you use `eval`, which is described in Chapter 10.

You can also use backslash sequences to specify characters with their hexadecimal or octal value:

```
set escape \0x1b
set escape \033
```

The value of variable `escape` is the ASCII ESC character, which has character code `27`. The table on page 18 summarizes backslash substitutions.

A common use of backslashes is to continue long commands on multiple lines. This is necessary because a newline terminates a command unless an argument is being grouped as described in the next section. A backslash as the last character in a line is converted into a space. In addition, all the white space at the beginning of the next line is replaced by this substitution. The backslash in the next example is required; otherwise the `expr` command gets terminated by the newline after the plus sign.

Example 1–8 Continuing long lines with backslashes.

```
set totalLength [expr [string length $one] + \
      [string length $two]]
```

Grouping with Braces and Double Quotes

Double quotes and curly braces are used to group words together into one argument. The difference between double quotes and curly braces is that quotes allow substitutions to occur in the group, while curly braces prevent substitutions. This rule applies to command, variable, and backslash substitutions.

Example 1–9 Grouping with double quotes vs. braces.

```
set s Hello
=> Hello
puts stdout "The length of $s is [string length $s]."
=> The length of Hello is 5.
puts stdout {The length of $s is [string length $s].}
=> The length of $s is [string length $s].
```

In the second command of Example 1–9, the Tcl interpreter does variable and command substitution on the second argument to `puts`. In the third command, substitutions are prevented so the string is printed as-is.

In practice, grouping with curly braces is used when substitutions on the argument must be delayed until a later time (or never done at all). Examples include loops, conditional statements, and procedure declarations. Double quotes are useful in simple cases like the `puts` command previously shown.

Another common use of quotes is with the `format` command. This is similar to the C `printf` function. The first argument to `format` is a format specifier that often includes special characters like newlines, tabs, and spaces. The easiest way to specify these characters is with backslash sequences (e.g., `\n` for newline and `\t` for tab). The backslashes must be substituted before the `format` command is called, so you need to use quotes to group the format specifier.

```
puts [format "Item: %s\t%5.3f" $name $value]
```

Here `format` is used to align a name and a value with a tab. The `%s` and `%5.3f` indicate how the remaining arguments to `format` are to be formatted. Note that the trailing `\n` usually found in a C `printf` call is not needed because `puts` provides one for us. For more information about the `format` command, see page 46.

Square Brackets Do Not Group

The square bracket syntax used for command substitution does not provide grouping. Instead, a nested command is considered part of the current group. In the command below the double quotes group the last argument, and the nested command is just part of that group.

```
puts stdout "The length of $s is [string length $s]."
```

In the next example the last argument is a nested command. There is no need to explicitly group the nested command because the Tcl parser treats the whole nested command as part of the group.

```
puts stdout [string length $s]
```

In general, you can place a bracketed command or variable reference anywhere. The following computes a command name:

```
[findCommand $x] arg arg
```

Grouping before Substitution

The Tcl parser makes a single pass through a command as it makes grouping decisions and performs string substitutions. Grouping decisions are made before substitutions are performed, which is an important property of Tcl. This means that the values being substituted do not affect grouping because the grouping decisions have already been made.

The following example demonstrates how nested command substitution affects grouping. A nested command is treated as an unbroken sequence of characters, regardless of its internal structure. It is included with the surrounding group of characters when collecting arguments for the main command.

Example 1–10 Embedded command and variable substitution.

```
set x 7; set y 9
puts stdout $x+$y=[expr $x + $y]
=> 7+9=16
```

In the example the second argument to `puts` is:

```
$x+$y=[expr $x + $y]
```

The white space inside the nested command is ignored for the purposes of grouping the argument. By the time Tcl encounters the left bracket, it has already done some variable substitutions to obtain:

```
7+9=
```

When the left bracket is encountered, the interpreter calls itself recursively to evaluate the nested command. Again, the `$x` and `$y` are substituted before calling `expr`. Finally, the result of `expr` is substituted for everything from the left bracket to the right bracket. The `puts` command gets the following as its second argument:

```
7+9=16
```

Grouping before substitution.

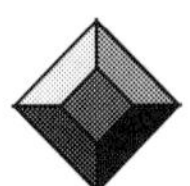

The point of this example is that the grouping decision about `puts`'s second argument is made before the command substitution is done. Even if the result of the nested command contained spaces or other special characters, they would be ignored for the purposes of grouping the arguments to the outer command. Grouping and variable substitution interact the same as grouping and command substitution. Spaces or special characters in variable values do not affect grouping decisions because these decisions are made before the variable values are substituted.

If you want the output to look nicer in the example, with spaces around the `+` and `=`, then you can use double quotes to explicitly group the argument to `puts`:

```
puts stdout "$x + $y = [expr $x + $y]"
```

The double quotes are used for grouping in this case to allow the variable and command substitution on the argument to `puts`. Note that it is never necessary to explicitly group a nested command with double quotes if it makes up the whole argument. The following is a redundant use of double quotes:

```
puts stdout "[expr $x + $y]"
```

Procedures

Tcl uses the `proc` command to define procedures. Once defined, a Tcl procedure is used just like any of the built-in Tcl commands. The basic syntax to define a procedure is:

```
proc name arglist body
```

The first argument is the name of the procedure being defined. The second argument is a list of parameters to the procedure. The third argument is a *command body* that is one or more Tcl commands.

The procedure name is case sensitive, and in fact it can contain any characters. Procedure names and variable names do not conflict with each other. As a convention, this book begins procedure names with uppercase letters and it begins variable names with lowercase letters. Good programming style is important as your Tcl scripts get larger. Tcl coding style is discussed in Chapter 12.

Example 1–11 Defining a procedure.

```
proc Diag {a b} {
    set c [expr sqrt($a * $a + $b * $b)]
    return $c
}
puts "The diagonal of a 3, 4 right triangle is [Diag 3 4]"
=> The diagonal of a 3, 4 right triangle is 5.0
```

The `Diag` procedure defined in the example computes the length of the diagonal side of a right triangle given the lengths of the other two sides. The `sqrt` function is one of many math functions supported by the `expr` command. The variable `c` is local to the procedure; it is only defined during execution of `Diag`. Variable scope is discussed further in Chapter 7. It is not really necessary to use the variable `c` in this example. The procedure could also be written as:

```
proc Diag {a b} {
    return [expr sqrt($a * $a + $b * $b)]
}
```

The `return` command is used to return the result of the prodecure. The return `command` is optional in this example because the Tcl interpreter returns the value of the last command in the body as the value of the procedure. So, the procedure could be reduced to:

```
proc Diag {a b} {
    expr sqrt($a * $a + $b * $b)
}
```

Note the stylized use of curly braces in the example. The curly brace at the end of the first line starts the third argument to `proc`, which is the command body. In this case, the Tcl interpreter sees the opening left brace, causing it to ignore newline characters and scan the text until a matching right brace is found. *Double quotes have the same property*. They group characters, including newlines, until another double quote is found. The result of the grouping is that the third argument to `proc` is a sequence of commands. When they are evaluated later, the embedded newlines will terminate each command. The other crucial effect of the curly braces around the procedure body is to delay any substitutions in the body until the time the procedure is called. For example, the variables `a`, `b`, and `c` are not defined until the procedure is called, so we do not want to do variable substitution at the time `Diag` is defined.

The `proc` command supports additional features such as having variable numbers of arguments and default values for arguments. These are described in detail in Chapter 7.

A Factorial Example

To reinforce what we have learned so far, here is a longer example that uses a `while` loop to compute the factorial function:

Example 1–12 A `while` loop to compute factorial.

```
proc Factorial {x} {
    set i 1; set product 1
    while {$i <= $x} {
        set product [expr $product * $i]
        incr i
    }
    return $product
}
Factorial 10
=> 3628800
```

The semicolon is used on the first line to remind you that it is a command terminator just like the newline character.

The `while` loop is used to multiply all the numbers from one up to the value of `x`. The first argument to `while` is a boolean expression, and its second argument is a command body to execute. The `while` command evaluates the boolean expression, and then executes the body if the expression is true (non-zero). The `while` command continues to test the expression and evaluate the command body until the expression is false (zero). Other control structures are described in Chapter 6.

The same math expression evaluator used by the `expr` command is used by `while` to evaluate the boolean expression. There is no need to explicitly use the `expr` command in the first argument to `while`, even if you have a much more complex expression.

The loop body and the procedure body are grouped with curly braces in the same way. The opening curly brace has to be on the same line as `proc` and `while`. If you like to put opening curly braces on the line after a `while` or `if` statement, you have to escape the newline with a backslash:

```
while {$i < $x} \
{
    set product ...
}
```

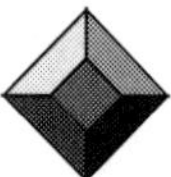

Always group expressions and command bodies with curly braces.

Curly braces around the boolean expression are crucial because they delay variable substitution until the `while` command implementation tests the expression. The following example is an infinite loop:

```
set i 1; while $i<=10 {incr i}
```

The loop will run indefinitely. The reason is that the Tcl interpreter will substitute for `$i` *before* `while` is called, so `while` gets a constant expression `1<=10` that will always be true. You can avoid these kinds of errors by adopting a consistent coding style that groups expressions with curly braces:

```
set i 1; while {$i<=10} {incr i}
```

The `incr` command is used to increment the value of the loop variable `i`. This is a handy command that saves us from the longer command:

```
set i [expr $i + 1]
```

The `incr` command can take an additional argument, a positive or negative integer by which to change the value of the variable. Using this form it is possible to eliminate the loop variable `i` and just modify the parameter `x`. The loop body can be written like this:

```
while {$x > 1} {
    set product [expr $product * $x]
    incr x -1
}
```

More about Variables

The `set` command will return the value of a variable if it is only passed a single argument. It treats that argument as a variable name and returns the current value of the variable. The dollar-sign syntax used to get the value of a variable is really just an easy way to use the `set` command.

Example 1–13 Using `set` to return a variable value.

```
set var {the value of var}
=> the value of var
set name var
=> var
set name
=> var
```

```
set $name
=> the value of var
```

This is a somewhat tricky example. In the last command, `$name` gets substituted with `var`. Then the `set` command returns the value of `var`, which is `the value of var`. Nested `set` commands provide another way to achieve a level of indirection. The last `set` command above can be written as follows:

```
set [set name]
=> the value of var
```

Using a variable to store the name of another variable may seem overly complex. However, there are some times when it is very useful. There is even a special command, `upvar`, that makes this sort of trick easier. The `upvar` command is described in detail on page 79 in Chapter 7.

Funny Variable Names

The Tcl interpreter makes some assumptions about variable names that make it easy to embed variable references into other strings. By default, it assumes that variable names only contain letters, digits, and the underscore. The construct `$foo.o` represents a concatenation of the value of `foo` and the literal ".o".

If the variable reference is not delimited by punctuation or white space, then you can use curly braces to explicitly delimit the variable name (e.g., `${x}`). You can also use this to reference variables with funny characters in their name, although you probably do not want variables named like that. If you find yourself using funny variable names, or computing the names of variables, then you may want to use the `upvar` command.

Example 1–14 Embedded variable references.

```
set foo filename
set object $foo.o
=> filename.o
set a AAA
set b abc${a}def
=> abcAAAdef
set .o yuk!
set x ${.o}y
=> yuk!y
```

The `unset` Command

You can delete a variable with the `unset` command:

```
unset varName varName2 ...
```

Any number of variable names can be passed to the `unset` command. However, `unset` will raise an error if a variable is not already defined.

Using info to Find Out about Variables

The existence of a variable can be tested with the info exists command. For example, because incr requires that a variable exist, you might have to test for the existence of the variable first.

Example 1–15 Using info to determine if a variable exists.

```
if {![info exists foobar]} {
   set foobar 0
} else {
   incr foobar
}
```

In Chapter 7, page 80, there is an example that implements a new version of incr, which handles this case.

More about Math Expressions

This section describes a few fine points about math in Tcl scripts. In Tcl 7.6 and earlier versions math is not that efficient because of conversions between strings and numbers. The expr command must convert its arguments from strings to numbers. It then does all its computations with double precision floating point values. The result is formatted into a string that has, by default, six significant digits. This can be changed by setting the tcl_precision variable to the number of significant digits desired. Seventeen digits of precision are enough to ensure that no information is lost when converting back and forth between a string and an IEEE double precision number:

Example 1–16 Controlling precision with tcl_precision.

```
expr 1 / 3
=> 0
expr 1 / 3.0
=> 0.333333
set tcl_precision 17
=> 17
expr 1 / 3.0
# The trailing 1 is the IEEE rounding digit
=> 0.33333333333333331
```

In Tcl 8.0 and later versions the overhead of conversions is eliminated in most cases by the built-in compiler. The use of tcl_precision is also eliminated so values are always printed with full precision. Even so, Tcl was not designed to support math intensive applications. You may want to implement math-intensive code in a compiled language and register the function as a Tcl command as described in Chapter 41.

There is support for string comparisons by `expr`, so you can test string values in `if` statements. You must use quotes so that `expr` knows to do string comparisons:

```
if {$answer == "yes"} { ... }
```

However, the `string compare` command described in Chapter 4 is more reliable because `expr` may do conversions on strings that look like numbers. This area has improved in Tcl 8.0. The issues with string operations and `expr` are discussed on page 45.

Expressions can include variable and command substitutions and still be grouped with curly braces. This is because an argument to `expr` is subject to two rounds of substitution: one by the Tcl interpreter, and a second by `expr` itself. Ordinarily this is not a problem because math values do not contain the characters that are special to the Tcl interpreter. The second round of substitutions is needed to support commands like `while` and `if` that use the expression evaluator internally. You may see uses of `expr` that group the expression into one argument, which was necessary in early versions of Tcl:

```
set y [expr {$x + $y}]
```

Comments

Tcl uses the pound character, `#`, for comments. Unlike many languages, the `#` must occur at the beginning of a command. A `#` that occurs elsewhere is not treated specially. An easy trick to append a comment to the end of a command is to precede the `#` with a semicolon to terminate the previous command:

```
# Here are some parameters
set rate 7.0        ;# The interest rate
set months 60       ;# The loan term
```

One subtle effect to watch out for is that a backslash effectively continues a comment line onto the next line of the script. In addition, a semicolon inside a comment is not significant. Only a newline terminates comments:

```
# Here is the start of a Tcl comment \
and some more of it; still in the comment
```

The behavior of a backslash in comments is pretty obscure, but it can be exploited as shown in Example 2–3 on page 25.

Substitution and Grouping Summary

The following rules summarize the fundamental mechanisms of grouping and substitution that are performed by the Tcl interpreter before it invokes a command:

- Command arguments are separated by white space, unless arguments are grouped with curly braces or double quotes as described below.
- Grouping with curly braces, `{ }`, prevents substitutions. Braces nest. The interpreter includes all characters between the matching left and right brace in the group, including newlines, semicolons, and nested braces. The enclosing (i.e., outermost) braces are not included in the group's value.
- Grouping with double quotes, `" "`, allows substitutions. The interpreter groups everything until another double quote is found, including newlines and semicolons. The enclosing quotes are not included in the group of characters. A double-quote character can be included in the group by quoting it with a backslash, (e.g. `\"`).
- Grouping decisions are made before substitutions are performed. This means that the values of variables or command results do not affect grouping.
- A dollar sign, `$`, causes variable substitution. Variable names can be any length, and case is significant. If variable references are embedded into other strings, or if they include characters other than letters, digits, and the underscore, they can be distinguished with the `${`*`varname`*`}` syntax.
- Square brackets, `[ ]`, cause command substitution. Everything between the brackets is treated as a command, and everything including the brackets is replaced with the result of the command. Nesting is allowed.
- The backslash character, `\`, is used to quote special characters. You can think of this as another form of substitution in which the backslash and the next character or group of characters are replaced with a new character.
- Substitutions can occur anywhere unless prevented by curly brace grouping. Part of a group can be a constant string, and other parts of it can be the result of substitutions. Even the command name can be affected by substitutions.
- A single round of substitutions is performed before command invocation. The result of a substitution is not interpreted a second time. This rule is important if you have a variable value or a command result that contains special characters such as spaces, dollar signs, square brackets, or braces. Because only a single round of substitution is done, you do not have to worry about special characters in values causing extra substitutions.

Fine Points

- A common error is to forget a space between arguments when grouping with braces or quotes. This is because white space is used as the separator, while the braces or quotes only provide grouping. If you forget the space, you will get syntax errors about unexpected characters after the closing brace or quote. The following is an error because of the missing space between `}` and `{`:

```
if {$x > 1}{puts "x = $x"}
```

- A double quote is only used for grouping when it comes after white space. This means you can include a double quote in the middle of a group without quoting it with a backslash. This requires that curly braces or white space delimit the group. I do not recommend using this obscure feature, but this is what it looks like:

```
set silly a"b
```

- When double quotes are used for grouping, the special effect of curly braces is turned off. Substitutions occur everywhere inside a group formed with double quotes. In the next command, the variables are still substituted:

```
set x xvalue
set y "foo {$x} bar"
=> foo {xvalue} bar
```

- Spaces are *not* required around the square brackets used for command substitution. For the purposes of grouping, the interpreter considers everything between the square brackets as part of the current group. The following sets `x` to the concatenation of two command results because there is no space between `]` and `[`.

```
set x [cmd1][cmd2]
```

- Newlines and semicolons are ignored when grouping with braces or double quotes. They get included in the group of characters just like all the others. The following sets `x` to a string that contains newlines:

```
set x "This is line one.
This is line two.
This is line three."
```

- During command substitution, newlines and semicolons *are* significant as command terminators. If you have a long command that is nested in square brackets, put a backslash before the newline if you want to continue the command on another line. This was illustrated in Example 1–8 on page 7.
- A dollar sign followed by white space is treated as a literal dollar sign. The following sets `x` to the single character `$`.

```
set x $
```

Reference

Backslash Sequences

Table 1–1 Backslash sequences.

\a	Bell. (0x7)
\b	Backspace. (0x8)
\f	Form feed. (0xc)
\n	Newline. (0xa)
\r	Carriage return. (0xd)
\t	Tab (0x9)
\v	Vertical tab. (0xb)
\<newline>	Replace the newline and the leading white space on the next line with a space.
\\	Backslash. ('\')
ooo	Octal specification of character code. 1, 2, or 3 digits.
\x*hh*	Hexadecimal specification of character code. 1 or 2 digits.
c	Replaced with literal *c* if *c* is not one of the cases listed above. In particular, \$, \", \{, \}, \], and \[are used to obtain these characters.

Arithmetic Operators

Table 1–2 Arithmetic operators from highest to lowest precedence.

- ~ !	Unary minus, bitwise NOT, logical NOT.
* / %	Multiply, divide, remainder.
+ -	Add, subtract.
<< >>	Left shift, right shift.
< > <= >=	Comparison: less, greater, less or equal, greater or equal.
== !=	Equal, not equal.
&	Bitwise AND.
^	Bitwise XOR.
|	Bitwise OR.
&&	Logical AND.

Table 1–2 Arithmetic operators from highest to lowest precedence. (Continued)

`||`	Logical OR.
x?*y*:*z*	If *x* then *y* else *z*.

Built-in Math Functions

Table 1–3 Built-in math functions.

`acos(x)`	Arc-cosine of *x*.
`asin(x)`	Arc-sine of *x*.
`atan(x)`	Arc-tangent of *x*.
`atan2(y,x)`	Rectangular `(x,y)` to polar `(r,th)`. `atan2` gives *th*.
`ceil(x)`	Least integral value greater than or equal to *x*.
`cos(x)`	Cosine of *x*.
`cosh(x)`	Hyperbolic cosine of *x*.
`exp(x)`	Exponential, e^x.
`floor(x)`	Greatest integral value less than or equal to *x*.
`fmod(x,y)`	Floating point remainder of *x*/*y*.
`hypot(x,y)`	Returns `sqrt(x*x + y*y)`. *r* part of polar coordinates.
`log(x)`	Natural log of *x*.
`log10(x)`	Log base 10 of *x*.
`pow(x,y)`	*x* to the *y* power, x^y.
`sin(x)`	Sine of *x*.
`sinh(x)`	Hyperbolic sine of *x*.
`sqrt(x)`	Square root of *x*.
`tan(x)`	Tangent of *x*.
`tanh(x)`	Hyperbolic tangent of *x*.
`abs(x)`	Absolute value of *x*.
`double(x)`	Promote *x* to floating point.
`int(x)`	Truncate *x* to an integer.
`round(x)`	Round *x* to an integer.
`rand()`	Return a random floating point value between 0.0 and 1.0.
`srand(x)`	Set the seed for the random number generator to the integer *x*.

Core Tcl Commands

The pages given in Table 1–4 are the primary reference for the command.

Table 1–4 Built-in Tcl commands.

Command	Pg.	Description
`after`	178	Schedule a Tcl command for later execution.
`append`	45	Append arguments to a variable's value. No spaces added.
`array`	85	Query array state and search through elements.
`binary`	49	Convert between strings and binary data.
`break`	71	Premature loop exit.
`catch`	71	Trap errors.
`cd`	106	Change working directory.
`clock`	145	Get the time and format date strings.
`close`	106	Close an open I/O stream.
`concat`	55	Concatenate arguments with spaces between. Splices lists.
`console`	26	Control the console used to enter commands interactively.
`continue`	71	Continue with next loop iteration.
`error`	73	Raise an error.
`eof`	101	Check for end of file.
`eval`	113	Concatenate arguments and evaluate them as a command.
`exec`	91	Fork and execute a UNIX program.
`exit`	108	Terminate the process.
`expr`	6	Evaluate a math expression.
`fblocked`	182	Poll an I/O channel to see if data is ready.
`fconfigure`	181	Set and query I/O channel properties.
`fcopy`	197	Copy from one I/O channel to another.
`file`	94	Query the file system.
`fileevent`	179	Register callback for event-driven I/O.
`flush`	101	Flush output from an I/O stream's internal buffers.
`for`	70	Loop construct similar to C `for` statement.
`foreach`	67	Loop construct over a list, or lists, of values.
`format`	46	Format a string similar to C `sprintf`.
`gets`	104	Read a line of input from an I/O stream.

Table 1–4 Built-in Tcl commands. (Continued)

glob	106	Expand a pattern to matching file names.
global	78	Declare global variables.
history	155	Command-line history control.
if	64	Conditional command. Allows else and elseif clauses.
incr	11	Increment a variable by an integer amount.
info	148	Query the state of the Tcl interpreter.
interp	204	Create additional Tcl interpreters.
join	59	Concatenate list elements with a given separator string.
lappend	55	Add elements to the end of a list.
lindex	57	Fetch an element of a list.
linsert	57	Insert elements into a list.
list	55	Create a list out of the arguments.
llength	57	Return the number of elements in a list.
load	523	Load shared libraries that define Tcl commands.
lrange	57	Return a range of list elements.
lreplace	57	Replace elements of a list.
lsearch	58	Search for an element of a list that matches a pattern.
lsort	58	Sort a list.
namespace	172	Create and manipulate namespaces.
open	101	Open a file or process pipeline for I/O.
package	138	Provide or require code packages.
pid	108	Return the process ID.
proc	75	Define a Tcl procedure.
puts	104	Output a string to an I/O stream.
pwd	106	Return the current working directory.
read	105	Read blocks of characters from an I/O stream.
regexp	124	Regular expression matching.
regsub	127	Substitutions based on regular expressions.
rename	76	Change the name of a Tcl command.
return	74	Return a value from a procedure.
scan	48	Parses a string according to a format specification.

Table 1–4 Built-in Tcl commands. (Continued)

`socket`	186	Open a TCP/IP network connection.
`source`	24	Evaluate the Tcl commands in a file.
`split`	59	Chop a string up into list elements.
`string`	43	Operate on strings.
`subst`	120	Substitutions without command evaluation.
`switch`	65	Multi-way branch.
`tell`	106	Return the current seek offset of an I/O stream.
`time`	162	Measure the execution time of a command.
`trace`	153	Monitor variable assignments.
`unknown`	141	Unknown command handler.
`unset`	12	Delete variables.
`uplevel`	118	Execute a command in a different scope.
`upvar`	79	Reference a variable in a different scope.
`vwait`	180	Wait for a variable to be modified.
`while`	67	A loop construct.

CHAPTER 2

Getting Started

This chapter explains how to run Tcl and Tk on different operating system platforms: UNIX, Windows, and Macintosh. Tcl commands: `source` and `info`.

This chapter explains how to run Tcl scripts on different computer systems. While you can write Tcl scripts that are portable among UNIX, Windows, and the Macintosh, the details about getting started are different on each system.

The main Tcl/Tk program is *wish*. *Wish* stands for windowing shell, and with it you can create graphical applications that run on all these platforms. The name of the program is a little different on UNIX, Windows, and Macintosh systems. On UNIX it is just *wish*. On Windows you will find *wish.exe*, and on the Macintosh the application name is *Wish*. A version number may also be part of the name, such as *wish4.1*, *wish42.exe*, or *Wish 8.0*. The differences among versions are introduced on page xl, and described in more detail in Part VII of the book. This book will just use *wish* to refer to all of these possibilities.

Tk adds Tcl commands that are used to create graphical user interfaces, and it is described in Part III. You can run Tcl without Tk if you do not need a graphical interface, such as with the CGI script in Chapter 3. In this case the program is *tclsh*, *tclsh.exe* or *Tclsh*.

When you run *wish* it displays an empty window and prompts for a Tcl command with a % prompt. You can enter Tcl commands interactively and experiment with the examples in this book. On Windows and Macintosh, a console window is used to prompt for Tcl commands. On UNIX, your terminal window is used. As described later, you can also set up stand-alone Tcl/Tk scripts that are self contained applications.

The source Command

You can enter Tcl commands interactively at the % prompt. It is a good idea to try out the examples in this book as you read along. For longer examples you can find them on the CD-ROM and edit the scripts in your favorite editor. Save your examples to a file and then execute them with the Tcl `source` command:

```
source filename
```

The `source` command reads Tcl commands from a file and evaluates them just as if you had typed them interactively.

Chapter 3 develops a sample application. To get started, just open an editor on a file named `cgi1.tcl`. Each time you update this file you can save it, reload it into Tcl with the `source` command, and test it again. Development goes quickly because you do not wait for things to compile!

UNIX Tcl Scripts

On UNIX you can create a stand-alone Tcl or Tcl/Tk script much like an `sh` or `csh` script. The trick is in the first line of the file that contains your script. If the first line of a file begins with `#!pathname`, then UNIX uses `pathname` as the interpreter for the rest of the script. The "Hello, World!" program from Chapter 1 is repeated in Example 2–1 with the special starting line:

Example 2–1 A stand-alone Tcl script on UNIX.

```
#!/usr/local/bin/tclsh
puts stdout {Hello, World!}
```

Similarly, the Tk hello world program from Chapter 18 is shown in Example 2–2:

Example 2–2 A stand-alone Tk script on UNIX.

```
#!/usr/local/bin/wish
button .hello -text Hello -command {puts "Hello, World!"}
pack .hello -padx 10 -pady 10
```

The actual pathname for *tclsh* and *wish* may be different on your system. If you get the pathname for the interpreter wrong, you get a confusing "command not found" error. You can find out the complete pathname of the Tcl interpreter with the `info nameofexecutable` command. This is what I get on my system:

```
info nameofexecutable
=> /proj/tcl/install/5.x-sparc/bin/tclsh8.0
```

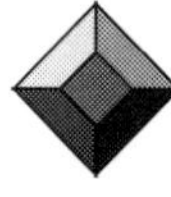

Watch out for long pathnames.

On most UNIX systems this special first line is limited to 32-characters, including the `#!`. If the pathname is too long you may end up with `/bin/sh` trying to interpret your script, giving you syntax errors. You might try using a symbolic link from a short name to the true, long name of the interpreter. However, watch out for systems like Solaris in which the script interpreter cannot be a symbolic link. Fortunately Solaris doesn't impose a 32 character limit on the pathname, so you can just use a long pathname.

The next example shows a trick that works around the pathname length limitation in all cases. The trick comes from a posting to `comp.lang.tcl` by Kevin Kenny. It takes advantage of a difference between comments in Tcl and the Bourne shell. Tcl comments are described on page 15. In the example, the Bourne shell command that runs the Tcl interpreter is hidden in a comment as far as Tcl is concerned, but it is visible to `/bin/sh`:

Example 2–3 Using `/bin/sh` to run a Tcl script.

```
#!/bin/sh
# The backslash makes the next line a comment in Tcl \
exec /some/very/long/path/to/wish "$0" ${1+"$@"}
#   ... Tcl script goes here ...
```

You do not even have to know the complete pathname of *tclsh* or *wish* to use this trick. You can just do this:

```
#!/bin/sh
# Run wish from the users PATH \
exec wish -f "$0" ${1+"$@"}
```

The drawback of an incomplete pathname is that many sites have different versions of *wish* and *tclsh* that correspond to different versions of Tcl and Tk. In addition, some users may not have these programs in their PATH.

If you have Tk version 3.6 or earlier, its version of *wish* requires a `-f` argument to make it read the contents of a file. The `-f` switch is ignored in Tk 4.0 and higher versions. The `-f`, if required, is also counted in the 32-character limit on `#!` lines.

```
#!/usr/local/bin/wish -f
```

Windows 95 Start Menu

You can add your Tcl/Tk programs to the Windows start menu. The command is the complete name of the *wish.exe* program and the name of the script. The trick is that the name of *wish.exe* has a space in it in the default configuration, so you must use quotes. Your start command will look something like this:

```
"c:\Program Files\TCL76\wish.exe" c:\your\script.tcl
```

This starts `c:\your\script.tcl` as a stand-alone Tcl/Tk program.

The Macintosh and *ResEdit*

If you want to create a self-contained Tcl/Tk application on Macintosh you must copy the *Wish* program and add a Macintosh resource named `tclshrc` that has the start-up Tcl code. The Tcl code can be a single `source` command that reads your script file. Here are step by step instructions to create the resource using *ResEdit*:

- First, make a copy of *Wish* and open the copy in *ResEdit*.
- Pull down the `Resource` menu and select `Create New Resource` operation to make a new `TEXT` resource.
- *ResEdit* opens a window and you can type in text. Type in a `source` command that names your script:

```
source "Hard Disk:Tcl/Tk 4.1:Applications:MyScript.tcl"
```

- Set the name of the resource to be `tclshrc`. You do this through the `Get Resource Info` dialog under the `Resources` menu in *ResEdit*.

If you have a Macintosh development environment you can build a version of *Wish* that has additional resources built right in. You add the resources to the `applicationInit.r` file. If a resource contains Tcl code, you use it like this:

```
source -rcrc resource
```

If you don't want to edit resources, you can just use the *Wish* `Source` menu to select a script to run.

The `console` Command

The Windows and Macintosh platforms have a built-in console that is used to enter Tcl commands interactively. You can control this console with the `console` command. The console is visible by default. Hide the console like this:

```
console hide
```

Display the console like this:

```
console show
```

The console is implemented by a second Tcl interpreter. You can evaluate Tcl commands in that interpreter with:

```
console eval command
```

Command-Line Arguments

If you run a script from the command line, for example from a UNIX shell, you can pass the script command-line arguments. You can also specify these arguments in the shortcut command in Windows. For example, under UNIX you could type this at a shell:

```
% myscript.tcl arg1 arg2 arg3
```

In Windows, you can have a shortcut that runs *wish* on your script and also passes additional arguments:

```
"c:\Program Files\TCL76\wish.exe" c:\your\script.tcl arg1
```

The Tcl shells pass the command-line arguments to the script as the value of the `argv` variable. The number of command-line arguments is given by the `argc` variable. The name of the program, or script, is not part of `argv` nor is it counted by `argc`. Instead, it is put into the `argv0` variable. Table 2–2 lists all the predefined variables in the Tcl shells. `argv` is a list, so you can use the `lindex` command described in Chapter 5 to extract items from it:

```
set arg1 [lindex $argv 0]
```

The following script prints its arguments (`foreach` is described on page 67):

Example 2–4 The `EchoArgs` script.

```
# Tcl script to echo command line arguments
puts "Program: $argv0"
puts "Number of arguments: $argc"
set i 0
foreach arg $argv {
   puts "Arg $i: $arg"
   incr i
}
```

Command-Line Options to *Wish*

Some command-line options are interpreted by *wish*, and they do not appear in the `argv` variable. The general form of the *wish* command line is:

```
wish ?options? ?script? ?arg1 arg2?
```

If no script is specified, then *wish* just enters an interactive command loop. Table 2–1 lists the options that *wish* supports:

Table 2–1 Wish command line options.

`-colormap new`	Use a new private colormap. See page 456.
`-display` *`display`*	Use the specified X *`display`*. UNIX only.
`-geometry` *`geometry`*	The size and position of the window. See page 488.
`-name` *`name`*	Specify the Tk application name. See page 478.
`-sync`	Run X synchronously. UNIX only.
`-use` *`id`*	Use the window specified by *`id`* for the main window. See page 496.
`-visual` *`visual`*	Specify the visual for the main window. See page 456.
`--`	Terminate options to *wish*.

Predefined Variables

Table 2–2 Variables defined by *tclsh* and *wish*.

`argc`	The number of command-line arguments
`argv`	A list of the command-line arguments
`argv0`	The name of the script being executed. If being used interactively, `argv0` is the name of the shell program.
`embed_args`	The list of arguments in the `<EMBED>` tag. Tcl applets only. See page 607.
`env`	An array of the environment variables. See page 108.
`tcl_interactive`	True (one) if the *tclsh* is prompting for commands.
`tcl_library`	The script library directory.
`tcl_patchLevel`	Modified version number, e.g., 8.0b1
`tcl_platform`	Array containing operating system information. See page 152.
`tcl_pkgPath`	List of directories to search for packages.
`tcl_prompt1`	If defined, this is a command that outputs the prompt.
`tcl_prompt2`	If defined, this is a command that outputs the prompt if the current command is not yet complete.
`tcl_version`	Version number.
`auto_path`	The search path for script library directories. See page 136.
`auto_index`	A map from command name to a Tcl command that defines it.
`auto_noload`	If set, the library facility is disabled.
`auto_noexec`	If set, the auto execute facility is disabled.
`geometry`	(*wish* only). The value of the `-geometry` argument.

CHAPTER 3

The Guestbook CGI Application

This chapter presents a simple Tcl program that computes a Web page. The chapter provides a brief background to HTML and the CGI interface to Web servers.

This chapter presents a complete, but simple guestbook program that computes an HTML document, or Web page, based on the contents of a simple database. The basic idea is that a user with a Web browser visits a page that is computed by the program. The details of how the page gets from your program to the user with the Web browser vary from system to system. You can use these scripts on your own Web server, but you will need help from your Webmaster to set things up. The goal of the examples in the chapter are to demonstrate a few non-trivial programming techniques with a real example.

The chapter provides a very brief introduction to HTML and CGI programming. HTML is a way to specify text formatting, including hypertext links to other pages on the World Wide Web. CGI is a standard for communication between a Web server that delivers documents and a program that computes documents for the server. There are many books on these subjects alone. *CGI Developers Resource, Web Programming with Tcl and Perl* (Prentice Hall, 1997) by John Ivler is a good reference for details that are left unexplained here.

A guestbook is a place for visitors to sign their name and perhaps provide other information. We will build a guestbook that takes advantage of the World Wide Web. Our guests can leave their address as a Universal Resource Location (URL). The guestbook will be presented as a page that has hypertext links to all these URLs so that other guests can visit them. The program works by keeping a simple database of the guests, and it generates the guestbook page from the database.

The Tcl scripts described in this chapter use commands and techniques that are described in more detail in later chapters. The goal of the examples is to demonstrate the power of Tcl without explaining every detail. If the examples in this chapter raise questions, you can follow the references to examples in other chapters that do go into more depth.

A Quick Introduction to HTML

Web pages are written in a text markup language called HTML (HyperText Markup Language). The idea of HTML is that you annotate, or mark up, regular text with special tags that indicate structure and formatting. For example, the title of a Web page is defined like this:

```
<TITLE>My Home Page</TITLE>
```

The tags provide general formatting guidelines, but the browsers that display HTML pages have freedom in how they display things. This keeps the markup simple. The general syntax for HTML tags is:

```
<tag parameters>normal text</tag>
```

As shown here, the tags usually come in pairs. The open tag may have some parameters, and the close tag name begins with a slash. The case of a tag is not considered, so `<title>`, `<Title>`, and `<TITLE>` are all valid and mean the same thing. The corresponding close tag could be `</title>`, `</Title>`, `</TITLE>`, or even `</TiTlE>`.

The `<A>` tag defines hypertext links that reference other pages on the Web. The hypertext links connect pages into a Web so you can move from page to page to page and find related information. It is the flexibility of the links that make the Web so interesting. The `<A>` tag takes an `HREF` parameter that defines the destination of the link. If you wanted to link to the Sun home page, you would put this in your page:

```
<A HREF="http://www.sun.com/">Sun Microsystems</A>
```

When this construct appears in a Web page, your browser typically displays "Sun Microsystems" in blue underlined text. When you click on that text, your browser switches to the page at the address "http://www.sun.com/". There is a lot more to HTML, of course, but this should give you a basic idea of what is going on in the examples. The following list summarizes the HTML tags that will be used in the examples:

Table 3–1 HTML tags used in the examples.

HTML	Main tag that surrounds the whole document.
HEAD	Delimits head section of the HTML document.
TITLE	Defines the title of the page.
BODY	Delimits the body section. Lets you specify page colors.

Table 3–1 HTML tags used in the examples. (Continued)

`H1 - H6`	HTML defines 6 heading levels: `H1`, `H2`, `H3`, `H4`, `H5`, `H6`.
`P`	Start a new paragraph.
`B`	Bold text.
`I`	Italic text.
`A`	Used for hypertext links.
`IMG`	Specify an image.
`DL`	Definition list.
`DT`	Term clause in a definition list.
`DD`	Definition clause in a definition list.
`FORM`	Defines a data entry form.
`INPUT`	A one-line entry field, checkbox, radio button, or submit button.
`TEXTAREA`	A multiline text field.

CGI for Dynamic Pages

There are two classes of pages on the Web, static and dynamic. A static page is written and stored on a Web server, and the same thing is returned each time a user views the page. This is the easy way to think about Web pages. You have some information to share, so you compose a page and tinker with the HTML tags to get the information to look good. If you have a home page, it is probably in this class.

In contrast, a dynamic page is computed each time it is viewed. This is how pages that give up-to-the-minute stock prices work, for example. A dynamic page does not mean it includes animations; it just means that a program computes the page contents when a user visits the page. The advantage of this approach is that a user might see something different each time they visit the page. As we shall see, it is also easier to maintain information in a database of some sort and generate the HTML formatting for the data with a program.

A CGI (Common Gateway Interface) program is used to compute Web pages. The CGI standard defines how inputs are passed to the program and a way to identify different types of results, such as images, plain text, or HTML markup. A CGI program simply writes the contents of the document to its standard output, and the Web server takes care of delivering the document to the user's Web browser. The following is a very simple CGI script:

Example 3–1 A simple CGI script.

```
puts "Content-Type: text/html"
puts ""
puts "<TITLE>The Current Time</TITLE>"
puts "The time is <B>[clock format [clock seconds]]</B>"
```

The program computes a simple HTML page that has the current time. Each time a user visits the page they will see the current time on the server. The server that has the CGI program and the user viewing the page might be on different sides of the planet. The output of the program starts with a `Content-Type` line that tells your Web browser what kind of data comes next. This is followed by a blank line and then the contents of the page.

The `clock` command is used twice: once to get the current time in seconds, and a second time to format the time into a nice looking string. The `clock` command is described in detail on page 145. Fortunately there is no conflict between the markup syntax used by HTML and the Tcl syntax for embedded commands, so we can mix the two in the argument to the `puts` command. Double quotes are used to group the argument to `puts` so that the `clock` commands will be executed. When run, the output of the program will look like this:

Example 3–2 Output of Example 3–1.

```
Content-Type: text/html

<TITLE>The Current Time</TITLE>
The time is <B>Wed Oct 16 11:23:43  1996</B>
```

This example is a bit sloppy in its use of HTML, but it should display properly in most Web browsers. The next example include all the required tags for a proper HTML document.

The `guestbook.cgi` Script

The `guestbook.cgi` script computes a page that lists all the registered guests. The example is shown first, and then each part of it is discussed in more detail later. One thing to note right away is that the HTML tags are generated by procedures that hide the details of the HTML syntax. The first lines of the script use the UNIX trick to have *tclsh* interpret the script. This trick is described on page 24:

Example 3–3 The `guestbook.cgi` script.

```
#!/bin/sh
# guestbook.cgi
# \
```

```
exec tclsh "$0" ${1+"$@"}

# Implement a simple guestbook page.
# The set of visitors is kept in a simple database.
# The newguest.cgi script will update the database.
#
source /usr/local/lib/cgilib.tcl

Cgi_Header "Brent's Guestbook" {BGCOLOR=white TEXT=black}
P
set datafile [file join \
   [file dirname [info script]] guestbook.data]
if {![file exists $datafile]} {
   puts "No registered guests, yet."
   P
   puts "Be the first [Link {registered guest!} newguest.html]"
} else {
   puts "The following folks have registered in my GuestBook."
   P
   puts [Link Register newguest.html]
   H2 Guests
   catch {source $datafile}
   foreach name [lsort [array names Guestbook]] {
      set item $Guestbook($name)
      set homepage [lindex $item 0]
      set markup [lindex $item 1]
      H3 [Link $name $homepage]
      puts $markup
   }
}
Cgi_End
```

Beginning the HTML Page

The script uses a number of Tcl procedures that make working with HTML and the CGI interface easier. These procedures are kept in the cgilib.tcl file. You must update the complete pathname of this file to match your system. The script starts by sourcing the cgilib.tcl file and generating the standard information that comes at the beginning of an HTML page:

```
source /usr/local/lib/cgilib.tcl
Cgi_Header {Brent's GuestBook} {bgcolor=white text=black}
```

The Cgi_Header procedure takes as arguments the title for the page and some optional parameters for the HTML <Body> tag that set the page background and text color. Here we specify black text on a white background to avoid the standard grey background of most browsers. An empty default value is specified for the bodyparams so you do not have to pass those to Cgi_Header. Default values for procedure parameters are described on page 75.

Example 3–4 The `Cgi_Header` procedure.

```
proc Cgi_Header {title {bodyparams {}}} {
    puts stdout \
"Content-Type: text/html

<HTML>
<HEAD>
<TITLE>$title</TITLE>
</HEAD>
<BODY $bodyparams>
<H1>$title</H1>"
}
```

The `Cgi_Header` procedure just contains a single `puts` command that generates the standard boilerplate that appears at the beginning of the output. Note that several lines are grouped together with double quotes. Double quotes are used so that the variable references mixed into the HTML are substituted properly.

The output begins with the CGI content-type information, a blank line, and then the HTML. The HTML is divided into a head and body part. The `<TITLE>` tag goes in the head section of an HTML document. Finally, browsers display the title in a different place than the rest of the page, so I always want to repeat the title as a level-one heading (i.e., `H1`) in the body of the page.

Simple Tags and Hypertext Links

The next thing the program does is see if there are any registered guests or not. The `file` command, which is described in detail on page 94, is used to see if there is any data:

```
if [file exists $datafile] {
```

If the database file does not exist, a different page is displayed to encourage a registration. The page includes a hypertext link to a registration page. The `newguest.html` page will be described in more detail later:

```
puts "No registered guests, yet."
P
puts "Be the first [Link {registered guest!} newguest.html]"
```

The `P` command generates the HTML for a paragraph break. This trivial procedure saves us a few keystrokes:

```
proc P {} {
   puts <P>
}
```

The `Link` command formats and returns the HTML for a hypertext link. Instead of printing the HTML directly, it is returned so you can include it in-line with other text you are printing:

Example 3–5 The Link command formats a hypertext link.

```
proc Link {text url} {
    return "<A HREF=\"$url\">$text</A>"
}
```

The output of the program would be this if there were no data:

Example 3–6 Initial output of guestbook.cgi

```
Content-Type: text/html

<HTML>
<HEAD>
<TITLE>Brent's Guestbook</TITLE>
</HEAD>
<BODY BGCOLOR=white TEXT=black>
<H1>Brent's Guestbook</H1>
<P>
No registered guests.
<P>
Be the first <A HREF="newguest.cgi">registered guest!</A>
</BODY>
</HTML>
```

If the database file exists, then the real work begins. We first generate a link to the registration page, and a level-two header to separate that from the guest list:

```
puts [Link Register newguest.html]
H2 Guests
```

The H2 procedure handles the detail of including the matching close tag:

```
proc H2 {string} {
    puts "<H2>$string</H2>"
}
```

Using a Tcl Array for the Database

The datafile contains Tcl commands that define an array that holds the guestbook data. If this file is kept in the same directory as the guestbook.cgi script, then you can compute its name. The info script command returns the file name of the script. The file dirname and file join commands manipulate file names in a platform-independent way. They are described on page 94:

```
set datafile [file join \
    [file dirname [info script]] guestbook.data]
```

By using Tcl commands to represent the data, we can load the data with the source command. The catch command is used to protect the script from a bad data file, which will show up as an error from the source command. Catching errors is described in detail on page 73:

```
catch {source $datafile}
```

The `Guestbook` variable is the array defined in `guestbook.data`. Array variables are the topic of Chapter 8. Each element of the array is defined with a Tcl command that looks like this:

```
set {Guestbook(Brent Welch)} {
     http://www.beedub.com/
     {<img src=http://www.beedub.com/welch.gif>}
}
```

The person's name is the array index, or key. The value of the array element is a Tcl list with two elements: their URL and some additional HTML markup that they can include in the guestbook. Tcl lists are the topic of Chapter 5. The spaces in the name result in some awkward syntax that is explained on page 84. Do not worry about this now. We will see on page 40 that all the braces in the previous statement are generated automatically. The main point is that the person's name is the key, and the value is a list with two elements.

The `array names` command returns all the indices, or keys, in the array, and the `lsort` command sorts these alphabetically. The `foreach` command loops over the sorted list, setting the loop variable `x` to each key in turn:

```
foreach name [lsort [array names Guestbook]] {
```

Given the key, we get the value like this:

```
set item $Guestbook($name)
```

The two list elements are extracted with `lindex`, which is described on page 57.

```
set homepage [lindex $item 0]
set markup [lindex $item 1]
```

We generate the HTML for the guestbook entry as a level-three header that contains a hypertext link to the guest's home page. We follow the link with any HTML markup text that the guest has supplied to embellish their entry. The `H3` procedure is similar to the `H2` procedure already shown, except it generates `<H3>` tags;

```
H3 [Link $name $homepage]
puts $markup
```

Sample Output

The last thing the script does is call `Cgi_End` to output the proper closing tags. An example of the output of the `guestbook.cgi` script is shown in Example 3–7:

Example 3–7 Output of `guestbook.cgi`.

```
Content-Type: text/html

<HTML>
<HEAD>
<TITLE>Brent's Guestbook</TITLE>
</HEAD>
<BODY BGCOLOR=white TEXT=black>
<H1>Brent's Guestbook</H1>
<P>
The following folks have registered in my guestbook.
<P>
<A HREF="newguest.cgi">Register</A>
<H2>Guests</H2>
<H3><A HREF="http://www.beedub.com/">Brent Welch</A></H3>
<IMG SRC="http://www.beedub.com/welch.gif">
</BODY>
</HTML>
```

Defining Forms and Processing Form Data

The `guestbook.cgi` script only generates output. The other half of CGI deals with input from the user. Input is more complex for two reasons. First, we have to define another HTML page that has a form for the user to fill out. Second, the data from the form is organized and encoded in a standard form that must be decoded by the script. Example 3–8 on page 38 defines a very simple form, and the procedure that decodes the form data is described in detail in Example 11–4 on page 129.

The guestbook page contains a link to `newguest.html`. This page contains a form that lets a user register their name, home page URL, and some additional HTML markup. The form has a submit button. When a user clicks that button in their browser, the information from the form is passed to the `newguest.cgi` script. This script updates the database and computes another page for the user that acknowledges their contribution.

The `newguest.html` Form

An HTML form is defined with tags that define data entry fields, buttons, checkboxes, and other elements that let the user specify values. For example, a one-line entry field that is used to enter the home page URL is defined like this:

```
<INPUT TYPE=text NAME=url>
```

The `INPUT` tag is used to define several kinds of input elements, and its `type` parameter indicates what kind. In this case, `TYPE=text` creates a one-line text entry field. The submit button is defined with a `INPUT` tag that has `TYPE=submit`, and the `VALUE` parameter becomes the text that appears on the button:

```
<INPUT TYPE=submit NAME=submit VALUE=Register>
```

A general type-in window is defined with the TEXTAREA tag. This creates a multiline, scrolling text field that is useful for specifying lots of information, such as a free-form comment. In our case we will let guests type in HTML that will appear with their guestbook entry. The text between the open and close TEXTAREA tags is inserted into the type-in window when the page is first displayed.

```
<TEXTAREA NAME=markup ROWS=10 COLS=50>Hello.</TEXTAREA>
```

A common parameter to the form tags is NAME=*something*. This name identifies the data that will come back from the form. The tags also have parameters that affect their display, such as the label on the submit button and the size of the text area. Those details are not important for our example. The complete form is shown in Example 3–8:

Example 3–8 The newguest.html form.

```
<!Doctype HTML PUBLIC "-//IETF//DTD HTML 2.0//EN">
<HTML>
<HEAD>
<TITLE>Register in my Guestbook</TITLE>
<!-- Author: bwelch -->
<META HTTP-Equiv=Editor Content="SunLabs WebTk 1.0beta 10/
11/96">
</HEAD>
<BODY>

<FORM ACTION="newguest.cgi" METHOD="POST">

<H1>Register in my Guestbook</H1>
<UL>
<LI>Name <INPUT TYPE="text" NAME="name" SIZE="40">
<LI>URL  <INPUT TYPE="text" NAME="url" SIZE="40">
<P>
If you don't have a home page, you can use an email URL like
"mailto:welch@acm.org"
<LI>Additional HTML to include after your link:
<BR>

<TEXTAREA NAME="html" COLS="60" ROWS="15">
</TEXTAREA>
<LI><INPUT TYPE="submit" NAME="new" VALUE="Add me to your
guestbook">
<LI><INPUT TYPE="submit" NAME="update" VALUE="Update my
guestbook entry">
</UL>
</FORM>

</BODY>
</HTML>
```

The `newguest.cgi` Script

When the user clicks the Submit button in their browser, the data from the form is passed to the program identified by the `Action` parameter of the form tag. That program takes the data, does something useful with it and then returns a new page for the browser to display. In our case the `FORM` tag names `newguest.cgi` as the program to handle the data:

```
<FORM ACTION=newguest.cgi METHOD=POST>
```

The CGI specification defines how the data from the form is passed to the program. The data is encoded and organized so that the program can figure out the values the user specified for each form element. The encoding is handled rather nicely with some regular expression tricks that are done in `Cgi_Parse`. `Cgi_Parse` saves the form data, and you use `Cgi_Value` to get a form value in your script. These procedures are described in Example 11–4 on page 129. Example 3–9 starts out by calling `Cgi_Parse`:

Example 3–9 The `newguest.cgi` script.

```
#!/bin/sh
# \
exec tclsh "$0" ${1+"$@"}
# source cgilib.tcl from the same directory as newguest.cgi
source [file join \
    [file dirname [info script]] cgilib.tcl]

set datafile [file join \
    [file dirname [info script]] guestbook.data]

Cgi_Parse

# Open the datafile in append mode

if [catch {open $datafile a} out] {
    Cgi_Header "Guestbook Registration Error" \
        {BGCOLOR=black TEXT=red}
    P
    puts "Cannot open the data file"
    P
    puts $out;# the error message
    exit 0
}

# Append a Tcl set command that defines the guest's entry

puts $out ""
puts $out [list set Guestbook([Cgi_Value name]) \
    [list [Cgi_Value url] [Cgi_Value html]]]
close $out

# Return a page to the browser

Cgi_Header "Guestbook Registration Confirmed" \
```

```
    {BGCOLOR=white TEXT=black}

puts "
<DL>
<DT>Name
<DD>[Cgi_Value name]
<DT>URL
<DD>[Link [Cgi_Value url] [Cgi_Value url]]
</DL>
[Cgi_Value html]
"

Cgi_End
```

The main idea of the `newguest.cgi` script is that it saves the data to a file as a Tcl command that defines an element of the `Guestbook` array. This lets the `guestbook.cgi` script simply load the data by using the Tcl `source` command. This trick of storing data as a Tcl script saves us from the chore of defining a new file format and writing code to parse it. Instead, we can rely on the well-tuned Tcl implementation to do the hard work for us efficiently.

The script opens the datafile in append mode so it can add a new record to the end. Opening files is described in detail on page 101. The script uses a `catch` command to guard against errors. If an error occurs, a page explaining the error is returned to the user. Working with files is one of the most common sources of errors (permission denied, disk full, file-not-found, and so on), so I always open the file inside a `catch` statement:

```
if [catch {open $datafile a} out] {
    # an error occurred
} else {
    # open was ok
}
```

In this command, the variable `out` gets the result of the `open` command, which is either a file descriptor or an error message. This style of using `catch` is described in detail in Example 6–14 on page 71.

The script writes the data as a Tcl `set` command. The `list` command is used to format the data properly:

```
puts $out [list set Guestbook([Cgi_Value name]) \
    [list [Cgi_Value url] [Cgi_Value html]]]
```

There are two lists. First the url and html are formatted into one list. This list will be the value of the array element. Then, the whole Tcl command is formed as a list. In simplified form, the command is generated from this:

```
list set variable value
```

Using the `list` command ensures that the result will always be a valid Tcl command that sets the variable to the given value. The `list` command is described in more detail on page 55.

Next Steps

There are a number of details that could be added to this example. A user may want to update their entry, for example. They could do that now, but they would have to retype everything. They might also like a chance to check the results of their registration and make changes before committing them. This requires another page that displays their guest entry as it would appear on a page, and also has the fields that let them update the data.

The details of how a CGI script is hooked up with a Web server vary from server to server. You should ask your local Webmaster for help if you want to try this out on your Web site.

Don Libes has created a nice package for CGI scripts, `cgi.tcl`, and you can find it on the web at `http://expect.nist.gov/cgi.tcl/`.

The next few chapters describe basic Tcl commands and data structures. We return to this example in Chapter 11 on regular expressions.

CHAPTER 4

String Processing in Tcl

This chapter describes string manipulation and simple pattern matching. Tcl commands described: `string`, `append`, `format`, `scan`, and `binary`.

Strings are the basic data item in Tcl, so it should not be surprising that there are a large number of commands to manipulate strings. A closely related topic is pattern matching, in which string comparisons are made more powerful by matching a string against a pattern. This chapter describes a simple pattern matching mechanism that is similar to that used in many shell languages. Chapter 11 describes a more complex and powerful regular expression pattern matching mechanism.

The `string` Command

The `string` command is really a collection of operations you can perform on strings. The first argument to `string` determines the operation. You can ask `string` for valid operations by giving it a bad one:

```
string junk
=> bad option "junk": should be compare, first, index,
last, length, match, range, tolower, toupper, trim, trim-
left, trimright, wordend, or wordstart
```

The following example gets the length of the value of variable `name`.

```
set name "Brent Welch"
string length $name
=> 11
```

Table 4–1 summarizes the `string` command.

Table 4–1 The `string` command.

`string compare` *str1 str2*	Compare strings lexicographically. Returns 0 if equal, -1 if *str1* sorts before *str2*, else 1.
`string first` *str1 str2*	Return the index in *str2* of the first occurrence of *str1*, or -1 if *str1* is not found.
`string index` *string index*	Return the character at the specified *index*.
`string last` *str1 str2*	Return the index in *str2* of the last occurrence of *str1*, or -1 if *str1* is not found.
`string length` *string*	Return the number of characters in *string*.
`string match` *pattern str*	Return 1 if *str* matches the *pattern*, else 0. Glob-style matching is used. See page 48.
`string range` *str i j*	Return the range of characters in *str* from *i* to *j*.
`string tolower` *string*	Return *string* in lower case.
`string toupper` *string*	Return *string* in upper case.
`string trim` *string* ?*chars*?	Trim the characters in *chars* from both ends of *string*. *chars* defaults to whitespace.
`string trimleft` *string* ?*chars*?	Trim the characters in *chars* from the beginning of *string*. *chars* defaults to whitespace.
`string trimright` *string* ?*chars*?	Trim the characters in *chars* from the end of *string*. *chars* defaults to whitespace.
`string wordend` *str ix*	Return the index in *str* of the character after the word containing the character at index *ix*.
`string wordstart` *str ix*	Return the index in *str* of the first character in the word containing the character at index *ix*.

These are the string operations I use most:

- The `compare` operation, which is shown in Example 4–1 on page 45.
- String `match`. This pattern matching operation is described on page 48.
- The `tolower` and `toupper` operations convert case.
- The `trim`, `trimright`, and `trimleft` operations are handy for cleaning up strings.

There are several operations that pick apart strings: `first`, `last`, `wordstart`, `wordend`, `index`, and `range`. If you find yourself using combinations of these operations to pick apart data, it will be faster if you can do it with the regular expression pattern matcher described in Chapter 11. These operations involve character indices into the string that count from zero. The `end` keyword refers to the last character in a string:

```
string range abcd 1 end
=> bcd
```

Strings and Expressions

Strings can be compared with `expr` using the comparison operators. However, there are a number of subtle issues that can cause problems. First, you must quote the string value so the expression parser can identify it as a string type. Then you must group the expression with curly braces to prevent the double quotes from being stripped off by the main interpreter:

```
if {$x == "foo"}
```

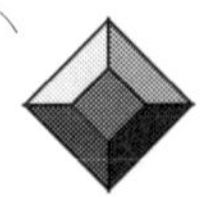

`expr` *is unreliable for string comparison before Tcl 8.0.*

Ironically, despite the quotes, the expression evaluator first converts items to numbers if possible, and then converts them back if it detects a case of string comparison. Before Tcl 8.0, the conversion back was always done as a decimal number. This could lead to unexpected conversions between strings that look like hexadecimal or octal numbers:

```
if {"0xa" == "10"} { puts stdout ack! }
=> ack!
```

A safe way to compare strings is the `string compare` command. This command also operates faster because the unnecessary conversions are eliminated. Like the C library `strcmp` function, `string compare` returns 0 if the strings are equal, -1 if the first string is lexicographically less than the second, or 1 if the first string is greater than the second:

Example 4–1 Comparing strings.

```
if {[string compare $s1 $s2] == 0} {
    # strings are equal
}
```

The append Command

The `append` command takes a variable name as its first argument, and concatenates its remaining arguments onto the current value of the named variable. The variable is created if it does not already exist:

```
set foo z
append foo a b c
set foo
=> zabc
```

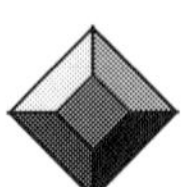

append is efficient.

The `append` command provides an efficient way to add items to the end of a string. It modifies a variable directly so it can exploit the memory allocation scheme used internally by Tcl. Using the `append` command like this:

```
append x " some new stuff"
```

is always faster than this:

```
set x "$x some new stuff"
```

The `lappend` command described on page 55 has similar performance benefits when working with Tcl lists.

The `format` Command

The `format` command is similar to the C `printf` function. It formats a string according to a format specification:

```
format spec value1 value2 ...
```

The `spec` argument includes literals and keywords. The literals are placed in the result as-is, while each keyword indicates how to format the corresponding argument. The keywords are introduced with a percent sign, `%`, followed by zero or more modifiers, and terminate with a conversion specifier. Example keywords include `%f` for floating point, `%d` for integer, and `%s` for string format. Use `%%` to obtain a single percent character. The most general keyword specification for each argument contains up to six parts:

- position specifier
- flags
- field width
- precision
- word length
- conversion character.

These components are explained by a series of examples. The examples use double quotes around the `format` specification. This is because often the format contains white space, so grouping is required, as well as backslash substitutions like `\t` or `\n`, and the quotes allow substitution of these special characters. Table 4–2 lists the conversion characters:

Table 4–2 Format conversions.

`d`	Signed integer.
`u`	Unsigned integer.
`i`	Signed integer. The argument may be in hex (0x) or octal (0) format.
`o`	Unsigned octal.
`x` or `X`	Unsigned hexadecimal. 'x' gives lowercase results.
`c`	Map from an integer to the ASCII character it represents.
`s`	A string.
`f`	Floating point number in the format `a.b`.
`e` or `E`	Floating point number in scientific notation, `a.bE+-c`.
`g` or `G`	Floating point number in either `%f` or `%e` format, whichever is shorter.

A position specifier is *i*$, which means take the value from argument *i* as opposed to the normally corresponding argument. The position counts from 1. If a position is specified for one format keyword, the position must be used for all of them. If you group the format specification with double quotes, you need to quote the $ with a backslash:

```
set lang 2
format "%${lang}\$s" one un uno
=> un
```

The position specifier is useful for picking a string from a set, such as this simple language-specific example. The position is also useful if the same value is repeated in the formatted string.

The flags in a format are used to specify padding and justification. In the following examples, the # causes a leading 0x to be printed in the hexadecimal value. The zero in 08 causes the field to be padded with zeros. Table 4–3 summarizes the format flag characters.

```
format "%#x" 20
=> 0x14
format "%#08x" 10
=> 0x0000000a
```

Table 4–3 Format flags.

-	Left justify the field.
+	Always include a sign, either + or -.
space	Precede a number with a space, unless the number has a leading sign. Useful for packing numbers close together.
0	Pad with zeros.
#	Leading 0 for octal. Leading 0x for hex. Always include a decimal point in floating point. Do not remove trailing zeros (%g).

After the flags you can specify a minimum field width value. The value is padded to this width with spaces, or with zeros if the 0 flag is used:

```
format "%-20s %3d" Label 2
=> Label                  2
```

You can compute a field width and pass it to format as one of the arguments by using * as the field width specifier. In this case the next argument is used as the field width instead of the value, and the argument after that is the value that gets formatted.

```
set maxl 8
format "%-*s = %s" $maxl Key Value
=> Key      = Value
```

The precision comes next, and it is specified with a period and a number. For `%f` and `%e` it indicates how many digits come after the decimal point. For `%g` it indicates the total number of significant digits used. For `%d` and `%x` it indicates how many digits will be printed, padding with zeros if necessary.

```
format "%6.2f %6.2d" 1 1
=>   1.00     01
```

The storage length part comes last, but it is rarely useful because Tcl maintains all floating point values in double-precision, and all integers as long words.

The scan Command

The `scan` command parses a string according to a format specification and assigns values to variables. It returns the number of successful conversions it made. The general form of the command is:

```
scan string format var ?var? ?var? ...
```

The format for `scan` is nearly the same as in the `format` command. There is no `%u` scan format. The `%c` scan format converts one character to its decimal value.

The `scan` format includes a set notation. Use square brackets to delimit a set of characters. The set matches one or more characters that are copied into the variable. A dash is used to specify a range. The following scans a field of all lowercase letters.

```
scan abcABC {%[a-z]} result
=> 1
set result
=> abc
```

If the first character in the set is a right square bracket, then it is considered part of the set. If the first character in the set is `^`, then characters *not* in the set match. Again, put a right square bracket right after the `^` to include it in the set. Nothing special is required to include a left square bracket in the set. As in the previous example, you will want to protect the format with braces, or use backslashes, because square brackets are special to the Tcl parser.

String Matching

The `string match` command implements *glob*-style pattern matching that is modeled after the file name pattern matching done by various UNIX shells. There are just three constructs used in glob patterns: match any number of any characters (`*`), match any single character (`?`), or match one of a set of characters (`[abc]`).* Any other characters in a pattern are taken as literals that must match the input exactly. To match all strings that begin with `a`:

```
string match a* alpha
=> 1
```

To match all two-letter strings:

```
string match ?? XY
=> 1
```

To match all strings that begin with either a or b:

```
string match {[ab]*} cello
=> 0
```

Be careful! Square brackets are also special to the Tcl interpreter, so you will need to wrap the pattern up in curly braces to prevent it from being interpreted as a nested command. Another approach is to put the pattern into a variable:

```
set pat {[ab]*x}
string match $pat box
=> 1
```

The pattern specifies a range of characters with the syntax `[x-y]`. For example, `[a-z]` represents the set of all lower-case letters, and `[0-9]` represents all the digits. You can include more than one range in a set. Any letter, digit, or the underscore is matched with:

```
string match {[a-zA-Z0-9_]} $char
```

The set only matches a single character. To match more complicated patterns, like one or more characters from a set, then you need to use regular expression matching, which is described on page 124.

If you need to include a literal `*`, `?`, or bracket in your pattern, preface it with a backslash:

```
string match {*\?} what?
=> 1
```

In this case the pattern is quoted with curly braces because the Tcl interpreter is also doing backslash substitutions. Without the braces, you would have to use two backslashes. They are replaced with a single backslash by Tcl before `string match` is called.

```
string match *\\? what?
```

The `binary` Command

Tcl 8.0 adds support for binary strings. Previous versions of Tcl used null-terminated strings internally, which foils the manipulation of some types of data. Tcl 8.0 uses counted strings so it can tolerate a null byte in a string value without truncating it.

This section describes the `binary` command that provides conversions between strings and packed binary data representations. The `binary format` command takes values and packs them according to a template. The resulting

* The `string match` function does not support alternation in a pattern, such as the `{a,b,c}` syntax of the C shell. The `glob` command, however, does support this form.

binary value is returned:

```
binary format template value ?value ...?
```

The `binary scan` command extracts values from a binary string according to a similar template. It assigns values to a set of Tcl variables:

```
binary scan value template variable ?variable ...?
```

Format Templates

The template consists of type keys and counts. The types are summarized in Table 4–4. In the table, *count* is the optional count following the type letter.

Table 4–4 Binary conversion types.

`a`	A character string of length *count*. Padded with nulls in `binary format`.
`A`	A character string of length *count*. Padded with spaces in `binary format`. Trailing nulls and blanks are discarded in `binary scan`.
`b`	A binary string of length *count*. Low-to-high order.
`B`	A binary string of length *count*. High-to-low order.
`h`	A hexadecimal string of length *count*. Low-to-high order.
`H`	A hexadecimal string of length *count*. High-to-low order.
`c`	An 8-bit character code. The *count* is for repetition.
`s`	A 16-bit integer in little-endian byte order. The *count* is for repetition.
`S`	A 16-bit integer in big-endian byte order. The *count* is for repetition.
`i`	A 32-bit integer in little-endian byte order. The *count* is for repetition.
`I`	A 32-bit integer in big-endian byte order. The *count* is for repetition.
`f`	Single-precision floating point value in native format. *count* is for repetition.
`d`	Double-precision floating point value in native format. *count* is for repetition.
`x`	Pack *count* null bytes with `binary format`. Skip *count* bytes with `binary scan`.
`X`	Backup *count* bytes.
`@`	Skip to absolute position specified by *count*. If *count* is `*`, skip to the end.

The count is interpreted differently depending on the type. For types like integer (`i`) and double (`d`), the count is a repetition count (e.g., `i3` means three integers). For strings, the count is a length (e.g., `a3` means a three character string). If no count is specified, it defaults to 1. If count is `*`, then `binary scan` uses all the remaining bytes in the value.

Several type keys can be specified in a template. Each key-count combination moves an imaginary cursor through the binary data. There are special type keys to move the cursor. The x key generates null bytes in binary format and it skips over bytes in binary scan. The @ key uses its *count* as an absolute byte offset to which to set the cursor. As a special case, @* skips to the end of the data. The X key backs up *count* bytes.

Numeric types have a particular byte order that determines how their value is laid out in memory. The type keys are lowercase for little-endian byte order (e.g., Intel) and uppercase for big-endian byte order (e.g., SPARC and Motorola). Different integer sizes are 16-bit (s or S), 32-bit (i or I), and possibly 64-bit (l or L) on those machines that support it. Note that the official byte order for data transmitted over a network is big-endian. Floating point values are always machine-specific so it only makes sense to format and scan these values on the same machine.

There are three string types: character (a or A), binary (b or B), and hexadecimal (h or H). With these types the *count* is the length of the string. The a type pads its value to the specified length with null bytes in binary format and the A type pads its value with spaces. If the value is too long, it is truncated. In binary scan, the A type strips trailing blanks and nulls.

A binary string consists of zeros and ones. The b type specifies bits from low-to-high order and the B type specifies bits from high-to-low order. A hexadecimal string specifies 4 bits (i.e., nybbles) with each character. The h type specifies nybbles from low-to-high order and the H type specifies nybbles from high-to-low order. The B and H formats match the way you normally write out numbers.

Examples

When you experiment with binary format and binary scan, remember that Tcl treats things as strings by default. A "6", for example, is the letter 6 with character code 54 or 0x36. The c type returns these character codes:

```
binary scan 6 c 6val
set 6val
=> 54
```

You can scan several character codes at a time:

```
binary scan abc c3 aval bval cval
```

Use the H format to get hexadecimal values:

```
binary scan 6 H2 6val
set 6val
=> 36
```

Use the a and A formats to extract fixed width fields. Here the * count is used to get all the rest of the string. Note that A trims trailing spaces:

```
binary scan "hello world " a3x2A* first second
puts "\"$first\" \"$second\""
=> "hel" " world"
```

Use the @ key to seek to a particular offset in a value. This command gets the second double-precision number from a vector. Assume the vector is read from a binary data file:

```
binary scan $value "@8d" double
```

With `binary format`, the `a` and `A` types create fixed width fields. `A` pads its field with spaces, if necessary. The value is truncated if the string is too long:

```
binary format "A9A3" hello world
=> hello    wor
```

An array of floating point values can be created with this command:

```
binary format "f*" 1.2 3.45 7.43 -45.67 1.03e4
```

Remember that floating point values are always in native format so you have to read them on the same type of machine that they were created. With integer data you specify either big-endian or little-endian formats. The `tcl_platform` variable described on page 153 can tell you the byte order of the current platform.

Related Chapters

- To learn more about manipulating data in Tcl, read Chapter 5 on lists and Chapter 8 on arrays.
- For more about pattern matching, read Chapter 11 on regular expressions.

CHAPTER 5

Tcl Lists

This chapter describes Tcl lists. Tcl commands described: `list`, `lindex`, `llength`, `lrange`, `lappend`, `linsert`, `lreplace`, `lsearch`, `lsort`, `concat`, `join`, and `split`.

Lists in Tcl have the same structure as Tcl commands. All the rules you learned about grouping arguments in Chapter 1 apply to creating valid Tcl lists. However, when you work with Tcl lists, it is best to think of lists in terms of operations instead of syntax. Tcl commands provide operations to put values into a list, get elements from lists, count the elements of lists, replace elements of lists, and so on. The syntax can sometimes be confusing, especially when you have to group arguments to the list commands themselves.

Lists are used with commands such as `foreach` that take lists as arguments. In addition, lists are important when you are building up a command to be evaluated later. Delayed command evaluation with `eval` is described in Chapter 10, and similar issues with Tk callback commands are described in Chapter 24.

However, Tcl lists are not that great for building complicated data structures in Tcl. Use arrays instead, which are the topic of Chapter 8. List operations are also not right for handling unstructured data such as user input. Use regular expressions instead, which are described in Chapter 11.

Tcl Lists

A Tcl list has the same structure as a Tcl command. A list is simply a string with list elements separated by white space. Braces or quotes can be used to group words with white space into a single list element. Because of the relationship between lists and commands, the list-related commands described in this chapter are used often when constructing Tcl commands.

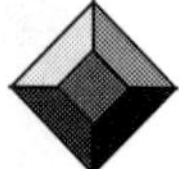

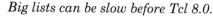

Big lists can be slow before Tcl 8.0.

Unlike list data structures in other languages, Tcl lists are just strings with a special interpretation. The string representation must be parsed on each list access, so be careful when you use large lists. A list with a few elements will not slow down your code much. A list with hundreds or thousands of elements can be very slow. If you find yourself maintaining large lists that must be frequently accessed, consider changing your code to use arrays instead.

The performance of lists is improved by the Tcl compiler in Tcl 8.0. They are stored in an internal format that requires constant time to access. Accessing the first element costs the same as accessing any other element in the list. Before Tcl 8.0, the cost of accessing an element is proportional to the number of elements before it in the list. The internal format also records the number of list elements, so getting the length of a list is cheap. Before Tcl 8.0, computing the length required reading the whole list.

Table 5–1 briefly describes the Tcl commands related to lists.

Table 5–1 List-related commands.

`list` *`arg1 arg2`* `...`	Creates a list out of all its arguments.
`lindex` *`list i`*	Returns the *`i`*th element from *`list`*.
`llength` *`list`*	Returns the number of elements in *`list`*.
`lrange` *`list i j`*	Returns the *`i`*th through *`j`*th elements from *`list`*.
`lappend` *`listVar arg arg`* ...	Append elements to the value of *`listVar`*.
`linsert` *`list index arg arg`* ...	Insert elements into *`list`* before the element at position *`index`*. Returns a new list.
`lreplace` *`list i j arg arg`* `...`	Replace elements *`i`* through *`j`* of *`list`* with the *`args`*. Returns a new list.
`lsearch ?`*`mode`*`?` *`list value`*	Return the index of the element in *`list`* that matches the *`value`* according to the *`mode`*, which is `-exact`, `-glob`, or `-regexp`. `-glob` is the default. Return -1 if not found.
`lsort ?`*`switches`*`?` *`list`*	Sort elements of the list according to the switches: `-ascii`, `-integer`, `-real`, `-dictionary`, `-increasing`, `-decreasing`, `-index` *`ix`*, `-command` *`command`*. Returns a new list.
`concat` *`list list list`* `...`	Join multiple lists together into one list.
`join` *`list joinString`*	Merge the elements of a list together by separating them with *`joinString`*.
`split` *`string splitChars`*	Split a string up into list elements, using the characters in *`splitChars`* as boundaries between list elements.

Constructing Lists

Constructing a list can be tricky because you must maintain proper list syntax. In simple cases you can do this by hand. In more complex cases, however, you should use Tcl commands that take care of quoting so the syntax comes out right.

The `list` command

The `list` command constructs a list out of its arguments so that there is one list element for each argument. If any of the arguments contain special characters, the `list` command adds quoting to ensure they are parsed as a single element of the resulting list. The automatic quoting is very useful, and the examples in this book use the `list` command frequently. The next example uses `list` to create a list with three values, two of which contain special characters.

Example 5–1 Constructing a list with the `list` command.

```
set x {1 2}
=> 1 2
set y foo
=> foo
set l1 [list $x "a b" $y]
=> {1 2} {a b} foo
set l2 "\{$x\} {a b} $y"
=> {1 2} {a b} foo
```

The `list` command does automatic quoting.

Compare the use of `list` with doing the quoting by hand in Example 5–1. The assignment of `l2` requires carefully constructing the first list element by using quoted braces. The braces have to be turned off so `$x` can be substituted, but we need to group the result so it remains a single list element. We also have to know in advance that `$x` contains a space so that quoting is required. We are taking a risk by not quoting `$y` because we know it doesn't contain spaces. If its value changes in the future, the structure of the list can change and even become invalid. In contrast, when you use the `list` command it takes care of all these details automatically.

When I first experimented with Tcl lists, I got confused by the treatment of curly braces. In the assignment to `x`, for example, the curly braces disappear. However, they come back again when `$x` is put into a bigger list. Also, the double quotes around `a b` get changed into curly braces. What's going on? Remember there are two steps. In the first step, the Tcl parser groups arguments. In the grouping process the braces and quotes are syntax that define groups. These syntax characters get stripped off. The braces and quotes are not part of the value. In the second step the `list` command creates a valid Tcl list. This may require quoting to get the list elements into the right groups. The `list` command uses curly braces to group values back into list elements.

The lappend Command

The lappend command is used to append elements to the end of a list. The first argument to lappend is the name of a Tcl variable, and the rest of the arguments are added to the variable's value as new list elements. Like list, lappend preserves the structure of its arguments. It may add braces to group the values of its arguments so they retain their identity as list elements when they are appended onto the string representation of the list.

Example 5–2 Using lappend to add elements to a list.

```
lappend new 1 2
=> 1 2
lappend new 3 "4 5"
=> 1 2 3 {4 5}
set new
=> 1 2 3 {4 5}
```

The lappend command is unique among the list-related commands because its first argument is the name of a list-valued variable, while all the other commands take list values as arguments. You can call lappend with the name of an undefined variable and the variable will be created.

The lappend command is implemented efficiently to take advantage of the way that Tcl stores lists internally. It is always more efficient to use lappend than to try and append elements by hand.

The concat Command

The concat command is useful for splicing lists together. It works by concatenating its arguments, separating them with spaces. This joins multiple lists into one list where the top-level list elements in each input list become top-level list elements in the resulting list:

Example 5–3 Using concat to splice lists together.

```
set x {4 5 6}
set y {2 3}
set z 1
concat $z $y $x
=> 1 2 3 4 5 6
```

Double quotes behave much like the concat command. Example 5–4 compares the use of list, concat, and double quotes:

Example 5–4 Double quotes compared to the list command.

```
set x {1 2}
=> 1 2
```

```
set y "$x 3"
=> 1 2 3
set y [concat $x 3]
=> 1 2 3
set z [list $x 3]
=> {1 2} 3
```

The distinction between `list` and `concat` becomes important when Tcl commands are built dynamically. The basic rule is that `list` and `lappend` preserve list structure, while `concat` (or double quotes) eliminate one level of list structure. The distinction can be subtle because there are examples where `list` and `concat` return the same results. Unfortunately, this can lead to data-dependent bugs. Throughout the examples of this book you will see the `list` command used to safely construct lists. This issue is discussed more in Chapter 10.

Getting List Elements: llength, lindex, and lrange

The `llength` command returns the number of elements in a list.

```
llength {a b {c d} "e f g" h}
=> 5
llength {}
=> 0
```

The `lindex` command returns a particular element of a list. It takes an index; list indices count from zero. You can use the keyword `end` to specify the last element of a list.

```
set x {1 2 3}
lindex $x 1
=> 2
```

The `lrange` command returns a range of list elements. It takes a list and two indices as arguments.

```
lrange {1 2 3 {4 5}} 2 end
=> 3 {4 5}
```

Modifying Lists: linsert and lreplace

The `linsert` command inserts elements into a list value at a specified index. If the index is zero or less, then the elements are added to the front. If the index is equal to or greater than the length of the list, then the elements are appended to the end. Otherwise, the elements are inserted before the element that is currently at the specified index.

`lreplace` replaces a range of list elements with new elements. If you don't specify any new elements, you effectively delete elements from a list.

Note: `linsert` and `lreplace` do not modify an existing list. Instead, they return a new list value. In the following example, the `lreplace` command does not change the value of `x`:

Example 5–5 Modifying lists with `linsert` and `lreplace`.

```
linsert {1 2} 0 new stuff
=> new stuff 1 2
set x [list a {b c} e d]
=> a {b c} e d
lreplace $x 1 2 B C
=> a B C d
lreplace $x 0 0
=> {b c} e d
```

Searching Lists: `lsearch`

`lsearch` returns the index of a value in the list, or -1 if it is not present. `lsearch` supports pattern matching in its search. Glob-style pattern matching is the default, and this can be disabled with the `-exact` flag. The semantics of glob pattern matching is described on page 48 in Chapter 4. The `-regexp` option lets you specify the list value with a regular expression. Regular expressions are described in Chapter 11 starting on page 122. In the following example, the glob pattern `l*` matches the value `list`.

```
lsearch {here is a list} l*
=> 3
```

Example 5–6 uses `lreplace` and `lsearch` to delete a list element by value. The value is found with `lsearch`. The value is removed with an `lreplace` that does not specify any replacement list elements:

Example 5–6 Deleting a list element by value.

```
proc ldelete { list value } {
    set ix [lsearch -exact $list $value]
    if {$ix >= 0} {
        return [lreplace $list $ix $ix]
    } else {
        return $list
    }
}
```

Sorting Lists: `lsort`

You can sort a list in a variety of ways with `lsort`. The list is not sorted in place. Instead, a new list value is returned. The basic types of sorts are specified with the `-ascii`, `-dictionary`, `-integer`, or `-real` options. The `-increasing` or

-decreasing option indicate the sorting order. The default option set is -ascii -increasing. An ascii sort uses character codes, and a dictionary sort folds together case and treats digits like numbers. For example:

```
lsort -ascii {a Z n2 n100}
=> Z a n100 n2
lsort -dictionary {a Z n2 n100}
=> a n2 n100 Z
```

You can provide your own sorting function for special-purpose sorting. For example, suppose you have a list of names, where each element is itself a list containing the person's first name, middle name (if any), and last name. The default sorts by everyone's first name. If you want to sort by their last name, you need to supply a sorting command.

Example 5–7 Sorting a list using a comparison function.

```
proc NameCompare {a b} {
    set alast [lindex $a end]
    set blast [lindex $b end]
    set res [string compare $alast $blast]
    if {$res != 0} {
        return $res
    } else {
        return [string compare $a $b]
    }
}
set list {{Brent B. Welch} {John Ousterhout} {Miles Davis}}
=> {Brent B. Welch} {John Ousterhout} {Miles Davis}
lsort -command NameCompare $list
=> {Miles Davis} {John Ousterhout} {Brent B. Welch}
```

The NameCompare procedure extracts the last element from each of its arguments and compares those. If they are equal, then it just compares the whole of each argument.

Tcl 8.0 adds a -index option to lsort that can be used to sort lists on an index. Instead of using NameCompare, you could do this:

```
lsort -index end $list
```

The split Command

The split command takes a string and turns it into a list by breaking it at specified characters and ensuring that the result has the proper list syntax. The split command provides a robust way to turn input lines into proper Tcl lists:

```
set line {welch:*:28405:100:Brent Welch:/usr/welch:/bin/csh}
split $line :
=> welch * 28405 100 {Brent Welch} /usr/welch /bin/csh
lindex [split $line :] 4
=> Brent Welch
```

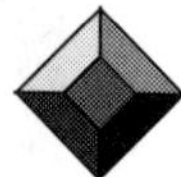

Do not use list operations on arbitrary data.

Even if your data has space-separated words, you should be careful when using list operators on arbitrary input data. Otherwise, stray double quotes or curly braces in the input can result in invalid list structure and errors in your script. The next example shows what happens when input is not a valid list. The syntax error, an unmatched quote, occurs in the middle of the list. You can get away with accessing the beginning of the list as a list, but run into an error if Tcl has to parse the whole line as a list. With the compiler in Tcl 8.0, the error in the data will be found with the first attempt to use it as a list.

Example 5–8 Use `split` to turn input data into Tcl lists.

```
set line {this is "not a tcl list}
lindex $line 1
=> is
lindex $line 2
=> unmatched open quote in list
lindex [split $line] 2
=> "not
```

The default separator character for `split` is white space, which is spaces, tabs, and newlines. If there are multiple separator characters in a row, these result in empty list elements; the separators are not collapsed. The following command splits on commas, periods, spaces, and tabs. The backslash-space sequence is used to include a space in the set of characters. You could also group the argument to `split` with double quotes:

```
set line "\tHello, world."
split $line \ ,.\t
=> {} Hello {} world {}
```

A trick that splits each character into a list element is to specify an empty string as the split character. This lets you get at individual characters with list operations:

```
split abc {}
=> a b c
```

However, if you write scripts that process data a character at a time it may be pretty slow. Read Chapter 11 about regular expressions for hints on really efficient string processing.

The `join` Command

The `join` command is the inverse of `split`. It takes a list value and reformats it with specified characters separating the list elements. In doing so, it removes any curly braces from the string representation of the list that are used to group the top-level elements. For example:

```
join {1 {2 3} {4 5 6}} :
=> 1:2 3:4 5 6
```

If the treatment of braces is puzzling, you can think of `join` in terms of this implementation;

Example 5–9 Implementing `join` in Tcl.

```
proc join {list sep} {
    set s {}  ;# s is the current separator
    set result {}
    foreach x $list {
        append result $s $x
        set s $sep
    }
    return $result
}
```

Related Chapters

- Arrays are the other main data structure in Tcl. They are described in Chapter 8.
- List operations are used when generating Tcl code dynamically. Chapter 10 describes these techniques when using the `eval` command.
- The `foreach` command loops over the values in a list. It is described on page 67 in Chapter 6.

CHAPTER 6

Control Structure Commands

This chapter describes the Tcl commands that implement control structures: `if`, `switch`, `foreach`, `while`, `for`, `break`, `continue`, `catch`, `error`, and `return`.

Control structure in Tcl is achieved with commands, just like everything else. There are looping commands: `while`, `foreach`, and `for`. There are conditional commands: `if` and `switch`. There is an error handling command: `catch`. Finally, there are some commands to fine-tune control structures: `break`, `continue`, `return`, and `error`.

A control structure command often has a command body that is executed later, either conditionally or in a loop. In this case, it is important to group the command body with curly braces to avoid substitutions at the time the control structure command is invoked. Group with braces, and let the control structure command trigger evaluation at the proper time. A control structure command returns the value of the last command it chose to execute.

Another pleasant property of curly braces is that they group things together while including newlines. The examples use braces in a way that is both readable and convenient for extending the control structure commands across multiple lines.

Commands like `if`, `for`, and `while` involve boolean expressions. They use the `expr` command internally, so there is no need for you to invoke `expr` explicitly to evaluate their boolean test expressions.

If Then Else

The `if` command is the basic conditional command. If an expression is true then execute one command body; otherwise execute another command body. The second command body (the `else` clause) is optional. The syntax of the command is:

```
if boolean ?then? body1 ?else? ?body2?
```

The `then` and `else` keywords are optional. In practice, I omit `then`, but use `else` as illustrated in the next example. I always use braces around the command bodies, even in the simplest cases:

Example 6–1 A conditional `if then else` command.

```
if {$x == 0} {
   puts stderr "Divide by zero!"
} else {
   set slope [expr $y/$x]
}
```

Curly brace positioning is important.

The style of this example takes advantage of the way the Tcl interpreter parses commands. Recall that newlines are command terminators, except when the interpreter is in the middle of a group defined by braces or double quotes. The stylized placement of the opening curly brace at the end of the first and third line exploits this property to extend the `if` command over multiple lines.

The first argument to `if` is a boolean expression. As a matter of style this expression is grouped with curly braces. The expression evaluator performs variable and command substitution on the expression. Using curly braces ensures that these substitutions are performed at the proper time. It is possible to be lax in this regard, with constructs such as:

```
if $x break continue
```

This is a sloppy, albeit legitimate, `if` command that will either break out of a loop or continue with the next iteration depending on the value of variable `x`. This style is fragile and error prone. Instead, always use braces around the command bodies to avoid trouble later when you modify the command. It also improves the readability of your code. The following is much better (use `then` if it suites your taste):

```
if {$x} {
     break
} else {
     continue
}
```

You can create chained conditionals by using the `elseif` keyword. Again, note the careful placement of curly braces that create a single `if` command:

Example 6–2 Chained conditional with `elseif`.

```
if {$key < 0} {
   incr range 1
} elseif {$key == 0} {
   return $range
} else {
   incr range -1
}
```

Any number of conditionals can be chained in this manner. However, the `switch` command provides a more powerful way to test multiple conditions.

Switch

The `switch` command is used to branch to one of many command bodies depending on the value of an expression. The choice can be made on the basis of pattern matching as well as simple comparisons. Pattern matching is discussed in more detail in Chapter 4 and Chapter 11. The general form of the command is:

`switch` *`flags value pat1 body1 pat2 body2`* `...`

Any number of pattern-body pairs can be specified. If multiple patterns match, only the body of the first matching pattern is evaluated. You can also group all the pattern-body pairs into one argument:

`switch` *`flags value`* `{` *`pat1 body1 pat2 body2`* `... }`

The first form allows substitutions on the patterns but will require backslashes to continue the command onto multiple lines. This is shown in Example 6–4 on page 66. The second form groups all the patterns and bodies into one argument. This makes it easy to group the whole command without worrying about newlines, but it suppresses any substitutions on the patterns. This is shown in Example 6–3. In either case, you should always group the command bodies with curly braces so that substitution occurs only on the body with the pattern that matches the value.

There are four possible flags that determine how *`value`* is matched.

`-exact`	Match the *`value`* exactly to one of the patterns. This is the default.
`-glob`	Use glob-style pattern matching. See page 48.
`-regexp`	Use regular expression pattern matching. See page 122.
`--`	No flag (or end of flags). Necessary when *`value`* can begin with `-`.

The `switch` command raises an error if any other flag is specified or if the *`value`* begins with `-`. In practice I always use the `--` flag before *`value`* so I don't have to worry about that problem.

If the pattern associated with the last body is `default`, then this command body is executed if no other patterns match. The `default` keyword only works on the last pattern-body pair. If you use the `default` pattern on an earlier body, it will be treated as a pattern to match the literal string `default`:

Example 6–3 Using `switch` for an exact match.

```
switch -exact -- $value {
    foo { doFoo; incr count(foo) }
    bar { doBar; return $count(foo)}
    default { incr count(other) }
}
```

If you have variable references or backslash sequences in the patterns, then you cannot use braces around all the pattern-body pairs. You must use backslashes to escape the newlines in the command:

Example 6–4 Using `switch` with substitutions in the patterns.

```
switch -regexp -- $value \
    ^$key { body1 }\
    \t### { body2 }\
    {[0-9]*} { body3 }
```

In this example the first and second patterns have substitutions performed to replace `$key` with its value and `\t` with a tab character. The third pattern is quoted with curly braces to prevent command substitution; square brackets are part of the regular expression syntax, too. (See page 122.)

If the body associated with a pattern is just a dash, `-`, then the `switch` command "falls through" to the body associated with the next pattern. You can tie together any number of patterns in this manner.

Example 6–5 A `switch` with "fall through" cases.

```
switch -glob -- $value {
    X* -
    Y* { takeXorYaction $value }
}
```

Comments in `switch` Commands

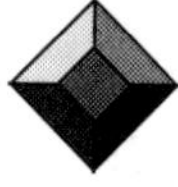

A comment can only occur where the Tcl parser expects a command to begin. This restricts the location of comments in a `switch` command. You must put them inside the command body associated with a pattern. If you put a comment at the same level as the patterns, the `switch` command will try to interpret the comment as one or more pattern-body pairs. The following example is incorrect:

Example 6–6 Comments in switch commands.

```
switch -- $value {
   # this comment confuses switch
   pattern { # this comment is ok }
}
```

While

The while command takes two arguments, a test and a command body:

```
while booleanExpr body
```

The while command repeatedly tests the boolean expression and then executes the body if the expression is true (non-zero). Because the test expression is evaluated again before each iteration of the loop, it is crucial to protect the expression from any substitutions before the while command is invoked. The following is an infinite loop (see also Example 1–12 on page 11):

```
set i 0 ; while $i<10 {incr i}
```

The following behaves as expected:

```
set i 0 ; while {$i<10} {incr i}
```

It is also possible to put nested commands in the boolean expression. The following example uses gets to read standard input. The gets command returns the number of characters read, returning -1 upon end of file. Each time through the loop the variable line contains the next line in the file:

Example 6–7 A while loop to read standard input.

```
set numLines 0 ; set numChars 0
while {[gets stdin line] >= 0} {
   incr numLines
   incr numChars [string length $line]
}
```

Foreach

The foreach command loops over a command body assigning one or more loop variables to each of the values in one or more lists. Multiple loop variables were introduced in Tcl 7.5. The syntax for the simple case of a single variable and a single list is:

```
foreach loopVar valueList commandBody
```

The first argument is the name of a variable, and the command body is executed once for each element in the list with the loop variable taking on successive values in the list. The list can be entered explicitly, as in the next example:

Example 6–8 Looping with `foreach`.

```
set i 1
foreach value {1 3 5 7 11 13 17 19 23} {
    set i [expr $i*$value]
}
set i
=> 111546435
```

It is also common to use a list-valued variable or command result instead of a static list value. The next example loops through command-line arguments. The variable `argv` is set by the Tcl interpreter to be a list of the command-line arguments given when the interpreter was started:

Example 6–9 Parsing command-line arguments.

```
# argv is set by the Tcl shells
# possible flags are:
# -max integer
# -force
# -verbose
set state flag
set force 0
set verbose 0
set max 10
foreach arg $argv {
    switch -- $state {
        flag {
            switch -glob -- $arg {
                -f*    {set force 1}
                -v*    {set verbose 1}
                -max   {set state max}
                default {error "unknown flag $arg"}
            }
        }
        max {
            set max $arg
            set state flag
        }
    }
}
```

The loop uses the `state` variable to keep track of what is expected next, which in this example is either a flag or the integer value for `-max`. The `--` flag to `switch` is *required* in this example because the `switch` command complains about a bad flag if the pattern begins with a `-` character. The `-glob` option lets the user abbreviate the `-force` and `-verbose` options.

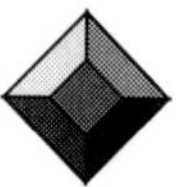

If the list of values is to contain variable values or command results, then the `list` command should be used to form the list. Avoid double quotes because if any values or command results contain spaces or braces, the list structure will be reparsed, which can lead to errors or unexpected results.

Example 6–10 Using `list` with `foreach`.

```
foreach x [list $a $b [foo]] {
   puts stdout "x = $x"
}
```

The loop variable `x` will take on the value of `a`, the value of `b`, and the result of the `foo` command, regardless of any special characters or whitespace in those values.

Multiple Loop Variables

You can have more than one loop variable with `foreach`. Suppose you have two loop variables, `x` and `y`. In the first iteration of the loop `x` gets the first value from the value list, and `y` gets the second value. In the second iteration, `x` gets the third value and `y` gets the fourth value. This continues until there are no more values. If there are not enough values to assign to all the loop variables, the extra variables get the empty string as their value.

Example 6–11 Multiple loop variables with `foreach`.

```
foreach {key value} {orange 55 blue 72 red 24 green} {
   puts "$key: $value"
}
orange: 55
blue: 72
red: 24
green:
```

If you have a command that returns a short list of values, then you can abuse the `foreach` command to assign the results of the commands to several variables all at once. For example, suppose the command `MinMax` returns two values: the minimum and maximum values in a list. Here is one way to get the values:

```
set result [MinMax $list]
set min [lindex $result 0]
set max [lindex $result 1]
```

The `foreach` command lets us do this much more compactly:

```
foreach {min max} [MinMax $list] {break}
```

The `break` in the body of the `foreach` loop guards against the case where the command returns more values than we expected. This trick is encapsulated into the `lassign` procedure in Example 10–3 on page 119.

Multiple Value Lists

The `foreach` command has the ability to loop over multiple value lists in parallel. In this case each value list can also have one or more variables. The `foreach` command keeps iterating until all values are used from all value lists. If a value list runs out of values before the last iteration of the loop, its corresponding loop variables just get the empty string for their value.

Example 6–12 Multiple value lists with `foreach`.

```
foreach {k1 k2} {orange blue red green black} value {55 72 24} {
    puts "$k1 $k2: $value"
}
orange blue: 55
red green: 72
black : 24
```

For

The `for` command is similar to the C `for` statement. It takes four arguments:

```
for initial test final body
```

The first argument is a command to initialize the loop. The second argument is a boolean expression that determines if the loop body will execute. The third argument is a command to execute after the loop body:

Example 6–13 A `for` loop.

```
for {set i 0} {$i < 10} {incr i 3} {
    lappend aList $i
}
set aList
=> 0 3 6 9
```

You could use `for` to iterate over a list, but you should really use `foreach` instead. Code like the following is slow and cluttered:

```
for {set i 0} {$i < [llength $list]} {incr i} {
    set value [lindex $list $i]
}
```

This is the same as:

```
foreach value $list {
}
```

Break and Continue

You can control loop execution with the `break` and `continue` commands. The `break` command causes immediate exit from a loop, while the `continue` command causes the loop to continue with the next iteration. There is no `goto` command in Tcl.

Catch

Until now we have ignored the possibility of errors. In practice, however, a command will raise an error if it is called with the wrong number of arguments, or if it detects some error condition particular to its implementation. An uncaught error aborts execution of a script.* The `catch` command is used to trap such errors. It takes two arguments:

```
catch command ?resultVar?
```

The first argument to `catch` is a command body. The second argument is the name of a variable that will contain the result of the command, or an error message if the command raises an error. `catch` returns zero if there was no error caught, or a non-zero error code if it did catch an error.

You should use curly braces to group the command instead of double quotes because `catch` invokes the full Tcl interpreter on the command. If double quotes are used, an extra round of substitutions occurs before `catch` is even called. The simplest use of `catch` looks like the following:

```
catch { command }
```

A more careful `catch` phrase saves the result and prints an error message:

Example 6–14 A standard `catch` phrase.

```
if [catch { command arg1 arg2 ... } result] {
   puts stderr $result
} else {
   # command was ok, result contains the return value
}
```

A more general `catch` phrase is shown in the next example. Multiple commands are grouped into a command body. The `errorInfo` variable is set by the Tcl interpreter after an error to reflect the stack trace from the point of the error:

* More precisely, the Tcl script unwinds and the current `Tcl_Eval` procedure in the C runtime library returns `TCL_ERROR`. There are three cases. In interactive use, the Tcl shell prints the error message. In Tk, errors that arise during event handling trigger a call to `bgerror`, a Tcl procedure you can implement in your application. In your own C code you should check the result of `Tcl_Eval` and take appropriate action in the case of an error.

Example 6–15 A longer `catch` phrase.

```
if [catch {
    command1
    command2
    command3
} result] {
    global errorInfo
    puts stderr $result
    puts stderr "*** Tcl TRACE ***"
    puts stderr $errorInfo
} else {
    # command body ok, result of last command is in result
}
```

These examples have not grouped the call to `catch` with curly braces. This is acceptable because `catch` always returns an integer, so the `if` command will parse correctly. However, if we had used `while` instead of `if`, then curly braces would be necessary to ensure that the `catch` phrase was evaluated repeatedly.

Catching More Than Errors

The `catch` command catches more than just errors. If the command body contains `return`, `break`, or `continue` commands, these terminate the command body and are reflected by `catch` as non-zero return codes. You need to be aware of this if you try to isolate troublesome code with a `catch` phrase. An innocent looking `return` command will cause the `catch` to signal an apparent error. The next example uses `switch` to find out exactly what `catch` returns. Non-error cases are passed up to the surrounding code by invoking `return`, `break`, or `continue`:

Example 6–16 There are several possible return values from `catch`.

```
switch [catch {
    command1
    command2
    ...
} result] {
    0 {                    # Normal completion }
    1 {                    # Error case }
    2 { return $result    ;# return from procedure}
    3 { break             ;# break out of the loop}
    4 { continue          ;# continue loop}
    default {              # User-defined error codes }
}
```

Error

The `error` command raises an error condition that terminates a script unless it is trapped with the `catch` command. The command takes up to three arguments:

```
error message ?info? ?code?
```

The *message* becomes the error message stored in the result variable of the `catch` command.

If the *info* argument is provided, then the Tcl interpreter uses this to initialize the `errorInfo` global variable. That variable is used to collect a stack trace from the point of the error. If the *info* argument is not provided, then the `error` command itself is used to initialize the `errorInfo` trace.

Example 6–17 Raising an error.

```
proc foo {} {
   error bogus
}
foo
=> bogus
set errorInfo
=> bogus
   while executing
"error bogus"
   (procedure "foo" line 2)
   invoked from within
"foo"
```

In the previous example, the `error` command itself appears in the trace. One common use of the `info` argument is to preserve the `errorInfo` that is available after a `catch`. In the next example, the information from the original error is preserved:

Example 6–18 Preserving `errorInfo` when calling `error`.

```
if [catch {foo} result] {
   global errorInfo
   set savedInfo $errorInfo
   # Attempt to handle the error here, but cannot...
   error $result $savedInfo
}
```

The *code* argument specifies a concise, machine-readable description of the error. It is stored into the global `errorCode` variable. It defaults to `NONE`. Many of the file system commands return an `errorCode` that has three elements: `POSIX`, the error name (e.g., `ENOENT`), and the associated error message:

```
POSIX ENOENT {No such file or directory}
```

In addition, your application can define error codes of its own. Catch phrases could examine the code in the global `errorCode` variable and decide how to respond to the error.

Return

The `return` command is used to return from a procedure. It is needed if return is to occur before the end of the procedure body, or if a constant value needs to be returned. As a matter of style, I also use `return` at the end of a procedure, even though a procedure returns the value of the last command executed in the body.

Exceptional return conditions can be specified with some optional arguments to `return`. The complete syntax is:

```
return ?-code c? ?-errorinfo i? ?-errorcode ec? string
```

The `-code` option value is one of `ok`, `error`, `return`, `break`, `continue`, or an integer. `ok` is the default if `-code` is not specified.

The `-code error` option makes `return` behave much like the `error` command. The `-errorcode` option sets the global `errorCode` variable, and the `-errorinfo` option initializes the `errorInfo` global variable. When you use `return -code error` there is no `error` command in the stack trace. Compare Example 6–17 with Example 6–19:

Example 6–19 Raising an error with `return`.

```
proc bar {} {
    return -code error bogus
}
catch {bar} result
=> 1
set result
=> bogus
set errorInfo
=> bogus
    while executing
"bar"
```

The `return`, `break`, and `continue` code options take effect in the caller of the procedure doing the exceptional return. If `-code return` is specified, then the calling procedure returns. If `-code break` is specified, then the calling procedure breaks out of a loop, and if `-code continue` is specified, then the calling procedure continues to the next iteration of the loop. These `-code` options to `return` enable the construction of new control structures entirely in Tcl. The following example implements the `break` command with a Tcl procedure:

```
proc break {} {
    return -code break
}
```

CHAPTER 7

Procedures and Scope

Procedures encapsulate a set of commands, and they introduce a local scope for variables. Commands covered: `proc`, `global`, and `upvar`.

Procedures parameterize a commonly used sequence of commands. In addition, each procedure has a new local scope for variables. The scope of a variable is the range of commands over which it is defined. Originally Tcl had one global scope for shared variables, local scopes within procedures, and one global scope for procedures. Tcl 8.0 added *namespaces* that provide new scopes for procedures and global variables. For simple applications you can ignore namespaces and just use the global scope. Namespaces are described in Chapter 14.

The `proc` Command

A Tcl procedure is defined with the `proc` command. It takes three arguments:

```
proc name params body
```

The first argument is the procedure name, which is added to the set of commands understood by the Tcl interpreter. The name is case sensitive and can contain any characters. Procedure names do not conflict with variable names. The second argument is a list of parameter names. The last argument is the body of the procedure.

Once defined, a Tcl procedure is used just like any other Tcl command. When it is called, each argument is assigned to the corresponding parameter and the body is evaluated. The result of the procedure is the result returned by the last command in the body. The `return` command can be used to return a specific value.

Procedures can have default parameters so the caller can leave out some of the command arguments. A default parameter is specified with its name and default value, as shown in the next example:

Example 7–1 Default parameter values.

```
proc P2 {a {b 7} {c -2} } {
    expr $a / $b + $c
}
P2 6 3
=> 0
```

Here the procedure `P2` can be called with one, two, or three arguments. If it is called with only one argument, then the parameters `b` and `c` take on the values specified in the `proc` command. If two arguments are provided, then only `c` gets the default value, and the arguments are assigned to `a` and `b`. At least one argument and no more than three arguments can be passed to `P2`.

A procedure can take a variable number of arguments by specifying the `args` keyword as the last parameter. When the procedure is called, the `args` parameter is a list that contains all the remaining values:

Example 7–2 Variable number of arguments.

```
proc ArgTest {a {b foo} args} {
    foreach param {a b args} {
        puts stdout "\t$param = [set $param]"
    }
}
set x one
set y {two things}
set z \[special\$
ArgTest $x
=> a = one
    b = foo
    args =
ArgTest $y $z
=> a = two things
    b = [special$
    args =
ArgTest $x $y $z
=> a = one
    b = two things
    args = {[special$}
ArgTest $z $y $z $x
=> a = [special$
    b = two things
    args = {[special$} one
```

The effect of the list structure in `args` is illustrated by the treatment of variable `z` in Example 7–2. The value of `z` has special characters in it. When `$z` is passed as the value of parameter b, its value comes through to the procedure unchanged. When $z is part of the optional parameters, quoting is automatically added to create a valid Tcl list as the value of args. Example 10–2 on page 116 illustrates a technique that uses eval to undo the effect of the added list structure.

Changing Command Names with rename

The rename command changes the name of a command. There are two main uses for rename. The first is to augment an existing procedure. Before you redefine it with proc, rename the existing command:

```
rename foo foo.orig
```

From within the new implementation of foo you can invoke the original command as foo.orig. Existing users of foo will transparently use the new version.

The other thing you can do with rename is completely hide a command by renaming it to the empty string. For example, you might not want users to execute UNIX programs, so you could disable exec with the following command:

```
rename exec {}
```

Scope

By default there is a single, global scope for procedure names. This means you can use a procedure anywhere in your script. Variables defined outside any procedure are global variables. However, as described below, global variables are not automatically visible inside procedures. There is a different name space for variables and procedures, so you could have a procedure and a global variable with the same name without conflict. You can use the namespace facility described in Chapter 7 to manage procedures and global variables.

Each procedure has a local scope for variables. That is, variables introduced in the procedure only live for the duration of the procedure call. After the procedure returns, those variables are undefined. Variables defined outside the procedure are not visible to a procedure, unless the upvar or global scope commands are used. You can also use qualified names to name variables in a namespace scope. The global and upvar commands are described later in this chapter. Qualified names are described on page 167. If the same variable name exists in an outer scope, it is unaffected by the use of that variable name inside a procedure.

In Example 7–3, the variable a in the global scope is different than the parameter a to P1. Similarly, the global variable b is different than the variable b inside P1:

Example 7–3 Variable scope and Tcl procedures.

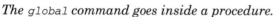

```
set a 5
set b -8
proc P1 {a} {
    set b 42
    if {$a < 0} {
        return $b
    } else {
        return $a
    }
}
P1 $b
=> 42
P1 [expr $a*2]
=> 10
```

The `global` Command

Global scope is the toplevel scope. This scope is outside of any procedure. Variables defined at the global scope must be made accessible to the commands inside a procedure by using the `global` command. The syntax for `global` is:

```
global varName1 varName2 ...
```

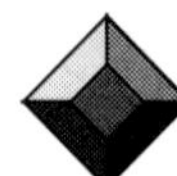

The `global` command goes inside a procedure.

The `global` command adds a global variable to the current scope. A common mistake is to have a single `global` command and expect that to apply to all procedures. However, a `global` command in the global scope has no effect. Instead, you must put a `global` command in all procedures that access the global variable. The variable can be undefined at the time the `global` command is used. When the variable is defined, it becomes visible in the global scope.

The following example shows a random number generator. The state has to persist between calls to `random`, so it is kept in a global variable. The choice of `randomSeed` as the name of the global variable associates it with the random number generator. It is important to pick names of global variables carefully to avoid conflict with other parts of your program. For comparison, Example 14–1 on page 166 uses namespaces to hide the state variable:

Example 7–4 A random number generator.*

```
proc RandomInit { seed } {
    global randomSeed
    set randomSeed $seed
}
proc Random {} {
```

* Adapted from *Exploring Expect* by Don Libes, O'Reilly & Associates, Inc., 1995, and from *Numerical Recipes in C* by Press et al., Cambridge University Press, 1988

```
    global randomSeed
    set randomSeed [expr ($randomSeed*9301 + 49297) % 233280]
    return [expr $randomSeed/double(233280)]
}
proc RandomRange { range } {
    expr int([Random]*$range)
}
RandomInit [pid]
=> 5049
Random
=> 0.517686899862825 79
Random
=> 0.217176783264746 24
RandomRange 100
=> 17
```

Call by Name Using upvar

Use the `upvar` command when you need to pass the name of a variable into a procedure, as opposed to its value. The `upvar` command associates a local variable with a variable in a scope up the Tcl call stack. The syntax of the `upvar` command is:

`upvar ?level? varName localvar`

The *level* argument is optional, and it defaults to 1, which means one level up the Tcl call stack. You can specify some other number of frames to go up, or you can specify an absolute frame number with a `#number` syntax. Level `#0` is the global scope, so the `global foo` command is equivalent to:

`upvar #0 foo foo`

The variable in the uplevel stack frame can be either a scalar variable, an array element, or an array name. In the first two cases, the local variable is treated like a scalar variable. In the case of an array name, then the local variable is treated like an array. The use of `upvar` and arrays is discussed further in Chapter 8 on page 86. The following procedure uses `upvar` to print the value of a variable given its name.

Example 7–5 Print variable by name.

```
proc PrintByName { varName } {
    upvar $varName var
    puts stdout "$varName = $var"
}
```

You can use `upvar` to fix the `incr` command. One drawback of the built-in `incr` is that it raises an error if the variable does not exist. We can define a new version of `incr` that initializes the variable if it does not already exist:

Example 7–6 Improved `incr` procedure.

```
proc incr { varName {amount 1}} {
    upvar $varName var
    if [info exists var] {
        set var [expr $var + $amount]
    } else {
        set var $amount
    }
    return $var
}
```

Variable Aliases with upvar

The `upvar` command is useful in any situation where you have the name of a variable stored in another variable. In Example 7–2 on page 76 the loop variable `param` holds the names of other variables. Their value is obtained with this construct:

```
puts stdout "\t$param = [set $param]"
```

Another way to do this is to use `upvar`. It eliminates the need to use awkward constructs like `[set $param]`. If the variable is in the same scope, use 0 as the scope number with `upvar`. The following is equivalent:

```
upvar 0 $param x
puts stdout "\t$param = $x"
```

Associating State with Data

Suppose you have a program that maintains state about a set of objects like files, URLs, or people. You can use the name of these objects as the name of a variable that keeps state about the object. The `upvar` command makes this more convenient:

```
upvar #0 $name state
```

Using the name directly like this is somewhat risky. If there were an object named `x`, then this trick might conflict with an unrelated variable named `x` elsewhere in your program. You can modify the name a bit to make this trick more robust:

```
upvar #0 state$name state
```

This approach reserves all variables with a name that begins with `state`. Your code can pass *name* around as a handle on an object, then use this `upvar` construct to get access to the data associated with the object. Your code is just written to use the `state` variable, which is an alias to the state variable for the current object. This technique is illustrated in Example 16–6 on page 192.

Commands That Take Variable Names

Several Tcl commands involve variable names. For example, the Tk widgets can be associated with a global Tcl variable. The `vwait` and `tkwait` commands also take variable names as arguments.

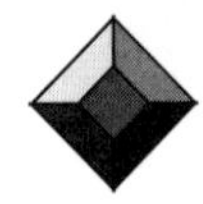

`Upvar` aliases do not work with text variables.

The aliases created with `upvar` do not work with these commands, nor do they work if you use `trace`, which is described on page 153. Instead, you must use the actual name of the global variable. To continue the above example where `state` is an alias, you cannot:

```
vwait state(foo)
button .b -textvariable state(foo)
```

Instead, you must

```
vwait state$name\(foo)
button .b -textvariable state$name\(foo)
```

The backslash turns off the array reference so Tcl does not try to access `name` as an array. You do not need to worry about special characters in `$name`, except parentheses. Once the name has been passed into the Tk widget it will be used directly as a variable name.

CHAPTER 8

Tcl Arrays

This chapter describes Tcl arrays, which provide a flexible mechanism to build many other data structures in Tcl. Tcl commands described: `array`.

An array is a Tcl variable with a string-valued index. You can think of the index as a key, and the array as a collection of related data items identified by different keys. The index, or key, can be any string value. Internally an array is implemented with a hash table, so the cost of accessing each array element is about the same. Before Tcl 8.0, arrays had a performance advantage over lists that took time to access proportional to the size of the list.

The flexibility of arrays makes them an important tool for the Tcl programmer. A common use of arrays is to manage a collection of variables, much as you use a C struct or Pascal record. This chapter shows how to create several simple data structures using Tcl arrays.

Array Syntax

The index of an array is delimited by parentheses. The index can have any string value, and it can be the result of variable or command substitution. Array elements are defined with `set`:

```
set arr(index) value
```

The value of an array element is obtained with `$` substitution:

```
set foo $arr(index)
```

Example 8–1 uses the loop variable value `$i` as an array index. It sets `arr(x)` to the product of `1 * 2 * ... * x`:

Example 8–1 Using arrays.

```
set arr(0) 1
for {set i 1} {$i <= 10} {incr i} {
   set arr($i) [expr $i * $arr([expr $i-1])]
}
```

Complex Indices

An array index can be any string, like `orange`, `5`, `3.1415`, or `foo,bar`. The examples in this chapter, and this book, often use indices that are pretty complex strings to create flexible data structures. As a rule of thumb, you can use any string for an index, but avoid using a string that contains spaces.

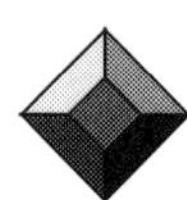

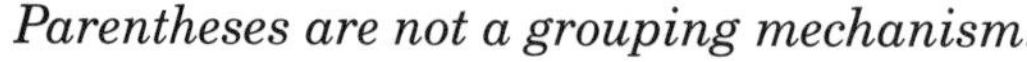

Parentheses are not a grouping mechanism.

The main Tcl parser does not know about array syntax. All the rules about grouping and substitution described in Chapter 1 are still the same in spite of the array syntax described here. Parentheses do not group like curly braces or quotes, which is why a space causes problems. If you have complex indices, use a comma to separate different parts of the index. If you use a space in an index instead, then you have a quoting problem. The space in the index needs to be quoted with a backslash, or the whole variable reference needs to be grouped:

```
set {arr(I'm asking for trouble)} {I told you so.}
set arr(I'm\ asking\ for\ trouble) {I told you so.}
```

If the array index is stored in a variable, then there is no problem with spaces in the variable's value. The following works well:

```
set index {I'm asking for trouble}
set arr($index) {I told you so.}
```

Array Variables

You can use an array element as you would a simple variable. For example, you can test for its existence with `info exists`, increment its value with `incr`, and append elements to it with `lappend`:

```
if [info exists stats($event)] {incr stats($event)}
```

You can delete an entire array, or just a single array element with `unset`. Using `unset` on an array is a convenient way to clear out a big data structure.

It is an error to use a variable as both an array and a normal variable. The following is an error:

```
set arr(0) 1
set arr 3
=> can't set "arr": variable is array
```

The name of the array can be the result of a substitution. This is a tricky situation as shown in Example 8–2:

Example 8–2 Referencing an array indirectly.

```
set name TheArray
=> TheArray
set ${name}(xyz) {some value}
=> some value
set x $TheArray(xyz)
=> some value
set x ${name}(xyz)
=> TheArray(xyz)
set x [set ${name}(xyz)]
=> some value
```

A better way to deal with this situation is to use the `upvar` command, which is introduced on page 79. The previous example is much cleaner when `upvar` is used:

Example 8–3 Referencing an array indirectly using `upvar`.

```
set name TheArray
=> TheArray
upvar 0 $name a
set a(xyz) {some value}
=> some value
set x $TheArray(xyz)
=> some value
```

The `array` Command

The `array` command returns information about array variables. The `array names` command returns the index names that are defined in the array. If the array variable is not defined, then `array names` just returns an empty list. It allows easy iteration through an array with a `foreach` loop:

```
foreach index [array names arr pattern] {
    # use arr($index)
}
```

The order of the names returned by `array names` is arbitrary. It is essentially determined by the hash table implementation of the array. You can limit what names are returned by specifying a *pattern* that matches indices. The pattern is the kind supported by the `string match` command, which is described on page 48.

It is also possible to iterate through the elements of an array one at a time using the search-related commands listed in Table 8–1. The ordering is also random, and in practice I find the `foreach` over the results of `array names` much more convenient. If your array has an extremely large number of elements, or if you need to manage an iteration over a long period of time, then the array search operations might be more appropriate. Table 8–1 summarizes the `array` command:

Table 8–1 The `array` command.

`array exists arr`	Returns 1 if *arr* is an array variable.
`array get arr ?pattern?`	Returns a list that alternates between an index and the corresponding array value. *pattern* selects matching indices. If not specified, all indices and values are returned.
`array names arr ?pattern?`	Return the list of all indices defined for *arr*, or those that match the string match *pattern*.
`array set arr list`	Initialize the array *arr* from *list*, which has the same form as the list returned by `array get`.
`array size arr`	Return the number of indices defined for *arr*.
`array startsearch arr`	Return a search token for a search through *arr*.
`array nextelement arr id`	Return the value of the next element in *array* in the search identified by the token *id*. Returns an empty string if no more elements remain in the search.
`array anymore arr id`	Returns 1 if more elements remain in the search.
`array donesearch arr id`	End the search identified by *id*.

Converting Arrays to Lists

The `array get` and `array set` operations are used to convert between an array and a list. The list returned by `array get` has an even number of elements. The first element is an index, and the next is the corresponding array value. The list elements continue to alternate between index and value. The list argument to `array set` must have the same structure.

```
set fruit(best) kiwi
set fruit(worst) peach
set fruit(ok) banana
array get fruit
=> ok banana best kiwi worst peach
```

Another way to loop through the contents of an array is to use `array get` and the two-variable form of the `foreach` command. This requires Tcl 7.5 or later.

```
foreach {key value} [array get fruit] {
    # key is ok, best, or worst
    # value is some fruit
}
```

Passing Arrays by Name

The `upvar` command works on arrays. You can pass an array name to a procedure and use the `upvar` command to get an indirect reference to the array variable in the caller's scope. This is illustrated in Example 8–4 that inverts an array. As with `array names`, you can specify a pattern to `array get` to limit what part of the array is returned. This example uses `upvar` because the array names are passed into the `ArrayInvert` procedure. The inverse array does not need to exist before you call `ArrayInvert`.

Example 8–4 `ArrayInvert` inverts an array.

```
proc ArrayInvert {arrName inverseName {pattern *}} {
    upvar $arrName array $inverseName inverse
    foreach {index value} [array get array $pattern] {
        set inverse($value) $index
    }
}
```

Building Data Structures with Arrays

This section describes several data structures you can build with Tcl arrays. These examples are presented as procedures that implement access functions to the data structure. Wrapping up your data structures in procedures is good practice. It shields the user of your data structure from the details of its implementation.

Use arrays to collect related variables.

A good use for arrays is to collect together a set of related variables for a module, much as one would use a record in other languages. By collecting these together in an array that has the same name as the module, name conflicts between different modules are avoided. Also, in each of the module's procedures, a single `global` statement will suffice to make all the state variables visible. You can also use `upvar` to manage a collection of arrays as shown in Example 8–8 on page 89.

Simple Records

Suppose we have a database of information about people. One approach uses a different array for each class of information. The name of the person is the index into each array:

Example 8–5 Using arrays for records, version 1.

```
proc Emp_AddRecord {id name manager phone} {
    global employeeID employeeManager \
        employeePhone employeeName
    set employeeID($name) $id
    set employeeManager($name) $manager
    set employeePhone($name) $phone
    set employeeName($id) $name
}
```

```
proc Emp_Manager {name} {
    global employeeManager
    return $employeeManager($name)
}
```

Simple procedures are defined to return fields of the record, which hides the implementation so you can change it more easily. The employeeName array provides a secondary key. It maps from the employee ID to the name so that the other information can be obtained if you have an ID instead of a name. Another way to implement the same little database is to use a single array with more complex indices:

Example 8–6 Using arrays for records, version 2.

```
proc Emp_AddRecord {id name manager phone} {
    global employee
    set employee(id,$name) $id
    set employee(manager,$name) $manager
    set employee(phone,$name) $phone
    set employee(name,$id) $name
}
proc Emp_Manager {name} {
    global employee
    return $employee(manager,$name)
}
```

The difference between these two approaches is partly a matter of taste. Using a single array can be more convenient because there are fewer variables to manage. In any case you should hide the implementation in a small set of procedures.

A Stack

A stack can be implemented with either a list or an array. If you use a list then the push and pop operations have a runtime cost that is proportional to the size of the stack. If the stack has a few elements this is fine. If there is lots of data in a stack, you may wish to use arrays instead. There is no real performance difference in Tcl 8.0.

In these examples the name of the stack is a parameter, and upvar is used to convert that into the data used for the stack. The variable is a list in Example 8–7 and an array in Example 8–8. The user of the stack module does not have to know.

Example 8–7 Using a list to implement a stack.

```
proc Push { stack value } {
    upvar $stack list
    lappend list $value
```

```
}
proc Pop { stack } {
	upvar $stack list
	set value [lindex $list end]
	set list [lrange $list 0 [expr [llength $list]-2]]
	return $value
}
```

The array implementation of a stack uses one array element to record the number of items in the stack. The other elements of the array have the stack values. The `Push` and `Pop` procedures both guard against a non-existent array with the `info exists` command. When the first assignment to `S(top)` is done by `Push`, the array variable is created in the caller's scope. The example uses array indices in two ways. The `top` index records the depth of the stack. The other indices are numbers, so the construct `$S($S(top))` is used to reference the top of the stack.

Example 8–8 Using an array to implement a stack.

```
proc Push { stack value } {
	upvar $stack S
	if ![info exists S(top)] {
		set S(top) 0
	}
	set S($S(top)) $value
	incr S(top)
}
proc Pop { stack } {
	upvar $stack S
	if ![info exists S(top)] {
		return {}
	}
	if {$S(top) == 0} {
		return {}
	} else {
		incr S(top) -1
		set x $S($S(top))
		unset S($S(top))
		return $x
	}
}
```

A List of Arrays

Suppose you have many arrays that each stores some data, and you want to maintain an overall ordering among the data sets. One approach is to keep a Tcl list with the name of each array in order. Example 8–9 defines `RecordInsert` to add an array to the list, and an iterator function, `RecordIterate`, that applies a script to each array in order. The iterator uses `upvar` to make `data` an alias for the current array. The script is executed with `eval`, which is described in detail in Chapter 10. The Tcl commands in `script` can reference the arrays with the name `data`:

Example 8–9 A list of arrays.

```
proc RecordAppend {listName arrayName} {
    upvar $listName list
    lappend list $arrayName
}
proc RecordIterate {listName script} {
    upvar $listName list
    foreach arrayName $list {
        upvar #0 $arrayName data
        eval $script
    }
}
```

Another way to implement this list-of-records structure is to keep references to the arrays that come before and after each record. Example 8–10 shows the insert function and the iterator function when using this approach. Once again, `upvar` is used to set up `data` as an alias for the current array in the iterator. In this case the loop is terminated by testing for the existence of the next array. It is perfectly OK to make an alias with `upvar` to a non-existent variable. It is also OK to change the target of the `upvar` alias. One detail that is missing from the example is the initialization of the very first record so that its `next` element is the empty string:

Example 8–10 A list of arrays.

```
proc RecordInsert {recName afterThis} {
    upvar $recName record $afterThis after
    set record(next) $after(next)
    set after(next) $recName
}
proc RecordIterate {firstRecord body} {
    upvar #0 $firstRecord data
    while {[info exists data]} {
        eval $body
        upvar #0 $data(next) data
    }
}
```

## CHAPTER 9

Working with Files and Programs

This chapter describes how to run programs, examine the file system, and access environment variables through the `env` array. Tcl commands: `exec`, `file`, `open`, `close`, `read`, `write`, `puts`, `gets`, `flush`, `seek`, `tell`, `glob`, `pwd`, `cd`, `exit`, and `pid`.

This chapter describes how to run programs and access the file system from Tcl. These commands were designed for UNIX. In Tcl 7.5 they were implemented in the Tcl ports to Windows and Macintosh. There are facilities for naming files and manipulating file names in a platform-independent way so you can write scripts that are portable across systems. These capabilities enable your Tcl script to be a general-purpose glue that assembles other programs into a tool that is customized for your needs.

Running Programs with exec

The `exec` command runs programs from your Tcl script.[*] For example:

```
set d [exec date]
```

The standard output of the program is returned as the value of the `exec` command. However, if the program writes to its standard error channel or exits with a non-zero status code, then `exec` raises an error. If you do not care about the exit status, or you use a program that insists on writing to standard error, then you can use `catch` to mask the errors:

```
catch {exec program arg arg} result
```

[*] Unlike other UNIX shell `exec` commands, the Tcl `exec` does not replace the current process with the new one. Instead, the Tcl library forks first and executes the program as a child process.

The `exec` command supports a full set of *I/O redirection* and *pipeline* syntax. Each process normally has three I/O channels associated with it: standard input, standard output, and standard error. With I/O redirection you can divert these I/O channels to files or to I/O channels you have opened with the Tcl `open` command. A pipeline is a chain of processes that have the standard output of one command hooked up to the standard input of the next command in the pipeline. Any number of programs can be linked together into a pipeline.

Example 9–1 Using `exec` on a process pipeline.

```
set n [exec sort < /etc/passwd | uniq | wc -l 2> /dev/null]
```

Example 9–1 uses `exec` to run three programs in a pipeline. The first program is `sort`, which takes its input from the file `/etc/passwd`. The output of `sort` is piped into `uniq`, which suppresses duplicate lines. The output of `uniq` is piped into `wc`, which counts the lines. The error output of the command is diverted to the null device to suppress any error messages.

Table 9–1 provides a summary of the syntax understood by the `exec` command.

Table 9–1 Summary of the `exec` syntax for I/O redirection.

`-keepnewline`	(First argument.) Do not discard trailing newline from the result.
`|`	Pipe standard output from one process into another.
`|&`	Pipe both standard output and standard error output.
`<` *`fileName`*	Take input from the named file.
`<@` *`fileId`*	Take input from the I/O channel identified by *`fileId`*.
`<<` *`value`*	Take input from the given *`value`*.
`>` *`fileName`*	Overwrite *`fileName`* with standard output.
`2>` *`fileName`*	Overwrite *`fileName`* with standard error output.
`>&` *`fileName`*	Overwrite *`fileName`* with both standard error and standard out.
`>>` *`fileName`*	Append standard output to the named file.
`2>>` *`fileName`*	Append standard error to the named file.
`>>&` *`fileName`*	Append both standard error and standard output to the named file.
`>@` *`fileId`*	Direct standard output to the I/O channel identified by *`fileId`*.
`2>@` *`fileId`*	Direct standard error to the I/O channel identified by *`fileId`*.
`>&@` *`fileId`*	Direct both standard error and standard output to the I/O channel.
`&`	As the last argument, indicates pipeline should run in background.

Note that a trailing `&` causes the program to run in the background. In this case the process identifier is returned by the `exec` command. Otherwise, the `exec` command blocks during execution of the program and the standard output of the program is the return value of `exec`. The trailing newline in the output is trimmed off, unless you specify `-keepnewline` as the first argument to `exec`.

If you look closely at the I/O redirection syntax, you'll see that it is built up from a few basic building blocks. The basic idea is that | stands for pipeline, > for output, and < for input. The standard error is joined to the standard output by `&`. Standard error is diverted separately by using `2>`. You can use your own I/O channels by using `@`.

The auto_noexec Variable

The Tcl shell programs are set up during interactive use to attempt to execute unknown Tcl commands as programs. For example, you can get a directory listing by typing:

```
ls
```

instead of:

```
exec ls
```

This is handy if you are using the Tcl interpreter as a general shell. It can also cause unexpected behavior when you are just playing around. To turn this off, define the `auto_noexec` variable:

```
set auto_noexec anything
```

Limitations of exec on Windows

Windows 3.1 has an unfortunate combination of special cases that stem from console-mode programs, 16-bit programs, and 32-bit programs. In addition, pipes are really just simulated by writing output from one process to a temporary file and then having the next process read from that file. If `exec` or a process pipeline fails it is because of a fundamental limitation of Windows. (In Tcl 7.5, there were still bugs in some cases, but those were fixed in Tcl 7.6.)

The good news is that Windows 95 and Windows NT clean up most of these problems. Windows NT 4.0 is the most robust.

Limitations of exec on Macintosh

The `exec` command is not provided on the Macintosh. The proper way to execute other programs is via AppleScript. Tcl 8.0 ships with an AppleScript extension that lets you control other Macintosh applications. As of this writing, the Tcl interface to the AppleScript extension is not finalized. You can find documentation at `http://sunscript.sun.com/mac/AppleScript.html`.

The `file` Command

The `file` command provides several ways to check the status of files in the file system. For example, you can find out if a file exists, what type of file it is, and other file attributes. There are facilities for manipulating files in a platform-independent manner. Table 9–2 provides a summary of the various forms of the `file` command. They are described in more detail later. Note that the `split`, `join`, and `pathtype` operations were added in Tcl 7.5. The `copy`, `delete`, `mkdir`, and `rename` operations were added in Tcl 7.6. The `attributes` operation was added in Tcl 8.0.

Table 9–2 The `file` command options.

`file atime` *name*	Return access time as a decimal string.
`file attributes` *name ?option? ?value?* ...	Query or set file attributes. (Tcl 8.0)
`file copy ?-force?` *source destination*	Copy file *source* to file *destination*. The *source* and *destination* can be directories. (Tcl 7.6)
`file delete ?-force?` *name*	Delete the named file. (Tcl 7.6)
`file dirname` *name*	Return parent directory of file *name*.
`file executable` *name*	Return 1 if *name* has execute permission, else 0.
`file exists` *name*	Return 1 if *name* exists, else 0.
`file extension` *name*	Return the part of *name* from the last dot (i.e., `.`) to the end. The dot is included in the return value.
`file isdirectory` *name*	Return 1 if *name* is a directory, else 0.
`file isfile` *name*	Return 1 if *name* is not a directory, symbolic link, or device, else 0.
`file join` *path path...*	Join pathname components into a new pathname. (Tcl 7.5)
`file lstat` *name var*	Place attributes of the link *name* into *var*.
`file mkdir` *name*	Create directory *name*. (Tcl 7.6)
`file mtime` *name*	Return modify time of *name* as a decimal string.
`file nativename` *name*	Return the platform-native version of *name*. (Tk 8.0).
`file owned` *name*	Return 1 if current user owns the file *name*, else 0.
`file pathtype` *name*	`relative`, `absolute`, or `driverelative`. (Tcl 7.5)
`file readable` *name*	Return 1 if *name* has read permission, else 0.
`file readlink` *name*	Return the contents of the symbolic link *name*.

Table 9–2 The `file` command options. (Continued)

`file rename ?-force? old new`	Change the name of *old* to *new*. (Tcl 7.6)
`file rootname name`	Return all but the extension of *name* (i.e., up to but not including the last `.` in *name*).
`file size name`	Return the number of bytes in *name*.
`file split name`	Split *name* into its pathname components. (Tcl 7.5)
`file stat name var`	Place attributes of *name* into array *var*. The elements defined for *var* are listed in Table 9–3.
`file tail name`	Return the last pathname component of *name*.
`file type name`	Return type identifier, which is one of: `file`, `directory`, `characterSpecial`, `blockSpecial`, `fifo`, `link`, or `socket`.
`file writable name`	Return 1 if *name* has write permission, else 0.

Cross-Platform File Naming

Files are named differently on UNIX, Windows, and Macintosh. UNIX separates file name components with a forward slash (/), Macintosh separates components with a colon (:), and Windows separates components with a backslash (\). In addition, the way that absolute and relative names are distinguished is different. For example, these are absolute pathnames for the Tcl script library (i.e., `$tcl_library`) on Macintosh, Windows, and UNIX, respectively:

```
Disk:System Folder:Extensions:Tool Command Language:tcl7.6
c:\Program Files\Tcl\lib\Tcl7.6
/usr/local/tcl/lib/tcl7.6
```

The good news is that Tcl provides operations that let you deal with file pathnames in a platform-independent manner. The file operations described in this chapter allow either native format or the UNIX naming convention. The backslash used in Windows pathnames is especially awkward because the backslash is special to Tcl. Happily, you can use forward slashes instead:

```
c:/Program Files/Tcl/lib/Tcl7.6
```

There are some ambiguous cases that can only be specified with native pathnames. On my Macintosh, Tcl and Tk are installed in a directory that has a slash in it. You can only name it with the native Macintosh name:

```
Disk:Applications:Tcl/Tk 4.2
```

Another construct to watch out for is a leading `//` in a file name. This is the Windows syntax for network names that reference files on other computers. You can avoid accidentally constructing a network name by using the `file join` command described next. Of course, you can use network names to access remote files.

If you have to communicate with external programs, you may need to construct a file name in the native syntax for the current platform. You can construct these names with `file join` described later. You can also convert a UNIX-like name to a native name with `file nativename`.

Several of the `file` operations operate on pathnames as opposed to returning information about the file itself. You can use the `dirname`, `extension`, `join`, `pathtype`, `rootname`, `split`, and `tail` operations on any string; there is no requirement that the pathnames refer to an existing file.

Building up Pathnames: `file join`

You can get into trouble if you try to construct file names by simply joining components with a slash. If part of the name is in native format, joining things with slashes will result in incorrect pathnames on Macintosh and Windows. The same problem arises when you accept user input. The user is likely to provide file names in native format. For example, this construct will not create a valid pathname on the Macintosh because `$tcl_library` is in native format:

```
set file $tcl_library/init.tcl
```

Use `file join` to construct file names.

The platform-independent way to construct file names is with `file join`. The following command returns the name of the `init.tcl` file in native format:

```
set file [file join $tcl_library init.tcl]
```

The `file join` operation can join any number of path name components. In addition, it has the feature that an absolute pathname overrides any previous components. For example (on UNIX), `/b/c` is an absolute pathname, so it overrides any paths that come before it in the arguments to `file join`:

```
file join a b/c d
=> a/b/c/d
file join a /b/c d
=> /b/c/d
```

On Macintosh, a relative pathname starts with a colon, and an absolute pathname does not. To specify an absolute path you put a trailing colon on the first component so it is interpreted as a volume specifier. These relative components are joined into a relative pathname:

```
file join a :b:c d
=> :a:b:c:d
```

In the next case, `b:c` is an absolute pathname with `b:` as the volume specifier. The absolute name overrides the previous relative name:

```
file join a b:c d
=> b:c:d
```

The file join operation converts UNIX-style pathnames to native format. For example, on Macintosh you get this:

```
file join /usr/local/lib
=> usr:local:lib
```

Chopping Pathnames: split, dirname, tail

The file split command divides a pathname into components. It is the inverse of file join. The split operation detects automatically if the input is in native or UNIX format. The results of file split may contain some syntax to help resolve ambiguous cases when the results are passed back to file join. For example, on Macintosh a UNIX-style pathname is split on slash separators. The Macintosh syntax for a volume specifier (Disk:) is returned on the leading component:

```
file split "/Disk/System Folder/Extensions"
=> Disk: {System Folder} Extensions
```

Common reasons to split up pathnames are to divide a pathname into the directory part and the file part. These special cases are handled directly by the dirname and tail operations. The dirname operation returns the parent directory of a pathname, while tail returns the trailing component of the pathname:

```
file dirname /a/b/c
=> /a/b
file tail /a/b/c
=> c
```

For a pathname with a single component, the dirname option returns ".", on UNIX and Windows, or ":" on Macintosh. This is the name of the current directory.

The extension and root options are also complementary. The extension option returns everything from the last period in the name to the end (i.e., the file suffix including the period.) The root option returns everything up to, but not including, the last period in the pathname:

```
file root /a/b.c
=> /a/b
file extension /a/b.c
=> .c
```

Manipulating Files and Directories

Tcl 7.6 added file operations to copy files, delete files, rename files, and create directories. In earlier versions it was necessary to exec other programs to do these things, except on Macintosh where cp, rm, mv, mkdir, and rmdir were built in. These commands are no longer supported on the Macintosh. Your scripts should use the file command operations described below to manipulate files in a platform-independent way.

File name patterns are not directly supported by the file operations. Instead, you can use the glob command described on page 106 to get a list of file names that match a pattern.

Copying Files

The `file copy` operation copies files and directories. The following example copies *file1* to *file2*. If *file2* already exists, the operation raises an error unless the `-force` option is specified:

```
file copy ?-force? file1 file2
```

Several files can be copied into a destination directory. The names of the source files are preserved. The `-force` option indicates that files under *directory* can be replaced:

```
file copy ?-force? file1 file2 ... directory
```

Directories can be recursively copied. The `-force` option indicates that files under *dir2* can be replaced:

```
file copy ?-force? dir1 dir2
```

Creating Directories

The `file mkdir` operation creates one or more directories:

```
file mkdir dir dir ...
```

It is *not* an error if the directory already exists. Furthermore, intermediate directories are created if needed. This means you can always make sure a directory exists with a single `mkdir` operation. Suppose `/tmp` has no subdirectories at all. The following command creates `/tmp/sub1` and `/tmp/sub1/sub2`:

```
file mkdir /tmp/sub1/sub2
```

The `-force` option is not understood by `file mkdir`, so the following command accidentally creates a folder named `-force`, as well as one named `oops`.

```
file mkdir -force oops
```

Deleting Files

The `file delete` operation deletes files and directories. It is *not* an error if the files do not exist. A non-empty directory is not deleted unless the `-force` option is specified, in which case it is recursively deleted:

```
file delete ?-force? name name ...
```

To delete a file or directory named `-force`, you must specify a non-existent file before the `-force` to prevent it from being interpreted as a flag (`-force -force` won't work):

```
file delete xyzzy -force
```

Renaming Files and Directories

The `file rename` operation changes a file's name from *old* to *new*. The `-force` option causes *new* to be replaced if it already exists.

```
file rename ?-force? old new
```

Using `file rename` is the best way to update an existing file. First generate the new version of the file in a temporary file. Then use `file rename` to replace the old version with the new version. This ensures that any other programs that access the file will not see the new version until it is complete.

File Attributes

There are several file operations that return specific file attributes: `atime`, `executable`, `exists`, `isdirectory`, `isfile`, `mtime`, `owned`, `readable`, `readlink`, `size` and `type`. Refer to Table 9–2 on page 94 for their function. The following command uses `file mtime` to compare the modify times of two files. If you have ever resorted to piping the results of *ls -l* into *awk* in order to derive this information in other shell scripts, you will appreciate this example:

Example 9–2 Comparing file modify times.

```
proc newer { file1 file2 } {
    if ![file exists $file2] {
        return 1
    } else {
        # Assume file1 exists
        expr [file mtime $file1] > [file mtime $file2]
    }
}
```

The `stat` and `lstat` operations return a collection of file attributes. They take a third argument that is the name of an array variable, and they initialize that array with elements that contain the file attributes. If the file is a symbolic link, then the `lstat` operation returns information about the link itself and the `stat` operation returns information about the target of the link. The array elements are listed in Table 9–3. All the element values are decimal strings, except for `type`, which can have the values returned by the `type` option. These are based on the UNIX `stat` system call. Use the `file attributes` command described later to get other platform-specific attributes:

Table 9–3 Array elements defined by `file stat`.

`atime`	The last access time, in seconds.
`ctime`	The last change time (not the create time), in seconds.
`dev`	The device identifier, an integer.
`gid`	The group owner, an integer.
`ino`	The file number (i.e., inode number), an integer.
`mode`	The permission bits.
`mtime`	The last modify time, in seconds.

Table 9–3 Array elements defined by `file stat`.

`nlink`	The number of links, or directory references, to the file.
`size`	The number of bytes in the file.
`type`	`file`, `directory`, `characterSpecial`, `blockSpecial`, `fifo`, `link`, or `socket`.
`uid`	The owner's user ID, an integer.

Example 9–3 uses the device (`dev`) and inode (`ino`) attributes of a file to determine if two pathnames reference the same file.

Example 9–3 Determining if pathnames reference the same file.

```
proc fileeq { path1 path2 } {
    file stat $path1 stat1
    file stat $path2 stat2
    expr $stat1(ino) == $stat2(ino) && \
          $stat1(dev) == $stat2(dev)
}
```

The `file attributes` operation was added in Tcl 8.0 to provide access to platform-specific attributes. The `attributes` operation lets you set and query attributes. The interface uses option-value pairs. With no options, all the current values are returned.

```
file attributes book.doc
=> -creator FRAM -hidden 0 -readonly 0 -type MAKR
```

These Macintosh attributes are explained in Table 9–4. The 4-character type codes used on Macintosh are illustrated on page 432. With a single option, just that value is returned:

```
file attributes book.doc -readonly
=> 0
```

The attributes are modified by specifying one or more option-value pairs. Setting attributes can raise an error if you do not have the right permissions:

```
file attributes book.doc -readonly 1 -hidden 0
```

Table 9–4 Platform-specific file attributes.

`-permissions` *`mode`*	File permission bits. *`mode`* is a number with bits defined by the `chmod` system call. (UNIX)
`-group` *`ID`*	The group owner of the file. (UNIX)
`-owner` *`ID`*	The owner of the file. (UNIX)
`-archive` *`bool`*	The archive bit, which is set by backup programs. (Windows)

Table 9–4 Platform-specific file attributes. (Continued)

`-hidden bool`	If set, then the file does not appear in listings. (Windows, Macintosh)
`-readonly bool`	If set, then you cannot write the file. (Windows, Macintosh)
`-system bool`	If set, then you cannot remove the file. (Windows)
`-creator type`	*type* is 4-character code of creating application. (Macintosh)
`-type type`	*type* is 4-character type code. (Macintosh)

Input/Output Command Summary

The following sections describe how to open, read, and write files. The basic model is that you open a file, read and/or write it, then close the file. Network sockets also use the commands described here. Socket programming is discussed in Chapter 16, and more advanced *event-driven* I/O is described in Chapter 15. Table 9–5 lists the basic commands associated with file I/O:

Table 9–5 Tcl commands used for file access.

`open what ?access? ?permissions?`	Return channel ID for a file or pipeline.
`puts ?-nonewline? ?channel? string`	Write a string.
`gets channel ?varname?`	Read a line.
`read channel ?numBytes?`	Read `numBytes` bytes, or all data.
`read -nonewline channel`	Read all bytes and discard the last `\n`.
`tell channel`	Return the seek offset.
`seek channel offset ?origin?`	Set the seek offset. `origin` is one of `start`, `current`, or `end`.
`eof channel`	Query end-of-file status.
`flush channel`	Write buffers of a channel.
`close channel`	Close an I/O channel.

Opening Files for I/O

The `open` command sets up an I/O channel to either a file or a pipeline of processes. The return value of `open` is an identifier for the I/O channel. Store the result of `open` in a variable and use the variable as you used the `stdout`, `stdin`, and `stderr` identifiers in the examples so far. The basic syntax is:

```
open what ?access? ?permissions?
```

The *what* argument is either a file name or a pipeline specification similar to that used by the exec command. The *access* argument can take two forms, either a short character sequence that is compatible with the fopen library routine, or a list of POSIX access flags. Table 9–6 summarizes the first form, while Table 9–7 summarizes the POSIX flags. If *access* is not specified, it defaults to read. The *permissions* argument is a value used for the permission bits on a newly created file. The default permission bits are 0666, which grant read/write access to everybody. Example 9–4 specifies 0600 so that the file is only readable and writable by the owner. Remember to specify the leading zero to get an octal number as used in the *chmod* documentation. Consult the manual page on the UNIX *chmod* command for more details about permission bits.

Example 9–4 Opening a file for writing.

```
set fileId [open /tmp/foo w 0600]
puts $fileId "Hello, foo!"
close $fileId
```

Table 9–6 Summary of the open access arguments.

r	Open for reading. The file must exist.
r+	Open for reading and writing. The file must exist.
w	Open for writing. Truncate if it exists. Create if it does not exist.
w+	Open for reading and writing. Truncate or create.
a	Open for writing. Data is appended to the file.
a+	Open for reading and writing. Data is appended.

Table 9–7 Summary of POSIX flags for the access argument.

RDONLY	Open for reading.
WRONLY	Open for writing.
RDWR	Open for reading and writing.
APPEND	Open for append.
CREAT	Create the file if it does not exist.
EXCL	If CREAT is also specified, then the file cannot already exist.
NOCTTY	Prevent terminal devices from becoming the controlling terminal.
NONBLOCK	Do not block during the open.
TRUNC	Truncate the file if it exists.

The following example illustrates how to use a list of POSIX access flags to open a file for reading and writing, creating it if needed, and not truncating it. This is something you cannot do with the simpler form of the access argument:

```
set fileId [open /tmp/bar {RDWR CREAT}]
```

Catch errors from open.

In general you should check for errors when opening files. The following example illustrates a catch phrase used to open files. Recall that catch returns 1 if it catches an error, otherwise it returns zero. It treats its second argument as the name of a variable. In the error case it puts the error message into the variable. In the normal case it puts the result of the command into the variable:

Example 9–5 A more careful use of open.

```
if [catch {open /tmp/data r} fileId] {
   puts stderr "Cannot open /tmp/data: $fileId"
} else {
   # Read and process the file, then...
   close $fileId
}
```

Opening a Process Pipeline

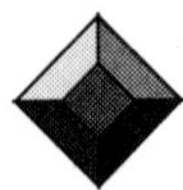

You can open a process pipeline by specifying the pipe character, |, as the first character of the first argument. The remainder of the pipeline specification is interpreted just as with the exec command, including input and output redirection. The second argument determines which end of the pipeline open returns. The following example runs the UNIX *sort* program on the password file, and it uses the split command to separate the output lines into list elements:

Example 9–6 Opening a process pipeline.

```
set input [open "|sort /etc/passwd" r]
set contents [split [read $input] \n]
close $input
```

You can open a pipeline for both read and write by specifying the r+ access mode. In this case you need to worry about buffering. After a puts, the data may still be in a buffer in the Tcl library. Use the flush command to force the data out to the spawned processes before you try to read any output from the pipeline. You can also use the fconfigure command described on page 182 to force line buffering. Remember that read-write pipes will not work at all with Windows 3.1 because pipes are simulated with files. On UNIX, the *expect* extension, which is described in *Exploring Expect* (Libes, O'Reilly & Associates, Inc., 1995), provides a much more powerful way to interact with other programs.

Event-driven I/O is also very useful with pipes. It means you can do other processing while the pipeline executes, and just respond when the pipe generates data. This is described in Chapter 15.

Reading and Writing

The standard I/O channels are already open for you. There is a standard input channel, a standard output channel, and a standard error output channel. These channels are identified by `stdin`, `stdout`, and `stderr`, respectively. Other I/O channels are returned by the `open` command, and by the `socket` command described on page 186.

There may be cases when the standard I/O channels are not available. Windows has no standard error channel. Some UNIX window managers close the standard I/O channels when you start programs from window manager menus. You can also close the standard I/O channels with `close`.

The `puts` and `gets` Commands

The `puts` command writes a string and a newline to the output channel. There are a couple of details about the `puts` command that we have not yet used. It takes a `-nonewline` argument that prevents the newline character that is normally appended to the output channel. This will be used in the prompt example below. The second feature is that the channel identifier is optional, defaulting to `stdout` if not specified.

Example 9–7 Prompting for input.

```
puts -nonewline "Enter value: "
flush stdout ;# Necessary in Tcl 7.5 and Tcl 7.6
set answer [gets stdin]
```

The `gets` command reads a line of input, and it has two forms. In the previous example, with just a single argument, `gets` returns the line read from the specified I/O channel. It discards the trailing newline from the return value. If end of file is reached, an empty string is returned. You must use the `eof` command to tell the difference between a blank line and end-of-file. `eof` returns 1 if there is end of file. Given a second *`varName`* argument, `gets` stores the line into a named variable and returns the number of bytes read. It discards the trailing newline, which is not counted. A -1 is returned if the channel has reached the end of file.

Example 9–8 A read loop using `gets`.

```
while {[gets $channel line] >= 0} {
    # Process line
}
close $channel
```

The `read` Command

The `read` command reads blocks of data, which is often more efficient. There are two forms for `read`: you can specify the `-nonewline` argument or the *`numBytes`* argument, but not both. Without *`numBytes`*, the whole file (or what is left in the I/O channel) is read and returned. The `-nonewline` argument causes the trailing newline to be discarded. Given a byte count argument, `read` returns that amount, or less if there is not enough data in the channel. The trailing newline is not discarded in this case.

Example 9–9 A read loop using `read` and `split`.

```
foreach line [split [read $channel] \n] {
   # Process line
}
close $channel
```

For moderate-sized files it is about 10 percent faster to loop over the lines in a file using the read loop in the second example. In this case, `read` returns the whole file, and `split` chops the file into list elements, one for each line. For small files (less than 1K) it doesn't really matter. For large files (megabytes) you might induce paging with this approach.

Platform-Specific End of Line Characters

Tcl automatically detects different end of line conventions. On UNIX, text lines are ended with a newline character (`\n`). On Macintosh they are terminated with a carriage return (`\r`). On Windows they are terminated with a carriage return, newline sequence (`\r\n`). Tcl accepts any of these, and the line terminator can even change within a file. All these different conventions are converted to the UNIX style so that once read, text lines are always terminated with a newline character (`\n`). Both the `read` and `gets` commands do this conversion.

During output, text lines are generated in the platform-native format. The automatic handling of line formats means that it is easy to convert a file to native format. You just need to read it in and write it out:

```
puts -nonewline $out [read $in]
```

To suppress conversions, use the `fconfigure` command, which is described in more detail on page 183.

Example 9–10 demonstrates a `File_Copy` procedure that translates files to native format. It is complicated because it handles directories:

Example 9–10 Copy a file and translate to native format.

```
proc File_Copy {src dest} {
   if [file isdirectory $src] {
      file mkdir $dest
      foreach f [glob -nocomplain [file join $src *]] {
         File_Copy $f [file join $dest [file tail $f]]
```

```
        }
        return
    }
    if [file isdirectory $dest] {
        set dest [file join $dest [file tail $src]]
    }
    set in [open $src]
    set out [open $dest w]
    puts -nonewline $out [read $in]
    close $out ; close $in
}
```

Random Access I/O

The `seek` and `tell` commands provide random access to I/O channels. Each channel has a current position called the *seek offset*. Each read or write operation updates the seek offset by the number of bytes transferred. The current value of the offset is returned by the `tell` command. The `seek` command sets the seek offset by an amount, which can be positive or negative, from an origin which is either `start`, `current`, or `end`.

Closing I/O channels

The `close` command is just as important as the others because it frees operating system resources associated with the I/O channel. If you forget to close a channel, it will be closed when your process exits. However, if you have a long-running program, like a Tk script, you might exhaust some operating system resources if you forget to close your I/O channels.

The `close` command can raise an error.

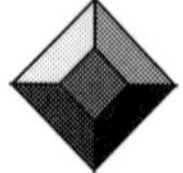

If the channel was a process pipeline and any of the processes wrote to their standard error channel, then Tcl believes this is an error. The error is raised when the channel to the pipeline is finally closed. Similarly, if any of the processes in the pipeline exit with a non-zero status, `close` raises an error.

The Current Directory — `cd` and `pwd`

Every process has a current directory that is used as the starting point when resolving a relative pathname. The `pwd` command returns the current directory, and the `cd` command changes the current directory. Example 9–11 uses these commands.

Matching File Names with `glob`

The `glob` command expands a pattern into the set of matching file names. The general form of the `glob` command is:

```
glob ?flags? pattern ?pattern? ...
```

The pattern syntax is similar to the `string match` patterns:

- `*` matches zero or more characters
- `?` matches a single character
- `[abc]` matches a set of characters.
- `{a,b,c}` matches any of *a*, *b*, or *c*.
- All other characters must match themselves.

The `-nocomplain` flag causes `glob` to return an empty list if no files match the pattern. Otherwise `glob` raises an error if no files match.

The `--` flag must be used if the *pattern* begins with a `-`.

Unlike the glob matching in *csh*, the Tcl `glob` command only matches the names of existing files. In *csh*, the `{a,b}` construct can match non-existent names. In addition, the results of `glob` are not sorted. Use the `lsort` command to sort its result if you find it important.

Example 9–11 Finding a file by name.

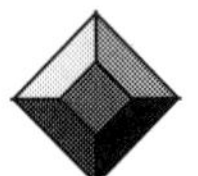

```
proc FindFile { startDir namePat } {
    set pwd [pwd]
    if [catch {cd $startDir} err] {
        puts stderr $err
        return
    }
    foreach match [glob -nocomplain -- $namePat]{
        puts stdout [file join $startDir $match]
    }
    foreach file [glob -nocomplain *] {
        if [file isdirectory $file] {
            FindFile [file join $startDir $file] $namePat
        }
    }
    cd $pwd
}
```

The `FindFile` procedure traverses the file system hierarchy using recursion. At each iteration it saves its current directory and then attempts to change to the next subdirectory. A `catch` guards against bogus names. The `glob` command matches file names.

Expanding Tilde in File Names

The `glob` command also expands a leading tilde (~) in filenames. There are two cases:

- `~/` expands to the current user's home directory.
- `~user` expands to the home directory of *user*.

If you have a file that starts with a literal tilde, you can avoid the tilde expansion by adding a leading `./` (e.g., `./~foobar`).

The `exit` and `pid` Commands

The `exit` command terminates your script. Note that `exit` causes termination of the whole process that was running the script. If you supply an integer-valued argument to `exit`, then that becomes the exit status of the process.

The `pid` command returns the process ID of the current process. This can be useful as the seed for a random number generator because it changes each time you run your script. It is also common to embed the process ID in the name of temporary files.

You can also find out the process IDs associated with a process pipeline with `pid`:

```
set pipe [open "|command"]
set pids [pid $pipe]
```

There is no built-in mechanism to control processes in Tcl. On UNIX systems you can `exec` the *kill* program to terminate a process:

```
exec kill $pid
```

Environment Variables

Environment variables are a collection of string-valued variables associated with each process. The process's environment variables are available through the global array `env`. The name of the environment variable is the index, (e.g., `env(PATH)`), and the array element contains the current value of the environment variable. If assignments are made to `env`, they result in changes to the corresponding environment variable. Environment variables are inherited by child processes, so programs run with the `exec` command inherit the environment of the Tcl script. The following example prints the values of environment variables.

Example 9–12 Printing environment variable values.

```
proc printenv { args } {
    global env
    set maxl 0
    if {[llength $args] == 0} {
        set args [lsort [array names env]]
    }
    foreach x $args {
        if {[string length $x] > $maxl} {
            set maxl [string length $x]
        }
    }
    incr maxl 2
    foreach x $args {
```

```
        puts stdout [format "%*s = %s" $maxl $x $env($x)]
    }
}
printenv USER SHELL TERM
=>
USER   = welch
SHELL  = /bin/csh
TERM   = tx
```

Note: Environment variables can be initialized for Macintosh applications by editing a resource of type STR# whose name is "Tcl Environment Variables". This resource is part of the *tclsh* and *wish* applications. Follow the directions on page 26 for using *ResEdit*. The format of the resource values is *NAME=VALUE*.

P A R T II

Advanced Tcl

Part II describes advanced programming techniques that support sophisticated applications. The Tcl interfaces remain simple, so you can quickly construct powerful applications.

Chapter 10 describes `eval`, which lets you create Tcl programs on the fly. There are tricks with using `eval` correctly, and a few rules of thumb to make your life easier.

Chapter 11 describes regular expressions. This is the most powerful string processing facility in Tcl. This chapter includes a cookbook of useful regular expressions.

Chapter 12 describes the library and package facility used to organize your code into reusable modules.

Chapter 13 describes introspection and debugging. Introspection provides information about the state of the Tcl interpreter.

Chapter 14 describes namespaces that partition the global scope for variables and procedures. Namespaces help you structure large Tcl applications.

Chapter 15 describes event-driven I/O programming. This lets you run process pipelines in the background. It is also very useful with network socket programming, which is the topic of Chapter 16.

Chapter 17 describes Safe-Tcl and using multiple Tcl interpreters. You can create multiple Tcl interpreters for your application. If an interpreter is safe, then you can grant it restricted functionality. This is ideal for supporting network applets that are downloaded from untrusted sites.

C H A P T E R 10

Eval

This chapter describes explicit calls to the interpreter with the `eval` command. An extra round of substitutions is performed that results in some useful effects. The chapter describes the potential problems with `eval` and the ways to avoid them. The `uplevel` command evaluates commands in a different scope. The `subst` command does substitutions but no command invocation.

Evaluation involves substitutions, and it is sometimes useful to go through an extra round of substitutions. This is achieved with the `eval` and `subst` commands. In addition, there are commands like `after`, `uplevel`, and the Tk `send` command that have similar properties to `eval`, except that the command evaluation occurs later or in a different context.

The `eval` command is used to re-interpret a string as a command. It is very useful in certain cases, but it can be tricky to assemble a command so it is evaluated properly by `eval`. The root of the quoting problems is the internal use of `concat` by `eval` and similar commands to put their arguments into one command string. The `concat` can lose some important list structure so that arguments are not passed through as you expect. One general strategy to avoid these problems is to use `list` and `lappend` to explicitly form the command as a single, well-structured list.

There are also times when the loss of list structure is exactly what you need. This is often true with the list-valued `args` parameter to procedures. The `concat` by `eval` command is used to undo a level of list structure in order to make up a single command.

Construct Commands with `list`

The `eval` command results in another call to the Tcl interpreter. If you construct a command dynamically, you must use `eval` to interpret it. For example, suppose we want to construct the following command now but execute it later:

```
puts stdout "Hello, World!"
```

In this case, it is sufficient to do the following:

```
set cmd {puts stdout "Hello, World!"}
=> puts stdout "Hello, World!"
# sometime later...
eval $cmd
=> Hello, World!
```

In this case the value of `cmd` is passed to Tcl. All the standard grouping and substitution are done again on the value, which is a `puts` command. However, suppose that part of the command is stored in a variable, but that variable will not be defined at the time `eval` is used. We can artificially create this situation like this:

```
set string "Hello, World!"
set cmd {puts stdout $string}
=> puts stdout $string
unset string
eval $cmd
=> can't read "string": no such variable
```

In this case the command contains `$string`. When this is processed by `eval`, the interpreter looks for the current value of `string`, which is undefined. This example is contrived, but the same problem occurs if `string` is a local variable, and `cmd` will be evaluated later in the global scope.

Many folks choose to use double quotes in this case. That will let `$string` be substituted now. However, this works if string has a simple value, but fails if the value of `string` contains spaces or other Tcl special characters:

```
set cmd "puts stdout $string"
=> puts stdout Hello, World!
eval $cmd
=> bad argument "World!": should be "nonewline"
```

The problem is that we have lost some important structure. The identity of `$string` as a single argument gets lost in the second round of parsing by `eval`. The solution to this problem is to construct the command using `list`, as shown in the following example:

Example 10–1 Using `list` to construct commands.

```
set string "Hello, World!"
set cmd [list puts stdout $string]
=> puts stdout {Hello, World!}
unset string
eval $cmd
=> Hello, World!
```

The trick is that list has formed a list containing three elements: puts, stdout, and the value of string. The substitution of $string occurs before list is called, and list takes care of grouping that value for us. In contrast, using double quotes is equivalent to:

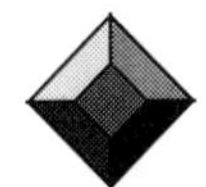

```
set cmd [concat puts stdout $string]
```

Double quotes lose list structure.

The problem here is that concat does not preserve list structure. The main lesson is that you should use list to construct commands if they contain variable values or command results that must substituted now. If you use double quotes, the values are substituted but you lose proper command structure. If you use curly braces, then values are not substituted until later, which may not be in the right context.

Exploiting the concat inside eval

The previous section warns about the danger of the concat done by eval. However, it is done for good reason. This section illustrates cases where the concat done by eval is useful in assembling a command by concatenating multiple lists into one list. A concat is done internally by eval if it gets more than one argument:

```
eval list1 list2 list3 ...
```

The effect of concat is to join all the lists into one list; a new level of list structure is *not* added. This is useful if the lists are fragments of a command. It is common to use this form of eval with the args construct in procedures. Use the args parameter to pass optional arguments through to another command. Invoke the other command with eval and the values in $args get concatenated onto the command properly.

This technique is illustrated with a simple Tk example. In Tk, the button command creates a button in the user interface. The button command can take many arguments that specify different button attributes. You do not have to specify everything, and commonly you just specify the text of the button and the Tcl command that is executed when the user clicks on the button:

```
button .foo -text Foo -command foo
```

After a button is created, it is made visible by packing it into the display. The pack command can also take many arguments to control screen placement. Here we just specify a side and let the packer take care of the rest of the details:

```
pack .foo -side left
```

Even though this is only two Tcl commands to create a user interface button, we will write a procedure that replaces the two commands with one. Our first version might be:

```
proc PackedButton {name txt cmd} {
	button $name -text $txt -command $cmd
	pack $name -side left
}
```

This is not a very flexible procedure. The main problem is that it hides the full power of the Tk `button` command, which can really take about 20 widget configuration options such as `-background`, `-cursor`, `-relief`, and more. They are listed on page 309. You can easily make a red button like this:

```
button .foo -text Foo -command foo -background red
```

A better version of `PackedButton` uses `args` to pass through extra configuration options to the `button` command. The `args` parameter is a list of all the extra arguments passed to the Tcl procedure. My first attempt to use `$args` looked like this, but it was not correct:

```
proc PackedButton {name txt cmd args} {
    button $name -text $txt -command $cmd $args
    pack $name -side left
}
PackedButton .foo "Hello, World!" {exit} -background red
=> unknown option "-background red"
```

The problem is that `$args` is a list value, and `button` gets the whole list as a single argument. Instead, `button` needs to get the elements of `$args` as individual arguments. In this case, you can use `eval` because it concatenates its arguments to form a single list before evaluation. The single list is, by definition, the same as a single Tcl command, so the `button` command parses correctly. Here we give `eval` two lists, which it joins into one command:

```
eval {button $name -text $txt -command $cmd} $args
```

The use of the braces in this command is discussed below. We also generalize our procedure to take some options to the `pack` command. This argument, `pack`, has to be a list of packing options. The final version of `PackedButton` is shown in Example 10–2:

Example 10–2 Using `eval` with `$args`.

```
# PackedButton creates and packs a button.
proc PackedButton {path txt cmd {pack {-side right}} args} {
    eval {button $path -text $txt -command $cmd} $args
    eval {pack $path} $pack
}
```

In `PackedButton`, both `pack` and `args` are list-valued parameters that are used as parts of a command. The internal `concat` done by `eval` is perfect for this situation. The simplest call to `PackedButton` is:

```
PackedButton .new "New" { New }
```

The quotes and curly braces are redundant in this case but are retained to convey some type information. The `pack` argument takes on its default value, and the `args` variable is an empty list. The two commands executed by `PackedButton` are:

```
button .new -text New -command New
pack .new -side right
```

PackedButton creates a horizontal stack of buttons by default. The packing can be controlled with a packing specification:

```
PackedButton .save "Save" { Save $file } {-side left}
```

The two commands executed by PackedButton are:

```
button .new -text Save -command { Save $file }
pack .new -side left
```

The remaining arguments, if any, are passed through to the button command. This lets the caller fine-tune some of the button attributes:

```
PackedButton .quit Quit { Exit } {-side left -padx 5} \
    -background red
```

The two commands executed by PackedButton are:

```
button .quit -text Quit -command { Exit } -background red
pack .quit -side left -padx 5
```

Double Quotes and **eval**

What about the peculiar placement of braces in PackedButton? By using braces we control the number of times different parts of the command are seen by the Tcl evaluator. Without any braces everything goes through two rounds of substitution. The braces prevent one of those rounds. In the following command, only $args is substituted twice.

```
eval {button $name -text $txt -command $cmd} $args
```

Do not use double quotes with eval.

You may be tempted to use double quotes instead of curly braces in your uses of eval. *Don't give in!* Using double quotes is, mostly likely, wrong. Suppose the first eval command is written like this:

```
eval "button $path -text $txt -command $cmd $args"
```

This happens to work with the following because txt and cmd have one-word values with no special characters in them:

```
PackedButton .quit Quit { Exit }
```

The button command is:

```
button .quit -text Quit -command { Exit }
```

In the next call an error is raised:

```
PackedButton .save "Save" { Save $file }
=> can't read "file": no such variable
```

This is because the button command is this:

```
button .save -text Save -command Save $file
```

The real problem is that the structure of the button command is now wrong. It shows up with this error because file is not defined inside PackedButton. The worst part is that sometimes using double quotes works, and sometimes it fails. The success of this approach depends on the value of the parameters. The value of txt and the value of cmd are subject to another round of substitutions and parsing. When those values contain spaces or special characters, the command gets parsed incorrectly.

To repeat, the safe construct is:

```
eval {button $path -text $txt -command $cmd} $args
```

As you may be able to tell, this was one of the more difficult lessons I learned, despite three uses of the word "concatenate" in the `eval` man page!

More Examples

Example 13–5 on page 151 shows how to use `eval` with command *callbacks*. A callback is a Tcl command that is passed into another procedure and executed later, perhaps with additional arguments.

The `uplevel` Command

The `uplevel` command is similar to `eval`, except that it evaluates a command in a different scope than the current procedure. It is useful for defining new control structures entirely in Tcl. The syntax for `uplevel` is:

```
uplevel ?level? command
```

As with `upvar`, the *level* parameter is optional and defaults to 1, which means to execute the command in the scope of the calling procedure. The other common use of level is `#0`, which means to evaluate the command in the global scope.

When you specify the *command* argument, you have to be aware of any substitutions that might be performed by the Tcl interpreter before `uplevel` is called. If you are entering the command directly, protect it with curly braces so that substitutions occur in the other scope. The following affects the variable `x` in the caller's scope:

```
uplevel {set x [expr $x + 1]}
```

However, the following will use the value of `x` in the current scope to define the value of `x` in the calling scope, which is probably not what was intended:

```
uplevel "set x [expr $x + 1]"
```

It is common to have the command in a variable. This is the case when the command has been passed into your new control flow procedure as an argument. In this case you should evaluate the command one level up:

```
uplevel $cmd
```

Example 10–3 does list assignment using the `foreach` trick described on Page 69. List assignment is useful if a command returns several values in a list. The `lassign` procedure assigns the list elements to several variables. The `lassign` procedure hides the foreach trick, but it must use the `uplevel` command so the loop variables get assigned in the correct scope. The `list` command is used to construct the command that is executed in the caller's scope. This is necessary so that `$variables` and `$values` gets substituted before the command is evaluated in the other scope.

Example 10–3 `lassign`: list assignment with `foreach`.

```
proc lassign {variables values} {
    uplevel 1 [list \
        foreach $variables $values { break } \
    ]
}
```

Another common scenario is reading commands from users as part of an application. In this case, you should evaluate the command at the global scope:

```
uplevel #0 $cmd
```

Example 10–4 reads commands from standard input. It uses `info complete` to determine when a complete Tcl command is ready to be evaluated:

Example 10–4 Reading commands from standard input.

```
proc CommandRead {} {
    set cmd {}
    while {![eof stdin]} {
        append cmd [gets stdin]
        if [info complete $cmd] {
            uplevel #0 $cmd
            set cmd {}
            break
        }
    }
}
```

If you are assembling a command from a few different lists, such as the `args` parameter, then you can use `concat` to form the command:

```
uplevel [concat $cmd $args]
```

The lists in `$cmd` and `$args` are concatenated into a single list, which is a valid Tcl command. Like `eval`, `uplevel` uses `concat` internally if it is given extra arguments, so you can leave out the explicit use of `concat`:

```
uplevel $cmd $args
```

Commands That Concatenate Their Arguments

The `uplevel` command and two other commands, `after` and `send`, concatenate their arguments into a command and execute it later in a different context. Whenever I discover such a command I put it on my danger list and make sure I explicitly form a single command argument with `list` instead of letting the command `concat` items for me. Get in the habit now:

```
after 100 [list doCmd $param1 $param2]
send $interp [list doCmd $param1 $param2];# Safe!
```

The worst part of this is `concat` and `list` can result in the same thing, so you can be led down the rosy garden path, only to get errors later when values change. The two previous examples always work. The next two work only if `param1` and `param2` have values that are single list elements:

```
after 100 doCmd $param1 $param2
send $interp doCmd $param1 $param2;# Unsafe!
```

If you use other Tcl extensions that provide `eval`-like functionality, carefully check their documentation to see if they contain commands that `concat` their arguments into a command. For example, Tcl-DP, which provides a network version of `send`, `dp_send`, also uses `concat`.

The `subst` Command

The `subst` command is used to do command and variable substitution, but without invoking any command. It is similar to `eval` in that it does a round of substitutions for you. However, it doesn't try to interpret the result as a command.

```
set a "foo bar"
subst {a=$a date=[exec date]}
=> a=foo bar date=Thu Dec 15 10:13:48 PST 1994
```

The `subst` command does not honor the quoting effect of curly braces. It does substitutions regardless of braces:

```
subst {a=$a date={[exec date]}}
=> a=foo bar date={Thu Dec 15 10:15:31 PST 1994}
```

You can use backslashes to prevent variable and command substitution.

```
subst {a=\$a date=\[exec date]}
=> a=$a date=[exec date]
```

The `subst` command takes flags that limit which substitutions it will perform. The flags are `-nobackslashes`, `-nocommands`, or `-novariables`. You can specify one or more of these flags before the string that needs to be substituted:

```
subst -novariables {a=$a date=[exec date]}
=> a=$a date=Thu Dec 15 10:15:31 PST 1994
```

String Processing with `subst`

The `subst` command can be used with the `regsub` command to do efficient, two-step string processing. In the first step `regsub` is used to rewrite an input string into data with embedded Tcl commands. In the second step, `subst` or `eval` replaces the Tcl commands with their result. By artfully mapping the data into Tcl commands you can dynamically construct a Tcl script that processes the data. The processing is efficient because the Tcl parser and the regular expression processor have been highly tuned. Chapter 11 has several examples that use this technique.

CHAPTER 11

Regular Expressions

This chapter describes regular expression pattern matching and string processing based on regular expression substitutions. Tcl commands described: `regexp` and `regsub`.

Regular expressions are a formal way to describe string patterns. They provide a powerful and compact way to specify patterns in your data. Even better, there is a very efficient implementation of the regular expression mechanism due to Henry Spenser. If your script does much string processing, it is worth the effort to learn about regular expressions. Your Tcl scripts will be compact and efficient. This chapter includes a large set of canned regular expressions you can pick up and use.

Regular expression substitution is a mechanism that lets you rewrite a string based on regular expression matching. This is another powerful tool, and this chapter includes several examples that do a lot of work in just a few Tcl commands. Stephen Uhler has shown me several ways to transform input data into a Tcl script and then use `subst` or `eval` to process the data. The idea takes a moment to get used to, but it provides a very efficient way to process strings.

One of the stumbling blocks with regular expressions is that they use some of the same special characters as Tcl. When you construct regular expressions in Tcl programs, you must be aware of this. In many cases you can group the regular expression with curly braces so Tcl pays no attention to it. In other cases you need Tcl to do substitutions on part of the pattern, and then you need to worry about quoting the special characters in the regular expression. The first section of this chapter ignores this issue. The working examples take into account any necessary quoting.

Regular Expression Syntax

A regular expression is a sequence of the following items:

- A literal character.
- A matching character.
- A repetition clause.
- An alternation clause.
- A subpattern grouped with parentheses.

Table 11–1 summarizes the syntax of regular expressions:

Table 11–1 Regular expression syntax.

`.`	Matches any character.
`*`	Matches zero or more instances of the previous pattern item.
`+`	Matches one or more instances of the previous pattern item.
`?`	Matches zero or one instances of the previous pattern item.
`( )`	Groups a subpattern. The repetition and alternation operators apply to the whole proceeding subpattern.
`|`	Alternation.
`[ ]`	Delimit a set of characters. Ranges are specified as [*x*-*y*]. If the first character in the set is ^, then there is a match if the remaining characters in the set are *not* present.
`^`	Anchor the pattern to the beginning of the string. Only when first.
`$`	Anchor the pattern to the end of the string. Only when last.

A number of examples of regular expressions follow. Any pattern that contains brackets, dollar signs, or spaces must be handled specially when used in a Tcl command. It is unfortunate, but there is a clash between the Tcl special characters and the regular expression special characters. The patterns in this section ignore this problem. The sample expressions in Table 11–2 are quoted for use within Tcl scripts.

The general wild-card character is the period, "`.`". It matches any single character. The following pattern matches all two-character strings:

```
..
```

The matching character can be restricted to a set of characters with the `[`*xyz*`]` syntax. Any of the characters between the two brackets is allowed to match. For example, the following matches either `Hello` or `hello`:

```
[Hh]ello
```

The matching set can be specified as a range over the ASCII character set with the `[`*x*-*y*`]` syntax. There is also the ability to specify the complement of a set. That is, the matching character can be anything except what is in the set. This is achieved with the `[^xyz]` syntax. Ranges and complements can be combined. The following matches anything except the uppercase and lowercase letters:

```
[^a-zA-Z]
```

Repetition is specified with `*`, for zero or more, `+`, for one or more, and `?`, for zero or one. These operators apply to the previous item, which is either a matching character, which could involve the set syntax, or a subpattern grouped with parentheses. The following matches a string that contains `b` followed by zero or more `a`'s:

```
ba*
```

The following matches a string that has one or more sequences of `ab`:

```
(ab)+
```

The pattern that matches anything is:

```
.*
```

Alternation is specified with `|`, a pipe symbol. Another way to match either `Hello` or `hello` is:

```
hello|Hello
```

By default a pattern does not have to match the whole string. There can be unmatched characters before and after the match. You can anchor the match to the beginning of the string by starting the pattern with `^`, or to the end of the string by ending the pattern with `$`. You can force the pattern to match the whole string by using both. All strings that begin with spaces or tabs are matched with:

```
^[ \t]+
```

If a pattern can match several parts of a string, the matcher takes the match that occurs earliest in the input string. Then, if there is more than one match from that same point, the matcher takes the longest possible match. The rule of thumb is: *first, then longest.*

A Pattern to Match URLs

Let's try one complex pattern to match a URL. Our sample input string will be:

```
http://www.sun.com:80/index.html
```

The regular expression is:

```
[^:]+://[^:/]+(:[0-9]+)?/.*
```

Let's look at the pattern one piece at a time. The first part looks for the protocol, which is separated by a colon from the rest of the URL. The first part of the pattern is one or more characters that are not a colon, followed by a colon. This matches the `http:` part of the URL:

```
[^:]+:
```

The next part of the pattern looks for the server name, which comes after two slashes. The server name is either followed by a colon and a port number, or by a slash. The pattern uses a complementary set that specifies one or more characters that are *not* a colon or a slash. This matches the `//www.sun.com` part of the URL:

```
//[^:/]+
```

The port number is optional, so a subpattern is delimited with parentheses and followed by a question mark. This matches the `:80` part of the URL:

```
(:[0-9]+)?
```

The last part of the pattern is everything else, starting with a slash. This matches the `/index.html` part of the URL:

```
/.*
```

Use subpatterns to parse strings.

To make this pattern really useful we delimit several subpatterns with parentheses:

```
([^:]+)://([^:/]+)(:([0-9]+))?(/.*)
```

These parentheses do not change the way the pattern matches. Only the optional port number really needs the parentheses in this example. However, the `regexp` command described next gives us access to the strings that match these subpatterns. In one step `regexp` can test for a valid URL and divide it into the protocol part, the server, the port, and the trailing path. This is shown later in Example 11–2 on page 126.

The `regexp` Command

The `regexp` command provides direct access to the regular expression matcher. Not only does it tell you if a string matches a pattern, it can also extract one or more matching substrings. The return value is 1 if some part of the string matches the pattern; it is 0 otherwise. Its syntax is:

```
regexp ?flags? pattern string ?match sub1 sub2...?
```

The *flags* are optional and constrain the match as follows:

- If `-nocase` is specified, then lowercase characters in *pattern* can match either lowercase or uppercase letters in *string*.
- If `-indices` is specified, then the match variables each contain a pair of numbers that are the indices delimiting the match within *string*. Otherwise, the matching string itself is copied into the match variables.
- If your pattern begins with `-`, then you can use `--` to separate the flags from the pattern.

The *pattern* argument is a regular expression as described in the previous section. If this contains `$` or `[`, you must be careful. The easiest thing to do is group your patterns with curly braces. However, if your pattern contains backslash sequences like `\n` or `\t`, you must group with double quotes so the Tcl interpreter can do those substitutions. In that case, use `\[` and `\$` in your patterns.

If *string* matches *pattern*, then the results of the match are stored in the variables named in the command. These match variable arguments are optional. If present, *match* is set to be the part of the string that matched the pattern. The remaining variables are set to be the substrings of *string* that matched the corresponding subpatterns in *pattern*. The correspondence is based on the order of left parentheses in the pattern to avoid ambiguities that can arise from nested subpatterns.

Example 11–1 uses regexp to pick the hostname out of the DISPLAY environment variable, which has the form:

hostname:display.screen

Example 11–1 Using regular expressions to parse a string.

```
set env(DISPLAY) sage:0.1
regexp {([^:]*):} $env(DISPLAY) match host
=> 1
set match
=> sage:
set host
=> sage
```

The pattern involves a complementary set, [^:], to match anything except a colon. It uses repetition, *, to repeat that zero or more times. It groups that part into a subexpression with parentheses. The literal colon ensures that the DISPLAY value matches the format we expect. The part of the string that matches the complete pattern is stored into the match variable. The part that matches the subpattern is stored into host. The whole pattern has been grouped with braces to quote the square brackets. Without braces it would be:

```
regexp (\[^:\]*): $env(DISPLAY) match host
```

This is quite a powerful statement, and it is efficient. If we had only had the string command to work with, we would have needed to resort to the following, which takes roughly twice as long to interpret:

```
set i [string first : $env(DISPLAY)]
if {$i >= 0} {
    set host [string range $env(DISPLAY) 0 [expr $i-1]]
}
```

Example 11–2 demonstrates a pattern with several subpatterns that extract the different parts of a URL. There are lots of subpatterns, and you can determine which match variable is associated with which subpattern by counting the left parenthesis. Note that the port number uses a nested subpattern. The subpattern (:([0-9]+))? uses the zero-or-more pattern character ? because the port specification is optional. However, this puts a colon into the match variable x, so another subpattern is used to just get the digits of the port number into the port match variable:

Example 11–2 A pattern to match URLs.

```
set url http://www.sun.com:80/index.html
regexp {([^:]+)://([^:/]+)(:([0-9]+))?(/.*)} $url \
   match protocol server x port path
=> 1
set match
=> http://www.sun.com:80/index.html
set protocol
=> http
set server
=> www.sun.com
set x
=> :80
set port
=> 80
set path
=> /index.html
```

Useful Regular Expressions

Table 11–1 lists regular expressions as you would use them in Tcl commands. Most are quoted with curly braces to turn off the special meaning of square brackets and dollar sign. Others patterns are grouped with double quotes and use backslash quoting because the patterns include backslash sequences like `\n` and `\t` that must be substituted by Tcl before the `regexp` command is called.

Table 11–2 Simple regular expressions

<table>
<tr><td><code>{^[yY]}</code></td><td>Begins with y or Y, as in a Yes answer.</td></tr>
<tr><td><code>{^(yes|YES|Yes)$}</code></td><td>Exactly "yes", "Yes", or "YES".</td></tr>
<tr><td><code>"^\[^ \t:\]+:"</code></td><td>Begins with colon-delimited field that has no spaces or tabs.</td></tr>
<tr><td><code>"^\[\t]*$"</code></td><td>A blank line.</td></tr>
<tr><td><code>{^[A-Za-z]+$}</code></td><td>Only letters.</td></tr>
<tr><td><code>{^[A-Za-z0-9_]+$}</code></td><td>Letters, digits, and the underscore.</td></tr>
<tr><td><code>{[][${}\\]}</code></td><td>The set of Tcl special characters:] [$ { } \</td></tr>
<tr><td><code>"\[^\n\]*\n"</code></td><td>Everything up to a newline.</td></tr>
<tr><td><code>{\.}</code></td><td>A period.</td></tr>
<tr><td><code>{[][$^\?\+*\(\)\|\\}</code></td><td>The set of regular expression special characters:
] [$ ^ ? + * ( ) | \</td></tr>
<tr><td><code>"(^|\n)to:\[^\n\]+\n"</code></td><td>A line that begins with "to:". The (^|\n) matches the beginning of string or a newline before the line.</td></tr>
</table>

The regsub Command

The regsub command does string substitution based on pattern matching. Its syntax is:

```
regsub ?switches? pattern string subspec varname
```

The regsub command returns the number of matches and replacements, or 0 if there was no match. regsub copies *string* to *varname*, replacing occurrences of *pattern* with the substitution specified by *subspec*. If the pattern does not match, then *string* is copied to *varname* without modification. The optional switches include:

- -all, which means to replace all occurrences of the pattern. Otherwise only the first occurrence is replaced.
- The -nocase switch means that lower-case characters in the *pattern* can match either lower or upper case letters in *string*.
- The -- switch separates the pattern from the switches, which is necessary if your pattern begins with a -.

The replacement pattern, *subspec*, can contain literal characters as well as the following special sequences:

- & is replaced with the string that matched the pattern.
- \1 through \9 are replaced with the strings that match the corresponding subpatterns in *pattern*. Nine subpatterns are supported. The correspondence is based on the order of left parentheses in the pattern specification.

The following replaces a user's home directory with a ~:

```
regsub ^$env(HOME)/ $pathname ~/ newpath
```

The following constructs a C compile command line given a filename:

```
regsub {([^\.]*)\.c} file.c {cc -c & -o \1.o} ccCmd
```

The \. is used to specify a match against period. The & is replaced with file.c, and \1 is replaced with file, which matches the pattern between the parentheses. The value assigned to ccCmd is:

```
cc -c file.c -o file.o
```

The regsub command can count things for us. The following command counts the newlines in some text. In this case the substitution is not important:

```
set numLines [regsub -all \n $text {} ignore]
```

Transforming Data to Tcl with regsub

One of the most powerful combinations of Tcl commands is regsub and subst. This section describes a few examples that use regsub to transform data into Tcl commands, and then use subst to replace those commands with a new version of the data. This technique is very efficient because it relies on two subsystems that are written in highly optimized C code: the regular expression engine and the Tcl parser. These examples are primarily written by Stephen Uhler.

URL Decoding

When a URL is transmitted over the network, it is encoded by replacing special characters with a `%xx` sequence, where *xx* is the hexadecimal code for the character. In addition, spaces are replaced with a plus (+). It would be tedious and very inefficient to scan a URL one character at a time with Tcl statements to undo this encoding. It would be more efficient to do this with a custom C program, but still very tedious. Instead, a combination of `regsub` and `subst` can do it efficiently in just a few Tcl commands.

Replacing the + with spaces requires quoting the + because it is the one-or-more special character in regular expressions:

```
regsub -all {\+} $url { } url
```

The `%xx` are replaced with a `format` command that will generate the right character:

```
regsub -all {%([0-9a-fA-F][0-9a-fA-F])} $url \
    {[format %c 0x\1]} url
```

The `%c` directive to `format` tells it to generate the character from a character code number. We force a hexadecimal interpretation with a leading `0x`. The resulting string is passed to `subst` to get the `format` commands substituted:

```
set url [subst $url]
```

For example, if the input is `%7ewelch`, the result of the `regsub` is:

```
[format %c 0x7e]welch
```

And then subst generates:

```
~welch
```

Example 11–3 encapsulates this trick in the `Url_Decode` procedure.

Example 11–3 The `Url_Decode` procedure.

```
proc Url_Decode {url} {
    regsub -all {\+} $url { } url
    regsub -all {%([0-9a-fA-F][0-9a-fA-F])} $url \
        {[format %c 0x\1]} url
    return [subst $url]
}
```

CGI Argument Parsing

Example 11–4 builds upon `Url_Decode` to decode the inputs to a CGI program that processes data from an HTML form. Each form element is identified by a name, and the value is URL encoded. All the names and encoded values are passed to the CGI program in the following format:

```
name1=value1&name2=value2&name3=value3
```

Example 11–4 uses `split` to get back a list of names and values, and then it decodes them with `Url_Decode`. The values are stored in the `cgi` array with the name as the key:

Example 11–4 The Cgi_Parse and Cgi_Value procedures.

```
proc Cgi_Parse {} {
    global cgi env
    if [info exists env(QUERY_STRING)] {
        # This comes from GET-style forms
        set query $env(QUERY_STRING)
    } elseif {[info exists env(CONTENT_LENGTH)]} {
        # This comes from POST-style forms
        set query [read stdin $env(CONTENT_LENGTH)]
    } else {
        # No content-length so it is only safe to read one line
        gets stdin query
    }
    foreach {name value} [split $query &=] {
        lappend cgi([Url_Decode $name]) [Url_Decode $value]
    }
}
proc Cgi_Value {name} {
    global cgi
    if ![info exists cgi($name)] {
        return {}
    } elseif {[llength $cgi($name)] == 1} {
        # Strip a level of listing for convenience
        return [lindex $cgi($name) 0]
    } else {
        # Return the whole list of values
        return $cgi($name)
    }
}
```

An HTML form can have several form elements with the same name, and this can result in more than one value for each name. This is why Cgi_Parse uses lappend to assign to the array. The list structure makes it a bit awkward to get the values back, so the Cgi_Value procedure is added to make this more convenient. In the normal case of a single value for a name, Cgi_value eliminates the list structure.

Decoding HTML Entities

The next example is a decoder for HTML *entities*. In HTML, special characters are encoded as entities. If you want a literal < or > in your document, you encode them to avoid conflict with the <tag> syntax used in HTML. HTML syntax is briefly described in Chapter 3 on page 30. The < and > characters are encoded as the entities < and >, respectively. Characters with codes above 127 like copyright © and egrave è are also encoded. There are named entities, like < for < and è for è. You can also use decimal-valued entities like © for ©. Finally, the trailing semicolon is optional, so < or < can both be used to encode <.

The entity decoder is similar to `Url_Decode`. In this case, however, we need to be more careful with `subst`. The text passed to the decoder could contain special characters like a square bracket or dollar sign. With `Url_Decode` we can rely on those special characters being encoded as, for example `%24`. Entity encoding is different (do not ask me why URLs and HTML have different encoding standards), and dollar signs and square brackets are not necessarily encoded. This requires an additional pass to quote these characters. This `regsub` puts a backslash in front of all the brackets, dollar signs, and backslashes.

```
regsub -all {([][$\\])} $text {\\\1} new
```

The decimal encoding (e.g., `©`) is also more awkward than the hexadecimal encoding used in URLs. We cannot force a decimal interpretation of a number in Tcl. In particular, if the entity has a leading zero (e.g., `
`) then Tcl interprets the value (e.g., `010`) as octal. The `scan` command is used to do a decimal interpretation:

```
regsub -all {&#([0-9][0-9]?[0-9]?);?}  $new \
    {[format %c [scan \1 %d tmp;set tmp]]} new
```

The named entities are converted with an array that maps from the entity names to the special character. The only detail is that unknown entity names (e.g., `&foobar;`) are not converted. This mapping is done inside `HtmlMapEntity`, which guards against invalid entities.

```
regsub -all {&([a-zA-Z]+)(;?)} $new \
    {[HtmlMapEntity \1 \\\2 ]} new
```

If the input text contained:

```
[x &lt; y]
```

then the `regsub` would transform this into:

```
\[x [HtmlMapEntity lt \; ] y\]
```

Finally, `subst` will result in:

```
[x < y]
```

Example 11–5 `Html_DecodeEntity`.

```
proc Html_DecodeEntity {text} {
    if {![regexp & $text]} {return $text}
    regsub -all {([][$\\])} $text {\\\1} new
    regsub -all {&#([0-9][0-9]?[0-9]?);?}  $new {\
        [format %c [scan \1 %d tmp;set tmp]]} new
    regsub -all {&([a-zA-Z]+)(;?)} $new \
        {[HtmlMapEntity \1 \\\2 ]} new
    return [subst $new]
}
proc HtmlMapEntity {text {semi {}}} {
    global htmlEntityMap
    set result $text$semi
    catch {set result $htmlEntityMap($text)}
    return $result
}
```

```
# Some of the htmlEntityMap
array set htmlEntityMap {
   lt <   gt >   amp &
   aring \xe5   atilde \xe3
   copy  \xa9   ecirc  \xea   egrave \xe8
}
```


A Simple HTML Parser

The following example is the brainchild of Stephen Uhler. It uses regsub to transform HTML into a Tcl script. When it is evaluated the script calls a procedure to handle each tag in an HTML document. This provides a general framework for processing HTML. Different callback procedures can be applied to the tags to achieve different effects. For example, the html_library package on the CD-ROM uses Html_Parse to display HTML in a Tk text widget.

Example 11–6 Html_Parse.

```
proc Html_Parse {html cmd {start {}}} {

   # Map braces and backslashes into HTML entities
   regsub -all \{ $html {\&ob;} html
   regsub -all \} $html {\&cb;} html
   regsub -all {\\} $html {\&bsl;} html

   # This pattern matches the parts of an HTML tag
   set w " \t\r\n"   ;# white space
   set exp <(/?)(\[^$w>]+)\[$w]*(\[^>]*)>

   # This generates a call to cmd with HTML tag parts
   # \1 is the leading /, if any
   # \2 is the HTML tag name
   # \3 is the parameters to the tag, if any
   # The curly braces at either end group of all the text
   # after the HTML tag, which becomes the last arg to $cmd.
   set sub "\}\n$cmd {\\2} {\\1} {\\3} \{"
   regsub -all $exp $html $sub html

   # This balances the curly braces,
   # and calls $cmd with $start as a pseudo-tag
   # at the beginning and end of the script.
   eval "$cmd {$start} {} {} {$html}"
   eval "$cmd {$start} / {} {}"
}
```

An example will help visualize the transformation. Given this HTML:

```
<Title>My Home Page</Title>
<Body bgcolor=white text=black>
<H1>My Home</H1>
This is my <b>home</b> page.
```

and a call to `Html_Parse` that looks like this:

```
Html_Parse $html {Render .text} hmstart
```

then the generated program is this:

```
Render .text {hmstart} {} {} {}
Render .text {Title} {} {} {My Home Page}
Render .text {Title} {/} {} {
}
Render .text {Body} {} {bgcolor=white text=black} {
}
Render .text {H1} {} {} {My Home}
Render .text {H1} {/} {} {
This is my }
Render .text {b} {} {} {home}
Render .text {b} {/} {} { page.
}
Render .text {hmstart} / {} {}
```

One overall point to make about this example is the difference between using `eval` and `subst` with the generated script. The decoders shown in Examples 11–3 and 11–5 use `subst` to selectively replace encoded characters while ignoring the rest of the text. In `Html_Parse` we must process all the text. The main trick is to replace the matching text (e.g., the HTML tag) with some Tcl code that ends in an open curly brace and starts with a close curly brace. This effectively groups all the unmatched text.

When `eval` is used this way you must do something with any braces and backslashes in the unmatched text. Otherwise the resulting script does not parse correctly. In this case these special characters are encoded as HTML entities. We can afford to do this because the `cmd` that is called must deal with encoded entities already. It is not possible to quote these special characters with backslashes because all this text is inside curly braces so no backslash substitution is performed. If you try that the backslashes will be seen by the `cmd` callback.

Finally, I must admit that I am always surprised that this works:

```
eval "$cmd {$start} {} {} {$html}"
```

I always forget that `$start` and `$html` are substituted in spite of the braces. This is because double quotes are being used to group the argument, so the quoting effect of braces is turned off. Try this:

```
set x hmstart
set y "foo {$x} bar"
=> foo {hmstart} bar
```

Stripping HTML Comments

The `Html_Parse` procedure does not correctly handle HTML comments. The problem is that the syntax for HTML commands allows tags inside comments, so there can be > characters inside the comment. HTML comments are also used to hide Javascript inside pages, which can also contain >. We can fix this with a pass that eliminates the comments.

The comment syntax is this:

```
<!-- HTML comment -->
```

It is awkward to match the closing `-->` without getting stuck on embedded `>` characters, or without matching too much and going all the way to the end of the last comment. This is because the regular expression matcher uses a greedy algorithm. Time for another trick:

```
regsub -all --> $html \x81 html
```

This replaces all the end comment sequences with a single character that is not allowed in HTML. Now you can delete the comments like this:

```
regsub -all "<--\[^\x81\]*\x81" $html {} html
```

Other Commands That Use Regular Expressions

Several Tcl commands use regular expressions.

- `lsearch` takes a `-regexp` flag so you can search for list items that match a regular expression. The `lsearch` command is described on page 58.
- `switch` takes a `-regexp` flag so you can branch based on a regular expression match instead of an exact match or a `string match` style match. The `switch` command is described on page 65.
- The Tk text widget can search its contents based on a regular expression match. Searching in the text widget is described on page 379.
- The `expect` command that is part of the `expect` Tcl extension can match the output of a program with regular expressions. Expect is the subject of its own book, *Exploring Expect* (Don Libes, O'Reilly & Associates, Inc., 1995).

## CHAPTER 12

Script Libraries and Packages

Collections of Tcl commands are kept in libraries and organized into packages. Tcl automatically loads libraries as an application uses their commands. Tcl commands: `package`, `pkg_mkIndex`, `auto_mkIndex`, and `unknown`.

Libraries group useful sets of Tcl procedures so they can be used by multiple applications. For example, you could use any of the code examples that come with this book by creating a script library and then directing your application to check in that library for missing procedures. One way to structure a large application is to have a short main script and a library of support scripts. The advantage of this approach is that not all the Tcl code needs to be loaded to get the application started. Applications start up quickly, and as new features are accessed the code that implements them is loaded automatically.

A package facility was added in Tcl 7.5. It supports version numbers and has a *provide/require* model of use. Typically each file in a library provides one package with a particular version number. Packages also work with shared object libraries that implement Tcl commands in compiled code, which are described on page 523. A package can be provided by a combination of script files and object files. Applications specify which packages they require and the libraries are loaded automatically. The package facility is an alternative to the auto loading scheme used in earlier versions of Tcl. You can use either mechanism, and this chapter describes them both.

If you create a package you may wish to use the namespace facility to avoid conflicts between procedures and global variables used in different packages. Namespaces are the topic of Chapter 14. Before Tcl 8.0 you had to use your own conventions to avoid conflicts. This chapter explains a simple coding convention for large Tcl programs. I use this convention in *exmh*, a mail user interface that

that has grown from about 2,000 to over 25,000 lines of Tcl code. Easily half of the code has been contributed by the *exmh* user community. Such growth might not have been possible without a module system.

Locating Packages: The `auto_path` Variable

The package facility assumes that Tcl libraries are kept in well-known directories. The list of well-known directories is kept in the `auto_path` Tcl variable. This is initialized by *tclsh* and *wish* to include the Tcl script library directory, the Tk script library directory (for *wish*), and the parent directory of the Tcl script library directory. For example, on my Macintosh `auto_path` is a list of these three directories:

```
Disk:System Folder:Extensions:Tool Command Language:tcl7.6
Disk:System Folder:Extensions:Tool Command Language
Disk:System Folder:Extensions:Tool Command Language:tk4.2
```

On my Windows 95 machine the `auto_path` lists these directories:

```
c:\Program Files\Tcl\lib\Tcl7.6
c:\Program Files\Tcl\lib
c:\Program Files\Tcl\lib\Tk4.2
```

On my UNIX workstation the `auto_path` lists these directories:

```
/usr/local/tcl/lib/tcl7.6
/usr/local/tcl/lib
/usr/local/tcl/lib/tk4.2
```

The package facility searches these directories and their subdirectories for packages. The easiest way to manage your own packages is to create a directory at the same level as the Tcl library. Packages in this location, for example, will be found automatically because the `auto_path` list includes `/usr/local/tcl/lib`:

```
/usr/local/tcl/lib/welchbook
```

You can also add directories to the `auto_path` explicitly:

```
lappend auto_path directory
```

Using Packages

Each script file in a library declares what package it implements with the `package provide` command:

```
package provide name version
```

The *name* identifies the package, and the *version* has a *major.minor* format. The convention is that the minor version number can change and the package implementation will still be compatible. If the package changes in an incompatible way, then the major version number should change. For example, Chapter 16 defines several procedures that use the HTTP network protocol.

These include `Http_Open`, `Http_Get`, and `Http_Validate`. The file that contains the procedures starts with this command:

```
package provide Http 1.0
```

More than one file can contribute to the same package simply by specifying the same *name* and *version*. In addition, different versions of the same package can be kept in the same directory but in different files.

An application specifies the packages it needs with the `package require` command:

```
package require name ?version? ?-exact?
```

If the *version* is left off, then the highest available version is loaded. Otherwise the highest version with the same major number is loaded. For example, if the client requires version 1.1, version 1.2 could be loaded if it exists, but version 1.0 would not be loaded. You can restrict the package to a specific version with the `-exact` flag. If no matching version can be found, then the `package require` command raises an error.

Loading Packages Automatically

The `package require` command does not load procedures directly. Instead, the commands implemented by a package are loaded into your application when they are used the first time. The automatic loading depends on an index to record which files implement which packages. The index must be maintained by you, your project librarian, or your system administrator when packages change. The index is computed by a Tcl procedure, `pkg_mkIndex`, and the results are put into the `pkgIndex.tcl` file in each library directory. The `pkg_mkIndex` command takes the name of a directory and one or more *glob* patterns that specify files within that directory. File name patterns are described on page 106. For example:

```
pkg_mkIndex /usr/local/lib/welchbook *.tcl
```

The `pkg_mkIndex` command sources all the files matched by the pattern, detects what packages they provide, and computes the index. You should be aware of this behavior because it only works well for libraries. If the `pkg_mkIndex` command hangs or starts random applications, it is because it sourced an application file instead of a library file.

Packages Implemented in C Code

The files in a library can be either script files that define Tcl procedures, or binary files in shared library format that define Tcl commands in compiled code (i.e., a Dynamic Link Library (DLL)). Chapter 41 describes how to implement Tcl commands in C. There is a C API to the package facility that you use to declare the package name for your commands. This is shown in Example 41–1 on page 523. Chapter 37 also describes the Tcl `load` command that is used instead of `source` to link in shared libraries. The `pkg_mkIndex` command also handles shared libraries:

```
pkg_mkIndex directory *.tcl *.so *.shlib *.dll
```

In this example, `.so`, `.shlib`, and `.dll` are file suffixes for shared libraries on UNIX, Macintosh, and Windows systems, respectively. You can have packages that have some of their commands implemented in C, and some implemented as Tcl procedures. The script files and the shared library just have to declare that they implement the same package. The `pkg_mkIndex` procedure will detect this and set up the `auto_index` so some commands are defined by sourcing scripts, and some are defined by loading shared libraries.

If your file servers support more than one machine architecture, such as Solaris and Linux systems, you probably keep the shared library files in machine-specific directories. In this case the `auto_path` should also list the machine-specific directory so the shared libraries there can be loaded automatically. If your system administrator configured the Tcl installation properly, this should already be set up. If not, or you have your shared libraries in a non-standard place, you must append the location to the `auto_path` variable.

The package Command

The `package` command has several operations that are used primarily by the `pkg_mkIndex` procedure and the automatic loading facility. These operations are summarized in Table 12–1. The basic structure of package loading works like this:

- An application does a `package require` command.
- The package facility checks to see if it knows about the package. If it does, then it sets up the `auto_index` so the commands in the package will be automatically loaded.
- If the package is unknown, the `tclPkgUnknown` procedure is called to find it. Actually, you can specify what procedure to call to do the lookup with the `package unknown` command, but the standard one is `tclPkgUnknown`.
- The `tclPkgUnknown` procedure looks through the `auto_path` directories, and their subdirectories for `pkgIndex.tcl` files. It sources those to build an internal database of packages and version information. The `pkgIndex.tcl` files contain calls to `package ifneeded` that specify what to do to set up automatic loading of the package. The standard action is to call the `tclPkgSetup` procedure.
- The `tclPkgSetup` procedure defines the `auto_index` array to contain the correct `source` or `load` commands to define each command in the package. Automatic loading and the `auto_index` array are described in more detail later.

Table 12–1 The package command.

package forget *package*	Delete registration information for package.
package ifneeded *package* ?*command*?	Query or set the command used to set up automatic loading of a package.
package names	Return the set of registered packages.
package provide *package* *version*	Declare that a script file defines commands for *package* with the given *version*.
package require *package* ?*version*? ?-exact?	Declare that a script uses commands from *package*. The -exact flag specifies that the exact version must be loaded. Otherwise the highest matching version is loaded.
package unknown ?*command*?	Query or set the *command* used to locate packages.
package vcompare *v1* *v2*	Compare version *v1* and *v2*. Returns 0 if they are equal, -1 if *v1* is less than *v2*, or 1 if *v1* is greater than *v2*.
package versions *package*	Returns which versions of the package are registered.
package vsatisfies *v1* *v2*	Returns 1 if *v1* is greater or equal to *v2* and still has the same major version number. Otherwise returns 0.

Libraries Based on the tclIndex File

You can create libraries without using the package command. The basic idea is that a directory has a library of script files, and an index of the Tcl commands defined in the library is kept in a tclIndex file. The drawback is that versions are not supported and you may need to adjust the auto_path to list your library directory. The main advantage of this approach is that this mechanism has been part of Tcl since the earliest versions. If you currently maintain a library using tclIndex files, it will still work.

When you create a script library without packages, you must generate the index that records what procedures are defined in the library. The auto_mkindex procedure creates the index, which is stored in a file named tclIndex that is kept in the script library directory. Suppose all the examples from this book are in the directory /usr/local/tcl/welchbook. You can make the examples into a script library by creating the tclIndex file:

```
auto_mkindex /usr/local/tcl/welchbook *.tcl
```

You will need to update the tclIndex file if you add procedures or change any of their names. A conservative approach to this is shown in the next example. It is conservative because it re-creates the index if anything in the library has changed since the tclIndex file was last generated, whether or not the change added or removed a Tcl procedure.

Example 12–1 Maintaining a `tclIndex` file.

```
proc Library_UpdateIndex { libdir } {
    set index [file join $libdir tclIndex]
    if ![file exists $index] {
        set doit 1
    } else {
        set age [file mtime $index]
        set doit 0
        # Changes to directory may mean files were deleted
        if {[file mtime $libdir] > $age} {
            set doit 1
        } else {
            # Check each file for modification
            foreach file [glob [file join $libdir *.tcl]] {
                if {[file mtime $file] > $age} {
                    set doit 1
                    break
                }
            }
        }
    }
    if { $doit } {
        auto_mkindex $libdir *.tcl
    }
}
```

Tcl uses the `auto_path` variable to record a list of directories to search for unknown commands. To continue our example, you can make the procedures in the book examples available by putting this command at the beginning of your scripts:

```
lappend auto_path /usr/local/tcl/welchbook
```

This has no effect if you have not created the `tclIndex` file. If you want to be extra careful, you can call `Library_UpdateIndex`. This will update the index if you add new things to the library.

```
lappend auto_path /usr/local/tcl/welchbook
Library_UpdateIndex /usr/local/tcl/welchbook
```

This will not work if there is no `tclIndex` file at all because Tcl won't be able to find the implementation of `Library_UpdateIndex`. Once the `tclIndex` has been created for the first time, then this will ensure that any new procedures added to the library will be installed into `tclIndex`. In practice, if you want this sort of automatic update it is wise to include something like the `Library_UpdateIndex` procedure directly into your application as opposed to loading it from the library it is supposed to be maintaining.

The unknown Command

Automatic loading of Tcl commands is implemented by the unknown command. Whenever the Tcl interpreter encounters a command that it does not know about, it calls the unknown command with the name of the missing command. The unknown command is implemented in Tcl, so you are free to provide your own mechanism to handle unknown commands. This chapter describes the behavior of the default implementation of unknown, which can be found in the init.tcl file in the Tcl library. The location of the library is returned by the info library command. In order to bootstrap the library facility, the Tcl shells (*tclsh* and *wish*) invoke the following Tcl command:

```
source [file join [info library] init.tcl]
```


How Auto Loading Works

The unknown command uses an array named auto_index. One element of the array is defined for each procedure that can be automatically loaded. The auto_index array is initialized by the package mechanism or by tclIndex files. The value of an auto_index element is a command that defines the procedure. Typical commands are:

```
source [file join $dir bind_ui.tcl]
load [file join $dir mime.so] Mime
```

The $dir gets substituted with the name of the directory that contains the library file, so the result is a source or load command that defines the missing Tcl command. The substitution is done with eval, so you could initialize auto_index with any commands at all. Example 12–2 is a simplified version of the code that reads the tclIndex file.

Example 12–2 Loading a tclIndex file.

```
# This is a simplified part of the auto_load command.
# Go through auto_path from back to front.
set i [expr [llength $auto_path]-1]
for {} {$i >= 0} {incr i -1} {
   set dir [lindex $auto_path $i]
   if [catch {open [file join $dir tclIndex]} f] {
      # No index
      continue
   }
   # eval the file as a script. Because eval is
   # used instead of source, an extra round of
   # substitutions is performed and $dir gets expanded
   # The real code checks for errors here.
   eval [read $f]
   close $f
}
```

Disabling the Library Facility: auto_noload

If you do not want the unknown procedure to try and load procedures, you can set the auto_noload variable to disable the mechanism:

```
set auto_noload anything
```

Interactive Conveniences

The unknown command provides a few other conveniences. These are only used when you are typing commands directly. They are disabled once execution enters a procedure or if the Tcl shell is not being used interactively. The convenience features are automatic execution of programs, command history, and command abbreviation. These options are tried, in order, if a command implementation cannot be loaded from a script library.

Auto Execute

The unknown procedure implements a second feature: automatic execution of external programs. This makes a Tcl shell behave more like other UNIX shells that are used to execute programs. The search for external programs is done using the standard PATH environment variable that is used by other shells to find programs. If you want to disable the feature all together, set the auto_noexec variable:

```
set auto_noexec anything
```

History

The history facility described in Chapter 13 is implemented by the unknown procedure.

Abbreviations

If you type a unique prefix of a command, unknown recognizes it and executes the matching command for you. This is done after automatic program execution is attempted and history substitutions are performed.

Tcl Shell Library Environment

It may help to understand how the Tcl shells initialize their library environment. The first toehold on the environment is made when the shells are compiled. At that point the default pathname of the library directory is defined. For Tcl, this pathname is put into the tcl_library variable. This value is also returned by the info library command for backward compatibility with early versions of Tcl:

```
info library
```

As of Tcl 7.6, another variable is also defined when Tcl is compiled. The tcl_packagePath variable is defined and is used as the initial value of the auto_path variable. It contains a list of the Tcl script library directory, its parent directory, and the directory containing compiled shared libraries. Changing tcl_packagePath has no effect after auto_path is initialized.

A Tcl shell initializes itself by sourcing init.tcl:

```
source [file join $tcl_library init.tcl]
```

The primary thing defined by init.tcl is the implementation of the unknown procedure. It also initializes auto_path from the value of tcl_packagePath.

The Tk library pathname is defined by the tk_library variable. For Tk, *wish* also does this:

```
source [file join $tk_library tk.tcl]
```

This initializes the scripts that support the Tk widgets. There are still more scripts, and they are organized as a library. So, the tk.tcl script sets up the auto_path variable so the Tk script library is accessible. It does this:

```
lappend auto_path $tk_library
```

To summarize, the bootstrap works as follows:

- The Tcl C library defines the pathname stored in the $tcl_library variable. This default can be overridden with the TCL_LIBRARY environment variable.
- The Tcl C library defines the tcl_pkgPath variable, and this default can be overridden with the TCL_PACKAGE_PATH environment variable.
- The Tcl interpreter sources init.tcl to define the unknown command and initialize auto_path from tcl_pkgPath.
- The Tk C library defines a pathname and stores it into tk_library, a Tcl variable. The default can be overridden with the TK_LIBRARY environment variable.
- The Tk interpreter sources init.tcl as above, and tk.tcl.
- The Tk initialization script appends $tk_library to auto_path.

Normally these details are taken care of by the proper installation of the Tcl and Tk software, but I find it helps to understand things when you see all the steps in the initialization process. If you have only a binary distribution of Tcl and Tk (e.g., a Linux shared library) you may need to adjust TCL_LIBRARY and TK_LIBRARY to reflect the location of the libraries on your system.

Coding Style

If you supply a package, you need to follow some simple coding conventions to make your library easier to use by other programmers. You can use the namespace facility introduced in Tcl 8.0. You can also just use some conventions to avoid name conflicts with other library packages and the main application. This section describes the conventions I developed before namespaces were added to Tcl.

A Module Prefix for Procedure Names

The first convention is to choose an identifying prefix for the procedures in your package. For example, the preferences package in Chapter 39 uses `Pref` as its prefix. All the procedures provided by the library begin with `Pref`. This convention is extended to distinguish between private and exported procedures. An exported procedure has an underscore after its prefix, and it is acceptable to call this procedure from the main application or other library packages. Examples include `Pref_Add`, `Pref_Init`, and `Pref_Dialog`. A private procedure is meant for use only by the other procedures in the same package. Its name does not have the underscore. Examples include `PrefDialogItem` and `PrefXres`.

This naming convention precludes casual names like `doit`, `setup`, `layout`, and so on. There is no way to hide procedure names, so you must maintain the naming convention for all procedures in a package.

A Global Array for State Variables

You should use the same prefix on the global variables used by your package. You can alter the capitalization, just keep the same prefix. I capitalize procedure names and use lowercase for variables. By sticking with the same prefix you identify what variables belong to the package and you avoid conflict with other packages.

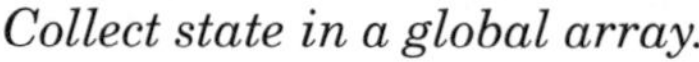

Collect state in a global array.

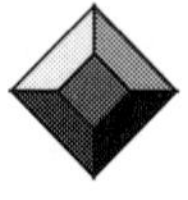

In general I try to use a single global array for a package. The array provides a convenient place to collect a set of related variables, much as a struct is used in C. For example, the preferences package uses the `pref` array to hold all its state information. It is also a good idea to keep the use of the array private. It is better coding practice to provide exported procedures than to let other modules access your data structures directly. This makes it easier to change the implementation of your package without affecting its clients.

If you do need to export a few key variables from your module, use the underscore convention to distinguish exported variables. If you need more than one global variable, just stick with the prefix convention to avoid conflicts.

## CHAPTER 13

Reflection and Debugging

II. Advanced Tcl

This chapter describes commands that give you a view into the interpreter. The `history` command and a simple debugger are useful during development and debugging. The `info` command provides a variety of information about the internal state of the Tcl interpreter. The `time` command measures the time it takes to execute a command. Tcl commands: `info`, `history`, `time`, and `clock`.

Reflection provides feedback to a script about the internal state of the interpreter. This is useful in a variety of cases, from testing to see if a variable exists to dumping the state of the interpreter. This chapter starts with a description of the `info` command that provides lots of different information about the interpreter.

Interactive command history is the second topic of the chapter. The history facility can save you some typing if you spend a lot of time entering commands interactively.

Debugging is the last topic. The old-fashioned approach of adding `puts` commands to your code is often quite useful. It takes so little time to add code and run another test that this is much less painful than if you had to wait for a long compilation every time you changed a print command. The *tkinspect* program is an inspector that lets you look into the state of a Tk application. It can hook up to any Tk application dynamically, so it proves quite useful. Don Libes has implemented a Tcl debugger that lets you set breakpoints and step through your script. His debugger is described at the end of the chapter.

The `clock` Command

The `clock` command has facilities for getting the current time, formatting time values, and scanning printed time strings to get an integer time value. The `clock` command was added in Tcl 7.5. Table 13–1 summarizes the `clock` command:

Table 13–1 The `clock` command.

`clock clicks`	A system-dependent high resolution counter.
`clock format` *value* `?-format` *str*`?`	Format a clock value according to *str*.
`clock scan` *string* `?-base` *clock*`? ?-gmt` *boolean*`?`	Parse date *string* and return seconds value. The *clock* value determines the date.
`clock seconds`	Return the current time in seconds.

The following command prints the current time:

```
clock format [clock seconds]
=> Sun Nov 24 14:57:04  1996
```

The `clock seconds` command returns the current time, in seconds since a starting epoch. The `clock format` command formats an integer value into a date string. It takes an optional argument that controls the format. The format strings contains % keywords that are replaced with the year, month, day, date, hours, minutes, and seconds, in various formats. The default string is:

```
%a %b %d %H:%M:%S %Z %Y
```

Table 13–2 summarizes the `clock` formatting strings:

Table 13–2 Clock formatting keywords.

`%%`	Insert a `%`.
`%a`	Abbreviated weekday name (Mon, Tue, etc.).
`%A`	Full weekday name (Monday, Tuesday, etc.).
`%b`	Abbreviated month name (Jan, Feb, etc.).
`%B`	Full month name.
`%c`	Locale specific date and time (e.g., `Nov 24 16:00:59 1996`).
`%d`	Day of month (01 - 31).
`%H`	Hour in 24-hour format (00 - 23).
`%I`	Hour in 12-hour format (01 - 12).
`%j`	Day of year (001 - 366).
`%m`	Month number (01 - 12).
`%M`	Minute (00 - 59).
`%p`	AM/PM indicator.
`%S`	Seconds (00 - 59).
`%U`	Week of year (00 - 52) when Sunday starts the week.

Table 13–2 Clock formatting keywords. (Continued)

%w	Weekday number (Sunday = 0).
%W	Week of year (01 - 52) when Monday starts the week.
%x	Locale specific date format (e.g., Feb 19 1997).
%X	Locale specific time format (e.g., 20:10:13).
%y	Year without century (00 - 99).
%Y	Year with century (e.g. 1997).
%Z	Time zone name.
	The following work only on UNIX.
%D	Date as %m/%d/%y (e.g., 02/19/97).
%e	Day of month (1 - 31), no leading zeros.
%h	Abbreviated month name.
%n	Insert a newline.
%r	Time as %I:%M:%S %p (e.g., 02:39:29 PM).
%R	Time as %H:%M (e.g., 14:39).
%t	Insert a tab.
%T	Time as %H:%M:%S (e.g., 14:34:29).

The clock clicks command returns the value of the system's highest resolution clock. The units of the clicks are not defined. The main use of this command is to measure the relative time of different performance tuning trials. The following command counts the clicks per second over 10 seconds, which will vary from system to system:

Example 13–1 Calculating clicks per second.

```
set t1 [clock clicks]
after 10000 ;# See page 178
set t2 [clock clicks]
puts "[expr ($t2 - $t1)/10] Clicks/second"
=> 1001313 Clicks/second
```

The clock scan command parses a date string and returns a seconds value. The command handles a variety of date formats. If you leave off the year, the current year is assumed. Tcl implements the standard interpretation of 2-digit year values, which is that 70-99 are 1970-1999, 00-38 are 2000-2038, and other values are undefined. If you leave out a date, the current date is assumed. You can also use the -base option to specify a date. The following example uses the current time as the base, which is redundant:

```
clock scan "10:30:44 PM" -base [clock seconds]
=> 2931690644
```

The date parser allows modifiers: `year`, `month`, `fortnight` (2 weeks), `week`, `day`, `hour`, `minute`, `second`. You can put a positive or negative number in front of a modifier as a multiplier. For example:

```
clock format [clock scan "10:30:44 PM 1 week"]
=> Sun Dec 01 22:30:44  1996
clock format [clock scan "10:30:44 PM -1 week"]
Sun Nov 17 22:30:44  1996
```

You can also use `tomorrow`, `yesterday`, `today`, `now`, `last`, `this`, `next`, and `ago`, as modifiers.

```
clock format [clock scan "3 years ago"]
=> Wed Nov 24 17:06:46  1993
```

Both `clock format` and `clock scan` take a `-gmt` option that uses Greenwich Mean Time. Otherwise the local time zone is used.

```
clock format [clock seconds] -gmt true
=> Sun Nov 24 09:25:29  1996
clock format [clock seconds] -gmt false
=> Sun Nov 24 17:25:34  1996
```

The `info` Command

Table 13–3 summarizes the `info` command. The operations are described in more detail later.

Table 13–3 The `info` command.

`info args` *procedure*	A list of *procedure*'s arguments.
`info body` *procedure*	The commands in the body of *procedure*.
`info cmdcount`	The number of commands executed so far.
`info commands ?`*pattern*`?`	A list of all commands, or those matching *pattern*. Includes built-ins and Tcl procedures.
`info complete` *string*	True if *string* contains a complete Tcl command.
`info default` *proc arg var*	True if *arg* has a default parameter value in procedure *proc*. The default value is stored into *var*.
`info exists` *variable*	True if *variable* is defined.
`info globals ?`*pattern*`?`	A list of all global variables, or those matching *pattern*.
`info hostname`	The name of the machine. This may be the empty string if networking is not initialized.

Table 13–3 The info command. (Continued)

`info level`	The stack level of the current procedure, or 0 for the global scope.
`info level` *`number`*	A list of the command and its arguments at the specified level of the stack.
`info library`	The pathname of the Tcl library directory.
`info loaded ?`*`interp`*`?`	A list of the libraries loaded into the interpreter named *`interp`*, which defaults to the current one.
`info locals ?`*`pattern`*`?`	A list of all local variables, or those matching *`pattern`*.
`info nameofexecutable`	The file name of the program (e.g., of *tclsh* or *wish*).
`info patchlevel`	The release patch level for Tcl.
`info procs ?`*`pattern`*`?`	A list of all Tcl procedures, or those that match *`pattern`*.
`info script`	The name of the file being processed, or the empty string.
`info sharedlibextension`	The file name suffix of shared libraries.
`info tclversion`	The version number of Tcl.
`info vars ?`*`pattern`*`?`	A list of all visible variables, or those matching *`pattern`*.

Variables

There are three categories of variables: *local*, *global*, and *visible*. Information about these categories is returned by the `locals`, `globals`, and `vars` operations, respectively. The local variables include procedure arguments as well as locally defined variables. The global variables include all variables defined at the global scope. The visible variables include locals, plus any variables made visible via `global` or `upvar` commands. A pattern can be specified to limit the returned list of variables to those that match the pattern. The pattern is interpreted according to the rules of `string match`, which is described on page 48:

```
info globals auto*
=> auto_index auto_noexec auto_path
```

Namespaces, which are the topic of the next chapter, partition global variables into different scopes. You query the variables visible in a namespace with:

```
info vars namespace::*
```

Remember that a variable may not be defined yet even though a `global` or `upvar` command has declared it visible in the current scope. Use the `info exists` command to test whether a variable or an array element is defined or not. An example is shown on page 53.

Procedures

You can find out everything about a Tcl procedure with the `args`, `body`, and `default` operations. This is illustrated in the following `Proc_Show` example. The `puts` commands use the `-nonewline` flag because the newlines in the procedure body, if any, are retained:

Example 13–2 Printing a procedure definition.

```
proc Proc_Show {{namepat *} {file stdout}} {
    foreach proc [info procs $namepat] {
        set space ""
        puts -nonewline $file "proc $proc {"
        foreach arg [info args $proc] {
            if [info default $proc $arg value] {
                puts -nonewline $file "$space{$arg $value}"
            } else {
                puts -nonewline $file $space$arg
            }
            set space " "
        }
        # No newline needed because info body may return a
        # value that starts with a newline
        puts -nonewline $file "} {"
        puts -nonewline $file [info body $proc]
        puts $file "}"
    }
}
```

The `info commands` operation returns a list of all commands, which includes both built-in commands defined in C and Tcl procedures. There is no operation that just returns the list of built-in commands. Example 13–3 finds the built-in commands by removing all the procedures from the list of commands:

Example 13–3 Finding built-in commands.

```
proc Command_Info {{pattern *}} {
    set cmds [info commands $pattern]
    foreach proc [info procs $pattern] {
        set ix [lsearch $cmds $proc]
        if {$ix >= 0} {
            set cmds [lreplace $cmds $ix $ix]
        }
    }
    return [lsort $cmds]
}
```

The Call Stack

The `info level` operation returns information about the Tcl evaluation stack, or *call stack*. The global level is numbered zero. A procedure called from the global level is at level one in the call stack. A procedure it calls is at level two, and so on. The `info level` command returns the current level number of the stack if no level number is specified.

If a positive level number is specified (e.g., `info level 3`) then the command returns the procedure name and argument values at that level in the call stack. If a negative level is specified, then it is relative to the current call stack. Relative level -1 is the level of the current procedure's caller, and relative level 0 is the current procedure. The following example prints the call stack. The `Call_trace` procedure avoids printing information about itself by starting at one less than the current call stack level:

Example 13–4 Getting a trace of the Tcl call stack.

```
proc Call_Trace {{file stdout}} {
    puts $file "Tcl Call Trace"
    for {set x [expr [info level]-1]} {$x > 0} {incr x -1} {
        puts $file "$x: [info level $x]"
    }
}
```

Command Evaluation

If you want to know how many Tcl commands are executed, use the `info cmdcount` command. This counts all commands, not just top-level commands. The counter is never reset, so you need to sample it before and after a test run if you want to know how many commands are executed during a test.

The `info complete` operation figures out if a string is a complete Tcl command. This is useful for command interpreters that need to wait until the user has typed in a complete Tcl command before passing it to `eval`. Example 13–5 defines `Command_Process` that gets a line of input and builds up a command. When the command is complete, the command is executed at the global scope. `Command_Process` takes two *callbacks* as arguments. The `inCmd` is evaluated to get the line of input, and the `outCmd` is evaluated to display the results. Chapter 10 describes why `eval` is used as it is in this example:

Example 13–5 A procedure to read and evaluate commands.

```
proc Command_Process {inCmd outCmd} {
    global command
    append command(line) [eval $inCmd]
    if [info complete $command(line)] {
        set code [catch {uplevel #0 $command(line)} result]
        eval $outCmd {$result $code}
        set command(line) {}
```

```
    }
}
proc Command_Read {{in stdin}} {
    if [eof $in] {
        if {$in != "stdin"} {
            close $in
        }
        return {}
    }
    return [gets $in]
}
proc Command_Display {file result code} {
    puts stdout $result
}
while {![eof stdin]} {
    Command_Process {Command_Read stdin} \
        {Command_Display stdout}
}
```

Scripts and the Library

The name of the current script file is returned with the `info script` command. For example, if you use the `source` command to read commands from a file, then `info script` returns the name of that file if it is called during execution of the commands in that script. This is true even if the `info script` command is called from a procedure that is not defined in the script.

The pathname of the Tcl library is stored in the `tcl_library` variable, and it is also returned by the `info library` command. While you could put scripts into this directory, it might be better to have a separate directory and use the script library facility described in Chapter 12. This makes it easier to deal with new releases of Tcl and to package up your code if you want other sites to use it.

Version Numbers

Each Tcl release has a version number such as 7.4 or 8.0. This number is returned by the `info tclversion` command. If you want your script to run on a variety of Tcl releases, you may need to test the version number and take different actions in the case of incompatibilities between releases.

The Tcl release cycle starts with one or two alpha and beta releases before the final release, and there may even be a patch release after that. The `info patchlevel` command returns a qualified version number, like 8.0b1 for the first beta release of 8.0, or 7.4p1, for the first patch release after the final 7.4 release. The patch level is the same as the version number for the final release.

Execution Environment

The file name of the program being executed is returned with `info nameofexecutable`. This is more precise than the name in the `argv0` variable, which could be a relative name or a name found in a command directory on your command search path. It is still possible for `info nameofexecutable` to return a relative pathname if the user runs your program as `./foo`, for example. The following construct always returns the absolute pathname of the current program. If `info nameofexecutable` returns an absolute pathname, then the value of the current directory is ignored. The `pwd` command is described on page 106:

```
file join [pwd] [info nameofexecutable]
```

A few operations support dynamic loading of shared libraries, which are described in Chapter 41. The `info sharedlibextension` returns the file name suffix of dynamic link libraries. The `info loaded` command returns a list of libraries that have been loaded into an interpreter. Multiple interpreters are described in Chapter 17.

Cross-Platform Support

Tcl is designed so you can write scripts that run unchanged on UNIX, Macintosh, and Windows platforms. In practice, you may need a small amount of code that is specific to a particular platform. You can find out information about the platform via the `tcl_platform` variable. This is an array with these elements defined:

- `tcl_platform(platform)` is one of `unix`, `macintosh`, or `windows`.
- `tcl_platform(os)` identifies the operating system. Examples include `MacOS`, `Solaris`, `Linux`, `Win32s` (Windows 3.1 with the Win32 subsystem), `Windows 95`, `Windows NT`, and `SunOS`.
- `tcl_platform(osVersion)` gives the version number of the operating system.
- `tcl_platform(machine)` identifies the hardware. Examples include `ppc` (Power PC), `68k` (68000 family), `sparc`, `intel`, `mips`, and `alpha`.

On some platforms a *hostname* is defined. If available, it is returned with the `info hostname` command. This command may return an empty string.

One of the most significant areas affected by cross-platform portability is the file system and the way files are named. This topic is discussed on page 95.

Tracing Variable Values

The `trace` command registers a command to be called whenever a variable is accessed, modified, or unset. This form of the command is:

```
trace variable name ops command
```

The *name* is a Tcl variable name, which can be a simple variable, an array, or an array element. If a whole array is traced, the trace is invoked when any element is used according to *ops*. The *ops* argument is one or more of the letters `r`, for read traces, `w`, for write traces, and `u`, for unset traces. The *command* is executed when one of these events occurs. It is invoked as:

command name1 name2 op

The *name1* argument is the variable or array name. The *name2* argument is the name of the array index, or null if the trace is on a simple variable. If there is an unset trace on an entire array and the array is unset, *name2* is also null. The value of the variable is not passed to the procedure. The traced variable is one level up the Tcl call stack. The `upvar`, `uplevel`, or `global` commands need to be used to make the variable visible in the scope of *command*. These commands are described in more detail in Chapter 7.

A read trace is invoked before the value of the variable is returned, so if it changes the variable itself, the new value is returned. A write trace is called after the variable is modified. The unset trace is called after the variable is unset.

Example 13–6 uses traces to implement a read-only variable. The value is modified before the trace procedure is called, so another variable (or some other mechanism) is needed to preserve the original value. When a variable is unset the traces are automatically removed, so the unset trace action reestablishes the trace explicitly. Note that the `upvar` alias cannot be used to set up the trace:

Example 13–6 Tracing variables.

```
set x-orig $x
trace variable x wu FixupX
proc FixupX { varName index op } {
    upvar $varName var
    global x-orig
    switch $op {
        w {set var $x-orig}
        u {set var $x-orig
            # Re-establish the trace using the true name
            trace variable $varName wu FixupX}
    }
}
```

This example merely overrides the new value with the saved valued. Another alternative is to raise an error with the `error` command. This will cause the command that modified the variable to return the error. Another common use of `trace` is to update a user interface widget in response to a variable change. Several of the Tk widgets have this feature built into them.

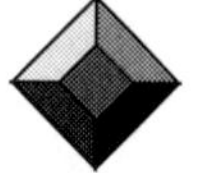

If more than one trace is set on a variable, then they are invoked in the reverse order; the most recent trace is executed first. If there is a trace on an array and on an array element, then the trace on the array is invoked first. The next example uses an array trace to dynamically create array elements:

Example 13–7 Creating array elements with array traces.

```
# make sure variable is an array
set dynamic() {}
trace variable dynamic r FixupDynamic
```

```
proc FixupDynamic {name index op} {
    global dynamic;# We know this is $name
    if ![info exists dynamic($index)] {
        set dynamic($index) 0
    }
}
```

Information about traces on a variable is returned with the `vinfo` option:

```
trace vinfo dynamic
=> {r FixupDynamic}
```

A trace is deleted with the `vdelete` option, which has the same form as the `variable` option. The trace in the previous example can be removed with the following command:

```
trace vdelete dynamic r FixupDynamic
```


Interactive Command History

The Tcl shell programs keep a log of the commands that you type by using a history facility. The log is controlled and accessed via the `history` command. The history facility uses the term *event* to mean an entry in its history log. The events are just commands, and they have an event ID that is their index in the log. You can also specify an event with a negative index that counts backwards from the end of the log. Event -1 is the previous event. Table 13–4 summarizes the Tcl `history` command. In the table, *event* defaults to -1.

In practice you will want to take advantage of the ability to abbreviate the history options and even the name of the `history` command itself. For the command, you need to type a unique prefix, and this depends on what other commands are already defined. For the options, there are unique one-letter abbreviations for all of them. For example, you could reuse the last word of the previous command with `[hist w $]`. This works because a `$` that is not followed by alphanumerics or an open brace is treated as a literal `$`.

Several of the history operations update the history list. They remove the actual `history` command and replace it with the command that resulted from the history operation. The `event`, `redo`, `substitute`, and `words` operations all behave in this manner. This makes perfect sense because you would rather have the actual command in the history, instead of the history command used to retrieve the command.

Table 13–4 The `history` command.

`history`	Short for `history info` with no *count*.
`history add command ?exec?`	Add the command to the history list. If `exec` is specified, then execute the command.
`history change` *new* `?`*event*`?`	Change the command specified by *event* to *new* in the command history.

Table 13–4 The `history` command. (Continued)

`history event ?event?`	Returns the command specified by *event*.
`history info ?count?`	Returns a formatted history list of the last *count* commands, or of all commands.
`history keep count`	Limit the history to the last *count* commands.
`history nextid`	Returns the number of the next event.
`history redo ?event?`	Repeat the specified command.
`history substitute old new ?event?`	Globally replace *old* with *new* in the command specified by *event*, then execute the result.
`history words selector ?event?`	Return list elements from the event according to *selector*. List items count from zero. `$` is the last item. A range is specified as *a-b*, e.g., *1-$*.

History Syntax

Some extra syntax is supported when running interactively to make the history facility more convenient to use. Table 13–5 shows the special history syntax supported by *tclsh* and *wish*.

Table 13–5 Special `history` syntax.

`!!`	Repeat the previous command.
`!n`	Repeat command number *n*. If *n* is negative it counts backward from the current command. The previous command is event -1.
`!prefix`	Repeat the last command that begins with *prefix*.
`!pattern`	Repeat the last command that matches *pattern*.
`^old^new`	Globally replace *old* with *new* in the last command.

The next example shows how some of the history operations work:

Example 13–8 Interactive `history` usage.

```
% set a 5
5
% set a [expr $a+7]
12
% history
    1 set a 5
    2 set a [expr $a+7]
    3 history
% !2
19
% !!
26
```

```
% ^7^13
39
% !h
    1 set a 5
    2 set a [expr $a+7]
    3 history
    4 set a [expr $a+7]
    5 set a [expr $a+7]
    6 set a [expr $a+13]
    7 history
```


A Comparison to C Shell History Syntax

The history syntax shown in the previous example is simpler than the history syntax provided by the C shell. Not all of the history operations are supported with special syntax. The substitutions (using `^old^new`) are performed globally on the previous command. This is different than the quick-history of the C shell. Instead, it is like the `!:gs/old/new/` history command. So, for example, if the example had included `^a^b` in an attempt to set `b` to `39`, an error would have occurred because the command would have used `b` before it was defined:

```
set b [expr $b+7]
```

If you want to improve the history syntax, you will need to modify the `unknown` command, which is where it is implemented. This command is discussed in more detail in Chapter 12. Here is the code from the `unknown` command that implements the extra history syntax. The main limitation in comparison with the C shell history syntax is that the `!` substitutions are only performed when `!` is at the beginning of the command:

Example 13–9 Implementing special history syntax.

```
# Excerpts from the standard unknown command
# uplevel is used to run the command in the right context
if {$name == "!!"} {
    return [uplevel {history redo}]
}
if [regexp {^!(.+)$} $name dummy event] {
    return [uplevel [list history redo $event]]
}
if [regexp {^\^([^^]*)\^([^^]*)\^?$} $name dummy old new] {
    return [uplevel [list history substitute $old $new]]
}
```

Debugging

The rapid turnaround with Tcl coding means that it is often sufficient to add a few `puts` statements to your script to gain some insight about its behavior. This solution doesn't scale too well, however. A slight improvement is to add a `Debug` procedure that can have its output controlled better. You can log the information to a file, or turn it off completely. In a Tk application, it is simple to create a text widget to hold the contents of the log so you can view it from the application. Here is a simple `Debug` procedure. To enable it you need to set the `debug(enable)` variable. To have its output go to your terminal, set `debug(file)` to `stderr`.

Example 13–10 A `Debug` procedure.

```
proc Debug { args } {
    global debug
    if ![info exists debug(enabled)] {
        # Default is to do nothing
        return
    }
    puts $debug(file) [join $args " "]
}
proc DebugOn {{file {}}} {
    global debug
    set debug(enabled) 1
    if {[string length $file] == 0} {
        set debug(file) stderr
    } else {
        if [catch {open $file w} fileID] {
            puts stderr "Cannot open $file: $fileID"
            set debug(file) stderr
        } else {
            puts stderr "Debug info to $file"
            set debug(file) $fileID
        }
    }
}
proc DebugOff {} {
    global debug
    if [info exists debug(enabled)] {
        unset debug(enabled)
        flush $debug(file)
        if {$debug(file) != "stderr" &&
             $debug(file) != "stdout"} {
            close $debug(file)
            unset $debug(file)
        }
    }
}
```

Don Libes' Debugger

Don Libes at the National Institute of Standards and Technology has built a Tcl debugger that lets you set breakpoints and step through your scripts interactively. He is also the author of the *expect* program that is described in the O'Reilly book, *Exploring Expect*. The debugger requires a modified Tcl shell because the debugger needs a few more built-in commands to support it. This section assumes you have it built into your shell already. The *expect* program includes the debugger, and creating a custom shell that includes the debugger is described in Chapter 41 on page 540.

The most interesting feature of the debugger is that you set breakpoints by specifying patterns that match commands. The reason for this is that Tcl doesn't keep around enough information to map from file line numbers to Tcl commands in scripts. The pattern matching is a clever alternative, and it opens up lots of possibilities.

The debugger defines several one-character command names. The commands are only defined when the debugger is active, and you should not have one-letter commands of your own so there should not be conflicts :-) The way you enter the debugger in the first place is left up to the application. The *expect* shell enters the debugger when you generate a keyboard interrupt. Example 41–10 on page 542 shows how to set this up. Table 13–6 summarizes the commands.

Table 13–6 Debugger commands.

`s ?n?`	Step. Goes into procedures. Step once, or *n* times.
`n ?n?`	Step. Skips over procedures. Step once, or *n* times.
`r`	Return from a procedure.
`b ?options?`	Set, clear, or show a breakpoint.
`c`	Continue execution to next breakpoint or interrupt.
`w ?-w width? ?-c X?`	Show the call stack, limiting each line to *width* characters. `-c` 1 displays control characters as escape sequences. -c 0 displays control characters normally.
`u ?level?`	Move scope up the call stack one level, or to level *level*.
`d ?level?`	Move scope down the call stack one level, or to level *level*.
`h`	Display help information.

When you are at the debugger prompt, you are talking to your Tcl interpreter so you can issue any Tcl command. There is no need to define new commands to look at variables. Just use `set`!

The `s` and `n` commands step through your script. They take an optional parameter that indicates how many steps to take before stopping again. The `r` command completes execution of the current procedure and stops right after the procedure returns.

The `w` command prints the call stack. Each level is preceded by its number, with level 0 being the top of the stack. An asterisk is printed by the current scope, which you can change as described next. Each line of the stack trace can get quite long because of argument substitutions. Control the output width with the -w argument.

The u and d commands change the current scope. They move up and down the Tcl call stack, where "up" means toward the calling procedures. The very top of the stack is the global scope. You need to use these commands to easily examine variables in different scopes. They take an optional parameter that specifies what level to go to. If the level specifier begins with #, then it is an absolute level number and the current scope changes to that level. Otherwise the scope moves up or down the specified number of levels.

Breakpoints by Pattern Matching

The b command manipulates breakpoints. The location of a breakpoint is specified by a pattern. When a command that matches the pattern is executed, the breakpoint occurs. Eventually it will be possible to specify breakpoints by line number, but the Tcl interpreter doesn't keep around enough information to make that easy to do. The general form of the command to set a breakpoint is shown below:

```
b ?-re regexp? ?if condition? ?then action?
b ?-glob pattern? ?if condition? ?then action?
```

The b command supports both glob patterns and regular expressions. Patterns will be discussed later in more detail. A breakpoint can have a test associated with it. The breakpoint will only occur if the condition is met. A breakpoint can have an action, independent of a condition. The action provides a way to patch code into your script. Finally, the pattern itself is also optional, so you can have a breakpoint that is just a conditional. A breakpoint that just has an action will trigger on every command.

Here are several examples:

```
b -re ^foobar
```

This breaks whenever the foobar command is invoked. The ^ in the regular expression ensures that foobar is the first word in the command. In contrast, the next breakpoint occurs whenever foobar is about to be called from within another command. A glob pattern is used for comparison. A glob pattern has to match the whole command string, hence the asterisk at the beginning and end of the pattern:

```
b -glob {*\[foobar *}
```

The subpattern matching of the regular expression facility is supported. If you have subpatterns, the parts of the string that match are stored in the dbg(1) through dbg(9) array elements. The string that matched the whole pattern is stored in dbg(0). The following breakpoint stops when the crunch command is about to be called with its first argument greater than 1024:

```
b -re {^crunch ([0-9]+)} if {$dbg(1) > 1024}
```

If you just want to print information and keep going, you can put a c, s, n, or r command into the action associated with a breakpoint. The following breakpoint traces assignments to a variable:

```
b -re {^set a ([^ ]+)} then {
    puts "a changing from $a to $dbg(1)"
    c
}
```

The breakpoint is called before the command executes, so in this case `$a` refers to the old value, and the pattern extracts the new value. If an error occurs inside the action, the error is discarded and the rest of the action is skipped.

Deleting Break Points

The `b` command with no arguments lists the defined breakpoints. Each breakpoint is preceded by an ID number. To delete a breakpoint, give the breakpoint number preceded by a minus sign:

```
b -N
```

Debugging Tk Scripts

You can use the techniques outlined so far to debug Tk scripts. There are some additional techniques, too. Instead of logging error messages to a file, you can log them to a text widget and view them from within your application. You can also use the ability to send Tcl commands between Tk applications to look at the state of your application.

The *tkinspect* Program

The *tkinspect* program is a Tk application that lets you look at the state of other Tk applications. It displays procedures, variables, and the Tk widget hierarchy. With *tkinspect* you can issue commands to another application in order to change variables or test out commands. This turns out to be a very useful way to debug Tk applications. It was written by Sam Shen and is available on the CD-ROM. The current FTP address for this is:

```
ftp.neosoft.com:/pub/tcl/sorted/devel/tkinspect-5.1.6.tar.gz
```

The *tdebug* Program

The *tdebug* program is a debugger written purely in Tcl. It sets breakpoints by rewriting Tcl procedures to contain extra calls to the debugger. A small amount of support code is loaded into your application automatically, and the debugger application can set breakpoints, watch variables, and trace execution. It was written by Gregor Schmid and is available on the CD-ROM. The current FTP address for this package is:

```
ftp.neosoft.com:/pub/tcl/sorted/devel/tdebug-1.0.tar.gz
```

The `bgerror` Command

When a Tcl script encounters an error during background processing, such as handling file events or during the command associated with a button, it signals the error by calling the `bgerror` procedure. A default implementation displays a dialog and gives you an opportunity to view the Tcl call stack at the point of the error. You can supply your own version of `bgerror`. For example, when my *exmh* mail application gets an error it offers to send mail to me with a few words of explanation from the user and a copy of the stack trace. I get interesting bug reports from all over the world!

The `bgerror` command is called with one argument that is the error message. The global variable `errorInfo` contains the stack trace information. There is an example `tkerror` implementation in the on-line sources associated with this book.

The `tkerror` Command

The `bgerror` command used to be called `tkerror`. When event processing shifted from Tk into Tcl with Tcl 7.5 and Tk 4.1, the name `tkerror` was changed to `bgerror`. Backwards compatibility is provided so that if `tkerror` is defined, then it is called instead of `bgerror`. I have run into problems with the compatibility setup and have found it more reliable to update my applications to use `bgerror` instead of `tkerror`. If you have an application that runs under either Tk 4.0 or Tk 4.1, you can just define both:

```
proc bgerror [info args tkerror] [info body tkerror]
```

Performance Tuning

The `time` command measures the execution time of a Tcl command. It takes an optional parameter that is a repetition count:

```
time {set a "Hello, World!"} 1000
=> 28 microseconds per iteration
```

If you need the result of the command being timed, use `set` to capture the result:

```
puts $log "command: [time {set result [command]}]"
```

Time stamps in a Log

Another way to gain insight into the performance of your script is to generate log records that contain time stamps. The `clock seconds` value is too coarse, but you can couple it with the `clock clicks` value to get higher resolution measurements. Use the code shown in Example 13–1 on page 147 to calibrate the clicks per second on your system. Example 13–11 writes log records that contain the current time and the number of clicks since the last record. There will be occasional glitches in the clicks value when the system counter wraps around or is reset by the system clock, but it will normally give pretty accurate results. The `Log` procedure adds overhead, too, so you should take several measurements in a tight loop to see how long each `Log` call takes:

Example 13–11 Time Stamps in log records.

```
proc Log {args} {
    global log
    if [info exists log(file)] {
        set now [clock clicks]
        puts $log(file) [format "%s (%d)\t%s" \
            [clock format [clock seconds]] \
            [expr $now - $log(last)] \
            [join $args " "]]
        set log(last) $now
    }
}
proc Log_Open {file} {
    global log
    catch {close $log(file)}
    set log(file) [open $file w]
    set log(last) [clock clicks]
}
proc Log_Flush {} {
    global log
    catch {flush $log(file)}
}
proc Log_Close {} {
    global log
    catch {close $log(file)}
    catch {unset log(file)}
}
```

A more advanced `profile` command is part of the Extended Tcl (Tclx) package, which is described in *Tcl/Tk Tools* (Mark Harrison, ed. O'Reilly & Associates, Inc., 1997). The Tclx `profile` command monitors the number of calls, the CPU time, and the elapsed time spent in different procedures.

Tcl 8.0

The built-in compiler that comes with Tcl 8.0 improves performance in the following ways:

- Tcl scripts are converted into an internal byte-code format that is efficient to process. The byte codes are saved so that cost of compiling is only paid the first time you execute a procedure or loop. After that, execution proceeds much faster. Compilation is done as needed, so unused code is never compiled. If you redefine a procedure it is recompiled the next time it is executed.

- Variables and command arguments are kept in a native format as long as possible and only converted to strings when necessary. There are several native types, including integers, floating point numbers, Tcl lists, byte codes, and arrays. There are C APIs for implementing new types. Tcl is still dynamically typed, so a variable can contain different types during its lifetime.
- Expressions and control structures are compiled into special byte codes so they are executed more efficiently.

The operation of the compiler is essentially transparent to scripts, but there are some differences in lists and expressions. These are described in Chapter 47. With lists, the good news is that large lists are more efficient. The problem is that lists are parsed more aggressively, so syntax errors at the end of a list will be detected even if you only access the beginning of the list.

Namespaces

Namespaces group procedures and variables into separate name spaces. Namespaces were added in Tcl 8.0. This chapter describes the `namespace` and `variable` commands.

Namespaces provide new scopes for procedures and global variables. Originally Tcl had one global scope for shared variables, local scopes within procedures, and one global name space for procedures. The single global scope for procedures and global variables can become unmanageable as your Tcl application grows. I describe some simple naming conventions on page 143 that I have used successfully in large programs. However, Tcl 8.0 adds a more elegant namespace facility that partitions the global scope for procedure names and global variables.

Namespaces help structure large Tcl applications, but they add complexity. In particular, command callbacks may have to be handled specially so they execute in the proper namespace. You choose whether or not you need the extra structure and learning curve of namespaces. If your applications are small, then you can ignore the namespace facility.

Using Namespaces

Namespaces can be nested, so you can create a hierarchy of scopes. Namespaces add new syntax to procedure and variable names. A double-colon, `::`, separates the namespace name from the variable or procedure name. You use this syntax to reference procedures and variables in a different namespace. The `namespace import` command lets you name things in other namespaces without the extra syntax. These concepts are explained in more detail in the rest of this chapter.

Example 14–1 repeats the random number generator from Example 7–4 on page 78 using namespaces:

Example 14–1 Random number generator using namespaces.

```
namespace eval Random {
   # Create a variable inside the namespace
   variable seed [clock seconds]

   # Make the procedures visible to namespace import
   namespace export Init Random Range

   # Create procedures inside the namespace
   proc Init { value } {
      variable seed
      set seed $value
   }
   proc Random {} {
      variable seed
      set seed [expr ($seed*9301 + 49297) % 233280]
      return [expr $seed/double(233280)]
   }
   proc Range { range } {
      expr int([Random]*$range)
   }
}
```

Example 14–1 defines three procedures and a variable inside the namespace `Random`. From inside the namespace you can use these procedures and variables directly. From outside the namespace you use the `::` syntax for namespace qualifiers. For example, the state variable is just `seed` within the namespace, but you use `Random::seed` to refer to the variable from outside the namespace. Using the procedures looks like this:

```
Random::Random
=> 0.3993355624142661
Random::Range 10
=> 4
```

If you use a package a lot you can *import* its procedures. A package declares what procedures can be imported with the `namespace export` command. Importing and exporting are described in more detail later. Once you import a procedure you can use it without a qualified name:

```
namespace import Random::Random
Random
=> 0.54342849794238679
```

Namespace Variables

The `variable` command defines a variable inside a namespace. It is like the `set` command because it can define a value for the variable. You can declare several namespace variables with one `variable` command. The general form is:

```
variable name ?value? ?name value? ...
```

If you have an array, do not assign a value in the `variable` command. Instead, use regular Tcl commands after you declare the variable. You can put any commands inside a `namespace` block:

```
namespace eval foo {
    variable arr
    array set arr {name value name2 value2}
}
```

A namespace variable is similar to a global variable because it is outside the scope of any procedures. Procedures use the `variable` command or qualified names to reference namespace variables. For example, the `Random` procedure has a `variable` command that brings the namespace variable into the current scope:

```
variable seed
```

You do not have to have a `variable` command inside the namespace block. It is only useful there to give the namespace variable an initial value. If a procedure has a `variable` command that names a new variable, it is created in the namespace when it is first `set`.

Qualified Names

A fully qualified name begins with `::`, which is the name for the global namespace. A fully qualified name unambiguously names a procedure or a variable. The fully qualified name works anywhere. If you use a fully qualified variable name, it is *not* necessary to use a `global` command. For example, suppose namespace `foo` has a namespace variable `x`, and there is also a global variable `x`. The global variable `x` can be named with this:

```
::x
```

The `::` syntax does not affect variable substitutions. You can get the value of the global variable `x` with `$::x`. Name the namespace variable `x` with this:

```
::foo::x
```

A partially qualified name does not have a leading `::`. In this case the name is resolved from the current namespace. For example, the following also names the namespace variable `x`:

```
foo::x
```

You can use qualified names with `global`. Once you do this, you can access the variable with its short name:

```
global ::foo::x
set x 5
```

Command Lookup

A command is looked up first in the current name space. If it is not found there, then it is looked up in the global namespace. This means you can use all the built-in Tcl commands inside a namespace with no special effort.

You can play games by redefining commands within a namespace. For example, a namespace could define a procedure named `set`. To get the built-in `set` you could use `::set`, while `set` referred to the `set` defined inside namespace. Obviously you need to be quite careful when you do this.

You can use qualified names when defining procedures. This eliminates the need to put the `proc` commands inside a `namespace` block. Example 14–2 repeats the random number generator using qualified names. `Random::Init` does not need a `variable` command because it uses a qualified name for `seed`:

Example 14–2 Random number generator using qualified names.

```
namespace eval Random {
    # Create a variable inside the namespace
    variable seed [clock seconds]
}
# Create procedures inside the namespace
proc Random::Init { seed } {
    set ::Random::seed $seed
}
proc Random::Random {} {
    variable seed
    set seed [expr ($seed*9301 + 49297) % 233280]
    return [expr $seed/double(233280)]
}
proc Random::Range { range } {
    expr int([Random]*$range)
}
```

Nested Namespaces

Namespaces can be nested inside other namespaces. Example 14–3 shows three namespaces that each have their own variable `x`. The fully qualified names for these variables are `::foo::x`, `::bar::x`, and `::bar::foo::x`.

Example 14–3 Nested namespaces.

```
namespace eval foo {
    variable x 1     ;# ::foo::x
}
namespace eval bar {
    variable x 2     ;# ::bar::x
    namespace foo {
        variable x 3 ;# ::bar::foo::x
```

```
    }
    puts $foo::x      ;# prints 3
}
puts $foo::x          ;# prints 1
```

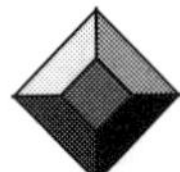

Partially qualified names can refer to two different objects.

In Example 14–3 the partially qualified name `foo::x` can reference one of two variables depending on the current namespace. From the global scope the name `foo::x` refers to the namespace variable `x` inside `::foo`. From the `::bar` namespace, `foo::x` refers to the variable `x` inside `::bar::foo`.

If you want to unambiguously name a variable in the current namespace, you have two choices. The simplest is to bring the variable into scope with the `variable` command:

```
variable x
set x something
```

If you need to give out the name of the variable, then you can use the `namespace current` command to create a fully qualified name:

```
trace variable [namespace current]::x r \
    [namespace current]::traceproc
```

Importing Procedures

Commands can be imported from namespaces to make it easier to name them. An imported command can be used without its namespace qualifier. Each namespace specifies exported procedures that can be the target of an import. Variables cannot be imported. Note that importing is only a convenience; you can always use qualified names to access any procedure.

The `namespace export` command goes inside the namespace block, and it specifies what procedures a namespace exports. The specification is a list of `string match` patterns that are compared against the set of commands defined in a namespace. The export list can be defined before the procedures being exported. You can do more than one `namespace export` to add more procedures, or patterns, to the export list for a namespace. Use the `-clear` flag if you need to reset the export list.

```
namespace export ?-clear? ?pat? ?pat? ...
```

The `namespace import` command makes commands in another namespace visible in the current namespace. An `import` can cause conflicts with commands in the current namespace. The `namespace import` command raises an error if there is a conflict. You can override this with the `-force` option. The general form of the command is:

```
namespace import ?-force? namespace::pat ?namespace::pat?...
```

The *`pat`* is a `string match` type pattern that is matched against *exported* commands defined in *`namespace`*. You cannot use patterns to match *`namespace`*. The *`namespace`* can be a fully or partially qualified name of a namespace.

If you are lazy, you can import all procedures from a namespace:

```
namespace import Random::*
```

The drawback of this approach is that `Random` exports an `Init` procedure, which might conflict with another module you import in the same way. It is safer to `import` just the procedures you plan on using:

```
namespace import Random::Random Random::Range
```

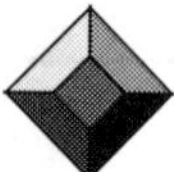

A `namespace import` takes a snapshot.

If the set of procedures in a namespace changes, or if its export list changes, then this has no effect on any imports that have already occurred from that namespace.

Other Namespaces

Several subsystems have their own namespaces for their objects. These other namespaces are independent of the procedure and variable namespaces. Named objects include Tcl interpreters, which are described on page 205, Tk widgets, which are introduced on page 228, and Tk images, which are introduced on page 458. For each instance of the object, a Tcl command is created with the same name as the object. These are always global command names, even if the code that creates the object is in a namespace. You can use `rename` to move one of these global commands into a namespace, but the name of the object does not change.

Callbacks and Namespaces

Commands like `after`, `bind`, and `button` take arguments that are Tcl scripts that are evaluated later. These *callback* commands execute later in the global scope by default. If you want a callback to be evaluated in a particular namespace, you can construct the callback with `namespace code`. This command does not execute the callback. Instead, it generates a Tcl command that will execute in the current namespace scope when it is evaluated later. For example, suppose `::current` is the current namespace. The `namespace code` command determines the current scope and adds that to the `namespace inscope` command it generates:

```
set callback [namespace code {set x 1}]
=> namespace inscope ::current {set x 1}
# sometime later ...
eval $callback
```

When you evaluate `$callback` later, it executes in the `::current` namespace. In particular, if there is a namespace variable `::current::x`, then that variable is modified. Compare this without namespaces:

```
set callback {set x 1}
# sometime later ...
eval $callback
```

If you need substitutions to occur on the command when you define it, use list to construct it. Using list is discussed in more detail on pages 114 and 305. Example 14–4 wraps up the list and the namespace inscope into the code procedure, which is handy because you almost always want to use list when constructing callbacks. The uplevel in code ensures that the correct namespace is captured; you can use code anywhere:

Example 14–4 The code procedure to wrap callbacks.

```
proc code {args} {
   set namespace [uplevel {namespace current}]
   return [list namespace inscope $namespace $args]
}
namespace eval foo {
   variable y "y value" x {}
   set callback [code set x $y]
   => namespace inscope ::foo {set x {y value}}
}
```

The example defines a callback that will set ::foo::x to y value. If you want to set x to the value that y has at the time of the callback, then you do not want to do any substitutions. In that case, the original namespace code is what you want:

```
set callback [namespace code {set x $y}]
=> namespace inscope ::foo {set x $y}
```

If the callback has additional arguments added by the caller, namespace inscope correctly adds them. For example, the scrollbar protocol described on page 347 adds parameters to the callback that controls a scrollbar.

Introspection

The info commands operation returns all the commands that are currently visible. It is described in more detail on page 150. You can limit the information returned with a string match pattern. You can also include a namespace specifier in the pattern to see what is visible in a namespace. Remember that global commands and imported commands are visible, so info commands returns more than just what is defined by the namespace. Example 14–5 uses namespace origin, which returns the original name of imported commands, to sort out the commands that are really defined in a namespace:

Example 14–5 Listing commands defined by a namespace.

```
proc Namespace_List {{namespace {}}} {
   if {[string length $namespace] == 0} {
      # Determine the namespace of our caller
      set namespace [uplevel {namespace current}]
   }
   set result {}
```

```
    foreach cmd [info commands ${namespace}::*] {
        if {[namespace origin $cmd] == $cmd} {
            lappend result $cmd
        }
    }
    return $result
}
```

The namespace Command

Table 14–1 summarizes the `namespace` operations:

Table 14–1 The `namespace` command.

`namespace current`	Return the current namespace.
`namespace children ?`*name*`? ?`*pat*`?`	Return names of nested namespaces. *name* defaults to current namespace. *pat* is a `string match` pattern that limits what is returned.
`namespace code script`	Generate a `namespace inscope` command that will eval *script* in the current namespace.
`namespace delete` *name* `?`*name*`? ...`	Delete the variables and commands from the specified namespaces.
`namespace eval` *name cmd* `?`*args*`? ...`	Concatenate *args*, if present, onto *cmd* and evaluate it in *name* namespace.
`namespace export ?-clear? ?`*pat*`? ?`*pat*`? ...`	Add patterns to the export list for current namespace. Returns export list if no patterns.
`namespace forget` *pat* `?`*pat*`? ...`	Undo the `import` of names matching patterns.
`namespace import ?-force?` *pat* `?`*pat*`? ...`	Add the names matching the patterns to the current namespace.
`namespace inscope` *name cmd* `?`*args*`? ...`	Append *args*, if present, onto *cmd* as list elements and evaluate it in *name* namespace.
`namespace origin` *cmd*	Return the original name of *cmd*.
`namespace parent ?`*name*`?`	Return the parent namespace of *name*., or of the current namespace.
`namespace qualifiers` *name*	Return the part of *name* up to the last `::` in it.
`namespace which ?`*flag*`?` *name*	Return the fully qualified version of *name*. The *flag* is one of `-command`, `-variable`, or `-namespace`.
`namespace tail` *name*	Return the last component of *name*.

Wrapping Existing Packages

Suppose you have an existing set of Tcl procedures that you want to wrap in a namespace. Obviously, you start by surrounding your existing code in a namespace block. However, you need to consider three things: global variables, exported procedures, and callbacks.

- Global variables remain global until you change your code to use `variable` instead of `global`. Some variables may make sense to leave at the global scope. Remember that the variables that Tcl defines are global, including `env`, `tcl_platform`, and the others listed in Table 2–2 on page 28. If you use the `upvar #0` trick described on page 80, you can adapt this to namespaces by doing this instead:

```
upvar #0 [namespace current]::$instance state
```

- Exporting procedures makes it more convenient for users of your package. It is not strictly necessary because they can always use qualified names to reference your procedures. An export list is a good hint about which procedures are expected to be used by other packages.
- Callbacks execute at the global scope. If you use variable traces and variables associated with Tk widgets, these are also treated as global variables. If you want a callback to invoke a namespace procedure, or if you give out the name of a namespace variable, then you must construct fully qualified variable and procedure names with `namespace current`:

```
button .foo -command [namespace current]::callback \
    -textvariable [namespace current]::textvar
```

[incr Tcl] Object System

The Tcl namespace facility was proposed by Michael Mclennan based on his experiences with [incr Tcl], which is the most widely used object-oriented extension for Tcl. The Tcl namespace facility does not directly provide classes and inheritance. It just provides new scopes and a way to hide procedures and variables inside a scope. There are Tcl C APIs that support hooks in variable name and command lookup for object systems so they can implement classes and inheritence. The goal is that various object systems can be added to Tcl as shared libraries.

[incr Tcl] provides classes, inheritance, and protected variables and commands. If you are familiar with C++, [incr Tcl] should feel similar. A complete treatment of [incr Tcl] is not made in this book. *Tcl/Tk Tools* (Mark Harrison, O'Reilly & Associates, Inc., 1997) is an excellent source of information. You can find a version of [incr Tcl] on the CD-ROM. The [incr Tcl] home page is `http://www.tcltk.com/itcl/`.

Notes

The namespace facility is brand new. I have participated in the design, but I do not have much experience using it, yet. This book goes to press slightly before the final release of Tcl 8.0. It is possible that last minute changes to namespaces will result in corrections to this book at a later time. You can always consult my on-line errata at `http://www.beedub.com/book/`.

Auto Loading

Currently there is no special interaction between `namespace import` and the auto loading mechanism described in Chapter 12. Make sure the target package is loaded before doing `namespace import`.

Namespaces and `uplevel`

Namespaces affect the Tcl call frames just like procedures. If you walk the call stack with `info level`, the namespace frames are visible. This means you can get access to all variables with `uplevel` and `upvar`. Level `#0` is still the absolute global scope, outside any namespace or procedure. Try out `Call_Trace` from Example 13–4 on page 151 on your code that uses namespaces to see the effect.

Naming Quirks

When you name a namespace, you are allowed to have extra colons at the end. You can also have two or more colons as the separator between namespace name components. These rules make it easier to assemble names by adding to the value returned from `namespace current`. These all name the same namespace:

```
::foo::bar
::foo::bar::
::foo:::bar
```

The name of the global namespace can be either `::` or the empty string. This follows from the treatment of `::` in namespace names.

When you name a variable or command, a trailing `::` is treated differently. In the following command a variable inside the `::foo::bar` namespace is modified. The variable has an empty string for its name:

```
set ::foo::bar:: 3
```

If you want to embed a reference to a variable just before two colons, use a backslash to turn off the variable name parsing before the colons:

```
set x xval
set y $x\::foo
=> xval::foo
```

Miscellaneous

You can remove names you have imported:

```
namespace forget Random::Init
```

You can `rename` imported procedures to modify their names:

```
rename Range range
```

You can even move a procedure into another namespace with `rename`:

```
rename Random::Init myspace::Init
```

CHAPTER 15

Event-Driven Programming

This chapter describes event-driven programming using timers and asynchronous I/O facilities. The `after` command causes Tcl commands to occur at a time in the future, and the `fileevent` command registers a command to occur in response to file input/output (I/O). Tcl commands: `after`, `fblocked`, `fconfigure`, `fileevent`, and `vwait`.

Event-driven programming is used in long-running programs like network servers and graphical user interfaces. This chapter introduces event-driven programming in Tcl. Tcl provides an easy model in which you register Tcl commands and the system calls those commands when a particular event occurs. The `after` command is used to execute Tcl commands at a later time, and the `fileevent` command is used to execute Tcl commands when the system is ready for I/O. The `vwait` command is used to wait for events. During the wait Tcl automatically calls Tcl commands that are associated with different events.

The event model is also used when programming user interfaces using Tk. Originally, event processing was only associated with Tk. The event loop moved from Tk to Tcl in the Tcl 7.5/Tk 4.1 release.

The Tcl Event Loop

An event loop is built into Tcl. Tcl checks for events and calls out to handlers that have been registered for different types of events. Some of the events are processed internally to Tcl. You can register Tcl commands to be called in response to events. There are also C APIs to event loop, which are described on page 558. Event processing is active all the time in Tk applications. If you do not use Tk, you can start the event loop with the `vwait` command as shown in Example 15–2 on page 180. The four event classes are handled in the following order:

- Window events. These include keystrokes and button clicks. Handlers are set up for these automatically by the Tk widgets, and you can register window event handlers with the `bind` command described in Chapter 23
- File events. The `fileevent` command registers handlers for these events.
- Timer events. The `after` command registers commands to occur at specific times.
- Idle events. These events are processed when there is nothing else to do. The Tk widgets use idle events to display themselves. The `after idle` command registers a command to run at the next idle time.

The `after` Command

The `after` command sets up commands to happen in the future. In its simplest form it just pauses the application for a specified time, in milliseconds. The example below waits for half a second:

```
after 500
```

During this time the application processes no events. You can use the `vwait` command as shown on page 180 to keep the Tcl event loop active during the waiting period.

The `after` command can register a Tcl command to occur after a period of time, in milliseconds:

```
after milliseconds cmd arg arg...
```

The `after` command treats its arguments like `eval`; if you give it extra arguments it concatenates them to form a single command. If your argument structure is important, use `list` to build the command. The following example always works, no matter what the value of `myvariable` is:

```
after 500 [list puts $myvariable]
```

The return value of `after` is an identifier for the registered command. You can cancel this command with the `after cancel` operation. You specify either the identifier returned from `after`, or the command string. In the latter case the event that matches the command string exactly is canceled.

Table 15–1 summarizes the `after` command:

Table 15–1 The `after` command.

`after` *`milliseconds`*	Pause for *`milliseconds`*.
`after` *`ms arg ?arg...?`*	Concatenate the *`args`* into a command and execute it after *`ms`* milliseconds. Immediately returns an ID.
`after cancel` *`id`*	Cancel the command registered under *`id`*.
`after cancel` *`command`*	Cancel the registered *`command`*.
`after idle` *`command`*	Run *`command`* at the next idle moment.
`after info ?`*`id`*`?`	Return a list of IDs for outstanding `after` events, or the command associated with *`id`*.

The fileevent Command

The fileevent command registers a procedure that is called when an I/O channel is ready for read or write events. For example, you can open a pipeline or network socket for reading, and then process the data from the pipeline or socket using a command registered with fileevent. Using network sockets is described in Chapter 15. The advantage of this approach is that your application can do other things, like update the user interface, while waiting for data from the pipeline or socket. You can use fileevent on stdin and stdout, too.

The command registered with fileevent uses the regular Tcl commands to read or write data on the I/O channel. For example, if the pipeline generates line-oriented output, you should use gets to read a line of input. If you try and read more data than is available, your application may block waiting for more input. For this reason you should read one line in your fileevent handler, assuming the data is line-oriented. If you know the pipeline will generate data in fixed-sized blocks, then you can use the read command to read one block.

The fconfigure command described on page 181 can put a channel into non-blocking mode. This is not strictly necessary when using fileevent. The pros and cons of non-blocking I/O are discussed later.

End of file makes a channel readable.

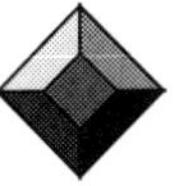

You should check for end of file in your read handler because it will be called when end of file occurs. It is important to close the channel inside the handler because closing the channel automatically unregisters the handler. If you forget to close the channel, your read event handler will be called repeatedly.

There can be at most one read handler and one write handler for an I/O channel. If you register a handler and one is already registered, then the old registration is removed. If you call fileevent without a command argument it returns the currently registered command, or null if there is none. If you register the empty string, it deletes the current file handler.

The following example shows a read event handler. Example 19–1 on page 234 also uses fileevent to read from a pipeline. A pipeline is opened for reading and its command executes in the background. The Reader command is invoked when data is available on the pipe. The end of file condition is checked, and then a single line of input is read and processed.

Example 15–1 A read event file handler.

```
set pipe [open "|some command"]
fileevent $pipe readable [list Reader $pipe]
proc Reader { pipe } {
    if [eof $pipe] {
        catch {close $pipe}
        return
    }
    gets $pipe line
    # Process one line
}
```

Table 15–2 summarizes the `fileevent` command.

Table 15–2 The `fileevent` command.

`fileevent` *`fileId`* `readable` ?*`command`*?	Query or register *`command`* to be called when *`fileId`* is readable.
`fileevent` *`fileId`* `writable` ?*`command`*?	Query or register *`command`* to be called when *`fileId`* is writable.

The `vwait` Command

The `vwait` command waits until a variable is modified. For example, you can set variable `x` at a future time, and then wait for that variable to be set with `vwait`.

```
set x 0
after 500 {set x 1}
vwait x
```

Waiting with `vwait` causes Tcl to enter the event loop. Tcl will process events until the variable `x` is modified. The `vwait` command completes when some Tcl code runs in response to an event and modifies the variable. In this case the event is a timer event, and the Tcl code is simply:

```
set x 1
```

In some cases `vwait` is only used to start the event loop. The following example sets up a file event handler for `stdin` that will read and execute commands. Once this is set up, `vwait` is used to enter the event loop and process commands until the input channel is closed. The process exits at that point, so the `vwait` variable `forever` is not used:

Example 15–2 Using `vwait` to activate the event loop.

```
fileevent stdin readable StdinRead
proc StdinRead {} {
    global command prompt
    if [eof stdin] {
        exit
    }
    append command(line) [gets stdin]
    if [info complete $command(line)] {
        catch {uplevel #0 $command(line)} result
        puts $result
        puts -nonewline $prompt
        flush stdout
        set command(line) {}
    }
}
puts -nonewline $prompt
flush stdout
vwait forever
```

The fconfigure Command

The fconfigure command sets and queries several properties of I/O channels. The default settings are suitable for most cases. If you do event-driven I/O you probably want to set your channel into non-blocking mode. If you handle binary data, you can turn off end of line translations. You can query the channel parameters like this:

```
fconfigure stdin
-blocking 1 -buffering none -buffersize 4096 -eofchar {}
-translation lf
```

Table 15–3 summarizes the properties controlled by fconfigure. They are discussed in more detail below.

Table 15–3 I/O channel properties controlled by fconfigure.

-blocking	Block until I/O channel is ready: 0 or 1.
-buffering	Buffer mode: none, line, or full.
-buffersize	Number of characters in the buffer.
-eofchar	Special end of file character. Control-z (\x1a) for DOS. Null otherwise.
-translation	End of line translation: auto, lf, cr, crlf, binary.
-mode	Serial devices only. Format: *baud,parity,data,stop*
-peername	Sockets only. IP address of remote host.
-peerport	Sockets only. Port number of remote host.

Non-Blocking I/O

By default, I/O channels are *blocking*. A gets or read will wait until data is available before returning. A puts may also wait if the I/O channel is not ready to accept data. This behavior is OK if you are using disk files, which are essentially always ready. If you use pipelines or network sockets, however, the blocking behavior can hang up your application.

The fconfigure command can set a channel into *non-blocking mode*. A gets or read command may return immediately with no data. This occurs when there is no data available on a socket or pipeline. A puts to a non-blocking channel will accept all the data and buffer it internally. When the underlying device (i.e., a pipeline or socket) is ready, then Tcl automatically writes out the buffered data. Non-blocking channels are useful so your application can do something else while waiting for the I/O channel. You can also manage several non-blocking I/O channels at once. Non-blocking channels should be used with the fileevent command described earlier. The following command puts a channel into non-blocking mode:

```
fconfigure fileID -blocking 0
```

II. Advanced Tcl

It is not strictly necessary to put a channel into non-blocking mode if you use `fileevent`. However, if the channel is in blocking mode, then it is still possible for the `gets` or `read` done by your `fileevent` procedure to block. For example, an I/O channel might have some data ready, but not a complete line. In this case a `gets` would block, unless the channel is non-blocking. Perhaps the best motivation for a non-blocking channel is the buffering behavior of a non-blocking `puts`. You can even `close` a channel that has buffered data, and Tcl will automatically write out the buffers as the channel becomes ready. For these reasons, it is common to use a non-blocking channel with `fileevent`. Example 15–3 shows a `fileevent` handler for a non-blocking channel. As described above, the `gets` may not find a complete line, in which case it doesn't read anything and returns -1.

Example 15–3 A read event file handler for a non-blocking channel.

```
set pipe [open "|some command"]
fileevent $pipe readable [list Reader $pipe]
fconfigure $pipe -blocking 0
proc Reader { pipe } {
    if [eof $pipe] {
        catch {close $pipe}
        return
    }
    if {[gets $pipe line] < 0} {
        # We blocked anyway because only part of a line
        # was available for input
    } else {
        # Process one line
    }
}
```

The `fblocked` Command

The `fblocked` command returns 1 if a channel does not have data ready. Normally the `fileevent` command takes care of waiting for data, so I have only seen `fblocked` useful in testing channel implementations.

Buffering

By default, Tcl buffers data so I/O is more efficient. The underlying device is accessed less frequently so there is less overhead. In some cases you may want data to be visible immediately and buffering gets in the way. The following turns off all buffering:

```
fconfigure fileID -buffering none
```

Full buffering means that output data is accumulated until a buffer fills, then a write is performed. For reading, Tcl attempts to read a whole buffer each time more data is needed. The read-ahead for buffering will not block. The `-buffersize` parameter controls the buffer size:

```
fconfigure fileID -buffering full -buffersize 8192
```

Line buffering is used by default on stdin and stdout. Each newline in an output channel causes an write operation. Read buffering is the same as full buffering. The following command turns on line buffering:

```
fconfigure fileID -buffering line
```

End of Line Translations

On UNIX, text lines end with a newline character (\n). On Macintosh they end with a carriage return (\r). On Windows they end with a carriage return, newline sequence (\r\n). Network sockets also use the carriage return, newline sequence. By default, Tcl accepts any of these, and the line terminator can even change within a channel. All of these different conventions are converted to the UNIX style so that once read, text lines always end with a newline character (\n). Both the read and gets commands do this conversion. By default, text lines are generated in the platform-native format during output.

The default behavior is almost always what you want, but you can control the translation with fconfigure. Table 15–4 shows settings for -translation:

Table 15–4 End of line translation modes.

binary	No translation at all.
lf	UNIX-style, which also means no translations.
cr	Macintosh style. On input, carriage returns are converted to newlines. On output, newlines are converted to carriage returns.
crlf	Windows and Network style. On input, carriage return, newline is converted to a newline. On output, a newline is converted to a carriage return, newline sequence.
auto	The default behavior. On input, all end of line conventions are converted to a newline. Output is in native format.

End of File Character

In DOS file systems, there may be a Control-z character (\x1a) at the end of a text file. By default, this character is ignored on the Windows platform if it occurs at the end of the file, and this character is output when you close the file. You can turn this off by specifying an empty string for the end of file character:

```
fconfigure fileID -eofchar {}
```

Serial Devices

The -mode attribute specifies the baud rate, parity mode, the number of data bits, and the number of stop bits:

```
set tty [open /dev/ttya]
fconfigure $tty -mode
=> 9600,0,8,2
```

Windows has some special device names that always connect you to the serial line devices when you use `open`. They are `com1` through `com8`. The system console is named `con`. The null device is `nul`.

UNIX has names for serial devices in `/dev`. The serial devices are `/dev/ttya`, `/dev/ttyb`, and so on. The system console is `/dev/console`. The current terminal is `/dev/tty`. The null device is `/dev/null`.

Macintosh needs a special command to open serial devices. As of this writing the command is not implemented. Check your Tcl release for a `serial` command that will open serial devices on all platforms.

Configuring Read-Write Channels

If you have a channel that is used for both input and output, you can set the channel parameters independently for input and output. In this case you can specify a two-element list for the parameter value. The first element is for the input side of the channel, and the second element is for the output side of the channel. If you only specify a single element, it applies to both input and output. For example, the following command forces output end of line translations to be `crlf` mode, leaves the input channel on automatic, and sets the buffer size for both input and output:

```
fconfigure pipe -translation {auto crlf} -buffersize 4096
```

CHAPTER 16

Socket Programming

This chapter shows how to use sockets for programming network clients and servers. Advanced I/O techniques for sockets are described, including non-blocking I/O and control over I/O buffering. Tcl command: `socket`.

Sockets are network communication channels. The sockets described in this chapter use the TCP network protocol, although you can find Tcl extensions that create sockets using other protocols. TCP provides a reliable byte stream between two hosts connected to a network. TCP handles all the issues about routing information across the network, and it automatically recovers if data is lost or corrupted along the way. TCP is the basis for other protocols like Telnet, FTP, and HTTP.

A Tcl script can use a network socket just like an open file or pipeline. Instead of using the Tcl `open` command, you use the `socket` command to open a socket. Then you use `gets`, `puts`, and `read` to transfer data. The `close` command closes a network socket.

Network programming distinguishes between clients and servers. A server is a process or program that runs for long periods of time and controls access to some resource. For example, an FTP server governs access to files, and an HTTP server provides access to hypertext pages on the World Wide Web. A client typically connects to the server for a limited time in order to gain access to the resource. For example, when a Web browser fetches a hypertext page, it is acting as a client. The extended examples in this chapter show how to program the client side of the HTTP protocol.

Client Sockets

A client opens a socket by specifying the *host address* and *port number* for the server of the socket. The host address gives the network location (i.e., which computer) and the port selects a particular server from all the possible servers that may be running on that host. For example, HTTP servers typically use port 80, while FTP servers use port 20. The following example shows how to open a client socket to a Web server:

```
set s [socket www.sun.com 80]
```

There are two forms for host names. The previous example uses a *domain name*: `www.sun.com`. You can also specify raw IP addresses, which are specified with 4 dot-separated integers (e.g., `128.15.115.32`). A domain name is mapped into a raw IP address by the system software, and it is almost always a better idea to use a domain name in case the IP address assignment for the host changes. This can happen when hosts are upgraded or they move to a different part of the network. As of Tcl 8.0, there is no direct access from Tcl to the DNS service that maps host names to IP addresses. The Scotty Tcl extension provides DNS access and other network protocols. Its home page is:

```
http://wwwsnmp.cs.utwente.nl/~schoenw/scotty/
```

Some systems also provide symbolic names for well-known port numbers, too. For example, instead of using `20` for the FTP service, you can use `ftp`. On UNIX systems the well-known port numbers are listed in the file named `/etc/services`.

Client Socket Options

The `socket` command accepts some optional arguments when opening the client-side socket. The general form of the command is:

```
socket ?-async? ?-myaddr address? ?-myport myport? host port
```

Ordinarily the address and port on the client side are chosen automatically. If your computer has multiple network interfaces you can select one with the `-myaddr` option. The *`address`* value can be a domain name or an IP address. If your application needs a specific client port, it can choose one with the `-myport` option. If the port is in use, the `socket` command will raise an error.

In some cases it can take a long time to open the connection to the server. The `-async` option causes connection to happen in the background, and the `socket` command returns immediately. The socket becomes writable when the connection completes, or fails. You can use `fileevent` to get a callback when this occurs. If you use the socket before the connection completes, and the socket is in blocking mode, then Tcl automatically blocks and waits for the connection to complete. If the socket is in non-blocking mode, attempts to use the socket return immediately. The `gets` and `read` commands would return -1, and `fblocked` would return 1 in this situation. The following example illustrates `-async`. One advantage of this approach is that the Tcl event loop is active while your application waits for the connection:

```
set sock [socket -async host port]
fileevent $sock w {set connected 1}
global connected
vwait connected
```


Server Sockets

A server socket is a little more complex because it has to allow for multiple clients. The way this works is that the `socket` command creates a listening socket, and then new sockets are created when clients make connections to the server. Tcl takes care of all the details and makes this easy to use. You give the socket command a *callback* to execute when a client connects to your server socket. The callback is just a Tcl command. It gets as arguments the new socket and the address and port number of the connecting client. A simple example is shown below:

Example 16–1 Opening a server socket.

```
set mainSocket [socket -server Accept 2540]
proc Accept {newSock addr port} {
   puts "Accepted $newSock from $addr port $port"
}
vwait forever
```

This example creates a server socket and specifies the `Accept` command as the server callback. In this simple example, `Accept` just prints out its arguments. The last argument to the `socket` command is the server's port number. For your own unofficial servers, you'll need to pick port numbers higher than 1024 to avoid conflicts with existing services. UNIX systems prevent user programs from opening server sockets with port numbers less than 1024.

The `vwait` command puts Tcl into its event loop so it can do the background processing necessary to accept connections. The `vwait` command will wait until the `forever` variable is modified, which won't happen in this simple example. The key point is that Tcl processes other events (e.g., network connections and other file I/O) while it waits. If you have a Tk application (e.g., *wish*), then it already has an event loop to handle window system events, so you do not need to use `vwait`. The Tcl event loop is discussed on page 177

Server Socket Options

By default, Tcl lets the operating system choose the network interface used for the server socket, and you just supply the port number. If your computer has multiple interfaces you may want to specify a particular one. Use the `-myaddr` option for this. The general form of the command to open server sockets is:

```
socket -server callback ?-myaddr address? port
```

The Echo Service

This section presents a simple echo server. The echo server accepts connections from clients. It reads data from the clients and writes that data back. The example uses `fileevent` to wait for data from the client, and it uses `fconfigure` to adjust the buffering behavior of the network socket. You can use this example as a template for more interesting services.

Example 16–2 The echo service.

```
proc Echo_Server {port} {
    global echo
    set echo(main) [socket -server EchoAccept $port]
}
proc EchoAccept {sock addr port} {
    global echo
    puts "Accept $sock from $addr port $port"
    set echo(addr,$sock) [list $addr $port]
    fconfigure $sock -buffering line
    fileevent $sock readable [list Echo $sock]
}
proc Echo {sock} {
    global echo
    if {[eof $sock] || [catch {gets $sock line}]} {
        # end of file or abnormal connection drop
        close $sock
        puts "Close $echo(addr,$sock)"
        unset echo(addr,$sock)
    } else {
        if {[string compare $line "quit"] == 0} {
            # Prevent new connections.
            # Existing connections stay open.
            close $echo(main)
        }
        puts $sock $line
    }
}
```

The `Echo_Server` procedure opens the socket and saves the result in `echo(main)`. When this socket is closed later, the server stops accepting new connections but existing connections won't be affected. If you want to experiment with this server, start it and wait for connections like this:

```
Echo_Server 2540
vwait forever
```

The `EchoAccept` procedure uses the `fconfigure` command to set up line buffering. This means that each `puts` by the server results in a network transmission to the client. The importance of this will be described in more detail later. A complete description of the `fconfigure` command is given on page 181. The `EchoAccept` procedure uses the `fileevent` command to register a procedure that handles I/O on the socket. In this example, the `Echo` procedure will be called whenever the socket is readable. Note that it is not necessary to put the socket into non-blocking mode when using the `fileevent` callback. The effects of non-blocking mode are discussed on page 181.

`EchoAccept` saves information about each client in the `echo` array. This is just used to print out a message when a client closes its connection. In a more sophisticated server, however, you may need to keep more interesting state about each client. The name of the socket provides a convenient handle on the client. In this case it is used as part of the array index.

The `Echo` procedure first checks to see if the socket has been closed by the client or there is an error when reading the socket. The `if` expression only does the `gets` if the `eof` does not return true:

```
if {[eof $sock] || [catch {gets $sock line}]} {
```

Closing the socket automatically clears the `fileevent` registration. If you forget to close the socket upon the end of file condition, the Tcl event loop will invoke your callback repeatedly. It is important to close it when you detect end of file.

In the normal case the server simply reads a line with `gets` and then writes it back to the client with `puts`. If the line is "quit," then the server closes its main socket. This prevents any more connections by new clients, but it doesn't affect any clients that are already connected.

Example 16–3 A client of the echo service.

```
proc Echo_Client {host port} {
	set s [socket $host $port]
	fconfigure $s -buffering line
	return $s
}
set s [Echo_Client localhost 2540]
puts $s "Hello!"
gets $s
=> Hello!
```

Example 16–3 shows a sample client of the `Echo` service. The main point is to ensure the socket is line buffered so that each `puts` by the client results in a network transmission. (Or, more precisely, each newline character results in a network transmission.) If you forget to set line buffering with `fconfigure`, the client's `gets` command will probably hang because the server will not get any data; it will be stuck in buffers on the client.

Fetching a URL with HTTP

The HyperText Transport Protocol (HTTP) is the protocol used on the World Wide Web. This section presents a procedure to fetch pages or images from a server on the Web. Items in the Web are identified with a Universal Resource Location (URL) that specifies a host, port, and location on the host. The basic outline of HTTP is that a client sends a URL to a server, and the server responds with some header information and some content data. The header information describes the content, which can be hypertext, images, postscript, and more.

Example 16–4 Opening a connection to an HTTP server.

```
proc Http_Open {url} {
    global http
    if {![regexp -nocase {^(http://)?([^:/]+)(:([0-9])+)?(/.*)} \
            $url x protocol server y port path]} {
        error "bogus URL: $url"
    }
    if {[string length $port] == 0} {
        set port 80
    }
    set sock [socket $server $port]
    puts $sock "GET $path HTTP/1.0"
    puts $sock "Host: $server"
    puts $sock "User-Agent: Tcl/Tk Http_Open"
    puts $sock ""
    flush $sock
    return $sock
}
```

The `Http_Open` procedure uses `regexp` to pick out the server and port from the URL. This regular expression is described in detail on page 123. The leading `http://` is optional, and so is the port number. If the port is left off, then the standard port 80 is used. If the regular expression matches, then a `socket` command opens the network connection.

The protocol begins with the client sending a line that identifies the command (`GET`), the path, and the protocol version. The path is the part of the URL after the server and port specification. The rest of the request is lines in the following format:

`key: value`

The `Host` identifies the server, which supports servers that implement more than one server name. The `User-Agent` identifies the client program, which is often a browser like *Netscape Navigator* or *Internet Explorer*. The key-value lines are terminated with a blank line. This data is flushed out of the Tcl buffering system with the `flush` command. The server will respond by sending the URL contents back over the socket. This is described shortly, but first we consider proxies.

Proxy Servers

A *proxy* is used to get through firewalls that many organizations set up to isolate their network from the Internet. The proxy accepts HTTP requests from clients inside the firewall and then forwards the requests outside the firewall. It also relays the server's response back to the client. The protocol is nearly the same when using the proxy. The difference is that the complete URL is passed to the GET command so the proxy can locate the server. Example 16–5 uses a proxy if one is defined:

Example 16–5 Opening a connection to an HTTP server.

```
# Http_Proxy sets or queries the proxy
proc Http_Proxy {{new {}}} {
    global http
    if ![info exists http(proxy)] {
        return {}
    }
    if {[string length $new] == 0} {
        return $http(proxy):$http(proxyPort)
    } else {
        regexp {^([^:]+):([0-9]+)$} $new x \
            http(proxy) http(proxyPort)
    }
}

proc Http_Open {url {command GET} {query {}}} {
    global http
    if {![regexp -nocase {^(http://)?([^:/]+)(:([0-9])+)?(/.*)} \
            $url x protocol server y port path]} {
        error "bogus URL: $url"
    }
    if {[string length $port] == 0} {
        set port 80
    }
    if {[info exists http(proxy)] &&
            [string length $http(proxy)]} {
        set sock [socket $http(proxy) $http(proxyPort)]
        puts $sock "$command http://$server:$port$path HTTP/
1.0"
    } else {
        set sock [socket $server $port]
        puts $sock "$command $path HTTP/1.0"
    }
    puts $sock "User-Agent: Tcl/Tk Http_Open"
    puts $sock "Host: $server"
    if {[string length $query] > 0} {
        puts $sock "Content-Length: [string length $query]"
        puts $sock ""
        puts $sock $query
    }
    puts $sock ""
    flush $sock
    fconfigure $sock -blocking 0
    return $sock
}
```

The HEAD Request

Example 16–5 parameterizes the HTTP protocol so the user of `Http_Open` can perform different operations. The `GET` operation fetches the contents of a URL. The `HEAD` operation just fetches the description of a URL, which is useful to validate a URL. The `POST` operation transmits query data to the server (e.g., values from a form) and also fetches the contents of the URL. All of these operations follow a similar protocol. The reply from the server is a status line followed by lines that have key-value pairs. This format is similar to the client's request. The reply header is followed by content data with `GET` and `POST` operations. Example 16–6 implements the `HEAD` command, which does not involve any reply data:

Example 16–6 `Http_Head` validates a URL.

```
proc Http_Head {url} {
    upvar #0 $url state
    catch {unset state}
    set state(sock) [Http_Open $url HEAD]
    fileevent $state(sock) readable [list HttpHeader $url]
    # Specify the real name, not the upvar alias, to vwait
    vwait $url\(status)
    catch {close $state(sock)}
    return $state(status)
}
proc HttpHeader {url} {
    upvar #0 $url state
    if [eof $state(sock)] {
        set state(status) eof
        close $state(sock)
        return
    }
    if [catch {gets $state(sock) line} nbytes] {
        set state(status) error
        lappend state(headers) [list error $nbytes]
        close $state(sock)
        return
    }
    if {$nbytes < 0} {
        # Read would block
        return
    } elseif {$nbytes == 0} {
        # Header complete
        set state(status) head
    } elseif {![info exists state(headers)]} {
        # Initial status reply from the server
        set state(headers) [list http $line]
    } else {
        # Process key-value pairs
        regexp {^([^:]+): *(.*)$} $line x key value
        lappend state(headers) [string tolower $key] $value
    }
}
```

The `Http_Head` procedure uses `Http_Open` to contact the server. The `HttpHeader` procedure is registered as a `fileevent` handler to read the server's reply. A global array keeps state about each operation. The URL is used in the array name, and `upvar` is used to create an alias to the name (`upvar` is described on page 80):

```
upvar #0 $url state
```

You cannot use the `upvar` alias as the variable specified to `vwait`. Instead, you must use the actual name. The backslash turns off the array reference in order to pass the name of the array element to `vwait`, otherwise Tcl tries to reference `url` as an array:

```
vwait $url\(status)
```

The `HttpHeader` procedure checks for special cases: end of file, an error on the `gets`, or a short read on a non-blocking socket. The very first reply line contains a status code from the server that is in a different format than the rest of the header lines:

```
code message
```

The code is a 3-digit numeric code. `200` is OK. Codes in the `400`'s and `500`'s indicate an error. The codes are explained fully in RFC 1945 that specifies HTTP 1.0. The first line is saved with the key `http`:

```
set state(headers) [list http $line]
```

The rest of the header lines are parsed into key-value pairs and appended onto `state(headers)`. This format can be used to initialize an array:

```
array set header $state(headers)
```

When `HttpHeader` gets an empty line, the header is complete and it sets the `state(status)` variable, which signals `Http_Head`. Finally, `Http_Head` returns the status to its caller. The complete information about the request is still in the global array named by the URL. Example 16–7 illustrates the use of `Http_Head`:

Example 16–7 Using `Http_Head`.

```
set url http://www.sun.com/
set status [Http_Head $url]
=> eof
upvar #0 $url state
array set info $state(headers)
parray info
info(http)           HTTP/1.0 200 OK
info(server)         Apache/1.1.1
info(last-modified) Nov ...
info(content-type)   text/html
```

The GET and POST Requests

Example 16–8 shows `Http_Get` that implements the `GET` and `POST` requests. The difference between these is that `POST` sends query data to the server after the request header. Both operations get a reply from the server that is divided into a descriptive header and the content data. The `Http_Open` procedure sends the request and the query, if present, and reads the reply header. `Http_Get` reads the content.

The descriptive header returned by the server is in the same format as the client's request. One of the key-value pairs returned by the server specifies the `Content-Type` of the URL. The content-types come from the MIME standard, which is described in RFC 1521. Typical content-types are:

- `text/html` — HyperText Markup Language (HTML), which is introduced on page 30.
- `text/plain` — plain text with no markup.
- `image/gif` — image data in GIF format.
- `image/jpeg` — image data in JPEG format.
- `application/postscript` — a postscript document.
- `application/x-tcl` — a Tcl program! This type is discussed in Chapter 48.

Example 16–8 `Http_Get` fetches the contents of a URL.

```
proc Http_Get {url {query {}}} {
    upvar #0 $url state        ;# Alias to global array
    catch {unset state}        ;# Aliases still valid.
    if {[string length $query] > 0} {
        set state(sock) [Http_Open $url POST $query]
    } else {
        set state(sock) [Http_Open $url GET]
    }
    set sock $state(sock)
    fileevent $sock readable [list HttpHeader $url]
    # Specify the real name, not the upvar alias, to vwait
    vwait $url\(status)
    set header(content-type) {}
    set header(http) "500 unknown error"
    array set header $state(headers)
    # Check return status.
    # 200 is OK, other codes indicate a problem.
    regsub "HTTP/1.. " $header(http) {} header(http)
    if {![string match 2* $header(http)]} {
        catch {close $sock}
        if {[info exists header(location)] &&
                [string match 3* $header(http)]} {
            # 3xx is a redirection to another URL
            set state(link) $header(location)
            return [Http_Get $header(location) $query]
        }
        return -code error $header(http)
    }
    # Set up to read the content data
    switch -glob -- $header(content-type) {
        text/*    {
            # Read HTML into memory
            fileevent $sock readable [list HttpGetText $url]
```

```
            }
            default     {
                # Copy content data to a file
                fconfigure $sock -translation binary
                set state(filename) [File_TempName http]
                if [catch {open $state(filename) w} out] {
                    set state(status) error
                    set state(error) $out
                    close $sock
                    return $header(content-type)
                }
                set state(fd) $out
                fileevent $sock readable [list HttpCopyData $url]
            }
        }
        vwait $url\(status)
        return $header(content-type)
}
```

`Http_Get` uses `Http_Open` to initiate the request, and then it looks for errors. It handles redirection errors that occur if a URL has changed. These have error codes that begin with `3`. A common case of this is when a user omits the trailing slash on a URL (e.g., `http://www.sun.com`). Most servers respond with:

```
302 Document has moved
Location: http://www.sun.com/
```

If the content-type is text, then `Http_Get` sets up a `fileevent` handler to read this data into memory. The socket is in non-blocking mode so the read handler can read as much data as possible each time it is called. This is more efficient than using `gets` to read a line at a time. The text will be stored in the `state(body)` variable for use by the caller of `Http_Get`. Example 16–9 shows the `HttpGetText fileevent` handler:

Example 16–9 `HttpGetText` reads `text` URLs.

```
proc HttpGetText {url} {
    upvar #0 $url state
    if [eof $state(sock)] {
        # Content complete
        set state(status) done
        close $state(sock)
    } elseif {[catch {read $state(sock)} block]} {
        set state(status) error
        lappend state(headers) [list error $block]
        close $state(sock)
    } else {
        append state(body) $block
    }
}
```

The content may be in binary format. This poses a problem for Tcl 7.6 and earlier. A null character will terminate the value, so values with embedded nulls cannot be processed safely by Tcl scripts. Tcl 8.0 supports strings and variable values with arbitrary binary data. Example 16–10 shows `HttpCopyData` that is used by `Http_Get` to copy non-text content data to a file. `HttpCopyData` uses an undocumented Tcl command, `unsupported0`, to copy data from one I/O channel to another without storing it in Tcl variables. This command has been replaced with `fcopy` in Tcl 8.0.

Example 16–10 `HttpCopyData` copies content to a file.

```
rename unsupported0 copychannel
proc HttpCopyData {url} {
    upvar #0 $url state
    if [eof $state(sock)] {
        # Content complete
        set state(status) done
        close $state(sock)
        close $state(fd)
    } elseif {[catch {copychannel $state(sock) $state(fd)} x]} {
        set state(status) error
        lappend state(headers) [list error $x]
        close $state(sock)
        close $state(fd)
    }
}
```

The user of `Http_Get` uses the information in the `state` array to determine the status of the fetch and where to find the content. There are four cases to deal with:

- There was an error, which is indicated by the presence of the `state(error)` element.
- There was a redirection, in which case the new URL is in `state(link)`. The client of `Http_Get` should change the URL and look at its state instead. You can use `upvar` to redefine the alias for the `state` array:

  ```
  upvar #0 $state(link) state
  ```

- There was text content. The content is in `state(body)`.
- There was another content type that was copied to `state(filename)`.

The `unsupported0` Command

Officially, the `copychannel` command is named `unsupported0` because it was not guaranteed to stay around. It was introduced in Tcl 7.5 along with the `socket` command. It was still present in the alpha 2 version of Tcl 8.0, but it was then replaced by an `fcopy` command in the final version of Tcl 8.0. I insisted on having the `copychannel` functionality so Tcl scripts could implement HTTP and other protocols that use binary data without needing an extension. The general form of the command is:

```
unsupported0 input output ?chunksize?
```

The command reads from the *input* channel and writes to the *output* channel. The number of bytes transferred is returned. If *chunksize* is specified, then at most this many bytes are read from *input*. If *input* is in blocking mode, then unsupported0 will block until *chunksize* bytes are read, or until end of file. If *input* is non-blocking, all available data from *input* is read, up to *chunksize* bytes, and copied to *output*. If *output* is non-blocking, then unsupported0 queues all the data read from *input* and returns. Otherwise, unsupported0 could block when writing to output.

The fcopy Command

The official replacement for unsupported0 is fcopy, which has improved semantics. The fcopy command can do a complete copy in the background; the unsupported0 command only does the output half of the copy in the background. The fcopy command also manages its buffers more efficiently. The general form of the command is:

```
fcopy input output ?-size size? ?-command callback?
```

The -command argument makes fcopy work in the background. When the copy is complete or an error occurs, the *callback* is invoked with one or two additional arguments: the number of bytes copied, and, in the case of an error, it is also passed an error string:

```
proc CopyDone {in out bytes {error {}} {
   close $in ; close $out
}
```

With a background copy, the fcopy command transfers data from *input* until end of file or *size* bytes have been transferred. If no -size argument is given, then the copy goes until end of file. It is not safe to do other I/O operations with *input* or *output* during a background fcopy. If either *input* or *output* get closed while the copy is in progress, the current copy is stopped. If the *input* is closed, then all data already queued for *output* is written out.

Without a -command argument, the fcopy command is much like the unsupported0 command. It reads as much as possible depending on the blocking mode of *input* and the optional *size* parameter. Everything it reads is queued for output before fcopy returns. If *output* is blocking, then fcopy returns after the data is written out. If *input* is blocking, then fcopy can block attempting to read *size* bytes or until end of file.

The http Package

Tcl 8.0 includes a new version of the code in this chapter. The interface is slightly different and this section documents the http package that is part of the Tcl library. I wrote this chapter before the http package was adopted, and I think you can still learn from the examples. You should also look at http.tcl in the Tcl 8.0 library, which I also wrote.

http_config

The http_config command is used to set the proxy information, time-outs, and the User-Agent and Accept headers that are generated in the HTTP request. You can specify the proxy host and port, or you can specify a Tcl command that is run to determine the proxy. With no arguments, http_config returns the current settings:

```
http_config
=> -accept */* -proxyfilter httpProxyRequired -proxyhost
{} -proxyport {} -timeout unlimited
-useragent {Tcl http client package 1.0}
```

If you specify just one option, its value is returned:

```
http_config -proxyfilter
=> httpProxyRequired
```

You can set one or more options:

```
http_config -proxyhost webcache.eng -proxyport 8080
```

The default proxy filter just returns the -proxyhost and -proxyport values if they are set. You can supply a smarter filter that picks a proxy based on the host in the URL. The proxy filter is called with the hostname and should return a list of two elements, the proxy host and port. If no proxy is required, return an empty list.

The -timeout value limits the time the transaction can take. Its value is unlimited for no timeout, or a seconds value. You can specify 0.5, for example, to have a 500 millisecond timeout.

http_get

The http_get procedure does a GET, POST, or HEAD transaction depending on its arguments. By default, http_get blocks until the request completes and it returns a token that represents the transaction. As described below, you use the token to get the results of the transaction. If you supply a -command *callback* option, then http_get returns immediately and invokes *callback* when the transaction completes. The callback is passed the token that represents the transaction. Table 16–1 lists the options to http_get:

Table 16–1 Options to the http_get command.

-blocksize *num*	Block size when copying to a channel.
-channel *fileID*	The *fileID* is an open file or socket. The URL data is copied to this channel instead of saving it in memory.
-command *callback*	Call *callback* when the transaction completes. The token from http_get is passed to *callback*.
-handler *command*	Called from the event handler to read data from the URL.

Table 16–1 Options to the `http_get` command.

`-headers` *keyvaluelist*	The *keyvaluelist* specifies a set of headers that are included in the HTTP request. The list alternates between header keys and values.
`-progress` *command*	Call *command* after each block is copied to a channel. It gets called with three parameters: *command token totalsize currentsize*
`-query` *codedstring*	Issue a POST request with the *codedstring* form data.
`-validate` *bool*	If *bool* is true, a HEAD request is made.

For simple applications you can just block on the transaction:

```
set token [http_get www.sun.com/index.html]
=> http#1
```

The leading `http://` in the URL is optional. The return value is a token that is also the name of a global array that contains state about the transaction. Names like `http#1` are used instead of using the URL as the array name. You can use `upvar` to convert the return value from `http_get` to an array variable:

```
upvar #0 $token state
```

By default, the URL data is saved in `state(body)`. The elements of the state array are described in Table 16–2:

Table 16–2 The `http_get` state array.

`body`	The contents of the URL.
`currentsize`	The current number of bytes transferred.
`error`	An explanation of why the transaction was aborted.
`http`	The HTTP reply status.
`meta`	A list of the keys and values in the reply header.
`status`	The current status: `pending`, `ok`, `eof`, or `reset`.
`totalsize`	The expected size of the returned data.
`type`	The content type of the returned data.
`url`	The URL of the request.

A handful of access functions are provided so you can avoid using the state array directly. These are listed in Table 16–3:

Table 16–3 The `http` support procedures.

`http_data $token`	Return `state(body)`
`http_status $token`	Return `state(status)`
`http_error $token`	Return `state(error)`
`http_code $token`	Return `state(http)`
`http_wait $token`	Block until the transaction completes.

You can take advantage of the asynchronous interface by specifying a command that is called when the transaction completes. The callback is passed the token returned from `http_get` so it can access the transaction state:

```
http_get $url -command [list Url_Display $text $url]
proc Url_Display {text url token} {
    upvar #0 $token state
    # Display the url in text
}
```

You can have `http_get` copy the URL to a file or socket with the `-channel` option. This is useful for downloading large files or images. In this case you can get a progress callback so you can provide user feedback during the transaction. Example 16–11 shows a simple downloading script:

Example 16–11 Downloading files with http_get.

```
#!/usr/local/tclsh8.0
if {$argc < 2} {
    puts stderr "Usage: $argv0 url file"
    exit 1
}
set url [lindex $argv 0]
set file [lindex $argv 1]
set out [open $file w]

proc progress {token total current} {
    puts -nonewline "."
}
http_config -proxyhost webcache.eng -proxyport 8080
set token [http_get $url -progress progress \
    -headers {Pragma no-cache} -channel $out]
close $out

# Print out the return header information
puts ""
upvar #0 $token state
puts $state(http)
foreach {key value} $state(meta) {
    puts "$key: $value"
}
exit 0
```

http_formatQuery

If you specify form data with the -query option, then http_get does a POST transaction. You need to encode the form data for safe transmission. The http_formatQuery procedure takes set of keys and values and encodes them in x-www-url-encoded format. Pass this result as the query data:

```
http_formatQuery name "Brent Welch" title "Tcl Program-
mer"
=> name=Brent+Welch&title=Tcl+Programmer
```

http_reset

You can cancel an outstanding transaction with http_reset:

```
http_reset $token
```

This is done automatically when you setup a -timeout with http_config.

The Namespace Version

Tcl 8.0 has two versions of the http package. Version 1 is described above. Version 2 has the same functionality but uses the ::http namespace. The procedures in the interface are:

```
http::geturl
http::config
http::formatQuery
http::reset
http::data
http::status
http::error
http::code
http::wait
```

The state arrays are inside the ::http namespace, too, but you can use the same upvar #0 trick to make an alias to the array.

In either case you must use package require before using any of the procedures in the package.

```
package require http 1.0    ;# http_get
package require http 2.0    ;# http::geturl
```

## CHAPTER 17

Multiple Interpreters and Safe-Tcl

This chapter describes how to create more than one Tcl interpreter in your application. A child interpreter can be made safe so it can execute untrusted scripts without compromising your application or your computer. Command aliases, hidden commands, and shared I/O channels enable communication among interpreters. Tcl command: `interp`. This feature was added in Tcl 7.5.

Safe-Tcl was invented by Nathaniel Borenstein and Marshall Rose so they could send Tcl scripts via email and have the recipient safely execute the script without worry of viruses or other attacks. Safe-Tcl works by removing dangerous commands like `exec` and `open` that would let an untrusted script damage the host computer. You can think of this restricted interpreter as a "padded cell" in which it is safe to execute untrusted scripts. To continue the analogy, if the untrusted code wants to do anything potentially unsafe, it must ask permission. This works by adding additional commands, or *aliases*, that are implemented by a different Tcl interpreter. For example, a `safeopen` command could be implemented by limiting file space to a temporary directory that is deleted when the untrusted code terminates.

The key concept of Safe-Tcl is that there are two Tcl interpreters in the application, a trusted one and an untrusted (or "safe") one. The trusted interpreter can do anything, and it is used for the main application (e.g., the Web browser or email user interface). When the main application receives a message containing an untrusted script, it evaluates that script in the context of the untrusted interpreter. The restricted nature of the untrusted interpreter means the application is safe from attack. This model is much like user mode and kernel mode in a multi-user operating system like UNIX or Windows/NT. In these systems, applications run in user mode and trap into the kernel to access resources like files and the network. The kernel implements access controls so that users cannot read and write each others files, or hijack network services. In Safe-Tcl the application implements access controls for untrusted scripts.

The dual interpreter model of Safe-Tcl has been generalized in Tcl 7.5 and made accessible to Tcl scripts. A Tcl script can create other interpreters, destroy them, create command aliases among them, share I/O channels among them, and evaluate scripts in them.

The `interp` Command

The `interp` command is used to create and manipulate interpreters. The interpreter being created is called a *slave*, and the interpreter that creates it is called the *master*. The master has complete control over the slave. The `interp` command is summarized in Table 17–1.

Table 17–1 The `interp` command.

`interp aliases` *`slave`*	List aliases that are defined in *`slave`*.
`interp alias` *`slave cmd1`*	Return the target command and arguments for the alias *`cmd1`* in *`slave`*.
`interp alias` *`slave cmd1 master cmd2 arg ...`*	Define *`cmd1`* in *`slave`* that is an alias to *`cmd2`* in *`master`* with additional *`args`*.
`interp create ?-safe?` *`slave`*	Create an interpreter named *`slave`*.
`interp delete` *`slave`*	Destroy interpreter *`slave`*.
`interp eval` *`slave cmd args ...`*	Evaluate *`cmd`* and *`args`* in *`slave`*.
`interp exists` *`slave`*	Returns 1 if *`slave`* is an interpreter, else 0.
`interp expose` *`slave cmd`*	Expose hidden command *`cmd`* in *`slave`*.
`interp hide` *`slave cmd`*	Hide *`cmd`* from *`slave`*.
`interp invokehidden` *`slave cmd arg ...`*	Invoke hidden command *`cmd`* and *`args`* in *`slave`*.
`interp issafe` *`slave`*	Returns 1 if *`slave`* was created with `-safe` flag.
`interp share` *`master file slave`*	Share the I/O descriptor named *`file`* in *`master`* with *`slave`*.
`interp slaves` *`master`*	Return the list of slave interpreters of *`master`*.
`interp target` *`slave cmd`*	Return the name of the interpreter that is the target of alias *`cmd`* in *`slave`*.
`interp transfer` *`master file slave`*	Transfer the I/O descriptor named *`file`* from *`master`* to *`slave`*.

Creating Interpreters

Here is a simple example that creates an interpreter, evaluates a couple of commands in it, and then deletes the interpreter:

Example 17–1 Creating and deleting an interpreter.

```
interp create foo
=> foo
interp eval foo {set a 5}
=> 5
set sum [interp eval foo {expr $a + $a}]
=> 10
interp delete foo
```

In Example 17–1 the interpreter is named `foo`. Two commands are evaluated in the `foo` interpreter:

```
set a 5
expr $a + $a
```

Note that curly braces are used to protect the commands from any interpretation by the main interpreter. The variable `a` is defined in the `foo` interpreter and does not conflict with variables in the main interpreter. The set of variables and procedures in each interpreter is completely independent.

The Interpreter Hierarchy

A slave interpreter can itself create interpreters, resulting in a hierarchy. The next examples illustrates this, and it shows how the grandparent of an interpreter can reference the grandchild by name. The example uses `interp slaves` to query the existence of child interpreters.

Example 17–2 Creating a hierarchy of interpreters.

```
interp create foo
=> foo
interp eval foo {interp create bar}
=> bar
interp create {foo bar2}
=> foo bar2
interp slaves
=> foo
interp slaves foo
=> bar bar2
interp delete bar
=> interpreter named "bar" not found
interp delete {foo bar}
```

The example creates `foo`, and then it creates two children of `foo`. The first one is created by `foo` with this command:

```
interp eval foo {interp create bar}
```

The second child is created by the main interpreter. In this case the grandchild must be named by a two-element list to indicate it is a child of a child. The same naming convention is used when the grandchild is deleted:

```
interp create {foo bar2}
interp delete {foo bar2}
```

The `interp slaves` operation returns the names of child (i.e., slave) interpreters. The names are relative to their parent, so the slaves of `foo` are reported simply as `bar` and `bar2`. The name for the current interpreter is the empty list, or `{}`. This is useful in command aliases and file sharing described later. For security reasons, it is not possible to name the master interpreter from within the slave.

The Interpreter Name as a Command

After interpreter *slave* is created, a new command is available in the main interpreter, also called *slave*, that operates on the child interpreter. The following two forms are equivalent most operations:

```
slave operation args ...
interp operation slave args ...
```

For example, the following are equivalent commands:

```
foo eval {set a 5}
interp eval foo {set a 5}
```

And so are these:

```
foo issafe
interp issafe foo
```

However, the operations `delete`, `exists`, `share`, `slaves`, `target`, and `transfer` cannot be used with the per interpreter command. In particular, there is no `foo delete` operation; you must use `interp delete foo`.

If you have a deep hierarchy of interpreters, the command corresponding to the slave is only defined in the parent. For example, if a master creates `foo`, and `foo` creates `bar`, then the master must operate on `bar` with the `interp` command. There is no "`foo bar`" command defined in the master.

Use `list` with `interp eval`

The `interp eval` command treats its arguments like `eval`. If there are extra arguments they are all concatenated together first. This can lose important structure as described in Chapter 10. To be safe, use `list` to construct your commands. For example, to safely define a variable in the slave, you should do this:

```
interp eval slave [list set var $value]
```

Safe Interpreters

A child can be created either safe (i.e., untrusted) or fully functional. In the examples so far, the children have been trusted and fully functional; they have all the basic Tcl commands available to them. An interpreter is made safe by eliminating certain commands. Table 17–2 lists the commands removed from safe interpreters. As described later, these commands can be used by the master on behalf of the safe interpreter. To create a safe interpreter, use the `-safe` flag:

```
interp create -safe untrusted
```

Table 17–2 Commands removed from safe interpreters.

`cd`	Change directory.
`exec`	Execute another program.
`exit`	Terminate the process.
`fconfigure`	Set modes of an I/O stream.
`file`	Query file attributes.
`glob`	Pattern match on file names.
`load`	Dynamically load object code.
`open`	Open files and process pipelines.
`pwd`	Determine the current directory.
`socket`	Open network sockets.
`source`	Load scripts.

A safe interpreter does not have commands to manipulate the file system and other programs (e.g., `cd`, `open`, and `exec`). This ensures that untrusted scripts cannot harm the host computer. The `socket` command is removed so untrusted scripts cannot access the network. The `exit`, `source`, and `load` commands are removed so an untrusted script cannot harm the hosting application. Note that commands like `puts` and `gets` are *not* removed. A safe interpreter can still do I/O, but it cannot create an I/O channel. We will show how to pass an I/O channel to a child interpreter on page 211.

The initial state of a safe interpreter is very safe, but it is too limited. The only thing a safe interpreter can do is compute a string and return that value to the parent. By creating command aliases, a master can give a safe interpreter controlled access to resources. A *security policy* implements a set of command aliases that add controlled capabilities to a safe interpreter. We will show, for example, how to provide limited network and file system access to untrusted slaves. Tcl provides a framework to manage several security policies, which is described later.

Command Aliases

A *command alias* is a command in one interpreter that is implemented by a command in another interpreter. The master interpreter installs command aliases in its slaves. The command to create an alias has the following general form:

```
interp alias slave cmd1 target cmd2 ?arg arg ...?
```

This creates *cmd1* in *slave* that is an alias for *cmd2* in *target*. When *cmd1* is invoked in *slave*, *cmd2* is invoked in *target*. The alias mechanism is transparent to the slave. Whatever *cmd2* returns, the slave sees as the return value of *cmd1*. If *cmd2* raises an error, the error is propagated to the slave.

Name the current interpreter with `{}`.

If *target* is the current interpreter, name it with `{}`. The empty list is the way to name yourself as the interpreter. This is the most common case, although *target* could be a different slave. The *slave* and *target* can even be the same interpreter.

The arguments to *cmd1* are passed to *cmd2*, after any additional arguments to *cmd2* that were specified when the alias was created. These hidden arguments provide a safe way to pass extra arguments to an alias. For example, it is quite common to pass the name of the slave to the alias. In Example 17–3, `exit` in the interpreter `foo` is an alias that is implemented in the current interpreter (i.e., `{}`). When the slave executes `exit`, the master executes:

```
interp delete foo
```

Example 17–3 A command alias for `exit`.

```
interp create foo
interp alias foo exit {} interp delete foo
interp eval foo exit
# Child foo is gone.
```

Alias Introspection

You can query what aliases are defined for a child interpreter. The `interp aliases` command lists the aliases; the `interp alias` command can also return the value of an alias, and the `interp target` command tells you what interpreter implements an alias. These are illustrated in the following examples:

Example 17–4 Querying aliases.

```
proc Interp_ListAliases {name out} {
    puts $out "Aliases for $name"
    foreach alias [interp aliases $name] {
        puts $out [format "%-20s => (%s) %s" $alias \
                [interp target $name $alias] \
                [interp alias $name $alias]]
    }
}
```

Example 17–4 generates output in a human readable format. Example 17–5 generates the aliases as Tcl commands that can be used to re-create them later:

Example 17–5 Dumping aliases as Tcl commands.

```
proc Interp_DumpAliases {name out} {
    puts $out "# Aliases for $name"
    foreach alias [interp aliases $name] {
        puts $out [format "interp alias %s %s %s %s" \
            $name $alias [list [interp target $name $alias]] \
            [interp alias $name $alias]]
    }
}
```


Hidden Commands

The commands listed in Table 17–2 are *hidden* instead of being completely removed. A hidden command can be invoked in a slave by its master. For example, a master can load Tcl scripts into a slave by using its hidden `source` command:

```
interp create -safe slave
interp invokehidden slave source filename
```

Without hidden commands the master has to do a bit more work to achieve the same thing. It must open and read the file and `eval` the contents of the file in the slave. File operations are described in Chapter 9.

```
interp create -safe slave
set in [open filename]
interp eval slave [read $in]
close $in
```

Hidden commands were added in Tcl 7.7 in order to better support the Tcl/Tk browser plug-in described in Chapter 48. In some cases hidden commands are strictly necessary; it is not possible to simulate them any other way. The best examples are in the context of Safe-Tk, where the master creates widgets or does potentially dangerous things on behalf of the slave. These will be discussed in more detail later.

A master can hide and expose commands using the `interp hide` and `interp expose` operations, respectively. You can even hide Tcl procedures. However, the commands inside the procedure run with the same privilege as the slave. For example, if you are really paranoid you might not want an untrusted interpreter to read the clock or get timing information. You can hide the `clock` and `time` commands:

```
interp create -safe slave
interp hide slave clock
interp hide slave time
```

You can remove commands from the slave entirely like this:

```
interp eval slave [list rename clock {}]
interp eval slave [list rename time {}]
```

Substitutions

You must be aware of Tcl parsing and substitutions when commands are invoked in other interpreters. There are three cases corresponding to `interp eval`, `interp invokehidden`, and command aliases.

With `interp eval` the command is subject to a complete round of parsing and substitutions in the target interpreter. This occurs after the parsing and substitutions for the `interp eval` command itself. In addition, if you pass several arguments to `interp eval`, those are concatenated before evaluation. This is similar to the way the `eval` command works as described on page 113. The most reliable way to use `interp eval` is to construct a list to ensure the command is well structured:

```
interp eval slave [list cmd arg1 arg2]
```

With hidden commands, the command and arguments are taken directly from the arguments to `interp invokehidden`, and there are no substitutions done in the target interpreter. This means that the master has complete control over the command structure, and nothing funny can happen in the other interpreter. For this reason you should not create a list. If you do that, the whole list will be interpreted as the command name! Instead, just pass separate arguments to `interp invokehidden` and they are passed straight through to the target:

```
interp invokehidden slave command arg1 arg2
```

Never `eval` alias arguments.

With aliases, all the parsing and substitutions occur in the slave before the alias is invoked in the master. The alias implementation should never `eval` or `subst` any values it gets from the slave to avoid executing arbitrary code.

For example, suppose there is an alias to open files. The alias does some checking and then invokes the hidden `open` command. An untrusted script might pass `[exit]` as the name of the file to open in order to create mischief. The untrusted code is hoping that the master will accidentally `eval` the filename and cause the application to exit. This attack has nothing to do with opening files; it just hopes for a poor alias implementation. Example 17–6 shows an alias that is not subject to this attack:

Example 17–6 Substitutions and hidden commands.

```
interp alias slave open {} safeopen slave
proc safeopen {slave filename {mode r}} {
   # do some checks, then...
   interp invokehidden $slave open $filename $mode
}
interp eval slave {open \[exit\]}
```

The command in the slave starts out as:

```
open \[exit\]
```

The master has to quote the brackets in its `interp eval` command or else the slave will try to invoke `exit` because of command substitution. Presumably `exit` isn't defined, or it is defined to terminate the slave. Once this quoting is done, the value of `filename` is `[exit]` and it is not subject to substitutions. It is safe to use `$filename` in the `interp invokehidden` command because it is only substituted once, in the master. The hidden `open` command also gets `[exit]` as its filename argument, which is never evaluated as a Tcl command.

I/O from Safe Interpreters

A safe child interpreter cannot open files or network sockets directly. An alias can create an I/O channel (i.e., open a file or socket) and give the child access to it. The parent can share the I/O channel with the child, or it can transfer the I/O channel to the child. If the channel is shared, both the parent and the child can use it. If the channel is transferred, the parent no longer has access to the channel. In general, transferring an I/O channel is simpler, but sharing an I/O channel gives the parent more control over an unsafe child. The differences are illustrated in Example 17–7 and Example 17–9.

There are three properties of I/O channels that are important to consider when choosing between sharing and transferring: the name, the seek offset, and the reference count.

- The name of the I/O channel (e.g., `file4`) is the same in all interpreters. If a parent transfers a channel to a child, it can close the channel by evaluating a `close` command in the child. Although names are shared, an interpreter cannot attempt I/O on a channel to which it has not been given access.
- The seek offset of the I/O channel is shared by all interpreters that share the I/O channel. An I/O operation on the channel updates the seek offset for all interpreters that share the channel. This means that if two interpreters share an I/O channel, their output will be cleanly interleaved in the channel. If they both read from the I/O channel, they will get different data. Seek offsets are explained in more detail on page 106.
- A channel has a reference count of all interpreters that share the I/O channel. The channel remains open until all references are closed. When a parent transfers an I/O channel, the reference count stays the same. When a parent shares an I/O channel, the reference count increments by one. When an interpreter closes a channel with `close`, the reference count is decremented by one. When an interpreter is deleted, all of its references to I/O channels are removed.

The syntax of commands to share or transfer an I/O channel is:

```
interp share interp1 chanName interp2
interp transfer interp1 chanName interp2
```

In these commands, *chanName* exists in *interp1* and is being shared or transferred to *interp2*. As with command aliases, if *interp1* is the current interpreter, name it with `{}`.

The following example creates a temporary file for an unsafe interpreter. The file is opened for reading and writing, and the slave can use it to store data temporarily.

Example 17–7 Opening a file for an unsafe interpreter.

```
proc TempfileAlias {slave} {
	set i 0
	while {[file exists Temp$slave$i]} {
		incr i
	}
	set out [open Temp$slave$i w+]
	interp transfer {} $out $slave
	return $out
}
proc TempfileExitAlias {slave} {
	foreach file [glob -nocomplain Temp$slave*] {
		file delete -force $file
	}
	interp delete $slave
}
interp create -safe foo
interp alias foo Tempfile {} TempfileAlias foo
interp alias foo exit {} TempfileExitAlias foo
```

The `TempfileAlias` procedure is invoked in the parent when the child interpreter invokes `Tempfile`. `TempfileAlias` returns the name of the open channel, and this becomes the return value from `Tempfile` so the child knows the name of the I/O channel. `TempfileAlias` uses `interp transfer` to pass the I/O channel to the child so the child has permission to access the I/O channel. In this example, it would also work to invoke the hidden `open` command to create the I/O channel directly in the slave.

Example 17–7 is not fully safe because the unsafe interpreter can still overflow the disk or create a million files. Because the parent has transferred the I/O channel to the child, it cannot easily monitor the I/O activity by the child. Example 17–9 addresses these issues.

The Safe Base

An safe interpreter created with `interp create -safe` has no script library environment and no way to source scripts. Tcl provides a *safe base* that extends a raw safe interpreter with the ability to source scripts and packages as described in Chapter 12. The safe base also defines an `exit` alias that terminates the slave like the one in Example 17–7. The safe base is implemented as Tcl scripts that are part of the standard Tcl script library. Create an interpreter that uses the safe base with `safe::interpCreate`:

```
safe::interpCreate foo
```

The safe base has `source` and `load` aliases that only access directories on an *access path* defined by the master interpreter. The master has complete control over what files can be loaded into a slave. In general it would be OK to source any Tcl program into an untrusted interpreter. However, untrusted scripts might learn things by sourcing arbitrary files. The safe base also has versions of the `package` and `unknown` commands that support the library facility.

Table 17–3 lists the Tcl procedures in the safe base:

Table 17–3 The safe base master interface.

`safe::interpCreate ?slave? ?options?`	Create a safe interpreter and initialize the security policy mechanism.
`safe::interpInit slave ?options?`	Initialize a safe interpreter so it can use security policies.
`safe::interpConfigure slave ?options?`	Options are `-accessPath pathlist`, `-nostatics`, `-deleteHook script`, `-nestedLoadOk`.
`safe::interpDelete slave`	Delete a safe interpreter.
`safe::interpAddToAccessPath slave directory`	Add a directory to the slave's access path.
`safe::interpFindInAccessPath`	Map from a directory to the token visible in the slave for that directory.
`safe::setLogCmd ?cmd arg ... ?`	Set or query the logging command used by the safe base.

Table 17–4 lists the aliases defined in a safe interpreter by the safe base.

Table 17–4 The safe base slave aliases.

`source`	Load scripts from directories in the access path
`load`	Load binary extensions from the slaves access path
`file`	Only the `dirname`, `join`, `extension`, `root`, `tail`, `pathname`, and `split` operations are allowed.
`exit`	Destroy the slave interpreter.

Security Policies

A *security policy* defines what a safe interpreter can do. Designing security policies that are secure is difficult. If you design your own, make sure to have your colleagues review the code. Give out prizes to folks who can break your policy. Good policy implementations are proven with lots of review and trial attacks.

The good news is that Safe-Tcl security policies can be implemented in relatively small amounts of Tcl code. This makes them easier to analyze and get correct. Here are a number of rules of thumb:

- Small policies are better than big, complex policies. If you do a lot of complex processing to allow or disallow access to resources, chances are there are holes in your policy. Keep it simple.
- Never `eval` arguments to aliases. If an alias accepts arguments that are passed by the slave, you must avoid being tricked into executing arbitrary Tcl code. The primary way to avoid this is to never `eval` arguments that are passed into an alias.
- Security policies do not compose. Each time you add a new alias to a security policy it changes the nature of the policy. Even if *alias1* and *alias2* are safe in isolation, there is no guarantee that they cannot be used together to mount an attack. Each addition to a security policy requires careful review.

Limited Socket Access

The `Safesock` security policy provides limited socket access. The policy is designed around a simple table of allowed hosts and ports. An untrusted interpreter can only connect to addresses listed in the table. For example, I would never let untrusted code connect to the *sendmail*, *ftp*, or *telnet* ports on my hosts. There are just too many attacks possible on these ports. On the other hand, I might want to let untrusted code fetch a URL from certain hosts, or connect to a database server for an intranet application. The goal of this policy is to have a simple way to specify exactly what hosts and ports a slave can access. Example 17–8 shows a simplified version of the `Safesock` security policy that is distributed with Tcl 8.0.

Example 17–8 The `Safesock` security policy.

```
# The index is a host name, and the
# value is a list of port specifications, which can be
# an exact port number
# a lower bound on port number: N-
# a range of port numbers, inclusive: N-M
array set safesock {
   sage.eng      3000-4000
   www.sun.com   80
   webcache.eng {80 8080}
   bisque.eng    {80 1025-}
}
proc Safesock_PolicyInit {slave} {
   interp alias $slave socket {} SafesockAlias $slave
}
proc SafesockAlias {slave host port} {
   global safesock
   if ![info exists safesock($host)] {
```

```
        error "unknown host: $host"
    }

    foreach portspec $safesock($host) {
        set low [set high ""]
        if {[regexp {^([0-9]+)-([0-9]*)$} $portspec x low high]} {
            if {($low <= $port && $high == "") ||
                    ($low <= $port && $high >= $port)} {
                set good $port
                break
            }
        } elseif {$port == $portspec} {
            set good $port
        }
    }

    if [info exists good] {
        set sock [interp invokehidden $slave socket $host $good]
        interp invokehidden $slave fconfigure $sock \
            -blocking 0
        return $sock
    }
    error "bad port: $port"
}
```


The policy is initialized with `Safesock_PolicyInit`. The name of this procedure follows a naming convention used by the safe base. In this case, a single alias is installed. The alias gives the slave a `socket` command that is implemented by `SafesockAlias` in the master.

The alias checks for a port that matches one of the port specifications for the host. If a match is found, then the `invokehidden` operation is used to invoke two commands in the slave. The `socket` command creates the network connection, and the `fconfigure` command puts the socket into non-blocking mode so `read` and `gets` by the slave do not block the application:

```
set sock [interp invokehidden $slave socket $host $good]
interp invokehidden $slave fconfigure $sock -blocking 0
```

The `socket` alias in the slave does not conflict with the hidden `socket` command. There are two distinct sets of commands, hidden and exposed. It is quite common for the alias implementation to invoke the hidden command after various permission checks are made.

The Tcl Web browser plug-in ships with a slightly improved version of the `Safesock` policy. It adds an alias for `fconfigure` so the `http` package can set end of line translations and buffering modes. The `fconfigure` alias does not let you change the blocking behavior of the socket. The policy has also been extended to classify hosts into trusted and untrusted hosts based on their address. A different table of allowed ports is used for the two classes of hosts. The classification is done with two tables: one table lists patterns that match trusted hosts and the other table lists hosts that should not be trusted even though they match the first table. The improved also version lets a downloaded script connect to the

Web server that it came from. The Web browser plug-in is described in Chapter 48.

Limited Temporary Files

Example 17–9 improves on Example 17–7 by limiting the number of temporary files and the size of the files. It is written to work with the safe base so it has a `Tempfile_PolicyInit` that takes the name of the slave as an argument. `TempfileOpenAlias` lets the child specify a file by name, yet it limits the files to a single directory.

The example demonstrates a shared I/O channel that gives the master control over output. `TempfilePutsAlias` restricts the amount of data that can be written to a file. By sharing the I/O channel for the temporary file the slave can use commands like `gets`, `eof`, and `close`, while the master does the `puts`. The need for shared I/O channels is somewhat reduced by hidden commands, which were added to Safe-Tcl more recently than shared I/O channels. For example, the `puts` alias can either write to a shared channel after checking the file size, or it could invoke the hidden `puts` in the slave. This alternative is shown in Example 17–10.

Example 17–9 The `Tempfile` security policy.

```
# Policy parameters:
#   directory is the location for the files
#   maxfile is the number of files allowed in the directory
#   maxsize is the max size for any single file.

array set tempfile {
	maxfile	4
	maxsize	65536
}
# tempfile(directory) is computed dynamically based on
# the source of the script

proc Tempfile_PolicyInit {slave} {
	global tempfile
	interp alias $slave open {} \
		TempfileOpenAlias $slave $tempfile(directory) \
			$tempfile(maxfile)
	interp alias $slave puts {} TempfilePutsAlias $slave \
		$tempfile(maxsize)
	interp alias $slave exit {} TempfileExitAlias $slave
}
proc TempfileOpenAlias {slave dir maxfile name {m r} {p 0777}} {
	global tempfile
	# remove sneaky characters
	regsub -all {|/:} [file tail $name] {} real
	set real [file join $dir $real]
	# Limit the number of files
	set files [glob -nocomplain [file join $dir *]]
	set N [llength $files]
```

```
    if {($N >= $maxfile) && (\
            [lsearch -exact $files $real] < 0)} {
        error "permission denied"
    }
    if [catch {open $real $m $p} out] {
        return -code error "$name: permission denied"
    }
    lappend tempfile(channels,$slave) $out
    interp share {} $out $slave
    return $out
}
proc TempfileExitAlias {slave} {
    global tempfile
    interp delete $slave
    if [info exists tempfile(channels,$slave)] {
        foreach out $tempfile(channels,$slave) {
            catch {close $out}
        }
        unset tempfile(channels,$slave)
    }
}
# See also the puts alias in Example 19-4 on page 245
proc TempfilePutsAlias {slave max chan args} {
    # max is the file size limit, in bytes
    # chan is the I/O channel
    # args is either a single string argument,
    # or the -nonewline flag plus the string.

    if {[llength $args] > 2} {
        error "invalid arguments"
    }
    if {[llength $args] == 2} {
        if {![string match -n* [lindex $argv 0]]} {
            error "invalid arguments"
        }
        set string [lindex $args 1]
    } else {
        set string [lindex $args 0]\n
    }
    set size [expr [tell $chan] + [string length $string]]
    if {$size > $max} {
        error "File size exceeded"
    } else {
        puts -nonewline $chan $string
    }
}
```

The `TempfileAlias` procedure is generalized in Example 17–9 to have parameters that specify the directory, name, and a limit to the number of files allowed. The `directory` and `maxfile` limit are part of the alias definition. Their existence is transparent to the slave. The slave only specifies the name and access mode (i.e., for reading or writing.) The `Tempfile` policy could be used by different slave interpreters with different parameters.

The master is careful to restrict the files to the specified directory. It uses `file tail` to strip off any leading pathname components that the slave might specify. The `tempfile(directory)` definition is not shown in the example. The application must choose a directory when it creates the safe interpreter. The `Browser` security policy described on page 611 chooses a directory based on the name of the URL containing the untrusted script.

The `TempfilePutsAlias` procedure implements a limited form of `puts`. It checks the size of the file with `tell` and measures the output string to see if the total exceeds the limit. The limit comes from a parameter defined when the alias is created. The file cannot grow past the limit, at least not by any action of the child interpreter. The `args` parameter is used to allow an optional `-nonewline` flag to `puts`. The value of `args` is checked explicitly instead of using the `eval` trick described in Example 10–2 on page 116. Never `eval` arguments to aliases or else a slave can attack you with arguments that contain embedded Tcl commands.

The master and slave share the I/O channel. The name of the I/O channel is recorded in `tempfile`, and `TempfileExitAlias` uses this information to close the channel when the child interpreter is deleted. This is necessary because both parent and child have a reference to the channel when it is shared. The child's reference is automatically removed when the interpreter is deleted, but the parent must close its own reference.

The shared I/O channel lets the master use `puts` and `tell`. It is also possible to implement this policy by using hidden `puts` and `tell` commands. The reason `tell` must be hidden is to prevent the slave from implementing its own version of `tell` that lies about the seek offset value. One advantage of using hidden commands is there is no need to clean up the tempfile state about open channels. You can also layer the puts alias on top of any existing puts implementation. For example, a script may define `puts` to be a procedure that inserts data into a text widget. Example x shows the difference when using hidden commands.

Example 17–10 Restricted `puts` using hidden commands.

```
proc Tempfile_PolicyInit {slave} {
    global tempfile
    interp alias $slave open {} \
        TempfileOpenAlias $slave $tempfile(directory) \
            $tempfile(maxfile)
    interp hide $slave tell
    interp alias $slave tell {} TempfileTellAlias $slave
    interp hide $slave puts
    interp alias $slave puts {} TempfilePutsAlias $slave \
        $tempfile(maxsize)
    # no special exit alias required
}
proc TempfileOpenAlias {slave dir maxfile name {m r} {p 0777}} {
    # remove sneaky characters
    regsub -all {|/:} [file tail $name] {} real
```

```
    set real [file join $dir $real]
    # Limit the number of files
    set files [glob -nocomplain [file join $dir *]]
    set N [llength $files]
    if {($N >= $maxfile) && (\
            [lsearch -exact $files $real] < 0)} {
        error "permission denied"
    }
    if [catch {interp invokehidden $slave \
            open $real $m $p} out] {
        return -code error "$name: permission denied"
    }
    return $out
}
proc TempfileTellAlias {slave chan} {
    interp invokehidden $slave tell $chan
}
proc TempfilePutsAlias {slave max chan args} {
    if {[llength $args] > 2} {
        error "invalid arguments"
    }
    if {[llength $args] == 2} {
        if {![string match -n* [lindex $args 0]]} {
            error "invalid arguments"
        }
        set string [lindex $args 1]
    } else {
        set string [lindex $args 0]\n
    }
    set size [interp invokehidden $slave tell $chan]
    incr size [string length $string]
    if {$size > $max} {
        error "File size exceeded"
    } else {
        interp invokehidden $slave \
            puts -nonewline $chan $string
    }
}
```


Safe `after` Command

The `after` command is unsafe because it can block the application for an arbitrary amount of time. This happens if you only specify a time but do not specify a command. In this case Tcl just waits for the time period and processes no events. This will stop all interpreters, not just the one doing the `after` command. This is a kind of *resource attack*. It doesn't leak information or damage anything, but it disrupts the main application.

Example 17–11 defines an alias that implements `after` on behalf of safe interpreters. The basic idea is to carefully check the arguments, and then do the `after` in the parent interpreter. As an additional feature, the number of outstanding `after` events is limited. The master keeps a record of each `after` event scheduled. Two IDs are associated with each event: one chosen by the master (i.e., `myid`), and the other chosen by the `after` command (i.e., `id`). The master keeps a map from `myid` to `id`. The map serves two purposes. The number of map entries counts the number of outstanding events. The map also hides the real `after` ID from the slave, which prevents a slave from attempting mischief by specifying invalid after IDs to `after cancel`. The `SafeAfterCallback` is the procedure scheduled. It maintains state and then invokes the original callback in the slave.

Example 17–11 A safe `after` command.

```
# SafeAfter_PolicyInit creates a child with
# a safe after command

proc SafeAfter_PolicyInit {slave max} {
    # max limits the number of outstanding after events
    global after
    interp alias $slave after {} SafeAfterAlias $slave $max
    interp alias $slave exit {} SafeAfterExitAlias $slave
    # This is used to generate after IDs for the slave.
    set after(id,$slave) 0
}

# SafeAfterAlias is an alias for after. It disallows after
# with only a time argument and no command.

proc SafeAfterAlias {slave max args} {
    global after
    set argc [llength $args]
    if {$argc == 0} {
        error "Usage: after option args"
    }
    switch -- [lindex $args 0] {
        cancel {
            # A naive implementation would just
            # eval after cancel $args
            # but something dangerous could be hiding in args.
            set myid [lindex $args 1]
            if {[info exists after(id,$slave,$myid)]} {
                set id $after(id,$slave,$myid)
                unset after(id,$slave,$myid)
                after cancel $id
            }
            return ""
        }
        default {
            if {$argc == 1} {
                error "Usage: after time command args..."
            }
            if {[llength [array names after id,$slave,*]]\
                    >= $max} {
                error "Too many after events"
            }
```

```
            # Maintain concat semantics
            set command [concat [lrange $args 1 end]]
            # Compute our own id to pass the callback.
            set myid after#[incr after(id,$slave)]
            set id [after [lindex $args 0] \
               [list SafeAfterCallback $slave $myid $command]]
            set after(id,$slave,$myid) $id
            return $myid
        }
    }
}

# SafeAfterCallback is the after callback in the master.
# It evaluates its command in the safe interpreter.

proc SafeAfterCallback {slave myid cmd} {
    global after
    unset after(id,$slave,$myid)
    if [catch {
        interp eval $slave $cmd
    } err] {
        catch {interp eval $slave bgerror $error}
    }
}

# SafeAfterExitAlias is an alias for exit that does cleanup.

proc SafeAfterExitAlias {slave} {
    global after
    foreach id [array names after id,$slave,*] {
        after cancel $after($id)
        unset after($id)
    }
    interp delete $slave
}
```

PART III

Tk Basics

Part III introduces Tk, the toolkit for building graphical user interfaces. The Tcl command interface to Tk makes it quick and easy to build powerful user interfaces. Tk is portable and your user interface code can work unchanged on UNIX, Windows, and the Macintosh.

Chapter 18 describes the basic concepts of Tk and provides an overview of its facilities.

Chapter 19 illustrates Tk with three example programs including a browser for the examples from this book. These examples use facilities that are described in more detail in later chapters.

Geometry managers implement the layout of a user interface. Chapters Chapter 20, Chapter 21, and Chapter 22 describe the `pack`, `grid`, and `place` geometry managers. The packer and gridder are general-purpose managers that use constraints to create flexible layouts with a small amount of code. The placer is a special purpose geometry manager that can be used for special effects.

Chapter 23 describes event bindings that associate Tcl commands with events like keystrokes and mouse motion.

CHAPTER 18

Tk Fundamentals

This chapter introduces the basic concepts used in the Tk graphical user interface toolkit. Tk adds about 35 Tcl commands that let you create and manipulate widgets in a graphical user interface. Tk works with the X window system, Windows, and Macintosh. The same script can run unchanged on all of these major platforms.

Tk is a toolkit for programming graphical user interfaces. It was designed for the X window system used on UNIX systems, and it was ported to the Macintosh and Windows environments in Tk 4.1. Tk shares many concepts with other windowing toolkits, but you do not need to know much about graphical user interfaces to get started with Tk.

Tk provides a set of Tcl commands that create and manipulate *widgets*. A widget is a window in a graphical user interface that has a particular appearance and behavior. The terms *widget* and *window* are often used interchangeably. Widget types include buttons, scrollbars, menus, and text windows. Tk also has a general-purpose drawing widget called a *canvas* that lets you create lighter-weight items such as lines, boxes, and bitmaps. The Tcl commands added by Tk are summarized at the end of this chapter.

Tk widgets are organized in a hierarchy. To an application, the window hierarchy means that there is a primary window, and inside that window there can be a number of children windows. The children windows can contain more windows, and so on. Just as a hierarchical file system has directories (i.e., folders) that are containers for files and directories, a hierarchical window system uses windows as containers for other windows. The hierarchy affects the naming scheme used for Tk widgets as described later, and it is used to help arrange widgets on the screen.

Widgets are under the control of a *geometry manager* that controls their size and location on the screen. Until a geometry manager learns about a widget, it will not be mapped onto the screen and you will not see it. Tk has powerful geometry managers that make it very easy to create nice screen layouts. The main trick with any geometry manager is that you use *frame* widgets as containers for other widgets. One or more widgets are created and then arranged in a frame by a geometry manager. By putting frames within frames you can create complex layouts. There are three different geometry managers you can use in Tk: `grid`, `pack`, and `place`. The Tk geometry managers are discussed in detail in Chapters 20, 21, and 22.

A Tk-based application has an *event-driven* control flow, like most window system toolkits. The Tk widgets handle most events automatically, so programming your application remains simple. For specialized behaviors, you use the `bind` command to register a Tcl command that runs when an event occurs. There are lots of events, including mouse motion, keystrokes, window resize, and window destruction. You can also define *virtual events*, like `Cut` and `Paste`, that are caused by different events on different platforms. Bindings are discussed in detail in Chapter 23. Chapter 15 describes I/O events and the Tcl event loop, while Chapter 42 describes C programming and the event loop.

Event bindings are grouped into classes, which are called *bindtags*. The `bindtags` command associates a widget with an ordered set of bindtags. The level of indirection between the event bindings and the widgets creates a flexible and powerful system for managing events. You can create your own bindtags and dynamically change the bindtags for a widget to support mode changes in your application.

A concept related to binding is *focus*. At any given time, one of the widgets has the input focus, and keyboard events are directed to it. There are two general approaches to focusing: give focus to the widget under the mouse, or explicitly set the focus to a particular widget. Tk provides commands to change focus so you can implement either style of focus management. To support modal dialog boxes, you can forcibly *grab* the focus away from other widgets. Chapter 33 describes focus, grabs, and dialogs.

The basic structure of a Tk script begins by creating widgets and arranging them with a geometry manager, and then binding actions to the widgets. After the interpreter processes the commands that initialize the user interface, the event loop is entered and your application begins running.

If you use *wish* interactively, it creates and displays an empty main window and gives you a command-line prompt. With this interface, your keyboard commands are handled by the event loop, so you can build your Tk interface gradually. As we will see, you will be able to change virtually all aspects of your application interactively.

Hello, World! in Tk

Our first Tk script is very simple. It creates a button that prints "Hello, World!" to standard output when you press it. Above the button widget is a title bar that is provided by the window manager, which in this case is *twm* under X windows:

Example 18–1 "Hello, World!" Tk program.

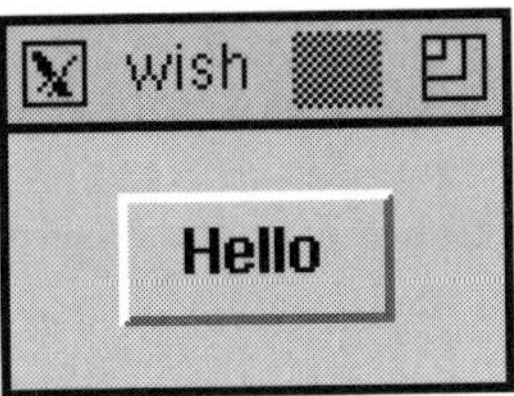


```
#!/usr/local/bin/wish
button .hello -text Hello \
    -command {puts stdout "Hello, World!"}
pack .hello -padx 20 -pady 10
```

The first line identifies the interpreter for the script:

```
#!/usr/local/bin/wish
```

This special line is necessary if the script is in a file that will be used like other UNIX command files. Chapter 2 describes how to set up scripts on different platforms.

There are two Tcl commands in the script: one to create the button, and one to make it visible on the display. The `button` command creates an instance of a button:

```
button .hello -text Hello \
    -command {puts stdout "Hello, World!"}
=> .hello
```

The name of the button is `.hello`. The label on the button is `Hello`, and the command associated with the button is:

```
puts stdout "Hello, World!"
```

The `pack` command maps the button onto the screen. Some padding parameters are supplied so there is space around the button:

```
pack .hello -padx 20 -pady 10
```

If you type these two commands into `wish`, you will not see anything happen when the `button` command is given. After the `pack` command, though, you will see the empty main window shrink to be just big enough to contain the button and its padding. The behavior of the packer will be discussed further in Chapters 19 and 20.

Tk uses an object-based system for creating and naming widgets. Associated with each class of widget (e.g., `Button`) is a command that creates instances of that class of widget. As the widget is created, a new Tcl command is defined that operates on that instance of the widget. Example 18–1 creates a button named `.hello`, and we can operate on the button using its name as a Tcl command. For example, we can cause the button to highlight a few times:

```
.hello flash
```

Or, we can run the command associated with the button:

```
.hello invoke
=> Hello, World!
```

Tk has widget classes and instances, but it is not fully object oriented. It is not possible to subclass a widget class and use inheritance. Instead, Tk provides very flexible widgets that can be configured in many different ways to tune their appearance. The resource database can store configuration information that is shared by many widgets, and new classes can be introduced to group resources. Widget behavior is shared by using binding tags that group bindings. Instead of building class hierarchies, Tk uses composition to assemble widgets with shared behavior and attributes.

Naming Tk Widgets

The period in the name of the button instance, `.hello`, is required. Tk uses a naming system for the widgets that reflects their position in a hierarchy of widgets. The root of the hierarchy is the main window of the application, and its name is simply a dot (i.e., .). This is similar to the naming convention for directories in UNIX where the root directory is named `/`, and then `/` is used to separate components of a file name. Tk uses a dot in the same way. Each widget that is a child of the main window is named something like `.foo`. A child widget of `.foo` would be `.foo.bar`, and so on. Just as file systems have directories that are containers for files and other directories, the Tk window hierarchy uses frame widgets that are containers for widgets and other frames.

Each component of a Tk pathname must start with a lowercase letter or a number. Obviously, a component cannot include a period, either. The lower case restriction avoids a conflict with resource class names that begin with an upper case letter. A resource name can include Tk pathname components and Tk widget classes, and case is used to distinguish them. Chapter 25 describes resources in detail.

Store widget names in variables.

There is one drawback to the Tk widget naming system. If your interface changes enough it can result in some widgets changing their position in the widget hierarchy. In that case they may need to change their name. You can insulate yourself from this programming nuisance by using variables to hold the names of important widgets. Use a variable reference instead of widget pathnames in case you need to change things, or if you want to reuse your code in a different interface.

Configuring Tk Widgets

Example 18–1 illustrates a style of named parameter passing that is prevalent in the Tk commands. Pairs of arguments specify the attributes of a widget. The attribute names begin with `-`, such as `-text`, and the next argument is the value of that attribute. Even the simplest Tk widget can have a dozen or more attributes that can be specified this way, and complex widgets can have 20 or more attributes. However, the beauty of Tk is that you only need to specify the attributes for which the default value is not good enough. This is illustrated by the simplicity of the `Hello, World` example.

Finally, each widget instance supports a `configure` operation, which can be abbreviated to `config`, that can query and change these attributes. The syntax for `config` uses the same named argument pairs used when you create the widget. For example, we can change the background color of the button to red even after it has been created and mapped onto the screen:

```
.hello config -background red
```

Widget attributes can be redefined any time, even the `text` and `command` that were set when the button was created. The following command changes `.hello` into a goodbye button:

```
.hello config -text Goodbye! -command exit
```

Widgets have a `cget` operation to query the current value of an attribute:

```
.hello cget -background
=> red
```

You can find out more details about a widget attribute by using `configure` without a value:

```
.hello config -background
=> -background background Background #ffe4c4 red
```

The returned information includes the command-line switch, the resource name, the class name, the default value, and the current value, which is last. The class and resource name have to do with the resource mechanism described in Chapter 25. If you only specify `configure` and no attribute, then a list of the configuration information for all widget attributes is returned. Example 18–2 uses this to print out all the information about a widget:

Example 18–2 Looking at all widget attributes.

```
proc Widget_Attributes {w {out stdout}} {
    puts $out [format "%-20s %-10s %s" Attribute Default Value]
    foreach item [$w configure] {
        puts $out [format "%-20s %-10s %s" \
            [lindex $item 0] [lindex $item 3] \
            [lindex $item 4]]
    }
}
```

Tk Widget Attributes and the Resource Database

A widget attribute can be named three different ways: by its command-line option, by its resource name, and by its resource class. The command-line option is the format you use in Tcl scripts. This form is always all lowercase and prefixed with a hyphen (e.g., `-offvalue`). The resource name for the attribute has no leading hyphen, and it has uppercase letters at internal word boundaries (e.g., offValue). The resource class begins with an uppercase letter and has uppercase letters at internal word boundaries. (e.g., OffValue).

The tables in this book list widget attributes by their resource name.

You need to know these naming conventions if you specify widget attributes via the resource mechanism. The command-line option can be derived from the resource name by mapping it to all lowercase. The primary advantage of using resources to specify attributes is that you do not have to litter your code with attribute specifications. With just a few resource database entries you can specify attributes for all your widgets. In addition, if attributes are specified with resources, users can provide alternate resource specifications in order to override the values supplied by the application. For attributes like colors and fonts, this feature can be important to users. Resource specifications are described in detail in Chapter 25.

The Tk Manual Pages

This book provides summaries for all the Tk commands, the widget attributes, and the default bindings. However, for the absolute truth, you may need to read the on-line manual pages that come with Tk. They provide a complete reference source for the Tk commands. You should be able to use the UNIX *man* program to read them:

```
% man button
```

The *tkman* program provides a very nice graphical user interface to the UNIX manual pages. On the Macintosh platform, the manual pages are formatted into HTML documents that you can find in the HTML Docs folder of the Tcl/Tk distribution. On Windows, the manual pages are formatted into Help documents.

There are a large number of attributes that are common across most of the Tk widgets. These are described in a separate man page under the name options. Each man page begins with a STANDARD OPTIONS section that lists which of these standard attributes apply, but you have to look at the options man page for the description. In contrast, the tables in this book always list all widget attributes.

Summary of the Tk Commands

The following tables list the Tcl commands added by Tk. Table 18–1 lists commands that create widgets. There are 15 different widgets in Tk, although 4 of them are variations on a button, and 5 are devoted to different flavors of text display. Table 18–2 lists commands that manipulate widgets and provide associated functions like input focus, event binding, and geometry management. Table 18–3 lists several support procedures that implement standard dialogs, option menus, and other facilities. The page number in the table is the primary reference for the command, and there are other references in the index.

Table 18–1 Tk widget-creation commands.

Command	Pg.	Description
`button`	304	Create a command button.
`checkbutton`	308	Create a toggle button that is linked to a Tcl variable.
`radiobutton`	308	Create one of a set of radio buttons linked to one variable.
`menubutton`	312	Create a button that posts a menu.
`menu`	312	Create a menu.
`canvas`	391	Create a canvas, which supports lines, boxes, bitmaps, images, arcs, text, polygons, and embedded widgets.
`label`	336	Create a read-only, one-line text label.
`entry`	353	Create a one-line text entry widget.
`message`	338	Create a read-only, multiline text message.
`listbox`	359	Create a line-oriented, scrolling text widget.
`text`	369	Create a general-purpose, editable text widget.
`scrollbar`	345	Create a scrollbar that can be linked to another widget.
`scale`	341	Create a scale widget that adjusts the value of a variable.
`frame`	333	Create a container widget used with geometry managers.
`toplevel`	333	Create a frame that is a new top level window.

Table 18–2 Tk widget-manipulation commands.

Command	Pg.	Description
`bell`	344	Ring the terminal bell device.
`bind`	285	Bind a Tcl command to an event.
`bindtags`	287	Create binding classes and control binding inheritance.
`clipboard`	426	Manipulate the clipboard.
`destroy`	437	Delete a widget.
`event`	297	Define and generate virtual events.
`focus`	434	Control the input focus.
`font`	471	Set and query font attributes and measurements.
`grab`	436	Steal the input focus from other widgets.
`grid`	274	Arrange widgets into a grid with constraints.
`image`	458	Create and manipulate images.
`lower`	265	Lower a window in the stacking order.

Table 18–2 Tk widget-manipulation commands. (Continued)

option	325	Set and query the resources database.
pack	264	Pack a widget in the display with constraints.
place	283	Place a widget in the display with positions.
raise	265	Raise a window in the stacking order.
selection	425	Manipulate the selection.
send	478	Send a Tcl command to another Tk application.
tk	498	Query or set the application name.
tkerror	162	Handler for background errors.
tkwait	436	Wait for an event.
update	440	Update the display by going through the event loop.
winfo	492	Query window state.
wm	487	Interact with the window manager.

Table 18–3 Tk support procedures.

Command	Pg.	Description
tk_bisque	453	Install bisque family of colors.
tk_chooseColor	433	Dialog to select a color. (Tk 4.2)
tk_dialog	431	Create simple dialogs.
tk_focusFollowsMouse	434	Install mouse-tracking focus model.
tk_focusNext	435	Focus on next widget in tab order.
tk_focusPrev	435	Focus on previous widget in tab order.
tk_getOpenFile	432	Dialog to open an existing file. (Tk 4.2)
tk_getSaveFile	432	Dialog to open a new file. (Tk 4.2)
tk_messageBox	432	Message dialog. (Tk 4.2)
tk_optionMenu	314	Create an option menu.
tk_popup	314	Create a pop-up menu.
tk_setPalette	453	Set the standard color palette. (Tk 4.2)

CHAPTER 19

Tk by Example

This chapter introduces Tk through a series of short examples. The ExecLog runs a program in the background and displays its output. The Example Browser displays the Tcl examples from the book. The Tcl Shell lets you type Tcl commands and execute them in a slave interpreter.

III. Tk Basics

Tk provides a quick and fun way to generate user interfaces. In this chapter we will go through a series of short example programs to give you a feel for what you can do. Some details are glossed over in this chapter and considered in more detail later. In particular, the `pack` geometry manager is covered in Chapter 20 and event bindings are discussed in Chapter 23. The Tk widgets are discussed in more detail in later chapters.

ExecLog

Our first example provides a simple user interface to running another program with the `exec` command. The interface consists of two buttons, `Run it` and `Quit`, an entry widget in which to enter a command, and a text widget in which to log the results of running the program. The script runs the program in a pipeline and uses the `fileevent` command to wait for output. This structure lets the user interface remain responsive while the program executes. You could use this to run *make*, for example, and it would save the results in the log. The complete example is given first, and then its commands are discussed in more detail.

Example 19–1 Logging the output of a program run with `exec`.

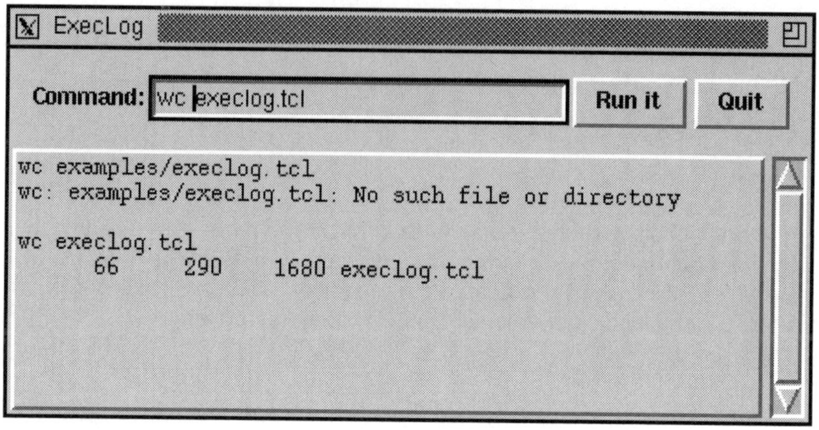

```
#!/usr/local/bin/wish
# execlog - run a program with exec and log the output
# Set window title
wm title . ExecLog

# Create a frame for buttons and entry.

frame .top -borderwidth 10
pack .top -side top -fill x

# Create the command buttons.

button .top.quit -text Quit -command exit
set but [button .top.run -text "Run it" -command Run]
pack .top.quit .top.run -side right

# Create a labeled entry for the command

label .top.l -text Command: -padx 0
entry .top.cmd -width 20 -relief sunken \
   -textvariable command
pack .top.l -side left
pack .top.cmd -side left -fill x -expand true

# Set up key binding equivalents to the buttons

bind .top.cmd <Return> Run
bind .top.cmd <Control-c> Stop
focus .top.cmd

# Create a text widget to log the output

frame .t
set log [text .t.log -width 80 -height 10 \
   -borderwidth 2 -relief raised -setgrid true \
```

```
    -yscrollcommand {.t.scroll set}]
scrollbar .t.scroll -command {.t.log yview}
pack .t.scroll -side right -fill y
pack .t.log -side left -fill both -expand true
pack .t -side top -fill both -expand true

# Run the program and arrange to read its input

proc Run {} {
    global command input log but
    if [catch {open "|$command |& cat"} input] {
        $log insert end $input\n
    } else {
        fileevent $input readable Log
        $log insert end $command\n
        $but config -text Stop -command Stop
    }
}

# Read and log output from the program

proc Log {} {
    global input log
    if [eof $input] {
        Stop
    } else {
        gets $input line
        $log insert end $line\n
        $log see end
    }
}

# Stop the program and fix up the button

proc Stop {} {
    global input but
    catch {close $input}
    $but config -text "Run it" -command Run
}
```


Window Title

The first command sets the title that appears in the title bar implemented by the window manager. Recall that dot (i.e., .) is the name of the main window:

```
wm title . ExecLog
```

The `wm` command communicates with the window manager. The window manager is the program that lets you open, close, and resize windows. It implements the title bar for the window and probably some small buttons to close or resize the window. Different window managers have a distinctive look; the figure shows a title bar from *twm*, a window manager for X.

A Frame for Buttons

A frame is created to hold the widgets that appear along the top of the interface. The frame has a border to provide some space around the widgets:

```
frame .top -borderwidth 10
```

The frame is positioned in the main window. The default packing side is the top, so `-side top` is redundant here, but it is used for clarity. The `-fill x` packing option makes the frame fill out to the whole width of the main window:

```
pack .top -side top -fill x
```

Command Buttons

Two buttons are created: one to run the command, the other to quit the program. Their names, `.top.quit` and `.top.run`, imply that they are children of the `.top` frame. This affects the `pack` command, which positions widgets inside their parent by default:

```
button .top.quit -text Quit -command exit
set but [button .top.run -text "Run it" \
    -command Run]
pack .top.quit .top.run -side right
```

A Label and an Entry

The label and entry are also created as children of the `.top` frame. The label is created with no padding in the X direction so it can be positioned right next to the entry. The size of the entry is specified in terms of characters. The `relief` attribute gives the entry some looks to set it apart visually on the display. The contents of the entry widget are linked to the Tcl variable `command`:

```
label .top.l -text Command: -padx 0
entry .top.cmd -width 20 -relief sunken \
    -textvariable command
```

The label and entry are positioned to the left inside the `.top` frame. The additional packing parameters to the entry allow it to expand its packing space and fill up that extra area with its display. The difference between packing space and display space is discussed in Chapter 20 on page 255:

```
pack .top.l -side left
pack .top.cmd -side left -fill x -expand true
```

Key Bindings and Focus

Key bindings are set up for the entry widget that provide an additional way to invoke the functions of the application. The `bind` command associates a Tcl command with an event in a particular widget. The `<Return>` event is generated when the user presses the `Return` key on the keyboard. The `<Control-c>` event is generated when the letter `c` is typed while the `Control` key is already held down. For the events to go to the entry widget, `.top.cmd`, input focus must be given to the widget. By default, an entry widget gets the focus when you click the left mouse button in it. The explicit `focus` command is helpful for users with the focus-follows-mouse model. As soon as the mouse is over the main window the user can type into the entry:

```
bind .top.cmd <Return> Run
bind .top.cmd <Control-c> Stop
focus .top.cmd
```

A Resizable Text and Scrollbar

A text widget is created and packed into a frame with a scrollbar. The width and height of the text widget are specified in characters and lines, respectively. The `setgrid` attribute of the text widget is turned on. This restricts the resize so that only a whole number of lines and average-sized characters can be displayed.

The scrollbar is a separate widget in Tk, and it can be connected to different widgets using the same setup as is used here. The text's `yscrollcommand` updates the display of the scrollbar when the text widget is modified, and the scrollbar's `command` scrolls the associated widget when the user manipulates the scrollbar:

```
frame .t
set log [text .t.log -width 80 -height 10 \
    -borderwidth 2 -relief raised -setgrid true\
    -yscrollcommand {.t.scroll set}]
scrollbar .t.scroll -command {.t.log yview}
pack .t.scroll -side right -fill y
pack .t.log -side left -fill both -expand true
pack .t -side top -fill both -expand true
```

A side effect of creating a Tk widget is the creation of a new Tcl command that operates on that widget. The name of the Tcl command is the same as the Tk pathname of the widget. In this script, the text widget command, `.t.log`, is needed in several places. However, it is a good idea to put the Tk pathname of an important widget into a variable because that pathname can change if you reorganize your user interface. The disadvantage of this is that you must declare the variable with `global` inside procedures. The variable `log` is used for this purpose in this example to demonstrate this style.

The `Run` Procedure

The `Run` procedure starts the program specified in the command entry. That value is available in the global `command` variable because of the `textvariable` attribute of the entry. The command is run in a pipeline so that it executes in the background. The leading | in the argument to `open` indicates that a pipeline is being created. The `catch` command guards against bogus commands. The variable `input` is set to an error message, or to the normal `open` return that is a file

III. Tk Basics

descriptor. The program is started like this:

```
if [catch {open "|$command |& cat"} input] {
```

Trapping errors from pipelines.

The pipeline diverts error output from the command through the *cat* program. If you do not use *cat* like this, then the error output from the pipeline, if any, shows up as an error message when the pipeline is closed. In this example it turns out to be awkward to distinguish between errors generated from the program and errors generated because of the way the `Stop` procedure is implemented. Furthermore, some programs interleave output and error output, and you might want to see the error output in order instead of all at the end.

If the pipeline is opened successfully, then a callback is set up using the `fileevent` command. Whenever the pipeline generates output, then the script can read data from it. The `Log` procedure is registered to be called whenever the pipeline is readable:

```
fileevent $input readable Log
```

The `command` (or the error message) is inserted into the log. This is done using the name of the text widget, which is stored in the `log` variable, as a Tcl command. The value of the command is appended to the log, and a newline is added so its output will appear on the next line.

```
$log insert end $command\n
```

The text widget's `insert` function takes two parameters: a *mark* and a string to insert at that mark. The symbolic mark `end` represents the end of the contents of the text widget.

The run button is changed into a stop button after the program begins. This avoids a cluttered interface and demonstrates the dynamic nature of a Tk interface. Again, because this button is used in a few different places in the script, its pathname has been stored in the variable `but`:

```
$but config -text Stop -command Stop
```

The Log Procedure

The `Log` procedure is invoked whenever data can be read from the pipeline, and when end of file has been reached. This condition is checked first, and the `Stop` procedure is called to clean things up. Otherwise, one line of data is read and inserted into the log. The text widget's `see` operation is used to position the view on the text so the new line is visible to the user:

```
if [eof $input] {
   Stop
} else {
   gets $input line
   $log insert end $line\n
   $log see end
}
```

The `Stop` Procedure

The `Stop` procedure terminates the program by closing the pipeline. The `close` is wrapped up with a `catch`. This suppresses the errors that can occur when the pipeline is closed prematurely on the process. Finally, the button is restored to its run state so that the user can run another command:

```
catch {close $input}
$but config -text "Run it" -command Run
```

In most cases, closing the pipeline is adequate to kill the job. On UNIX, this results in a signal, SIGPIPE, being delivered to the program the next time it does a write to its standard output. There is no built-in way to kill a process, but you can `exec` the UNIX *kill* program. The `pid` command returns the process IDs from the pipeline:

```
foreach pid [pid $input] {
    catch {exec kill $pid}
}
```

If you need more sophisticated control over another process, you should check out the *expect* Tcl extension, which is described in the book *Exploring Expect* (Don Libes, O'Reilly & Associates, Inc., 1995). *Expect* provides powerful control over interactive programs. You can write Tcl scripts that send interactive programs input and pattern match on their output. *Expect* is designed to automate the use of programs that were designed for interactive use.

Cross-Platform Issues

This script will run on UNIX and Windows, but not on Macintosh because there is no `exec` command. One other problem is the binding for `<Control-c>` to cancel the job. This is UNIX-like, while Windows users might expect `<Escape>` to cancel a job, and Macintosh users expect `<Command-.>`. `Platform_CancelEvent` defines a virtual event, `<<Cancel>>`, and `Stop` is bound to it:

Example 19–2 A platform-specific cancel event.

```
proc Platform_CancelEvent {} {
    global tcl_platform
    switch $tcl_platform(platform) {
        unix {
            event add <<Cancel>> <Control-c>
        }
        windows {
            event add <<Cancel>> <Escape>
        }
        macintosh {
            event add <<Cancel>> <Command-.>
        }
    }
}
bind .top.entry <<Cancel>> Stop
```

III. Tk Basics

There are other virtual events already defined by Tk. The `event` command and virtual events are described on page 297.

The Example Browser

Example 19–3 is a browser for the code examples that appear in this book. The basic idea is to provide a menu that selects the examples, and a text window to display the examples. Before you can use this sample program, you need to edit it to set the proper location of the `exsource` directory that contains all the example sources from the book. Example 19–4 on page 245 extends the browser with a shell that is used to test the examples.

Example 19–3 A browser for the code examples in the book.

```
#!/usr/local/bin/wish
#   Browser for the Tcl and Tk examples in the book.

# browse(dir) is the directory containing all the tcl files
# Please edit to match your system configuration.

switch $tcl_platform(platform) {
    "unix" {set browse(dir) /cdrom/tclbook2/exsource}
    "windows" {set browse(dir) D:/exsource}
    "macintosh" {set browse(dir) /tclbook2/exsource}
}

wm minsize . 30 5
wm title . "Tcl Example Browser"

# Create a row of buttons along the top

set f [frame .menubar]
pack $f -fill x
button $f.quit -text Quit -command exit
button $f.next -text Next -command Next
button $f.prev -text Previous -command Previous

# The Run and Reset buttons use EvalEcho that
# is defined by the Tcl shell in Example 19-4 on page 245

button $f.load -text Run -command Run
button $f.reset -text Reset -command Reset
pack $f.quit $f.reset $f.load $f.next $f.prev -side right

# A label identifies the current example

label $f.label -textvariable browse(current)
pack $f.label -side right -fill x -expand true

# Create the menubutton and menu
```

```
menubutton $f.ex -text Examples -menu $f.ex.m
pack $f.ex -side left
set m [menu $f.ex.m]

# Create the text to display the example
# Scrolled_Text is defined in Example 27-1 on page 346

set browse(text) [Scrolled_Text .body \
    -width 80 -height 10\
    -setgrid true]
pack .body -fill both -expand true

# Look through the example files for their ID number.

foreach f [lsort -dictionary [glob [file join $browse(dir) *]]] {
    if [catch {open $f} in] {
        puts stderr "Cannot open $f: $in"
        continue
    }
    while {[gets $in line] >= 0} {
        if [regexp {^# Example ([0-9]+)-([0-9]+)} $line \
                x chap ex] {
            lappend examples($chap) $ex
            lappend browse(list) $f
            # Read example title
            gets $in line
            set title($chap-$ex) [string trim $line "# "]
            set file($chap-$ex) $f
            close $in
            break
        }
    }
}

# Create two levels of cascaded menus.
# The first level divides up the chapters into chunks.
# The second level has an entry for each example.

option add *Menu.tearOff 0
set limit 8
set c 0; set i 0
foreach chap [lsort -integer [array names examples]] {
    if {$i == 0} {
        $m add cascade -label "Chapter $chap..." \
            -menu $m.$c
        set sub1 [menu $m.$c]
        incr c
    }
    set i [expr ($i +1) % $limit]
    $sub1 add cascade -label "Chapter $chap" -menu $sub1.sub$i
    set sub2 [menu $sub1.sub$i ]
    foreach ex [lsort -integer $examples($chap)] {
        $sub2 add command -label "$chap-$ex $title($chap-$ex)" \
            -command [list Browse $file($chap-$ex)]
```

```
    }
}

# Display a specified file. The label is updated to
# reflect what is displayed, and the text is left
# in a read-only mode after the example is inserted.

proc Browse { file } {
    global browse
    set browse(current) [file tail $file]
    set browse(curix) [lsearch $browse(list) $file]
    set t $browse(text)
    $t config -state normal
    $t delete 1.0 end
    if [catch {open $file} in] {
        $t insert end $in
    } else {
        $t insert end [read $in]
        close $in
    }
    $t config -state disabled
}

# Browse the next and previous files in the list

set browse(curix) -1
proc Next {} {
    global browse
    if {$browse(curix) < [llength $browse(list)] - 1} {
        incr browse(curix)
    }
    Browse [lindex $browse(list) $browse(curix)]
}
proc Previous {} {
    global browse
    if {$browse(curix) > 0} {
        incr browse(curix) -1
    }
    Browse [lindex $browse(list) $browse(curix)]
}

# Run the example in the shell

proc Run {} {
    global browse
    EvalEcho [list source \
        [file join $browse(dir) $browse(current)]]
}

# Reset the slave in the eval server

proc Reset {} {
    EvalEcho reset
}
```

More about Resizing Windows

This example uses the `wm minsize` command to put a constraint on the minimum size of the window. The arguments specify the minimum width and height. These values can be interpreted in two ways. By default they are pixel values. However, if an internal widget has enabled *geometry gridding*, then the dimensions are in grid units of that widget. In this case the text widget enables gridding with its `setgrid` attribute, so the minimum size of the window is set so that the text window is at least 30 characters wide by five lines high:

```
wm minsize . 30 5
```

In older versions of Tk, Tk 3.6, gridding also enabled interactive resizing of the window. Interactive resizing is enabled by default in Tk 4.0 and later.

Managing Global State

The example uses the `browse` array to collect its global variables. This makes it simpler to reference the state from inside procedures because only the array needs to be declared global. As the application grows over time and new features are added, that `global` command won't have to be adjusted. This style also serves to emphasize what variables are important. The `browse` array holds the name of the example directory (`dir`), the Tk pathname of the text display (`text`), and the name of the current file (`current`). The `list` and `curix` elements are used to implement the `Next` and `Previous` procedures.

Searching through Files

The browser searches the file system to determine what it can display. The `tcl_platform(platform)` variable is used to select a different example directory on different platforms. You may need to edit the on-line example to match your system. The example uses `glob` to find all the files in the `exsource` directory. The `file join` command is used to create the file name pattern in a platform-independent way. The result of `glob` is sorted explicitly so the menu entries are in the right order. Each file is read one line at a time with `gets`, and then `regexp` is used to scan for keywords. The loop is repeated here for reference:

```
foreach f [lsort -dictionary [glob [file join $browse(dir) *]]] {
   if [catch {open $f} in] {
      puts stderr "Cannot open $f: $in"
      continue
   }
   while {[gets $in line] >= 0} {
      if [regexp {^# Example ([0-9]+)-([0-9]+)} $line \
            x chap ex] {
         lappend examples($chap) $ex
         lappend browse(list) $f
         # Read example title
         gets $in line
         set title($chap-$ex) [string trim $line "# "]
         set file($chap-$ex) $f
```

III. Tk Basics

```
                close $in
                break
            }
        }
    }
```

The example files contain lines like this:

```
# Example 1-1
# The Hello, World! program
```

The regexp picks out the example numbers with the `([0-9]+)-([0-9]+)` part of the pattern, and these are assigned to the chap and ex variables. The x variable is assigned the value of the whole match, which is more than we are interested in. Once the example number is found, the next line is read to get the description of the example. At the end of the foreach loop the examples array has an element defined for each chapter, and the value of each element is a list of the examples for that chapter.

Cascaded Menus

The values in the examples array are used to build up a cascaded menu structure. First a menubutton is created that will post the main menu. It is associated with the main menu with its menu attribute. The menu must be a child of the menubutton for its display to work properly:

```
menubutton $f.ex -text Examples -menu $f.ex.m
set m [menu $f.ex.m]
```

There are too many chapters to put them all into one menu. The main menu has a cascade entry for each group of 8 chapters. Each of these submenus has a cascade entry for each chapter in the group. Finally, each chapter has a menu of all its examples. Once again, the submenus are defined as a child of their parent menu. Note the inconsistency between menu entries and buttons. Their text is defined with the -label option, not -text. Other than this they are much like buttons. Chapter 24 describes menus in more detail. The code is repeated here:

```
set limit 8 ; set c 0 ; set i 0
foreach key [lsort -integer [array names examples]] {
    if {$i == 0} {
        $m add cascade -label "Chapter $key..." \
            -menu $m.$c
        set sub1 [menu $m.$c]
        incr c
    }
    set i [expr ($i +1) % $limit]
    $sub1 add cascade -label "Chapter $key" -menu $sub1.sub$i
    set sub2 [menu $sub1.sub$i]
    foreach ex [lsort -integer $examples($key)] {
        $sub2 add command -label "$key-$ex $title($key-$ex)" \
            -command [list Browse $file($key-$ex)]
    }
}
```

A Read-Only Text Widget

The `Browse` procedure is fairly simple. It sets `browse(current)` to be the name of the file. This changes the main label because of its `textvariable` attribute that links it to this variable. The `state` attribute of the text widget is manipulated so that the text is read-only after the text is inserted. You have to set the `state` to `normal` before inserting the text; otherwise the `insert` has no effect. Here are a few commands from the body of `Browse`:

```
global browse
set browse(current) [file tail $file]
$t config -state normal
$t insert end [read $in]
$t config -state disabled
```

A Tcl Shell

This section demonstrates the text widget with a simple Tcl shell application. Instead of using some other terminal emulator, it provides its own terminal environment using a text widget. It uses a second Tcl interpreter to evaluate the commands you type. This dual interpreter structure is used by the console built into the Windows and Macintosh versions of *wish*. You can use the Tcl shell as a sandbox to try out Tcl examples.

Example 19–4 is written to be used with the browser from Example 19–3 in the same application. The browser's `Run` button runs the current example in the shell. An alternative is to have the shell run as a separate process and use the `send` command to communicate Tcl commands between separate applications. That alternative is shown in Example on page 481.

Example 19–4 A Tcl shell in a text widget.

```
#!/usr/local/bin/wish
# Simple evaluator. It executes Tcl in a slave interpreter

set t [Scrolled_Text .eval -width 80 -height 10]
pack .eval -fill both -expand true

# Text tags give script output, command errors, command
# results, and the prompt a different appearance

$t tag configure prompt -underline true
$t tag configure result -foreground purple
$t tag configure error -foreground red
$t tag configure output -foreground blue

# Insert the prompt and initialize the limit mark

set eval(prompt) "tcl> "
$t insert insert $eval(prompt) prompt
$t mark set limit insert
```

```
$t mark gravity limit left
focus $t
set eval(text) $t

# Key bindings that limit input and eval things. The break in
# the bindings skips the default Text binding for the event.

bind $t <Return> {EvalTypein ; break}
bind $t <BackSpace> {
	if {[%W tag nextrange sel 1.0 end] != ""} {
		%W delete sel.first sel.last
	} elseif {[%W compare insert > limit]} {
		%W delete insert-1c
		%W see insert
	}
	break
}
bind $t <Key> {
	if [%W compare insert < limit] {
		%W mark set insert end
	}
}

# Evaluate everything between limit and end as a Tcl command

proc EvalTypein {} {
	global eval
	$eval(text) insert insert \n
	set command [$eval(text) get limit end]
	if [info complete $command] {
		$eval(text) mark set limit insert
		Eval $command
	}
}

# Echo the command and evaluate it

proc EvalEcho {command} {
	global eval
	$eval(text) mark set insert end
	$eval(text) insert insert $command\n
	Eval $command
}

# Evaluate a command and display its result

proc Eval {command} {
	global eval
	$eval(text) mark set insert end
	if [catch {$eval(slave) eval $command} result] {
		$eval(text) insert insert $result error
	} else {
		$eval(text) insert insert $result result
	}
	if {[$eval(text) compare insert != "insert linestart"]} {
```

```
        $eval(text) insert insert \n
    }
    $eval(text) insert insert $eval(prompt) prompt
    $eval(text) see insert
    $eval(text) mark set limit insert
    return
}

# Create and initialize the slave interpreter

proc SlaveInit {slave} {
    interp create $slave
    load {} Tk $slave
    interp alias $slave reset {} ResetAlias $slave
    interp alias $slave puts {} PutsAlias $slave
    return $slave
}

# The reset alias deletes the slave and starts a new one

proc ResetAlias {slave} {
    interp delete $slave
    SlaveInit $slave
}

# The puts alias puts stdout and stderr into the text widget

proc PutsAlias {slave args} {
    if {[llength $args] > 3} {
        error "invalid arguments"
    }
    set newline "\n"
    if {[string match "-nonewline" [lindex $args 0]]} {
        set newline ""
        set args [lreplace $args 0 0]
    }
    if {[llength $args] == 1} {
        set chan stdout
        set string [lindex $args 0]$newline
    } else {
        set chan [lindex $args 0]
        set string [lindex $args 1]$newline
    }
    if [regexp (stdout|stderr) $chan] {
        global eval
        $eval(text) mark gravity limit right
        $eval(text) insert limit $string output
        $eval(text) see limit
        $eval(text) mark gravity limit left
    } else {
        puts -nonewline $chan $string
    }
}
set eval(slave) [SlaveInit shell]
```

Text Marks, Tags, and Bindings

The shell uses a text *mark* and some extra bindings to ensure that users only type new text into the end of the text widget. A mark represents a position in the text that is updated as characters are inserted and deleted. The `limit` mark keeps track of the boundary between the read-only area and the editable area. The `insert` mark is where the cursor is displayed. The `end` mark is always the end of the text. The `EvalTypein` procedure looks at all the text between `limit` and `end` to see if it is a complete Tcl command. If it is, it evaluates the command in the slave interpreter.

The `<Key>` binding checks to see where the `insert` mark is and bounces it to the `end` if the user tries to input text before the `limit` mark. The `puts` alias sets `right` gravity on `limit` so the mark is pushed along when program output is inserted right at `limit`. Otherwise, the `left` gravity on limit means that the mark does not move when the user inserts right at `limit`.

Text *tags* are used to give different regions of text difference appearances. A tag applies to a range of text. The tags are configured at the beginning of the script and they are applied when text is inserted.

Chapter 30 describes the text widget in more detail.

Multiple Interpreters

The `SlaveInit` procedure creates another interpreter to evaluate the commands. This prevents conflicts with the procedures and variables used to implement the shell. Initially the slave interpreter only has access to Tcl commands. The `load` command installs the Tk commands, and it creates a new top-level window that is "." for the slave interpreter. Example 48–1 on page 608 describes how to embed the window of the slave within other frames.

The `shell` interpreter is not created with the `-safe` flag, so it can do anything. For example, if you type `exit`, it will exit the whole application. The `SlaveInit` procedure installs an alias, `reset`, that just deletes the slave interpreter and creates a new one. You can use this to clean up after working in the shell for a while. Chapter 17 describes the `interp` command in detail.

Native Look and Feel

When you run a Tk script on different platforms, it uses native buttons, menus, and scrollbars. The text and entry widgets are tuned to give the application the native look and feel. The following screen shots show the combined browser and shell as it looks on Macintosh, Windows, and UNIX.

Example 19–5 Macintosh look and feel.

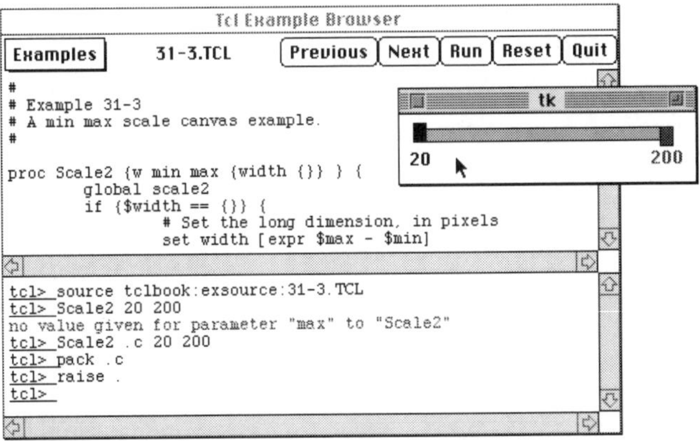

Example 19–6 Windows look and feel.

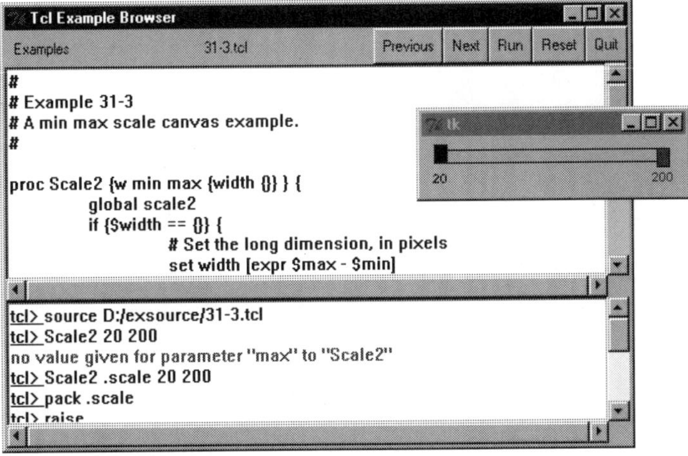

Example 19–7 UNIX look and feel.

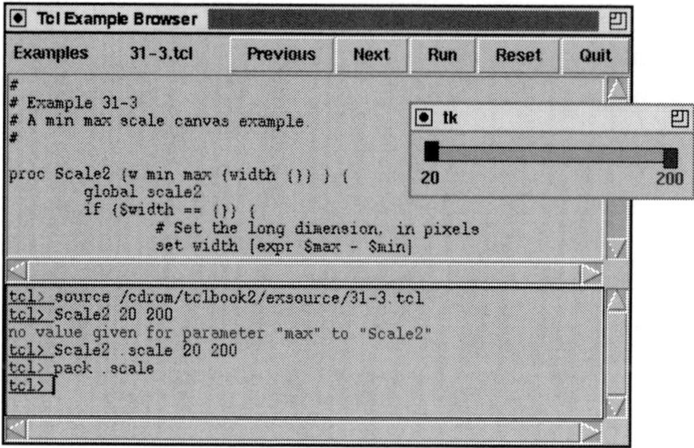

CHAPTER 20

The Pack Geometry Manager

This chapter explores the `pack` geometry manager that positions widgets on the screen.

Geometry managers arrange widgets on the screen. This chapter describes the `pack` geometry manager, which is a constraint-based system. The next two chapters describe the `grid` and `place` geometry managers. The `pack` and `grid` geometry managers are quite general, while `place` is used for special-purpose applications. This book uses `pack` a lot because it was the original geometry manager for Tk. The `grid` geometry manager was added in Tk 4.1.

A geometry manager uses one widget as a parent, and it arranges multiple children (also called slaves) inside the parent. The parent is almost always a frame, but this is not strictly necessary. A widget can only be managed by one geometry manager at a time, but you can use different managers to control different widgets in your user interface. If a widget is not managed, then it doesn't appear on your display at all.

The packer is a powerful constraint-based geometry manager. Instead of specifying in detail the placement of each window, the programmer defines some constraints about how windows should be positioned, and the packer works out the details. It is important to understand the algorithm the packer uses; otherwise the constraint-based results may not be what you expect.

This chapter explores the packer through a series of examples. The background of the main window is set to black, and the other frames are given different colors so you can identify frames and observe the effect of the different packing parameters. When consecutive examples differ by a small amount, the added command or option is printed in **`bold courier`** to highlight the addition.

Packing toward a Side

The following example creates two frames and packs them toward the top side of the main window. The upper frame, `.one`, is not as big and the main window shows through on either side. The children are packed toward the specified side in order, so `.one` is on top. The four possible sides are: `top`, `right`, `bottom`, and `left`. The `top` side is the default.

Example 20–1 Two frames packed inside the main frame.

```
# Make the main window black
. config -bg black
# Create and pack two frames
frame .one -width 40 -height 40 -bg white
frame .two -width 100 -height 50 -bg grey50
pack .one .two -side top
```

Shrinking Frames and `pack propagate`

In the previous example the main window shrank down to be just large enough to hold its two children. In most cases this is the desired behavior. If not, you can turn it off with the `pack propagate` command. Apply this to the parent frame, and it will not adjust its size to fit its children:

Example 20–2 Turning off geometry propagation.

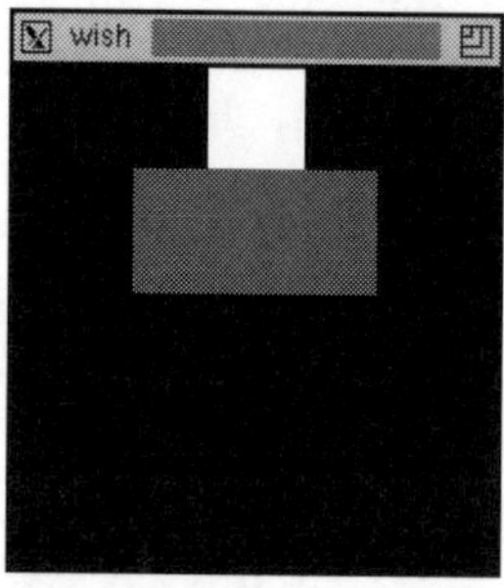


```
frame .one -width 40 -height 40 -bg white
frame .two -width 100 -height 50 -bg grey50
pack propagate . false
pack .one .two -side top
```

Horizontal and Vertical Stacking

In general you use either horizontal or vertical stacking within a frame. If you mix sides such as `left` and `top`, the effect might not be what you expect. Instead, you should introduce more frames to pack a set of widgets into a stack of a different orientation. For example, suppose we want to put a row of buttons inside the upper frame in the examples we have given so far:

Example 20–3 A horizontal stack inside a vertical stack.

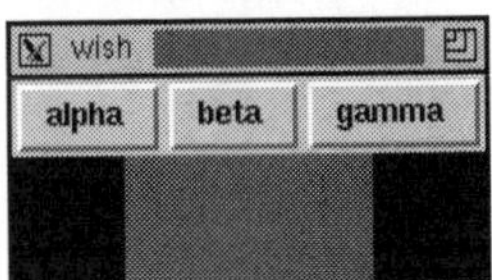


```
frame .one -bg white
frame .two -width 100 -height 50 -bg grey50
# Create a row of buttons
foreach b {alpha beta gamma} {
    button .one.$b -text $b
    pack .one.$b -side left
}
pack .one .two -side top
```

Example 20–4 Even more nesting of horizontal and vertical stacks.

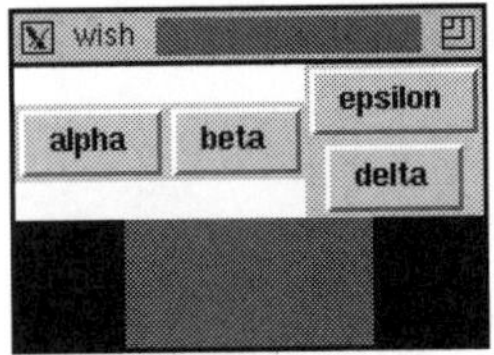


```
frame .one -bg white
frame .two -width 100 -height 50 -bg grey50
foreach b {alpha beta} {
    button .one.$b -text $b
    pack .one.$b -side left
}
# Create a frame for two more buttons
frame .one.right
foreach b {delta epsilon} {
    button .one.right.$b -text $b
    pack .one.right.$b -side bottom
}
pack .one.right -side right
pack .one .two -side top
```

You can build more complex arrangements by introducing nested frames and switching between horizontal and vertical stacking as you go. Within each frame pack all the children with either a combination of `-side left` and `-side right`, or `-side top` and `-side bottom`.

Example 20–4 replaces the `.one.gamma` button with a vertical stack of two buttons, `.one.right.delta` and `.one.right.epsilon`. These are packed toward the bottom of `.one.right`, so the first one packed is on the bottom.

The frame `.one.right` was packed to the right, and in the previous example the button `.one.gamma` was packed to the left. Despite the difference, they ended up in the same position relative to the other two widgets packed inside the `.one` frame. The next section explains why.

The Cavity Model

The packing algorithm is based on a *cavity model* for the available space inside a frame. For example, when the main *wish* window is created, the main frame is empty and there is an obvious space, or cavity, in which to place widgets. The primary rule about the packing cavity is *a widget occupies one whole side of the cavity.* To demonstrate this, pack three widgets into the main frame. Put the first two on the bottom, and the third one on the right:

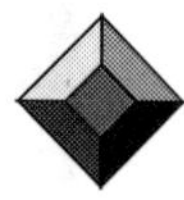

Example 20–5 Mixing bottom and right packing sides.

```
# pack two frames on the bottom.
frame .one -width 100 -height 50 -bg grey50
frame .two -width 40 -height 40 -bg white
pack .one .two -side bottom
# pack another frame to the right
frame .three -width 20 -height 20 -bg grey75
pack .three -side right
```

When we pack a third frame into the main window with `-side left` or `-side right`, the new frame is positioned inside the cavity, which is above the two frames already packed toward the bottom side. The frame does not appear to the right of the existing frames as you might have expected. This is because the `.two` frame occupies the whole bottom side of the packing cavity, even though its display does not fill up that side.

Can you tell where the packing cavity is after this example? It is to the left of the frame `.three`, which is the last frame packed toward the right, and it is above the frame `.two`, which is the last frame packed toward the bottom. This explains why there was no difference between the previous two examples when `.one.gamma` was packed to the left, but `.one.right` was packed to the right. At that point, packing to the left or right of the cavity had the same effect. However, it will affect what happens if another widget is packed into those two configurations. Try out the following commands after running Example 20–3 and Example 20–4 and compare the difference.*

```
button .one.omega -text omega
pack .one.omega -side right
```

Each packing parent has its own cavity, which is why introducing nested frames can help. If you use a horizontal or vertical arrangement inside any given frame, you can more easily simulate the packer's behavior in your head!

Packing Space and Display Space

The packer distinguishes between *packing* space and *display* space when it arranges the widgets. The display space is the area requested by a widget for the purposes of painting itself. The packing space is the area the packer allows for the placement of the widget. Because of geometry constraints, a widget may be allocated more (or less) packing space than it needs to display itself. The extra space, if any, is along the side of the cavity against which the widget was packed.

The `-fill` Option

The `-fill` packing option causes a widget to fill up the allocated packing space with its display. A widget can fill in the X or Y direction, or both. The default is not to fill, which is why the black background of the main window has shown through in the examples so far:

Example 20–6 Filling the display into extra packing space.

```
frame .one -width 100 -height 50 -bg grey50
frame .two -width 40 -height 40 -bg white
# Pack with fill enabled
pack .one .two -side bottom -fill x
frame .three -width 20 -height 20 -bg red
pack .three -side right -fill x
```

* Answer: After Example 20–3 the new button is to the right of all buttons. After Example 20–4 the new button is between `.one.beta` and `.one.right`.

This is just like Example 20–5, except that `-fill x` has been specified for all the frames. The `.two` frame fills, but the `.three` frame does not. This is because the fill does not expand into the packing cavity. In fact, after this example, the packing cavity is the part that shows through in black. Another way to look at this is that the `.two` frame was allocated the whole bottom side of the packing cavity, so its fill can expand the frame to occupy that space. The `.three` frame has only been allocated the right side, so a fill in the X direction will not have any effect.

Another use of fill is for a menu bar that has buttons at either end and some empty space between them. The frame that holds the buttons is packed toward the top. The buttons are packed into the left and right sides of the menu bar frame. Without fill, the menu bar shrinks to be just large enough to hold all the buttons, and the buttons are squeezed together. When fill is enabled in the X direction, the menu bar fills out the top edge of the display:

Example 20–7 Using horizontal fill in a menu bar.

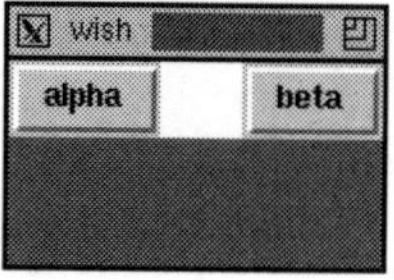


```
frame .menubar -bg white
frame .body -width 150 -height 50 -bg grey50
# Create buttons at either end of the menubar
foreach b {alpha beta} {
    button .menubar.$b -text $b
}
pack .menubar.alpha -side left
pack .menubar.beta -side right
# Let the menu bar fill along the top
pack .menubar -side top -fill x
pack .body
```

Internal Padding with `-ipadx` and `-ipady`

Another way to get more fill space is with the `-ipadx` and `-ipady` packing options that request more display space in the X and Y directions, respectively. Due to other constraints the request might not be offered, but in general you can use this to give a widget more display space. The next example is just like the previous one except that some internal padding has been added:

Example 20–8 The effects of internal padding (`-ipady`).

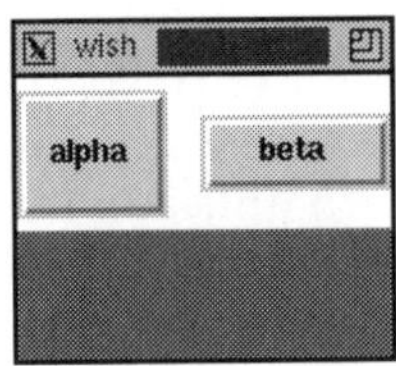


```
# Create and pack two frames
frame .menubar -bg white
frame .body -width 150 -height 50 -bg grey50
# Create buttons at either end of the menubar
foreach b {alpha beta} {
   button .menubar.$b -text $b
}
pack .menubar.alpha -side left -ipady 10
pack .menubar.beta -side right -ipadx 10
# Let the menu bar fill along the top
pack .menubar -side top -fill x -ipady 5
pack .body
```

The `alpha` button is taller and the `beta` button is wider because of the internal padding. The frame has internal padding, which reduces the space available for the packing cavity, so the `.menubar` frame shows through above and below the buttons.

Some widgets have attributes that result in more display space. For example, it would be hard to distinguish a frame with width `50` and no internal padding from a frame with width `40` and a `-ipadx 5` packing option. The packer would give the frame `5` more pixels of display space on either side for a total width of `50`.

Buttons have their own `-padx` and `-pady` options that give them more display space, too. This padding provided by the button is used to keep its text away from the edge of the button. The following example illustrates the difference. The `-anchor e` button option positions the text as far to the right as possible. Example 34–5 on page 449 provides another comparison of these options:

Example 20–9 Button padding vs. packer padding.

```
# Foo has internal padding from the packer
button .foo -text Foo -anchor e -padx 0 -pady 0
pack .foo -side right -ipadx 10 -ipady 10
# Bar has its own padding
button .bar -text Bar -anchor e -pady 10 -padx 10
pack .bar -side right -ipadx 0 -ipady 0
```

III. Tk Basics

External Padding with -padx and -pady

The packer can provide external padding that allocates packing space that cannot be filled. The space is outside of the border that widgets use to implement their 3D reliefs. Example 34–2 on page 446 shows the different reliefs. The look of a default button is achieved with an extra frame and some padding:

Example 20–10 The look of a default button.

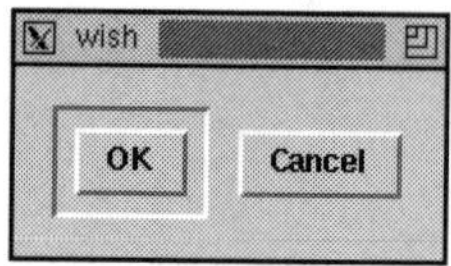


```
. config -borderwidth 10
# OK is the default button
frame .ok -borderwidth 2 -relief sunken
button .ok.b -text OK
pack .ok.b -padx 5 -pady 5
# Cancel is not
button .cancel -text Cancel
pack .ok .cancel -side left -padx 5 -pady 5
```

Even if the `.ok.b` button were packed with `-fill both`, it would look the same. The external padding provided by the packer will not be filled by the child widgets.

Example 20–10 handcrafts the look of a default button. Tk 8.0 has a `-default` attribute for buttons that gives them the right appearance for the default button on the current platform. It looks somewhat like this on UNIX, but the appearance is different on Macintosh and Windows.

Resizing and -expand

The `-expand true` packing option lets a widget expand its packing space into unclaimed space in the packing cavity. Example 20–6 could use this on the small frame on top to get it to expand across the top of the display, even though it is packed to the right side. The more common case occurs when you have a resizable window. When the user makes the window larger, the widgets have to be told to take advantage of the extra space. Suppose you have a main widget like a text, listbox, or canvas that is in a frame with a scrollbar. That frame has to be told to expand into the extra space in its parent (e.g., the main window) and then the main widget (e.g., the canvas) has to be told to expand into its parent frame. Example 19–1 on page 234 does this.

In nearly all cases the `-fill both` option is used along with `-expand true` so that the widget actually uses its extra packing space for its own display. The converse is not true. There are many cases where a widget should fill extra space, but not attempt to expand into the packing cavity. The examples below show the difference.

Now we can investigate what happens when the window is made larger. The next example starts like Example 20–7 on page 256 but the size of the main window is increased:

Example 20–11 Resizing without the `expand` option.

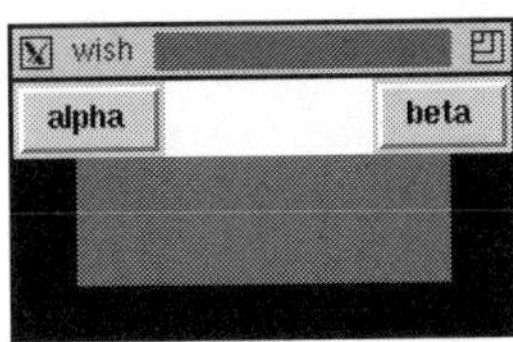


```
# Make the main window black
. config -bg black
# Create and pack two frames
frame .menubar -bg white
frame .body -width 150 -height 50 -bg grey50
# Create buttons at either end of the menubar
foreach b {alpha beta} {
   button .menubar.$b -text $b
}
pack .menubar.alpha -side left
pack .menubar.beta -side right
# Let the menu bar fill along the top
pack .menubar -side top -fill x
pack .body
# Resize the main window to be bigger
wm geometry . 200x100
# Allow interactive resizing
wm minsize . 100 50
```

The only widget that claims any of the new space is `.menubar` because of its `-fill x` packing option. The `.body` frame needs to be packed properly:

Example 20–12 Resizing with `expand` turned on.

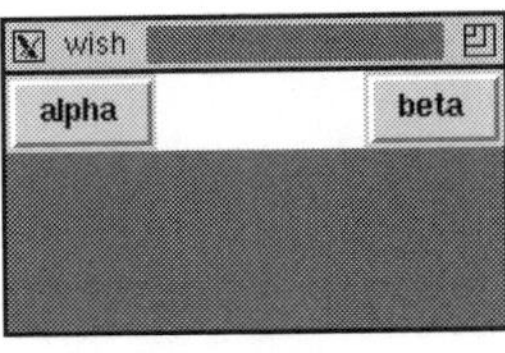


```
# Use all of Example 20-11 then repack .body
pack .body -expand true -fill both
```

If more than one widget inside the same parent is allowed to expand, then the packer shares the extra space between them proportionally. This is probably

III. Tk Basics

not the effect you want in the examples we have built so far. The .menubar, for example, is not a good candidate for expansion.

Example 20–13 More than one expanding widget.

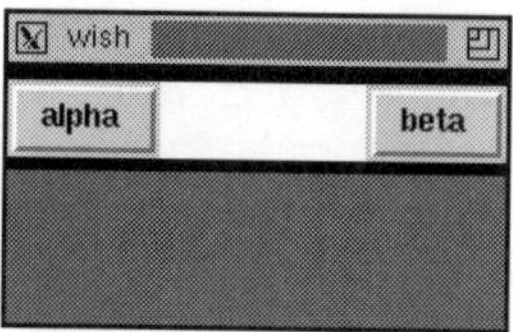


```
# Use all of Example 20-11 then repack .menubar and .body
pack .menubar -expand true -fill x
pack .body -expand true -fill both
```

Anchoring

If a widget is left with more packing space than display space, you can position it within its packing space using the -anchor packing option. The default anchor position is center. The other options correspond to points on a compass: n, ne, e, se, s, sw, w, and nw:

Example 20–14 Setup for anchor experiments.

```
# Make the main window black
. config -bg black
# Create two frames to hold open the cavity
frame .prop -bg white -height 80 -width 20
frame .base -width 120 -height 20 -bg grey50
pack .base -side bottom
# Float a label and the prop in the cavity
label .foo -text Foo
pack .prop .foo -side right -expand true
```

The .base frame is packed on the bottom. Then the .prop frame and the .foo label are packed to the right with expand set but no fill. Instead of being pressed up against the right side, the expand gives each of these widgets half of the extra space in the X direction. Their default anchor of center results in the positions shown. The next example shows some different anchor positions:

Example 20–15 The effects of non-center anchors.

```
. config -bg black
# Create two frames to hold open the cavity
frame .prop -bg white -height 80 -width 20
frame .base -width 120 -height 20 -bg grey50
pack .base -side bottom
# Float the label and prop
# Change their position with anchors
label .foo -text Foo
pack .prop -side right -expand true -anchor sw
pack .foo -side right -expand true -anchor ne
```

The `label` has room on all sides, so each of the different anchors will position it differently. The `.prop` frame only has room in the X direction, so it can only be moved into three different positions: left, center, and right. Any of the anchors `w`, `nw`, and `sw` result in the left position. The anchors `center`, `n`, and `s` result in the center position. The anchors `e`, `se`, and `ne` result in the right position.

If you want to see all the variations, type in the following commands to animate the different packing anchors. The `update idletasks` forces any pending display operations. The `after 500` causes the script to wait for `500` milliseconds:

Example 20–16 Animating the packing anchors.

```
foreach anchor {center n ne e se s sw w nw center} {
    pack .foo .prop -anchor $anchor
    # Update the display
    update idletasks
    # Wait half a second
    after 500
}
```

Packing Order

The packer maintains an order among the children that are packed into a frame. By default, each new child is appended to the end of the packing order. The most obvious effect of the order is that the children first in the packing order are closest to the side they are packed against. You can control the packing order with the `-before` and `-after` packing options, and you can reorganize widgets after they have already been packed:

Example 20–17 Controlling the packing order.

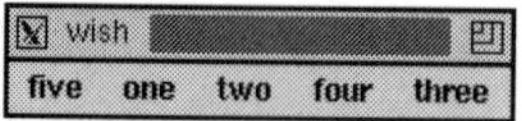


```
# Create five labels in order
foreach label {one two three four five} {
    label .$label -text $label
    pack .$label -side left -padx 5
}
# ShuffleUp moves a widget to the beginning of the order
proc ShuffleUp { parent child } {
    set first [lindex [pack slaves $parent] 0]
    pack $child -in $parent -before $first
}
# ShuffleDown moves a widget to the end of the order
proc ShuffleDown { parent child } {
    pack $child -in $parent
}
ShuffleUp . .five
ShuffleDown . .three
```

Introspection

The `pack slaves` command returns the list of children in their packing order. The `ShuffleUp` procedure uses this to find out the first child so it can insert another child before it. The `ShuffleDown` procedure is simpler because the default is to append the child to the end of the packing order.

When a widget is repacked, then it retains all its packing parameters that have already been set. If you need to examine the current packing parameters for a widget, use the `pack info` command.

```
pack info .five
=> -in . -anchor center -expand 0 -fill none -ipadx 0 \
     -ipady 0 -padx 0 -pady 0 -side left
```

Pack the Scrollbar First

The packing order also determines what happens when the window is made too small. If the window is made small enough the packer will clip children that come later in the packing order. This is why, when you pack a scrollbar and a text widget into a frame, you should pack the scrollbar first. Otherwise, when the window is made smaller the `text` widget takes up all the space and the scrollbar is clipped.

Choosing the Parent for Packing

In nearly all of the examples in this chapter a widget is packed into its parent frame. In general, it is possible to pack a widget into any descendent of its parent. For example, the `.a.b` widget could be packed into `.a`, `.a.c` or `.a.d.e.f`. The `-in` packing option lets you specify an alternate packing parent. One motivation for this is that the frames introduced to get the arrangement right can cause cluttered names for important widgets. In Example 20–4 on page 253 the buttons have names like `.one.alpha` and `.one.right.delta`, which is not consistent. Here is an alternate implementation of the same example that simplifies the button names and gives the same result:

Example 20–18 Packing into other relatives.

```
# Create and pack two frames
frame .one -bg white
frame .two -width 100 -height 50 -bg grey50
# Create a row of buttons
foreach b {alpha beta} {
    button .$b -text $b
    pack .$b -in .one -side left
}
# Create a frame for two more buttons
frame .one.right
foreach b {delta epsilon} {
    button .$b -text $b
    pack .$b -in .one.right -side bottom
}
pack .one.right -side right
pack .one .two -side top
```

When you do this, remember that the order in which you create widgets is important. Create the frames first, then create the widgets. The stacking order for windows will cause the later windows to obscure the windows created first. The following is a common mistake because the frame obscures the button:

```
button .a -text hello
frame .b
pack .a -in .b
```

If you cannot avoid this problem scenario, then you can use the `raise` command to fix things up. Stacking order is also discussed on page 265.

```
raise .a
```

Unpacking a Widget

The `pack forget` command removes a widget from the packing order. The widget gets unmapped so it is not visible. If you unpack a parent frame, the packing

III. Tk Basics

structure inside it is maintained, but all the widgets inside the frame get unmapped. Unpacking a widget is useful if you want to suppress extra features of your interface. You can create all the parts of the interface, and just delay packing them in until the user requests to see them. Then you can pack and unpack them dynamically.

Packer Summary

Keep these rules in mind about the packer:

- Pack vertically (`-side top` and `-side bottom`) or horizontally (`-side left` and `-side right`) within a frame. Only rarely will a different mixture of packing directions work out the way you want. Add frames to build more complex structures.
- By default, the packer puts widgets into their parent frame, and the parent frame must be created before the children that are packed into it.
- If you put widgets into other relatives, remember to create the frames first so the frames stay underneath the widgets packed into them.
- By default, the packer ignores `-width` and `-height` attributes of frames that have widgets packed inside them. It shrinks frames to be just big enough to allow for its border width and to hold the widgets inside them. Use `pack propagate` to turn off the shrink-wrap behavior.
- The packer distinguishes between packing space and display space. A widget's display might not take up all the packing space allocated to it.
- The `-fill` option causes the display to fill up the packing space in the X or Y directions, or both.
- The `-expand true` option causes the packing space to expand into any room in the packing cavity that is otherwise unclaimed. If more than one widget in the same frame wants to expand, then they share the extra space.
- The `-ipadx` and `-ipady` options allocate more display space inside the border, if possible.
- The `-padx` and `-pady` options allocate more packing space outside the border, if possible. This space is never filled by the widget's display.

The `pack` Command

Table 20–1 summarizes the `pack` command. Table 20–2 summarizes the packing options for a widget. These are set with the `pack configure` command, and the current settings are returned by the `pack info` command:

Table 20–1 The `pack` command.

`pack` *`win ?win ..? ?options?`*	This is just like `pack configure`.
`pack configure` *`win ?win ...? ?options?`*	Pack one or more widgets according to the *`options`*, which are given in Table 20–2.
`pack forget` *`win ?win...?`*	Unpack the specified windows.
`pack info` *`win`*	Return the packing parameters of *`win`*.
`pack propagate` *`win ?bool?`*	Query or set the geometry propagation of *`win`*, which has other widgets packed inside it.
`pack slaves` *`win`*	Return the list of widgets managed by *`win`*.

Table 20–2 Packing options.

`-after` *`win`*	Pack after *`win`* in the packing order.
`-anchor` *`anchor`*	Anchors: `center`, `n`, `ne`, `e`, `se`, `s`, `sw`, `w`, or `nw`.
`-before` *`win`*	Pack before *`win`* in the packing order.
`-expand` *`boolean`*	Control expansion into the unclaimed packing cavity.
`-fill` *`style`*	Control fill of packing space. Style: `x`, `y`, `both`, or `none`.
`-in` *`win`*	Pack inside *`win`*.
`-ipadx` *`amount`*	Horizontal internal padding, in screen units.
`-ipady` *`amount`*	Vertical internal padding, in screen units.
`-padx` *`amount`*	Horizontal external padding, in screen units.
`-pady` *`amount`*	Vertical external padding, in screen units.
`-side` *`side`*	Sides: `top`, `right`, `bottom`, or `left`.

III. Tk Basics

Window Stacking Order

The `raise` and `lower` commands control the window stacking order. The stacking order controls the display of windows. Windows higher in the stacking order obscure windows lower in the stacking order. By default, new windows are created at the top of the stacking order so they obscure older windows. Consider this sequence of commands:

```
button .one
frame .two
pack .one -in .two
```

If you do this, you do not see the button. The problem is that the frame is higher in the stacking order so it obscures the button. You can change the stacking order with the `raise` command:

```
raise .one .two
```

This puts `.one` just above `.two` in the stacking order. If `.two` was not specified, then `.one` would be put at the top of the stacking order.

The `lower` command has a similar form. With one argument it puts that window at the bottom of the stacking order. Otherwise it puts it just below another window in the stacking order.

You can use `raise` and `lower` on top-level windows to control their stacking order among all other top-level windows. For example, if a user requests a dialog that is already displayed, use `raise` to make it pop to the foreground of their cluttered desktop.

CHAPTER 21

The Grid Geometry Manager

This chapter explores the `grid` geometry manager that positions widgets on a grid that automatically adjusts its size. Grid was added in Tk 4.1.

The `grid` geometry manager arranges widgets on a grid with variable-sized rows and columns. You specify the rows and columns occupied by each widget, and the grid is adjusted to accommodate all the widgets it contains. This is ideal for creating table-like layouts. The manager also has sophisticated facilities for controlling row and column sizes and the dynamic resize behavior. By introducing subframes with grids of their own, you can create arbitrary layouts.

A Basic Grid

Example 21–1 uses `grid` to lay out a set of labels and frames in two parallel columns. It takes advantage of the relative placement feature of `grid`. You do not necessarily have to specify rows and columns. Instead, the order of `grid` commands and their arguments implies the layout. Each `grid` command starts a new row, and the order of the widgets in the `grid` command determines the column. In the example, there are two columns, and iteration of the loop adds a new row. `Grid` makes each column just wide enough to hold the biggest widget. Widgets that are smaller are centered in their cell. That's why the labels appear centered in their column:

Example 21–1 A basic grid.

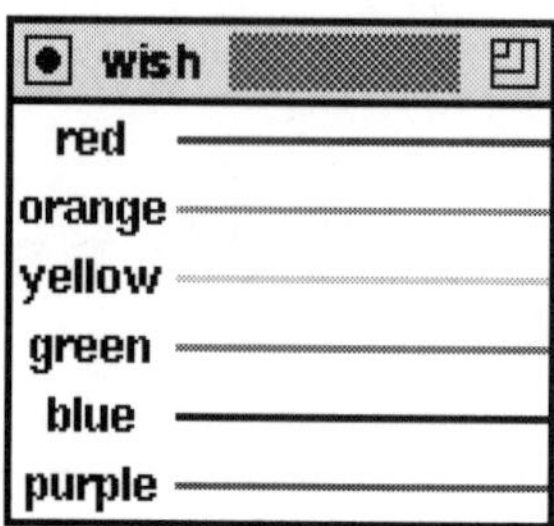


```
foreach color {red orange yellow green blue purple} {
    label .l$color -text $color -bg white
    frame .f$color -background $color -width 100 -height 2
    grid .l$color .f$color
}
```

The -sticky Setting

If a grid cell is larger than the widget inside it, you can control the size and position of the widget with the `-sticky` option. The `-sticky` option combines the functions of `-fill` and `-anchor` used with the `pack` geometry manager. You specify to which sides of its cell a widget sticks. You can specify any combination of `n`, `e`, `w`, and `s` to stick a widget to the top, right, left, and bottom sides of its cell. You can concatenate these letters together (e.g., `news`) or uses spaces or commas to separate them (e.g., `n,e,w,s`). Example 21–2 uses `-sticky w` to left justify the labels, and `-sticky ns` to stretch the color frames to the full height of their row:

Example 21–2 A grid with `sticky` settings.

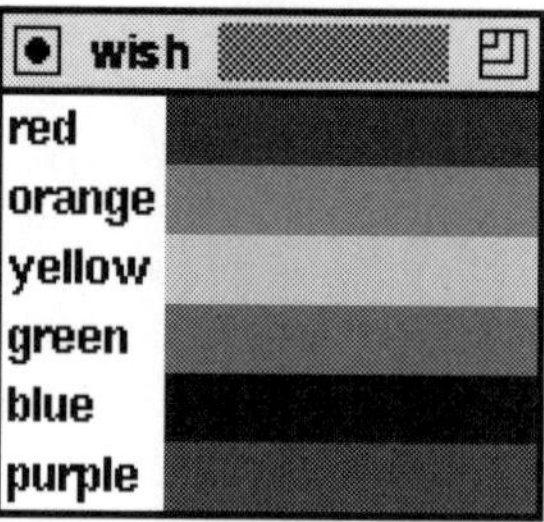


```
foreach color {red orange yellow green blue purple} {
    label .l$color -text $color -bg white
    frame .f$color -background $color -width 100 -height 2
    grid .l$color .f$color
    grid .l$color -sticky w
    grid .f$color -sticky ns
}
```

Example 21–2 uses `grid` in two ways. The first `grid` in the loop fixes the positions of the widgets because it is the first time they are assigned to the master. The next `grid` commands modify the existing parameters; they just adjust the `-sticky` setting because their row and column positions are already known.

You can specify row and column positions explicitly with the `-row` and `-column` attribute. This is generally more work than using the relative placement, but it is necessary if you need to dynamically move a widget into a different cell. Example 21–3 keeps track of rows and columns explicitly and achieves the same layout as Example 21–2:

Example 21–3 A grid with row and column specifications.

```
set row 0
foreach color {red orange yellow green blue purple} {
   label .l$color -text $color -bg white
   frame .f$color -background $color -width 100
   grid .l$color -row $row -column 0 -sticky w
   grid .f$color -row $row -column 1 -sticky ns
   incr row
}
```

External Padding with -padx and -pady

You can keep a widget away from the edge of its cell with the `-padx` and `-pady` settings. Example 21–4 uses external padding to shift the labels away from the left edge, and to keep some blank space between the color bars:

Example 21–4 A grid with external padding.

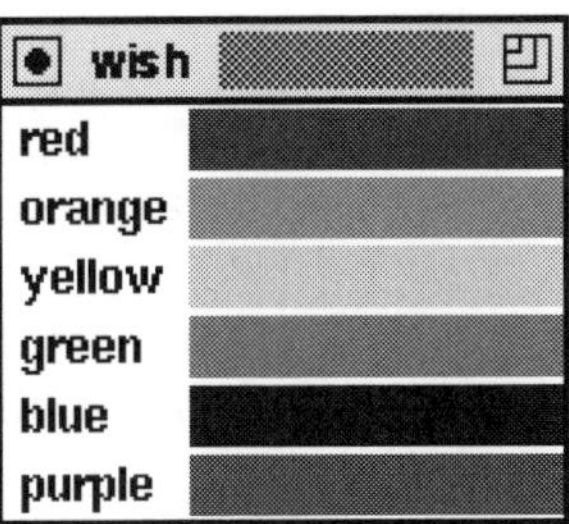


```
foreach color {red orange yellow green blue purple} {
   label .l$color -text $color -bg white
   frame .f$color -background $color -width 100 -height 2
   grid .l$color .f$color
   grid .l$color -sticky w -padx 3
   grid .f$color -sticky ns -pady 1
}
```

III. Tk Basics

Internal Padding with **-ipadx** and **-ipady**

You can give a widget more display space than it normally needs with internal padding. The internal padding increases the size of the grid. In contrast, a `-sticky` setting might stretch a widget, but it will not change the size of the grid. Example 21–5 makes the labels taller with `-ipady`:

Example 21–5 A grid with internal padding.

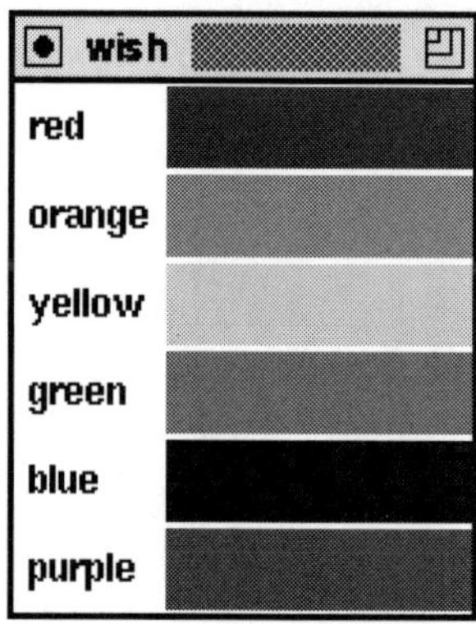


```
foreach color {red orange yellow green blue purple} {
    label .l$color -text $color -bg white
    frame .f$color -background $color -width 100 -height 2
    grid .l$color .f$color
    grid .l$color -sticky w -padx 3 -ipady 5
    grid .f$color -sticky ns -pady 1
}
```

Multiple Widgets in a Cell

Example 21–6 shows all possible `-sticky` settings. It uses the ability to put more than one widget into a grid cell. A large square frame is put in each cell, and then a label is put into the same cell with a different `-sticky` setting. It is important to create the frame first so it is below the label. Window stacking is discussed on page 265. External padding is used to keep the labels away from the edge so they do not hide the `-ridge` relief of the frames.

Example 21–6 All combinations of `-sticky` settings.

```
set index 0
foreach x {news ns ew  " " new sew wsn esn nw ne sw se n s w e} {
    frame .f$x -borderwidth 2 -relief ridge -width 40 -height 40
    grid .f$x  -sticky news \
        -row [expr $index/4] -column [expr $index%4]
    label .l$x -text $x -background white
    grid .l$x -sticky $x -padx 2 -pady 2 \
        -row [expr $index/4] -column [expr $index%4]
    incr index
}
```

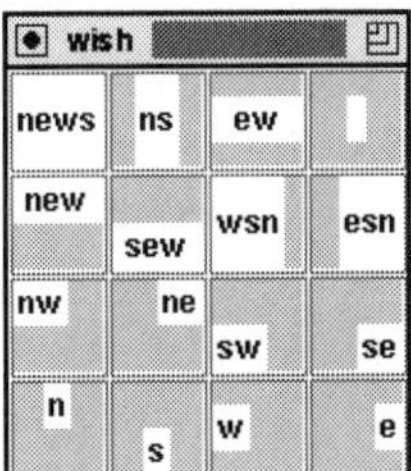

Spanning Rows and Columns

A widget can occupy more than one cell. The `-rowspan` and `-columnspan` attributes indicate how many rows and columns are occupied by a widget. Example 21–7 uses explicit `row`, `column`, `rowspan` and `columnspan` specifications:

Example 21–7 Explicit row and column span.

```
. config -bg white
foreach color {888 999 aaa bbb ccc fff} {
   frame .$color -bg #$color -width 40 -height 40
}
grid .888 -row 0 -column 0 -columnspan 3 -sticky news
grid .999 -row 1 -column 0 -rowspan 2 -sticky news
grid .aaa -row 1 -column 1 -columnspan 2 -sticky news
grid .bbb -row 2 -column 2 -rowspan 2 -sticky news
grid .ccc -row 3 -column 0 -columnspan 2 -sticky news
grid .fff -row 2 -column 1 -sticky news
```

You can also use special syntax in `grid` commands that imply row and column placement. Special characters represent a cell that is spanned or skipped:

- `-` represents a spanned column.
- `^` represents a spanned row.
- `x` represents a skipped cell.

A nice feature of the implicit row and column assignments is that it is easy to make minor changes to your layout. Example 21–8 achieves the same layout:

III. Tk Basics

Example 21–8 Grid syntax row and column span.

```
. config -bg white
foreach color {888 999 aaa bbb ccc ddd fff} {
   frame .$color -bg #$color -width 40 -height 40
}
grid .888 -      -      -sticky news
grid .999 .aaa   -      -sticky news
grid ^    .fff   .bbb   -sticky news
grid .ccc -      ^      -sticky news
```

Row and Column Constraints

The `grid` manager supports attributes on whole rows and columns. You can control the row and column sizes with a `-pad` and `-minsize` attribute. The `-weight` attribute controls resize behavior. The `grid` command has a `rowconfigure` and `columnconfigure` operation to set and query these attributes:

`grid columnconfigure` *`master col ?attributes?`*

`grid rowconfigure` *`master row ?attributes?`*

With no *`attributes`*, the current settings are returned. The *`row`* and *`col`* specifications can be lists instead of simple indices so you can configure several rows or columns at once.

Row and Column Padding

The `-pad` attribute increases a row or column size. The initial size of a row or column is determined by the largest widget, and `-pad` adds to this size. This padding can be filled by the widget by using the `-sticky` attribute. Row and column padding works like internal padding because it is extra space that can be occupied by the widget's display. In contrast, the `-pad` attribute on an individual widget acts like a spacer that keeps the widget away from the edge of the cell. Example 21–9 shows the difference. The row padding increases the height of the row, but the padding on `.f1` keeps it away from the edge of the cell:

Example 21–9 Row padding compared to widget padding.

```
. config -bg black
label .f1 -text left -bg #ccc
label .f2 -text right -bg #aaa
grid .f1 .f2 -sticky news
grid .f1 -padx 10 -pady 10
grid rowconfigure . 0  -pad 20
```

Minimum Size

The `-minsize` attribute restricts a column or row to be a minimum size. The row or column can grow bigger if its widget requests it, but they will not get smaller than the minimum. One useful application of `-minsize` is to create empty rows or columns, which is more efficient than creating an extra frame.

Managing Resize Behavior

If the master frame is bigger than the required size of the grid, it shrinks to be just large enough to contain the grid. You can turn off the shrink-wrap behavior with `grid propagate`. If geometry propagation is off, then the grid is centered inside the master. If the master frame is too small to fit the grid, then the grid is anchored to the upper-left corner of the master and clipped on the bottom-right.

By default, rows and columns do not resize when you grow the master frame. You enable resizing by specifying a `-weight` for a row or column that is an integer value greater than zero. Example 21–10 grids a text widget and two scrollbars. The protocol between the scrollbar and the text widget is described on page 347. The text widget is in row 0, column 0, and both of these can expand. The vertical scrollbar is in row 0, column 1, so it only grows in the Y direction. The horizontal scrollbar is in row 1, column 0, so it only grows in the X direction:

Example 21–10 Gridding a text widget and scrollbar.

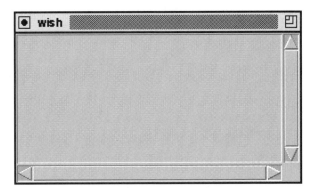

```
text .text -yscrollcommand ".yscroll set" \
   -xscrollcommand ".xscroll set"-width 40 -height 10
scrollbar .yscroll -command ".text yview" -orient vertical
scrollbar .xscroll -command ".text xview" -orient horizontal
grid .text .yscroll -sticky news
grid .xscroll -sticky ew
grid rowconfigure . 0 -weight 1
grid columnconfigure . 0 -weight 1
```

You can use different weights to let different rows and columns grow at different rates. However, there are some tricky issues because the resize behavior applies to extra space, not total space. For example, suppose there are 4 columns that have widths 10, 20, 30, and 40 pixels, for a total of 100. If the master frame is grown to 140 pixels wide, then there are 40 extra pixels. If each column has weight 1, then each column gets an equal share of the extra space, or 10 more pixels. Now suppose column 0 has weight 0, columns 1 and 2 have weight 1, and column 3 has weight 2. Column 0 will not grow, columns 1 and 2 will get 10 more pixels, and column 3 will get 20 more pixels. In most cases, weights of 0 or 1 make the most sense.

Weight works in reverse when shrinking.

If a row or column has to shrink, the weights are applied in reverse. A row or column with a higher weight will shrink more. For example, put two equal sized frames in columns with different weights. When the user makes the window bigger, the frame in the column with more weight gets larger more quickly. When the window is made smaller, that frame gets smaller more quickly.

The `grid` Command

Table 21–1 summarizes the usage of the `grid` command.

Table 21–1 The `grid` command.

`grid bbox` *`master ?c1 r1? ?c2 r2?`*	Return the bounding box, of the whole grid, the cell at *`c1`*, *`r1`*, or the cells from *`c1`*, *`r1`* to *`c2`*, *`r2`*.
`grid columnconfigure` *`master col ?options?`*	Set or query the configuration of *`col`*. Options are `-minsize`, `-weight`, and `-pad`.
`grid configure` *`win ?win ...? ?options?`*	Grid one or more widgets according to the *`options`*, which are given in Table 21–2.
`grid forget` *`win ?win...?`*	Unmap the specified windows.
`grid info` *`win`*	Return the grid parameters of *`win`*.
`grid location` *`master x y`*	Return the cell column and row under the point *`x`*, *`y`* in *`master`*.
`grid propagate` *`master ?boolean?`*	Enable or disable shrink-wrapping of *`master`*.
`grid rowconfigure` *`master row ?options?`*	Set or query the configuration of *`row`*. Options are `-minsize`, `-weight`, and `-pad`.
`grid remove` *`slave`*	Unmap *`slave`*, but remember its configuration.
`grid size master`	Return the number of columns and rows.
`grid slaves` *`win`* `?-row` *`r`*`? ?-column` *`c`*`?`	Return the list of widgets managed by *`win`*, or just those in the specified row or column.

Table 21–2 summarizes the grid options for a widget. These are set with the `grid configure` command, and the current settings are returned by the `grid info` command.

Table 21–2 Grid widget options.

`-in` *`win`*	Place inside *`win`*.
`-column` *`col`*	Column position. Columns count from zero.
`-columnspan` *`n`*	Span *n* columns.
`-ipadx` *`pixels`*	Internal widget padding in the X direction, in screen units.
`-ipady` *`pixels`*	Internal widget padding in the Y direction, in screen units..
`-padx` *`pixels`*	External widget padding in the X direction, in screen units..
`-pady` *`pixels`*	External widget padding in the Y direction, in screen units..
`-row` *`row`*	Row position. Rows count from zero.
`-rowspan` *`n`*	Span *n* rows.
`-sticky` *`how`*	Position widget next to any combination of north (`n`), south (`s`), east (`w`), and west (`e`) sides of the cell. Use `{}` for center.

CHAPTER 22

The Place Geometry Manager

This chapter explores the `place` geometry manager that positions widgets on the screen.

III. Tk Basics

The `place` geometry manager is much simpler than `pack` and `grid`. You specify the exact position and size of a window, or you specify the relative position and relative size of a widget. This is useful in a few situations, but it rapidly becomes tedious if you have to position lots of windows. The best application of `place` is to create special-purpose geometry managers using its relative constraints. A standard application of `place` is to adjust the boundary between two adjacent windows.

`place` Basics

The `place` command lets you specify the width and height of a window, and the X and Y locations of the window's anchor point. The size and location can be specified in absolute or relative terms. Relative specifications are more powerful. Example 22–1 uses `place` to center a window in its parent. You can use this command to position dialogs that you do not want to be detached top-level windows:

Example 22–1 Centering a window with `place`.

```
place $w -in $parent -relx 0.5 -rely 0.5 -anchor center
```

The `-relx` and `-rely` specify the relative X and Y positions of the anchor point of the widget `$w` in `$parent`. A relative X (or Y) value of zero corresponds to the left (or top) edge of `$parent`. A value of one corresponds to the right (or bottom) edge of `$parent`. A value of `0.5` specifies the middle. The anchor point determines what point in `$w` is positioned according to the specifications. In Example 22–1 the `center` anchor point is used so that the center of `$w` is centered in `$parent`.

The relative height and width settings are used to base a widget's size on another widget. Example 22–2 completely covers one window with another window. It uses the default anchor point for windows, which is their upper-left hand corner (`nw`):

Example 22–2 Covering a window with `place`.

```
place $w -in $parent -relwidth 1 -relheight 1 -x 0 -y 0
```

The absolute and relative size and position parameters are additive (e.g., `-width` and `-relwidth`). You can make a window slightly larger or smaller than the parent by specifying both parameters. In Example 22–3 a negative width and height are used to make a window smaller than another one:

Example 22–3 Combining relative and absolute sizes.

```
place $w -in $parent -relwidth 1 -relheight 1 -x 0 -y 0 \
    -width -4 -height -4
```

It is not necessary for `$parent` to actually be the parent widget of `$w`. The requirement is that `$parent` be the parent, or a descendent of the parent, of `$w`. It also has to be in the same top-level window. This guarantees that `$w` is visible whenever `$parent` is visible. These are the same restrictions imposed by the `pack` geometry manager.

It is not necessary to position a widget inside another widget, either. Example 22–4 positions a window five pixels above a sibling widget. If `$sibling` is repositioned, then `$w` moves with it. This approach is useful when you decorate a resizable window by placing other widgets at its corners or edges. When the window is resized, the decorations automatically move into place:

Example 22–4 Positioning a window above a sibling with `place`.

```
place $w -in $sibling -relx 0.5 -y -5 -anchor s \
    -bordermode outside
```

The `-bordermode outside` option is specified so that any decorative border in `$sibling` is ignored when positioning `$w`. In this case the position is relative to the outside edge of `$sibling`. By default, the border is taken into account to make it easy to position widgets inside their parent's border.

The parent widget does not have to be a `frame`. Example 22–1 can be used to place a dialog in the middle of a `text` widget. In Example 22–4, `$sibling` and `$w` can both be `label` widgets.

The Pane Manager

The relative size and placement parameters of the `place` command can be used to create custom geometry managers. Example 22–5 shows a paned layout manager. Two frames, or panes, are placed inside another frame. A small third frame represents a grip that is used to adjust the boundary between the two panes:

Example 22–5 `Pane_Create` sets up vertical or horizontal panes.

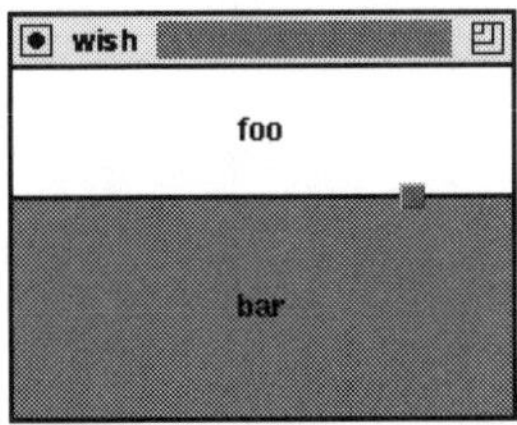


```
proc Pane_Create {f1 f2 args} {

    # Map optional arguments into array values
    set t(-orient) vertical
    set t(-percent) 0.5
    set t(-in) [winfo parent $f1]
    array set t $args

    # Keep state in an array associated with the master frame
    set master $t(-in)
    upvar #0 Pane$master pane
    array set pane [array get t]

    # Create the grip and set placement attributes that
    # will not change. A thin divider line is achieved by
    # making the two frames one pixel smaller in the
    # adjustable dimension and making the main frame black.

    set pane(1) $f1
    set pane(2) $f2
    set pane(grip) [frame $master.grip -background gray50 \
        -width 10 -height 10 -bd 1 -relief raised \
        -cursor crosshair]
    if {[string match vert* $pane(-orient)]} {
        set pane(D) Y;# Adjust boundary in Y direction
        place $pane(1) -in $master -x 0 -rely 0.0 -anchor nw \
            -relwidth 1.0 -height -1
        place $pane(2) -in $master -x 0 -rely 1.0 -anchor sw \
            -relwidth 1.0 -height -1
        place $pane(grip) -in $master -anchor c -relx 0.8
    } else {
        set pane(D) X ;# Adjust boundary in X direction
        place $pane(1) -in $master -relx 0.0 -y 0 -anchor nw \
            -relheight 1.0 -width -1
        place $pane(2) -in $master -relx 1.0 -y 0 -anchor ne \
```

```
        -relheight 1.0 -width -1
      place $pane(grip) -in $master -anchor c -rely 0.8
   }
   $master configure -background black

   # Set up bindings for resize, <Configure>, and
   # for dragging the grip.

   bind $master <Configure> [list PaneGeometry $master]
   bind $pane(grip) <ButtonPress-1> \
      [list PaneDrag $master %$pane(D)]
   bind $pane(grip) <B1-Motion> \
      [list PaneDrag $master %$pane(D)]
   bind $pane(grip) <ButtonRelease-1> \
      [list PaneStop $master]

   # Do the initial layout

   PaneGeometry $master
}
```

Parsing Arguments and Maintaining State

The `Pane_Create` procedure is given two widgets to manage, and an optional set of parameters. The general syntax of `Pane_Create` is:

`Pane_Create f1 f2 ?-orient` *`xy`*`? ?-percent` *`p`*`? ?-in` *`master`*`?`

All the optional arguments are available in `$args`. Its attribute-value structure is used to initialize a temporary array `t`. Default values are set before the assignment from `$args`. The following code is compact but doesn't check errors in the optional arguments.

```
set t(-orient) vertical
set t(-percent) 0.5
set t(-in) [winfo parent $f1]
array set t $args
```

Global state about the layout is kept in an array whose name is based on the master frame. The name of the master frame isn't known until after arguments are parsed, which is why `t` is used. After the `upvar` the argument values are copied from the temporary array into the global state array:

```
set master $t(-in)
upvar #0 Pane$master pane
array set pane [array get t]
```

Sticky Geometry Settings

Example 22–5 sets several `place` parameters on the frames when they are created. These are remembered, and other parameters are adjusted later to dynamically adjust the boundary between the frames. All Tk geometry managers retain settings like this. The initial settings for the vertical layout is shown here:

```
place $pane(1) -in $parent -x 0 -rely 0.0 -anchor nw \
    -relwidth 1.0 -height -1
place $pane(2) -in $parent -x 0 -rely 1.0 -anchor sw \
    -relwidth 1.0 -height -1
place $pane(grip) -in $parent -anchor c -relx 0.8
```

The position of the upper and lower frames is specified with an absolute X and a relative Y position, and the anchor setting is chosen to keep the frame visible inside the main frame. For example, the lower frame is positioned at the bottom-left corner of the container with `-x 0` and `-rely 1.0`. The `-anchor sw` attaches the lower-left corner of the frame to this position.

The size of the contained frames is also a combination of absolute and relative values. The width is set to the full width of the container with `-relwidth 1.0`. The height is set to minus one with `-height -1`. This value gets added to a relative height that is determined later. It will leave a little space between the two contained frames.

The resize grip is just a small frame positioned at the boundary. Initially it is just placed over toward one size with `-relx 0.8`. It gets positioned on the boundary with a `-rely` setting later. It has a different cursor to indicate it is active.

Event Bindings

The example uses some event bindings that are described in more detail in Chapter 23. The `<Configure>` event occurs when the containing frame is resized by the user. When the user presses the mouse button over the grip and drags it, there is a `<ButtonPress-1>` event, one or more `<B1-Motion>` events, and finally a `<ButtonRelease-1>` event. Tcl commands are bound to these events:

```
bind $parent <Configure> [list PaneGeometry $parent]
bind $pane(grip) <ButtonPress-1> \
    [list PaneDrag $parent %$pane(D)]
bind $pane(grip) <B1-Motion> \
    [list PaneDrag $parent %$pane(D)]
bind $pane(grip) <ButtonRelease-1> [list PaneStop $parent]
```

Managing the Layout

The code is set up to work with either horizontal or vertical layouts. The `pane(D)` variable is either `X`, for a horizontal layout, or `Y`, for a vertical layout. This value is used in the bindings to get `%X` or `%Y`, which are replaced with the X and Y screen positions of the mouse when the bindings fire. This value is passed to `PaneDrag` as the parameter `D`. The `PaneDrag` procedure remembers the previous position in `pane(lastD)` and uses that to update the percentage split between the two contained panes:

Example 22–6 `PaneDrag` adjusts the percentage.

```
proc PaneDrag {master D} {
    upvar #0 Pane$master pane
    if [info exists pane(lastD)] {
        set delta [expr double($pane(lastD) - $D) \
                                    / $pane(size)]
        set pane(-percent) [expr $pane(-percent) - $delta]
        if {$pane(-percent) < 0.0} {
            set pane(-percent) 0.0
        } elseif {$pane(-percent) > 1.0} {
            set pane(-percent) 1.0
        }
        PaneGeometry $master
    }
    set pane(lastD) $D
}
proc PaneStop {master} {
    upvar #0 Pane$master pane
    catch {unset pane(lastD)}
}
```

The `PaneGeometry` procedure adjusts the positions of the frames. It is called when the main window is resized, so it updates `pane(size)`. It is also called as the user drags the grip. For a vertical layout, the grip is moved by setting its relative Y position. The size of the two contained frames is set with a relative height. Remember this is combined with the fixed height of -1 to get some space between the two frames:

Example 22–7 `PaneGeometry` updates the layout.

```
proc PaneGeometry {master} {
    upvar #0 Pane$master pane
    if {$pane(D) == "X"} {
        place $pane(1) -relwidth $pane(-percent)
        place $pane(2) -relwidth [expr 1.0 - $pane(-percent)]
        place $pane(grip) -relx $pane(-percent)
        set pane(size) [winfo width $master]
    } else {
        place $pane(1) -relheight $pane(-percent)
        place $pane(2) -relheight [expr 1.0 - $pane(-percent)]
        place $pane(grip) -rely $pane(-percent)
        set pane(size) [winfo height $master]
    }
}
proc PaneTest {{p .p} {orient vert}} {
    catch {destroy $p}
    frame $p -width 200 -height 200
    label $p.1 -bg blue -text foo
    label $p.2 -bg green -text bar
    pack $p -expand true -fill both
```

```
    pack propagate $p off
    Pane_Create $p.1 $p.2 -in $p -orient $orient -percent 0.3
}
```

The place Command

Table 22–1 summarizes the usage of the `place` command.

Table 22–1 The `place` command.

`place` *win* `?`*win* `..?` `?`*options*`?`	This is just like `place configure`.
`place configure` *win* `?`*win* `...? ?`*options*`?`	Place one or more widgets according to the *options*, which are given Table 22–2.
`place forget` *win* `?`*win*`...?`	Unmap the specified windows.
`place info` *win*	Return the placement parameters of *win*.
`place slaves` *win*	Return the list of widgets managed by *win*.

Table 22–2 summarizes the placement options for a widget. These are set with the `place configure` command, and the current settings are returned by the `place info` command.

Table 22–2 Placement options.

`-in` *win*	Place inside (or relative to) *win*.
`-anchor` *where*	Anchors: `center`, `n`, `ne`, `e`, `se`, `s`, `sw`, `w`, or `nw`. Default: `nw`.
`-x` *coord*	X position, in screen units, of the anchor point.
`-relx` *offset*	Relative X position. 0.0 is the left edge. 1.0 is the right edge.
`-y` *coord*	Y position, in screen units, of the anchor point.
`-rely` *offset*	Relative Y position. 0.0 is the top edge. 1.0 is the bottom edge.
`-width size`	Width of the window, in screen units.
`-relwidth size`	Width relative to parent's width. 1.0 is full width.
`-height size`	Height of the window, in screen units.
`-relheight size`	Height relative to the parent's height. 1.0 is full height.
`-bordermode mode`	If mode is `inside`, then size and position are inside the parent's border. If mode is `outside`, then size and position are relative to the outer edge of the parent. The default is `inside`.

CHAPTER 23

Binding Commands to Events

This chapter introduces the event binding mechanism in Tk. Bindings associate a Tcl command with an event like a mouse click or a key stroke. There are also facilities to define virtual events like <<Cut>> and <<Paste>> that are associated with different keystrokes on different platforms. Tcl commands: `bind`, `bindtags`, and `event`.

Bindings associate a Tcl command with a sequence of events from the window system. Events include key press, key release, button press, button release, mouse entering a window, mouse leaving, window changing size, window open, window close, focus in, focus out, and widget destroyed. The bindings are defined on *binding tags*, and each widget is associated with an ordered set of binding tags. The binding tags provide a level of indirection between bindings and widgets that creates a flexible and powerful system.

Virtual events were introduced in Tk 4.2 to support a different look and feel on different platforms. A virtual event is a higher-level name, like `<<Copy>>`, for a lower-level event name like `<Control-c>` or `<Key-F6>`. A virtual event hides the different keystrokes used on different platforms for the same logical operation. Tk defines a few virtual events, and applications can define their own.

The bind Command

The `bind` command creates event bindings, and it returns information about current bindings. The general form of the command is:

```
bind bindingTag ?eventSequence? ?command?
```

If all arguments are present, a binding from *eventSequence* to *command* is defined for *bindingTag*. The *bindingTag* is typically a widget class name (e.g., `Button`) or a widget instance name (e.g., `.buttons.foo`). Binding tags are described in more detail later. Called with a single argument, a binding tag, bind returns the events for which there are command bindings:

```
bind Menubutton
=> <Key-Return> <Key-space> <ButtonRelease-1>
   <B1-Motion> <Motion> <Button-1> <Leave> <Enter>
```

The events in this example are keystroke and mouse events. <Button-1> is the event generated when the user presses the first, or left-hand, mouse button. <B1-Motion> is generated when the user moves the mouse while holding down the first mouse button. The <Key-space> event occurs when the user presses the space bar. The surrounding angle brackets delimit a single event, and you can define bindings for a sequence of events. The event syntax is described on page 289, and event sequences are described on page 295.

If bind is given a binding tag and an event sequence, it returns the Tcl command bound to that event sequence:

```
bind Menubutton <B1-Motion>
=> tkMbMotion %W down %X %Y
```

The Tcl commands in event bindings support an additional syntax for event keywords. These keywords begin with a percent sign and have one more character that identifies some attribute of the event. The keywords are substituted with event-specific data before the Tcl command is evaluated. For example, %W is replaced with the widget's pathname. The %X and %Y keywords are replaced with the coordinates of the event relative to the screen. The %x and %y keywords are replaced with the coordinates of the event relative to the widget. The event keywords are summarized on page 298.

The % substitutions are performed throughout the entire command bound to an event, without regard to other quoting schemes. You must use %% to obtain a single percent sign. For this reason you should make your binding commands short, adding a new procedure if necessary (e.g., tkMbMotion), instead of littering percent signs throughout your code.

A new binding is created by specifying a binding tag, an event sequence, and a command:

```
bind Menubutton <B1-Motion> {tkMbMotion %W down %X %Y}
```

If the first character of the binding command is +, the command (without the +) is added to the commands, if any, for that event and binding tag:

```
bind bindingTag event {+ command args}
```

To delete a binding for an event, bind the event to the null string:

```
bind bindingTag event {}
```

Bindings execute in the global scope.

When a binding is triggered, the command is evaluated at the global scope. A very common mistake is to confuse the scope that is active when the bind command creates a binding, and the scope that is active when the binding is triggered. The same problem crops up with the commands associated with buttons, and it is discussed in more detail at the beginning of Chapter 24.

The bindtags Command

A binding tag groups related bindings, and each widget is associated with an ordered set of binding tags. The level of indirection between widgets and bindings lets you group functionality on binding tags and compose widget behavior from different binding tags.

For example, the `all` binding tag has bindings on `<Tab>` that change focus among widgets. The `Text` binding tag has bindings on keystrokes that insert and edit text. Only text widgets use the `Text` binding tag, but all widgets share the `all` binding tag. You can introduce new binding tags and change the association of widgets to binding tags dynamically. The result is a powerful and flexible way to manage bindings.

The `bindtags` command sets or queries the binding tags for a widget. The general form of the `bindtags` command is:

```
bindtags widget ?tagList?
```

The following command returns the binding tags for text widget `.t`:

```
bindtags .t
=> .t Text . all
```

You can change the binding tags and their order. The *tagList* argument to `bindtags` must be a proper Tcl list. The following command reorders the binding tags for `.t` and eliminates the `.` binding tag:

```
bindtags .t [list all Text .t]
```

By default, all the Tk widgets, except a top-level, have four binding tags in the following order:

- The widget's Tk pathname (e.g., `.t`). Use this binding tag to provide special behavior to a particular widget. There are no bindings on this bindtag by default.
- The widget's class (e.g., `Text`). The class for a widget is derived from the name of the command that creates it. A button widget has the class `Button`, a text has the class `Text`, and so on. The Tk widgets define their default behavior with bindings on their class.
- The Tk pathname of the widget's top-level window (e.g., .). This is redundant in the case of a top-level widget, so it is not used twice. There are no bindings on this bindtag by default. The bindings on a top-level window can be used in dialog boxes to handle keyboard accelerators.
- The global binding tag `all`. The default bindings on `all` are used to change focus among widgets. They are described on page 440.

When there is more than one binding tag on a widget, then one binding from each binding tag can match an event. The bindings are processed in the order of the binding tags. By default, the most specific binding tag comes first, and the most general binding tag comes last.

Example 23–1 has two frame widgets that have the following behavior. When the mouse enters them, they turn red. They turn white when the mouse leaves. When the user types `<Control-c>`, the frame under the mouse is destroyed. One of the frames, `.two`, reports the coordinates of mouse clicks:

Example 23–1 Bindings on different binding tags.

```
frame .one -width 30 -height 30
frame .two -width 30 -height 30
bind Frame <Enter> {%W config -bg red}
bind Frame <Leave> {%W config -bg white}
bind .two <Button> {puts "Button %b at %x %y"}
pack .one .two -side left
bind all <Control-c> {destroy %W}
bind all <Enter> {focus %W}
```

The `Frame` class has a binding on `<Enter>` and `<Leave>` that change a frame's background color when the mouse moves in and out of the window. This binding is shared by all the frames. There is also a binding on `all` for `<Enter>` that sets the keyboard focus. Both bindings will trigger when the mouse enters a frame.

Focus and Key Events

The binding on `<Control-c>` is shared by all widgets. The binding destroys the target widget. Because this is a keystroke, it is important to get the keyboard *focus* directed at the proper widget. By default, focus is on the main window, and destroying it terminates the entire application. The global binding for `<Enter>` gives focus to a widget when you move the mouse over the widget. In this example, moving the mouse into a widget and then typing `<Control-c>` destroys the widget. Bind the `focus` command to `<Button>` instead of `<Enter>` if you prefer a click-to-type focus model. Focus is described in Chapter 33.

Using `break` and `continue` in Bindings

The `break` and `continue` commands control the progression through the set of binding tags. The `break` command stops the current binding and suppresses the bindings from any remaining tags in the binding set order. The `continue` command in a binding stops the current binding and continues with the command from the next binding tag.

For example, the `Entry` binding tag has bindings that insert and edit text in a one-line entry widget. You can put a binding on `<Return>` that executes a Tcl command using the value of the widget. The following example runs *`Some Command`* before the `\r` character is added to the entry widget. The binding is on the name of the widget, which is first in the set of binding tags, so the `break` suppresses the `Entry` binding that inserts the character:

```
bind .entry <Return> {Some Command ; break}
```

Note that you cannot use the `break` or `continue` commands inside a procedure that is called by the binding. This is because the procedure mechanism will not propagate the `break` or `continue` signal. Instead, you could use the `-code` option to `return`, which is described on page 74:

```
return -code break
```

Defining New Binding Tags

You introduce new binding tags just by using them in a `bind` or `bindtags` command. Binding tags are useful for grouping bindings into different sets, such as specialized bindings for different modes of an editor. One way to emulate the *vi* editor, for example, is to use two bind tags, one for insert mode and one for command mode. The user types `i` to enter insert mode, and they type `<Escape>` to enter command mode:

```
bindtags $t [list ViInsert Text $t all]
bind ViInsert <Escape> {bindtags %W {ViCmd %W all}}
bind ViCmd <Key-i> {bindtags %W {ViInsert Text %W all}}
```

The `Text` class bindings are used in insert mode. The command to put the widget into command mode is put on a new binding tag, `ViInsert`, instead of changing the default `Text` bindings. The `bindtag` command changes the mode by changing the set of binding tags for the widget. The `%W` is replaced with the name of the widget, which is the same as `$t` in this example. Of course, you need to define many more bindings to fully implement all the *vi* commands.

Binding Precedence in Tk 3.6

In versions of Tk 3.6 and earlier the set of binding tags for a widget is fixed, and only one source of bindings for an event is used. If there is a binding on a widget instance for an event sequence, that binding overrides any class-specific or global bindings for that event sequence. Similarly, if there is a class-specific binding, that overrides an `all` binding.

There are two problems in this scheme. First, `all` bindings are not that useful because they are almost always overridden. Second, if you add custom behavior to a widget instance, you suppress the default bindings on the class. Even the + syntax on a binding at the instance level does not preserve the class bindings; they are still overridden. The following trick adds a new instance binding while preserving the class binding.

```
bind .list <Button-1> "[bind Listbox <Button-1>] ; Doit"
```

Event Syntax

The `bind` command uses the following syntax to describe events:

```
<modifier-modifier-type-detail>
<<Event>>
```

The first form is for physical events like keystrokes and mouse motion. The second form is for *virtual events* like Cut and Paste, which correspond to different physical events on different platforms. Physical events are described in this section. Virtual events are described in more detail on page 297.

The primary part of the description is the *type*, (e.g., `Button` or `Motion`). The *detail* is used in some events to identify keys or buttons, (.e.g., `Key-a` or

`Button-1`). A *`modifier`* is another key or button that is already pressed when the event occurs, (e.g., `Control-Key-a` or `B2-Motion`). There can be multiple modifiers (e.g., `Control-Shift-x`). The < and > delimit a single event.

Table 23–1 briefly describes all the physical event types. When two event types are listed together (e.g., `ButtonPress` and `Button`) they are equivalent.

Table 23–1 Event types.

`Activate`	The application has been activated. (Macintosh)
`ButtonPress, Button`	A button is pressed (down).
`ButtonRelease`	A button is released (up).
`Circulate`	The stacking order of the window changed.
`Colormap`	The color map has changed.
`Configure`	The window has changed size, position, border, or stacking order.
`Deactivate`	The application has been deactivated. (Macintosh)
`Destroy`	The window has been destroyed.
`Enter`	The mouse has entered the window.
`Expose`	The window has been exposed.
`FocusIn`	The window has received focus.
`FocusOut`	The window has lost focus.
`Gravity`	The window has moved because of a change in size of its parent window.
`KeyPress, Key`	A key is pressed (down).
`KeyRelease`	A key is released (up).
`Motion`	The mouse is moving in the window.
`Leave`	The mouse is leaving the window.
`Map`	The window has been mapped (opened).
`Property`	A property on the window has been changed or deleted.
`Reparent`	A window has been reparented.
`Unmap`	The window has been unmapped (iconified).
`Visibility`	The window has changed visibility.

Keyboard Events

The `KeyPress` type is distinguished from `KeyRelease` so that you can have different bindings for each of these events. `KeyPress` can be abbreviated `Key`, and `Key` can be left off altogether if a detail is given to indicate what key. Finally, as a special case for KeyPress events, the angle brackets can also be left out. The following are all equivalent event specifications:

```
<KeyPress-a>
<Key-a>
<a>
a
```

The detail for a key is also known as the *keysym*, which refers to the graphic printed on the key of the keyboard. For punctuation and non-printing characters, special keysyms are defined. Case is significant in keysyms, but unfortunately there is no consistent scheme. In particular BackSpace has a capital B and a capital S. Commonly encountered keysyms include:

```
Return, Escape, BackSpace, Tab, Up, Down, Left, Right,
comma, period, dollar, asciicircum, numbersign, exclam
```

The keysyms are defined by the window system implementation, and on UNIX systems they are affected by a dynamic keyboard map, the X modmap. You may find the next binding useful to determine just what the keysym for a particular key is on your system:

```
bind $w <KeyPress> {puts stdout {%%K=%K %%A=%A}}
```

The %K keyword is replaced with the keysym from the event. The %A is replaced with the printing character that results from the event and any modifiers like Shift. The %% is replaced with a single percent sign. Note that these substitutions occur in spite of the curly braces used for grouping. If the user types a capital Q, there are two KeyPress events, one for the Shift key, and one for the q key. The output is:

```
%K=Shift_R %A={}
%K=Q %A=Q
```

The Shift_R keysym indicates the right-hand shift key was pressed. The %A keyword is replaced with {} when modifier keys are pressed. You can check for this in <KeyPress> bindings to avoid doing anything if only a modifier key is pressed. On Macintosh, there is no event at all when the modifier keys are pressed. The following can be used with a text widget. The double quotes are necessary to force a string comparison:

```
bind $w <KeyPress> {
    if {"%A" != "{}"} {%W insert insert %A}
}
```

Detecting Modifiers in Tk 3.6

In Tk 3.6 and earlier, the %A keyword is substituted with an empty string instead of the literal {}. In addition, you must use the Any event modifier to allow any key sequence to match. The previous example must be changed to this if you are using Tk 3.6:

```
bind $w <Any-Key> {
    if {"%A" != ""} {%W insert insert %A}
}
```

Mouse Events

Button events also distinguish between ButtonPress, (or Button), and ButtonRelease. Button can be left off if a detail specifies a button by number. The following are equivalent:

```
<ButtonPress-1>
<Button-1>
<1>
```

Note: The event <1> implies a ButtonPress event, while the event 1 implies a KeyPress event. To avoid confusion, always specify the Key or Button type.

The mouse is tracked by binding to the Enter, Leave, and Motion events. Enter and Leave are triggered when the mouse comes into and exits out of the widget, respectively. A Motion event is generated when the mouse moves within a widget.

The coordinates of the mouse event are represented by the %x and %y keywords in the binding command. The coordinates are widget-relative, with the origin at the upper-left hand corner of a widget's window. The keywords %X and %Y represent the coordinates relative to the screen:

```
bind $w <Enter>  {puts stdout "Entered %W at %x %y"}
bind $w <Leave>  {puts stdout "Left %W at %x %y"}
bind $w <Motion> {puts stdout "%W %x %y"}
```

A mouse drag event is a Motion event that occurs when the user holds down a mouse button. In this case the mouse button is a modifier, which is discussed in more detail on page 293. The binding looks like this:

```
bind $w <B1-Motion> {puts stdout "%W %x %y"}
```

Other Events

The <Map> and <Unmap> events are generated when a window is opened and closed, or when a widget is packed or unpacked by its geometry manager.

The <Activate> and <Deactivate> events are generated when an application is activated by the operating system. This applies to Macintosh systems, and it occurs when the user clicks in the application window.

The <Configure> event is generated when the window changes size. A canvas that computes its display based on its size can bind a redisplay procedure to the <Configure> event, for example. The <Configure> event can be caused by interactive resizing. It can also be caused by a configure widget command that changes the size of the widget. You should not reconfigure a widget's size while processing a <Configure> event to avoid an indefinite sequence of these events.

The <Destroy> event is generated when a widget is destroyed. You can intercept requests to delete windows, too. See also the description of the wm command on page 490.

Chapter 33 presents some examples that use the <FocusIn> and <FocusOut> events. The remaining events in Table 23–1 have to do with dark corners of the X protocol, and they are seldom used. More information can be found on these events in the Event Reference section of the *Xlib Reference Manual* (Adrian Nye, O'Reilly & Associates, Inc., 1992).

Bindings on Top-level Windows

Be careful when binding events to top-level windows because their name is used as a binding tag on all the widgets contained in them. For example, the following binding fires when the user destroys the main window, which means the application is about to exit:

```
bind . <Destroy> {puts "goodbye"}
```

Unfortunately, all widgets inside the main window are destroyed as a side effect, and they all share the name of their toplevel widget as a binding tag. So, this binding fires when every widget inside the main window is destroyed. Typically you only want to do something one time. The following binding checks the identity of the widget before doing anything:

```
bind . <Destroy> {if {"%W" == "."} {puts "goodbye"}}
```

Modifiers

A modifier indicates that another key or button is being held down at the time of the event. Typical modifiers are the `Shift` and `Control` keys. The mouse buttons can also be used as modifiers. If an event does not specify any modifiers, the presence of a modifier key is ignored by the event dispatcher. However, if there are two possible matching events, the more accurate match will be used. For example, consider these three bindings:

```
bind $w <KeyPress> {puts "key=%A"}
bind $w <Key-c> {puts "just a c"}
bind $w <Control-Key-c> {exit}
```

The last event is more specific than the others. Its binding will be triggered when the user types `c` with the `Control` key held down. If the user types `c` with the `Meta` key held down, the second binding will be triggered. The `Meta` key is ignored because it does not match any binding. If the user types something other than a `c`, the first binding is triggered. If the user presses the `Shift` key, then the keysym that is generated is `C`, not `c`, so the last two events do not match.

There are eight possible modifier keys. The `Control`, `Shift`, and `Lock` modifiers are found on nearly all keyboards. The `Meta` and `Alt` modifiers tend to vary from system to system, and they may not be defined at all. They are commonly mapped to be the same as `Mod1` or `Mod2`, and Tk will try to determine how the mappings are set. The Macintosh has a `Command` modifier that corresponds to the clover-leaf or apple key. The remaining modifiers, `Mod3` through `Mod5`, are sometimes mapped to other special keys. In OpenLook environments, for example, the `Paste` function key is also mapped to the `Mod5` modifier.

The button modifiers, `B1` through `B5`, are most commonly used with the `Motion` event to distinguish different mouse dragging operations. For example,

<B1-Motion> is the event generated when the user drags the mouse with the first mouse button held down.

Double-click warning.

The Double and Triple events match on repetitions of an event within a short period of time. These are commonly used with mouse events. Be careful: The binding for the regular press event will match on the first press of the Double. Then the command bound to the Double event will match on the second press. Similarly, a Double event will match on the first two presses of a Triple event. Verify this by trying out the following bindings:

```
bind . <1> {puts stdout 1}
bind . <Double-1> {puts stdout 2}
bind . <Triple-1> {puts stdout 3}
```

If you click the first mouse button several times quickly, you will see a 1, 2, and then a few 3's output. Your bindings must take into consideration that more than one binding might match a Double or Triple event. This effect is compatible with an interface that selects an object with the first click, and then operates on the selected object with a Double event. In an editor, character, word, and line selection on a single, double, and triple click, respectively, is a good example.*

Table 23–2 summarizes the modifiers.

Table 23–2 Event modifiers.

Control	The control key.
Shift	The shift key.
Lock	The caps-lock key.
Command	The command key. (Macintosh)
Meta, M	Defined to be what ever modifier (M1 through M5) is mapped to the Meta_L and Meta_R keysyms.
Alt	Defined to be the modifier mapped to Alt_L and Alt_R.
Mod1, M1	The first modifier.
Mod2, M2, Alt	The second modifier.
Mod3, M3	Another modifier.
Mod4, M4	Another modifier.
Mod5, M5	Another modifier.
Button1, B1	The first mouse button (left).

* If you really want to disable this, you can experiment with using after to postpone processing of one event. The time constant in the bind implementation of <Double> is 500 milliseconds. At the single-click event, schedule its action to occur after 600 milliseconds, and verify at that time that the <Double> event has not occurred.

Table 23–2 Event modifiers. (Continued)

`Button2, B2`	The second mouse button (middle).
`Button3, B3`	The third mouse button (right).
`Button4, B4`	The fourth mouse button.
`Button5, B5`	The fifth mouse button.
`Double`	Matches double-press event.
`Triple`	Matches triple-press event.
`Any`	Matches any combination of modifiers. (Before Tk 4.0)

The UNIX *xmodmap* program returns the current mappings from keys to these modifiers. The first column of its output lists the modifier. The rest of each line identifies the keysym(s) and low-level keycodes that are mapped to each modifier. The *xmodmap* program can also be used to change mappings. The following example shows the mappings on my system. Your setup may be different.

Example 23–2 Output from the UNIX *xmodmap* program.

```
xmodmap: up to 3 keys per modifier,
       (keycodes in parentheses):
shift Shift_L (0x6a), Shift_R (0x75)
lock Caps_Lock (0x7e)
control Control_L (0x53)
mod1 Meta_L (0x7f), Meta_R (0x81)
mod2 Mode_switch (0x14)
mod3 Num_Lock (0x69)
mod4 Alt_L (0x1a)
mod5 F13 (0x20), F18 (0x50), F20 (0x68)
```

Modifiers in Tk 3.6

In Tk Version 3.6 and earlier, extra modifier keys prevent events from matching. If you want your bindings to be liberal about what modifiers are in effect, you must use the `Any` modifier. This modifier is a wild card that matches if zero or more modifiers are in effect. You can still use `Any` in scripts that use Tk 4.0 or higher, but it has no effect.

Event Sequences

The `bind` command accepts a sequence of events in a specification, and most commonly this is a sequence of key events. In the following examples, the `Key` events are abbreviated to just the character detail, and so `abc` is a sequence of three `Key` events:

```
bind . a {puts stdout A}
bind . abc {puts stdout C}
```

With these bindings in effect, both bindings are executed when the user types `abc`. The binding for `a` is executed when `a` is pressed, even though this event is also part of a longer sequence. This is similar to the behavior with `Double` and `Triple` event modifiers. For this reason you must be careful when binding sequences. You can use `break` in the binding for the prefix to ensure that it does not do anything:

```
bindtags $w [list $w Text [winfo toplevel $w] all]
bind $w <Control-x> break
bind $w <Control-x><Control-s> {Save ; break}
bind $w <Control-x><Control-c> {Quit ; break}
```

The `break` ensures that the default `Text` binding that inserts characters does not trigger. This trick is embodied by `BindSequence` in the next example. If a sequence is detected, then a `break` binding is added for the prefix. The procedure also supports the *emacs* convention that `<Meta-x>` is equivalent to `<Escape>x`. This convention arose because `Meta` is not that standard across keyboards. There is no meta key at all on Windows and Macintosh keyboards. The `regexp` command is used to pick out the detail from the `<Meta>` event.

Example 23–3 Emacs-like binding convention for `Meta` and `Escape`.

```
proc BindSequence { w seq cmd } {
    bind $w $seq $cmd
    # Double-bind Meta-key and Escape-key
    if [regexp {<Meta-(.*)>} $seq match letter] {
        bind $w <Escape><$letter> $cmd
    }
    # Make leading keystroke harmless
    if [regexp {(<.+>)<.+>} $seq match prefix] {
        bind $w $prefix break
    }
}
```

The use of `break` and `continue` in bindings is not supported in Tk 3.6 and earlier. This is because only a single binding tag can match an event. To make a prefix of a sequence harmless in Tk 3.6, bind a space to it:

```
bind $w $prefix { }
```

This installs a binding for the widget, which suppresses the class binding in Tk 3.6. The space is different than a null string, `{}`. Binding to a null string deletes the current binding instead of replacing it with a harmless one.

Virtual Events

A virtual event corresponds to one or more event sequences. When any of the event sequences occurs, then the virtual event occurs. The next example shows the default virtual events for each platform:

Example 23–4 Virtual events for cut, copy, and paste.

```
switch $tcl_platform(platform) {
     "unix" {
        event add <<Cut>> <Control-Key-x> <Key-F20>
        event add <<Copy>> <Control-Key-c> <Key-F16>
        event add <<Paste>> <Control-Key-v> <Key-F18>
    }
    "windows" {
        event add <<Cut>> <Control-Key-x> <Shift-Key-Delete>
        event add <<Copy>> <Control-Key-c> <Control-Key-Insert>
        event add <<Paste>> <Control-Key-v> <Shift-Key-Insert>
    }
    "macintosh" {
        event add <<Cut>> <Control-Key-x> <Key-F2>
        event add <<Copy>> <Control-Key-c> <Key-F3>
        event add <<Paste>> <Control-Key-v> <Key-F4>
    }
}
```

You can define more than one physical event that maps to the same virtual event:

```
event add <<Cancel>> <Control-c> <Escape> <Command-.>
```

With this definition any of the physical events will trigger a `<<Cancel>>`. This would be convenient if the same user commonly used your application on different platforms. However, it is also possible that the physical bindings on different platforms overlap in conflicting ways.

By default, virtual event definitions add to existing definitions for the same virtual event. The previous command could be replaced with these three:

```
event add <<Cancel>> <Control-c>
event add <<Cancel>> <Escape>
event add <<Cancel>> <Command-.>
```

The `event` command is summarized in Table 23–3.

Table 23–3 The event command.

`event add` *virt phys1 phy2* ...	Add a mapping from one or more physical events to virtual event *virt*.
`event delete` *virt*	Delete virtual event *virt*.
`event info`	Return the defined virtual events.
`event info` *virt*	Return the physical events that map to *virt*.
`event generate` *win event ?opt val?* ...	Generate *event* for window *win*. The options are listed in Table 23–4.

Event Keywords

Table 23–4 lists the percent keywords and the corresponding option to the `event generate` command. Remember that keyword substitutions occur throughout the command, regardless of other Tcl quoting conventions. Keep your binding commands short, introducing procedures if needed. For the details about various event fields, consult the *Xlib Reference Manual* (O'Reilly & Associates, Inc.). The string values for the keyword substitutions are listed after a short description of the keyword. If no string values are listed, the keyword has an integer value like a coordinate or a window ID.

Table 23–4 A summary of the `event` keywords.

`%%`		Use this to get a single percent sign. All events.
`%#`	`-serial` *num*	The serial number for the event. All events.
`%a`	`-above` *win*	The above field from the event. `Configure` event.
`%b`	`-button` *num*	Button number. Events: `ButtonPress` and `ButtonRelease`.
`%c`	`-count` *num*	The count field. Events: `Expose` and `Map`.
`%d`	`-detail` *value*	The detail field. Values: `NotifyAncestor`, `NotifyNonlinearVirtual`, `NotifyDetailNone`, `NotifyPointer`, `NotifyInferior`, `NotifyPointerRoot`, `NotifyNonlinear`, or `NotifyVirtual`. Events: `Enter`, `Leave`, `FocusIn`, and `FocusOut`.
`%f`	`-focus` *boolean*	The focus field (0 or 1). Events: `Enter` and `Leave`.
`%h`	`-height` *num*	The height field. Events: `Configure` and `Expose`.
`%k`	`-keycode` *num*	The keycode field. Events: `KeyPress` and `KeyRelease`.
`%m`	`-mode` *value*	The mode field. Values: `NotifyNormal`, `NotifyGrab`, `NotifyUngrab`, or `NotifyWhileGrabbed`. Events: `Enter`, `Leave`, `FocusIn`, and `FocusOut`.
`%o`	`-override` *boolean*	The override_redirect field. Events: `Map`, `Reparent`, and `Configure`.
`%p`	`-place` *value*	The place field. Values: `PlaceOnTop`, `PlaceOnBottom`. `Circulate` event.
`%s`	`-state` *value*	The state field. A decimal string for events: `ButtonPress`, `ButtonRelease`, `Enter`, `Leave`, `KeyPress`, `KeyRelease`, `and Motion`. Values for the `Visibility` event: `VisibilityUnobscured`, `VisibilityPartiallyObscured`, or `VisibilityFullyObscured`.
`%t`	`-time` *num*	The time field. All events.
`%v`		The value_mask field. `Configure` event.

Table 23–4 A summary of the `event` keywords. (Continued)

`%w`	`-width` *num*	The width field. Events: `Configure` and `Expose`.
`%x`	`-x` *pixel*	The X coordinate, widget relative. Mouse events.
`%y`	`-y` *pixel*	The Y coordinate, widget relative. Mouse events.
`%A`		The printing character from the event, or `{}`. Events: `KeyPress` and `KeyRelease`.
`%B`	`-borderwidth` *num*	The border width. `Configure` event.
`%E`	`-sendevent` *bool*	The send_event field. All events.
`%K`	`-keysym` *symbol*	The keysym from the event. Events: `KeyPress` and `KeyRelease`.
`%N`		The keysym as a decimal number. Events: `KeyPress` and `KeyRelease`.
`%R`	`-root` *win*	The root window ID. All events.
`%S`	`-subwindow` *win*	The subwindow ID. All events.
`%T`		The type field. All events.
`%W`		The Tk pathname of the widget receiving the event. All events.
`%X`	`-rootx` *pixel*	The x_root field. Relative to the (virtual) root window. Events: `ButtonPress`, `ButtonRelease`, `KeyPress`, `KeyRelease`, and `Motion`.
`%Y`	`-rooty` *pixel*	The y_root field. Relative to the (virtual) root window. Events: `ButtonPress`, `ButtonRelease`, `KeyPress`, `KeyRelease`, and `Motion`.

PART IV

Tk Widgets

Part IV describes the Tk widgets. These are the components you use to build up your graphical user interface. Tk widgets are simple to use so you can rapidly develop your interface. At the same time, they have sophisticated features that you can use to fine-tune your interface in response to user feedback.

Chapter 24 describes buttons and menus. Tk 8.0 adds native look and feel to these widgets, so a single script will look different depending on the platform it is running on.

Associated with the widgets is a resource database that stores settings like colors and fonts. Chapter 25 describes the resource database and generalizes it to store button and menu configurations.

Chapter 26 describes a few simple widgets. The frame and toplevel are containers for other widgets. The label displays a text string. The message formats a long text string onto multiple lines. The scale represents a numeric value. The bell command rings the terminal bell.

Chapter 27 describes scrollbars, which can be attached in a general way to other widgets.

Chapter 28 describes entry widgets that provide one line of editable text.

Chapter 29 describes the listbox widget that displays several lines of text. The lines are manipulated as units.

Chapter 30 describes the general-purpose text widget. It can display multiple fonts and have binding tags on ranges of text.

Chapter 31 describes the canvas widget. The canvas manages objects like lines, boxes, images, arcs, and text labels. You can have binding tags on these objects and classes of objects.

CHAPTER 24

Buttons and Menus

Buttons and menus are the primary way that applications expose functions to users. This chapter describes how to create and manipulate buttons and menus.

A button widget is associated with a Tcl command that invokes an action in the application. The checkbutton and radiobutton widgets affect an application indirectly by controlling a Tcl variable. A menu elaborates on this concept by organizing button-like items into related sets, including cascaded menus. The menubutton widget is a special kind of button that displays a menu when you click on it.

Tk 8.0 provides a cross-platform menu bar facility. The menu bar is really just a menu that is displayed horizontally along the top of your application's main window. On the Macintosh, the menu bar appears at the top of the screen. You define the menu bar the same on all platforms. Tk 8.0 also uses native button and menu widgets on the Windows and Macintosh platforms. This contributes to a native look and feel for your application. In earlier versions, Tk displayed the widgets identically on all platforms.

Associating a command to a button is usually quite simple, as illustrated by the Tk "Hello, World!" example:

```
button .hello -command {puts stdout "Hello, World!"}
```

This chapter describes a few useful techniques for setting up the commands in more general cases. If you use variables inside button commands, you have to understand the scoping rules that apply. This is the first topic of the chapter. Once you get scoping figured out, then the other aspects of buttons and menus are quite straightforward.

Button Commands and Scope Issues

Perhaps the trickiest issue with button commands has to do with variable scoping. A button command is executed at the global scope, which is outside of any procedure. If you create a button while inside a procedure, then the button command executes in a different scope later. The commands used in event bindings also execute later at the global scope.

I think of this as the "now" (i.e., button definition) and "later" (i.e., button use) scope problem. For example, you may want to use the values of some variables when you define a button command but use the value of other variables when the button command is used. When these two contexts are mixed, it can be confusing. The next example illustrates the problem. The button's command involves two variables: `x` and `val`. The global variable `x` is needed later, when the button's command executes. The local variable `val` is needed now, in order to define the command. Example 24–1 shows this awkward mixture of scopes:

Example 24–1 A troublesome button command.

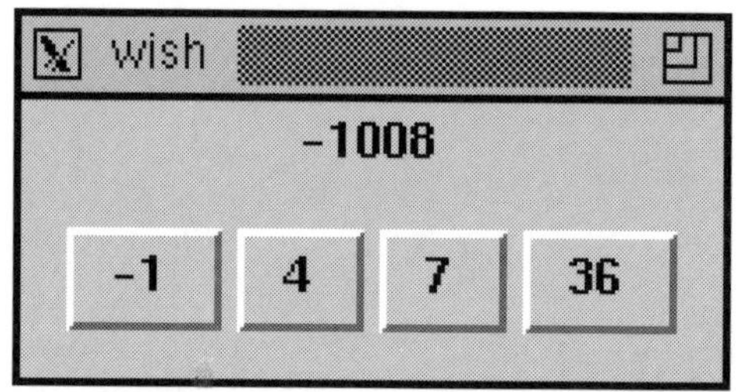


```
proc Trouble {args} {
    set b 0
    # Display the value of x, a global variable
    label .label -textvariable x
    set f [frame .buttons -borderwidth 10]
    # Create buttons that multiply x by their value
    foreach val $args {
        button $f.$b -text $val \
            -command "set x \[expr \$x * $val\]"
        pack $f.$b -side left
        incr b
    }
    pack .label $f
}
set x 1
Trouble -1 4 7 36
```

The example uses a label widget to display the current value of `x`. The `textvariable` attribute is used so that the label displays the current value of the variable, which is always a global variable. It is not necessary to have a `global` command inside `Trouble` because the value of `x` is not used there. The button's command is executed later at the global scope.

The definition of the button's command is ugly, though. The value of the loop variable `val` is needed when the button is defined, but the rest of the substitutions need to be deferred until later. The variable substitution of `$x` and the command substitution of `expr` are suppressed by quoting with backslashes:

```
set x \[expr \$x * $val\]
```

In contrast, the following command assigns a constant expression to `x` each time the button is clicked, and it depends on the current value of `x`, which is not defined the first time through the loop. Clearly, this is incorrect:

```
button $f.$b -text $val \
    -command "set x [expr $x * $val]"
```

Another incorrect approach is to quote the whole command with braces. This defers too much, preventing the value of `val` from being used at the correct time.

Use procedures for button commands.

The general technique for dealing with these sorts of scoping problems is to introduce Tcl procedures for use as the button commands. Example 24–2 introduces a little procedure to encapsulate the expression:

Example 24–2 Fixing the troublesome situation.

```
proc LessTrouble { args } {
   set b 0
   label .label -textvariable x
   set f [frame .buttons -borderwidth 10]
   foreach val $args {
      button $f.$b -text $val \
         -command "UpdateX $val"
      pack $f.$b -side left
      incr b
   }
   pack .label $f
}
proc UpdateX { val } {
   global x
   set x [expr $x * $val]
}
set x 1
LessTrouble -1 4 7 36
```

It may seem just like extra work to introduce the helper procedure, `UpdateX`. However, it makes the code clearer in two ways. First, you do not have to struggle with backslashes to get the button command defined correctly. Second, the code is much clearer about the function of the button. Its job is to update the global variable `x`.

You can generalize `UpdateX` to work on any variable by passing the name of the variable to update. Now it becomes much like the `incr` command:

```
button $f.$b -text $val -command "Update x $val"
```

The definition of `Update` uses `upvar`, which is explained on page 79, to manipulate the named variable in the global scope:

```
proc Update {varname val} {
    upvar #0 $varname x
    set x [expr $x * $val]
}
```

Double quotes are used in the button command to allow `$val` to be substituted. Whenever you use quotes like this, you have to be aware of the possible values for the substitutions. If you are not careful, the command you create may not be parsed correctly. The safest way to generate the command is with `list`:

```
button $f.$b -text $val -command [list UpdateX $val]
```

Using `list` ensures that the command is a list of two elements, `UpdateX` and the value of `val`. This is important because `UpdateX` takes only a single argument. If `val` contained white space then the resulting command would be parsed into more words than you expected. Of course, in this case we plan to always call `LessTrouble` with an integer value, which does not contain white space.

Example 24–3 provides a more straightforward application of procedures for button commands. In this case the advantage of the procedure `MaxLineLength` is that it creates a scope for the local variables used during the button action. This ensures that the local variables do not accidentally conflict with global variables used elsewhere in the program. There is also the standard advantage of a procedure, which is that you may find another use for the action in another part of your program.

Example 24–3 A button associated with a Tcl procedure.

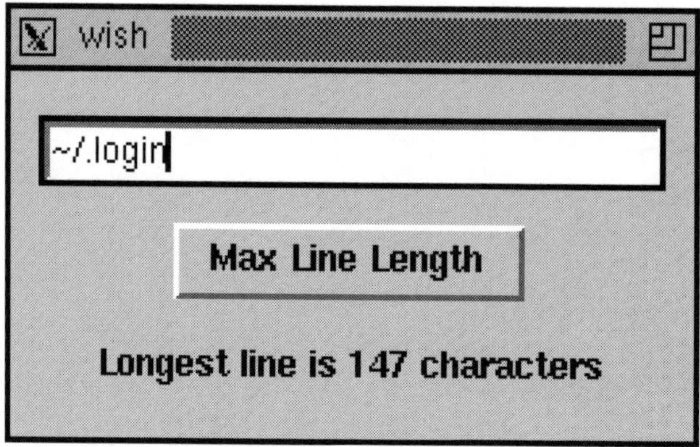


```
proc MaxLineLength { file } {
    set max 0
    if [catch {open $file} in] {
        return $in
    }
    foreach line [split [read $in] \n] {
        set len [string length $line]
```

```
        if {$len > $max} {
            set max $len
        }
    }
    return "Longest line is $max characters"
}
# Create an entry to accept the file name,
# a label to display the result
# and a button to invoke the action
. config -borderwidth 10
entry .e -width 30 -bg white -relief sunken
button .doit -text "Max Line Length" \
    -command {.label config -text [MaxLineLength [.e get]]}
label .label -text "Enter file name"
pack .e .doit .label -side top -pady 5
```

The example is centered around the `MaxLineLength` procedure. This opens a file and loops over the lines finding the longest one. The file `open` is protected with `catch` in case the user enters a bogus file name. In that case, the procedure returns the error message from `open`. Otherwise, the procedure returns a message about the longest line in the file. The local variables `in`, `max`, and `len` are hidden inside the scope of the procedure.

The user interface has three widgets: an entry for user input, the button, and a label to display the result. These are packed into a vertical stack, and the main window is given a border. Obviously this simple interface can be improved in several ways. There is no `Quit` button, for example.

All the action happens in the button command:

```
.label config -text [MaxLineLength [.e get]]
```

Braces are used when defining the button command so that the command substitutions all happen when the button is clicked. The value of the entry widget is obtained with `.e get`. This value is passed into `MaxLineLength`, and the result is configured as the text for the label. This command is still a little complex for a button command. For example, suppose you wanted to invoke the same command when the user pressed `<Return>` in the entry. You would end up repeating this command in the entry binding. It might be better to introduce a one-line procedure to capture this action so it is easy to bind the action to more than one user action. Here is how that might look:

```
proc Doit {} {
    .label config -text [MaxLineLength [.e get]]
}
button .doit -text "Max Line Length" -command Doit
bind .e <Return> Doit
```

Chapter 23 describes the `bind` command in detail, Chapter 26 describes the label widget, and Chapter 29 describes the entry widget.

Buttons Associated with Tcl Variables

The checkbutton and radiobutton widgets are associated with a global Tcl variable. When one of these buttons is clicked, a value is assigned to the Tcl variable. In addition, if the variable is assigned a value elsewhere in the program, the appearance of the checkbutton or radiobutton is updated to reflect the new value. A set of radiobuttons all share the same global variable. The set represents a choice among mutually exclusive options. In contrast, each checkbutton has its own global variable.

The `ShowChoices` example uses a set of radiobuttons to display a set of mutually exclusive choices in a user interface. The `ShowBooleans` example uses checkbutton widgets:

Example 24–4 Radiobuttons and checkbuttons.

```
proc ShowChoices { parent varname args } {
    set f [frame $parent.choices -borderwidth 5]
    set b 0
    foreach item $args {
        radiobutton $f.$b -variable $varname \
            -text $item -value $item
        pack $f.$b -side left
        incr b
    }
    pack $f -side top
}
proc ShowBooleans { parent args } {
    set f [frame $parent.booleans -borderwidth 5]
    set b 0
    foreach item $args {
        checkbutton $f.$b -text $item -variable $item
        pack $f.$b -side left
        incr b
    }
    pack $f -side top
}
set choice kiwi
ShowChoices {} choice apple orange peach kiwi strawberry
set Bold 1 ; set Italic 1
ShowBooleans {} Bold Italic Underline
```

The `ShowChoices` procedure takes as arguments the parent frame, the name of a variable, and a set of possible values for that variable. If the parent frame is null, `{}`, then the interface is packed into the main window. `ShowChoices` creates a radiobutton for each value, and it puts the value into the text of the button. It also has to specify the value to assign to the variable when the button is clicked because the default value associated with a radiobutton is the empty string.

The `ShowBooleans` procedure is similar to `ShowChoices`. It takes a set of variable names as arguments, and it creates a checkbutton for each variable. The default values for the variable associated with a checkbutton are zero and one, which is fine for this example. If you need particular values, you can specify them with the `-onvalue` and `-offvalue` options.

Radiobuttons and checkbuttons can have commands associated with them, just like ordinary buttons. The command is invoked after the associated Tcl variable has been updated. Remember that the Tcl variable associated with the button is defined in the global scope. For example, you could log the changes to variables as shown in the next example.

Example 24–5 A command on a radiobutton or checkbutton.

```
proc PrintByName { varname } {
    upvar #0 $varname var
    puts stdout "$varname = $var"
}
checkbutton $f.$b -text $item -variable $item \
    -command [list PrintByName $item]
radiobutton $f.$b -variable $varname \
    -text $item -value $item \
    -command [list PrintByName $varname]
```


Button Attributes

Table 24–1 lists the attributes for the button, checkbutton, menubutton, and radiobutton widgets. Unless otherwise indicated, the attributes apply to all of these widget types. Chapters 34, 35, and 36 discuss many of these attributes in more detail. Some attributes are ignored on the Windows and Macintosh platforms because they are not supported by the native button widgets.

The table uses the resource name for the attributes, which has capitals at internal word boundaries. In Tcl commands the attributes are specified with a dash and they are all lowercase. Compare:

```
option add *Menubutton.activeBackground: red
.mb configure -activebackground red
```

The first command defines a resource database entry that covers all menubuttons and gives them a red active background. This only affects menubuttons created after the database entry is added. The second command changes an existing menubutton (.mb) to have a red active background. Note the difference in capitalization of background in the two commands. The resource database is introduced on page 229, and Chapter 25 explains how to use the resource database in more detail.

Table 24–1 Resource names of attributes for all button widgets.

activeBackground	Background color when the mouse is over the button.
activeForeground	Text color when the mouse is over the button.
anchor	Anchor point for positioning the text.
background	The normal background color.
bitmap	A bitmap to display instead of text.
borderWidth	Width of the border around the button.
command	Tcl command to invoke when button is clicked.
cursor	Cursor to display when mouse is over the widget.
default	active displays as a default button. normal and disabled display as normal button. See page 603 (Tk 8.0).
direction	up, down, left, right, active. Offset direction for posting menus. menubutton. (Tk 8.0).
disabledForeground	Foreground (text) color when button is disabled.
font	Font for the text.
foreground	Foreground (text) color. (Also fg).
height	Height, in lines for text, or screen units for images.
highlightBackground	Focus highlight color when widget does not have focus.
highlightColor	Focus highlight color when widget has focus.
highlightThickness	Width of highlight border.
image	Image to display instead of text or bitmap.
indicatorOn	Boolean that controls if the indicator is displayed: checkbutton, menubutton, or radiobutton.
justify	Text justification: center, left, or right.
menu	Menu posted when menubutton is clicked.
offValue	Value for Tcl variable when checkbutton is not selected.
onValue	Value for Tcl variable when checkbutton is selected.
padX	Extra space to the left and right of the button text.
padY	Extra space above and below the button text.

Table 24–1 Resource names of attributes for all button widgets. (Continued)

`relief`	`flat`, `sunken`, `raised`, `groove`, `solid` or `ridge`.
`selectColor`	Color for selector. `checkbutton` or `radiobutton`.
`selectImage`	Alternate graphic image for selector: `checkbutton` or `radiobutton`.
`state`	Enabled (`normal`) or deactivated (`disabled`).
`takeFocus`	Control focus changes from keyboard traversal.
`text`	Text to display in the button.
`textVariable`	Tcl variable that has the value of the text.
`underline`	Index of text character to underline.
`value`	Value for Tcl variable when `radiobutton` is selected.
`variable`	Tcl variable associated with the button: `checkbutton` or `radiobutton`.
`width`	Width in characters for text, or screen units for image.
`wrapLength`	Maximum character length before text is wrapped, *in screen units.*

Button Operations

Table 24–2 summarizes the operations on button widgets. In the table `$w` is a button, checkbutton, radiobutton, or menubutton, except when noted. For the most part these operations are used by the script libraries that implement the bindings for buttons. The `cget` and `configure` operations are the most commonly used by applications.

Table 24–2 Button operations.

`$w cget` *`option`*	Return the value of the specified attribute.
`$w configure ?`*`option`*`? ?`*`value`*`? ...`	Query or manipulate the configuration information for the widget.
`$w deselect`	Deselect the `radiobutton` or `checkbutton`. Set the `radiobutton` variable to the null string. Set the `checkbutton` variable to the off value.
`$w flash`	Redisplay the button several times in alternate colors.
`$w invoke`	Invoke the command associated with the button.
`$w select`	Select the `radiobutton` or `checkbutton`, setting the associated variable appropriately.

Menus and Menubuttons

A menu presents a set of button-like *menu entries* to users. A menu entry is not a full fledged Tk widget. Instead, you create a menu widget and then add entries to the menu as shown in the following examples. There are several kinds of menu entries:

- Command entries are like buttons.
- Check entries are like checkbuttons.
- Radio entries are like radiobuttons.
- Separator entries are used to visually set apart entries.
- Cascade entries are used to post submenus.
- Tear-off entries are used to detach a menu from its menu button so that it becomes a new top-level window.

A menubutton is a special kind of button that posts (i.e., displays) a menu when you press it. If you click on a menubutton, then the menu is posted and remains posted until you click on a menu entry to select it, or click outside the menu to dismiss it. If you press and hold the menubutton, then the menu is unposted when you release the mouse. If you release the mouse over the menu, it selects the menu entry that was under the mouse.

You can have a command associated with a menubutton, too. The command is invoked *before* the menu is posted, which means you can compute the menu contents when the user presses the menubutton.

Our first menu example creates a sampler of the different entry types:

Example 24–6 A menu sampler.

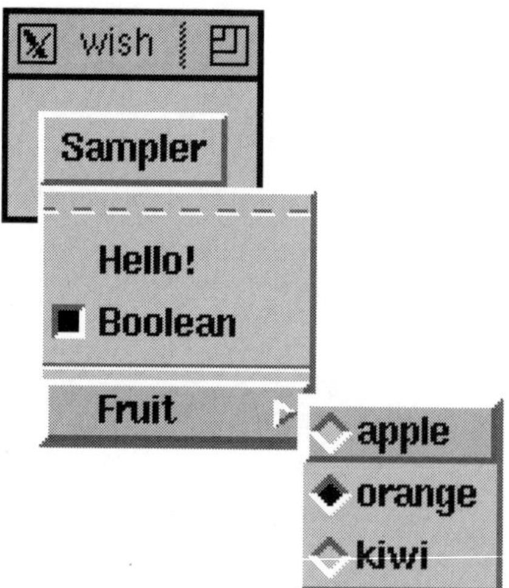


```
menubutton .mb -text Sampler -menu .mb.menu
pack .mb -padx 10 -pady 10
set m [menu .mb.menu -tearoff 1]
```

```
$m add command -label Hello! -command {puts "Hello, World!"}
$m add check -label Boolean -variable foo \
    -command {puts "foo = $foo"}
$m add separator
$m add cascade -label Fruit -menu $m.sub1
set m2 [menu $m.sub1 -tearoff 0]
$m2 add radio -label apple -variable fruit -value apple
$m2 add radio -label orange -variable fruit -value orange
$m2 add radio -label kiwi -variable fruit -value kiwi
```

The example creates a menubutton and two menus. The main menu `.mb.menu` is a child of the menubutton `.mb`. This relationship is necessary so the menu displays correctly when the menubutton is selected. Similarly, the cascaded submenu `.mb.menu.sub1` is a child of the main menu. The first menu entry is represented by the dashed line. This is a tear-off entry that, when selected, makes a copy of the menu in a new top-level window. This is useful if the menu operations are invoked frequently. The `-tearoff 0` argument is used when creating the submenu to eliminate its tear-off entry.

The command, radio, and check entries are similar to the corresponding button types. The configuration options for menu entries are similar to those for buttons. The main difference is that the text string in the menu entry is defined with the `-label` option, not `-text`. Table 24–6 gives the complete set of options for menu entries.

The cascade menu entry is associated with another menu. It is distinguished by the small right arrow in the entry. When you select the entry, the submenu is posted. It is possible to have several levels of cascaded menus. There is no limit to the number of levels, except that your users will complain if you nest too many menus.

A Menu Bar

You can create a menu bar manually by packing several menubuttons into a frame. The default bindings on menubuttons are such that you can drag your mouse over the menu bar and the different menus will display as you drag over their menubutton.

Tk 8.0 lets you create a menu bar as a horizontal menu that is associated with a top-level window. On Windows and UNIX the menu is displayed along the top of the window. On Macintosh this menu replaces the main menu along the top of the screen when the window is activated. The menu bar menu should have all cascade entries so that when you select an entry another menu is displayed. This is illustrated in Example 24–7. It defines variables that store the names of the menu widgets:

```
set $m [menu .menubar.m$m]
```

This creates a variable named `File`, `Edit`, and `Help` that store the names of the menu widgets. This trick is generalized on page 318 in a package that hides the menu widget names.

Example 24–7 A menu bar in Tk 8.0

```
menu .menubar
# attach it to the main window
. config -menu .menubar
# Create more cascade menus
foreach m {File Edit Help} {
    set $m [menu .menubar.m$m]
    .menubar add cascade -label $m -menu .menubar.m$m
}
$File add command -label Quit -command exit
# add more menu items...
```

System Menus

The Tk 8.0 menu bar implementation can add entries to the Windows system menu, the Macintosh Apple menu, and the Help menu on all platforms. This works by recognizing special names. For example, if the menu bar is `.menubar`, then the special names are `.menubar.system`, `.menubar.apple`, and `.menubar.help`. The Help menu is right justified on all platforms. The Apple menu is normally used by applications for their `About...` entry. The entries you add to the Apple menu are added to the top of the menu. The System menu appears in the Windows title bar and has entries such as `Close` and `Minimize`.

Pop-Up Menus

A pop-up menu is not associated with a menubutton. Instead, it is posted in response to a keystroke or other event in the application. The `tk_popup` command posts a pop-up menu:

`tk_popup` *`menu x y ?entry?`*

The last argument specifies the entry to activate when the menu is posted. It is an optional parameter that defaults to 1, which avoids the tear-off entry in position zero. The menu is posted at the specified X and Y coordinates in its parent widget.

Option Menus

An option menu represents a choice with a set of radio entries, and it displays the current choice in the text of the menubutton. The `tk_optionMenu` command creates a menubutton and a menu full of radio entries:

`tk_optionMenu` *`w varname firstValue ?value value ...?`*

The first argument is the pathname of the menubutton to create. The second is the variable name. The third is the initial value for the variable, and the rest are the other choices for the value. The menubutton displays the current choice and a small symbol, the indicator, to indicate it is an option menu.

Multicolumn Palette Menus

Tk 8.0 adds a `-columnbreak` menu entry attribute that puts the entry at the top of a new column. This is most useful when the menu consists of several images that are arranged as a palette. Set the entry's image with the `-image` attribute. You can create checkbutton and radiobutton entries that have images and no indicator by using the `-hidemargin` attribute. In this case, a selected entry is indicated by drawing a solid rectangle around it.

Keyboard Traversal

The default bindings for menus allow for keyboard selection of menu entries. The selection process is started by pressing `<Alt-x>` where *x* is the distinguishing letter for a menubutton. The `underline` attribute of a menubutton is used to highlight the appropriate letter. The `underline` value is a number that specifies a character position, and the count starts at zero. For example, a `File` menu with a highlighted `F` is created like this:

```
menubutton .menubar.file -text File -underline 0 \
	-menu .menubar.file.m
```

When the user types `<Alt-f>` over the main window, the menu is posted. The case of the highlighted letter is not important.

After a menu is posted, the arrow keys change the selected entry. The `<Up>` and `<Down>` keys move within a menu, and the `<Left>` and `<Right>` keys move between adjacent menus. The bindings assume that you create your menus from left to right.

If any of the menu entries have a letter highlighted with the `-underline` option, typing that letter invokes that menu entry. For example, an `Export` entry that is invoked by typing `x` can be created like this:

```
.menubar.file.m add command -label Export -underline 1 \
	-command File_Export
```

The `<space>` and `<Return>` keys invoke the menu entry that is currently selected. The `<Escape>` key aborts the menu selection and removes the menu.

Manipulating Menus and Menu Entries

There are a number of operations that apply to menu entries. We have already introduced the `add` operation. The `entryconfigure` operation is similar to the `configure` operation for widgets. It accepts the same attribute-value pairs used when the menu entry was added. The `delete` operation removes a range of menu entries. The rest of the operations are used by the library scripts that implement the standard bindings for menus.

A menu entry is referred to by an *index*. The index can be numerical, counting from zero, or symbolic. Table 24–3 summarizes the index formats. One of the most useful indices is a pattern that matches the `label` in the menu entry. The

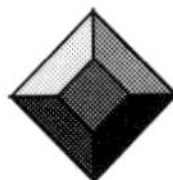

pattern matching is done with the rules of `string match`. Using a pattern eliminates the need to keep track of the numerical indices.

Table 24–3 Menu entry index keywords

index	A numerical index counting from zero.
`active`	The activated entry, either because it is under the mouse or has been activated by keyboard traversal.
`end`	The last menu entry.
`last`	The same as `end`.
`none`	No entry at all.
`@`*ycoord*	The entry under the given Y coordinate. Use `@%y` in bindings.
pattern	A `string match` pattern to match the label of a menu entry.

Table 24–4 summarizes the complete set of menu operations. In the table, `$w` is a menu widget.

Table 24–4 Menu operations.

`$w activate` *index*	Highlight the specified entry.
`$w add` *type ?option value? ...*	Add a new menu entry of the specified type with the given values for various attributes.
`$w cget` *option*	Return the value for the configuration *option*.
`$w clone`	Make a linked copy of the menu. This is used to implement tear-offs and menu bars.
`$w configure` *?option? ?value? ...*	Return the configuration information for the menu.
`$w delete` *i1 ?i2?*	Delete the menu entries from index *i1* to *i2*.
`$w entrycget` *index option*	Return the value of *option* for the specified entry.
`$w entryconfigure` *index ?option? ?value? ...*	Query or modify the configuration information for the specified menu entry.
`$w index` *index*	Return the numerical value of *index*.
`$w insert` *type index ?option value? ...*	Like `add`, but insert the new entry after the specified *index*.
`$w invoke` *index*	Invoke the command associated with the entry.
`$w post` *x y*	Display the menu at the specified coordinates.
`$w postcascade index`	Display the cascade menu from entry *index*.
`$w type` *index*	Return the type of the entry at *index*.

Table 24–4 Menu operations. (Continued)

`$w unpost`	Unmap the menu.
`$w ypostion` *`index`*	Return the Y coordinate of the top of the entry.

Menu Attributes

A menu has a few global attributes, and then each menu entry has many button-like attributes that describe its appearance and behavior. Table 24–5 specifies the attributes that apply globally to the menu, unless overridden by a per entry attribute. The table uses the X resource names, which may have a capital at interior word boundaries. In Tcl commands use all lowercase and a leading dash.

Table 24–5 Menu attribute resource names.

`activeBackground`	Background color when the mouse is over a menu entry.
`activeForeground`	Text color when the mouse is over a menu entry.
`activeBorderWidth`	Width of the raised border around active entries.
`background`	The normal background color for menu entries.
`borderWidth`	Width of the border around all the menu entries.
`cursor`	Cursor to display when mouse is over the menu.
`disabledForeground`	Foreground (text) color when menu entries are disabled.
`font`	Default font for the text.
`foreground`	Foreground color. (Also `fg`).
`postCommand`	Tcl command to run just before the menu is posted.
`selectColor`	Color for selector in check and radio type entries.
`takeFocus`	Control focus changes from keyboard traversal.
`tearOff`	True if menu should contain a tear-off entry.
`tearOffCommand`	Command to execute when menu is torn off. Two arguments are added: the original menu and the new tear-off.
`type`	(Read-only) `normal`, `menubar`, or `tearoff`. (Tk 8.0).

Table 24–6 describes the attributes for menu entries, as you would use them in a Tcl command (i.e., all lowercase with a leading dash.) The attributes for menu entries are not supported directly by the resource database. However, Example 25–6 on page 329 describes how you can use the resource database for menu entries.

Table 24–6 Attributes for menu entries.

`-activebackground`	Background color when the mouse is over the entry.
`-activeforeground`	Foreground (text) color with mouse is over the entry.
`-accelerator`	Text to display as a reminder about keystroke binding.
`-background`	The normal background color.
`-bitmap`	A bitmap to display instead of text.
`-columnbreak`	Put the entry at the start of a new column. (Tk 8.0).
`-command`	Tcl command to invoke when entry is invoked.
`-font`	Default font for the text.
`-foreground`	Foreground color. (Also `fg`).
`-hidemargin`	Supress the margin reserved for button indicators. (Tk 8.0).
`-image`	Image to display instead of text or bitmap.
`-label`	Text to display in the menu entry.
`-justify`	Text justification: `center`, `left`, or `right`.
`-menu`	Menu posted when `cascade` entry is invoked.
`-offvalue`	Variable value when `check` entry is not selected.
`-onvalue`	Value for Tcl variable when `check` entry is selected.
`-selectcolor`	Color for selector: `check` and `radio` entries.
`-state`	The state: `normal`, `active`, or `disabled`
`-underline`	Index of text character to underline.
`-value`	Value for Tcl variable when `radiobutton` entry is selected.
`-variable`	Tcl variable associated with the `check` or `radio` entry.

A Menu by Name Package

If your application supports extensible or user-defined menus, then it can be tedious to expose all the details of the Tk menus. The examples in this section create a little package that lets users refer to menus and entries by name. In addition, the package keeps keystroke accelerators for menus consistent with bindings.

The `Menu_Setup` procedure initializes the package. It creates a frame to hold the set of menu buttons, and it initializes some state variables: the frame for the menubuttons and a counter used to generate widget pathnames. All the global state for the package is kept in the array called `menu`.

The `Menu` procedure creates a menubutton and a menu. It records the association between the text label of the menubutton and the menu that was created for it. This mapping is used throughout the rest of the package so that the client of the package can refer to the menu by its label (e.g., `File`) as opposed to the internal Tk pathname, (e.g., `.top.menubar.file.menu`).

Example 24–8 A simple menu by name package.

```
proc Menu_Setup { menubar } {
    global menu
    frame $menubar
    pack $menubar -side top -fill x
    set menu(menubar) $menubar
    set menu(uid) 0
}
proc Menu { label } {
    global menu
    if [info exists menu(menu,$label)] {
        error "Menu $label already defined"
    }
    # Create the menubutton and its menu
    set name $menu(menubar).mb$menu(uid)
    set menuName $name.menu
    incr menu(uid)
    set mb [menubutton $name -text $label -menu $menuName]
    pack $mb -side left
    menu $menuName -tearoff 1
    # Remember the name to menu mapping
    set menu(menu,$label) $menuName
}
```


These procedures are repeated in Example 24–9, except they use the Tk 8.0 menu bar mechanism. The rest of the procedures in the package are the same with either version of menu bars.

Example 24–9 Using the Tk 8.0 menu bar facility.

```
proc Menu_Setup { menubar } {
    global menu
    menu $menubar
    # Associated menu with its main window
    set top [winfo parent $menubar]
    $top config -menu $menubar
    set menu(menubar) $menubar
    set menu(uid) 0
}
proc Menu { label } {
    global menu
    if [info exists menu(menu,$label)] {
        error "Menu $label already defined"
    }
    # Create the cascade menu
    set menuName $menu(menubar).mb$menu(uid)
    incr menu(uid)
```

```
    menu $menuName -tearoff 1
    $menu(menubar) add cascade -label $label -menu $menuName
    # Remember the name to menu mapping
    set menu(menu,$label) $menuName
}
```

Once the menu is set up, the `menu` array is used to map from a menu name, like `File`, to the Tk widget name such as `.menubar.mb3`. Even though this can be done with a couple lines of Tcl code, the mapping is put inside the `MenuGet` procedure to hide the implementation. `MenuGet` uses `return -code error` if the menu name is unknown, which changes the error reporting slightly as shown in Example 6–19 on page 74. If the user specifies a bogus menu name, the undefined variable error is caught and a more informative error is raised instead. `MenuGet` is private to the package, so it does not have an underscore in its name.

Example 24–10 `MenuGet` maps from name to menu.

```
proc MenuGet {menuName} {
    global menu
    if [catch {set menu(menu,$menuName)} m] {
        return -code error "No such menu: $menuName"
    }
    return $m
}
```

The procedures `Menu_Command`, `Menu_Check`, `Menu_Radio`, and `Menu_Separator` are simple wrappers around the basic menu commands. They use `MenuGet` to map from the menu label to the Tk widget name.

Example 24–11 Adding menu entries.

```
proc Menu_Command { menuName label command } {
    set m [MenuGet $menuName]
    $m add command -label $label -command $command
}

proc Menu_Check { menuName label var { command {} } } {
    set m [MenuGet $menuName]
    $m add check -label $label -command $command \
        -variable $var
}

proc Menu_Radio { menuName label var {val {}} {command {}} }
{
    set m [MenuGet $menuName]
    if {[string length $val] == 0} {
        set val $label
    }
    $m add radio -label $label -command $command \
        -value $val -variable $var
}
```

```
proc Menu_Separator { menuName } {
   [MenuGet $menuName] add separator
}
```

Creating a cascaded menu also requires saving the mapping between the label in the cascade entry and the Tk pathname for the submenu. This package imposes a restriction that different menus, including submenus, cannot have the same label.

Example 24–12 A wrapper for cascade entries.

```
proc Menu_Cascade { menuName label } {
   global menu
   set m [MenuGet $menuName]
   if [info exists menu(menu,$label)] {
      error "Menu $label already defined"
   }
   set sub $m.sub$menu(uid)
   incr menu(uid)
   menu $sub -tearoff 0
   $m add cascade -label $label -menu $sub
   set menu(menu,$label) $sub
}
```

Creating the sampler menu with this package looks like this:

Example 24–13 Using the menu by name package.

```
Menu_Setup .menubar
Menu Sampler
Menu_Command Sampler Hello! {puts "Hello, World!"}
Menu_Check Sampler Boolean foo {puts "foo = $foo"}
Menu_Separator Sampler
Menu_Cascade Sampler Fruit
Menu_Radio Fruit apple fruit
Menu_Radio Fruit orange fruit
Menu_Radio Fruit kiwi fruit
```


Menu Accelerators

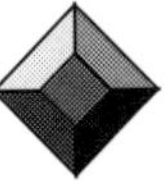

The final touch on the menu package is to support accelerators in a consistent way. A menu entry can display another column of information that is assumed to be a keystroke identifier to remind users of a binding that also invokes the menu entry. However, there is no guarantee that this string is correct, or that if the user changes the binding that the menu will be updated. Example 24–14 shows the `Menu_Bind` procedure that takes care of this.

Example 24–14 Keeping the accelerator display up to date.

```
proc Menu_Bind { what sequence menuName label } {
    global menu
    set m [MenuGet $menuName]
    if [catch {$m index $label} index] {
        error "$label not in menu $menuName"
    }
    set command [$m entrycget $index -command]
    bind $what $sequence $command
    $m entryconfigure $index -accelerator $sequence
}
```

The `Menu_Bind` command uses the `index` operation to find out what menu entry has the given label. It gets the command for that entry with `entrycget` and uses this command in a binding. It updates the display of the accelerator using the `entryconfigure` operation. This approach has the advantage of keeping the keystroke command consistent with the menu command, as well as updating the display. To try `Menu_Bind`, add an empty frame to the sampler example, and bind a keystroke to it and one of the menu commands, like this:

```
frame .body -width 100 -height 50
pack .body ; focus .body
Menu_Bind .body <space> Sampler Hello!
```

CHAPTER 25

The Resource Database

This chapter describes the use of the resource database, and how users can define buttons and menus via resource specifications. This chapter describes the `option` command.

Tk supports a resource database that holds specifications of widget attributes such as fonts and colors. You can control all attributes of the Tk widgets through the resource database. It can also be used as a more general database of application-specific parameter settings.

Because a Tk application can use Tcl for customization, it might not seem necessary to use the resource database. The resource database is, however, a useful tool for your Tk application. A developer can make global changes with just a few database entries. In addition, it lets users and site administrators customize applications without modifying the code.

An Introduction to Resources

When a Tk widget is created, its attributes are set by one of three sources. It is important to note that Tcl command specifications have priority over resource database specifications:

- The most evident source of attributes are the options in Tcl commands, such as the `-text quit` attribute specification for a button.
- If an attribute is not specified on the command line, then the resource database is queried as described later.
- If there is nothing in the resource database, then a hard-coded value from the widget implementation is used.

The resource database consists of a set of keys and values. Unlike many databases, however, the keys are patterns that are matched against the names of widgets and attributes. This makes it possible to specify attribute values for a large number of widgets with just a few database entries. In addition, the resource database can be shared by many applications, so users and administrators can define common attributes for their whole set of applications.

The resource database is maintained in main memory by the Tk toolkit. On UNIX the database is initialized from the `RESOURCE_MANAGER` property on the root window, or the `.Xdefaults` file in your home directory. On Windows and Macintosh there are a few resources added by the `tk.tcl` library file. Additional files can be explicitly loaded with the `option readfile` command, and individual database entries are added with the `option add` Tcl command.

The initialization of the database is different from the Xt toolkit, which loads specifications from as many as five different files to allow per-user, per-site, per-application, per-machine, and per-user-per-application specifications. You can achieve the same effect in Tk, but you must do it yourself. Example 39–1 on page 500 gives a partial solution.

Resource Patterns

The pattern language for the keys is related to the naming convention for Tk widgets. Recall that a widget name reflects its position in the hierarchy of windows. You can think of the resource names as extending the hierarchy one more level at the bottom to account for all the attributes of each individual widget. There is also a new level of the hierarchy at the top to specify the application by name. For example, the database could contain an entry like the following in order to define a font for the `quit` button in a frame called `.buttons`:

```
Tk.buttons.quit.font: fixed
```

The leading `Tk.` matches the default class name for Tcl/Tk applications. You could also specify a more specific application name, such as `exmh`, or an asterisk to match any application:

```
*buttons.quit.font: fixed
```

Resource keys can also specify *classes* of widgets and attributes as opposed to individual instances. The `quit` button, for example, is an instance of the `Button` class. Class names for widgets are the same as the Tcl command used to create them, except for a leading capital. A class-oriented specification that would set the font for all buttons in the `.buttons` frame would be:

```
Tk.buttons.Button.font: fixed
```

Patterns let you replace one or more components of the resource name with an asterisk (`*`). For example, to set the font for all the widgets packed into the `.buttons` frame, you could use the resource name `*buttons*font`. Or, you could specify the font for all buttons with the pattern `*Button.font`. In these examples we have replaced the leading `Tk.` with an asterisk as well. It is the ability to collapse several layers of the hierarchical name with a single asterisk that makes it easy to specify attributes for many widgets with just a few database entries.

The tables in this book list attributes by their resource name. The resource names use a capital letter at the internal word boundaries. For example, if the command line switch is `-offvalue`, then the corresponding resource name is `offValue`. There are also class names for attributes, which are distinguished with a leading capital (e.g., `OffValue`).

Warning: Order is Important!

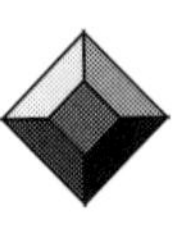

The matching between a widget name and the patterns in the database can be ambiguous. It is possible that multiple patterns can match the same widget. The way this is resolved in Tk is by the ordering of database entries, with later entries taking precedence. (This is different from the Xt toolkit, in which longer matching patterns have precedence, and instance specifications have priority over class specifications.) Suppose the database contained just two entries, in this order:

```
*Text*foreground: blue
*foreground: red
```

Despite the more specific `*Text*foreground` entry, all widgets will have a red foreground, even `text` widgets. For this reason you should list your most general patterns early in your resource files and give the more specific patterns later.

Tk also supports different priorities among resources as described in the next section. The ordering precedence described here applies to all resources with the same priority.

Loading Option Database Files

The `option` command manipulates the resource database. The first form of the command loads a file containing database entries:

```
option readfile filename ?priority?
```

The *`priority`* distinguishes different sources of resource information and gives them different priorities. Priority levels are numeric, from 0 to 100. However, symbolic names are defined for standard priorities. From lowest to highest, the standard priorities are `widgetDefault` (20), `startupFile` (40), `userDefault` (60), and `interactive` (80). These names can be abbreviated. The default priority is `interactive`.

Example 25–1 Reading an option database file.

```
if [file exists $appdefaults] {
    if [catch {option readfile $appdefaults startup} err] {
        puts stderr "error in $appdefaults: $err"
    }
}
```

The format of the entries in the file is:

```
key: value
```

The key has the pattern format previously described. The value can be anything, and there is no need to group multi-word values with any quoting characters. In fact, quotes will be picked up as part of the value.

Comment lines are introduced by the exclamation mark (!).

Example 25–2 A file containing resource specifications.

```
!
! Grey color set
! These values match those used by the Tk widgets on UNIX
!
*background:            #d9d9d9
*foreground:            black
*activeBackground:      #ececec
*activeForeground:      black
*selectColor:           #b03060
*selectBackground:      #c3c3c3
*troughColor:           #c3c3c3
*disabledforeground:#a3a3a3
```

The example resource file specifies the color scheme for the Tk widget set on UNIX that is based on a family of gray levels. Color highlighting shows up well against this backdrop. These colors are applied generically to all the widgets. The hexadecimal values for the colors specify two digits (eight bits) each for red, green, and blue. Chapter 35 describes the use of color in detail.

Adding Individual Database Entries

You can enter individual database entries with the `option add` Tcl command. This is appropriate to handle special cases, or if you do not want to manage a separate per application resource specification file. The command syntax is:

```
option add pattern value ?priority?
```

The *priority* is the same as that used with `option readfile`. The *pattern* and *value* are the same as in the file entries, except that the key does not have a trailing colon when specified in an `option add` command. If *value* contains spaces or special characters, you will need to group it like any other argument to a Tcl command. Some of the specifications from the last example could be added as follows:

```
option add *foreground black
option add *selectBackground #bfdfff
```

You can clear the option database:

```
option clear
```

However, on UNIX the database will be initialized from your `~/.Xdefaults` file, or the `RESOURCE_MANAGER` property on the root window, the next time the database is accessed.

Accessing the Database

Often it is sufficient to just set up the database and let the widget implementations use the values. However, it is also possible to record application-specific information in the database. To fetch a resource value, use `option get`:

```
option get window name class
```

The *window* is a Tk widget pathname. The *name* is a resource name. In this case, it is not a pattern or a full name. Instead, it is the resource name as specified in the tables in this book. Similarly, the *class* is a simple class name. It is possible to specify a null name or class. If there is no matching database entry, `option get` returns the empty string.

It is not possible to enumerate the database, nor can you detect the difference between a value that is the empty string and the absense of a value. You can work around this by introducing well-known resource names that list other resources. This trick is used in the next section.

User-Defined Buttons

Suppose you want users to be able to define a set of their own buttons for frequently executed commands. Or, perhaps users can augment the application with their own Tcl code. The following scheme, which is based on an idea from John LoVerso, lets them define buttons to invoke their own code or their favorite commands.

The application creates a special frame to hold the user-defined buttons and places it appropriately. Assume the frame is created like this:

```
frame .user -class User
```

The class specification for the frame means that we can name resources for the widgets inside the frame relative to `*User`. Users specify the buttons that go in the frame via a personal file containing resource specifications.

The first problem is that there is no means to enumerate the database, so we must create a resource that lists the names of the user-defined buttons. We use the name `buttonlist` and make an entry for `*User.buttonlist` that specifies which buttons are being defined. It is possible to use artificial resource names (e.g., `buttonlist`), but they must be relative to an existing Tk widget.

Example 25–3 Using resources to specify user-defined buttons.

```
*User.buttonlist: save search justify quit
*User.save.text: Save
*User.save.command: File_Save
*User.search.text: Search
*User.search.command: Edit_Search
*User.justify.text: Justify
*User.justify.command: Edit_Justify
*user.quit.text: Quit
*User.quit.command: File_Quit
*User.quit.background: red
```

In this example, we have listed four buttons and specified some of the attributes for each, most importantly the `text` and `command` attributes. We are assuming, of course, that the application manual publishes a set of commands that users can invoke safely. In this simple example the commands are all one word, but there is no problem with multi-word commands. There is no interpretation done of the value, so it can include references to Tcl variables and nested command calls. The following code uses these resource specifications to define the buttons.

Example 25–4 `Resource_ButtonFrame` defines buttons based on resources.

```
proc Resource_ButtonFrame { f class } {
    frame $f -class $class -borderwidth 2
    pack $f -side top -fill x
    foreach b [option get $f buttonlist {}] {
        if [catch {button $f.$b}] {
            button $f.$b -font fixed
        }
        pack $f.$b -side right
    }
}
```

The `catch` phrase is introduced to handle a common problem with fonts and widget creation. If the user's resources specify a bogus or missing font, then the widget creation command will fail. The `catch` phrase guards against this case by falling back to the `fixed` font, which is guaranteed to exist. This problem is fixed in Tk 8.0 because the font mechanism will search for alternate fonts.

Example 25–5 assumes the resource specifications from Example 25–2 are in the file `button.resources`. It creates the user-defined buttons in the `.users` frame.

Example 25–5 Using `Resource_ButtonFrame`.

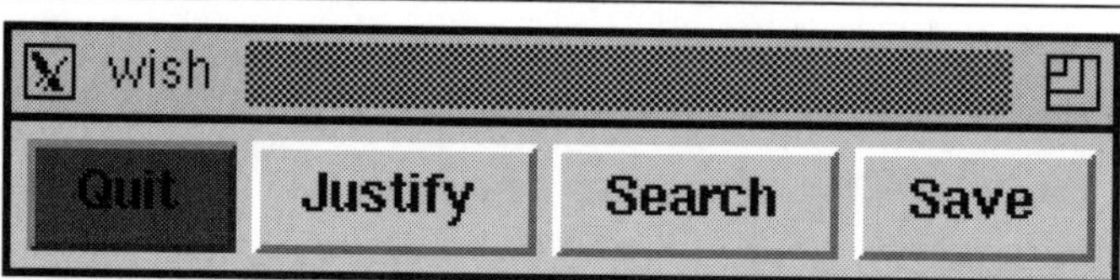


```
option readfile button.resources
Resource_ButtonFrame .user User
```

User-Defined Menus

User-defined menus can be set up with a similar scheme. However, it is more complex because there are no resources for specific menu entries. We must use more artificial resources to emulate this. We use `menulist` to name the set of menus. Then, for each of these, we define an `entrylist` resource. Finally, for each entry we define a few more resources. The name of the entry has to be combined with some type information, which leads to the following convention:

- `l_`*entry* is the label for the entry.
- `t_`*entry* is the type of the entry.
- `c_`*entry* is the command associated with the entry.
- `v_`*entry* is the variable associated with the entry.
- `m_`*entry* is the menu associated with the entry.

Example 25–6 Specifying menu entries via resources.

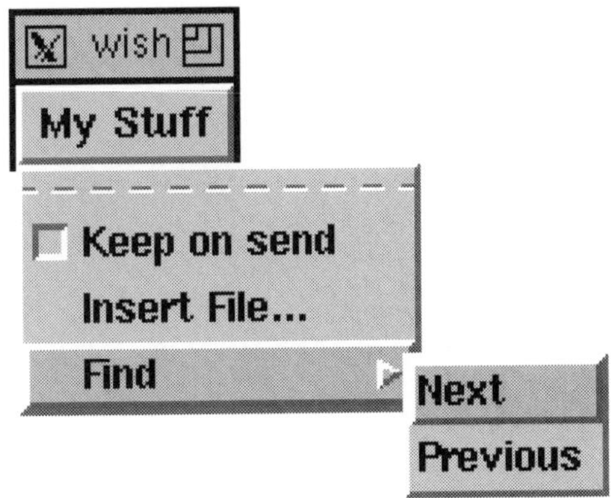


```
*User.menulist: stuff
*User.stuff.text: My stuff
*User.stuff.m.entrylist: keep insert find
*User.stuff.m.l_keep: Keep on send
*User.stuff.m.t_keep: check
*User.stuff.m.v_keep: checkvar
*User.stuff.m.l_insert: Insert File...
*User.stuff.m.c_insert: InsertFileDialog
*User.stuff.m.l_find: Find
*User.stuff.m.t_find: cascade
*User.stuff.m.m_find: find
*User.stuff.m.find.entrylist: next prev
*User.stuff.m.find.tearoff: 0
*User.stuff.m.find.l_next: Next
*User.stuff.m.find.c_next: Find_Next
*User.stuff.m.find.l_prev: Previous
*User.stuff.m.find.c_prev: Find_Previous
```

In the example, `.user.stuff` is a Tk menubutton. It has a menu as its child, `.user.stuff.m`, where the menu `.m` is set by convention. You will see this later in the code for `Resource_Menubar`. The `entrylist` for the menu is similar in spirit to the `buttonlist` resource. For each entry, however, we have to be a little creative with the next level of resource names. The following does not work:

```
*User.stuff.m.keep.label: Keep on send
```

The problem is that Tk does not directly support resources for menu entries, so it assumes `.stuff.m.keep` is a widget pathname, but it is not. You can add the resource, but you cannot retrieve it with `option get`. Instead, we must combine the attribute information (i.e., label) with the name of the entry:

```
*User.stuff.m.l_keep: Keep on send
```

You must do something similar if you want to define resources for items on a canvas, too, because that is not supported directly by Tk. The code to support menu definition by resources is shown in the next example:

Example 25–7 Defining menus from resource specifications.

```
proc Resource_Menubar { f class } {
    set f [frame $f -class $class]
    pack $f -side top
    foreach b [option get $f menulist {}] {
        set cmd [list menubutton $f.$b -menu $f.$b.m \
                    -relief raised]
        if [catch $cmd t] {
            eval $cmd {-font fixed}
        }
        if [catch {menu $f.$b.m}] {
            menu $f.$b.m -font fixed
        }
        pack $f.$b -side left
        ResourceMenu $f.$b.m
    }
}
proc ResourceMenu { menu } {
    foreach e [option get $menu entrylist {}] {
        set l [option get $menu l_$e {}]
        set c [option get $menu c_$e {}]
        set v [option get $menu v_$e {}]
        switch -- [option get $menu t_$e {}] {
            check {
                $menu add checkbutton -label $l -command $c \
                    -variable $v
            }
            radio {
                $menu add radiobutton -label $l -command $c \
                    -variable $v -value $l
            }
            separator {
                $menu add separator
            }
            cascade {
                set sub [option get $menu m_$e {}]
```

```
                if {[string length $sub] != 0} {
                    set submenu [menu $menu.$sub]
                    $menu add cascade -label $1 -command $c \
                        -menu $submenu
                    ResourceMenu $submenu
                }
            }
            default {
                $menu add command -label $1 -command $c
            }
        }
    }
}
```

Application and User Resources

The examples presented here are subset of a package I use in some large applications, *exmh* and *webtk*. The applications define nearly every button and menu via resources, so users and site administrators can redefine them. The `buttonlist`, `menulist`, and `entrylist` resources are generalized into user, site, and application lists. The application uses the application lists for the initial configuration. The site and user lists can add and remove widgets. For example:

- `buttonlist` - the application list of buttons
- `l-buttonlist` - the site-specific list of buttons to remove
- `lbuttonlist` - the site-specific list of buttons to add
- `u-buttonlist` - the per-user list of buttons to remove
- `ubuttonlist` - the per-user list of buttons to add

This idea and the initial implementation was contributed to *exmh* by Achim Bonet. The `Resource_GetFamily` procedure merges five sets of resources shown above. It can replace the option get commands for the `buttonlist`, `menulist`, and `entrylist` resources in Examples 25–4 and 25–7:

Example 25–8 `Resource_GetFamily` merges user and application resources.

```
proc Resource_GetFamily { w resname } {
    set res    [option get $w $resname {}]
    set lres   [option get $w l$resname {}]
    set ures   [option get $w u$resname {}]
    set l-res  [option get $w l-$resname {}]
    set u-res  [option get $w u-$resname {}]
    # Site-local deletions from application resources
    set list [lsubtract $res ${l-res}]
    # Site-local additions
    set list [concat $list $lres]
    # Per-user deletions
    set list [lsubtract $list ${u-res}]
    # Per-user additions
    return [concat $list $ures]
```

```
}
proc lsubtract { orig nuke } {
    # Remove elements in $nuke from $orig
    foreach x $nuke {
        set ix [lsearch $orig $x]
        if {$ix >= 0} {
            set orig [lreplace $orig $ix $ix]
        }
    }
    return $orig
}
```

Expanding Variables

If the command resource contains subsitution syntax like `$` and `[]`, then these are evaluated later when the command is invoked by the button or menu. This is because there is no interpretation of the command value when the widgets are created. However, it may be that you want variables substituted when the buttons and menus are defined. You can use the `subst` command to do this:

```
set cmd [$button cget -command]
$button config -command [subst $cmd]
```

Choosing the scope for the `subst` can be tricky. The previous command does the `subst` in the current scope. If this is the `Resource_ButtonFrame` procedure, then there are no interesting application-specific variables defined. The next command uses `uplevel` to do the `subst` in the scope of the caller of `Resource_ButtonFrame`. The `list` is necessary so that `uplevel` preserves the structure of the original `subst` command.

```
$button config -command [uplevel [list subst $cmd]]
```

If you do a `subst` in `ResourceMenu`, then you need to keep track of the recursion level to get back to the scope of the caller of `Resource_Menubar`. The next few lines show what changes in `RersourceMenu`:

```
proc ResourceMenu { menu {level 1} } {
    foreach e [option get $menu entrylist {}] {
        # code omitted
        set c [option get $menu c_$e {}]
        set c [uplevel $level [list subst $c]]
        # And the recursive call is
        ResourceMenu $submenu [expr $level+1]
        # more code omitted
    }
}
```

If you want the `subst` to occur in the global scope, use this:

```
$button config -command [uplevel #0 [list subst $cmd]]
```

However, the global scope may not be much different when you define the button than when the button is invoked. In practive, I have used `subst` to capture variables defined in the procedure that calls `Resource_Menubar`.

CHAPTER 26

Simple Tk Widgets

This chapter describes several simple Tk widgets: the `frame`, `label`, `message`, and `scale`. In general, these widgets require minimal setup to be useful in your application. The `bell` command rings the terminal bell.

This chapter describes four simple widgets and the `bell` command.

- The `frame` is a building block for widget layout. A `toplevel` is a frame that is detached from the main window.
- The `label` provides a line of read-only text.
- The `message` provides a read-only block of text that gets formatted onto several lines.
- The `scale` is a slider-like widget used to set a numeric value.
- The `bell` command rings the terminal bell.

Chapter 34, 35, and 36 go into more detail about some of the generic widget attributes shared by the widgets presented in this chapter. The examples in this chapter use the default widget attributes in most cases.

Frames and Toplevel Windows

Frames have been introduced before for use with the geometry managers. There is not much to a frame, except for its background color and border. You can also specify a colormap and visual type for a frame. Chapter 35 describes visual types and colormaps on page 456.

A toplevel widget is like a frame, except that it is created as a new main window. That is, it is not positioned inside the main window of the application.

This is useful for dialog boxes, for example. A toplevel has the same attributes as a frame, plus `screen` and `menu` attributes. The `menu` attribute is used to create menubars along the top edge of a toplevel. This feature was added in Tk 8.0, and it is described on page 313. On UNIX, the `screen` option lets you put the toplevel on any X display. The value of the `screen` option has the following format:

host:*display*.*screenNum*

For example, I have one X server on my workstation `sage` that controls two screens. My two screens are named `sage:0.0` and `sage:0.1`. If the *screenNum* specifier is left off, it defaults to `0`.

Attributes for Frames and Toplevels

Table 26–1 lists the attributes for the frame and toplevel widgets. The attributes are named according to their resource name, which includes a capital letter at internal word boundaries. When you specify an attribute in a Tcl command when creating or reconfiguring a widget, however, you specify the attribute with a dash and all lowercase letters. Chapter 25 explains how to use resource specifications for attributes. Chapters 34, 35, and 36 discuss many of these attributes in more detail.

Table 26–1 Attributes for frame and toplevel widgets.

`background`	Background color (also `bg`).
`borderWidth`	Extra space around the edge of the frame.
`class`	Resource class and binding class name.
`colormap`	The value is `new` or the name of a window.
`container`	If `true`, frame embeds another application.
`cursor`	Cursor to display when mouse is over the frame.
`height`	Height, in screen units.
`highlightBackground`	Focus highlight color when widget does not have focus.
`highlightColor`	Focus highlight color when widget has focus.
`highlightThickness`	Thickness of focus highlight rectangle.
`menu`	The menu to use for the menubar. Toplevel only.
`relief`	`flat`, `sunken`, `raised`, `groove`, `solid` or `ridge`.
`screen`	An X display specification. (Toplevel only, and this cannot be specified in the resource database).
`takeFocus`	Control focus changes from keyboard traversal.
`use`	A window ID from `winfo id`. This embeds the frame or toplevel into the specified window.

Table 26–1 Attributes for frame and toplevel widgets. (Continued)

`visual`	Type: `staticgrey`, `greyscale`, `staticcolor`, `pseudocolor`, `directcolor`, or `truecolor`.
`width`	Width, in screen units.

You cannot change the `class`, `colormap`, `visual`, or `screen` attributes after the frame or toplevel has been created. These settings are so fundamental that you need to destroy the frame and start over if you must change them.

Embedding Other Applications

The `container` and `use` attributes support application embedding. Embedding puts another application's window into a Tk frame or puts a Tk frame into another application. The `use` attribute specifies the ID of a window that will contain a Tk frame. *Wish* supports a `-use` command line argument that is used for the same pupose. Set the `container` attribute if you want to embed another window. For example, here is how to run another *wish* application and embed its window in one of your frames:

```
frame .embed -container 1 -bd 4 -bg red
exec wish somescript.tcl -use [winfo id .embed] &
```


Toplevel Window Styles

On Windows and Macintosh there are several styles of toplevel windows. They differ in their appearance and their behavior. On UNIX, toplevel windows are usually decorated by the window manager, which is a separate application. Chapter 38 describes how to interact with the window manager.

On Macintosh, Tk has an `unsupported1` command that you can use to set the window style:

```
unsupported1 style window style
```

The possible values for *`style`* include `documentProc`, `dBoxProc`, `plainDBox`, `altDBoxProc`, `movableDBoxProc`, `zoomDocProc`, `rDocProc`, `floatProc`, `floatZoomProc`, `floatSideProc`, or `floatSideZoomProc`. The `dBoxProc`, `plainDBox`, and `altDBoxProc` styles have no title bar, so there is no close box on them. The other styles have different title bars, a close box, and possibly a full-sized zoom box. The default style is `documentProc`. I used the following code to see what each looked like:

Example 26–1 Macintosh window styles.

```
set x {documentProc dBoxProc plainDBox altDBoxProc \
   movableDBoxProc zoomDocProc rDocProc floatProc \
   floatZoomProc floatSideProc floatSideZoomProc}
foreach y $x {
   toplevel .$y
```

```
        label .$y.l -text $y
        pack .$y.l -padx 40 -pady 20
        if [catch {unsupported1 style .$y $y} err] {
            puts "$y: $err"
        }
    }
```

This feature may appear as part of the `wm` command in future releases of Tk. On Windows you can get a couple different styles by using `transient` and `overrideredirect` windows, which are described on page 492.

The Label Widget

The label widget provides a read-only text label, and it has attributes that let you control the position of the label within the display space. Most commonly, however, you just need to specify the text for the label:

```
label .version -text "MyApp v1.0"
```

The text can be specified indirectly by using a Tcl variable to hold the text. In this case the label is updated whenever the value of the Tcl variable changes. The variable is used from the global scope, even if there happens to be a local variable by the same name when you create the widget inside a procedure:

```
set version "MyApp v1.0"
label .version -textvariable version
```

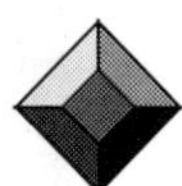

You can change the appearance of a label dynamically by using the `configure` widget operation. If you change the text or font of a label, you are liable to change the size of the widget, and this causes the packer to shuffle window positions. You can avoid this by specifying a width for the label that is large enough to hold all the strings you plan to display in it. The width is specified in characters, not screen coordinates:

Example 26–2 A label that displays different strings.

```
proc FixedWidthLabel { name values } {
    # name is a widget name to be created
    # values is a list of strings
    set maxWidth 0
    foreach value $values {
        if {[string length $value] > $maxWidth} {
            set maxWidth [string length $value]
        }
    }
    # Use -anchor w to left-justify short strings
    label $name -width $maxWidth -anchor w \
        -text [lindex $values 0]
    return $name
}
```

The `FixedWidthLabel` example is used to create a label with a width big enough to hold a set of different strings. It uses the `-anchor w` attribute to left justify strings that are shorter than the maximum. You can change the text for the label later by using the `configure` widget operation, which can be abbreviated to `config`:

```
FixedWidthLabel .status {OK Busy Error}
.status config -text Busy
```

A label can display a bitmap or image instead of a text string, which is described in Chapter 35 and the section on *Bitmaps and Images*.

This example could use the font metrics facilities of Tk 8.0 to get more accurate sizes of the text for different strings. It is possible, for example, that a three-character string like **OOO** is wider than a four-character string like **llll** in a variable-width font. The `font metrics` command is described on page 470.

Label Width and Wrap Length

When a label is displaying text, its `width` attribute is interpreted as a number of characters. The label is made wide enough to hold this number of averaged width characters in the label's font. However, if the label is holding a bitmap or an image, then the `width` is in pixels or another screen unit.

The `wrapLength` attribute determines when a label's text is wrapped onto multiple lines. *The wrap length is always screen units.* If you need to compute a `wrapLength` based on the font metrics, then you can use the `font metrics` command. If you use Tk 4.2 or earlier, then you have to measure text using a `text` widget with the same font. Chapter 30 describes the `text` widget operations that return size information for characters.

You can force line breaks by including newlines (`\n`) in the label's text. This lets you create labels that have multiple lines of text.

Label Attributes

Table 26–2 lists the widget attributes for the label widget. The attributes are named according to their resource name, which includes a capital letter at internal word boundaries. When you specify an attribute as an option in a Tcl command when creating or reconfiguring a widget, however, you specify the attribute with a dash and all lowercase letters. Chapter 25 explains how to use resource specifications for attributes. Chapters 34, 35, and 36 discuss many of these attributes in more detail.

Table 26–2 Label Attributes.

`anchor`	Relative position of the label within its packing space.
`background`	Background color (also `bg`).
`bitmap`	Name of a bitmap to display instead of a text string.

Table 26–2 Label Attributes. (Continued)

`borderWidth`	Extra space around the edge of the label.
`cursor`	Cursor to display when mouse is over the label.
`font`	Font for the label's text.
`foreground`	Foreground color (also `fg`).
`height`	In screen units for bitmaps, in lines for text.
`highlightBackground`	Focus highlight color when widget does not have focus.
`highlightColor`	Focus highlight color when widget has focus.
`highlightThickness`	Thickness of focus highlight rectangle.
`image`	Specifies image to display instead of bitmap or text.
`justify`	Text justification: `left`, `right`, or `center`.
`padX`	Extra space to the left and right of the label.
`padY`	Extra space above and below the label.
`relief`	`flat`, `sunken`, `raised`, `groove`, `solid` or `ridge`.
`takeFocus`	Control focus changes from keyboard traversal.
`text`	Text to display.
`textVariable`	Name of Tcl variable. Its value is displayed.
`underline`	Index of character to underline.
`width`	Width. In characters for text labels.
`wrapLength`	Length at which text is wrapped *in screen units*.

The Message Widget

The message widget displays a long text string by formatting it onto several lines. It is designed for use in dialog boxes. It can format the text into a box of a given width, in screen units, or a given *aspect ratio*. The aspect ratio is defined to be the ratio of the width to the height, times 100. The default is 150, which means the text will be one and a half times as wide as it is high.

Example 26–3 creates a message widget with one long line of text. Backslashes are used to continue the text string without embedding any newlines. (You can also just type a long line into your script.) Note that backslash-newline collapses white space after the newline into a single space.

Example 26–3 The message widget formats long lines of text.

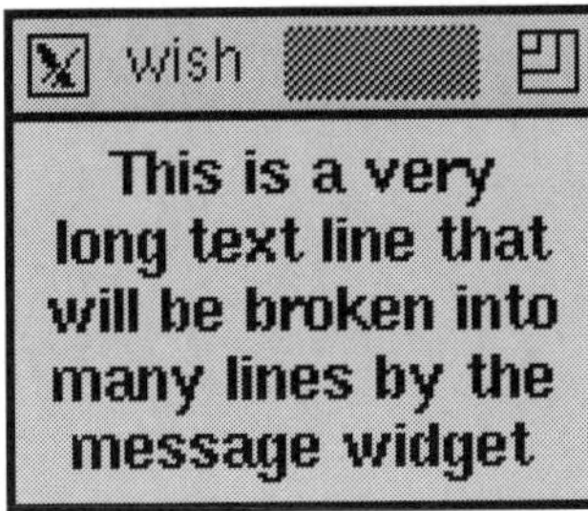


```
message .msg -justify center -text "This is a very long text\
    line that will be broken into many lines by the\
    message widget"
pack .msg
```

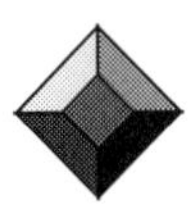

A newline in the string forces a line break in the message display. You can retain exact control over the formatting by putting newlines into your string and specifying a very large aspect ratio. In Example 26–4, grouping with double quotes is used to continue the string over more than one line. The newline character between the quotes is included in the string, and it causes a line break:

Example 26–4 Controlling the text layout in a message widget.

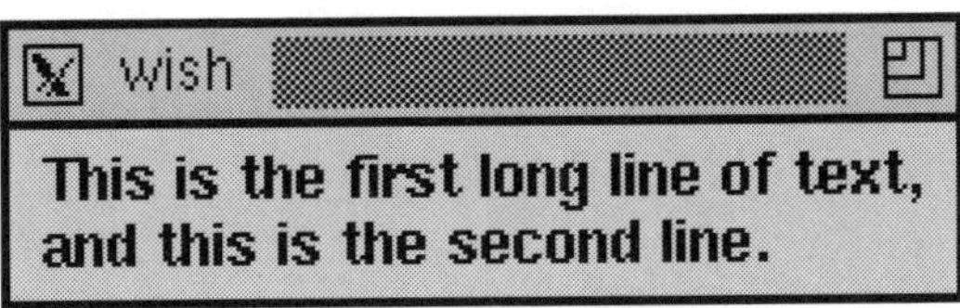


```
message .msg -aspect 1000 -justify left -text \
"This is the first long line of text,
and this is the second line."
pack .msg
```


One disadvantage of a message widget is that, by default, you cannot select the text it displays. Chapter 32 describes how to define custom selection handlers, so you could define one that returned the message string. The message widget predates the text widget, which has many more features and can emulate the message widget. If selections, multiple fonts, and other formatting are important, use a text widget instead of a message widget. Text widgets are described in Chapter 30.

Message Attributes

Table 26–3 lists the attributes for the message widget. The table lists the resource name, which has capitals at internal word boundaries. In Tcl commands these options are specified with a dash and all lowercase:

Table 26–3 Message Attributes

`anchor`	Relative position of the text within its packing space.
`aspect`	100 * width / height. Default 150.
`background`	Background color (also `bg`).
`borderWidth`	Extra space around the edge of the text.
`cursor`	Cursor to display when mouse is over the widget.
`font`	Font for the message's text.
`foreground`	Foreground color (also `fg`).
`highlightBackground`	Focus highlight color when widget does not have focus.
`highlightColor`	Focus highlight color when widget has focus.
`highlightThickness`	Thickness of focus highlight rectangle.
`justify`	Justification: `left`, `center`, or `right`.
`padX`	Extra space to the left and right of the text.
`padY`	Extra space above and below the text.
`relief`	`flat`, `sunken`, `raised`, `groove`, `solid` or `ridge`.
`takeFocus`	Control focus changes from keyboard traversal.
`text`	Text to display.
`textVariable`	Name of Tcl variable. Its value is displayed.
`width`	Width, in screen units.

Arranging Labels and Messages

Both the label and message widgets have attributes that control the position of their text in much the same way that the packer controls the position of widgets within a frame. These attributes are `padX`, `padY`, `anchor` and `borderWidth`. The `anchor` takes effect when the size of the widget is larger than the space needed to display its text. This happens when you specify the `-width` attribute or if you pack the widget with fill enabled and there is extra room. See Chapter 34 and the section on *Padding and Anchors* for more details.

The Scale Widget

The scale widget displays a *slider* in a *trough*. The trough represents a range of numeric values, and the slider position represents the current value. The scale can have an associated label, and it can display its current value next to the slider. The value of the scale can be used in three different ways:

- Explicitly get and set the value with widget commands.
- Associate the scale with a Tcl variable. The variable is kept in sync with the value of the scale, and changing the variable affects the scale.
- Register a Tcl command to be executed after the scale value changes. You specify the initial part of the Tcl command, and the scale implementation adds the current value as another argument to the command.

Example 26–5 A scale widget.

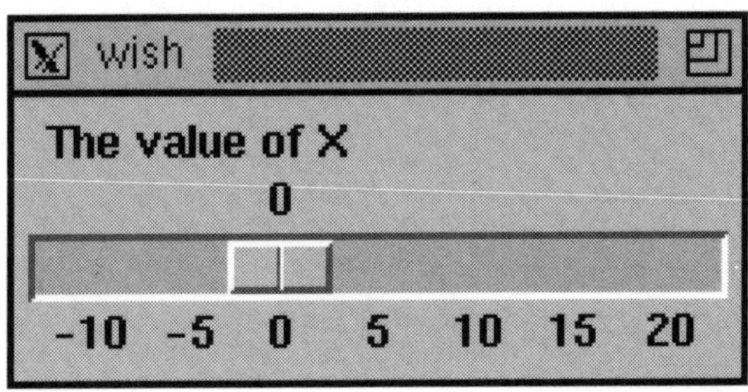


```
scale .scale -from -10 -to 20 -length 200 -variable x \
    -orient horizontal -label "The value of X" \
    -tickinterval 5 -showvalue true
pack .scale
```

Example 26–5 shows a scale for a variable that ranges in value from -10 to +20. The variable `x` is defined at the global scope. The `tickinterval` option results in the labels across the bottom, and the `showvalue` option causes the current value to be displayed. The `length` of the scale is in screen units (i.e., pixels).

Scale Bindings

Table 26–4 lists the bindings for scale widgets. You must direct focus to a scale explicitly for the key bindings like `<Up>` and `<Down>` to take effect.

Table 26–4 Bindings for scale widgets.

`<Button-1>`	Clicking on the trough moves the slider by one unit of resolution toward the mouse click.
`<Control-Button-1>`	Clicking on the trough moves the slider all the way to the end of the trough toward the mouse click.

Table 26–4 Bindings for scale widgets. (Continued)

<Left> <Up>	Move the slider toward the left (top) by one unit.
<Control-Left> <Control-Up>	Move the slider toward the left (top) by the value of the bigIncrement attribute.
<Right> <Down>	Move the slider toward the right (bottom) one unit.
<Control-Right> <Control-Down>	Move the slider toward the right (bottom) by the value of the bigIncrement attribute.
<Home>	Move the slider all the way to the left (top).
<End>	Move the slider all the way to the right (bottom).

Scale Attributes

Table 26–5 lists the scale widget attributes. The table uses the resource name, which has capitals at internal word boundaries. In Tcl commands the attributes are specified with a dash and all lowercase.

Table 26–5 Attributes for scale widgets.

activeBackground	Background color when the mouse is over the slider.
background	The background color (also bg in commands).
bigIncrement	Coarse grain slider adjustment value.
borderWidth	Extra space around the edge of the widget.
command	Command to invoke when the value changes. The current value is appended as another argument
cursor	Cursor to display when mouse is over the widget.
digits	Number of significant digits in scale value.
from	Minimum value. The left or top end of the scale.
font	Font for the label.
foreground	Foreground color (also fg).
highlightBackground	Focus highlight color when widget does not have focus.
highlightColor	Focus highlight color when widget has focus.
highlightThickness	Thickness of focus highlight rectangle.
label	A string to display with the scale.
length	The length, in screen units, of the long axis of the scale.
orient	horizontal or vertical.
relief	flat, sunken, raised, groove, solid or ridge.

Table 26–5 Attributes for scale widgets. (Continued)

`repeatDelay`	Delay before keyboard auto-repeat starts. Auto-repeat is used when pressing `<Button-1>` on the trough.
`repeatInterval`	Time period between auto-repeat events.
`resolution`	The value is rounded to a multiple of this value.
`showValue`	If true, value is displayed next to the slider.
`sliderLength`	The length, in screen units, of the slider.
`sliderRelief`	The relief of the slider.
`state`	`normal`, `active`, or `disabled`.
`takeFocus`	Control focus changes from keyboard traversal.
`tickInterval`	Spacing between tick marks. Zero means no marks.
`to`	Maximum value. Right or bottom end of the scale.
`troughColor`	The color of the bar on which the slider sits.
`variable`	Name of Tcl variable. Changes to the scale widget are reflected in the Tcl variable value, and changes in the Tcl variable are reflected in the scale display.
`width`	Width of the trough, or slider bar.

Programming Scales

The scale operations are primarily used by the default bindings and you do not need to program the scale directly. Table 26–6 lists the operations supported by the scale. In the table, `$w` is a scale widget.

Table 26–6 Operations on the scale widget.

`$w cget` *`option`*	Return the value of the configuration option.
`$w configure ...`	Query or modify the widget configuration.
`$w coords ?`*`value`*`?`	Returns the coordinates of the point in the trough that corresponds to *`value`*, or the scale's value.
`$w get ?x y?`	Return the value of the scale, or the value that corresponds to the position given by *x* and *y*.
`$w identify` *`x y`*	Returns `trough1`, `slider`, or `trough2` to indicate what is under the position given by *x* and *y*.
`$w set` *`value`*	Set the value of the scale.

The `bell` Command

The `bell` command rings the terminal bell. The bell is associated with the display; even if you are executing your program on a remote machine, the bell is heard by the user. If your application has windows on multiple displays, you can direct the bell to the display of a particular window with the `-displayof` option. The syntax for the `bell` command is given below:

```
bell ?-displayof window?
```

UNIX has an *xset* program that controls the bell's duration, pitch, and volume. The volume is in percent of a maximum, for example, 50. In practice, many keyboard bells only support a variable duration; the pitch and volume are fixed. The arguments of *xset* that control the bell are shown below.

```
exec xset b ?volume? ?hertz? ?milliseconds?
```

The `b` argument by itself resets the bell to the default parameters. You can turn the bell off with `-b`, or you can use the `on` or `off` arguments.

```
exec xset -b
exec xset b ?on? ?off?
```

## CHAPTER 27

Scrollbars

This chapter describes the Tk `scrollbar`. Scrollbars have a general protocol that is used to attach them to one or more other widgets.

Scrollbars control other widgets through a standard protocol based around Tcl commands. A scrollbar uses a Tcl command to ask a widget to display part of its contents. The scrollable widget uses a Tcl command to tell the scrollbar what part of its contents are visible. The Tk widgets designed to work with scrollbars are: entry, listbox, text, and canvas. The scrollbar protocol is general enough to use with new widgets, or collections of widgits. This chapter explains the protocol between scrollbars and the widgets they control, but you don't need to know the details to use a scrollbar. All you need to know is how to set things up, and then these widgets take care of themselves.

Using Scrollbars

The following commands create a text widget and two scrollbars that scroll it horizontally and vertically:

```
scrollbar .yscroll -command {.text yview} -orient vertical
scrollbar .xscroll -command {.text xview} -orient horizontal
text .text -yscrollcommand {.yscroll set} \
   -xscrollcommand {.xscroll set}
```

The scrollbar's `set` operation is designed to be called from other widgets when their display changes. The scrollable widget's `xview` and `yview` operations are designed to be called by the scrollbar when the user manipulates them. Additional parameters are passed to these operations as described later. In most cases you can ignore the details of the protocol and just set up the connection between the scrollbar and the widget.

Example 27–1 A text widget and two scrollbars.

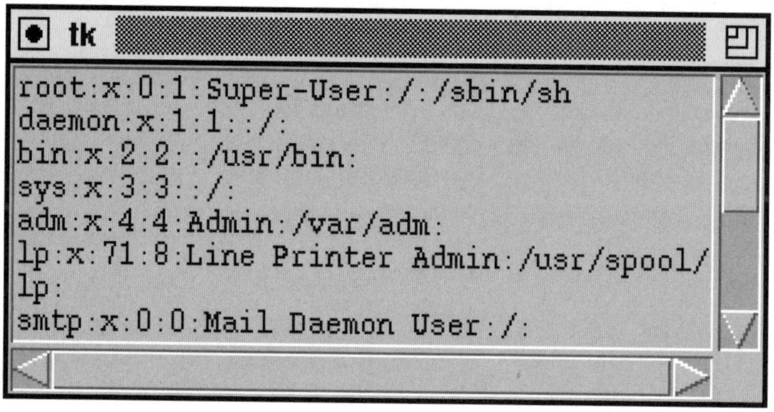

```
root:x:0:1:Super-User:/:/sbin/sh
daemon:x:1:1::/:
bin:x:2:2::/usr/bin:
sys:x:3:3::/:
adm:x:4:4:Admin:/var/adm:
lp:x:71:8:Line Printer Admin:/usr/spool/
lp:
smtp:x:0:0:Mail Daemon User:/:
```

```
proc Scrolled_Text { f args } {
    frame $f
    eval {text $f.text -wrap none \
        -xscrollcommand [list $f.xscroll set] \
        -yscrollcommand [list $f.yscroll set]} $args
    scrollbar $f.xscroll -orient horizontal \
        -command [list $f.text xview]
    scrollbar $f.yscroll -orient vertical \
        -command [list $f.text yview]
    grid $f.text $f.yscroll -sticky news
    grid $f.xscroll -sticky news
    grid rowconfigure $f 0 -weight 1
    grid columnconfigure $f 0 -weight 1
    return $f.text
}
set t [Scrolled_Text .f -width 40 -height 8]
pack .f -side top -fill both -expand true
set in [open /etc/passwd]
$t insert end [read $in]
close $in
```

Example 27–1 defines `Scrolled_Text` that creates a text widget with two scrollbars. It reads and inserts the password file into the text widget. There is not enough room to display all the text, and the scrollbars indicate how much text is visible. Chapter 30 describes the text widget in more detail.

The `list` command constructs the `-command` and `-xscrollcommand` values. Even though one could use double quotes here, you should make a habit of using `list` when constructing values that are used later as Tcl commands. Example

27–1 uses `args` to pass through extra options to the text widget. The use of `eval` and `args` is explained in Example 10–2 on page 116. The scrollbars and the text widget are lined up with the `grid` geometry manager as explained in Example 21–10 on page 273.

The Scrollbar Protocol

When the user manipulates the scrollbar, it calls its registered `command` with some additional parameters that indicate what the user said to do. The associated widget responds to this command (e.g., its `xview` operation) by changing its display. After the widget changes its display, it calls the scrollbar by using its registered `xscrollcommand` or `yscrollcommand` (e.g., the `set` operation) with some parameters that indicate the new relative size and position of the display. The scrollbar updates its appearance to reflect this information.

The protocol supports widgets that change their display by themselves, such as when more information is added to the widget. Scrollable widgets also support a binding to `<B2-Motion>` (i.e., "middle drag") that scrolls the widget. When anything happens to change the view on a widget, the scrollable widgets use their scroll commands to update the scrollbar.

The Scrollbar `set` Operation

The scrollbar `set` operation takes two floating point values between zero and one, *`first`* and *`last`*, that indicate the relative position of the top and bottom (or left and right) of the widget's display. The scrollable widget adds these values when they use their `yscrollcommand` or `xscrollcommand`. For example, the text widget would issue the following command to indicate that the first quarter of the widget is displayed:

```
.yscroll set 0.0 0.25
```

If the two values are 0.0 and 1.0, it means the widget's contents are fully visible, and a scrollbar is not necessary. You can monitor the protocol by using a Tcl wrapper, `Scroll_Set`, instead of the `set` operation directly. `Scroll_Set` waits for the scrollbar to be necessary before mapping it with a geometry manager command. It is not safe to unmap the scrollbar because that can change the size of the widget and create the need for a scrollbar. That leads to an infinite loop.

Example 27–2 `Scroll_Set` manages optional scrollbars.

```
proc Scroll_Set {scrollbar geoCmd offset size} {
    if {$offset != 0.0 || $size != 1.0} {
        eval $geoCmd    ;# Make sure it is visible
    }
    $scrollbar set $offset $size
}
```

Scroll_Set takes a geometry management command as an argument, which it uses to make the scrollbar visible. Example 27–3 uses Scroll_Set with a listbox. Note that it does not grid the scrollbars directly. Instead, it lets Scroll_Set do the geometry command the first time it is necessary.

Example 27–3 Listbox with optional scrollbars.

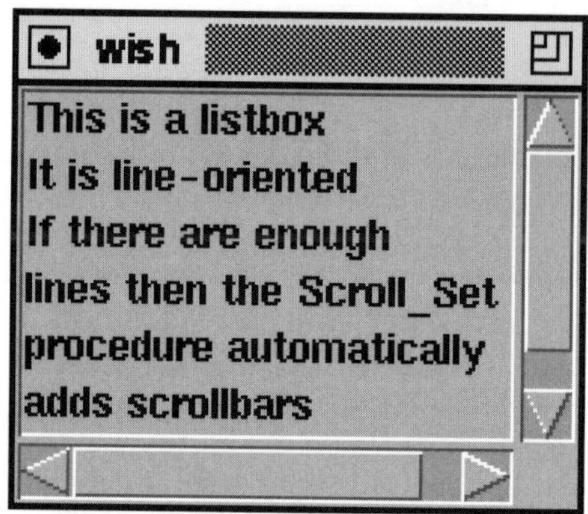


```
proc Scrolled_Listbox { f args } {
    frame $f
    listbox $f.list \
        -xscrollcommand [list Scroll_Set $f.xscroll \
            [list grid $f.xscroll -row 1 -column 0 -sticky we]] \
        -yscrollcommand [list Scroll_Set $f.yscroll \
            [list grid $f.yscroll -row 0 -column 1 -sticky ns]]
    eval {$f.list configure} $args
    scrollbar $f.xscroll -orient horizontal \
        -command [list $f.list xview]
    scrollbar $f.yscroll -orient vertical \
        -command [list $f.list yview]
    grid $f.list -sticky news
    grid rowconfigure $f 0 -weight 1
    grid columnconfigure $f 0 -weight 1
    return $f.list
}
```

Scrolled_Listbox takes optional parameters for the listbox. It uses eval to configure the listbox with these arguments. The style of using eval shown here is explained in Example 10–2 on page 116. Example 40–4 on page 514 associates two listboxes with one scrollbar.

The `xview` and `yview` Operations

The `xview` and `yview` operations are designed to be called from scrollbars, and they work the same for all scrollable widgets. You can use them to scroll the widgets for any reason, not just when the scrollbar is used. The following examples use a text widget named `.text` for illustration.

The `xview` and `yview` operations return the current *first* and *last* values that would be passed to a scrollbar `set` command:

```
.text yview
=> 0.2 0.55
```

When the user clicks on the arrows at either end of the scrollbar, the scrollbar adds `scroll` *num* `units` to its command, where *num* is positive to scroll down, and negative to scroll up. Scrolling up one line is indicated with this command:

```
.text yview scroll -1 units
```

When the user clicks above or below the elevator of the scrollbar, the scrollbar adds `scroll` *num* `pages` to its command. Scrolling down one page is indicated with this command:

```
.text yview scroll 1 pages
```

You can position a widget so that the top (or left) edge is at a particular offset from the beginning of the widget's contents. The offset is expressed as a floating point value between zero and one. To view the beginning of the contents:

```
.text yview moveto 0.0
```

If the offset is 1.0, the last part of the widget content's is displayed. The Tk widgets always keep the end of the widget contents at the bottom (or right) edge of the widget, unless the widget is larger than necessary to display all the contents. You can exploit this with the one-line entry widget to view the end of long strings:

```
.entry xview moveto 1.0
```

The Tk 3.6 Protocol

The protocol between the scrollbar and its associated widget changed in Tk 4.0. The scrollbar is backward compatible. The Tk 3.6 protocol had four parameters in the `set` operation: *totalUnits*, *windowUnits*, *firstUnit*, and *lastUnit*. If a scrollbar is updated with this form of a `set` command, then the `get` operation also changes to return this information. When the scrollbar makes the callback to the other widget (e.g., an `xview` or `yview` operation), it passes a single extra parameter that specifies what *unit* to display at the top (left) of the associated widget. The Tk widgets' `xview` and `yview` operations are also backward compatible with this interface.

The Scrollbar Widget

Tk 8.0 uses native scrollbar widgets on Macintosh and Windows. While the use of scrollbars with other widgets is identical on all platforms, the interpretation of the attributes and the details of the bindings vary across platforms. This section describes the Tk scrollbar on UNIX. The default bindings and attributes are fine on all platforms, so the differences should not be important.

The scrollbar is made up of five components: `arrow1`, `trough1`, `slider`, `trough2`, and `arrow2`. The arrows are on either end, with `arrow1` being the arrow to the left for horizontal scrollbars, or the arrow on top for vertical scrollbars. The slider represents the relative position of the information displayed in the associated widget, and the size of the slider represents the relative amount of the information displayed. The two trough regions are the areas between the slider and the arrows. If the slider covers all of the trough area, you can see all the information in the associated widget.

Scrollbar Bindings

Table 27–1 lists the default bindings for scrollbars on UNIX. Button 1 and button 2 of the mouse have the same bindings. You must direct focus to a scrollbar explicitly for the key bindings like `<Up>` and `<Down>` to take effect.

Table 27–1 Bindings for the scrollbar widget.

`<Button-1> <Button-2>`	Clicking on the arrows scrolls by one unit. Clicking on the trough moves by one screenful.
`<B1-Motion> <B2-Motion>`	Dragging the slider scrolls dynamically.
`<Control-Button-1>` `<Control-Button-2>`	Clicking on the trough or arrow scrolls all the way to the beginning (end) of the widget.
`<Up> <Down>`	Scroll up (down) by one unit.
`<Control-Up>` `<Control-Down>`	Scroll up (down) by one screenful.
`<Left> <Right>`	Scroll left (right) by one unit.
`<Control-Left>` `<Control-Right>`	Scroll left (right) by one screenful.
`<Prior> <Next>`	Scroll back (forward) by one screenful.
`<Home>`	Scroll all the way to the left (top).
`<End>`	Scroll all the way to the right (bottom).

Scrollbar Attributes

Table 27–2 lists the scrollbar attributes. The table uses the resource name for the attribute, which has capitals at internal word boundaries. In Tcl commands the attributes are specified with a dash and all lowercase.

There is no `length` attribute for a scrollbar. Instead, a scrollbar is designed to be packed next to another widget with a fill option that lets the `scrollbar` display grow to the right size. Only the relief of the active element can be set. The `background` color is used for the slider, the arrows, and the border. The slider and arrows are displayed in the `activeBackground` color when the mouse is over them. The trough is always displayed in the `troughColor`.

Table 27–2 Attributes for the scrollbar widget.

`activeBackground`	Color when the mouse is over the slider or arrows.
`activeRelief`	Relief of slider and arrows when mouse is over them.
`background`	The background color (also `bg` in commands).
`borderWidth`	Extra space around the edge of the scrollbar.
`command`	Prefix of the command to invoke when the scrollbar changes. Typically this is a `xview` or `yview` operation.
`cursor`	Cursor to display when mouse is over the widget.
`elementBorderWidth`	Border width of arrow and slider elements.
`highlightBackground`	Focus highlight color when widget does not have focus.
`highlightColor`	Focus highlight color when widget has focus.
`highlightThickness`	Thickness of focus highlight rectangle.
`elementBorderWidth`	Width of 3D border on arrows and slider.
`jump`	If true, dragging the elevator does not scroll dynamically. Instead, the display jumps to the new position.
`orient`	Orientation: `horizontal` or `vertical`.
`repeatDelay`	Milliseconds before auto-repeat starts. Auto-repeat is used when pressing `<Button-1>` on the trough or arrows.
`repeatInterval`	Milliseconds between auto-repeat events.
`troughColor`	The color of the bar on which the slider sits.
`width`	Width of the narrow dimension of the scrollbar.

Programming Scrollbars

The scrollbar operations are primarily used by the default bindings. Table 27–3 lists the operations supported by the scrollbar. In the table, `$w` is a scrollbar widget.

Table 27–3 Operations on the scrollbar widget.

`$w activate ?element?`	Query or set the active element, which can be `arrow1`, `arrow2`, or `slider`.
`$w cget option`	Return the value of the configuration option.
`$w configure ...`	Query or modify the widget configuration.
`$w delta dx dy`	Returns the change in the *first* argument to `set` required to move the scrollbar slider by *dx* or *dy*.
`$w fraction x y`	Return a number between 0 and 1 that indicates the relative location of the point in the trough.
`$s get`	Return *first* and *last* from the `set` operation.
`$w identify x y`	Returns `arrow1`, `trough1`, `slider`, `trough2`, or `arrow2`, to indicate what is under the point.
`$w set first last`	Set the scrollbar parameters. *first* is the relative position of the top (left) of the display. *last* is the relative position of the bottom (right) of the display.

CHAPTER 28

The Entry Widget

The entry widget provides a single line of text for use as a data entry field. The string in the entry can be linked to a Tcl variable.

Entry widgets are specialized text widgets that display a single line of editable text. It is a subset of the functionality of the general-purpose text widget described in Chapter 30. The entry is commonly used in dialog boxes when values need to be filled in, or as a simple command entry widget. A very useful feature of the entry is the ability to link it to a Tcl variable. The entry displays that variable's value, and editing the contents of the entry changes the Tcl variable.

Using Entry Widgets

The entry widget supports editing, scrolling, and selections, which make it more complex than label or message widgets. Fortunately, the default settings for an entry widget make it usable right away. You click with the left button to set the insert point and then type in text. Text is selected by dragging out a selection with the left button. The entry can be scrolled horizontally by dragging with the middle mouse button.

One common use of an entry widget is to associate a label with it, and a command to execute when `<Return>` is pressed in the entry. The grid geometry manager is ideal for lining up several entries and their labels. This is implemented in the following example:

Example 28–1 A command entry.

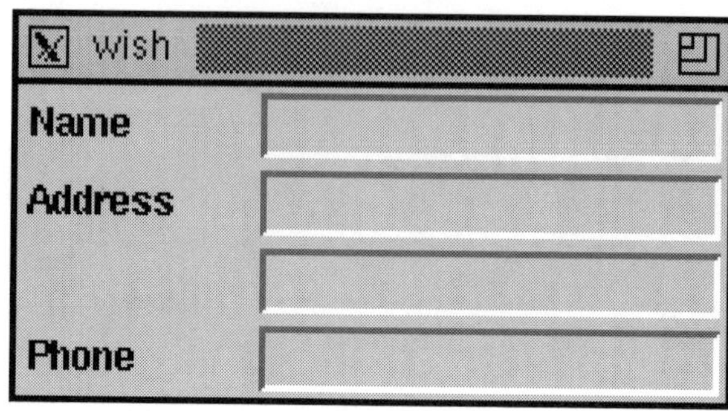


```
foreach field {Name Address1 Address2 Phone} {
    label .l$field -text $field -anchor w
    entry .e$field -textvariable address($field) -relief sunken
    grid .l$field .e$field -sticky news
    bind .e$field <Return> UpdateAddress
}
```

Example 28–1 creates four entries that are linked to variables with the `textvariable` attribute. The variables are elements of the `address` array. The `-relief sunken` for the entry widget sets them apart visually. Widget relief is described in more detail on page 446. The Tcl command `UpdateAddress` is bound to the `<Return>` keystroke. The `UpdateAddress` procedure, which is not shown, can get the current values of the entry widgets through the global array `address`.

Tips for Using Entry Widgets

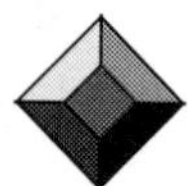

If you are displaying long strings in an entry, you can use the following command to keep the end of the string in view. The command requests that all the string be off screen to the left, but the widget implementation fills up the display; the scrolling is limited so that the tail of the string is visible:

```
$entry xview moveto 1.0
```

The `show` attribute is useful for entries that accept passwords or other sensitive information. If `show` is not empty, it is used as the character to display instead of the real value:

```
$entry config -show *
```

The `state` attribute determines if the contents of an entry can be modified. Set the `state` to `disabled` to prevent modification and set it to `normal` to allow modification.

```
$entry config -state disabled ;# read-only
$entry config -state normal   ;# editable
```

The middle mouse button (`<Button-2>`) is overloaded with two functions. If you click and release the middle button, the selection is inserted at the insert cursor. The location of the middle click does not matter. If you press and hold the middle button, you can scroll the contents of the entry by dragging the mouse to the left or right.

The Entry Widget

Table 28–1 gives the bindings for entry widgets. When the table lists two sequences, they are equivalent. The table does not list all the right arrow key bindings; there are corresponding bindings for the left and right arrow keys.

Table 28–1 Entry bindings.

`<Button-1>`	Set the insert point and start a selection.
`<B1-Motion>`	Drag out a selection.
`<Double-Button-1>`	Select a word.
`<Triple-Button-1>`	Select all text in the entry.
`<Shift-B1-Motion>`	Adjust the ends of the selection.
`<Control-Button-1>`	Set insert point, leaving selection as is.
`<Button-2>`	Paste selection at the insert cursor.
`<B2-Motion>`	Scroll horizontally.
`<Left> <Control-b>`	Move insert cursor one character left. Start selection.
`<Shift-Left>`	Move cursor left and extend selection.
`<Control-Left>`	Move cursor left one word. Start selection.
`<Meta-b>`	Same as `<Control-Left>`.
`<Control-Shift-Left>`	Move cursor left one word and extend the selection.
`<Right> <Control-f>`	Move right one character.
`<Meta-f> <Control-Right>`	Move right one word.
`<Home> <Control-a>`	Move cursor to beginning of entry.
`<Shift-Home>`	Move cursor to beginning and extend the selection.
`<End> <Control-e>`	Move cursor to end of entry.
`<Shift-End>`	Move cursor to end and extend the selection.
`<Select> <Control-Space>`	Anchor the selection at the insert cursor.
`<Shift-Select>` `<Control-Shift-Space>`	Adjust the selection to the insert cursor.
`<Control-slash>`	Select all the text in the entry.
`<Control-backslash>`	Clear the selection in the entry.

Table 28–1 Entry bindings. (Continued)

<Delete>	Delete the selection or delete next character.
<Backspace> <Control-h>	Delete the selection or delete previous character.
<Control-d>	Delete next character.
<Meta-d>	Delete next word.
<Control-k>	Delete to the end of the entry.
<Control-w>	Delete previous word.
<Control-x>	Delete the section, if it exists.
<Control-t>	Transpose characters.

Entry Attributes

Table 28–2 lists the entry widget attributes. The table lists the resource name, which has capitals at internal word boundaries. In Tcl commands these options are specified with a dash and are all lowercase.

Table 28–2 Entry attribute resource names.

background	Background color (also bg).
borderWidth	Extra space around the edge of the text (also bd).
cursor	Cursor to display when mouse is over the widget.
exportSelection	If true, selected text is exported via the X selection mechanism.
font	Font for the text.
foreground	Foreground color (also fg).
highlightBackground	Focus highlight color when widget does not have focus.
highlightColor	Focus highlight color when widget has focus.
highlightThickness	Thickness of focus highlight rectangle.
insertBackground	Background for area covered by insert cursor.
insertBorderWidth	Width of cursor border. Non-zero for 3D effect.
insertOffTime	Time, in milliseconds the insert cursor blinks off.
insertOnTime	Time, in milliseconds the insert cursor blinks on.
insertWidth	Width of insert cursor. Default is 2.
justify	Text justification: left, right, center.
relief	flat, sunken, raised, groove, solid or ridge.
selectBackground	Background color of selection.

Table 28–2 Entry attribute resource names. (Continued)

`selectForeground`	Foreground color of selection.
`selectBorderWidth`	Width of selection border. Non-zero for 3D effect.
`show`	A character (e.g., `*`) to display instead of contents.
`state`	State: `disabled` (read-only) or `normal`.
`takeFocus`	Control focus changes from keyboard traversal.
`textVariable`	Name of Tcl variable.
`width`	Width, in characters.
`xScrollCommand`	Connects entry to a scrollbar.

Programming Entry Widgets

The default bindings for entry widgets are fairly good. However, you can completely control the entry with a set of widget operations for inserting, deleting, selecting, and scrolling. The operations involve addressing character positions called *indices*. The indices count from zero. The entry defines some symbolic indices such as `end`. The index corresponding to an X coordinate is specified with `@`*`xcoord`*, such as `@26`. Table 28–3 lists the formats for indices.

Table 28–3 Entry indices.

`0`	Index of the first character.
`anchor`	The index of the anchor point of the selection.
`end`	Index just after the last character.
`number`	Index a character, counting from zero.
`insert`	The character right after the insertion cursor.
`sel.first`	The first character in the selection.
`sel.last`	The character just after the last character in the selection.
`@`*`xcoord`*	The character under the specified X coordinate.

Table 28–4 summarizes the operations on entry widgets. In the table, `$w` is an entry widget.

Table 28–4 Entry operations.

`$w cget` *`option`*	Return the value of the configuration option.
`$w configure ...`	Query or modify the widget configuration.

IV. Tk Widgets

Table 28–4 Entry operations.

`$w delete` *`first ?last?`*	Delete the characters from *`first`* to *`last`*, not including the character at *`last`*. The character at *`first`* is deleted if *`last`* is not specified.
`$w get`	Return the string in the entry.
`$w icursor` *`index`*	Move the insert cursor.
`$w index` *`index`*	Return the numerical index corresponding to *`index`*.
`$w insert` *`index string`*	Insert the *`string`* at the given *`index`*.
`$w scan mark` *`x`*	Start a scroll operation. *x* is a screen coordinate.
`$w scan dragto` *`x`*	Scroll from previous mark position.
`$w select adjust` *`index`*	Move the boundary of an existing selection.
`$w select clear`	Clear the selection.
`$w select from` *`index`*	Set the anchor position for the selection.
`$w select present`	Returns 1 if there is a selection in the entry.
`$w select range` *`start end`*	Select the characters from *`start`* to the one just before *`end`*.
`$w select to` *`index`*	Extend a selection.
`$w xview`	Return the offset and span of visible contents. These are both real numbers between 0 and 1.0.
`$w xview` *`index`*	Shift the display so the character at `index` is at the left edge of the display.
`$w xview moveto` *`fraction`*	Shift the display so that *`fraction`* of the contents are off the left edge of the display.
`$w xview scroll` *`num what`*	Scroll the contents by the specified number of *`what`*, which can be `units` or `pages`.

For example, the binding for `<Button-1>` includes the following commands:

```
%W icursor @%x
%W select from @%x
if {%W cget -state] == "normal"} {focus %W}
```

Recall that the `%` triggers substitutions in binding commands, and that `%W` is replaced with the widget pathname and `%x` is replaced with the X coordinate of the mouse event. Chapter 23 describes bindings and these substitutions in detail. These commands set the insert point to the point of the mouse click by using the `@%x` index, which will be turned into something like `@17` when the binding is invoked. The binding also starts a selection. If the entry is not in the disabled state, then keyboard focus is given to the entry so that it gets `KeyPress` events.

## CHAPTER 29

The Listbox Widget

The listbox provides a scrollable list of text lines. The listbox supports selections of one or more lines.

Listbox widgets display a set of text lines in a scrollable display. The basic text unit is a line. There are operations to insert, select, and delete lines, but there are no operations to modify the characters in a line. As such, the listbox is suitable for displaying a set of choices, such as in a file selection dialog. By default a user can select one item from a listbox, but you can select multiple items by setting the selection mode attribute.

Using Listboxes

The lines in a listbox are indexed from zero. The keyword index `end` addresses the last line. Other indices are described on page 361. The most common programming task for a listbox is to insert text. If your data is in a list, you can loop through the list and insert each element at the end:

```
foreach item $list {
    $listbox insert end $item
}
```

You can insert several items at once. The next command uses `eval` to concatenate the list onto a single `insert` command:

```
eval {$listbox insert end} $list
```

It is also common to react to mouse clicks on a listbox, although the default bindings handle most of the details of selecting items. The `nearest` operation finds the listbox entry that is closest to a mouse event. If the mouse is clicked beyond the last element, the index of the last element is returned:

```
set index [$list nearest $y]
```

Example 29–1 displays two listboxes. The `Scrolled_Listbox` procedure on page 348 is used to put scrollbars on the listboxes. When the user clicks on an item in the first listbox, it is copied into the second listbox. When an item in the second listbox is selected, it is removed. This example shows how to manipulate items selected from a listbox:

Example 29–1 Choosing items from a listbox.

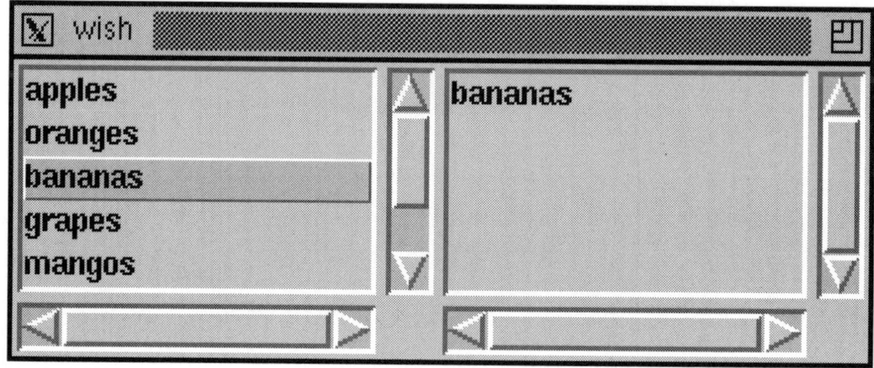


```
proc List_Select { parent values } {
    # Create two lists side by side
    frame $parent
    set choices [Scrolled_Listbox $parent.choices \
        -width 20 -height 5 ]
    set picked [Scrolled_Listbox $parent.picked \
        -width 20 -height 5]
    pack $parent.choices $parent.picked -side left \
        -expand true -fill both

    # Selecting in choices moves items into picked
    bind $choices <ButtonRelease-1> \
        [list ListTransferSel %W $picked]

    # Selecting in picked deletes items
    bind $picked <ButtonRelease-1> \
        {ListDeleteSel %W %y}

    # Insert all the choices
    foreach x $values {
        $choices insert end $x
    }
}
proc ListTransferSel {src dst} {
    foreach i [$src curselection] {
        $dst insert end [$src get $i]
    }
```

```
}
proc ListDeleteSel {w y} {
    foreach i [lsort -integer -decreasing [$w curselection]] {
        $w delete $i
    }
}
proc List_SelectValues {parent} {
    set picked $parent.picked.list
    set result {}
    foreach i [$w curselection] {
        lappend $result [$w get $i]
    }
}
List_Select .f {apples oranges bananas \
              grapes mangos peaches pears}
pack .f -expand true -fill both
```

Bindings are created to move items from `$choices` to `$picked`, and to delete items from `$picked`. Most of the work of selecting things in the listbox is done by the built-in bindings on the `Listbox` binding tag. The different selection models are described on page 364. Those bindings are on `<ButtonPress-1>` and `<B1-Motion>`. The selection is complete by the time the `<ButtonRelease-1>` event occurs. Consider the `<ButtonRelease-1>` binding for `$choices`:

```
bind $choices <ButtonRelease-1> \
    [list ListTransferSel %W $picked]
```

The `list` command is used to construct the Tcl command because we need to expand the value of `$picked` at the time the binding is created. The command will be evaluated later at the global scope, and `picked` will not be defined after the `List_Select` procedure returns. Or, worse yet, an existing global variable named `picked` will be used, which is unlikely to be correct!

Short procedures are used to implement the binding commands. This style has two advantages. First, it confines the `%` substitutions done by `bind` to a single command. Second, if there are any temporary variables, such as the loop counter `i`, they are hidden within the scope of the procedure.

The `ListTransferSel` gets the list of all the selected items and loops over this list to insert them into the other list. The `ListDeleteSel` procedure is similar. However, it sorts the selection indices in reverse order. It deletes items from the bottom up so the indices remain valid throughout the process.

Programming Listboxes

The listbox operations use indices to reference lines in the listbox. The lines are numbered starting at zero. Keyword indices are also used for some special lines. The listbox keeps track of an *active* element, which is displayed with underlined text. There is also a selection *anchor* that is used when adjusting selections. Table 29–1 summarizes the keywords used for indices.

Table 29–1 Listbox indices

`0`	Index of the first line.
`active`	The index of the activated line.
`anchor`	The index of the anchor point of the selection.
`end`	Index of the last line.
number	Index a line, counting from zero.
`@`*x*`,`*y*	The line closest to the specified X and Y coordinates.

Table 29–2 presents the operations for programming a listbox. In the table, `$w` is a listbox widget. Most of the operations have to do with the selection, and these operations are already programmed by the default bindings for the `Listbox` widget class:

Table 29–2 Listbox operations.

`$w activate` *index*	Activate the specified line.
`$w bbox` *index*	Return the bounding box of the text in the specified line in the form: *xoff yoff width height*.
`$w cget` *option*	Return the value of the configuration option.
`$w configure ...`	Query or modify the widget configuration.
`$w curselection`	Return a list of indices of the selected lines.
`$w delete` *first* ?*last*?	Delete the lines from *first* to *last*, including the line at *last*. The line at *first* is deleted if *last* is not given.
`$w get` *first* ?*last*?	Return the lines from *first* to *last* as a list.
`$w index` *index*	Return the numerical index corresponding to *index*.
`$w insert` *index* ?*string string string ...*?	Insert the *string* items before the line at *index*. If *index* is end, then append the items.
`$w nearest` *y*	Return the index of the line closest to the widget-relative Y coordinate.
`$w scan mark` *x y*	Start a scroll operation. *x* and *y* are widget-relative screen coordinates.
`$w scan dragto` *x y*	Scroll from previous mark position.
`$w see` *index*	Adjust the display so the line at *index* is visible.
`$w selection anchor` *index*	Anchor the selection at the specified line.
`$w selection clear` *start* ?*end*?	Clear the selection.

Table 29–2 Listbox operations. (Continued)

`$w selection includes` *`index`*	Returns 1 if the line at *`index`* is in the selection.
`$w selection set` *`start ?end?`*	Select the lines from *`start`* to *end*.
`$w xview`	Return the offset and span of visible contents. These are both real numbers between 0 and 1.
`$w xview` *`index`*	Shift the display so the character at *`index`* is at the left edge of the display.
`$w xview moveto` *`fraction`*	Shift the display so that *`fraction`* of the contents are off the left edge of the display.
`$w xview scroll` *`num what`*	Scroll the contents horizontally by the specified number of *`what`*, which can be `units` or `pages`.
`$w yview`	Return the offset and span of visible contents. These are both real numbers between 0 and 1.
`$w yview` *`index`*	Shift the display so the line at *`index`* is at the top edge of the display.
`$w yview moveto` *`fraction`*	Shift the display so that *`fraction`* of the contents are off the top of the display.
`$w yview scroll` *`num what`*	Scroll the contents vertically by the specified number of *`what`*, which can be `units` or `pages`.

Listbox Bindings

A listbox has an *active* element and it may have one or more *selected* elements. The active element is highlighted with an underline, and the selected elements are highlighted with a different color. There are a large number of key bindings for listboxes. You must set the input focus to the listbox for the key bindings to work. Chapter 33 describes focus. There are four selection modes for a listbox, and the bindings vary depending what mode the listbox is in. Table 29–3 lists the four possible `selectMode` settings:

Table 29–3 The values for the `selectMode` of a listbox.

`single`	A single element can be selected.
`browse`	A single element can be selected, and the selection can be dragged with the mouse. This is the default.
`multiple`	More than one element can be selected by toggling the selection state of items, but you only select or deselect one line at a time.
`extended`	More than one element can be selected by dragging out a selection with the shift or control keys.

Browse Select Mode

In browse selection mode, <Button-1> selects the item under the mouse and dragging with the mouse moves the selection, too. Table 29–4 gives the bindings for browse mode.

Table 29–4 Bindings for browse selection mode.

<Button-1>	Select the item under the mouse. This becomes the active element, too.
<B1-Motion>	Same as <Button-1>, the selection moves with the mouse.
<Shift-Button-1>	Activate the item under the mouse. The selection is not changed.
<Key-Up> <Key-Down>	Move the active item up (down) one line, and select it.
<Control-Home>	Activate and select the first element of the listbox.
<Control-End>	Activate and select the last element of the listbox.
<space> <Select> <Control-slash>	Select the active element.

Single Select Mode

In single selection mode, <Button-1> selects the item under the mouse, but dragging the mouse does not change the selection. When you release the mouse, the item under that point is activated. Table 29–5 specifies the bindings for single mode:

Table 29–5 Bindings for single selection mode.

<ButtonPress-1>	Select the item under the mouse.
<ButtonRelease-1>	Activate the item under the mouse.
<Shift-Button-1>	Activate the item under the mouse. The selection is not changed.
<Key-Up> <Key-Down>	Move the active item up (down) one line. The selection is not changed.
<Control-Home>	Activate and select the first element of the listbox.
<Control-End>	Activate and select the last element of the listbox.
<space> <Select> <Control-slash>	Select the active element.
<Control-backslash>	Clear the selection.

Extended Select Mode

In extended selection mode multiple items are selected by dragging out a selection with the first mouse button. Hold down the Shift key to adjust the ends of the selection. Use the Control key to make a disjoint selection. The Control key works in a toggle fashion, changing the selection state of the item under the mouse. If this starts a new part of the selection, then dragging the mouse extends the new part of the selection. If the toggle action cleared the selected item, then dragging the mouse continues to clear the selection. The extended mode is quite intuitive once you try it. Table 29–6 specifies the complete set of bindings for extended mode:

Table 29–6 Bindings for extended selection mode.

<Button-1>	Select the item under the mouse. This becomes the anchor point for adjusting the selection.
<B1-Motion>	Sweep out a selection from the anchor point.
<ButtonRelease-1>	Activate the item under the mouse.
<Shift-Button-1>	Adjust the selection from the anchor item to the item under the mouse.
<Shift-B1-Motion>	Continue to adjust the selection from the anchor.
<Control-Button-1>	Toggle the selection state of the item under the mouse, and make this the anchor point.
<Control-B1-Motion>	Set the selection state of the items from the anchor point to the item under the mouse to be the same as the selection state of the anchor point.
<Key-Up> <Key-Down>	Move the active item up (down) one line, and start a new selection with this item as the anchor point.
<Shift-Up> <Shift-Down>	Move the active element up (down) and extend the selection to include this element.
<Control-Home>	Activate and select the first element of the listbox.
<Control-Shift-Home>	Extend the selection to the first element.
<Control-End>	Activate and select the last element of the listbox.
<Control-Shift-End>	Extend the selection to the last element.
<space> <Select>	Select the active element.
<Escape>	Cancel the previous selection action.
<Control-slash>	Select everything in the listbox.
<Control-backslash>	Clear the selection.

Multiple Select Mode

In `multiple` selection mode you can select more than one item, but you can add or remove only one item at a time. Dragging the mouse does not sweep out a selection. If you click on a selected item it is deselected. Table 29–7 specifies the complete set of bindings for `multiple` selection mode.

Table 29–7 Bindings for `multiple` selection mode.

`<Button-1>`	Select the item under the mouse.
`<ButtonRelease-1>`	Activate the item under the mouse.
`<Key-Up> <Key-Down>`	Move the active item up (down) one line, and start a new selection with this item as the anchor point.
`<Shift-Up> <Shift-Down>`	Move the active element up (down).
`<Control-Home>`	Activate and select the first element of the listbox.
`<Control-Shift-Home>`	Activate the first element of the listbox.
`<Control-End>`	Activate and select the last element of the listbox.
`<Control-Shift-End>`	Activate the last element of the listbox.
`<space> <Select>`	Select the active element.
`<Control-slash>`	Select everything in the listbox.
`<Control-backslash>`	Clear the selection.

Scroll Bindings

There are a number of bindings that scroll the display of the listbox. In addition to the standard middle-drag scrolling, there are some additional key bindings for scrolling. Table 29–8 summarizes the the scroll-related bindings:

Table 29–8 Listbox scroll bindings.

`<Button-2>`	Mark the start of a scroll operation.
`<B2-Motion>`	Scroll vertically *and* horizontally.
`<Left> <Right>`	Scroll horizontally by one character.
`<Control-Left> <Control-Right>` `<Control-Prior> <Control-Next>`	Scroll horizontally by one screen width.
`<Prior> <Next>`	Scroll vertically by one screen height.
`<Home> <End>`	Scroll to left and right edges of the screen, respectively.

Listbox Attributes

Table 29–9 lists the listbox widget attributes. The table uses the resource name for the attribute, which has capitals at internal word boundaries. In Tcl commands these options are specified with a dash and all lowercase.

Table 29–9 Listbox attribute resource names.

`background`	Background color (also `bg`).
`borderWidth`	Extra space around the edge of the text.
`cursor`	Cursor to display when mouse is over the widget.
`exportSelection`	If `true`, then the selected text is exported via the X selection mechanism.
`font`	Font for the text.
`foreground`	Foreground color (also `fg`).
`height`	Number of lines in the listbox.
`highlightBack-ground`	Focus highlight color when widget does not have focus.
`highlightColor`	Focus highlight color when widget has focus.
`highlightThickness`	Thickness of focus highlight rectangle.
`relief`	`flat`, `sunken`, `raised`, `groove`, `solid` or `ridge`.
`selectBackground`	Background color of selection.
`selectForeground`	Foreground color of selection.
`selectBorderWidth`	Width of selection border. Non-zero for 3D effect.
`selectMode`	Mode: `browse`, `single`, `extended`, or `multiple`.
`setGrid`	Boolean. Set gridding attribute.
`takeFocus`	Control focus changes from keyboard traversal.
`width`	Width, in average character sizes.
`xScrollCommand`	Connects listbox to a horizontal scrollbar.
`yScrollCommand`	Connects listbox to a vertical scrollbar.

Geometry Gridding

The `setGrid` attribute affects interactive resizing of the window containing the listbox. By default, a window can be resized to any size. If gridding is turned on, the size is restricted so that a whole number of lines and a whole number of average-width characters is displayed. Gridding affects the user feedback during an interactive resize. Without gridding the size is reported in pixel dimensions. When gridding is turned on, then the size is reported in grided units.

CHAPTER 30

The Text Widget

Tk text widget is a general-purpose editable text widget with features for line spacing, justification, tags, marks, and embedded windows.

The Tk text widget is versatile, simple to use for basic text display and manipulation, and has many advanced features to support sophisticated applications. The line spacing and justification can be controlled on a line-by-line basis. Fonts, sizes, and colors are controlled with *tags* that apply to ranges of text. Edit operations use positional *marks* that keep track of locations in text, even as text is inserted and deleted.

Tags are the most important feature of the text widget. You can define attributes like font and justification for a tag. When that tag is applied to a range of text, the text uses those attributes. Text can pick up attributes from any number of tags, so you can compose different tags for justification, font, line spacing, and more. You can also define bindings for tags so ranges of text can respond to the mouse. Any interesting application of the text widget uses tags extensively.

Text Indices

The characters in a text widget are addressed by their line number and the character position within the line. Lines are numbered starting at one, while characters are numbered starting at zero. The numbering for lines was chosen to be compatible with other programs that number lines starting at one, like compilers that generate line-oriented error messages. Here are some examples of text indices:

`1.0`	The first character.
`1.1`	The second character on the first line.
`2.end`	The newline character on the second line.

There are also symbolic indices. The `insert` index is the position at which new characters are normally inserted when the user types in characters. You can define new indices called *marks*, too, as described later. Table 30–1 summarizes the various forms for a text index.

Table 30–1 Text indices.

line.char	Lines count from 1. Characters count from 0.
@*x,y*	The character under the specified screen position.
`current`	The character currently under the mouse.
`end`	Just after the very last character.
image	The position of the embedded *image*.
`insert`	The position right after the insert cursor.
mark	Just after the named *mark*.
tag.first	The first character in the range tagged with *tag*.
tag.last	Just after the last character tagged with *tag*.
window	The position of the embedded *window*.

Inserting and Deleting Text

You add text with the `insert` operation (`$t` is a text widget):

```
$t insert index string ?tagList? ?string tagList? ...
```

The *index* can be any of the forms listed in the table, or it can be an index expression as described in a moment. The tags, if any, are added to the newly inserted text. Otherwise, *string* picks up any tags present on both sides of *index*. Tags are described on page 373. Multiple strings with different tags can be inserted with one command.

The most common index at which to insert text is the `insert` index, which is where the insert cursor is displayed. The default bindings insert text at `insert` when you type. You must include a newline character explicitly to force a line break:

```
$t insert insert "Hello, World\n"
```

The `delete` operation takes one or two indices. If only one index is given, the character at that position is deleted. If there are two indices, all the characters up to the second index are deleted. The character at the second index is not deleted. For example, you can delete the first line with this command:

```
$t delete 1.0 2.0
```

Index Arithmetic

The text widget supports a simple sort of arithmetic on indices. You can specify "the end of the line with this index" and "three characters before this index", and so on. This is done by grouping a modifying expression with the index. For example, the `insert` index can be modified like this:

```
"insert lineend"
"insert -3 chars"
```

The interpretation of indices and their modifiers is designed to operate well with the `delete` and `tag add` operations of the `text` widget. These operations apply to a range of text defined by two indices. The second index refers to the character just after the end of the range. For example, the following command deletes the word containing the insert cursor:

```
$t delete "insert wordstart" "insert wordend"
```

If you want to delete a whole line, including the trailing newline, you need to use a "`lineend +1 char`" modifier. Otherwise the newline remains and you are left with a blank line. If you supply several modifiers to an index, they are applied in left to right order:

```
$t delete "insert linestart" "insert lineend +1 char"
```

Table 30–2 summarizes the set of index modifiers.

Table 30–2 Index modifiers for text widgets.

`+` *`count`* `chars`	*`count`* characters past the index.
`-` *`count`* `chars`	*`count`* characters before the index.
`+` *`count`* `lines`	*`count`* lines past the index, retaining character position.
`-` *`count`* `lines`	*`count`* lines before the index, retaining character position.
`linestart`	The beginning of the line.
`lineend`	The end of the line (i.e., the newline character).
`wordstart`	The first character of a word.
`wordend`	Just after the last character of a word.

Comparing Indices

The `compare` operation compares two text indices and index expressions. You must use `compare` for reliable comparisons because, for example, index 1.3 is less than index 1.13. If you try to compare indices as numbers, you get the wrong answer. The general form of the `compare` operation is:

```
$t compare ix1 op ix2
```

The comparison operator can be one of `<`, `<=`, `==`, `=>`, `>`, or `!=`. The indices can be simple indices in the forms listed in Table 30–1, and they can be index expressions. Example 30–6 on page 383 uses the `compare` operation.

Text Marks

A mark is a symbolic name for a position between two characters. Marks have the property that when text is inserted or deleted they retain their logical position, not their numerical index position. Marks are persistent: if you delete the text surrounding a mark, it remains intact. Marks are created with the `mark set` operation and must be explicitly deleted with the `mark unset` operation. Once defined, a mark can be used in operations that require indices. The following commands define a mark at the beginning of the word containing the insert cursor and delete from there up to the end of the line:

```
$t mark set foobar "insert wordstart"
$t delete foobar "foobar lineend"
$t mark unset foobar
```

When a mark is defined, it is set to be just before the character specified by the index expression. In the previous example, this is just before the first character of the word where the insert cursor is. When a mark is used in an operation that requires an index, it refers to the character just after the mark. So, in many ways the mark seems associated with the character right after it, except that the mark remains even if that character is deleted.

You can use almost any string for the name of a mark. However, do not use pure numbers and do not include spaces, plus (+) or minus (-). These characters are used in the mark arithmetic and may cause problems if you put them into mark names. The `mark names` operation returns a list of all defined marks.

The `insert` mark defines where the insert cursor is displayed. The `insert` mark is treated specially: you cannot remove it with the `mark unset` operation. Attempting to do so does not raise an error, though, so the following is a quick way to unset all marks. The `eval` is necessary to join the list of mark names into the `mark unset` command:

```
eval {$t mark unset} [$t mark names]
```

Mark Gravity

Each mark has a *gravity* that determines what happens when characters are inserted at the mark. The default gravity is `right`, which means that the mark sticks to the character that is to its right. Inserting text at a mark with `right` gravity causes the mark to be pushed along so it is always after the inserted text. With `left` gravity the mark stays with the character to its left, so inserted text goes after the mark and the mark does not move. In versions of Tk before 4.0, marks had only right gravity, which made some uses of marks awkward. The `mark gravity` operation is used to query and modify the gravity of a mark:

```
$t mark gravity foobar
=> right
$t mark gravity foobar left
```

Text Tags

A tag is a symbolic name that is associated with one or more ranges of characters. A tag has attributes that affect the display of text that is tagged with it. These attributes include fonts, colors, tab stops, line spacing and justification. A tag can have event bindings so you can create hypertext. A tag can also be used to represent application-specific information. The `tag names` and `tag ranges` operations described later tell you what tags are defined and where they are applied.

You can use almost any string for the name of a tag. However, do not use pure numbers, and do not include spaces, plus (+) or minus (-). These characters are used in the mark arithmetic and may cause problems if you use them in tag names.

A tag is added to a range with the `tag add` operation. The following command applies the tag `everywhere` to all the text in the widget:

```
$t tag add everywhere 1.0 end
```

You can add one or more tags when text is inserted, too:

```
$t insert insert "new text" {someTag someOtherTag}
```

If you do not specify tags when text is inserted, then the text picks up any tags that are present on the characters on both sides of the insertion point. (Before Tk 4.0, tags from the left-hand character were picked up.) If you specify tags in the `insert` operation, only those tags are applied to the text.

A tag is removed from a range of text with the `tag remove` operation. However, even if there is no text labeled with a tag, its attribute settings are remembered. All information about a tag can be removed with the `tag delete` operation:

```
$t tag remove everywhere 3.0 6.end
$t tag delete everywhere
```

Tag Attributes

The attributes for a tag are defined with the `tag configure` operation. Table 30–3 specifies the set of attributes for tags. For example, a tag for blue text is defined with the following command:

```
$t tag configure blue -foreground blue
```

Table 30–3 Attributes for text tags.

`-background` *`color`*	The background color for text.
`-bgstipple` *`bitmap`*	A stipple pattern for the background color.
`-borderwidth` *`pixels`*	The width for 3D border effects.
`-fgstipple` *`bitmap`*	A stipple pattern for the foreground color.
`-font` *`font`*	The font for the text.

Table 30–3 Attributes for text tags. (Continued)

`-foreground` *color*	The foreground color for text.
`-justify` *how*	Justification: `left`, `right`, or `center`.
`-lmargin1` *pixels*	Normal left indent for a line.
`-lmargin2` *pixels*	Indent for the part of a line that gets wrapped.
`-offset` *pixels*	Baseline offset. Positive for superscripts.
`-overstrike boolean`	Draw text with a horizontal line through it.
`-relief` *what*	`flat`, `sunken`, `raised`, `groove`, `solid` or `ridge`.
`-rmargin` *pixels*	Right-hand margin.
`-spacing1` *pixels*	Additional space above a line.
`-spacing2` *pixels*	Additional space above wrapped part of line.
`-spacing3` *pixels*	Additional space below a line.
`-tabs` *tabstops*	Specify tab stops.
`-underline` *boolean*	If true, the text is underlined.
`-wrap` *mode*	Line wrap: `none`, `char`, or `word`.

Note that some attributes can only be applied with tags; there is no global attribute for `-bgstipple`, `-fgstipple`, `-justify`, `-lmargin1`, `-lmargin2`, `-offset`, `-overstrike`, `-rmargin`, and `-underline`. Table 30–9 on page 389 lists the attributes for the text widget as a whole.

The `-relief` and `-borderwidth` attributes go together. If you only specify a relief, there is no visible effect. The default relief is `flat`, too, so if you specify a border width without a relief you won't see any effect either.

The stipple attributes require a bitmap argument. Bitmaps and colors are explained in more detail in Chapter 35. For example, to "grey out" text you could use a foreground stipple of `gray50`:

```
$t tag configure disabled -fgstipple gray50
```

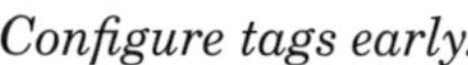

Configure tags early.

You can set up the appearance (and bindings) for tags once in your application, even before you have labeled any text with the tags. The attributes are retained until you explicitly delete the tag. If you are going to use the same appearance over and over again then it is more efficient to do the setup once so that Tk can retain the graphics context.

On the other hand, if you change the configuration of a tag, any text with that tag will be redrawn with the new attributes. Similarly, if you change a binding on a tag, all tagged characters are affected immediately.

The next example defines a few tags for character styles you might see in an editor. The example is uses the font naming system added in Tk 8.0, which is described on page 466:

Example 30–1 Tag configurations for basic character styles.

```
proc TextStyles { t } {
   $t tag configure bold -font {times 12 bold}
   $t tag configure italic -font {times 12 italic}
   $t tag configure fixed -font {courier 12}
   $t tag configure underline -underline true
   $t tag configure super -offset 6 -font {helvetica 8}
   $t tag configure sub -offset -6 -font {helvetica 8}
}
```

Mixing Attributes from Different Tags

A character can be labeled with more than one tag. For example, one tag could determine the font, another could determine the background color, and so on. If different tags try to supply the same attribute, a priority ordering is taken into account. The latest tag added to a range of text has the highest priority. The ordering of tags can be controlled explicitly with the `tag raise` and `tag lower` commands.

You can achieve interesting effects by composing attributes from different tags. In a mail reader, for example, the listing of messages in a mail folder can use one color to indicate messages that are marked for delete, and it can use another color for messages that are marked to be moved into another folder. The tags might be defined like this:

```
$t tag configure deleted -background grey75
$t tag configure moved -background yellow
```

These tags conflict, but they are never used on the same message. However, a selection could be indicated with an underline, for example:

```
$t tag configure select -underline true
```

You can add and remove the `select` tag to indicate what messages have been selected, and the underline is independent of the background color determined by the `moved` or `deleted` tag. If you look at the *exmh* implementation, the `ftocColor.tcl` file defines several text tags that are composed like this.

Line Spacing and Justification

The spacing and justification for text have several attributes. These settings are complicated by wrapped text lines. The text widget distinguishes between the first *display line* and the remaining display lines for a given text line. For example, if a line in the text widget has 80 characters but the window is only wide enough for 30, then the line may be wrapped onto three display lines. See Table 30–9 on page 389 for a description of the text widget's `wrap` attribute that controls this behavior.

Spacing is controlled with three attributes, and there are global spacing attributes as well as per-tag spacing attributes. The `-spacing1` attribute adds space above the first display line, while `-spacing2` adds space above the subsequent display lines that exist because of wrapping. The -spacing3 attribute adds space below the last display line, which could be the same as the first display line if the line is not wrapped.

The margin settings also distinguish between the first and remaining display lines. The -lmargin1 attribute specifies the indent for the first display line, while the -lmargin2 attribute specifies the indent for the rest of the display lines, if any. There is only a single attribute, -rmargin, for the right indent. These margin attributes are only tag attributes. The closest thing for the text widget as a whole is the -padx attribute, but this adds an equal amount of spacing on both sides:

Example 30–2 Line spacing and justification in the text widget.

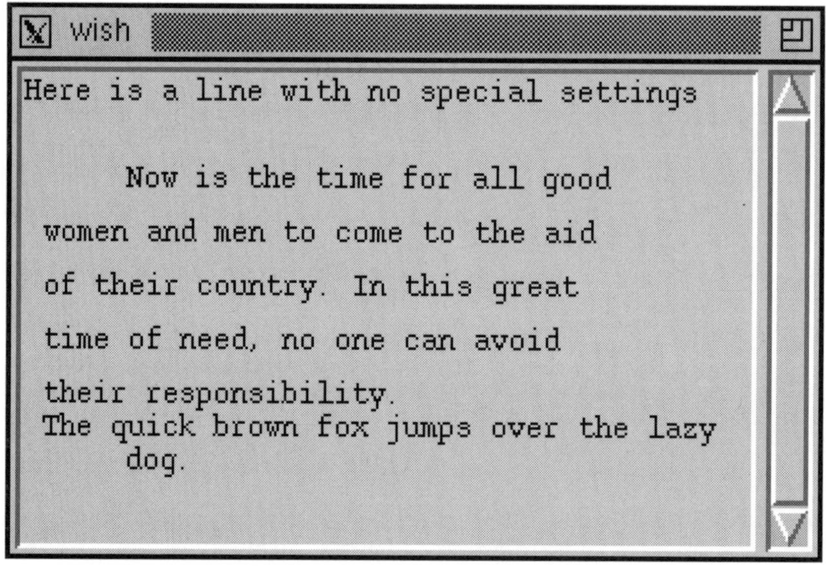


```
proc TextExample { f } {
    frame $f
    pack $f -side top -fill both -expand true
    set t [text $f.t -setgrid true -wrap word \
        -width 42 -height 14 \
        -yscrollcommand "$f.sy set"]
    scrollbar $f.sy -orient vert -command "$f.t yview"
    pack $f.sy -side right -fill y
    pack $f.t -side left -fill both -expand true

    $t tag configure para -spacing1 0.25i -spacing2 0.1i \
        -lmargin1 0.5i -lmargin2 0.1i -rmargin 0.5i
    $t tag configure hang -lmargin1 0.1i -lmargin2 0.5i

    $t insert end "Here is a line with no special settings\n"
    $t insert end "Now is the time for all good women and men
to come to the aid of their country. In this great time of
```

```
need, no one can avoid their responsibility.\n"
    $t insert end "The quick brown fox jumps over the lazy dog."

    $t tag add para 2.0 2.end
    $t tag add hang 3.0 3.end
}
```

The example defines two tags, `para` and `hang`, that have different spacing and margins. The `-spacing1` setting for `para` causes the white space before the second line. The `-spacing2` setting causes the white space between the wrapped portions of the second paragraph. The `hang` tag has no spacing attributes so the last paragraph starts right below the previous paragraph. You can also see the difference between the `-lmargin1` and `-lmargin2` settings.

The newline characters are inserted explicitly. Each newline character defines a new line for the purposes of indexing, but not necessarily for display, as this example shows. In the third line there is no newline. This means that if more text is inserted at the `end` mark, it will be on line three.

The values for the spacing and margin parameters are in screen units. Because different fonts are different sizes, you may need to compute the spacings as a function of the character sizes. The `bbox` operation returns the bounding box (x, y, width, height) for a given character:

```
$t insert 1.0 "ABCDE"
$t bbox 1.0
=> 4 4 8 12
```

The Tk 8.0 `font metrics` command, which is described on page 470, also gives detailed measurements:

```
font metrics {times 12}
-ascent 9 -descent 3 -linespace 12 -fixed 0
```

Text justification is limited to three styles: `left`, `right`, or `center`. There is no setting that causes the text to line up on both margins, which would have to be achieved by introducing variable spacing between words.

Tab Stops

Text widgets have adjustable tab stops. The `tabs` attribute is a list of tab stops, which are specified with a screen unit and optionally a keyword that indicates justification. The tab justification keywords are `left`, `right`, `center`, and `numeric`, and these can be abbreviated. The default is `left`. The following resource specification defines tab stops at 2-centimeter intervals with different justification:

```
*Text.tabs: 2c left 4c right 6c center 8c numeric
```

The `tabs` attribute applies to the whole text widget or to a tag. The last tab stop is extrapolated as needed. The following command defines a tag that has left justified tab stops every half inch:

```
$t tag configure foo -tabs ".5i left"
```

The Selection

The selection is implemented with a predefined tag named `sel`. If the application tags characters with `sel`, those characters are added to the selection. This is done as part of the default bindings on the text widget.

The `exportSelection` attribute of a text widget controls whether or not selected text is exported by the selection mechanism to other applications. By default the selection is exported. In this case, when another widget or application asserts ownership of the selection then the `sel` tag is removed from any characters that are tagged with it. Chapter 32 describes the selection mechanism in more detail.

You cannot delete the `sel` tag with the `tag delete` operation. However, it is not an error to do so. You can delete all the tags on the text widget with the following command. The `eval` command is used to join the list of tag names into the `tag delete` command:

```
eval {$t tag delete} [$t tag names]
```

Tag Bindings

You can associate a tag with bindings so when the user clicks on different areas of the text display, different things happen. The syntax for the `tag bind` command is similar to that of the main Tk `bind` command. You can both query and set the bindings for a tag. Chapter 23 describes the `bind` command and the syntax for events in detail.

The only events supported by the `tag bind` command are `Enter`, `Leave`, `ButtonPress`, `ButtonRelease`, `Motion`, `KeyPress`, and `KeyRelease`. `ButtonPress` and `KeyPress` can be shorted to `Button` and `Key` as in the regular `bind` command. The `Enter` and `Leave` events are triggered when the mouse moves in and out of characters with a tag, which is different than when the mouse moves in and out of the window.

If a character has multiple tags, then the bindings associated with all the tags will be invoked, in the order from lowest priority tag to highest priority tag. After all the tag bindings have run, the binding associated with the main widget is run, if any. The `continue` and `break` commands work inside tag bindings in a similar fashion as they work with regular command bindings. See Chapter 23 for the details.

Example 30–3 defines a text button that has a highlighted relief and an action associated with it. The example generates a new tag name so that each text button is unique. The relief and background are set for the tag to set it apart visually. The `winfo visual` command is used to find out if the display supports color before adding a colored background to the tag. On a black and white display, the button is displayed in reverse video (i.e., white on black.) The command is bound to `<Button-1>`, which is the same as `<ButtonPress-1>`.

The cursor is changed when the mouse is over the tagged area by binding to the `<Enter>` and `<Leave>` events. Upon leaving the tagged area, the cursor is restored. Another tag is used to remember the previous setting for the cursor. You could also use a global variable, but it is often useful to decorate the text with tags for your own purposes.

Example 30–3 An active text button.

```
proc TextButton { t start end command } {
   global textbutton
   if ![info exists textbutton(uid)] {
      set textbutton(uid) 0
   } else {
      incr textbutton(uid)
   }
   set tag button$textbutton(uid)
   $t tag configure $tag -relief raised -borderwidth 2
   if {[regexp color [winfo visual $t]]} {
      $t tag configure $tag -background thistle
   } else {
      $t tag configure $tag -background [$t cget -fg]
      $t tag configure $tag -foreground [$t cget -bg]
   }
   # Bind the command to the tag
   $t tag bind $tag <Button-1> $command
   $t tag add $tag $start $end
   # use another tag to remember the cursor
   $t tag bind $tag <Enter> \
      [list TextButtonChangeCursor %W $start $end tcross]
   $t tag bind $tag <Leave> {TextButtonRestoreCursor %W}
}
proc TextButtonChangeCursor {t start end cursor} {
   $t tag add cursor=[$t cget -cursor] $start $end
   $t config -cursor $cursor
}
proc TextButtonRestoreCursor {t} {
   regexp {cursor=([^ ]*)} [$t tag names] x cursor
   $t config -cursor $cursor
}
```

To behave even more like a button, the action should trigger upon `<Button-Release-1>`, and the appearance should change upon `<ButtonPress-1>`. If this is important to you, you can always embed a real Tk button. Embedding widgets is described later.

Searching Text

The `search` operation scans the text widget for a string that matches a pattern. The index of the text that matches the pattern is returned. The search starts at an index and covers all the text widget unless a stop index is supplied. You can use `end` as the stop index to prevent the search from wrapping back to the beginning of the document. The general form of the search operation is this:

```
$t search ?options? pattern index ?stopIndex?
```

Table 30–4 summarizes the `options` to the `search` operation:

Table 30–4 Options to the `search` operation.

`-forward`	Search forward from *index*. This is the default.
`-backward`	Search backward from *index*.
`-exact`	Match *pattern* exactly. This is the default.
`-regexp`	Use regular expression pattern matching.
`-nocase`	Lowercase letters in *pattern* can match upper case letters.
`-count varName`	Return in *varName* the number of characters that matched *pattern*.
`--`	End the options. Necessary if *pattern* begins with `-`.

If you use a regular expression to match a pattern, you may be interested in how much text matched so you can highlight the match. The `-count` option specifies a variable that gets the number of matching characters:

```
set start [$t search -count cnt -regexp -- $pattern 1.0 end]
$t tag add sel $start "$start +$cnt chars"
```

Embedded Widgets

The text widget can display embedded widgets as well as text. You can include a picture, for example, by constructing it in a canvas and then inserting the canvas into the text widget. An embedded widget takes up one character in terms of indices. You can address the widget by its index position or by the Tk pathname of the widget.

For example, suppose `$t` names a text widget. The following commands create a button and insert it into the text widget. The button behaves normally, and in this case it invokes the `Help` command when the user clicks on it:

```
button $t.help -bitmap questhead -command Help
$t window create end -window $t.help
```

By default an embedded widget is centered vertically on its text line. You can adjust this with the `-align` option to the `window create` command. This setting only takes effect if the image is smaller than the text in the line. I find that images are usually larger than the text line, and in that case the `-align` setting has no effect. The possible alignments are `top`, `center`, `baseline`, or `bottom`:

`top`	Top of widget lines up with top of text line.
`center`	Center of widget lines up with center of text line.

`baseline`	Bottom of widget lines up with text baseline.
`bottom`	Bottom of widget lines up with bottom of text line.

You can postpone the creation of the embedded widget by specifying a Tcl command that creates the window, instead of specifying the `-window` option. The delayed creation is useful if you have lots of widgets embedded in your text. In this case the Tcl command is evaluated just before the text widget needs to display the widget. In other words, when the user scrolls the text so the widget will appear, the Tcl command is run to create the widget:

Example 30–4 Delayed creation of embedded widgets.

```
$t window create end -create [list MakeGoBack $t]
proc MakeGoBack { t } {
    button $t.goback -text "Go to Line 1" \
        -command [list $t see 1.0]
}
```

The `MakeGoBack` procedure is introduced to eliminate potential quoting problems. If you need to execute more than one Tcl command to create the widget or if the embedded button has a complex command, the quoting can quickly get out of hand.

Table 30–5 gives the complete set of options for creating embedded widgets. You can change these later with the `window configure` operation. For example:

```
$t window configure $t.goback -padx 2
```

Table 30–5 Options to the `window create` operation.

`-align` *`where`*	Alignment: `top`, `center`, `bottom`, or `baseline`.
`-create` *`command`*	Tcl command to create the widget.
`-padx` *`pixels`*	Padding on either side of the widget.
`-pady` *`pixels`*	Padding above and below the widget.
`-stretch` *`boolean`*	If true, the widget is stretched vertically to match the spacing of the text line.
`-window` *`pathname`*	Tk pathname of the widget to embed.

You can specify the window to reconfigure by its pathname or the index where the window is located. In practice, naming the widget by its pathname is much more useful. Note that `end` is not useful for identifying an embedded window because the text widget treats `end` specially. You can insert a window at `end`, but `end` is always updated to be after the last item in the widget. Thus `end` will never name the position of an existing window.

Embedded Images

Tk 8.0 added embedded images that are much like embedded windows. They provide a more efficient way to add images than creating a canvas or label widget to hold the image. You can also put the same image into a text widget many times. Example 30–5 uses an image for the bullets in a bulleted list:

Example 30–5 Using embedded images for a bulleted list.

```
proc BList_Setup { t imagefile } {
    global blist
    set blist(image) [image create photo -file $imagefile]
    $t tag configure bulletlist -tabs ".5c center 1c left" \
        -lmargin1 0 -lmargin2 1c
}
proc BList_Item { t text {mark insert}} {
    global blist
    # Assume we are at the beginning of the line
    $t insert $mark \t bulletlist
    $t image create $mark -image $blist(image)
    $t insert $mark \t$text bulletlist
}
```

In Example 30–5, tabs are used to line up the bullet and the left edges of the text. The first tab centers the bullet over a point 0.5 centimeters from left margin. The second tab stop is the same as the `-lmargin2` setting so the text on the first line lines up with the text that wraps onto more lines.

If you update the image dynamically, all the instances of that image in the text widget are updated, too. This follows from the image model used in Tk, which is described in Chapter 35 on page 457.

The options for embedded images are mostly the same as those for embedded windows. One difference is that images have a `-name` option so you can reference an image without remembering its position in the text widget. You cannot use the image name directly because the same image can be embedded many times in the text widget. If you do not choose a name, the text widget assigns a name for you. The `image create` operation returns this name:

```
$t image create 1.0 -image image1
=> image1
$t image create end -image image1
=> image1#1
```

Table 30–6 gives the complete set of options for creating embedded images. You can change these later with the `image configure` operation.

Table 30–6 Options to the `image create` operation.

`-align` *where*	Alignment: `top`, `center`, `bottom`, or `baseline`. Only has effect if *image* is shorter than text line height.
`-image` *image*	The Tk image to add to the text widget.
`-name` *name*	A name for this instance of the image. A `#`*num* may be appended to generate a unique name.
`-padx` *pixels*	Padding on either side of the image.
`-pady` *pixels*	Padding above and below the image.

Looking inside the Text Widget

The text widget has several operations that let you examine its contents. The simplest is `get`, which returns a range of text from the widget. You can get all the text with this command:

```
$t get 1.0 end
```

Looking at Tags

The `tag names` command returns all the tag names, or the names of the tags at a specified index:

```
$t tag names ?index?
```

A text tag can be applied to many different ranges of text. The `tag ranges` operation returns a list of indices that alternate between the start and end of tag ranges. The `foreach` command with two loop variables makes it easy to iterate through all the ranges:

```
foreach {start end} [$t tag ranges $tag] {
   # start is the beginning of a range
   # end is the end of a range
}
```

The `tag nextrange` and `tag prevrange` operations return two indices that delimit the next and previous range of a tag. They take a starting index and an optional ending index. The `tag nextrange` operation skips to the next range if the tag is present at the starting index, unless the starting index is right at the start of a range. The `tag prevrange` operation is complementary. It does not skip the current range, unless the starting index is at the beginning of the range. These rules are used in Example 30–6 that defines a procedure to return the current range:

Example 30–6 Finding the current range of a text tag.

```
proc Text_CurrentRange { t tag mark } {
   set range [$t tag prevrange $tag $mark]
   set end [lindex $range 1]
```

```
    if {[llength $range] == 0 || [$t compare $end < $mark]} {
        # This occurs when the mark is at the
        # very beginning of the node
        set range [$t tag nextrange $tag $mark]
        if {[llength $range] == 0 ||
                [$t compare $mark < [lindex $range 0]]} {
            return {}
        }
    }
    return $range
}
```

Looking at Marks

The `mark names` operation returns the names of all the marks. Unlike `tag names`, you cannot supply an index to find out if there are marks there. You must use the `dump` operation described later. The `mark next` and `mark previous` operations search from a given index for a mark. The `mark next` operation will find a mark if it is at the starting index.

Dumping the Contents

The `dump` operation provides the most general way to examine the contents of the text widget. The general form of the command is:

`$t dump ?options? ix1 ?ix2?`

The `dump` operation returns information for the elements from *ix1* to *ix2*, or just for the elements at *ix1* if *ix2* is not specified. You can limit what information is returned with options that indicate what to return: `-text`, `-mark`, `-tag`, `-image`, `-window`, or `-all`.

Three pieces of information are returned for each element of the text widget: the type, the value, and the index. The possible types are `text`, `tagon`, `tagoff`, `mark`, `image`, and `window`. The information reflects the way the text widget represents its contents. Tags are represented as `tagon` and `tagoff` elements. Text is stored in segments that do not include any marks, tag elements, windows, or images. In addition, a newline ends a text segment.

Example 30–7 prints out the contents of the text widget:

Example 30–7 Dumping the text widget.

```
proc Text_Dump {t {start 1.0} {end end}} {
    foreach {key value index} [$t dump $start $end] {
        if {$key == "text"} {
            puts "$index \"$value\""
        } else {
            puts "$index $key $value"
        }
    }
}
```

Instead of having dump return all the information, you can have it call a Tcl command to process each element. The command gets passed three pieces of information for each element: the type, the value, and the index. Example 30–8 shows another way to print out the text widget contents:

Example 30–8 Dumping the text widget with a command callback.

```
proc Text_Dump {t {start 1.0} {end end}} {
    $t dump -command TextDump $start $end
}
proc TextDump {key value index} {
    if {$key == "text"} {
        puts "$index \"$value\""
    } else {
        puts "$index $key $value"
    }
}
```

Text Bindings

There is an extensive set of default bindings for text widgets. In general, the commands that move the insertion cursor also clear the selection. Often you can hold the Shift key down to extend the selection, or hold the Control key down to move the insertion cursor without affecting the selection. Table 30–7 lists the default bindings for the text widget:

Table 30–7 Bindings for the text widget.

<Any-Key>	Insert normal printing characters.
<Button-1>	Set the insert point, clear the selection, set focus.
<Control-Button-1>	Set the insert point without affecting the selection.
<B1-Motion>	Sweep out a selection from the insert point.
<Double-Button-1>	Select the word under the mouse.
<Triple-Button-1>	Select the line under the mouse.
<Shift-Button-1>	Adjust the end of selection closest to the mouse.
<Shift-B1-Motion>	Continue to adjust the selection.
<Button-2>	Paste the selection, or set the scrolling anchor.
<B2-Motion>	Scroll the window.
<Key-Left> <Control-b>	Move the cursor left one character. Clear selection.
<Shift-Left>	Move the cursor and extend the selection.
<Control-Left>	Move the cursor by words. Clear the selection.

Table 30–7 Bindings for the text widget. (Continued)

`<Control-Shift-Left>`	Move the cursor by words. Extend the selection.
`<Key-Right>` `<Control-f>`	`Right` bindings are analogous to `Left` bindings.
`<Meta-b>` `<Meta-f>`	Same as `<Control-Left>`, `<Control-Right>`.
`<Key-Up>` `<Control-p>`	Move the cursor up one line. Clear the selection.
`<Shift-Up>`	Move the cursor up one line. Extend the selection.
`<Control-Up>`	Move the cursor up by paragraphs, which are a group of lines separated by a blank line.
`<Control-Shift-Up>`	Move the cursor up by paragraph. Extend selection.
`<Key-Down>` `<Control-n>`	All `Down` bindings are analogous to `Up` bindings.
`<Next>` `<Prior>`	Move the cursor by one screen. Clear the selection.
`<Shift-Next>` `<Shift-Prior>`	Move the cursor by one screen. Extend the selection.
`<Home>` `<Control-a>`	Move the cursor to line start. Clear the selection.
`<Shift-Home>`	Move the cursor to line start. Extend the selection.
`<End>` `<Control-e>`	Move the cursor to line end. Clear the selection.
`<Shift-End>`	Move the cursor to line end. Extend the selection.
`<Control-Home>` `<Meta-less>`	Move the cursor to the beginning of text. Clear the selection.
`<Control-End>` `<Meta-greater>`	Move the cursor to the end of text. Clear the selection.
`<Select>` `<Control-space>`	Set the selection anchor to the position of the cursor.
`<Shift-Select>` `<Control-Shift-space>`	Adjust the selection to the position of the cursor.
`<Control-slash>`	Select everything in the text widget.
`<Control-backslash>`	Clear the selection.
`<Delete>`	Delete the selection, if any. Otherwise delete the character to the right of the cursor.
`<BackSpace>` `<Control-h>`	Delete the selection, if any. Otherwise delete the character to the left of the cursor.
`<Control-d>`	Delete character to the right of the cursor.
`<Meta-d>`	Delete word to the right of the cursor.
`<Control-k>`	Delete from cursor to end of the line. If you are at the end of line, delete the newline character.
`<Control-o>`	Insert a newline but do not advance the cursor.

Table 30–7 Bindings for the text widget. (Continued)

<Meta-Delete> <Meta-BackSpace>	Delete the word to the left of the cursor.
<Control-t>	Transpose the characters on either side of the cursor.
<<Copy>> <Meta-w>	Copy the selection to the clipboard.
<<Cut>> <Control-w>	Cut the selection and save on the clipboard.
<<Paste>> <Control-y>	Paste from the clipboard.

Text Operations

Table 30–8 describes the text widget operations, including some that are not discussed in this chapter. In the table, `$t` is a text widget:

Table 30–8 Operations for the text widget.

`$t bbox` *`index`*	Return the bounding box of the character at *`index`*. Four numbers are returned: *`x y width height`*.
`$t cget` *`option`*	Return the value of the configuration option.
`$t compare` *`i1 op i2`*	Perform index comparison. *`i1`* and *`i2`* are indexes. *`op`* is one of `< <= == >= > !=`
`$t configure ...`	Query or set configuration options.
`$t debug` *`boolean`*	Enable consistency checking for B-tree code.
`$t delete` *`i1 ?i2?`*	Delete from *`i1`* up to, but not including *`i2`*. Just delete the character at *`i1`* if *`i2`* is not specified.
`$t dlineinfo` *`index`*	Return the bounding box, in pixels, of the display for the line containing index. Five numbers are returned: *`x y width height baseline`*.
`$t dump` *`?options? i1 ?i2?`*	Return the marks, tags, windows, images, and text contained in the widget. Options are `-all`, `-command` *`command`*, `-image`, `-mark`, `-tag`, `-text`, and `-window`.
`$t get` *`i1 ?i2?`*	Return the text from *`i1`* to *`i2`*, or just the character at *`i1`* if *`i2`* is not specified.
`$t image cget` *`option`*	Return the value of the image *`option`*.
`$t image configure` *`?options?`*	Query or set the configuration of an embedded image.
`$t image create` *`option value ...`*	Create an embedded image. Options are described in Table 30–6 on page 383.

Table 30–8 Operations for the text widget. (Continued)

`$t image names`	Return the names of all embedded images.
`$t index` *index*	Return the numerical value of *index*.
`$t insert` *index chars ?tags? ?chars tags?* ...	Insert *chars* at the specified *index*. If *tags* are specified, they are added to the new characters.
`$t mark gravity` *name ?direction?*	Query or assign a gravity direction to the mark *name*. *direction*, if specified, is `left` or `right`.
`$t mark names`	Return a list of defined marks.
`$t mark next` *index*	Return the mark after *index*.
`$t mark previous` *index*	Return the mark before *index*.
`$t mark set` *name index*	Define a mark *name* at the given *index*.
`$t mark unset` *name1 ?name2 ...?*	Delete the named mark, or marks.
`$t scan mark` *x y*	Anchor a scrolling operation.
`$t scan dragto` *x y*	Scroll based on a new position.
`$t search` *?switches? pattern index ?stopIndex?*	Search for *pattern* starting at *index*. The index of the start of the match is returned. Switches are described in Table 30–4 on page 380.
`$t see` *index*	Position the display to view *index*.
`$t tag add` *name i1 ?i2? ?i1 i2? ?i1 i2? ...*	Add the tag to *i1* through, but not including *i2*, or just the character at *i1* if *i2* is not given.
`$t tag bind` *name ?sequence? ?script?*	Query or define bindings for the tag *name*.
`$t tag configure` *name ...*	Set or query the configuration of tag *name*.
`$t tag cget` *name option*	Return the value of *option* for tag *name*.
`$t tag delete` *tag1 ?tag2 ...?*	Delete information for the named tags.
`$t tag lower` *tag ?below?*	Lower the priority of *tag* to the lowest priority or to just below tag *below*.
`$t tag names` *?index?*	Return the names of the tags at the specified *index*, or in the whole widget, sorted from lowest to highest priority.
`$t tag nextrange` *tag i1 ?i2?*	Return a list of two indices that are the next range of text with tag that starts at or after *i1* and before index *i2*, or the end.
`$t tag prevrange` *tag i1 ?i2?*	Return a list of two indices that are the previous range of text with tag that ends at or before *i1* and at or after index *i2*, or 1.0.

Table 30–8 Operations for the text widget. (Continued)

`$t tag raise` *tag ?above?*	Raise the priority of *tag* to the highest priority, or to just above the priority of tag *above*.
`$t tag ranges` *tag*	Return a list describing all the ranges of tag.
`$t tag remove` *tag i1 ?i2? ?i1 i2? ?i1 i2? ...*	Remove *tag* from the range *i1* up to, but not including *i2*, or just at *i1* if *i2* is not specified.
`$t window config` *win ...*	Query or modify the configuration of the embedded window. *win* is a Tk pathname or an index.
`$t window cget` *win option*	Return the value of *option* for *win*.
`$t window create` *ix args*	Create an embedded window at *ix*.
`$t window names`	Return a list of windows embedded in `$t`.
`$t xview`	Return two fractions between zero and one that describes the amount of text off-screen to the left and the amount of text displayed.
`$t xview moveto` *fraction*	Position the text so *fraction* of the text is off screen to the left.
`$t xview scroll` *num what*	Scroll *num* of *what*, which is *units* or *pages*.
`$t yview`	Return two fractions between zero and one that describes the amount of text off-screen toward the beginning and the amount of text displayed.
`$t yview moveto` *fraction*	Position the text so *fraction* of the text is off-screen toward the beginning.
`$t yview scroll` *num what*	Scroll *num* of *what*, which is *units* or *pages*.
`$t yview ?-pickplace?` *ix*	Obsolete. Use the `see` operation, which is similar.
`$t yview` *num*	Obsolete. Position line *num* at the top of screen.

Text Attributes

Table 30–9 lists the attributes for the text widget. The table uses the resource name, which has capitals at internal word boundaries. In Tcl commands the attributes are specified with a dash and all lowercase:

Table 30–9 Text attribute resource names.

`background`	Background color (also `bg`).
`borderWidth`	Extra space around the edge of the text.
`cursor`	Cursor to display when mouse is over the widget.
`exportSelection`	If true, selected text is exported to the selection.

Table 30–9 Text attribute resource names. (Continued)

`font`	Default font for the text.
`foreground`	Foreground color (also `fg`).
`height`	Height, in text lines.
`highlightBackground`	Focus highlight color when widget does not have focus.
`highlightColor`	Color for input focus highlight border.
`highlightThickness`	Width of highlight border.
`insertBackground`	Color for the insert cursor.
`insertBorderWidth`	Size of 3D border for insert cursor.
`insertOffTime`	Milliseconds insert cursor blinks off.
`insertOnTime`	Milliseconds insert cursor blinks on.
`insertWidth`	Width of the insert cursor.
`padX`	Extra space to the left and right of the text.
`padY`	Extra space above and below the text.
`relief`	`flat`, `sunken`, `raised`, `groove`, `ridge`, or `solid`.
`selectBackground`	Background color of selected text.
`selectForeground`	Foreground color of selected text.
`selectBorderWidth`	Size of 3D border for selection highlight.
`setGrid`	Enable/disable geometry gridding.
`spacing1`	Extra space above each unwrapped line.
`spacing2`	Space between parts of a line that have wrapped.
`spacing3`	Extra space below an unwrapped line.
`state`	Editable (`normal`) or read-only (`disabled`).
`tabs`	Tab stops.
`takeFocus`	Control focus changes from keyboard traversal.
`width`	Width, in characters, of the text display.
`wrap`	Line wrap mode: `none`, `char`, or `word`.
`xScrollCommand`	Tcl command prefix for horizontal scrolling.
`yScrollCommand`	Tcl command prefix for vertical scrolling.

CHAPTER 31

The Canvas Widget

The canvas widget is a general-purpose widget that you can program to display a variety of objects including arcs, images, lines, ovals, polygons, rectangles, text, and embedded windows.

Canvas widgets display objects such as lines and images, and each object can have bindings that respond to user input, or be animated under program control. The objects can be labeled with *tags*, and the tags can be configured with display attributes and event bindings. This chapter describes all the predefined canvas object types. Chapter 42 outlines the C programming interface for creating new canvas objects.

Canvas Coordinates

The coordinate space of the canvas has 0, 0 at the top left corner. Larger X coordinates are to the right, and larger Y coordinates are downward. The position and possibly the size of a canvas object is determined by a set of coordinates. Different objects are characterized by different numbers of coordinates. For example, text objects have two coordinates, `x1 y1`, that specify their anchor point. A line can have many pairs of coordinates that specify the end points of its segments. The coordinates are set when the object is created, and they can be updated later with the `coords` operation. By default, coordinates are in pixels. Append a coordinate with one of the following letters to change the units:

```
c   centimeters
i   inches
m   millimeters
p   printer points (1/72 inches)
```

The tk scale command, which is described on page 498, changes the mapping from pixels to other screen measures. Use it before creating the canvas.

The width and height attributes of the canvas determine the size of the viewable area. The scrollRegion attribute of the canvas determines the boundaries of the canvas. Its value is four numbers that specify the upper-left and lower-right coordinates of the canvas. If you do not specify a scroll region, it defaults to the size of the viewable area. Example 31–1 creates a canvas that has a 1000 by 400 scrolling region, and a 300 by 200 viewing area. The canvas is connected to two scrollbars to provide horizontal and vertical scrolling:

Example 31–1 A large scrolling canvas.

```
proc Scrolled_Canvas { c args } {
    frame $c
    eval {canvas $c.canvas \
        -xscrollcommand [list $c.xscroll set] \
        -yscrollcommand [list $c.yscroll set] \
        -highlightthickness 0 \
        -borderwidth 0} $args
    scrollbar $c.xscroll -orient horizontal \
        -command [list $c.canvas xview]
    scrollbar $c.yscroll -orient vertical \
        -command [list $c.canvas yview]
    grid $c.canvas $c.yscroll -sticky news
    grid $c.xscroll -sticky ew
    grid rowconfigure $c 0 -weight 1
    grid columnconfigure $c 0 -weight 1
    return $c.canvas
}
Scrolled_Canvas .c -width 300 -height 200 \
    -scrollregion {0 0 1000 400}
=> .c.canvas
pack .c -fill both -expand true
```

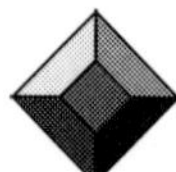

Borders are drawn in the canvas.

The highlight thickness and border width are set to 0 in Example 31–1. Otherwise these features occupy some of the canvas viewable area. If you want a raised border for your canvas, either use another frame, or remember to offset your positions to avoid having objects clipped by the borders.

Hello, World!

Example 31–2 creates an object that you can drag around with the mouse. It introduces the use of tags to classify objects. In this case the movable tag gets bindings that let you drag the item, so any item with the movable tag shares this behavior. The example uses Scrolled_Canvas from Example 31–1. When you use a scrolled canvas, you must map from the view coordinates reported by bindings to the canvas coordinates used to locate objects:

Example 31–2 The canvas "Hello, World!" example.

```
proc CanvasHello {} {
	set can [Scrolled_Canvas .c -width 400 -height 100 \
		-scrollregion {0 0 800 400}]
	pack .c -fill both -expand true
	# Create a text object on the canvas
	$can create text 50 50 -text "Hello, World!" -tag movable
	# Bind actions to objects with the movable tag
	$can bind movable <Button-1> {CanvasMark %x %y %W}
	$can bind movable <B1-Motion> {CanvasDrag %x %y %W}
}
proc CanvasMark { x y can} {
	global canvas
	# Map from view coordinates to canvas coordinates
	set x [$can canvasx $x]
	set y [$can canvasy $y]
	# Remember the object and its location
	set canvas($can,obj) [$can find closest $x $y]
	set canvas($can,x) $x
	set canvas($can,y) $y
}
proc CanvasDrag { x y can} {
	global canvas
	# Map from view coordinates to canvas coordinates
	set x [$can canvasx $x]
	set y [$can canvasy $y]
	# Move the current object
	set dx [expr $x - $canvas($can,x)]
	set dy [expr $y - $canvas($can,y)]
	$can move $canvas($can,obj) $dx $dy
	set canvas($can,x) $x
	set canvas($can,y) $y
}
```


Example 31–2 creates a `text` object and gives it a tag named `movable`:

```
.c create text 50 50 -text "Hello, World!" -tag movable
```

The first argument after `create` specifies the type, and the remaining arguments depend on the type of object being created. Each canvas object requires some coordinates, optionally followed by attribute value pairs. The complete set of attributes for canvas objects are presented later in this chapter. A `text` object needs two coordinates for its location.

Canvas Tags

The `create` operation returns an ID for the object being created, which would have been 1 in this case. However, the code manipulates the canvas objects by specifying a *tag* instead of an object ID. A tag is a more general handle on canvas objects. Many objects can have the same tag, and an object can have more than one tag. You can define bindings on tags, and you can define attributes for tags that will be picked up by objects with those tags.

A tag name can be almost any string, but you should avoid spaces that can cause parsing problems and pure numbers that get confused with object IDs. There are two predefined tags: `current` and `all`. The `current` tag applies to whatever object is under the mouse. The `all` tag applies to all the objects on the canvas.

The example defines behavior for objects with the `movable` tag. Pressing button 1 starts a drag, and dragging with the mouse button down moves the object. The pathname of the canvas (`%W`) is passed to `CanvasMark` and `CanvasDrag` so these procedures can be used on different canvases. The `%x` and `%y` keywords get substituted with the X and Y coordinate of the event:

```
$can bind movable <Button-1> {CanvasMark %x %y %W}
$can bind movable <B1-Motion> {CanvasDrag %x %y %W}
```

The `CanvasMark` and `CanvasDrag` procedures let you drag the object around the canvas. Because `CanvasMark` is applied to any object with the `movable` tag, it must first find the object that was clicked on. First the view coordinates are mapped into the canvas coordinates with the `canvasx` and `canvasy` operations:

```
set x [$can canvasx x]
set y [$can canvasy y]
```

Once you do this you can use the `find` operation:

```
set canvas($can,obj) [$can find closest $x $y]
```

The actual moving is done in `CanvasDrag` with the `move` operation:

```
$can move $canvas($can,obj) $dx $dy
```

Try creating a few other object types and dragging them around, too:

```
$can create rect 10 10 30 30 -fill red -tag movable
$can create line 1 1 40 40 90 60 -width 2 -tag movable
$can create poly 1 1 40 40 90 60 -fill blue -tag movable
```

The `CanvasMark` and `CanvasDrag` procedures can be used with any canvas. They use the global array `canvas` to keep their state, and they parameterize the indices with the canvas pathname to avoid conflict if there is more that one canvas in the application. If you get into this coding habit early, then you will find it easy to write reusable code.

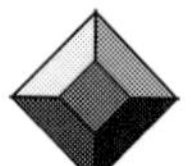

Canvas tags are not persistent.

Canvas tags do not work exactly like tags in the text widget. In the text widget, a tag is completely independent of the text. You can configure a text tag before it is applied to text, and the tag configuration is remembered even if you remove it from the text. A canvas tag, in contrast, must be applied to an object before you can configure it. If you configure a canvas tag that is not applied to any objects, those settings are forgotten. If you remove all the objects that share a tag, any settings associated with those tags are forgotten.

The Min Max Scale Example

This section presents Example 31–3 that constructs a scale-like object with two sliders. The sliders represent the minimum and maximum values for some parameter. Clearly, the minimum cannot be greater than the maximum, and vice versa. The example creates three rectangles on the canvas. One rectangle forms the long axis of the slider that represents the range of possible values. The other two rectangles are markers that represent the values. Two text objects float below the markers to give the current values of the minimum and maximum.

The example introduces four canvas operations: `bbox`, `coords`, `scale`, and `move`. The `bbox` operation returns the bounding box of an object or of all objects with a given tag. The `coords` operation sets or queries the coordinates of an object. The `scale` operation stretches an object, and the `move` operation translates the position of an object.

Use tags instead of object IDs.

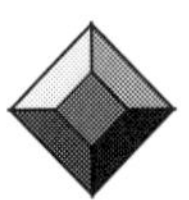

Many of the canvas operations take an argument that identifies objects. The value can be a tag name, or it can be the numerical object identifier returned by the `create` operation. Example 31–3 does not use object IDs. Instead, it gives each object a symbolic identifier with a tag, plus it introduces more tags to represent classes of objects. The example uses the `all` tag to move all the items and to find out the bounding box of the image. The left box and the left hanging text both have the `left` tag. They can be moved together, and they share the same bindings. Similarly, the `right` tag is shared by the right box and the right hanging text. Each item has its own unique tag so it can be manipulated individually, too. Those tags are `slider`, `lbox`, `lnum`, `rbox`, and `rnum`:

Example 31–3 A min max scale canvas example.

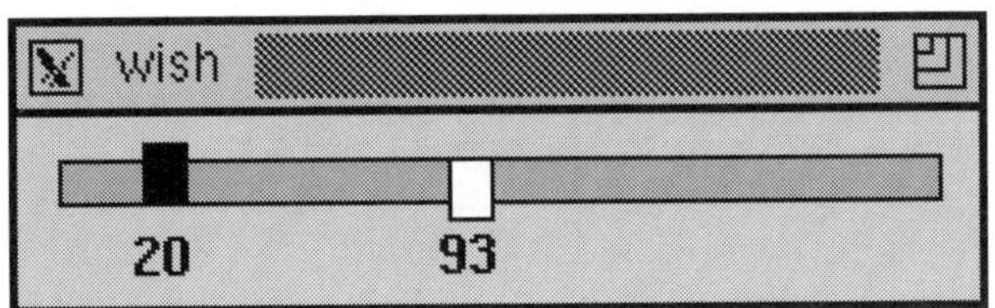


```
proc Scale2 {w min max {width {}} } {
    global scale2
    if {$width == {}} {
        # Set the long dimension, in pixels
        set width [expr $max - $min]
    }
    # Save parameters
    set scale2($w,scale) [expr ($max-$min)/$width.0]
    set scale2($w,min) $min;# Current minimum
    set scale2($w,max) $max
    set scale2($w,Min) $min ;# Lower bound to the scale
    set scale2($w,Max) $max
    set scale2($w,L) 10
```

```
    set scale2($w,R) [expr $width+10]

    # Build from 0 to 100, then scale and move it later.
    # Distance between left edges of boxes is 100.
    # The box is 10 wide, therefore the slider is 110 long.
    # The left box sticks up, and the right one hangs down.

    canvas $w
    $w create rect 0 0 110 10 -fill grey -tag slider
    $w create rect 0 -4 10 10 -fill black -tag {left lbox}
    $w create rect 100 0 110 14 -fill red -tag {right rbox}
    $w create text 5 16 -anchor n -text $min -tag {left lnum}
    $w create text 105 16 -anchor n -text $max \
        -tag {right rnum} -fill red

    # Stretch/shrink the slider to the right length
    set scale [expr ($width+10) / 110.0]
    $w scale slider 0 0 $scale 1.0

    # move the right box and text to match new length
    set nx [lindex [$w coords slider] 2]
    $w move right [expr $nx-110] 0
    # Move everything into view
    $w move all 10 10

    # Make the canvas fit comfortably around the image
    set bbox [$w bbox all]
    set height [expr [lindex $bbox 3]+4]
    $w config -height $height -width [expr $width+30]

    # Bind drag actions
    $w bind left  <Button-1> {Scale2Mark %W %x lbox}
    $w bind right <Button-1> {Scale2Mark %W %x rbox}
    $w bind left  <B1-Motion> {Scale2Drag %W %x lbox}
    $w bind right <B1-Motion> {Scale2Drag %W %x rbox}
}
```

The slider is constructed with absolute coordinates, and then it is scaled to the desired width. The alternative is to compute the coordinates based on the desired width. I have found it clearer to use numbers when creating the initial layout as opposed to using `expr` or introducing more variables. The `scale` operation stretches the slider bar to the correct length. The `scale` operation takes a reference point, which in our case is (0, 0), and independent scale factors for the X and Y dimensions. The scale factor is computed from the `width` parameter, taking into account the extra length added (10) so that the distance between the left edge of the slider boxes is `$width`:

```
set scale [expr ($width+10) / 110.0]
$w scale slider 0 0 $scale 1.0
```

The `move` operation repositions the right box and right hanging text. If the marker boxes are scaled, their shape gets distorted. The `coords` operation returns a list of four numbers: *x1 y1 x2 y2*. The distance to move is just the difference between the new right coordinate and the value used when constructing the slider initially. The box and text share the same tag, `right`, so they are both moved with a single `move` operation:

```
set nx [lindex [$w coords slider] 2]
$w move right [expr $nx-110] 0
```

After the slider is constructed, it is shifted away from (0, 0), which is the upper-left corner of the canvas. The `bbox` operation returns four coordinates: *x1 y1 x2 y2*, that define the bounding box of the items with the given tag. In the example, *y1* is zero, so *y2* gives us the height of the image. The information returned by `bbox` can be off by a few pixels, and the example needs a few more pixels of height to avoid clipping the text. The width is computed based on the extra length added for the marker box, the 10 pixels the whole image was shifted, and 10 more for the same amount of space on the right side:

```
set bbox [$w bbox all]
set height [expr [lindex $bbox 3]+4]
$w config -height $height -width [expr $width+30]
```

Bindings are defined for the box and hanging text. The general tags `left` and `right` are used for the bindings. This means you can drag either the box or the text to move the slider. The pathname of the canvas is passed into these procedures so you could have more than one double slider in your interface:

```
$w bind left  <Button-1> {Scale2Mark %W %x lbox}
$w bind right <Button-1> {Scale2Mark %W %x rbox}
$w bind left  <B1-Motion> {Scale2Drag %W %x lbox}
$w bind right <B1-Motion> {Scale2Drag %W %x rbox}
```


Example 31–4 Moving the markers for the min max scale.

```
proc Scale2Mark { w x what } {
	global scale2
	# Remember the anchor point for the drag
	set scale2($w,$what) $x
}
proc Scale2Drag { w x what } {
	global scale2

	# Compute delta and update anchor point
	set x1 $scale2($w,$what)
	set scale2($w,$what) $x
	set dx [expr $x - $x1]

	# Find out where the boxes are currently
	set rx [lindex [$w coords rbox] 0]
	set lx [lindex [$w coords lbox] 0]

	if {$what == "lbox"} {
		# Constrain the movement to be between the
		# left edge and the right marker.
		if {$lx + $dx > $rx} {
```

```
            set dx [expr $rx - $lx]
            set scale2($w,$what) $rx
        } elseif {$lx + $dx < $scale2($w,L)} {
            set dx [expr $scale2($w,L) - $lx]
            set scale2($w,$what) $scale2($w,L)
        }
        $w move left $dx 0

        # Update the minimum value and the hanging text
        set lx [lindex [$w coords lbox] 0]
        set scale2($w,min) [expr int($scale2($w,Min) + \
            ($lx-$scale2($w,L)) * $scale2($w,scale))]
        $w itemconfigure lnum -text $scale2($w,min)
    } else {
        # Constrain the movement to be between the
        # right edge and the left marker
        if {$rx + $dx < $lx} {
            set dx [expr $lx - $rx]
            set scale2($w,$what) $lx
        } elseif {$rx + $dx > $scale2($w,R)} {
            set dx [expr $scale2($w,R) - $rx]
            set scale2($w,$what) $scale2($w,R)
        }
        $w move right $dx 0

        # Update the maximum value and the hanging text
        set rx [lindex [$w coords right] 0]
        set scale2($w,max) [expr int($scale2($w,Min) + \
            ($rx-$scale2($w,L)) * $scale2($w,scale))]
        $w itemconfigure rnum -text $scale2($w,max)
    }
}
proc Scale2Value {w} {
    global scale2
    # Return the current values of the double slider
    return [list $scale2($w,min) $scale2($w,max)]
}
```

The `Scale2Mark` procedure initializes an anchor position, `scale2($w,$what)`, and `Scale2Drag` uses this to detect how far the mouse has moved. The change in position, `dx`, is constrained so that the markers cannot move outside their bounds. The anchor is updated if a constraint was used, and this means the marker will not move until the mouse is moved back over the marker. [Try commenting out the assignments to `scale2($w,$what)` inside the `if` statement.] After the marker and hanging text are moved, the value of the associated parameter is computed based on the parameters of the scale. The `Scale2Value` procedure queries the current values of the double slider.

Canvas Objects

The next several sections describe the built-in object types for the canvas: arc, bitmap, image, line, oval, polygon, rectangle, text, and window. Each object has its own set of attributes, and some attributes are found on most or all object types. Every object has a -tags attribute used to label the object with a list of symbolic names. Most objects, even text, specify their color with the -fill attribute. Only the bitmap uses -foreground and -background. If the object has a border, the color of the border is specified with -outline, and the thickness of the outline is specified with -width.

Arc Items

An arc is a section of an oval. The dimensions of the oval are determined by four coordinates that are its bounding box. The arc is then determined by two angles, the start angle and the extent. The region of the oval can be filled or unfilled, and there are three different ways to define the fill region. The pieslice style connects the arc with the center point of the oval. The chord style connects the two end points of the arc. The arc style just draws the arc itself and there is no fill. Example 31–5 shows three arcs with the same bounding box but different styles and angles:

Example 31–5 Canvas arc items.

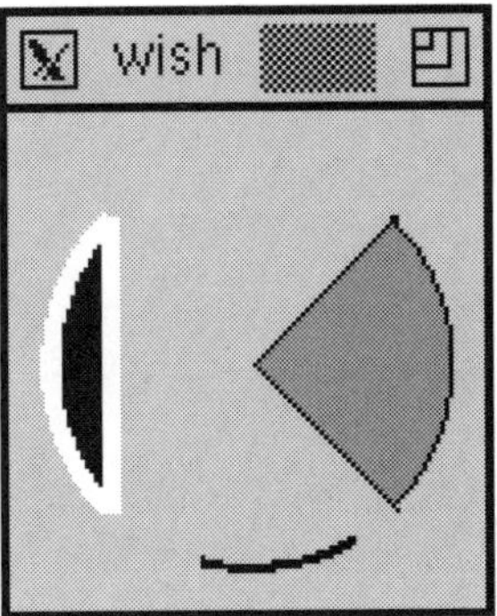


```
# $c is a canvas
$c create arc 10 10 100 100 -start 45 -extent -90 \
   -style pieslice -fill orange -outline black
$c create arc 10 10 100 100 -start 135 -extent 90 \
   -style chord -fill blue -outline white -width 4
$c create arc 10 10 100 100 -start 255 -extent 45 \
   -style arc -outline black -width 3
```

Table 31–1 specifies the complete set of arc attributes.

Table 31–1 Arc attributes.

`-extent` *degrees*	The length of the arc in the counter-clockwise direction.
`-fill` *color*	The color of the interior of the arc region.
`-outline` *color*	The color of the arc itself.
`-outlinestipple` *bmap*	The stipple pattern for the outline of the arc.
`-start` *degrees*	The starting angle of the arc.
`-stipple` *bitmap*	A stipple pattern for the fill.
`-style` *style*	`pieslice`, `chord`, `arc`.
`-tags` *tagList*	List of tags for the arc item.
`-width` *num*	Width, in canvas coordinates, of the arc and outline.

Bitmap Items

A bitmap is a simple graphic with a foreground and background color. One bit per pixel is used to choose between the foreground and the background. If you do not specify a background color, the background bits are clear and the canvas background shows through. A canvas `bitmap` item is positioned with two coordinates and an anchor position. Its size is determined by the bitmap data. The `bitmap` itself is specified with a symbolic name or by the name of a file that contains its definition. If the name begins with an `@`, it indicates a file name. The bitmaps built into wish are shown in the example below. Chapter 42 outlines the C interface for registering bitmaps under a name.

Example 31–6 Canvas `bitmap` items.

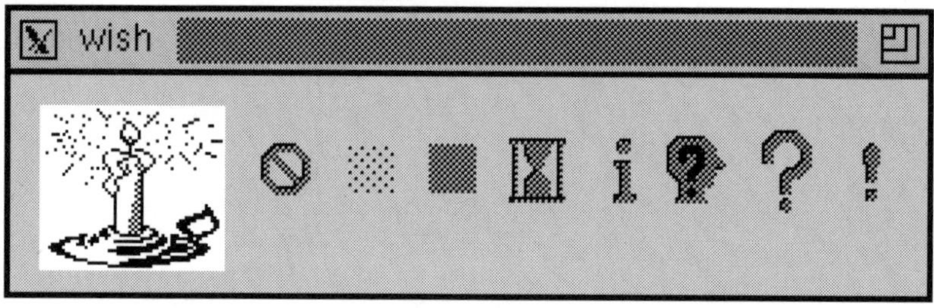


```
set o [$c create bitmap 10 10 -bitmap @candle.xbm -anchor nw\
    -background white -foreground blue]
set x [lindex [$c bbox $o] 2] ;# Right edge of bitmap
foreach builtin {error gray12 gray50 hourglass \
                info questhead question warning} {
    incr x 20
    set o [$c create bitmap $x 30 -bitmap $builtin -anchor c]
    set x [lindex [$c bbox $o] 2]
}
```

Table 31–2 specifies the complete set of `bitmap` attributes.

Table 31–2 Bitmap attributes.

`-anchor` *`position`*	Anchor: `c`, `n`, `ne`, `e`, `se`, `s`, `sw`, `w`, or `nw`.
`-background` *`color`*	The background color (for zero bits).
`-bitmap` *`name`*	A built-in bitmap.
`-bitmap @`*`filename`*	A bitmap defined by a file.
`-foreground` *`color`*	The foreground color (for one bits).
`-tags` *`tagList`*	List of tags for the bitmap item.

Image Items

The canvas `image` objects use the general image mechanism of Tk. You must first define an image using the `image` command, which is described in Chapter 35 in the section *Bitmaps and Images*. Once you have defined an image, all you need to specify for the canvas is its position, anchor point, and any tags. The size and color information is set when the image is defined. If an image is redefined, anything displaying that image automatically gets updated. Example 31–7 creates one image and puts six instances of it on a canvas:

Example 31–7 Canvas `image` items.

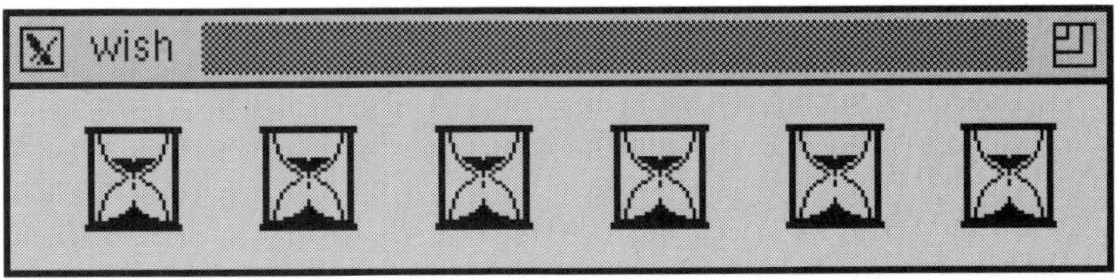


```
image create bitmap hourglass2 \
    -file hourglass.bitmap -maskfile hourglass.mask \
    -background white -foreground blue
for {set x 20} {$x < 300} {incr x 20} {
    $c create image $x 10 -image hourglass2 -anchor nw
    incr x [image width hourglass2]
}
```

Table 31–3 specifies the attributes for canvas `image` items.

Table 31–3 Image attributes.

`-anchor` *`position`*	Anchor: `c`, `n`, `ne`, `e`, `se`, `s`, `sw`, `w`, or `nw`.
`-image` *`name`*	The name of an image.
`-tags` *`tagList`*	List of tags for the image item.

IV. Tk Widgets

Line Items

A line has two or more sets of coordinates, where each set of coordinates defines an end point of a line segment. The segments can be joined in several different styles, and the whole line can be drawn with a spline fit as opposed to straight-line segments. The next example draws a line in two steps. In the first pass, single-segment lines are drawn. When the stroke completes, these are replaced with a single line segment that is drawn with a spline curve.

Example 31–8 A canvas stroke drawing example.

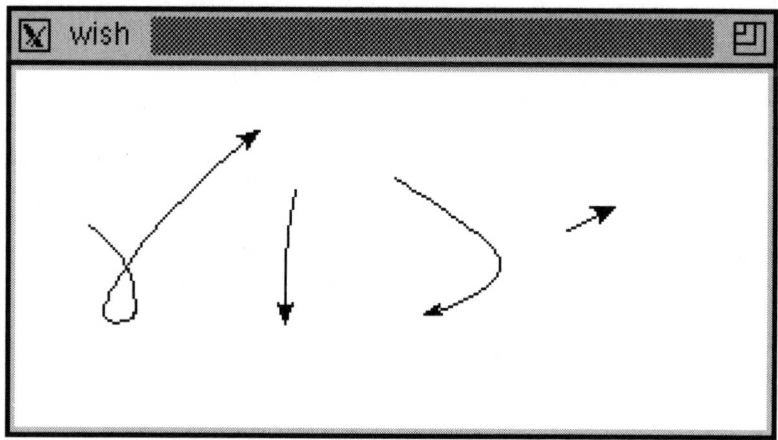


```
proc StrokeInit {} {
   canvas .c ; pack .c
   bind .c <Button-1> {StrokeBegin %W %x %y}
   bind .c <B1-Motion> {Stroke %W %x %y}
   bind .c <ButtonRelease-1> {StrokeEnd %W %x %y}
}
proc StrokeBegin { w x y } {
   global stroke
   catch {unset stroke}
   set stroke(N) 0
   set stroke(0) [list $x $y]
}
proc Stroke { w x y } {
   global stroke
   set coords $stroke($stroke(N))
   lappend coords $x $y
   incr stroke(N)
   set stroke($stroke(N)) [list $x $y]
   # eval gets the coordinates into individual arguments
   eval {$w create line} $coords {-tag segments}
}
proc StrokeEnd { w x y } {
   global stroke
   set coords {}
```

```
    for {set i 0} {$i <= $stroke(N)} {incr i} {
        append coords $stroke($i) " "
    }
    $w delete segments
    eval {$w create line} $coords \
        {-tag line -joinstyle round -smooth true -arrow last}
}
```

Example 31–8 uses the `stroke` array to hold the points of the line as it builds up the stroke. At the end of the stroke it assembles the points into a list. The `eval` command concatenates this list of points onto the `create line` command. Recall that `eval` uses `concat` if it gets multiple arguments. The other parts of the `create line` command are protected by braces so they get evaluated only once. Chapter 10 describes this trick in more detail on page 115

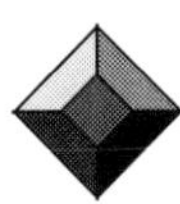

The arrow attribute adds an arrow head to the end of the stroke. If you try this example you will notice that the arrow is not always aimed as you expect. This is because there are often many points generated close together as you release the mouse button. In fact, the X and Y coordinates seen by `StrokeEnd` are always the same as those seen by the last `Stroke` call. If you add this duplicate point to the end of the list of points, no arrowhead is drawn at all. In practice you might want to make `Stroke` filter out points that are too close together.

Table 31–4 specifies the complete set of line attributes. The `capstyle` affects the way the ends of the line are drawn. The `joinstyle` affects the way line segments are joined together. The `capstyle` and `joinstyle` attributes are from the X window system and may not be implemented on the Macintosh and Windows platforms. Future versions of Tk may support dashed and dotted lines, too.

IV. Tk Widgets

Table 31–4 Line attributes.

`-arrow` *where*	Arrow location: `none`, `first`, `last`, or `both`.
`-arrowshape` *{a b c}*	Three parameters that describe the shape of the arrow. `c` is the width and `b` is the overall length. `a` is the length of the part that touches the line (e.g., `8 10 3`).
`-capstyle` *what*	Line ends: `butt`, `projecting`, or `round`.
`-fill` *color*	The color of the line.
`-joinstyle` *what*	Line joints: `bevel`, `miter`, or `round`.
`-smooth` *boolean*	If `true`, a spline curve is drawn.
`-splinesteps` *num*	Number of line segments that approximate the spline.
`-stipple` *bitmap*	Stipple pattern for line fill.
`-tags` *tagList*	Set of tags for the line item.
`-width` *width*	Width of the line, in screen units.

Oval Items

An `oval` is defined by two sets of coordinates that define its bounding box. If the box is square, a circle is drawn. You can set the color of the interior of the oval as well as the outline of the oval. A sampler of ovals is shown in Example 31–9.

Example 31–9 Canvas `oval` items.

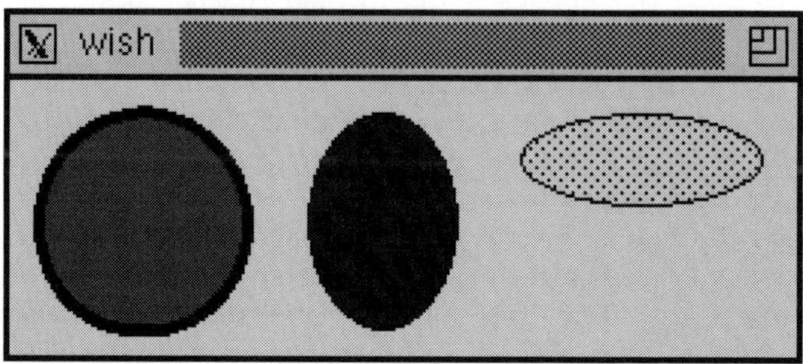


```
$c create oval 10 10 80 80 -fill red -width 4
$c create oval 100 10 150 80 -fill blue -width 0
$c create oval 170 10 250 40 -fill black -stipple gray12
```

Table 31–5 specifies the complete set of `oval` attributes.

Table 31–5 Oval attributes.

`-fill` *color*	The color of the interior of the oval.
`-outline` *color*	The color for the outline of the oval.
`-stipple` *bitmap*	Stipple pattern for oval fill.
`-tags` *tagList*	Set of tags for the oval item.
`-width` *width*	The thickness of the outline.

Polygon Items

A `polygon` is a closed shape specified by sets of points, one for each vertex of the polygon. The vertices can be connected with smooth or straight lines. Example 31–10 creates a stop sign. The picture is centered at (0, 0) and then moved fully onto the canvas:

Example 31–10 Canvas `polygon` items.

```
$c create poly 20 -40 40 -20 40 20 20 40 -20 40 \
   -40 20 -40 -20 -20 -40 -fill red \
   -outline white -width 5
$c create text 0 0 -text STOP -fill white \
   -font {helvetica 18 bold}
$c move all 50 50
```

Table 31–6 specifies the `polygon` attributes.

Table 31–6 Polygon attributes.

`-fill` *color*	The color of the polygon.
`-outline` *color*	The color of the polygon's outline.
`-smooth` *boolean*	If `true`, a spline curve is drawn around the points.
`-splinesteps` *num*	Number of line segments that approximate the spline.
`-stipple` *bitmap*	Stipple pattern for polygon fill.
`-tags` *tagList*	Set of tags for the line item.
`-width` *width*	The thickness of the outline.

Rectangle Items

A `rectangle` is specified with two coordinates that are its opposite corners. A rectangle can have a fill color and an outline color. If you do not specify a fill, then the background of the canvas (or other objects) show through. If you stipple the fill, the background also shows through the clear bits of the stipple pattern. You must use a second rectangle if you want the stippled fill to completely hide what is behind it. Example 31–11 drags out a box as the user drags the mouse. All it requires is remembering the last rectangle drawn so it can be deleted when the next box is drawn:

Example 31–11 Dragging out a box.

```
proc BoxInit {} {
	canvas .c -bg white ; pack .c
	bind .c <Button-1> {BoxBegin %W %x %y}
	bind .c <B1-Motion> {BoxDrag %W %x %y}
}
proc BoxBegin { w x y } {
	global box
	set box($w,anchor) [list $x $y]
	catch {unset box($w,last)}
}
proc BoxDrag { w x y } {
	global box
	catch {$w delete $box($w,last)}
	set box($w,last) [eval {$w create rect} $box($w,anchor) \
		{$x $y -tag box}]
}
```

The example uses `box($w,anchor)` to record the start of the box. This is a list with the X and Y coordinates. The `eval` command is used so that this list can be spliced into the `create rect` command. Table 31–7 specifies the complete set of rectangle attributes:

Table 31–7 Rectangle attributes.

`-fill` *color*	The color of the interior of the rectangle.
`-outline` *color*	The color for the outline of the rectangle.
`-stipple` *bitmap*	Stipple pattern for rectangle fill.
`-tags` *tagList*	Set of tags for the rectangle item.
`-width` *width*	The thickness of the outline.

Text Items

The canvas `text` item provides yet another way to display and edit text. It supports selection, editing, and can extend onto multiple lines. The position of a `text` item is specified by one set of coordinates and an anchor position. The size of the text is determined by the number of lines and the length of each line. A new line is started if there is a newline in the text string. If a `width` is specified, in screen units, then any line that is longer than this is wrapped onto multiple lines. The wrap occurs before a space character.

The editing and selection operations for `text` items use indices to specify positions within a given text item. These are very similar to those used in the entry widget. Table 31–8 summarizes the indices for canvas `text` items.

There are several canvas operations that manipulate text items. These are similar to some of the operations of the entry widget. The `dchars` and `select to` operations treat the second index differently than the corresponding operations

Table 31–8 Indices for canvas `text` items.

`0`	Index of the first character.
`end`	Index just past the last character.
`number`	Index a character, where *`number`* counts from zero.
`insert`	Index of the character right after the insertion cursor.
`sel.first`	Index of the first character in the selection.
`sel.last`	Index of the last character in the selection.
`@`*`x,y`*	Index of the character under the specified X and Y coordinate.

in the entry and text widget. The character at the second index *is* included in the operation (e.g., deleted), while in the entry and text widget it is not.

The canvas text operations are parameterized by the tag or ID of the canvas object being manipulated. If the tag refers to more than one object, then the operations apply to the first object in the display list that supports an insert cursor. The display list is described on page 412. Table 31–9 summarizes the operations on `text` items. In the table `$t` is a text item or tag and `$c` is a canvas.

Table 31–9 Canvas operations that apply to `text` items.

`$c dchars $t` *`first ?last?`*	Delete the characters from *`first`* through *`last`*, or just the character at *`first`*.
`$c focus ?$t?`	Set input focus to the specified item, or return the ID of the item with the focus if it is not given.
`$c icursor $t` *`index`*	Set the insert cursor to just before *`index`*.
`$c index $t` *`index`*	Return the numerical value of *`index`*.
`$c insert $t` *`index string`*	Insert the string just before *`index`*.
`$c select adjust $t` *`index`*	Move the boundary of an existing selection.
`$c select clear`	Clear the selection.
`$c select from $t` *`index`*	Start a selection.
`$c select item`	Returns the ID of the selected item, if any.
`$c select to $t` *`index`*	Extend the selection to the specified *`index`*.

There are no default bindings for canvas `text` items. Example 31–12 sets up some basic bindings for canvas text items. The `<Button-1>` and `<Button-2>` bindings are on the canvas as a whole. The rest of the bindings are on items with the `text` tag. You must add the `text` tag to text items that should share the editable text behavior. Small procedures are introduced for each binding to hide the details and any local variables needed in the operations.

Canvas `find overlapping` *vs.* `find closest`.

The `CanvasFocus` procedure uses the canvas `find overlapping` operation to see if a text object has been clicked. This must be used because `find closest` finds an object no matter how far away it is. It also uses the `type` operation to make sure only text objects are given the focus. If you want other object types to respond to key events, you should change that.

The `CanvasPaste` procedure does one of two things. It pastes the selection into the canvas item that has the focus. If no item has the focus, then a new `text` item is created with the selection as its value:

Example 31–12 Simple edit bindings for canvas `text` items.

```
proc Canvas_EditBind { c } {
    bind $c <Button-1> \
        {CanvasFocus %W [%W canvasx %x] [%W canvasy %y]}
    bind $c <Button-2> \
        {CanvasPaste %W [%W canvasx %x] [%W canvasy %y]}
    bind $c <<Cut>> {CanvasTextCopy %W; CanvasDelete %W}
    bind $c <<Copy>> {CanvasTextCopy %W}
    bind $c <<Paste>> {CanvasPaste %W}
    $c bind text <Button-1> \
        {CanvasTextHit %W [%W canvasx %x] [%W canvasy %y]}
    $c bind text <B1-Motion> \
        {CanvasTextDrag %W [%W canvasx %x] [%W canvasy %y]}
    $c bind text <Delete> {CanvasDelete %W}
    $c bind text <Control-d> {CanvasDelChar %W}
    $c bind text <Control-h> {CanvasBackSpace %W}
    $c bind text <BackSpace> {CanvasBackSpace %W}
    $c bind text <Control-Delete> {CanvasErase %W}
    $c bind text <Return> {CanvasNewline %W}
    $c bind text <Any-Key> {CanvasInsert %W %A}
    $c bind text <Key-Right> {CanvasMoveRight %W}
    $c bind text <Control-f> {CanvasMoveRight %W}
    $c bind text <Key-Left> {CanvasMoveLeft %W}
    $c bind text <Control-b> {CanvasMoveLeft %W}
}
proc CanvasFocus {c x y} {
    focus $c
    set id [$c find overlapping [expr $x-2] [expr $y-2] \
            [expr $x+2] [expr $y+2]]
    if {($id == {}) || ([$c type $id] != "text")} {
        set t [$c create text $x $y -text "" \
            -tags text -anchor nw]
        $c focus $t
        $c select clear
        $c icursor $t 0
    }
}
proc CanvasTextHit {c x y {select 1}} {
    $c focus current
    $c icursor current @$x,$y
    $c select clear
```

```
        $c select from current @$x,$y
    }
    proc CanvasTextDrag {c x y} {
        $c select to current @$x,$y
    }
    proc CanvasDelete {c} {
        if {[$c select item] != {}} {
            $c dchars [$c select item] sel.first sel.last
        } elseif {[$c focus] != {}} {
            $c dchars [$c focus] insert
        }
    }
    proc CanvasTextCopy {c} {
        if {[$c select item] != {}} {
            clipboard clear
            set t [$c select item]
            set text [$c itemcget $t -text]
            set start [$c index $t sel.first]
            set end [$c index $t sel.last]
            clipboard append [string range $text $start $end]
        } elseif {[$c focus] != {}} {
            clipboard clear
            set t [$c focus]
            set text [$c itemcget $t -text]
            clipboard append $text
        }
    }
    proc CanvasDelChar {c} {
        if {[$c focus] != {}} {
            $c dchars [$c focus] insert
        }
    }
    proc CanvasBackSpace {c} {
        if {[$c select item] != {}} {
            $c dchars [$c select item] sel.first sel.last
        } elseif {[$c focus] != {}} {
            set _t [$c focus]
            $c icursor $_t [expr [$c index $_t insert]-1]
            $c dchars $_t insert
        }
    }
    proc CanvasErase {c} {
        $c delete [$c focus]
    }
    proc CanvasNewline {c} {
        $c insert [$c focus] insert \n
    }
    proc CanvasInsert {c char} {
        $c insert [$c focus] insert $char
    }
    proc CanvasPaste {c {x {}} {y {}}} {
        if {[catch {selection get} _s] &&
             [catch {selection get -selection CLIPBOARD} _s]} {
            return ;# No selection
        }
```

```
        set id [$c focus]
        if {[string length $id] == 0 } {
            set id [$c find withtag current]
        }
        if {[string length $id] == 0 } {
            # No object under the mouse
            if {[string length $x] == 0} {
                # Keyboard paste
                set x [expr [winfo pointerx $c] - [winfo rootx $c]]
                set y [expr [winfo pointery $c] - [winfo rooty $c]]
            }
            CanvasFocus $c $x $y
        } else {
            $c focus $id
        }
        $c insert [$c focus] insert $_s
    }

    proc CanvasMoveRight {c} {
        $c icursor [$c focus] [expr [$c index current insert]+1]
    }
    proc CanvasMoveLeft {c} {
        $c icursor [$c focus] [expr [$c index current insert]-1]
    }
```

Table 31–10 specifies the complete set of attributes for `text` items. Note that there are no foreground and background attributes. Instead, the fill color specifies the color for the text. It is possible to stipple the text as well.

Table 31–10 Text attributes

`-anchor` *`position`*	Anchor: `c`, `n`, `ne`, `e`, `se`, `s`, `sw`, `w`, or `nw`.
`-fill` *`color`*	The foreground color for the text.
`-font` *`font`*	The font for the text.
`-justify` *`how`*	Justification: `left`, `right`, or `center`.
`-stipple` *`bitmap`*	Stipple pattern for the text fill.
`-tags` *`tagList`*	Set of tags for the rectangle item.
`-text` *`string`*	The string to display.
`-width` *`width`*	The width, in screen units, before text is wrapped

Window Items

A `window` item lets you position other Tk widgets on a canvas. The position is specified by one set of coordinates and an anchor position. You can also specify the width and height, or you can let the widget determine its own size. The following example uses a canvas to provide a scrolling surface for a large set of labeled entries. A frame is created and a set of labeled entry widgets are packed into it. This main frame is put onto the canvas as a single window item. This way we let `grid` take care of arranging all the labeled entries. The size of the canvas is set up so that a whole number of labeled entries are displayed. The scroll region and scroll increment are set up so that clicking on the scrollbar arrows brings one new labeled entry completely into view.

Example 31–13 Using a canvas to scroll a set of widgets.

```
proc Example31-13 { top title labels } {
   # Create a resizable toplevel window
   toplevel $top
   wm minsize $top 200 100
   wm title $top $title

   # Create a frame for buttons,
   # Only Dismiss does anything useful
   set f [frame $top.buttons -bd 4]
   button $f.quit -text Dismiss -command "destroy $top"
   button $f.save -text Save
   button $f.reset -text Reset
   pack $f.quit $f.save $f.reset -side right
   pack $f -side top -fill x

   # Create a scrolling canvas
   frame $top.c
   canvas $top.c.canvas -width 10 -height 10 \
      -yscrollcommand [list $top.c.yscroll set]
   scrollbar $top.c.yscroll -orient vertical \
      -command [list $top.c.canvas yview]
   pack $top.c.yscroll -side right -fill y
   pack $top.c.canvas -side left -fill both -expand true
   pack $top.c -side top -fill both -expand true

   Scrolled_EntrySet $top.c.canvas $labels
}
proc Scrolled_EntrySet { canvas labels } {
   # Create one frame to hold everything
   # and position it on the canvas
   set f [frame $canvas.f -bd 0]
   $canvas create window 0 0 -anchor nw -window $f

   # Create and grid the labeled entries
   set i 0
   foreach label $labels {
      label $f.label$i -text $label
      entry $f.entry$i
      grid $f.label$i $f.entry$i
      grid $f.label$i -sticky w
      grid $f.entry$i -sticky we
      incr i
   }
   set child $f.entry0
```

IV. Tk Widgets

```
        # Wait for the window to become visible and then
        # set up the scroll region based on
        # the requested size of the frame, and set
        # the scroll increment based on the
        # requested height of the widgets

        tkwait visibility $child
        set bbox [grid bbox $f 0 0]
        set incr [lindex $bbox 3]
        set width [winfo reqwidth $f]
        set height [winfo reqheight $f]
        $canvas config -scrollregion "0 0 $width $height"
        $canvas config -yscrollincrement $incr
        set max [llength $labels]
        if {$max > 10} {
            set max 10
        }
        set height [expr $incr * $max]
        $canvas config -width $width -height $height
}
Example31-13 .ex "An example" {
        alpha beta gamma delta epsilon zeta eta theta iota kappa
        lambda mu nu xi omicron pi rho sigma tau upsilon
        phi chi psi omega}
```

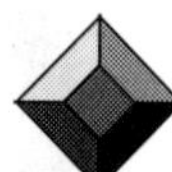

The `tkwait visibility` command is important to the example. It causes the script to suspend execution until the top-level window, `$top`, is displayed on the screen. The `tkwait` is necessary so the right information gets returned by the `grid bbox` commands. By waiting for a subframe of the main frame, `$child`, we ensure that grid has gone through all its processing to position the interior widgets. The canvas's scroll region is set to be just large enough to hold the complete frame. The scroll increment is set to the height of one of the grid cells. Each click on the scrollbar arrows brings one new grid row completely into view.

Canvas Operations

Table 31–11 summarizes the operations on canvas widgets. In the table, `$c` is a canvas and `$t` represents a canvas tag or numerical object ID. In some cases an operation only applies to a single object. In these cases, if a tag identifies several objects, the first object in the display list is operated on.

The canvas *display list* refers to the global order among canvas objects. New objects are put at the end of the display list. Objects later in the display list obscure objects earlier in the list. The term *above* refers to objects later in the display list.

Table 31–9 describes several of the canvas operations that only apply to `text` objects. They are `dchars`, `focus`, `index`, `icursor`, `insert`, and `select`. Table 31–11 does not repeat those operations.

Table 31–11 Operations on a `canvas` widget.

`$c addtag tag above $t`	Add *tag* to the item just above `$t` in the display list.
`$c addtag tag all`	Add *tag* to all objects in the canvas.
`$c addtag tag below $t`	Add *tag* to the item just below `$t` in the display list.
`$c addtag tag closest x y ?halo? ?start?`	Add *tag* to the item closest to the *x y* position. If more than one object is the same distance away, or if more than one object is within *halo* pixels, then the last one in the display list (uppermost) is returned. If *start* is specified, the closest object after *start* in the display list is returned.
`$c addtag tag enclosed x1 y1 x2 y2`	Add *tag* to the items completely enclosed in the specified region. *x1* <= *x2*, *y1* <= *y2*.
`$c addtag tag withtag $t`	Add *tag* to the items identified by `$t`.
`$c bbox $t ?tag tag ...?`	Return the bounding box of the items identified by the tag(s) in the form *x1 y1 x2 y2*
`$c bind $t ?sequence? ?command?`	Set or query the bindings of canvas items.
`$c canvasx screenx ?grid?`	Map from the X screen coordinate *screenx* to the X coordinate in canvas space, rounded to multiples of *grid* if specified.
`$c canvasy screeny ?grid?`	Map from screen Y to canvas Y.
`$c cget option`	Return the value of *option* for the canvas.
`$c configure ...`	Query or update the attributes of the canvas.
`$c coords $t ?x1 y1 ...?`	Query or modify the coordinates of the item.
`$c create type x y ?x2 y2 ...? ?opt value ...?`	Create a canvas object of the specified *type* at the specified coordinates.
`$c delete $t ?tag ...?`	Delete the item(s) specified by the tag(s) or ID(s).
`$c dtag $t ?deltag?`	Remove the specified tags from the items identified by `$t`. If *deltag* is omitted, it defaults to `$t`.
`$c find addtagSearch ...`	Return the IDs of the tags that match the search specification: `above`, `all`, `below`, `closest`, `enclosed`, and `withtag`, as for `addtag`.
`$c gettags $t`	Return the tags associated with the first item identified by `$t`.
`$c itemcget $t option`	Return the value of *option* for item `$t`.
`$c itemconfigure $t ...`	Query or reconfigure item `$t`.
`$c lower $t ?belowThis?`	Move the items identified by `$t` to the beginning of the display list, or just before *belowThis*.

Table 31–11 Operations on a `canvas` widget. (Continued)

`$c move $t` *dx dy*	Move `$t` by the specified amount.
`$c postscript ...`	Generate postscript. Table 31–12 lists options.
`$c raise $t ?`*aboveThis*`?`	Move the items identified by `$t` to the end of the display list, or just after *aboveThis*.
`$c scale $t` *x0 y0 xS yS*	Scale the coordinates of the items identified by `$t`. The distance between *x0* and a given X coordinate changes by a factor of *xS*. Similarly for Y.
`$c scan mark` *x y*	Set a mark for a scrolling operation.
`$c scan dragto` *x y*	Scroll the canvas from the previous mark.
`$c type $t`	Return the type of the first item identified by `$t`.
`$t xview`	Return two fractions between zero and one that describes the amount of the canvas off-screen to the left and the amount of the canvas displayed.
`$t xview moveto` *fraction*	Position the canvas so *fraction* of the scroll region is off-screen to the left.
`$t xview scroll` *num what*	Scroll *num* of *what*, which is *units* or *pages*.
`$t yview`	Return two fractions between zero and one that describes the amount of the canvas off-screen to the top and the amount of the canvas displayed.
`$t yview moveto` *fraction*	Position the text so *fraction* of the canvas scroll region is off-screen toward the top.
`$t yview scroll` *num what*	Scroll *num* of *what*, which is *units* or *pages*.

Generating Postscript

The `postscript` operation generates postscript based on the contents of a canvas. One limitation to note is that embedded windows are not captured in the postscript output. Table 31–12 summarizes all the options for generating postscript:

Table 31–12 Canvas `postscript` options.

`-colormap` *varName*	The index of *varName* is a named color, and the contents of each element is the postscript code to generate the RGB values for that color.
`-colormode` *mode*	*mode* is one of `color`, `grey`, or `mono`.
`-file` *name*	The file in which to write the postscript. If not specified, the postscript is returned as the result of the command.

Table 31–12 Canvas `postscript` options. (Continued)

`-fontmap` *`varName`*	The index of *`varName`* is an X font name. Each element contains a list of two items: a postscript font name and a point size.
`-height` *`size`*	Height of the area to print.
`-pageanchor` *`anchor`*	Anchor: `c`, `n`, `ne`, `e`, `se`, `s`, `sw`, `w`, or `nw`.
`-pageheight` *`size`*	Height of image on the output. A floating point number followed by `c` (centimeters), `i` (inches), `m` (millimeters), or `p` (printer points).
`-pagewidth` *`size`*	Width of image on the output.
`-pagex` *`position`*	The output X coordinate of the anchor point.
`-pagey` *`position`*	The output Y coordinate of the anchor point.
`-rotate` *`boolean`*	If true, rotate so that X axis is the long direction of the page (landscape orientation).
`-width` *`size`*	Width of the area to print.
`-x` *`position`*	Canvas X coordinate of left edge of the image.
`-y` *`position`*	Canvas Y coordinate of top edge of the image.

You control what region of the canvas is printed with the `-width`, `-height`, `-x`, and `-y` options. You control the size and location of this in the output with the `-pageanchor`, `-pagex`, `-pagey`, `-pagewidth`, and `-pageheight` options. The postscript is written to the file named by the `-file` option, or it is returned as the value of the postscript canvas operation.

You control fonts with a mapping from X screen fonts to postscript fonts. Define an array where the index is the name of the X font and the contents are the name and pointsize of a postscript font.

The next example positions a number of text objects with different fonts onto a canvas. For each different X font used, it records a mapping to a postscript font. The example has a fairly simple font mapping, and in fact the canvas would probably have guessed the same font mapping itself. If you use more exotic screen fonts you may need to help the canvas widget with an explicit font map.

The example positions the output at the upper-left corner of the printed page by using the `-pagex`, `-pagey`, and `-pageanchor` options. Recall that postscript has its origin at the lower-left corner of the page.

Example 31–14 Generating postscript from a canvas.

```
proc Setup {} {
    global fontMap
    canvas .c
    pack .c -fill both -expand true
    set x 10
    set y 10
```

```
    set last [.c create text $x $y -text "Font sampler" \
        -font fixed -anchor nw]

    # Create several strings in different fonts and sizes

    foreach family {times courier helvetica} {
        set weight bold
        switch -- $family {
            times { set fill blue; set psfont Times}
            courier { set fill green; set psfont Courier }
            helvetica { set fill red; set psfont Helvetica }
        }
        foreach size {10 14 24} {
            set y [expr 4+[lindex [.c bbox $last] 3]]

            # Guard against missing fonts
            if {[catch {.c create text $x $y \
                    -text $family-$weight-$size \
                    -anchor nw -fill $fill \
                    -font -*-$family-$weight-*-*-*-$size-*} \
            it] == 0} {
                set fontMap(-*-$family-$weight-*-*-*-$size-*)\
                    [list $psfont $size]
                set last $it
            }
        }
    }
    set fontMap(fixed) [list Courier 12]
}
proc Postscript { c file } {
    global fontMap
    # Tweak the output color
    set colorMap(blue) {0.1 0.1 0.9 setrgbcolor}
    set colorMap(green) {0.0 0.9 0.1 setrgbcolor}
    # Position the text at the upper-left corner of
    # an 8.5 by 11 inch sheet of paper
    $c postscript -fontmap fontMap -colormap colorMap \
        -file $file \
        -pagex 0.i -pagey 11.i -pageanchor nw
}
```

Canvas Attributes

Table 31–13 lists the attributes for the `canvas` widget. The table uses the resource name, which has capitals at internal word boundaries. In Tcl commands the attributes are specified with a dash and are all lowercase.

Table 31–13 Canvas attribute resource names.

`background`	The normal background color.
`borderWidth`	The width of the border around the canvas.
`closeEnough`	Distance from mouse to an overlapping object.
`confine`	Boolean. True constrains view to the scroll region.
`cursor`	Cursor to display when mouse is over the widget.
`height`	Height, in screen units, of canvas display.
`highlightBackground`	Focus highlight color when widget does not have focus.
`highlightColor`	Color for input focus highlight border.
`highlightThickness`	Width of highlight border.
`insertBackground`	Background for area covered by insert cursor.
`insertBorderwidth`	Width of cursor border. Non-zero for 3D effect.
`insertOffTime`	Time, in milliseconds the insert cursor blinks off.
`insertOnTime`	Time, in milliseconds the insert cursor blinks on.
`insertWidth`	Width of insert cursor. Default is 2.
`relief`	`flat`, `sunken`, `raised`, `groove`, `solid` or `ridge`.
`scrollIncrement`	The minimum scrolling distance.
`scrollRegion`	Left, top, right, and bottom coordinates of the canvas.
`selectBackground`	Background color of selection.
`selectForeground`	Foreground color of selection.
`selectBorderWidth`	Width of selection border. Non-zero for 3D effect.
`takeFocus`	Control focus changes from keyboard traversal.
`width`	Width in screen units for viewable area.
`xScrollCommand`	Tcl command prefix for horizontal scrolling.
`xScrollIncrement`	Distance for one scrolling unit in the X direction.
`yScrollCommand`	Tcl command prefix for vertical scrolling.
`yScrollIncrement`	Distance for one scrolling unit in the Y direction.

The scroll region of a canvas defines the boundaries of the canvas coordinate space. It is specified as four coordinates, *x1 y1 x2 y2* where (*x1, y1*) is the top-left corner and (*x2, y2*) is the lower-right corner. If the `confine` attribute is true, then the canvas cannot be scrolled outside this region. It is OK to position canvas objects partially or totally off the scroll region; they just may not be visible. The scroll increment attributes determine how much the canvas is scrolled when the user clicks on the arrows in the scrollbar.

The closeEnough attribute indicates how far away a position can be from an object and still be considered to overlap it. This applies to the overlapping search criteria.

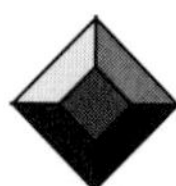

Hints

Screen Coordinates vs. Canvas Coordinates

The canvasx and canvasy operations map from a screen coordinate to a canvas coordinate. If the scroll region is larger than the display area, then you need to use these operations to map from the X and Y in an event (i.e., %x and %y) and the canvas coordinates. The typical use is:

```
set id [$c find closest [$c canvasx %x] [$c canvasy %y]]
```

Large Coordinate Spaces

Coordinates for canvas items are stored internally as floating point numbers, so the values returned by the coords operation will be floating point numbers. If you have a very large canvas, you may need to adjust the precision with which you see coordinates by setting the tcl_precision variable. This is an issue if you query coordinates, perform a computation on them, and then update the coordinates. (Tcl 8.0 changed the default tcl_precision from 6 to 12.)

Scaling and Rotation

The scale operation scales the coordinates of one or more canvas items. It is not possible to scale the whole coordinate space. The main problem with this is that you can lose precision when scaling and unscaling objects because their internal coordinates are actually changed by the scale operation. For simple cases this is not a problem, but in extreme cases it can show up.

The canvas does not support rotation.

Resources

There is no resource database support built into the canvas and its items. You can, however, define resources and query them yourself. For example, you could define:

```
*Canvas.foreground:   blue
```

This would have no effect by default. However, your code could look for this resource with option get, and specify this color directly for the -fill attribute of your objects:

```
set fg [option get $c foreground {}]
$c create rect 0 0 10 10 -fill $fg
```

The main reason to take this approach is to let your users customize the appearance of canvas objects without changing your code.

appearance of canvas objects without changing your code.

Objects with Many Points

The canvas implementation seems well optimized to handle lots of canvas objects. However, if an object like a line or a polygon has many points that define it, the implementation ends up scanning through these points linearly. This can adversely affect the time it takes to process mouse events in the area of the canvas containing such an item. Apparently any object in the vicinity of a mouse click is scanned to see if the mouse has hit it so that any bindings can be fired.

Selecting Canvas Items

Example 32–5 on page 428 implements cut and paste of canvas objects. The example exchanges the logical description of canvas objects with the selection mechanism.

PART V

Tk Details

Part V describes the rest of the Tk toolkit.

Chapter 32 describes the selection mechanism that is used for cut and paste between applications. It includes an example that implements cut and paste of graphical objects on a canvas.

Chapter 33 describes dialogs. Tk has several built-in dialogs that use the native platform look and feel. The chapter also describes how to build your own dialogs.

Chapter 34 is the first of three chapters that explain widget attributes in more detail. It describes size and layout attributes. Chapter 35 describes colors, images, and cursors. It explains how to use the bitmap and color photo image types. The chapter includes a complete map of the cursor font. Chapter 36 describes fonts and other text-related attributes. The extended example is a font selection application.

Chapter 37 describes the Tk `send` command that lets you send commands among Tk applications. It also presents a socket-based alternative that can be used among applications on different hosts and with the Safe-Tcl mechanism to limit the power of remotely invoked commands.

Chapter 38 explains how to interact with the window manager using the `wm` command. The chapter describes all the information available through the `winfo` command.

Chapter 39 builds upon Chapter 25 to create a user preferences package and an associated user interface. The preference package links a Tcl variable used in your application to a resource specification.

Chapter 40 presents a user interface to the binding mechanism. You can browse and edit bindings for widgets and classes with the interface.

CHAPTER 32

Selections and the Clipboard

Cut and paste allows information exchange between applications, and it is built upon a general purpose selection mechanism. The `CLIPBOARD` selection is used to implement cut and paste on all platforms. X Windows applications may also use the `PRIMARY` selection. This chapter describes the `selection` and `clipboard` commands.

Copy and paste is a basic way to transfer data between just about any two applications. In Tk, copy and paste is based on a general selection mechanism where the selection has a name, type, format, and value. For the most part you can ignore these details because they are handled by the Tk widgets. However, you can also control the selection explicitly. This chapter describes the selection model and the `selection` and `clipboard` commands. The last section of this chapter presents an example that implements copy and paste of graphical objects in a canvas.

The Selection Model

The Windows and Macintosh selection model is simpler than the selection model used in X windows. In the Macintosh and Windows there is one selection, although that selection may store different types of data like text or images. Users copy data from an application into a clipboard, and later they paste it into another application.

In X windows the selection model is generalized to support more than one selection, and they are identified by names like `PRIMARY` and `CLIPBOARD`. The `CLIPBOARD` selection is used for copy and paste as in Macintosh and Windows. The `PRIMARY` selection is described later. You could use other selection names, like `SECONDARY` or `FOOBAR`, but that only works if the other applications know about that selection name. The selection data has both a type and a format. These are described briefly later.

Data is not copied into a selection. Instead, an application asserts ownership of a selection, and other applications request the value of the selection from that owner. This model is used on all platforms. The window system keeps track of ownership, and applications are informed when some other application takes away ownership. Several of the Tk widgets implement selections and take care of asserting ownership and returning its value.

The X PRIMARY selection is used in a way that eliminates the explicit copy step in copy and paste user actions. Whenever you select an object in your application, your application automatically puts that value into the PRIMARY selection. The Tk entry, listbox, and text widgets do this with their text selections, although you can turn this off with the `exportSelection` widget attribute. Users typically insert the value of the PRIMARY selection by clicking with the middle mouse button. There is only one instance of the PRIMARY selection across all widgets and all applications. If the user makes a new selection it automatically overwrites the previous value of the PRIMARY selection.

The CLIPBOARD is cross-platform.

If you want a mechanism that works on all platforms, use the CLIPBOARD selection. The PRIMARY selection is implemented by Tk on all platforms, and you can use it within an application, but on Windows and Macintosh the non-Tk applications do not know about the PRIMARY selection. The main goal of copy and paste is to provide general interoperability among all applications, so stick with the CLIPBOARD.

Tk 3.6 and earlier only supported the PRIMARY selection. When Tk 4.0 added support for the CLIPBOARD, I tried to merge the two selections to "simplify" things for my users. Example 32–1 implements a `Paste` function that inserts either the PRIMARY or CLIPBOARD selection into a text widget. The `selection get` command is used to retrieve the selection value:

Example 32–1 Paste the PRIMARY or CLIPBOARD selection.

```
proc Paste { text } {
    if [catch {selection get} sel] {
        if [catch {selection get -selection CLIPBOARD} sel] {
            # no selection or clipboard data
            return
        }
    }
    $text insert insert $sel
}
```

This `Paste` function can be convenient, but it turns out that users still need to keep track of the difference between the two selections. If a user only understands the CLIPBOARD, then the use of PRIMARY is only surprising. I learned that it is best to have a separate paste user action for the two selections. The convention is that `<ButtonRelease-2>` sets the insert point and inserts the PRIMARY selection. (This convention is awkward with the one- and two-button mice on Macintosh and Windows.) The `<<Paste>>` event (e.g., the `Paste` key) simply inserts the CLIPBOARD selection at the current insert point. This convention is shown in Example 32–2, although these bindings are defined automatically for the text and entry widgets:

Example 32–2 Separate paste actions.

```
bind Text <<Paste>> {
    catch {%W insert insert \
        [selection get -selection CLIPBOARD]
    }
}
bind Text <ButtonRelease-2> {
    %W mark set insert @%x,%y
    catch {%W insert insert \
        [selection get -selection PRIMARY]
    }
}
```

The selection Command

There are two Tcl commands that deal with selections. The selection command is a general-purpose command that can set and get different selections. By default it manipulates the PRIMARY selection. The clipboard command stores data for later retrieval using the CLIPBOARD selection.

The selection command exposes the fully general selection model of different selections, types, and formats. You can define selection handlers that return selection values, and you can assert ownership of a selection and find out when you lose ownership to another application. Example 32–5 on page 428 shows a selection handler for a canvas.

A selection can have a type. The default is STRING. The type is different than the name of the selection (e.g., PRIMARY or CLIPBOARD). Each type can have a format, and the default format is also STRING. Ordinarily these defaults are fine. If you are dealing with non-Tk applications, however, you may need to ask for their selections by the right type (e.g., FILE_NAME). Formats include STRING, ATOM, and INTEGER. An ATOM is a name that is registered with the X server and identified by number. It is probably not a good idea to use non-STRING types and formats because it limits what other applications can use the information. The details about X selection types and formats are specified in the *Inter-Client Communication Conventions Manual* (David Rosenthal, Stuart Marks, X Consortium Standard). This is distributed with the X11 sources and can be found on the web at http://tronche.lri.fr:8000/gui/x/icccm/.

All of the selection operations take a -selection option that specifies the name of the selection being manipulated. This defaults to PRIMARY. Some of the operations take a -displayof option that specifies what display the selection is on. The value for this option is a Tk pathname of a window, and the selection on that window's display is manipulated. This is useful in X where applications can have their windows on remote displays. The default is to manipulate the selection on the display of the main window. Table 32–1 summarizes the `selection` command:

Table 32–1 The `selection` command.

`selection clear ?-displayof` *`win`*`? ?-selection` *`sel`*`?`	Clear the specified selection.
`selection get ?displayof` *`win`*`? ?-selection` *`sel`*`? ?-type` *`type`*`?`	Return the specified selection. Type defaults to `STRING`.
`selection handle ?-selection` *`sel`*`? ?-type` *`type`*`? ?-format` *`format`*`?` *`window command`*	Define *`command`* to be the handler for selection requests when *`window`* owns the selection.
`selection own ?-displayof` *`window`*`? ?-selection` *`sel`*`?`	Return the Tk pathname of the window that owns the selection, if it is in this application.
`selection own ?-command` *`command`*`? ?-selection` *`sel`*`?` *`window`*	Assert that *`window`* owns the *`sel`* selection. The *`command`* is called when ownership of the selection is taken away from *`window`*.

The `clipboard` Command

The `clipboard` command installs values into the `CLIPBOARD` selection. The `CLIPBOARD` is meant for values that have been recently or temporarily deleted. It is use for the copy and paste model of selections. You must use the `selection` command to retrieve values from the `CLIPBOARD` selection:

```
selection get -selection CLIPBOARD
```

Table 32–2 summarizes the `clipboard` command:

Table 32–2 The `clipboard` command.

`clipboard clear ?-displayof` *`win`*`?`	Clear the `CLIPBOARD` selection.
`clipboard append ?-displayof` *`win`*`? ?-format` *`format`*`? ?-type` *`type`*`? ?--?` *`data`*	Append *`data`* to the `CLIPBOARD` with the specified *`type`* and *`format`*, which both default to `STRING`.

Selection Handlers

The `selection handle` command registers a Tcl command to handle selection requests. The command is called to return the value of the selection to a requesting application. If the selection value is large, the command might be called several times to return the selection in pieces. The command gets two parameters that indicate the offset within the selection to start returning data, and the maximum number of bytes to return. If the command returns fewer than that many bytes, the selection request is assumed to be completed. Otherwise the command is called again to get the rest of the data, and the offset parameter is adjusted accordingly.

You can also get a callback when you lose ownership of the selection. At that time it is appropriate to unhighlight the selected object in your interface. The `selection own` command sets ownership and registers a callback for when you lose ownership.

A Canvas Selection Handler

Example 32–3 through Example 32–7 implement cut and paste for a canvas. The `CanvasSelect_Demo` procedure creates a canvas and sets up some bindings for cut and paste:

Example 32–3 Bindings for canvas selection.

```
proc CanvasSelect_Demo { c } {
    # Create a canvas with a couple of objects
    canvas $c
    pack $c
    $c create rect 10 10 50 50 -fill red -tag object
    $c create poly 100 100 100 30 140 50 -fill orange \
        -tag object
    # Set up cut and paste bindings
    $c bind object <Button-1> [list CanvasSelect $c %x %y]
    bind $c <Key-Delete> [list CanvasDelete $c]
    bind $c <<Cut>> [list CanvasCut $c]
    bind $c <<Copy>> [list CanvasCopy $c]
    bind $c <<Paste>> [list CanvasPaste $c]
    bind $c <Button-2> [list CanvasPaste $c %x %y]
    # Register the handler for selection requests
    selection handle $c [list CanvasSelectHandle $c]
}
```

The `CanvasSelect` procedure selects an object. It uses the `find closest` canvas operation to find out what object is under the mouse, which works because the binding is on canvas items with the `object` tag. If the binding were on the canvas as a whole, you would use the `find overlapping` operation to limit selection to objects near the mouse click. The `CanvasHighlight` procedure is used to highlight the selected object. It displays small boxes at the corners of the object's bounding box. Finally, the `CanvasSelectLose` procedure is registered to be called when another application asserts ownership of the `PRIMARY` selection.

Example 32–4 Selecting objects.

```
proc CanvasSelect { w x y } {
	# Select an item on the canvas.
	global canvas
	set id [$w find closest $x $y]
	set canvas(select,$w) $id
	CanvasHighlight $w $id
	# Claim ownership of the PRIMARY selection
	selection own -command [list CanvasSelectLose $w] $w
	focus $w
}
proc CanvasHighlight {w id {clear clear}} {
	if {$clear == "clear"} {
		$w delete highlight
	}
	foreach {x1 y1 x2 y2} [$w bbox $id] { # lassign }
	foreach x [list $x1 $x2] {
		foreach y [list $y1 $y2] {
			$w create rectangle [expr $x-2] [expr $y-2] \
				[expr $x+2] [expr $y+2] -fill black \
				-tag highlight
		}
	}
}
proc CanvasSelectLose { w } {
	# Some other app has claimed the selection
	global canvas
	$w delete highlight
	unset canvas(select,$w)
}
```

Once you claim ownership, Tk calls back to the `CanvasSelectHandle` procedure when another application, even yours, requests the selection. This uses `CanvasDescription` to compute a description of the canvas object. It uses canvas operations to query the object's configuration and store that as a command that will create the object:

Example 32–5 A canvas selection handler.

```
proc CanvasSelectHandle { w offset maxbytes } {
	# Handle a selection request
	global canvas
	if ![info exists canvas(select,$w)] {
		error "No selected item"
	}
	set id $canvas(select,$w)
	# Return the requested chunk of data.
	return [string range [CanvasDescription $w $id] \
		$offset [expr $offset+$maxbytes]]
}
proc CanvasDescription { w id } {
	# Generate a description of the object that can
```

```
    # be used to recreate it later.
    set type [$w type $id]
    set coords [$w coords $id]
    set config {}
    # Bundle up non-default configuration settings
    foreach conf [$w itemconfigure $id] {
        # itemconfigure returns a list like
        # -fill {} {} {} red
        set default [lindex $conf 3]
        set value [lindex $conf 4]
        if {[string compare $default $value] != 0} {
            lappend config [lindex $conf 0] $value
        }
    }
    return [concat CanvasObject $type $coords $config]
}
```

The CanvasCopy procedure puts the description of the selected item onto the clipboard with the clipboard append command. The CanvasDelete deletes an object and the highlighting, and CanvasCut is built from CanvasCopy and CanvasDelete:

Example 32–6 The copy and cut operations.

```
proc CanvasCopy { w } {
    global canvas
    if [info exists canvas(select,$w)] {
        set id $canvas(select,$w)
        clipboard clear
        clipboard append [CanvasDescription $w $id]
    }
}
proc CanvasDelete {w} {
    global canvas
    catch {
        $w delete highlight
        $w delete $canvas(select,$w)
        unset canvas(select,$w)
    }
}
proc CanvasCut { w } {
    CanvasCopy $w
    CanvasDelete $w
}
```

The CanvasPaste operation gets the value from the CLIPBOARD selection. The selection value has all the parameters needed for a canvas create operation. It gets the position of the new object from the <Button-2> event, or from the current mouse position if the <<Paste>> event is generated. If the mouse is out of the window, then the object is just put into the middle of the canvas. The original position and the new position are used to compute values for a canvas move:

Example 32–7 Pasting onto the canvas.

```
proc CanvasPaste { w {x {}} {y {}}} {
    # Paste the selection from the CLIPBOARD
    if [catch {selection get -selection CLIPBOARD} sel] {
        # no clipboard data
        return
    }
    if {[string length $x] == 0} {
        # <<Paste>>, get the current mouse coordinates
        set x [expr [winfo pointerx $w] - [winfo rootx $w]]
        set y [expr [winfo pointery $w] - [winfo rooty $w]]
        if {$x < 0 || $y < 0 ||
                $x > [winfo width $w] ||
                $y > [winfo height $w]} {
            # Mouse outside the window - center object
            set x [expr [winfo width $w]/2]
            set y [expr [winfo height $w]/2]
        }
    }
    if [regexp {^CanvasObject} $sel] {
        if [catch {eval {$w create} [lrange $sel 1 end]} id] {
            return;
        }
        # look at the first coordinate to see where to
        # move the object. Element 1 is the type, the
        # next two are the first coordinate
        set x1 [lindex $sel 2]
        set y1 [lindex $sel 3]
        $w move $id [expr $x-$x1] [expr $y-$y1]
    }
}
```

There is more you can do for a drawing program, of course. You'd like to be able to select multiple objects, create new ones, and more. The *canvas_ui* program on the CD-ROM was my first little effort at a canvas drawing program.

CHAPTER 33

Focus, Grabs, and Dialogs

Dialog boxes are a standard part of any user interface. Several dialog boxes are built into Tk. This chapter also describes how to build dialogs from scratch, which involves keyboard focus and grabs. Input focus directs keyboard events to different widgets. The grab mechanism lets a widget capture the input focus. This chapter describes the `focus`, `grab`, `tk_dialog`, and `tkwait` commands. Tk 4.2 adds `tk_getOpenFile`, `tk_getSaveFile`, `tk_chooseColor`, and `tk_messageBox`.

Dialog boxes are a common feature in a user interface. The application needs some user response before it can continue. A dialog box displays some information and some controls, and the user must interact with it before the application can continue. To implement this, the application *grabs* the input focus so the user can only interact with the dialog box. Tk has several built-in dialog boxes, including standard dialogs for finding files and selecting colors. A standard dialog has the same Tcl interface on all platforms, but it is implemented with platform-specific library routines to provide native look and feel. This chapter describes the dialogs built into Tk and then goes into the details of focus and grabs.

Standard Dialogs

The `tk_dialog` command presents a choice of buttons and returns a number indicating which one was clicked by the user. The general form of the command is:

```
tk_dialog win title text bitmap default ?label? ?label? ...
```

The *title* appears in the title bar, and the *text* appears in the dialog. The *bitmap* appears to the left of the text. Specify `{}` for the bitmap if you do not want one. The set of built-in bitmaps is given on page 459. The *label* arguments give labels that appear on buttons along the bottom of the dialog. The `default` argument gives the index of the default button, counting from zero. If there is no default, specify `{}` or `-1`.

Message Box

The tk_messageBox dialog is a limited form of tk_dialog that has native implementations on the different platforms. Like tk_dialog, it allows for a message, bitmap, and a set of buttons. However, the button sets are predefined, and the bitmaps are limited. The yesno button set, for example, displays a Yes and a No button. The abortretryignore button set displays Abort, Retry, and Ignore buttons. The tk_messageBox command returns the symbolic name of the selected button (e.g., yes or retry.) The yesnocancel message box could be used when trying to quit with unsaved changes:

```
set choice [tk_messageBox -type yesnocancel -default yes \
    -message "Save changes before quitting?" \
    -icon question]
```

The complete set of options to tk_messageBox is listed in Table 33–1:

Table 33–1 Options to tk_messageBox.

-default *name*	Default button name (e.g., yes)
-icon *name*	Name: error, info, question, or warning.
-message *string*	Message to display.
-parent *window*	Embed dialog in *window*.
-title *title*	Dialog title (UNIX and Windows)
-type *type*	Type: abortretrycancel, ok, okcancel, retrycancel, yesno, or yesnocancel

File Dialogs

There are two standard file dialogs, tk_getOpenFile and tk_getSaveFile. The tk_getOpenFile dialog is used to find an existing file, while tk_getSaveFile can be used to find a new file. These procedures return the selected file name, or the empty string if the user cancels the operation. These procedures take several options that are listed in Table 33–2:

Table 33–2 Options to the standard file dialogs.

-defaultextention *ext*	Append *ext* if an extension is not specified.
-filetypes *typelist*	The *typelist* defines a set of file types that the user can select to limit the files displayed in the dialog.
-initialdir *dir*	List contents of *dir* in the initial display.
-initialfile *file*	Default *file*, for tk_getSaveFile only.
-parent *window*	Create the dialog as an embedded child of *window*.
-title *string*	Display *string* in the title (UNIX and Windows).

The file dialogs can include a listbox that lists different file types. The file types are used to limit the directory listing to match only those types. The *typelist* option specifies a set of file extensions and Macintosh file types that correspond to a named file type. If you do not specify a *typelist*, users just see all the files in a directory. Each item in *typelist* is itself a list of three values:

name extensions ?mactypes?

The *name* is displayed in the list of file types. The *extensions* is a list of file extensions corresponding to that type. The empty extension "" matches files without an extension, and the extension * matches all files. The *mactypes* is an optional list of four-character Macintosh file types, which are ignored on other platforms. On the Macintosh, if you give both *extensions* and *mactypes*, the files must match both. If the *extensions* is an empty list, only the *mactypes* are considered. However, you can repeat *name* in the *typelist* and give *extensions* in one set and *mactypes* in another set. If you do this, then files that match either the *extensions* or *mactypes* are listed.

The following *typelist* matches Framemaker Interchange Files that have both a `.mif` extension *and* a `MIF` type:

```
set typelist {
    {"Maker Interchange Files" {".mif"} {"MIF "}}
}
```

The following typelist matches GIF image files that have either a `.gif` extension *or* the `GIFF` file type. Note that the *mactypes* are optional:

```
set typelist {
    {"GIF Image" {".gif"}}
    {"GIF Image" {} {"GIFF"}}}
}
```

The following typelist puts all these together, along with an entry for all files. The entry that comes first is displayed first:

```
set typelist {
    {"All Files" {*}}
    {"GIF Image" {".gif"}}
    {"GIF Image" {} {"GIFF"}}
    {"Maker Interchange Files" {".mif"} {"MIF "}}
}
```

Color Dialog

The `tk_chooseColor` dialog displays a color selection dialog. It returns a color, or the empty string if the user cancels the operation. The options to `tk_chooseColor` are listed in Table 33–3:

Table 33–3 Options to `tk_chooseColor`.

`-initialcolor` *color*	Initial color to display.
`-parent` *window*	Create the dialog as an embedded child of *window*.
`-title` *string*	Display *string* in the title (UNIX and Windows).

Custom Dialogs

When you create your own dialogs, you need to understand keyboard focus, focus grabs, and how to wait for the user to finish with a dialog. Here is the general structure of your code when creating a dialog:

```
# Create widgets, then
focus $toplevel
grab $toplevel
tkwait window $toplevel
```

This sequence of commands directs keyboard focus to the toplevel containing your dialog. The `grab` forces the user to interact with the dialog before using other windows in your application. The `tkwait` command returns when the toplevel window is destroyed, and this automatically releases the grab. This assumes that the button commands in the dialog destroy the toplevel. The following sections explain these steps in more detail, and Example 33–1 on page 437 illustrates a more robust sequence.

Input Focus

The window system directs keyboard events to the toplevel window that currently has the input focus. The application, in turn, directs the keyboard events to one of the widgets within that toplevel window. The `focus` command sets focus to a particular widget, and it is used by the default bindings for Tk widgets. Tk remembers what widget has focus within a toplevel window and automatically gives focus to that widget when the system gives focus to a toplevel window.

On Windows and Macintosh, the focus is given to an application when you click in its window. On UNIX, the window manager application gives focus to different windows, and window managers allow different conventions to shift focus. The click-to-type model is similar to Windows and Macintosh. There is also focus-follows-mouse which gives focus to the window under the mouse. One thing to note about click-to-type is that the application does not see the mouse click that gives the window focus.

Once the application has focus, you can manage the focus changes among your widgets any way you like. By default, Tk uses a click-to-type model. Text and entry widgets set focus to themselves when you click on them with the left mouse button. You can get the focus-follows-mouse model within your widgets by calling the `tk_focusFollowsMouse` procedure. However, in many cases you will find that an explicit focus model is actually more convenient for users. Carefully positioning the mouse over a small widget can be tedious.

The `focus` Command

Table 33–4 summarizes the `focus` command. The focus implementation supports multiple displays with a separate focus window on each display. This is useful on UNIX where X supports multiple displays. The `-displayof` option can be used to query the focus on a particular display. The `-lastfor` option finds out what widget last had the focus within the same toplevel as another window. Tk will restore focus to that window if the widget that has the focus is destroyed. The toplevel widget gets the focus if no widget claims it.

Table 33–4 The `focus` command.

`focus`	Return the widget that currently has the focus on the display of the application's main window.
`focus ?-force?` *`window`*	Set the focus to *`window`*. The `-force` option ignores the window manger, so use it sparingly.
`focus -displayof` *`win`*	Return the focus widget on the same display as *`win`*.
`focus -lastfor` *`win`*	Return the name of the last widget to have the focus in the same toplevel as *`win`*.

Keyboard Focus Traversal

Users can change focus among widgets with `<Tab>` and `<Shift-Tab>`. The creation order of widgets determines a traversal order for focus that is used by the `tk_focusNext` and `tk_focusPrev` procedures. There are global bindings for `<Tab>` and `<Shift-Tab>` that call these procedures:

```
bind all <Tab> {tk_focusNext %W}
bind all <Shift-Tab> {tk_focusPrev %W}
```

The Tk widgets highlight themselves when they have the focus. The highlight size is controlled with the `highlightThickness` attribute, and the color of the highlight is set with the `highlightColor` attribute. The Tk widgets, even buttons and scrollbars, have bindings that support keyboard interaction. A `<space>` invokes the command associated with a button, if the button has the input focus.

All widgets have a `takeFocus` attribute that the `tk_focusNext` and `tk_focusPrev` procedures use to determine if a widget will take the focus during keyboard traversal. There are four possible values to the attribute:

- `0` indicates the widget should not take focus.
- `1` indicates the widget should always take focus.
- An empty string means the traversal procedures `tk_focusNext` and `tk_focusPrev` should decide based on the widget's state and bindings.

- Otherwise the value is a Tcl command prefix. The command is called with the widget name as an argument, and it should return either `0`, `1`, or the empty string.

Grabbing the Focus

An input *grab* overrides the normal focus mechanism. For example, a dialog box can grab the focus so that the user cannot interact with other windows in the application. The typical scenario is that the application is performing some task but it needs user input. The grab restricts the user's actions so it cannot drive the application into an inconsistent state. A *global grab* prevents the user from interacting with other applications, too, even the window manager. Tk menus use a global grab, for example, which is how they unpost themselves no matter where you click the mouse. When an application prompts for a password, a global grab is also a good idea. This prevents the user from accidentally typing their password into a random window. Table 33–5 summarizes the `grab` command.

Table 33–5 The `grab` command.

`grab ?-global? window`	Set a grab to a particular window.
`grab current ?window?`	Query the grabs on the display of *window*, or on all displays if *window* is omitted.
`grab release window`	Release a grab on *window*.
`grab set ?-global? win`	Set a grab to a particular window.
`grab status window`	Returns `none`, `local`, or `global`.

In most cases you only need to use the `grab` and `grab release` commands. Note that the `grab set` command is equivalent to the `grab` command. The next section includes examples that use the `grab` command.

The `tkwait` Command

You wait for the user to interact with the dialog by using the `tkwait` command. The `tkwait` waits for something to happen, and while waiting it allows events to be processed. Like `vwait`, you can use `tkwait` to wait for a Tcl variable to change value. You can also wait for a window to become visible, or wait for a window to be destroyed. Table 33–6 summarizes the `tkwait` command.

Table 33–6 The `tkwait` command.

`tkwait variable varname`	Wait for the global variable *varname* to be set. This is just like the `vwait` command.
`tkwait visibility win`	Wait for the window *win* to become visible.
`tkwait window win`	Wait for the window *win* to be destroyed.

Use `tkwait` *with global variables.*

The variable specified in the `tkwait variable` command must be a global variable. Remember this if you use procedures to modify the variable. They must declare it global or the `tkwait` command will not notice the assignments.

The `tkwait visibility` waits for the visibility state of the window to change. Most commonly this is used to wait for a newly created window to become visible. For example, if you have any sort of animation in a complex dialog, you could wait until the dialog is displayed before starting the animation.

Destroying Widgets

The `destroy` command deletes one or more widgets. If the widget has children, all the children are destroyed, too. Chapter 38 describes a protocol on page 490 to handle destroy events that come from the window manager. You wait for a window to be deleted with the `tkwait window` command.

The `focus`, `grab`, `tkwait` sequence

In practice, I use a slightly more complex command sequence than just `focus`, `grab`, and `tkwait`. You can remember what widget had focus before the dialog is created so that focus can be restored after the dialog completes. When you do this, it is more reliable to restore focus before destroying the dialog. This prevents a tug of war between your application and the window manager. This sequence looks like:

```
set old [focus]
focus $toplevel
grab $toplevel
tkwait variable doneVar
grab release $toplevel
focus $old
destroy $toplevel
```

This sequence supports another trick I use, which is to unmap dialogs instead of destroying them. This way the dialogs appear more quickly the next time they are used. This makes creating the dialogs a little more complex because you need to see if the toplevel already exists. Chapter 38 describes the window manager commands used to map and unmap windows on page 490. Example 33–1 shows `Dialog_Create`, `Dialog_Wait`, and `Dialog_Dismiss` that capture all of these tricks:

Example 33–1 Procedures to help build dialogs.

```
proc Dialog_Create {top title args} {
    global dialog
    if [winfo exists $top] {
        switch -- [wm state $top] {
            normal {
                # Raise a buried window
```

V. Tk Details

```
            raise $top
        }
        withdrawn -
        iconified {
            # Open and restore geometry
            wm deiconify $top
            catch {wm geometry $top $dialog(geo,$top)}
        }
    }
    return 0
  } else {
    eval {toplevel $top} $args
    wm title $top $title
    return 1
  }
}
proc Dialog_Wait {top varName {focus {}}} {
  upvar $varName var

  # Poke the variable if the user nukes the window
  bind $top <Destroy> [list set $varName $var]

  # Grab focus for the dialog
  if {[string length $focus] == 0} {
    set focus $top
  }
  set old [focus -displayof $top]
  focus $focus
  catch {tkwait visibility $top}
  catch {grab $top}

  # Wait for the dialog to complete
  tkwait variable $varName
  catch {grab release $top}
  focus $old
}
proc Dialog_Dismiss {top} {
  global dialog
  # Save current size and position
  catch {
    # window may have been deleted
    set dialog(geo,$top) [wm geometry $top]
    wm withdraw $top
  }
}
```

The `Dialog_Wait` procedure allows a different focus widget than the toplevel. The idea is that you can start the focus out in the appropriate widget within the dialog, such as the first entry widget. Otherwise the user has to click in the dialog first.

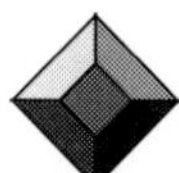

Grab can fail.

The `catch` statements in `Dialog_Wait` come from my experiences on different platforms. The `tkwait visibility` is sometimes required because `grab` can fail if the dialog is not yet visible. However, on other systems the `tkwait visibility` itself can fail in some circumstances. Tk reflects these errors, but in this case all that can go wrong is no grab. The user can still interact with the dialog without a grab so I just ignore these errors.

Prompter Dialog

The `Dialog_Prompt` dialog gets a value from the user, returning the value entered, or the empty string if the user cancels the operation. `Dialog_Prompt` uses the Tcl variable `prompt(ok)` to indicate the dialog is complete. The variable is set if the user presses the `OK` or `Cancel` buttons, or if they press `<Return>` or `<Control-c>` in the entry widget. The `Dialog_Wait` procedure waits on `prompt(ok)`, and it grabs and restores focus. If the `Dialog_Create` procedure returns 1, then the dialog is built: otherwise it already existed.

Example 33–2 A simple dialog.

```
proc Dialog_Prompt { string } {
    global prompt
    set f .prompt
    if [Dialog_Create $f "Prompt" -borderwidth 10] {
        message $f.msg -text $string -aspect 1000
        entry $f.entry -textvariable prompt(result)
        set b [frame $f.buttons]
        pack $f.msg $f.entry $f.buttons -side top -fill x
        pack $f.entry -pady 5
        button $b.ok -text OK -command {set prompt(ok) 1}
        button $b.cancel -text Cancel \
            -command {set prompt(ok) 0}
        pack $b.ok -side left
        pack $b.cancel -side right
        bind $f.entry <Return> {set prompt(ok) 1 ; break}
        bind $f.entry <Control-c> {set prompt(ok) 0 ; break}
    }
    set prompt(ok) 0
    Dialog_Wait $f prompt(ok) $f.entry
    Dialog_Dismiss $f
    if {$prompt(ok)} {
```

```
        return $prompt(result)
    } else {
        return {}
    }
}
Dialog_Prompt "Please enter a name"
```

Keyboard Shortcuts and Focus

Focus is set on the entry widget in the dialog with `Dialog_Wait`, and it is convenient if users can use special key bindings to complete the dialog. Otherwise they need to take their hands off the keyboard and use the mouse. The example defines bindings for `<Return>` and `<Control-c>` that invoke the `OK` and `Cancel` buttons, respectively. The bindings override all other bindings by including a `break` command. Otherwise, the `Entry` class bindings insert the short-cut keystroke into the entry widget.

Animation with the update Command

Suppose you want to entertain your user while your application is busy. By default, the user interface hangs until your processing completes. Even if you change a label or entry widget in the middle of processing, the updates to that widget are deferred until an idle moment. The user does not see your feedback, and the window is not refreshed if it gets obscured and uncovered. The solution is to use the `update` command that forces Tk to go through its event loop and update the display.

The next example shows a `Feedback` procedure that displays status messages. A read-only entry widget displays the messages, and the `update` command ensures that the user sees each new message. An entry widget is used because it won't change size based on the message length, and it can be scrolled by dragging with the middle mouse button. Entry widgets also work better with `update idletasks` as described later:

Example 33–3 A feedback procedure.

```
proc Feedback { message } {
    global feedback
    set e $feedback(entry)
    $e config -state normal
    $e delete 0 end
    $e insert 0 $message
    # Leave the entry in a read-only state
    $e config -state disabled
    # Force a display update
    update idletasks
}
```

The Tk widgets update their display at idle moments, which basically means after everything else is taken care of. This lets them collapse updates into one interaction with the window system. On UNIX, this improves the batching effects that are part of the X protocol. A call to `update idletasks` causes any pending display updates to be processed. Chapter 15 describes the Tk event loop in more detail.

Use `update idletasks` if possible.

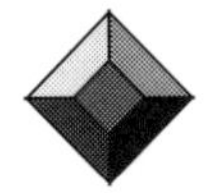

The safest way to use `update` is with its `idletasks` option. If you use the `update` command with no options, then all events are processed. In particular, user input events are processed. If you are not careful, it can have unexpected effects because another thread of execution is launched into your Tcl interpreter. The current thread is suspended and any callbacks that result from input events are executed. It is usually better to use the `tkwait` command if you need to process input because it pauses the main application at a well-defined point.

One drawback of `update idletasks` is that in some cases a widget's redisplay is triggered by window system events. In particular, when you change the text of a label, it can cause the size of the label to change. The widget is too clever for us in this case. Instead of scheduling a redisplay at idle time, it requests a different size and then waits for the `<Configure>` event from the window system. The `<Configure>` event indicates a size has been chosen by the geometry manager, and it is at that point that the label schedules its redisplay. So, changing the label's text and doing `update idletasks` does not work as expected.

CHAPTER 34

Tk Widget Attributes

Each Tk widget has a number of attributes that affect its appearance and behavior. This chapter describes attributes in general, and covers some of the size and appearance-related attributes. The next two chapters cover the attributes associated with colors, images, and text.

This chapter describes some of the attributes that are in common among many Tk widgets. A widget always provides a default value for its attributes, so you can avoid specifying most of them. If you want to fine-tune things, however, you'll need to know about all the widget attributes.

The native widgets used in Tk 8.0 ignore some of the original Tk attributes. This is because there is no support for them in the system widgets. For example, the buttons on Macintosh do not honor the `borderWidth` attribute, and they do not display a highlight focus. The native scrollbars on Windows and Macintosh have similar limitations. This chapter notes these limitations in the discussion of each attribute.

Configuring Attributes

You specify attributes for Tk widgets when you create them. You can also change them dynamically at any time after that. In both cases the syntax uses pairs of arguments. The first item in the pair identifies the attribute, the second provides the value. For example, a button can be created like this:

```
button .doit -text Doit -command DoSomething
```

The name of the button is `.doit`, and two attributes are specified: the `text` and the `command`. You can change the `.doit` button later with the `configure` widget operation:

```
.doit configure -text Stop -command StopIt
```

The current configuration of a widget can be queried with another form of the `configure` operation. If you just supply an attribute, the settings associated with that attribute are returned:

```
.doit configure -text
=> -text text Text { } Stop
```

This command returns several pieces of information: the command line switch, the resource name, the resource class, the default value, and the current value. If you don't give any options to configure, then the configuration information for all the attributes is returned. The following loop formats the information:

```
foreach item [$w configure] {
     puts "[lindex $item 0] [lindex $item 4]"
}
```

If you just want the current value, use the `cget` operation:

```
.doit cget -text
=> Stop
```

You can also configure widget attributes indirectly by using the resource database. An advantage of using the resource database is that users can reconfigure your application without touching the code. Otherwise, if you specify attribute values explicitly in the code, they cannot be overridden by resource settings. This is especially important for attributes like fonts and colors.

The tables in this chapter list the attributes by their resource name, which may have a capital letter at an internal word boundary (e.g., `activeBackground`). When you specify attributes in a Tcl command, use all lowercase instead, plus a leading dash. Compare:

```
option add *Button.activeBackground red
$button configure -activebackground red
```

The first command defines a resource that affects all buttons created after that point, and the second command changes an existing button. Command-line settings override resource database specifications. Chapter 25 describes the use of resources in detail.

Size

Most widgets have a `width` and `height` attribute that specifies their desired size, although there are some special cases. In all cases, the geometry manager for a widget might modify the size to some degree. The `winfo` operations described on page 489 return the current size of a widget.

Most of the text-related widgets interpret their sizes in units of characters for width and lines for height. All other widgets, including the `message` widget, interpret their dimensions in screen units, which are pixels by default. The `tk scale` command, which is described on page 498, controls the scale between pixels and the other measures. You can suffix the dimension with a unit specifier to get a particular measurement unit:

c	centimeters
i	inch
m	millimeters
p	printer points (1/72 inches)

Scales and scrollbars can have two orientations as specified by the `orient` attribute, so width and height are somewhat ambiguous. These widgets do not support a `height` attribute, and they interpret their `width` attribute to mean the size of their narrow dimension. The `scale` has a `length` attribute that determines its long dimension. Scrollbars do not even have a `length`. Instead, a `scrollbar` is assumed to be packed next to the widget it controls, and the `fill` packing attribute is used to extend the scrollbar to match the length of its adjacent widget. Example 27–1 on page 346 shows how to arrange scrollbars with another widget.

The `message` widget displays a fixed string on multiple lines, and it uses one of two attributes to constrain its size: its `aspect` or its `width`. The aspect ratio is defined to be 100*width/height, and it formats its text to honor this constraint. However, if a `width` is specified, it just uses that and uses as many lines (i.e., as much height) as needed. Example 26–3 on page 339 shows how message widgets display text. Table 34–1 summarizes the attributes used to specify the size for widgets:

Table 34–1 Size attribute resource names.

`aspect`	The aspect ratio of a `message` widget, which is 100 times the ratio of width divided by height.
`height`	Height, in text lines or screen units. Widgets: `button, canvas, checkbutton, frame, label, listbox, menubutton, radiobutton, text,` and `toplevel.`
`length`	The long dimension of a `scale`.
`orient`	Orientation for long and narrow widgets: `horizontal` or `vertical`. Widgets: `scale` and `scrollbar.`
`width`	Width, in characters or screen units. Widgets: `button, canvas, checkbutton, entry, frame, label, listbox, menubutton, message, radiobutton, scale, scrollbar, text,` and `toplevel.`

It is somewhat unfortunate that text-oriented widgets only take character- and line-oriented dimensions. These sizes change with the font used, and if you want a precise size you might be frustrated. Both `pack` and `grid` let the widgets decide how big to be. One trick is to put each widget, such as a label, in its own frame. Specify the size you want for the frame, and then pack the label and turn off size propagation. For example:

Example 34–1 Equal-sized labels.

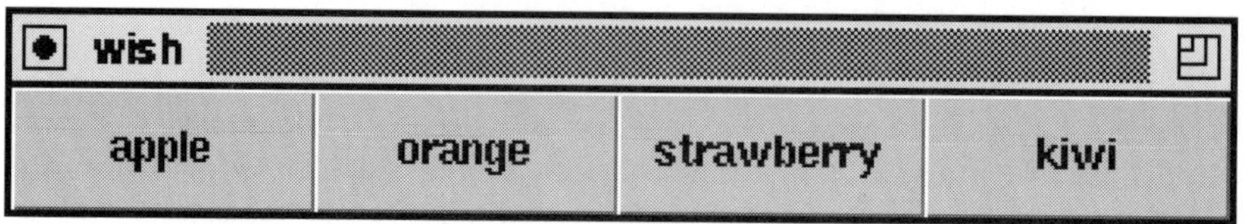


```
proc EqualSizedLabels { parent width height strings args } {
    set l 0
    foreach s $strings {
        frame $parent.$l -width $width -height $height
        pack propagate $parent.$l false
        pack $parent.$l -side left
        eval {label $parent.$l.l -text $s} $args
        pack $parent.$l.l -fill both -expand true
        incr l
    }
}
frame .f ; pack .f
EqualSizedLabels .f 1i 1c {apple orange strawberry kiwi} \
    -relief raised
```

The frames `$parent.$l` are all created with the same size. The `pack propagate` command prevents these frames from changing size when the labels are packed into them later. The labels are packed with `fill` and `expand` turned on so they fill up the fixed-sized frames around them.

Borders and Relief

The three dimensional appearance of widgets is determined by two attributes: `borderWidth` and `relief`. The `borderWidth` adds extra space around the edge of a widget's display, and this area can be displayed in a number of ways according to the `relief` attribute. Example 34–2 illustrates the different reliefs:

Example 34–2 3D relief sampler.

```
frame .f -borderwidth 10
pack .f
foreach relief {raised sunken flat ridge groove solid} {
    label .f.$relief -text $relief -relief $relief \
        -bd 2 -padx 3
```

```
    pack .f.$relief -side left -padx 4
}
```

The solid relief was added in Tk 8.0 to support the Macintosh look for entry widget, and it works well against white backgrounds. Macintosh and Windows buttons do not support different reliefs, and the Macintosh buttons do not honor border width.

The activeBorderWidth attribute is a special case for menus. It defines the border width for the menu entries. The relief of a menu is not configurable. It probably is not worth adjusting the menu border width attributes because the default looks OK. The native menus on Windows and Macintosh do not honor this attribute.

The activeRelief applies to the elements of a scrollbar (the elevator and two arrows) when the mouse is over them. The elementBorderWidth sets the size of the relief on these elements. Changing the activeRelief does not look good. The native scrollbars on Macintosh and Windows do not honor this attribute. Table 34–2 lists the attributes for borders and relief.

Table 34–2 Border and relief attribute resource names.

borderWidth	The width of the border around a widget, in screen units. Widgets: button, canvas, checkbutton, entry, frame, label, listbox, menu, menubutton, message, radiobutton, scale, scrollbar, text, and toplevel.
bd	Short for borderwidth. Tcl commands only.
elementBorderWidth	The width of the border on scrollbar and scale elements.
relief	The appearance of the border. Values: flat, raised, sunken, ridge, groove, or solid. Widgets: button, canvas, checkbutton, entry, frame, label, listbox, menubutton, message, radiobutton, scale, scrollbar, text, and toplevel.
activeBorderWidth	The border width for menu entries. UNIX only.
activeRelief	The relief for active scrollbar elements. UNIX only.

The Focus Highlight

Each widget can have a focus highlight indicating which widget currently has the input focus. This is a thin rectangle around each widget that is displayed in the highlight background color by default. When the widget gets the input focus, the highlight rectangle is displayed in an alternate color. The addition of the highlight adds a small amount of space outside the border described in the previous section. The attributes in Table 34–3 control the width and color of this rectangle. If the width is zero, no highlight is displayed.

By default, only the widgets that normally expect input focus have a non-zero width highlight border. This includes the `text`, `entry`, and `listbox` widgets. It also includes the `button` and `menu` widgets because there is a set of keyboard traversal bindings that focus input on these widgets, too. You can define non-zero highlight thicknesses for all widgets except Macintosh buttons.

Table 34–3 Highlight attribute resource names.

`highlightColor`	The color of the highlight when the widget has focus.
`highlightBackground`	The highlight color when the widget does not have focus.
`highlightThickness`	The width of the highlight border.

Padding and Anchors

Table 34–4 lists padding and anchor attributes that are similar in spirit to some packing attributes described in Chapter 20. However, they are distinct from the packing attributes, and this section explains how they work together with the packer.

Table 34–4 Layout attribute resource names.

`anchor`	The anchor position of the widget. Values: `n`, `ne`, `e`, `se`, `s`, `sw`, `w`, `nw`, or `center`. Widgets: `button`, `checkbutton`, `label`, `menubutton`, `message`, or `radiobutton`.
`padX`, `padY`	Padding space in the X or Y direction, in screen units. Widgets: `button`, `checkbutton`, `label`, `menubutton`, `message`, `radiobutton`, or `text`.

The padding attributes for a widget define space that is never occupied by the display of the widget's contents. For example, if you create a `label` with the following attributes and pack it into a frame by itself, you will see the text is still centered, despite the `anchor` attribute.

Example 34–3 Padding provided by labels and buttons.

```
label .foo -text Foo -padx 20 -anchor e
pack .foo
```

The `anchor` attribute only affects the display if there is extra room for another reason. One way to get extra room is to specify a `width` attribute that is longer than the text. The following label has right-justified text. You can see the default `padX` value for labels, which is one pixel:

Example 34–4 Anchoring text in a label or button.

```
label .foo -text Foo -width 10 -anchor e
pack .foo
```

Another way to get extra display space is with the `-ipadx` and `-ipady` packing parameters. The example in the next section illustrates this effect. Chapter 20 has several more examples of the packing parameters.

Putting It All Together

The number of different attributes that contribute to the size and appearance can be confusing. The example in this section uses a label to demonstrate the difference among size, borders, padding, and the highlight. Padding can come from the geometry manager, and it can come from widget attributes:

Example 34–5 Borders and padding.

wish
One
Two
pack -pady
pack -ipady
Attributes:
-padx
-pady
-highlightthickness
-borderwidth
-width

```
frame .f -bg white
label .f.one -text One -relief raised -bd 2 -padx 3m -pady 2m
pack .f.one -side top
label .f.two -text Two \
   -highlightthickness 4 -highlightcolor red \
   -borderwidth 5 -relief raised \
   -padx 0 -pady 0 \
   -width 10 -anchor nw
pack .f.two -side top -pady 10 -ipady 10 -fill both
focus .f.two
pack .f
```

The first label in the example uses a raised relief so you can see the two-pixel border. (The default border size changed in Tk 8.0 to one pixel to match the CDE look and feel.) There is no highlight on a label by default. There is internal padding so that the text is spaced away from the edge of the label. The second label adds a highlight rectangle by specifying a non-zero thickness. Widgets like buttons, entries, listboxes, and text have a highlight rectangle by default. The second label's padding attributes are reduced to zero. The anchor positions the text right next to the border in the upper-left (`nw`) corner. However, note the effect of the padding provided by the packer. There is both external and internal padding in the Y direction. The external padding (from `pack -pady`) results in unfilled space. The internal packing (`pack -ipady`) is used by the label for its display. This is different than the label's own `-pady` attribute, which keeps the text away from the top edge of the widget.

CHAPTER 35

Color, Images, and Cursors

This chapter describes the color attributes shared by the Tk widgets. Images and bitmaps can be displayed instead of text by several widgets. This chapter describes commands that create and manipulate images. The cursor attribute controls the shape and color of the mouse cursor when it is over a particular widget. This chapter includes a figure that shows all the cursors available in Tk.

Color is one of the most fun things to play with in a user interface. However, this chapter makes no attempt to improve your taste in color choices; it just describes the attributes that affect color. The tradition of having users change application colors is stronger in UNIX than on the other platforms. This is because all the X toolkits support color tuning via the resource database. Tk carries this tradition to Windows and Macintosh. However, if native look and feel is important, you should not change the default widget colors. On the other hand, tuning colors can provide a flair to your applications, and knowledge of colors is useful for canvas applications.

This chapter describes images, too. The image facility in Tk lets you create an image and then have other Tk widgets display it. The same image can be displayed by many different widgets, multiple times on a canvas, and multiple times within the text widget. If you redefine an image, its display is updated in whatever widgets are displaying it.

The last topic of the chapter is cursors. All widgets can control what the mouse cursor looks like when it is over them. In addition, the widgets that support text input define another cursor, the insert cursor. Its appearance is controlled with a few related attributes.

Colors

Table 35–1 lists the resource names for color attributes. The table indicates what widgets use the different color attributes. Remember to use all lowercase and a leading dash when specifying attributes in a Tcl command.

Table 35–1 Color attribute resource names.

`background`	The normal background color. All widgets.
`bg`	Short for background. Command line only.
`foreground`	The normal foreground color. Widgets: `button, checkbutton, entry, label, listbox, menu, menubutton, message, radiobutton, scale,` and `text`.
`fg`	Short for foreground. Command line only.
`activeBackground`	The background when a mouse button will take an action. Widgets: `button, checkbutton, menu, menubutton, radiobutton, scale,` and `scrollbar`.
`activeForeground`	The foreground when the mouse is over an active widget. Widgets: `button, checkbutton, menu, menubutton,` and `radiobutton`.
`disabledForeground`	The foreground when a widget is disabled. Widgets: `button, checkbutton, menu, menubutton,` and `radiobutton`.
`highlightBackground`	The highlight color when widget does not have focus. All widgets.
`highlightColor`	The highlight color when the widget has focus. All widgets.
`insertBackground`	The color of the insert cursor. Widgets: `canvas, entry,` and `text`.
`selectBackground`	The background of selected text. Widgets: `canvas, entry, listbox,` and `text`.
`selectColor`	The color of the selector indicator. Widgets: `checkbutton,` and `radiobutton`.
`selectForeground`	The foreground of selected text. Widgets: `canvas, entry, listbox,` and `text`.
`troughColor`	The trough part of scales and scrollbars.

The `foreground` color is used to draw an element, while the `background` color is used for the blank area behind the element. Text, for example, is painted with the foreground color. There are several variations on foreground and background that reflect different states for widgets or items they are displaying.

Each attribute also has a resource class. This is most useful for the variations on foreground and background colors. For example, Tk does not have a reverse video mode. However, with a couple of resource specifications you can convert a monochrome display into reverse video. The definitions are given in Example 35–1. The `Foreground` and `Background` resource class names are used, and the various foreground and background colors (e.g., `activeBackground`) have the correct resource class so these settings work. You have to set these resources before you create any widgets:

Example 35–1 Resources for reverse video.

```
proc ReverseVideo {} {
    option add *Foreground white
    option add *Background black
}
```

Color Palettes

The `tk_setPalette` command changes colors of existing widgets and installs resource values so new widgets have matching colors. If you give it a single argument, it treats this as the background and then computes new values for the other color resources. For example, if you do not like the standard Tk grey, you can lighten your spirits with a cool blue background:

```
tk_setPalette #0088cc
```

If you liked the light brown color scheme of Tk 3.6, you can restore that palette with the `tk_bisque` command:

```
tk_bisque
```

The `tk_setPalette` command can be used to change any of the color attributes. You can specify a set of name-value pairs, where the names are color resource names and the values are new color values:

```
tk_setPalette activeBackground red activeForeground white
```

Color Values

Color values are specified in two ways: symbolically (e.g., `red`), or by hexadecimal numbers (e.g., `#ff0000`). The leading `#` distinguishes the hexadecimal representation from the symbolic one. The number is divided into three equal-sized fields that give the red, green, and blue values, respectively. The fields can specify 4, 8, 12, or 16 bits of a color:

#*RGB*	4 bits per color
#*RRGGBB*	8 bits per color
#*RRRGGGBBB*	12 bits per color
#*RRRRGGGGBBBB*	16 bits per color

If you specify more resolution than is supported by the display, the low-order bits of each field are discarded. The different display types supported by Tk are described in the next section. Each field ranges from 0, which means no color, to a maximum, which is all ones in binary, or all `f` in hex, that means full color saturation. For example, pure red can be specified four ways:

```
#f00 #ff0000 #fff000000 #ffff00000000
```

There is a large collection of symbolic color names like "red," "blue," "green," "thistle," "medium sea green," and "yellow4." These names originate from X and UNIX, and Tk supports these colors on all platforms. You can find the list in the Tk sources in the `xlib/xcolor.c` file. Or, run the *xcolors* program that comes with the standard X distribution.

The Windows and Macintosh platforms have a small set of colors that are guaranteed to exist, and Tk defines names for these. The advantage of using these colors is that they are shared by all applications so the system can manage colors efficiently. Table 35–2 lists the system colors on Windows. Several of these colors map to the same RGB value. Table 35–3 lists the system colors on Macintosh

Table 35–2 Windows system colors.

`system3dDarkShadow`	Dark part of button 3D-relief.
`system3dLight`	Light part of button 3D-relief.
`systemActiveBorder`	Window border when activated.
`systemActiveCaption`	Caption (i.e., title bar) when activated.
`systemAppWorkspace`	Background for MDI workspaces.
`systemBackground`	Widget background.
`systemButtonFace`	Button background.
`systemButtonHighlight`	Lightest part of button 3D-relief.
`systemButtonShadow`	Darkest part of button 3D-relief.
`systemButtonText`	Button foreground.
`systemCaptionText`	Caption (i.e., title bar) text.
`systemDisabledText`	Text when disabled.
`systemGrayText`	Grey text color.
`systemHighlight`	Selection background.
`systemHighlightText`	Selection foreground.
`systemInactiveBorder`	Window border when not activated.
`systemInactiveCaption`	Caption background when not activated.
`systemInactiveCaptionText`	Caption text when not activated.
`systemInfoBackground`	Help pop-up background.
`systemInfoText`	Help pop-up text.

Table 35–2 Windows system colors. (Continued)

systemMenu	Menu background.
systemMenuText	Menu foreground.
systemScrollbar	Scrollbar background.
systemWindow	Text window background.
systemWindowFrame	Text window frame.
systemWindowText	Text window text color.

Table 35–3 Macintosh system colors.

systemHighlight	Selection background.
systemHighlightText	Selection foreground.
systemButtonFace	Button background.
systemButtonFrame	Button frame.
systemButtonText	Button foreground.
systemWindowBody	Widget background.
systemMenuActive	Selected menu item background.
systemMenuActiveText	Selected menu item foreground.
systemMenu	Menu background.
systemMenuDisabled	Disabled menu item background.
systemMenuText	Menu foreground.

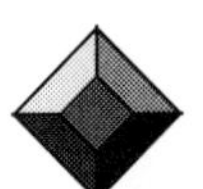

Getting RGB values.

The `winfo rgb` command maps from a color name (or value) to three numbers that are its red, green, and blue values. You can use this to compute variations on a color. The `ColorDarken` procedure shown below uses the `winfo rgb` command to get the red, green, and blue components of the input color. It reduces these amounts by 5 percent, and reconstructs the color specification using the `format` command.

Example 35–2 Computing a darker color.

```
proc ColorDarken { win color } {
    set rgb [winfo rgb $win $color]
    return [format "#%03x%03x%03x" \
        [expr round([lindex $rgb 0] * 0.95)] \
        [expr round([lindex $rgb 1] * 0.95)] \
        [expr round([lindex $rgb 2] * 0.95)]]
}
```

Colormaps and Visuals

Computer screens can display only a fixed number of different colors at one time. The best monitors can display 24 million colors, but it is common to find 256 color displays. Really old VGA displays only display 16 colors. If you run several applications at once, it is possible that more colors are requested than can be displayed. The Windows and Macintosh platforms manage this scenario automatically. X provides lower-level facilities that Tk uses on UNIX to do the management. So, for the most part you don't have to worry. However, if you need more control, especially under X, then you need to understand *colormaps* and the different *visual* types.

Each pixel on the screen is represented by one or more bits of memory. There are a number of ways to map from a value stored at a pixel to the color that appears on the screen at that pixel. The mapping is a function of the number of bits at each pixel, which is called the *depth* of the display, and the style of interpretation, or *visual class*. The six visual classes defined by X are listed in the following table. Some of the visuals use a *colormap* that maps from the value stored at a pixel to a value used by the hardware to generate a color. A colormap enables a compact encoding for a much richer color. For example, a 256-entry colormap can be indexed with 8 bits, but it may contain 24 bits of color information. The UNIX *xdpyinfo* program reports the different visual classes supported by your display. Table 35–4 lists the visual classes:

Table 35–4 Visual classes for displays.

`staticgrey`	Greyscale with a fixed colormap defined by the system.
`greyscale`	Greyscale with a writable colormap.
`staticcolor`	Color with a fixed colormap defined by the system.
`pseudocolor`	Color values determined by single writable colormap.
`truecolor`	Color values determined by three colormaps defined by the system: one each for red, green, and blue.
`directcolor`	Color values determined by three writable colormaps: one each for red, green, and blue.
`best`	Use the best visual for a given depth.

The frame and toplevel widgets support a `colormap` and `visual` attribute. You can query these attributes on all platforms. On Windows and Macintosh there is only one `visual` type at a time, and users may be able to change it for their whole system. On UNIX, the X server typically supports more than one visual class on the same display, and you can create frames and toplevels that use a particular visual class. The value of the `visual` attribute has two parts, a visual type and the desired depth of the display. The following example requests a greyscale visual with a depth of 4 bits per pixel:

```
toplevel .grey -visual "greyscale 4"
```

You can start *wish* with a `-visual` command line argument:

```
wish -visual "truecolor 24"
```

A visual is associated with a colormap. Windows and Macintosh have a single colormap that is shared by all applications. UNIX allows for private colormaps, which can be useful if you absolutely must have lots of colors. However, the drawback of a private colormap is that the display flashes as the mouse enters windows with their own colormap. This is because the monitor hardware really only has one colormap, so the X server must swap colormaps. Macintosh and Windows manage their colormap more gracefully, although if you use too many colors some flashing can occur. Tk can simulate private colormaps on Windows, but it is probably better to let the system manage the colormap. Tk on the Macintosh always uses a 24-bit `truecolor` visual, which is basically unlimited colors, and lets the operating system dither colors if necessary.

By default a widget inherits the colormap and visual from its parent widget. The value of the `colormap` attribute can be the keyword `new`, in which case the frame or toplevel gets a new private colormap, or it can be the name of another widget, in which case the frame or toplevel shares the colormap of that widget. When sharing colormaps, the other widget must be on the same screen and using the same visual class.

Bitmaps and Images

The label and all the button widgets have an `image` attribute that specifies a graphic image to display. Using an image takes two steps. In the first step the image is created via the `image create` command. This command returns an identifier for the image, and it is this identifier that is passed to widgets as the value of their image attribute.

Example 35–3 Specifying an image for a widget.

```
set im [image create bitmap \
   -file glyph.bitmap -maskfile glyph.mask \
   -background white -foreground blue]
button .foo -image $im
```

There are three things that can be displayed by labels and all the buttons: text, bitmaps, and images. If more than one of these attributes are specified, then the image has priority over the bitmap, and the bitmap has priority over the text. You can remove the image or bitmap attribute by specifying a null string for its value:

```
.foo config -image {}
```

The image Command

Table 35–5 summarizes the `image` command.

Table 35–5 Summary of the `image` command.

`image create` *`type ?name? ?options?`*	Create an image of the specified type. If *`name`* is not specified, one is made up. The remaining arguments depend on the *`type`* of image being created.
`image delete` *`name`*	Delete the named image.
`image height` *`name`*	Return the height of the image, in pixels.
`image names`	Return the list of defined images.
`image type` *`name`*	Return the type of the named image.
`image types`	Return the list of possible image types.
`image width` *`name`*	Return the width of the image, in pixels.

The exact set of options for `image create` depend on the image type. There are two built-in image types: `bitmap` and `photo`. Chapter 42 describes the C interface for defining new image types.

Bitmap Images

A `bitmap` image has a main image and an optional mask image. The main image is drawn in the foreground color. The mask image is drawn in the background color, unless the corresponding bit is set in the main image. The remaining bits are "clear" and the widget's normal background color shows through. Table 35–6 lists the options supported by the `bitmap` image type:

Table 35–6 Bitmap image options.

`-background` *`color`*	The background color (*no* `-bg` *equivalent).*
`-data` *`string`*	The contents of the bitmap as a string.
`-file` *`name`*	The name of the file containing a bitmap definition.
`-foreground` *`color`*	The foreground color (*no* `-fg` *equivalent*).
`-maskdata` *`string`*	The contents of the mask as a string.
`-maskfile` *`name`*	The name of the file containing the mask data.

The bitmap definition files are stylized C structure definitions that the Tk library parses. The files usually have a `.xbm` file name extension. These are generated by bitmap editors such as *bitmap* program, which comes with the standard X distribution. The `-file` and `-maskfile` options name a file that contains such a definition. The `-data` and `-maskdata` options specify a string in the same format as the contents of one of those files.

The `bitmap` Attribute

The label and all the button widgets also support a `bitmap` attribute, which is a special case of an image. This attribute is a little more convenient than the image attribute because the extra step of creating an image is not required. However, there are some power and flexibility with the `image` command, such as the ability to reconfigure a named image (e.g., for animation) that is not possible with a bitmap.

Example 35–4 Specifying a bitmap for a widget.

```
button .foo -bitmap @glyph.xbm -fg blue
```

The `@` syntax for the bitmap attribute signals that a file containing the bitmap is being specified. It is also possible to name built-in bitmaps. The predefined bitmaps are shown in the next figure along with their symbolic name. Chapter 42 describes the C interface for defining built in bitmaps.

Example 35–5 The built-in bitmaps.

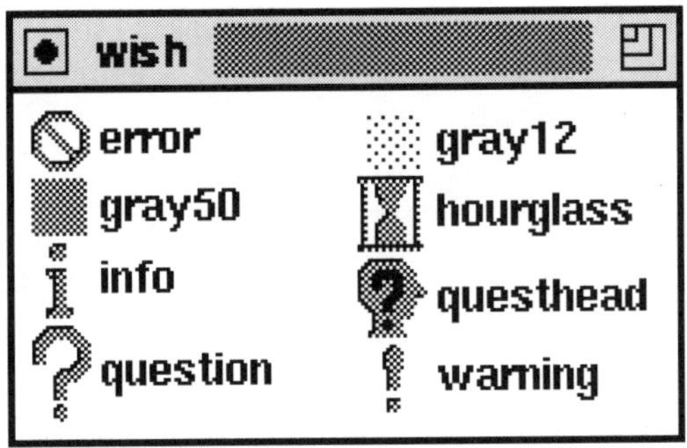


```
frame .f -bd 4; frame .g -bd 4 ; pack .f .g -side left
set parent .f ; set next .g
foreach name {error gray12 gray50 hourglass \
            info questhead question warning} {
    frame $parent.$name
    label $parent.$name.l -text $name -width 9 -anchor w
    label $parent.$name.b -bitmap $name
    pack $parent.$name.l -side right
    pack $parent.$name.b -side top
    pack $parent.$name -side top -expand true -fill x
    set tmp $parent ; set parent $next ; set next $tmp
}
```

Photo Images

The `photo` image type was contributed to Tk by Paul Mackerras. It displays full color images and can do dithering and gamma correction. Table 35–7 lists the attributes for photo images. These are specified in the `image create photo` command.

Table 35–7 Photo image attributes.

`-format` *format*	Specifies the data format for the file or data string.
`-data` *string*	The contents of the photo as a base64 coded string.
`-file` *name*	The name of the file containing a photo definition.
`-gamma` *value*	A gamma correction factor, which must be greater than zero. A value greater than one brightens an image.
`-height` *value*	The height, in screen units.
`-width` *value*	The width of the image, in screen units.
`-palette` *spec*	The number of shades of gray or color for the image.

The `format` indicates what format the data are in. The `photo` image supports different image formats. Tk 4.0 supports the PPM, PGM, and GIF formats. There is a C interface to define new photo formats. The CD-ROM has a "plus-patch" version of Tk that supports pixmaps and JPEG files. Normally you do not need to specify the format because the photo implementation will try all format handlers until it find one that accepts the data. An explicit format limits what handlers are tried. The format name is treated as a prefix that is compared against the names of handlers. Case is not significant in the format name.

The `palette` setting determines how many colors or graylevels are used when rendering an image. If a single number is specified, the image is rendered in greyscale with that many shades of gray. For full color, three numbers separated by slashes specify the number of shades of red, green, and blue, respectively. The more shades you specify the more room you take up in your colormap. The photo widget will switch to a private colormap if necessary. Multiply the number of red, green, and blue shades to determine how many different colors you use. If you have an 8-bit display, there are only 256 colors available. Reasonable palette settings that do not hog the colormap include `5/5/4` and `6/6/5`. You can use fewer shades of blue because the human eye is less sensitive to blue.

After you create an image you can operate on it. Table 35–8 lists the image instance operations. In the table, `$p` is a photo image handle returned by the `image create photo` command.

Table 35–9 lists the options available when you copy data from one image to another. The regions involved in the copy are specified by the upper-left and lower-right corners. If the lower-right corner of the source is not specified, then it

Table 35–8 Photo image operations.

`$p blank`	Clear the image. It becomes transparent.
`$p cget` *`option`*	Return the configuration attribute *`option`*.
`$p configure ...`	Reconfigure the photo image attributes.
`$p copy` *`source options`*	Copy another image. Table 35–9 lists the `copy` options.
`$p get` *`x y`*	Return the pixel value at position *x y*.
`$p put` *`data`* `?-to` *`x1 y1 x2 y2`*`?`	Insert *`data`* into the image. *`data`* is a list of rows, where each row is a list of colors.
`$p read` *`file options`*	Load an image from a file. Table 35–10 lists the read options.
`$p redither`	Reapply the dithering algorithm to the image.
`$p write file options`	Save the image to *`file`* according to *`options`*. Table 35–11 lists the `write` options.

defaults to the lower-right corner of the image. If the lower-right corner of the destination is not specified, then the size is determined by the area of the source. Otherwise, the source image may be cropped or replicated to fill the destination.

Table 35–9 Copy options for photo images.

`-from` *`x1 y1`* `?`*`x2 y2`*`?`	Specifies the location and area in the source image. If *x2* and *y2* are not given, they are set to the bottom-right corner.
`-to` *`x1 y1`* `?`*`x2 y2`*`?`	Specifies the location and area in the destination. If *x2* and *y2* are not given, the size is determined by the source. The source may be cropped or tiled to fill the destination.
`-shrink`	Shrink the destination so its bottom right corner matches the bottom right corner of the data copied in. This has no effect if the `width` and `height` have been set for the image.
`-zoom` *`x`* `?`*`y`*`?`	Magnify the source so each source pixel becomes a block of *x* by *y* pixels. *y* defaults to *x* if it is not specified.
`-subsample` *`x`* `?`*`y`*`?`	Reduce the source by taking every *x*th pixel in the X direction and every *y*th pixel in the Y direction. *y* defaults to *x*.

Table 35–10 lists the `read` options, and Table 35–11 lists the `write` options. The `-format` option is more important for writing, because the first format found is used. With reading, the format is determined automatically. If there are multiple image types that can read the same data, you may specify a read format.

Table 35–10 Read options for photo images.

`-format` *format*	Specifies the format of the data. By default, the format is determined automatically.
`-from` *x1 y1 ?x2 y2?*	Specifies a subregion of the source data. If *x2* and *y2* are not given, the size is determined by the data.
`-to` *x1 y1*	Specifies the top-left corner of the new data.
`-shrink`	Shrink the destination so its bottom-right corner matches the bottom-right corner of the data read in. This has no effect if the width and height have been set for the image.

Table 35–11 Write options for photo images.

`-format` *format*	Specifies the format of the data.
`-from` *x1 y1 ?x2 y2?*	Specifies a subregion of the data to save. If *x2* and *y2* are not given, they are set to the lower-right corner.

The Text Insert Cursor

The text, entry, and canvas widgets have a second cursor to mark the text insertion point. The text insert cursor is described by a set of attributes. These attributes can make the insert cursor vary from a thin vertical line to a large rectangle with its own relief. Table 35–12 lists these attributes. The default insert cursor is a two-pixel-wide vertical line. You may not like the look of a wide insert cursor. The cursor is centered between two characters, so a wide one does not look the same as the block cursors found in many terminal emulators. Instead of occupying the space of a single character, it partially overlaps the two characters on either side:

Table 35–12 Cursor attribute resource names.

`cursor`	The mouse cursor. See text for sample formats. All widgets.
`insertBackground`	Color for the text insert cursor. Widgets: `canvas`, `entry`, and `text`.
`insertBorderWidth`	Width for three dimensional appearance. Widgets: `canvas`, `entry`, and `text`.
`insertOffTime`	Milliseconds the cursor blinks off. (Zero disables blinking.) Widgets: `canvas`, `entry`, and `text`.
`insertOnTime`	Milliseconds the cursor blinks on. Widgets: `canvas`, `entry`, and `text`.
`insertWidth`	Width of the text insert cursor, in screen units. Widgets: `canvas`, `entry`, and `text`.

The Mouse Cursor

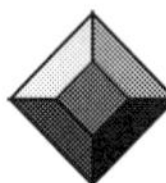

The `cursor` attribute defines the mouse cursor. Example 35–6 shows the cursors that come built into Tk:

Example 35–6 The Tk cursors.

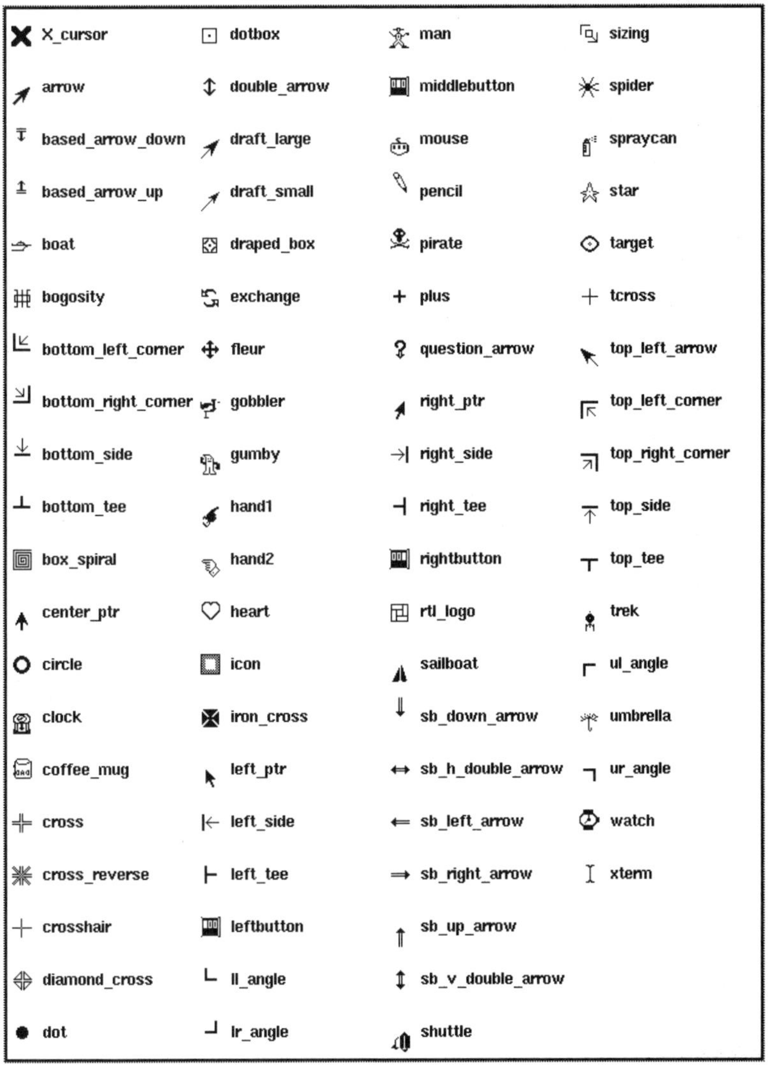

X_cursor	dotbox	man	sizing
arrow	double_arrow	middlebutton	spider
based_arrow_down	draft_large	mouse	spraycan
based_arrow_up	draft_small	pencil	star
boat	draped_box	pirate	target
bogosity	exchange	plus	tcross
bottom_left_corner	fleur	question_arrow	top_left_arrow
bottom_right_corner	gobbler	right_ptr	top_left_corner
bottom_side	gumby	right_side	top_right_corner
bottom_tee	hand1	right_tee	top_side
box_spiral	hand2	rightbutton	top_tee
center_ptr	heart	rtl_logo	trek
circle	icon	sailboat	ul_angle
clock	iron_cross	sb_down_arrow	umbrella
coffee_mug	left_ptr	sb_h_double_arrow	ur_angle
cross	left_side	sb_left_arrow	watch
cross_reverse	left_tee	sb_right_arrow	xterm
crosshair	leftbutton	sb_up_arrow	
diamond_cross	ll_angle	sb_v_double_arrow	
dot	lr_angle	shuttle	

A foreground and background color for the cursor can be specified. Here are some example cursor specifications:

```
$w config -cursor watch              ;# stop-watch cursor
$w config -cursor {gumby blue}       ;# blue gumby
$w config -cursor {X_cursor red white}  ;# red X on white
```

The other form for the cursor attribute specifies a file that contains the definition of the cursor bitmap. If two file names are specified, then the second specifies the cursor mask that determines what bits of the background get covered up. Bitmap editing programs like *idraw* and *iconedit* can be used to generate these files. Here are some example cursor specification using files. You need to specify a foreground color, and if you specify a mask file, then you also need to specify a background color:

```
$w config -cursor "@timer.xbm black"
$w config -cursor "@timer.xbm timer.mask black red"
```

The cursors shown in Example 35–6 are available on all platforms. However, on Windows and Macintosh some of the cursors are mapped to native cursors and appear differently. On Windows the following cursors are mapped to native cursors: `arrow`, `ibeam`, `icon`, `crosshair`, `fleur`, `sb_v_double_arrow`, `sb_h_double_arrow`, `center_ptr`, `watch`, and `xterm`. These additional cursors are defined on Windows: `starting`, `size`, `size_ne_sw`, `size_ns`, `size_nw_se`, `size_we`, `uparrow`, and `wait`. On Windows, use the `no` cursor to eliminate the cursor. On Macintosh the following cursors are mapped to native cursors: `ibeam`, `xterm`, `cross`, `crosshair`, `plus`, `watch`, `arrow`. These additional cursors are defined on Macintosh: `text` and `cross-hair`.

CHAPTER 36

Fonts and Text Attributes

This chapter describes the naming conventions for fonts. Tk 8.0 has a font object that you can dynamically configure and associate with widgets. This chapter describes other text-related attributes such as justification, anchoring, and geometry gridding.

Fonts describe how characters look on the screen. Tk widgets like buttons, labels, and listboxes have a `font` attribute that determines which font they use to display their text. The text widget has `font` attributes on tags that are applied to different regions of text. Tk 8.0 has a platform-independent way to name fonts (e.g., `times 12 bold`), plus it gracefully handles missing fonts. You can define named font objects and then associate those with widgets and text tags. When the font objects are reconfigured, the widgets using them update their display automatically. You can use the resource database to define the fonts used in your interface.

X font names (e.g., `-*-times-bold-r-normal-*-12-*`) were used in versions of Tk before 8.0, and the widgets would raise errors if a font could not be found. The X names have a pattern matching scheme that helps avoid some missing font errors. You can still use X font names in Tk 8.0, and the Tk font system now does font substitutions to avoid errors. Even so, you will find the platform independent names easier to work with.

After fonts are described, the chapter explains a few of the widget attributes that relate to fonts. This includes justification, anchors, and geometry gridding.

Naming a Font

There are two basic ways to name a font in Tk 8.0. You can use predefined font names (e.g., `system`), or you can specify a set of font attributes with a platform-independent name:

```
label .foo -text "Hello" -font {times 12 bold}
```

In this form the font is specified with a three element list. The first element is the font family, the second is the size, in points, and the third is a list of style parameters. The family determines the basic look, such as `courier` or helvetica. The complete set of style parameters are `normal`, `bold`, `roman`, `italic`, `underline`, and `overstrike`. For example, to specify both **bold** and *italic*:

```
label .foo -text "Hello" -font {times 12 {bold italic}}
```

The font size is points, which are 1/72 inch. Tk maintains a scale factor that maps from points to pixels. The default scale is 1, but you can change this with the `tk scale` command, which is described on page 498.

An alternate way to name font attributes uses name-value pairs. These are summarized in Table 36–1. The format is less compact, but it is useful for changing part of a font configuration because you do not need to specify everything. The same specification can be made like this:

```
label .foo -text "Hello" -font \
    {-family times -size 12 -weight bold -slant italic}
```

Table 36–1 Font attributes.

`-family` *name*	The *name* can be `times`, `courier`, `helvetica`, and others returned by the `font families` command.
`-size` *points*	The font size in points, which are 1/72 inch.
`-weight` *value*	The value is `bold` or `normal`.
`-slant` *value*	The value is `roman` or `italic`.
`-underline` *bool*	If *bool* is `true`, an underline is drawn.
`-overstrike` *bool*	If *bool* is `true`, an overstrike line is drawn.

Tk matches a font specification with the fonts available on your system. It will use the best possible font, but it may have to substitute some font parameters. Tk guarantees that the Times, `Courier`, and Helvetica families exist. It also understands the synonyms of Courier New for Courier, and Aerial or Geneva for Helvetica.The `font actual` command returns the parameters chosen to match a font specification:

```
font actual {times 13 bold}
-family Times -size 13 -weight bold -slant roman -under-
line 0 -overstrike 0
```

The Macintosh and Windows platforms have a system-defined default size.

You can get this size by specifying a size of 0 in your specification. The system font uses this:

```
font actual system
-family Chicago -size 0 -weight normal -slant roman
-underline 0 -overstrike 0
```

Named Fonts

You can define your own names for fonts with the `font create` command. Creating a named font provides a level of indirection between the font parameters and the widgets that use the fonts. If you reconfigure a named font, the widgets using it will update their display automatically. This makes it easy to support a user preference for font size. For example, we can define a font name `default` on all platforms:

```
font create default {-family times -size 12}
```

The `default` font can be made larger at anytime with `font configure`. Widgets using the fonts will update automatically:

```
font configure default -size 14
```

System Fonts

The Windows and Macintosh platforms have system-defined fonts that are used by most applications. When you query the configuration of the Tk widgets, you will see the system font names. The parameters for the system fonts can be tuned by the user via the system control panel. You can find out the attributes of the system font with `font actual`. These are the system fonts for each platform:

- The Windows platform supports `system`, `systemfixed`, `ansi`, `ansifixed`, `device`, `oemfixed`. The `fixed` suffix refers to a font where each character is the same size.
- The Macintosh platform has `system` and `application`.
- The UNIX platform has `fixed`. This is the only X font name that is guaranteed to exist. X font names are described in the next section.

V. Tk Details

X Font Names

Fonts can be specified with X font names on all platforms, and you must use X font names before Tk 8.0. The name `fixed` is an example of a short X font name. Other short names might include `6x12`, `9x15`, or `times12`. However, these aliases are site-dependent. In fact, all X font names are site dependent because different fonts may be installed on different systems. The only font guaranteed to exist on the UNIX platform is named `fixed`.

The more general form of an X font name has several components that describe the font parameters. Each component is separated by a dash, and the asterisk (`*`) is used for unspecified components. Short font names are system-defined aliases for these more complete specifications. Here is an example:

```
-*-times-medium-r-normal-*-18-*-*-*-*-*-iso8859-1
```

The components of X font names are listed in Table 36–2 in the order in which they occur in the font specification. The table gives the possible values for the components. If there is an ellipsis (...), then there are more possibilities, too.

Table 36–2 X Font specification components.

Component	Possible values
foundry	adobe xerox linotype misc ...
family	times helvetica lucida courier symbol ...
weight	bold medium demibold demi normal book light
slant	i r o
swidth	normal sans narrow semicondensed
adstyle	sans
pixels	8 10 12 14 18 24 36 48 72 144 ...
points	0 80 100 120 140 180 240 360 480 720 ...
resx	0 72 75 100
resy	0 72 75 100
space	p m c
avgWidth	73 94 124 ...
registry	iso8859 xerox dec adobe jisx0208.1983 ...
encoding	1 fontspecific dectech symbol dingbats

The most common attributes chosen for a font are its family, weight, slant, and size. The weight is usually **bold** or medium. The slant component is a bit cryptic, but `i` means *italic*, `r` means roman (i.e., normal), and `o` means *oblique*. A given font family might have an italic version, or an oblique version, but not both. Similarly, not all weights are offered by all font families. Size can be specified in pixels (i.e., screen pixels) or points. Points are meant to be independent of the screen resolution. On a 75dpi font, there are about 10 points per pixel. Note: these "points" are different than the printer points Tk uses in screen measurements. When you use X font names, the size of the font is not affected by the Tk scale factor described on page 498.

It is generally a good idea to specify just a few key components and use `*` for the remaining components. The X server attempts to match the font specification with its set of installed fonts, but it fails if there is a specific component that it cannot match. If the first or last character of the font name is an asterisk, then that can match multiple components. The following selects a 12-pixel times font:

```
*times-medium-r-*-*-12*
```

Two useful UNIX programs that deal with X fonts are *xlsfonts* and *xfontsel*. These are part of the standard X11 distribution. *xlsfonts* simply lists the available fonts that match a given font name. It uses the same pattern matching that the server does. Because asterisk is special to most UNIX shells, you need to quote the font name argument if you run *xlsfonts* from your shell. *xfontsel* has a graphical user interface and displays the font that matches a given font name.

Font Failures before Tk 8.0

Unfortunately, if a font is missing, versions of Tk before 8.0 do not attempt to substitute another font, not even `fixed`. (Tk 8.0 only does substitutions if you use platform-independent font names.) Before Tk 8.0, the widget creation or reconfiguration command raises an error if the font does not exist. The `FindFont` routine looks around for an existing font. It falls back to `fixed` if nothing else matches:

Example 36–1 `FindFont` matches an existing font.

```
proc FindFont { w {sizes 14} {weight medium} {slant r}} {
    foreach family {times courier helvetica} {
        foreach size $sizes {
            if {[catch {$w config -font \
                -*-$family-$weight-$slant-*-*-$size-*}] == 0} {
                return -*-$family-$weight-$slant-*-*-$size-*
            }
        }
    }
    $w config -font fixed
    return fixed
}
```

The `FindFont` proc takes the name of a widget, `w`, as an argument, plus some optional font characteristics. All five kinds of text widgets take a `-font` attribute specification, so you can use this routine on any of them. The `sizes` argument is a set of pixel sizes for the font (not points). The routine is written so you can supply a choice of sizes, but it fixes the set of families it uses and allows only a single weight and slant. Another approach is to loop through a set of more explicit font names, with `fixed` being your last choice. The font that works is returned by the procedure so that the search results can be saved and reused later. This is important because opening a font for the first time is a fairly heavyweight operation, and a failed font lookup is also expensive.

Another approach to the font problem is to create a wrapper around the Tk widget creation routines. The `FontWidget` procedure falls back to the `fixed` font if the widget creation command fails. It is careful to eliminate the font specified in `args`, if it exists. The explicit font overrides any setting from the resource database or the Tk defaults. Of course, widget creation might fail for some more legitimate reason, but that is allowed to happen in the backup case:

Example 36–2 `FontWidget` protects against font errors.

```
proc FontWidget { args } {
    # args is a Tcl command
    if [catch $args w] {
        # Delete the font specified in args, if any
        set ix [lsearch $args -font]
        if {$ix >= 0} {
            set args [lreplace $args $ix [expr $ix+1]]
        }
        # This font overrides the resource database
        set w [eval $args {-font fixed}]
    }
    return $w
}
FontWidget button .foo -text Foo -font garbage
```

Font Metrics

The `font metrics` command returns measurement information for fonts. It returns general information about all the characters in the font:

```
font metrics {times 10}
-ascent 9 -descent 2 -linespace 11 -fixed 0
```

The `fixed` setting is true for fonts where each character fits into the same sized bounding box. The `linespace` is the distance between the baselines of successive lines. The `ascent` and `descent` are illustrated in Example 36–3:

Example 36–3 Font metrics.

The `font measure` command returns the width of a string that will be displayed in a given font. The width does not account for heavily slanted letters that overhang their bounding box, nor does it do anything special with tabs or newlines in the string.

The font Command

Table 36–3 summarizes the font command. In the table, *font* is either a description of font parameters, a logical font name, a system font name, or an X font name. The -displayof option applies to X where you can have windows on different displays that could support different fonts. Note that when you delete a logical font name with font delete, the font is not really deleted if there are widgets that use that font.

Table 36–3 The font command.

font actual *font* ?-displayof *window*? ?*option*?	Return the actual parameters of *font*.
font configure *fontname* ?*option*? ?*value option value*?	Set or query the parameters for *fontname*.
font create ?*fontname*? ?*option value* ...?	Define *fontname* with the specified parameters.
font delete *fontname* ?*name2* ...?	Remove the definition for the named fonts.
font families ?-displayof *win*?	Return the list of font families supported on the display of *win*.
font measure *font* ?-displayof *win*? *text*	Return the width of *text* displayed in *win* with *font*.
font metrics *font* ?-displayof *win*? ?*option*?	The *option* can be -ascent, -descent, -linespace, or -fixed.
font names	Return the names of defined fonts.

Text Attributes

Layout

Table 36–4 summarizes two simple text layout attributes: justify and wrapLength. The text widget has several more layout-related attributes, and Chapter 30 describes those in detail. The two attributes described in this section apply to the various button widgets, the label, entry, and message widgets. Those widgets are described in Chapters 24, 26, and 28. The justify attribute causes text to be centered, left-justified, or right-justified. The default justification is center for all the widgets in the table, except for the entry widget, which is left-justified by default.

The wrapLength attribute specifies how long a line of text is before it is wrapped onto another line. It is used to create multiline buttons and labels. This attribute is specified in screen units, however, not string length. It is probably easier to achieve the desired line breaks by inserting newlines into the text for the button or label and specifying a `wrapLength` of 0, which is the default.

Table 36–4 Layout attribute resource names

`justify`	Text line justification. Values: `left`, `center`, or `right`. `Widgets: button, checkbutton, entry, label, menubutton, message, and radiobutton.`
`wrapLength`	Maximum line length for text, in screen units. Widgets: `button, checkbutton, label, menubutton,` and `radiobutton.`

Selection Attributes

Table 36–5 lists the selection-related attributes. The `exportSelection` attribute controls if the selection is exported for cut and paste to other widgets. The colors for selected text are set with `selectForeground` and `selectBackground`. The selection is drawn in a raised relief, and the `selectBorderWidth` attribute affects the 3D appearance. Choose a border width of zero to get a flat relief.

Table 36–5 Selection attribute resource names.

`exportSelection`	Share selection. Widgets: `entry, canvas, listbox, and text.`
`selectForeground`	Foreground of selected text.
`selectBackground`	Background of selected text.
`selectBorderWidth`	Width of 3D raised border for selection highlight.

Gridding, Resizing, and Geometry

The text, listbox, and canvas widgets support geometry gridding. This is an alternate interpretation of the main window geometry that is in terms of grid units, typically characters, as opposed to pixels. The `setGrid` attribute is a boolean that indicates if gridding should be turned on. The listbox and text widgets define a grid size that matches their character size. Example 38–1 on page 488 sets up gridding for a canvas.

When a widget is gridded, its size is constrained to have a whole number of grid units displayed. The height will be constrained to show a whole number of text lines, and the width will be constrained to show a whole number of average width characters. This affects interactive resizing by users, as well as the various window manger commands (`wm`) that relate to geometry. When gridding is turned on, the geometry argument (e.g., `24x80`) is interpreted as grid units; otherwise it is interpreted as pixels. The window manager geometry commands are summarized in Table 38–1on page 489.

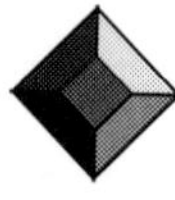

Gridding before Tk 4.0 enables resizing.

Before Tk 4.0, an important side effect of gridding was that it enabled interactive resizing. Setting the minimum size or maximum size of a window also enabled resizing. Otherwise, Tk windows were only resizable under program control. In Tk 4.0, this changed so that windows are always resizable by the user.

Try resizing the window in the following example with and without the `-setgrid` flag, and with and without the `wm minsize` command, which sets the minimum size of the window. The `Scrolled_Listbox` procedure is defined in Example 27–3 on page 348.

Example 36–4 A gridded, resizable listbox.

```
wm minsize . 5 3
button .quit -text Quit -command exit
pack .quit -side top -anchor e
Scrolled_Listbox .f -width 10 -height 5 -setgrid true
pack .f -side top -fill both -expand true
```

A Font Selection Application

This chapter concludes with an example that lets you select fonts. It is written as a dialog you can add to your application. The menus are tied to elements of the `font` array that are used in `font configure` commands. The actual settings of the font are shown above a sampler of what the font looks like. When the user clicks the OK button, the font configuration is returned:

Example 36–5 Font selection dialog.

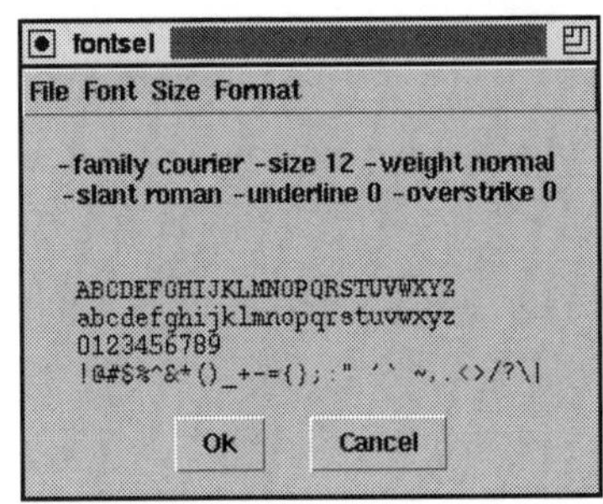


```
proc Font_Select {{top .fontsel}} {
	global font

	# Create the menus for the menu bar

	toplevel $top -class Fontsel -bd 10
	set menubar [menu $top.menubar]
	$top config -menu $menubar
	foreach x {File Font Size Format} {
		set menu [menu $menubar.[string tolower $x]]
```

```
    $menubar add cascade -menu $menu -label $x
}
$menubar.file add command -label Reset -command FontReset
$menubar.file add command -label OK \
    -command {set font(ok) 1}
$menubar.file add command -label Cancel \
    -command {set font(ok) 0}

# Build a cascaded family menu if there are lots of fonts

set allfonts [font families]
set numfonts [llength $allfonts]
set limit 20
if {$numfonts < $limit} {
    # Just a single level menu
    foreach family $allfonts {
        $menubar.font add radio -label $family \
            -variable font(-family) \
            -value $family \
            -command FontUpdate
    }
} else {
    set c 0 ; set l 0
    foreach family $allfonts {
        if {$l == 0} {
            $menubar.font add cascade -label $family... \
                -menu $menubar.font.$c
            set m [menu $menubar.font.$c]
            incr c
        }
        $m add radio -label $family \
            -variable font(-family) \
            -value $family \
            -command FontUpdate
        set l [expr ($l +1) % $limit]
    }
}

# Complete the other menus

foreach size {7 8 10 12 14 18 24 36 72} {
    $menubar.size add radio -label $size \
        -variable font(-size) \
        -value $size \
        -command FontUpdate
}
$menubar.size add command -label Other... \
        -command [list FontSetSize $top]
$menubar.format add check -label Bold \
        -variable font(-weight) \
        -onvalue bold -offvalue normal \
        -command FontUpdate
$menubar.format add check -label Italic \
        -variable font(-slant) \
        -onvalue italic -offvalue roman \
```

```
        -command FontUpdate
    $menubar.format add check -label underline \
        -variable font(-underline) \
        -command FontUpdate
    $menubar.format add check -label overstrike \
        -variable font(-overstrike) \
        -command FontUpdate

    FontReset

    # This label displays the current font
    label $top.font -textvar font(name) -bd 5

    # A message displays a string in the font.
    message $top.msg -aspect 1000 \
                -borderwidth 10 -font fontsel \
                -text  "
ABCDEFGHIJKLMNOPQRSTUVWXYZ
abcdefghijklmnopqrstuvwxyz
0123456789
!@#$%^&*()_+-=[]{};:\"'`~,.<>/?\\|
"

    # Lay out the dialog

    pack $top.font $top.msg  -side top
    set f [frame $top.buttons]
    button $f.ok -text Ok -command {set font(ok) 1}
    button $f.cancel -text Cancel -command {set font(ok) 0}
    pack $f.ok $f.cancel -padx 10 -side left
    pack $f -side top

    # Dialog_Wait is defined in Example 33-1 on page 437
    Dialog_Wait $top font(ok)
    destroy $top
    if {$font(ok)} {
        return [array get font -*]
    } else {
        return {}
    }
}
proc FontUpdate { } {
    global font

    # The elements of font that have a leading - are
    # used directly in the font configuration command.

    eval {font configure fontsel} [array get font -*]
    FontSet
}
proc FontReset {} {
    catch {font delete fontsel}
    font create fontsel
    FontSet
}
```

V. Tk Details

```
proc FontSet {} {
    global font

    # The name is the font configuration information
    # with a line break so it looks nicer

    set font(name) [font actual fontsel]
    regsub -- "-slant" $font(name) "\n-slant" font(name)

    # Save the actual parameters after any font substitutions

    array set font [font actual fontsel]
}
proc FontSetSize {top} {

    # Add an entry to enter a specific size.

    set f [frame $top.size -borderwidth 10]
    pack $f -side top -fill x
    label $f.msg -text "Size:"
    entry $f.entry -textvariable font(-size)
    bind $f.entry <Return> FontUpdate
    pack $f.msg -side left
    pack $f.entry -side top -fill x
}
```

CHAPTER 37

Send

This chapter describes the send command that invokes Tcl commands in other applications. This chapter also presents an alternative to send that uses network sockets.

The send command lets Tk applications on the same display send each other Tcl commands and cooperate in very flexible ways. A large application can be structured as a set of smaller tools that cooperate instead of one large monolith. This encourages reuse, and it exploits your workstation's multiprogramming capabilities.

The send facility provides a name space for Tk applications. The winfo interps command returns the names of all the Tk applications reachable with send. The send communication mechanism is limited to applications running on one display. Multiple screens on one workstation still count as the same display on X. In UNIX, send uses properties on the X display for communication and to record the application names. As of Tk 8.0, send is not yet implemented on Macintosh or Windows. There is an extension for Windows that uses DDE to emulate send.

This chapter also describes an alternative to send that uses network sockets. The facility is not limited to a single display, and can be used in conjunction with safe interpreters to limit the capabilities of remote operations. A number of Tcl extensions provide similar functionality, including *GroupKit* and *Tcl-DP*. You can find these extensions on the Tcl archive and the CD-ROM.

The send Command

The `send` command invokes a Tcl command in another application. The general form of the command is:

```
send options interp arg ?arg...?
```

The `send` command behaves like `eval`; if you give it extra arguments, it concatenates them to form a single command. If your argument structure is important, use `list` to build the command. Table 37–1 lists the options to `send`:

Table 37–1 Options to the `send` command.

`-async`	Do not wait for the remote command to complete.
`-displayof` *`window`*	Send to the application on the same display as *`window`*.
`--`	Delimits options from the *`interp`* argument. Useful if the *`interp`* begins with a dash.

The *`interp`* argument is the name of the other application. An application defines its own name when it creates its main window. The *wish* shell uses as its name the last component of the file name of the script. For example, when *wish* interprets `/usr/local/bin/exmh`, it sets its application name to `exmh`. However, if another instance of the `exmh` application is already running, *wish* chooses the name `exmh #2`, and so on. If *wish* is not executing from a file, its name is just `wish`. You may have noticed `wish #2` or `wish #3` in your window title bars, and this reflects the fact that multiple *wish* applications are running on your display. If you use Tk 3.6 or earlier and your application crashes, it can forget to unregister its name. The *tkinspect* program has a facility to clean up these old registrations.

A script can find out its own name, so you can pass names around or put them into files in order to set up communications. The `tk appname` command queries or changes the application name:

```
set myname [tk appname]
tk appname aNewName
```

In Tk 3.6 and earlier, you have to use the `winfo name` command to get the name of the application:

```
set myname [winfo name .]
```

Send and X Authority

The `send` command relies on the X authority mechanism for authorization. A command is rejected by the target interpreter if you do not have X authority set up. There are two ways around this problem. First, you can disable the access check by compiling the `tkSend.c` file with the `-DTK_NO_SECURITY` compile flag. If you must worry about malicious programs that send your programs commands, then you should not do this.

The second option is to start your X server with its `-auth` flag, which initializes the X authority mechanism. The details vary depending on your X server, and most modern X servers do this automatically. The general picture is that you generate a pseudo-random string and store it into a file, which is usually named `~/.Xauthority` and must be readable only by your account. The `-auth` flag specifies the name of this file to the X server. Each X application reads this file and sends the contents to the X server when opening the connection to the server. If the contents match what the server read when it started, then the connection is allowed. The system is slightly more complicated than described here. The file actually contains a sequence of records to support multiple displays and client hosts. Consult your local X guru or the documentation for the details particular to your system.

Your xhost list must be clear.

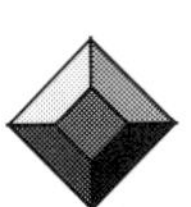

Tk also requires that the *xhost* list be empty. The *xhost* mechanism is the old, not-so-secure authentication mechanism in X. With *xhost* you allow all programs on a list of hosts to connect to your display. The problem with this is that multiuser workstations allow remote login, so essentially anybody could log in to a workstation on the *xhost* list and gain access to your display. The Xauthority mechanism is much stronger because it restricts access to your account, or to accounts that you explicitly give a secret token to. The problem is that even if Xauthority is set up, the user or a program can turn on *xhosts* and open up access to your display.

If you run the *xhost* program with no argument, it reports the status and what hosts are on the list. The following output is generated when access control is restricted, but programs running on `sage` are allowed to connect to the display:

```
exec xhost
=> Access control enabled: all hosts being restricted
sage
```

This is not good enough for Tk `send`. It will fail because `sage` is on the list. I work in an environment where old scripts and programs are constantly adding things to my *xhost* list for reasons that are no longer valid. I developed a version of `send` that checks for errors and then does the following to clean out the *xhost* list. You have to enable access control and then explicitly remove any hosts on the list. These are reported after an initial line that says whether or not hosts are restricted:

```
xhost - ;# enable access control in general
foreach host [lrange [split [exec xhost] \n] 1 end] {
    exec xhost -$host ;# clear out exceptions
}
```

V. Tk Details

The Sender Script

The following example is a general-purpose script that reads input and then sends it to another application. You can put this at the end of a pipeline to get a loopback effect to the main application, although you can also use `fileevent` for similar effects. One advantage of `send` over `fileevent` is that the sender and receiver can be more independent. A logging application, for example, can come and go independently of the applications that log error messages:

Example 37–1 The sender application.

```
#!/usr/local/bin/wish
# sender takes up to four arguments:
# 1) the name of the application to send to.
# 2) a command prefix.
# 3) the name of another application to notify
#    after the end of the data.
# 4) the command to use in the notification.

# Hide the unneeded window
wm withdraw .
# Process command line arguments
if {$argc == 0} {
   puts stderr "Usage: send name ?cmd? ?uiName? ?uiCmd?"
   exit 1
} else {
   set app [lindex $argv 0]
}
if {$argc > 1} {
   set cmd [lindex $argv 1]
} else {
   set cmd Send_Insert
}
if {$argc > 2} {
   set ui [lindex $argv 2]
   set uiCmd Send_Done
}
if {$argc > 3} {
   set uiCmd [lindex $argv 3]
}
# Read input and send it to the logger
while {[gets stdin input] >= 0} {
   # Ignore errors with the logger
   catch {send $app [concat $cmd [list $input\n]]}
}
# Notify the controller, if any
if [info exists ui] {
   if [catch {send $ui $uiCmd} msg] {
      puts stderr "send.tcl could not notify $ui\n$msg"
   }
}
# This is necessary to force wish to exit.
exit
```

The *sender* application supports communication with two processes. It sends all its input to a primary "logging" application. When the input finishes, it can send a notification message to another "controller" application. The logger and the controller could be the same application.

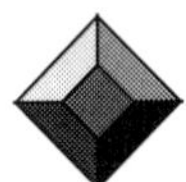

Use list to quote arguments to send.

Consider the `send` command used in the example:

```
send $app [concat $cmd [list $input\n]]
```

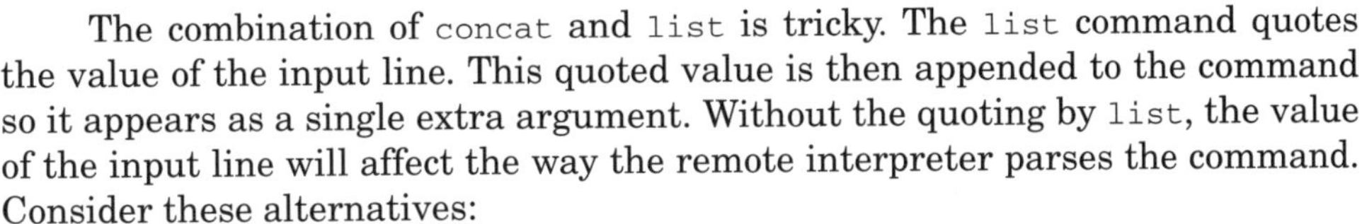

The combination of `concat` and `list` is tricky. The `list` command quotes the value of the input line. This quoted value is then appended to the command so it appears as a single extra argument. Without the quoting by `list`, the value of the input line will affect the way the remote interpreter parses the command. Consider these alternatives:

```
send $app [list $cmd $input]
```

This form is safe, except that it limits `$cmd` to a single word. If `cmd` contains a value like the ones given below, the remote interpreter will not parse it correctly. It will treat the whole multi-word value as the name of a command:

```
.log insert end
.log see end ; .log insert end
```

This is the most common wrong answer:

```
send $app $cmd $input
```

The `send` command concatenates `$cmd` and `$input` together, and the result will be parsed again by the remote interpreter. The success or failure of the remote command depends on the value of the input data. If the input included Tcl syntax like `$` or `[ ]`, errors or other unexpected behavior would result.

Communicating Processes

Chapter 19 presented two examples: a browser for the examples in this book, and a simple shell in which to try out Tcl commands. In that chapter they are put into the same application. The two examples shown below hook these two applications together using the `send` command. Example 37–2 changes the `Run` and `Reset` procedures to send Tcl commands the shell defined in Example 19–4 on page 245. The `StartEvalServer` procedure starts up the shell, if necessary.

Example 37–2 Hooking the browser to an `eval` server.

```
# Replace the Run and Reset procedures from
# Example 19-3 on page 240 with these procedures

# Start up the evalsrv.tcl script.
proc StartEvalServer {} {
   global browse
   # Start the shell and pass it our name.
   exec evalsrv.tcl [tk appname] &
   # Wait for evalsrv.tcl to send us its name
   tkwait variable browse(evalInterp)
}
proc Run {} {
   global browse
```

```
    set apps [winfo interps]
    set ix [lsearch -glob $apps evalsrv.tcl*]
    if {$ix < 0} {
        # No evalsrv.tcl application running
        StartEvalServer
    }
    if {![info exists browse(evalInterp)]} {
        # Hook up to already running eval server
        set browse(evalInterp) [lindex $apps $ix]
    }
    if [catch {send $browse(evalInterp) {info vars}} err] {
        # It probably died - restart it.
        StartEvalServer
    }
    # Send the command asynchronously. The two
    # list commands foil the concat done by send and
    # the uplevel in EvalServe
    send -async $browse(evalInterp) \
        [list EvalEcho [list source $browse(current)]]
}
# Reset the shell interpreter in the eval server
proc Reset {} {
    global browse
    send $browse(evalInterp) {EvalEcho reset}
}
```

The number of lists created before the `send` command may seem excessive, but they are all necessary. The `send` command concatenates its arguments, so instead of letting it do that, we pass it a single list. Similarly, `EvalServe` expects a single argument that is a valid command, so `list` is used to construct that.

The shell in Example 19–4 on page 245 has an `EvalEcho` procedure that we can use as the target of `send`. The only thing it needs is to complete the rendezvous with the browser. When the tcl shell starts up, it sends the browser its application name. The browser passes its own name on the command line that starts the shell, so the shell knows how to talk to the browser.

Example 37–3 Making the shell into an `eval` server.

```
# Add this to Example 19-4 on page 245
if {$argc > 0} {
    # Check in with the browser
    send [lindex $argv 0] \
        [list set browse(evalInterp) [tk appname]]
}
```

Remote `eval` through Sockets

Network sockets provide another communication mechanism you can use to evaluate Tcl commands in another application. The "name" of the application is just the host and port for the socket connection. There are a variety of schemes you can use to manage names. A crude, but effective way to manage host and ports for your servers is to record them in a file in your network file system. These examples ignore this problem. The server chooses a port and the client is expected to know what it is.

Example 37–4 implements `Eval_Server` that lets other applications connect and evaluate Tcl commands. The `interp` argument specifies the interpreter in which to evaluate the Tcl commands. If the caller of `Eval_Server` specifies `{}` for the interpreter, then the commands are evaluated in the current interpreter. The `openCmd` is called when the connection is made. It can do whatever setup or authentication is required. If it doesn't like the connection, it can close the socket:

Example 37–4 Remote `eval` using sockets.

```
proc Eval_Server {port {interp {}} {openCmd EvalOpenProc}} {
	socket -server [list EvalAccept $interp $openCmd] $port
}
proc EvalAccept {interp openCmd newsock addr port} {
	global eval
	set eval(cmdbuf,$newsock) {}
	fileevent $newsock readable [list EvalRead $newsock $interp]
	if [catch {
		interp eval $interp $openCmd $newsock $addr $port
	}] {
		close $newsock
	}
}
proc EvalOpenProc {sock addr port} {
	# do authentication here
	# close $sock to deny the connection
}
```

Example 37–5 shows `EvalRead` that reads commands and evaluates them in an interpreter. If the `interp` is `{}`, it causes the commands to execute in the current interpreter. In this case an `uplevel #0` is necessary to ensure the command is executed in the global scope. If you use `interp eval` to execute something in yourself, it executes in the current scope:

Example 37–5 Reading commands from a socket.

```
proc EvalRead {sock interp} {
	global eval errorInfo errorCode
	if [eof $sock] {
		close $sock
	} else {
		gets $sock line
		append eval(cmdbuf,$sock) $line\n
		if {[string length $eval(cmdbuf,$sock)] && \
				[info complete $eval(cmdbuf,$sock)]} {
```

```
            set code [catch {
                if {[string length $interp] == 0} {
                    uplevel #0 $eval(cmdbuf,$sock)
                } else {
                    interp eval $interp $eval(cmdbuf,$sock)
                }
            } result]
            set reply [list $code $result $errorInfo \
                $errorCode]\n
            # Use regsub to count newlines
            set lines [regsub -all \n $reply {} junk]
            # The reply is a line count followed
            # by a Tcl list that occupies that number of lines
            puts $sock $lines
            puts -nonewline $sock $reply
            flush $sock
            set eval(cmdbuf,$sock) {}
        }
    }
}
```

Example 37–6 presents `Eval_Open` and `Eval_Remote` that implement the client side of the eval connection. `Eval_Open` connects to the server and returns a token, which is just the socket. The main task of `Eval_Remote` is to preserve the information generated when the remote command raises an error

The network protocol is line-oriented. The `Eval_Remote` command writes the command on the socket. The `EvalRead` procedure uses `info complete` to detect the end of the command. The reply is more arbitrary, so server sends a line count and that number of lines. The `regsub` command counts up all the newlines because it returns the number of matches it finds. The reply is a list of error codes, results, and trace information. These details of the `return` command are described on page 74.

Example 37–6 The client side of remote evaluation.

```
proc Eval_Open {server port} {
    global eval
    set sock [socket $server $port]
    # Save this info for error reporting
    set eval(server,$sock) $server:$port
    return $sock
}
proc Eval_Remote {sock args} {
    global eval
    # Preserve the concat semantics of eval
    if {[llength $args] > 1} {
        set cmd [concat $args]
    } else {
        set cmd [lindex $args 0]
    }
    puts $sock $cmd
    flush $sock
```

```
    # Read return line count and the result.
    gets $sock lines
    set result {}
    while {$lines > 0} {
        gets $sock x
        append result $x\n
        incr lines -1
    }
    set code [lindex $result 0]
    set x [lindex $result 1]
    # Cleanup the end of the stack
    regsub "\[^\n]+$" [lindex $result 2] \
        "*Remote Server $eval(server,$sock)*" stack
    set ec [lindex $result 3]
    return -code $code -errorinfo $stack -errorcode $ec $x
}
proc Eval_Close {sock} {
    close $sock
}
```

If an error occurs in the remote command, then a stack trace is returned. This includes the command used inside EvalRead to invoke the command, which is either the uplevel or interp eval command. This is the very last line in the stack that is returned, and regsub is used to replace this with an indication of where control transferred to the remote server:

```
catch [Eval_Remote sock6 set xx]
=> 1
set errorInfo
=> can't read "xx": no such variable
    while executing
"set xx
"
    ("uplevel" body line 1)
    invoked from within
*Remote Server sage:4000*
    invoked from within
"catch [Eval_Remote sock6 set xx]"
```

CHAPTER 38

Window Managers and Window Information

The window manager controls the size and location of other applications' windows. The window manager is built into Windows and Macintosh, while it is a separate application on UNIX. The wm command provides an interface to the window manager. The winfo command returns information about windows.

Management of top-level windows is done by the *window manager*. The Macintosh and Windows platforms have the window manager built in to the operating system, but in UNIX the window manager is just another application. The window manager controls the position of top-level windows, provides a way to resize windows, open and close them, and implements a border and decorative title for windows. The wm command interacts with the window manager so the application can control its size, position, and iconified state.

If you need to fine-tune your display, you may need some detailed information about widgets. The winfo command returns all sorts of information about windows, including interior widgets, not just top-level windows.

V. Tk Details

The wm Command

The wm command has about 20 operations that interact with the window manager. The general form of the command is:

```
wm operation win ?args?
```

In all cases the *win* argument must be a toplevel. Otherwise, an error is raised. In many cases the operation either sets or queries a value. If a new value is not specified, then the current settings are returned. For example, this command returns the current window geometry:

```
wm geometry .
```

```
=> 300x200+327+20
```

This command defines a new geometry:

```
wm geometry . 400x200+0+0
```

There are lots of `wm` operations, and this reflects the complex protocol with UNIX window managers. The summary below lists the subset of operations that I find useful. The operations can be grouped into four main categories:

- *Size, placement and decoration of windows.* Use the `geometry` and `title` operations to position windows and set the title bar.
- *Icons.* Use the `iconify`, `deiconify`, and `withdraw` operations to open and close windows. On UNIX, closed windows are represented by an icon.
- *Long-term session state.* Use the `protocol` operation to get a callback when users destroy windows.
- *Miscellaneous.* Use the `transient` and `overrideredirect` operation to get specialized windows. Future versions of Tk may support a `style` operation to select different kinds of top-level windows.

Size, Placement, and Decoration

Each window has a title that appears in the title bar that the window manager places above the window. In a *wish* script, the default title of the main window is the last component of the file name of the script. Use the `wm title` command to change the title of the window. The title can also appear in the icon for your window, unless you specify another name with `wm iconname`.

```
wm title . "My Application"
```

Use the `wm geometry` command to adjust the position or size of your main windows. A geometry specification has the general form *W*x*H*+*X*+*Y*, where *W* is the width, *H* is the height, and *X* and *Y* specify the location of the upper-left corner of the window. The location `+0+0` is the upper-left corner of the display. You can specify a negative *X* or *Y* to position the bottom (right) side of the window relative to the bottom (right) side of the display. For example, `+0-0` is the lower-left corner, and `-100-100` is offset from the lower-right corner by 100 pixels in the X and Y direction. If you do not specify a geometry, then the current geometry is returned.

A window can have a gridded geometry, which means that the geometry is in terms of some unit other than pixels. For example, the text and listbox widgets set a grid based on the size of the characters they display. They have a `setgrid` attribute that turns on gridding, which is described on page 472. You can also define a grid with the `wm grid` command. The next example sets up gridded geometry for a canvas.

Example 38–1 Gridded geometry for a canvas.

```
canvas .c -width 300 -height 150
pack .c -fill both -expand true
wm geometry .
```

```
=> 300x200+678+477
wm grid . 30 15 10 10
wm geometry .
=> 30x20+678+477
```

The `wm resizable` command controls whether a user can resize a window. The following command allows a resize in the X direction, but not in the Y direction:

```
wm resizable . 1 0
```

You can constrain the minimum size, maximum size, and the aspect ratio of a toplevel. The aspect ratio is the width divided by the height. The constraint is applied when the user resizes the window interactively. The `minsize`, `maxsize`, and `aspect` operations apply these constraints.

Some window managers insist on having the user position windows. The `sizefrom` and `positionfrom` operations let you pretend that the user specified the size and position in order to work around this restriction.

Table 38–1 summarizes the `wm` commands that deal with size, decorations, placement:

Table 38–1 Size, placement and decoration window manager operations.

`wm aspect` *win ?a b c d?*	Constrain *win*'s ratio of width to height to be between (*a/b* and *c/d*).
`wm geometry` *win ?geometry?*	Query or set the geometry of *win*.
`wm grid` *win ?w h dx dy?*	Query or set the grid size. *w* and *h* are the base size, in grid units. *dx* and *dy* are the size, in pixels, of a grid unit.
`wm maxsize` *win ?width height?*	Constrain the maximum size of *win*.
`wm minsize` *win ?width height?*	Constrain the minimum size of *win*.
`wm positionfrom` *win ?who?*	Query or set *who* to be `program` or `user`.
`wm resizable` *win ?xok yok?*	Query or set ability to resize interactively.
`wm sizefrom` *win ?who?*	Query or set *who* to be `program` or `user`.
`wm title` *win ?string?*	Query or set the window title to *string*.

Icons

UNIX window managers let you close a window and replace it with an icon. The window still exists in your application, and users can open the window later. You can open and close a window yourself with the `deiconify` and `iconify` operations, respectively. Use the `withdraw` operation to unmap the window without replacing it with an icon. The `state` operation returns the current state, which is one of `normal`, `iconified`, or `withdrawn`. If you `withdraw` a window, you can restore it to the `normal` state with `deiconify`.

Windows and Macintosh do not implement icons for program windows. Instead, icons represent files and applications in the desktop environment. Tk does not provide facilities to set up desktop icons. When you `iconify` under Windows, the window gets *minimized* and users can open it by clicking on the taskbar at the bottom of the screen. When you `iconify` under Macintosh, the window simply gets withdrawn from the screen.

Windows and Macintosh applications have an additional state, `maximized`, which is not yet supported by Tk. This is a full-screen display mode. Future versions of Tk may support this state.

You can set the attributes of UNIX icons with the `iconname`, `iconposition`, `iconbitmap`, and `iconmask` operations. The icon's mask is used to get irregularly shaped icons. Chapter 35 describes how masks and bitmaps are defined. In the case of an icon, it is most likely that you have the definition in a file, so your command will look like this:

```
wm iconbitmap . @myfilename
```

Table 38–2 summarizes the `wm` operations that have to do with icons:

Table 38–2 Window manager commands for icons.

`wm deiconify` *win*	Open the window *win*.
`wm iconbitmap` *win ?bitmap?*	Query or define the bitmap for the icon. UNIX.
`wm iconify` *win*	Close the window *win*.
`wm iconmask` *win ?mask?*	Query or define the mask for the icon. UNIX.
`wm iconname` *win ?name?*	Query or set the name on the icon. UNIX.
`wm iconposition` *win ?x y?*	Query or set the location of the icon. UNIX.
`wm iconwindow` *win ?window?*	Query or specify an alternate window to display when in the iconified state. UNIX.
`wm state` *win*	Returns `normal`, `iconic`, or `withdrawn`.
`wm withdraw` *win*	Unmap the window. No icon is displayed.

Session State

The window manager lets users delete windows with a close operation. When the main Tk window gets deleted *wish* normally quits. If you have any special processing that must take place when the user deletes a window, you need to intercept the close action. Use the `wm protocol` operation to register a command that handles the `WM_DELETE_WINDOW` message from the window manager. This works on all platforms even though "delete" is a UNIX term and "close" is the Windows and Macintosh term:

```
wm protocol . WM_DELETE_WINDOW Quit
```

If you intercept close on the main Tk window (i.e., dot), you must eventually call `exit` to actually stop your application. However, you can also take the time to prompt the user about unsaved changes, or even let the user change their mind about quitting.

Other window manager messages that you can intercept are `WM_SAVE_YOURSELF` and `WM_TAKE_FOCUS`. The first is called periodically by some UNIX session managers, which are described below. The latter is used in the active focus model. Tk (and this book) assumes a passive focus model where the window manager assigns focus to a top-level window.

Saving session state.

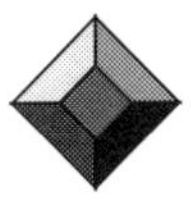

Some UNIX window managers support the notion of a *session* that lasts between runs of the window system. A session is implemented by saving state about the applications that are running, and using this information to restart the applications when the window system is restarted.

An easy way to participate in the session protocol is to save the command used to start your application. The `wm command` operation does this. The *wish* shell saves this information, so it is just a matter of registering it with the window manager. `argv0` is the command, and `argv` is the command-line arguments:

```
wm command . "$argv0 $argv"
```

If your application is typically run on a different host than the one with the display (like in an Xterminal environment), then you also need to record what host to run the application on. Use the `wm client` operation for this. You might need to use *hostname* instead of *uname* on your system:

```
wm client . [exec uname -n]
```

Table 38–3 describes the session-related window manager operations.

Table 38–3 Session-related window manager operations.

`wm client` *win* ?*name*?	Record the hostname in the `WM_CLIENT_MACHINE` property. UNIX.
`wm command` *win* ?*command*?	Record the start-up command in the `WM_COMMAND` property. UNIX.
`wm protocol` *win* ?*name*? ?*command*?	Register a *command* to handle the protocol request *name*, which can be `WM_DELETE_WINDOW`, `WM_SAVE_YOURSELF`, or `WM_TAKE_FOCUS`.

Miscellaneous

The UNIX window managers work by reparenting an application's window so it is a child of the window that forms the border and decorative title bar. The `wm frame` operation returns the window ID of the new parent, or the ID of the window itself if it has not been reparented. The `wm overrideredirect` operation can set a bit that overrides the reparenting. This means that no title or border will be drawn around the window, and you cannot control the window through the window manager.

The `wm group` operation defines groups of windows so the window manager can open and close them together. One window, typically the main window, is chosen as the leader. The other members of the group are iconified when it is iconified. This is not implemented on Windows and Macintosh, and not all UNIX window managers implement this, either.

The `wm transient` operation informs the window manager that this is a temporary window and there is no need to decorate it with the border and decorative title bar. This is used, for example, on pop-up menus. On Windows, a `transient` window is a toolbar window that does not appear in the task bar. On Macintosh, the `unsupported1` command, which is described on page 335, lets you create different styles of top-level windows.

Table 38–4 lists the remaining window manager operations:

Table 38–4 Miscellaneous window manager operations.

`wm colormapwindows` *`win`* `?`*`windowList`*`?`	Set or query the `WM_COLORMAP_WINDOWS` property that orders windows with different colormaps.
`wm focusmodel` *`win`* `?`*`what`*`?`	Set or query the focus model: `active` or `passive`. (Tk assumes the `passive` model.)
`wm frame` *`win`*	Return the ID of the parent of *`win`* if it has been reparented; otherwise return the ID of *`win`* itself.
`wm group` *`win`* `?`*`leader`*`?`	Query or set the group leader (a toplevel) for *`win`*. The window manager may unmap all the group at once.
`wm overrideredirect` *`win`* `?`*`boolean`*`?`	Set or query the override redirect bit that suppresses reparenting by the window manager.
`wm transient` *`win`* `?`*`leader`*`?`	Query or mark a window as a transient window working for *`leader`*, another widget.

The `winfo` Command

The `winfo` command has just over 40 operations that return information about a widget or the display. The operations fall into the following categories:

- Sending commands between applications.
- Family relationships.
- Size.
- Location.
- Virtual root coordinates.
- Atoms and IDs.
- Colormaps and visuals.

Sending Commands between Applications

Each Tk application has a name that is used when sending commands between applications using the send command, which is described in Chapter 37. The list of Tk applications is returned by the interps operation. The tk appname command is used to get the name of the application, and that command can also be used to set the application name. In Tk 3.6 and earlier, you had to use winfo name . to get the name of the application.

Example 38–2 shows how your application might connect up with several existing applications. It contacts each registered Tk interpreter and sends a short command that contains the application's own name as a parameter. The other application can use that name to communicate back.

Example 38–2 Telling other applications what your name is.

```
foreach app [winfo interps] {
   catch {send $app [list Iam [tk appname]]}
}
```

Table 38–5 summarizes these commands:

Table 38–5 send command information.

tk appname ?*newname*?	Query or set the name used with send.
winfo name .	Also returns the name used for send, for backward compatibility with Tk 3.6 and earlier.
winfo name *pathname*	Return the last component of *pathname*.
winfo ?-displayof *win*? interps	Return the list of registered Tk applications on the same display as *win*.

Family Relationships

The Tk widgets are arranged in a hierarchy, and you can use the winfo command to find out about the structure of the hierarchy. The winfo children operation returns the children of a window, and the winfo parent operation returns the parent. The parent of the main window is null (i.e., an empty string).

A widget is also a member of a class, which is used for bindings and as a key into the resource database. The winfo class operation returns this information. You can test for the existence of a window with winfo exists, and whether or not a window is mapped onto the screen with winfo viewable. Note that winfo ismapped is true for a widget that is managed by a geometry manager, but if the widget's top-level window is not mapped then the widget is not viewable.

The winfo manager operation tells you what geometry manager is controlling the placement of the window. This returns the name of the geometry manager command. Examples include pack, place, grid, canvas, and text. The last two indicate the widget is embedded into a canvas or text widget.

Table 38–6 summarizes these winfo operations:

Table 38–6 Window hierarchy information.

`winfo children` *win*	Return the list of children widgets of *win*.
`winfo class` *win*	Return the resource class of *win*.
`winfo exists` *win*	Returns 1 if *win* exists.
`winfo ismapped` *win*	Returns 1 if *win* is mapped onto the screen.
`winfo manager` *win*	Geometry manager: `pack`, `place`, `grid`, `canvas`, or `text`.
`winfo parent` *win*	Returns the parent widget of *win*.
`winfo viewable` *win*	Returns 1 if *win* and all its parent windows are mapped.

Size

The `winfo width` and `winfo height` operations return the width and height of a window, respectively. Alternatively, you can ask for the requested width and height of a window. Use `winfo reqwidth` and `winfo reqheight` for this information. The requested size may not be accurate, however, because the geometry manager may allocate more or less space, and the user may resize the window.

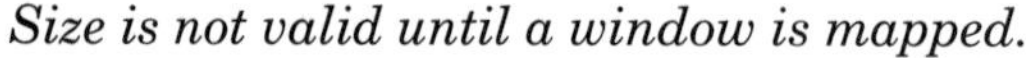

Size is not valid until a window is mapped.

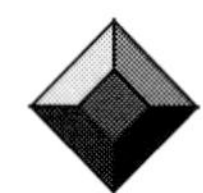

A window's size is not set until a geometry manager maps a window onto the display. Initially a window starts out with a width and height of 1. You can use `tkwait visibility` to wait for a window to be mapped before asking its width or height, or you can use `update` to give Tk a chance to update the display. There are some potential problems with `update` that are discussed on page 440. `Dialog_Wait` in Example 33–1 on page 437 uses `tkwait visibility`.

The `winfo geometry` operation returns the size and position of the window in the standard geometry format: *W*x*H*+*X*+*Y*. In this case the X and Y offsets are relative to the parent widget, or relative to the root window in the case of the main window.

You can find out how big the display is, too. The `winfo screenwidth` and `winfo screenheight` operations return this information in pixels. The `winfo screenmmwidth` and `winfo screenmmheight` return this information in millimeters.

You can convert between pixels and screen distances with the `winfo pixels` and `winfo fpixels` operations. Given a number of screen units such as `10m`, `3c`, or `72p`, these return the corresponding number of pixels. The first form rounds to a whole number, while the second form returns a floating point number. The correspondence between pixels and sizes may not be accurate because users can adjust the pixel size on their monitors, and Tk has no way of knowing about that. Chapter 34 explains screen units on page 444. For example:

```
set pixelsToInch [winfo pixels . 2.54c]
```

Table 38–7 summarizes these operations:

Table 38–7 Window size information.

`winfo fpixels` *`win num`*	Convert *num*, in screen units, to pixels. Returns a floating point number.
`winfo geometry` *`win`*	Return the geometry of *win*, in pixels and relative to the parent in the form *W*x*H*+*X*+*Y*
`winfo height` *`win`*	Return the height of *win*, in pixels.
`winfo pixels` *`win num`*	Convert *num* to a whole number of pixels.
`winfo reqheight` *`win`*	Return the requested height of *win*, in pixels.
`winfo reqwidth` *`win`*	Return the requested width of *win*, in pixels.
`winfo screenheight` *`win`*	Return the height of the screen, in pixels.
`winfo screenmmheight` *`win`*	Return the height of the screen, in millimeters.
`winfo screenmmwidth` *`win`*	Return the width of the screen, in millimeters.
`winfo screenwidth` *`win`*	Return the width of the screen, in pixels.
`winfo width` *`win`*	Return the width of *win*, in pixels.

Location

The `winfo x` and `winfo y` operations return the position of the upper-left corner of a window relative to its parent widget. In the case of the main window, this is its location on the screen. The `winfo rootx` and `winfo rooty` return the screen location of the upper-left corner of a widget, even if it is not a toplevel.

The `winfo containing` operation returns the pathname of the window that contains a point on the screen. This is useful in implementing menus and drag and drop applications.

The `winfo toplevel` operation returns the pathname of the toplevel that contains a widget. If the window is itself a toplevel, then this operation returns its own pathname.

The `winfo screen` operation returns the display identifier for the screen of the window.

Table 38–8 summarizes these operations:

Table 38–8 Window location information.

`winfo containing ?-displayof` *`win`*`?` *`win x y`*	Return the pathname of the window at *x* and *y*.
`winfo pointerx` *`win`*	Returns the X screen coordinate of the mouse.
`winfo pointery` *`win`*	Returns the Y screen coordinate of the mouse.
`winfo pointerxy` *`win`*	Returns the X and Y coordinates of the mouse.
`winfo rootx` *`win`*	Return the X screen position of *win*.
`winfo rooty` *`win`*	Return the Y screen position of *win*.

Table 38–8 Window location information. (Continued)

`winfo screen` *win*	Return the display identifier of *win*'s screen.
`winfo server` *win*	Returns the version string of the display server.
`winfo toplevel` *win*	Return pathname of toplevel that contains *win*.
`winfo x` *win*	Return the X position of *win* in its parent.
`winfo y` *win*	Return the Y position of *win* in its parent.

Virtual Root Window

Some window managers use a virtual root window to give the user a larger virtual screen. At any given time only a portion of the virtual screen is visible, and the user can change the view on the virtual screen to bring different applications into view. In this case, the `winfo x` and `winfo y` operations return the coordinates of a main window in the virtual root window (i.e., not the screen).

The `winfo vrootheight` and `winfo vrootwidth` operations return the size of the virtual root window. If there is no virtual root window, then these just return the size of the screen.

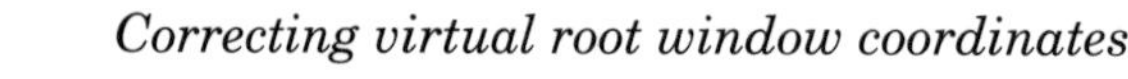

Correcting virtual root window coordinates.

The `winfo vrootx` and `winfo vrooty` are used to map from the coordinates in the virtual root window to screen-relative coordinates. These operations return 0 if there is no virtual root window. Otherwise they return a negative number. If you add this number to the value returned by `winfo x` or `winfo y`, it gives the screen-relative coordinate of the window:

```
set screenx [expr [winfo x $win] + [winfo vrootx $win]]
```

Table 38–9 summarizes these operations:

Table 38–9 Virtual root window information.

`winfo vrootheight` *win*	Return the height of the virtual root window for *win*.
`winfo vrootwidth` *win*	Return the width of the virtual root window for *win*.
`winfo vrootx` *win*	Return the X position of *win* in the virtual root.
`winfo vrooty` *win*	Return the Y position of *win* in the virtual root.

Atoms and IDs

An *atom* is an X technical term for an identifier that is registered with the X server. Applications map names into atoms, and the X server assigns each atom a 32-bit identifier that can be passed between applications. One of the few places this is used in Tk is when the selection mechanism is used to interface with different toolkits. In some cases the selection is returned as atoms, which appear as 32-bit integers. The `winfo atomname` operation converts that number into an atom (i.e., a string), and the `winfo atom` registers a string with the X server and returns the 32-bit identifier as a hexadecimal string

Each widget has an ID assigned by the window system. The `winfo id` command returns this identifier. The `winfo pathname` operation returns the Tk pathname of the widget that has a given ID, but only if the window is part of the same application.

Embedding applications.

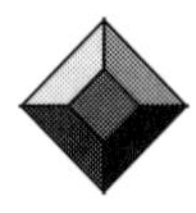

The `id` operation is useful if you need to embed another application into your window hierarchy. Wish takes a `-use` *`id`* command-line argument that causes it to use an existing window for its main window. Other toolkits provide similar functionality. For example, to embed another Tk app in a frame:

```
frame .embed -container true
exec wish -use [winfo id .embed] otherscript.tcl
```

Table 38–10 summarizes these operations:

Table 38–10 Atom and window ID information.

`winfo atom ?-displayof win? name`	Returns the 32-bit identifier for the atom *name*.
`winfo atomname ?-displayof win? id`	Returns the atom that corresponds to the 32-bit ID.
`winfo id win`	Returns the window ID of *win*.
`winfo pathname ?-displayof win? id`	Returns the Tk pathname of the window with *id*, or null.

Colormaps and Visuals

The `winfo depth` returns the number of bits used to represent the color in each pixel. The `winfo cells` command returns the number of colormap entries used by the visual class of a window. These two values are generally related. A window with 8 bits per pixel usually has 256 colormap cells. The `winfo screendepth` and `winfo screencells` return this information for the default visual class.

The `winfo visualsavailable` command returns a list of the visual classes and screen depths that are available. For example, a display with 8 bits per pixel might report the following visual classes are available:

```
winfo visualsavailable .
=> {staticgray 8} {grayscale 8} {staticcolor 8} \
   {pseudocolor 8}
```

The `winfo visual` operation returns the visual class of a window, and the `winfo screenvisual` returns the default visual class of the screen.

The `winfo rgb` operation converts from a color name or value to the red, green, and blue components of that color. Three decimal values are returned. Example 35–2 on page 455 uses this command to compute a slightly darker version of the same color.

Table 38–11 summarizes operations that return information about colormaps and visual classes, which are described in Chapter 35:

Table 38–11 Colormap and visual class information.

`winfo cells` *win*	Returns the number of colormap cells in *win*'s visual.
`winfo colormapfull` *win*	Returns 1 if the last color allocation failed.
`winfo depth` *win*	Return the number of bits per pixel for *win*.
`winfo rgb` *win color*	Return the red, green, and blue values for *color*.
`winfo screencells` *win*	Returns the number of colormap cells in the default visual.
`winfo screendepth` *win*	Returns the number of bits per pixel in the screen's default visual.
`winfo screenvisual` *win*	Returns the default visual of the screen.
`winfo visual` *win*	Returns the visual class of *win*.
`winfo visualsavailable` *win*	Returns a list of pairs that specify the visual type and bits per pixel of the available visual classes.

The `tk` Command

The `tk` command provides a few miscellaneous entry points into the Tk library. The `appname` operation is used to set or query the application name used with the Tk `send` command. If you define a new name and it is already in use by another application, (perhaps another instance of yourself), then a number is appended to the name (e.g., `#2`, `#3`, and so on). This is the syntax of the command:

```
tk appname ?name?
```

Fonts, canvas items, and widget sizes use screen units that are pixels, points, centimeters, millimeters, or inches. There are 72 points per inch. The `tk scaling` command, which was added in Tk 8.0, is used to set or query the mapping between pixels and points. A scale of 1.0 results in 72 pixels per inch. A scale of 1.25 results in 90 pixels per inch. This gives accurate sizes on a 90 dpi screen or it makes everything 25% larger on a 72 dpi screen. Changing the scale only affects widgets created after the change. This is the syntax of the command:

```
tk scaling ?num?
```

CHAPTER 39

Managing User Preferences

This chapter describes a user preferences package. The resource database stores preference settings. Applications specify Tcl variables that are initialized from the database entries. A user interface lets the user browse and change their settings.

User customization is an important part of any complex application. There are always design decisions that could go either way. A typical approach is to choose a reasonable default, but then let users change the default setting through a preferences user interface. This chapter describes a preference package that works by tying together a Tcl variable, which the application uses, and a resource specification, which the user sets. In addition, a user interface is provided so the user need not edit the resource database directly.

App-Defaults Files

We will assume that it is sufficient to have two sources of application defaults: a per-application database and a per-user database. In addition, we will allow for some resources to be specific to color and monochrome displays. The following example initializes the preference package by reading in the per-application and per-user resource specification files. There is also an initialization of the global array `pref` that will be used to hold state information about the preferences package. The `Pref_Init` procedure is called like this:

```
Pref_Init $library/foo-defaults ~/.foo-defaults
```

We assume `$library` is the directory holding support files for the `foo` application, and that per-user defaults will be kept in `~/.foo-defaults`. These are UNIX-oriented file names. When you write cross-platform Tk applications, you

V. Tk Details

will find that some file names are inherently platform-specific. The platform-independent operations described in Chapter 9 are great, but they do not change the fact that user preferences may be stored in `c:/webtk/userpref.txt` on Windows, `Hard Disk:System:Preferences:WebTk Prefs` on Macintosh, and `~/.webtk` on UNIX. I find it useful to have a small amount of platform-specific startup code that defines these pathnames. The preference package uses resource files that work on all platforms:

Example 39–1 Preferences initialization.

```
proc Pref_Init { userDefaults appDefaults } {
	global pref

	set pref(uid) 0;# for a unique identifier for widgets
	set pref(userDefaults) $userDefaults
	set pref(appDefaults) $appDefaults
	PrefReadFile $appDefaults startup
	if [file exists $userDefaults] {
		PrefReadFile $userDefaults user
	}
}
proc PrefReadFile { basename level } {
	if [catch {option readfile $basename $level} err] {
		Status "Error in $basename: $err"
	}
	if {[string match *color* [winfo visual .]]} {
		if [file exists $basename-color] {
			if [catch {option readfile \
					$basename-color $level} err] {
				Status "Error in $basename-color: $err"
			}
		}
	} else {
		if [file exists $basename-mono] {
			if [catch {option readfile $basename-mono \
					$level} err] {
				Status "Error in $basename-mono: $err"
			}
		}
	}
}
```

The `PrefReadFile` procedure reads a resource file and then looks for another file with the suffix `-color` or `-mono` depending on the characteristics of the display. With this scheme a UNIX user puts generic settings in `~/.foo-defaults`. They put color specifications in `~/.foo-defaults-color`. They put specifications for black and white displays in `~/.foo-defaults-mono`. You could extend `PrefReadFile` to allow for per-host files as well.

Throughout this chapter we assume that the `Status` procedure displays messages to the user. It could be as simple as:

```
proc Status { s } { puts stderr $s }
```

Defining Preferences

This section describes the `Pref_Add` procedure that an application uses to define preference items. A preference item defines a relationship between a Tcl variable and a resource name. If the Tcl variable is undefined at the time `Pref_Add` is called, then it is set from the value for the resource. If the resource is not defined, then the variable is set to the default value.

Hide simple data structures with Tcl procedures.

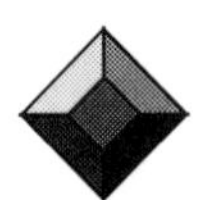

A default value, a label, and a more extensive help string are associated with each item, which is represented by a Tcl list of five elements. A few short routines hide the layout of the item lists and make the rest of the code read better:

Example 39–2 Adding preference items.

```
proc PrefVar { item } { lindex $item 0 }
proc PrefRes { item } { lindex $item 1 }
proc PrefDefault { item } { lindex $item 2 }
proc PrefComment { item } { lindex $item 3 }
proc PrefHelp { item } { lindex $item 4 }

proc Pref_Add { prefs } {
    global pref
    append pref(items) $prefs " "
    foreach item $prefs {
        set varName [PrefVar $item]
        set resName [PrefRes $item]
        set value [PrefValue $varName $resName]
        if {$value == {}} {
            # Set variables that are still not set
            set default [PrefDefault $item]
            switch -regexp -- $default {
                ^CHOICE {
                    PrefValueSet $varName [lindex $default 1]
                }
                ^OFF {
                    PrefValueSet $varName 0
                }
                ^ON {
                    PrefValueSet $varName 1
                }
                default {
                    # This is a string or numeric
                    PrefValueSet $varName $default
                }
            }
        }
    }
}
```

The procedures `PrefValue` and `PrefValueSet` are used to query and set the value of the named variable, which can be an array element or a simple variable. The `upvar #0` command sets the variable in the global scope.

Example 39–3 Setting preference variables.

```
# PrefValue returns the value of the variable if it exists,
# otherwise it returns the resource database value
proc PrefValue { varName res } {
   upvar #0 $varName var
   if [info exists var] {
      return $var
   }
   set var [option get . $res {}]
}
# PrefValueSet defines a variable in the global scope.
proc PrefValueSet { varName value } {
   upvar #0 $varName var
   set var $value
}
```

An important side effect of the `Pref_Add` call is that the variables in the preference item are defined at the global scope. It is also worth noting that `PrefValue` will honor any existing value for a variable, so if the variable is already set at the global scope, then neither the resource value nor the default value will be used. It is easy to change `PrefValue` to always set the variable if this is not the behavior you want. Here is a sample call to `Pref_Add`:

Example 39–4 Using the preferences package.

```
Pref_Add {
   {win(scrollside) scrollbarSide {CHOICE left right}
      "Scrollbar placement"
"Scrollbars can be positioned on either the left or
right side of the text and canvas widgets."}
   {win(typeinkills) typeinKills OFF
      "Type-in kills selection"
"This setting determines whether or not the selection
is deleted when new text is typed in."}
   {win(scrollspeed) scrollSpeed 15 "Scrolling speed"
"This parameter affects the scrolling rate when a selection
is dragged off the edge of the window. Smaller numbers
scroll faster, but can consume more CPU."}
}
```

Any number of preference items can be specified in a call to `Pref_Add`. The list-of-lists structure is created by proper placement of the curly braces, and it is preserved when the argument is appended to `pref(items)`, which is the master list of preferences. In this example `Pref_Add` gets passed a single argument that is a Tcl list with three elements. The Tcl variables are array elements, presumably related to the Win module of the application. The resource names are associated with the main application as opposed to any particular widget. They are specified in the database like this:

```
*scrollbarSide: left
*typeinKills: 0
*scrollSpeed: 15
```

The Preferences User Interface

The figure shows the interface for the items added with the Pref_Add command given in the previous section. The pop-up window with the extended help text appears after you click on "Scrollbar placement." The user interface to the preference settings is table-driven. As a result of all the Pref_Add calls, a single list of all the preference items is built. The interface is constructed by looping through this list and creating a user interface item for each:

Example 39–5 A user interface to the preference items.

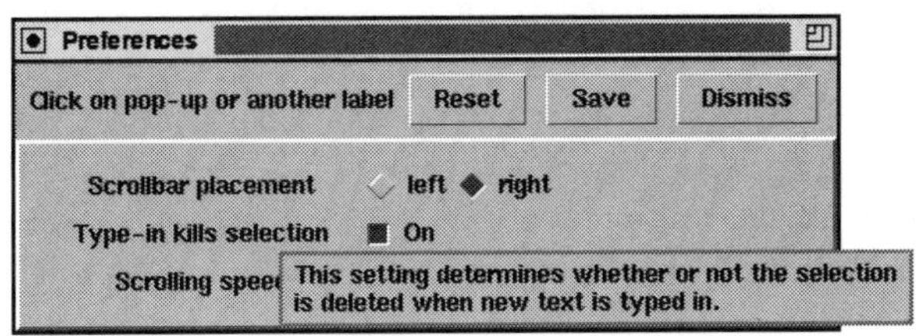


```
proc Pref_Dialog {} {
	global pref
	if [catch {toplevel .pref}] {
		raise .pref
	} else {
		wm title .pref "Preferences"
		set buttons [frame .pref.but -bd 5]
		pack .pref.but -side top -fill x
		button $buttons.quit -text Dismiss \
			-command {PrefDismiss}
		button $buttons.save -text Save \
			-command {PrefSave}
		button $buttons.reset -text Reset \
			-command {PrefReset ; PrefDismiss}
		label $buttons.label \
			 -text "Click labels for info on each item"
		pack $buttons.label -side left -fill x
		pack $buttons.quit $buttons.save $buttons.reset \
			-side right -padx 4

		frame .pref.b -borderwidth 2 -relief raised
		pack .pref.b -fill both
		set body [frame .pref.b.b -bd 10]
```

```
        pack .pref.b.b -fill both

        set maxWidth 0
        foreach item $pref(items) {
            set len [string length [PrefComment $item]]
            if {$len > $maxWidth} {
                set maxWidth $len
            }
        }
        set pref(uid) 0
        foreach item $pref(items) {
            PrefDialogItem $body $item $maxWidth
        }
    }
}
```

The interface supports three different types of preference items: boolean, choice, and general value. A boolean is implemented with a checkbutton that is tied to the Tcl variable, which will get a value of either 0 or 1. A boolean is identified by a default value that is either `ON` or `OFF`. A choice item is implemented as a set of radiobuttons, one for each choice. A choice item is identified by a default value that is a list with the first element equal to `CHOICE`. The remaining list items are the choices, with the first one being the default choice. A `regexp` is used to check for `CHOICE` instead of using list operations. This is because Tcl 8.0 will complain if the value is not a proper list, which could happen with arbitrary values. If neither of these cases, boolean or choice, are detected, then an entry widget is created to hold the general value of the preference item:

Example 39–6 Interface objects for different preference types.

```
proc PrefDialogItem { frame item width } {
    global pref
    incr pref(uid)
    set f [frame $frame.p$pref(uid) -borderwidth 2]
    pack $f -fill x
    label $f.label -text [PrefComment $item] -width $width
    bind $f.label <1> \
        [list PrefItemHelp %X %Y [PrefHelp $item]]
    pack $f.label -side left
    set default [PrefDefault $item]
    if {[regexp "^CHOICE " $default]} {
        foreach choice [lreplace $default 0 0] {
            incr pref(uid)
            radiobutton $f.c$pref(uid) -text $choice \
                -variable [PrefVar $item] -value $choice
            pack $f.c$pref(uid) -side left
        }
    } else {
        if {$default == "OFF" || $default == "ON"} {
            # This is a boolean
            set varName [PrefVar $item]
            checkbutton $f.check -variable $varName \
```

```
            -command [list PrefFixupBoolean $f.check $varName]
        PrefFixupBoolean $f.check $varName
        pack $f.check -side left
    } else {
        # This is a string or numeric
        entry $f.entry -width 10 -relief sunken
        pack $f.entry -side left -fill x -expand true
        set pref(entry,[PrefVar $item]) $f.entry
        set varName [PrefVar $item]
        $f.entry insert 0 [uplevel #0 [list set $varName]]
        bind $f.entry <Return> "PrefEntrySet %W $varName"
    }
  }
}
proc PrefFixupBoolean {check varname} {
   upvar #0 $varname var
   # Update the checkbutton text each time it changes
   if {$var} {
      $check config -text On
   } else {
      $check config -text Off
   }
}
proc PrefEntrySet { entry varName } {
   PrefValueSet $varName [$entry get]
}
```

In this interface, when the user clicks a radiobutton or a checkbutton, the Tcl variable is set immediately. To obtain a similar effect with the general preference item, the `<Return>` key is bound to a procedure that sets the associated Tcl variable to the value from the entry widget. `PrefEntrySet` is a one-line procedure that saves us from using the more awkward binding shown below. Grouping with double quotes allows substitution of `$varName`, but then we must quote the square brackets to postpone command substitution:

```
bind $f.entry <Return> "PrefValueSet $varName \[%W get\]"
```

The binding on `<Return>` is done as opposed to using the `-textvariable` option because it interacts with traces on the variable a bit better. With `trace` you can arrange for a Tcl command to be executed when a variable is changed. An example appears on page 508. For a general preference item it is better to wait until the complete value is entered before responding to its new value.

The other aspect of the user interface is the display of additional help information for each item. If there are lots of preference items, then there isn't enough room to display this information directly. Instead, clicking on the short description for each item brings up a toplevel with the help text for that item. The toplevel is marked `transient` so the window manager does not decorate it:

Example 39–7 Displaying the help text for an item.

```
proc PrefItemHelp { x y text } {
   catch {destroy .prefitemhelp}
```

```
    if {$text == {}} {
        return
    }
    set self [toplevel .prefitemhelp -class Itemhelp]
    wm title $self "Item help"
    wm geometry $self +[expr $x+10]+[expr $y+10]
    wm transient $self .pref
    message $self.msg -text $text -aspect 1500
    pack $self.msg
    bind $self.msg <1> {PrefNukeItemHelp .prefitemhelp}
    .pref.but.label configure -text \
        "Click on pop-up or another label"
}
proc PrefNukeItemHelp { t } {
    .pref.but.label configure -text \
        "Click labels for info on each item"
    destroy $t
}
```

Managing the Preferences File

The preference settings are saved in the per-user file. The file is divided into two parts. The tail is automatically rewritten by the preferences package. Users can manually add resource specifications to the beginning of the file and they will be preserved:

Example 39–8 Saving preferences settings to a file.

```
# PrefSave writes the resource specifications to the
# end of the per-user resource file,
proc PrefSave {} {
    global pref
    if [catch {
        set old [open $pref(userDefaults) r]
        set oldValues [split [read $old] \n]
        close $old
    }] {
        set oldValues {}
    }
    if [catch {open $pref(userDefaults).new w} out] {
        .pref.but.label configure -text \
        "Cannot save in $pref(userDefaults).new: $out"
        return
    }
    foreach line $oldValues {
        if {$line == \
                "!!! Lines below here automatically added"} {
            break
        } else {
            puts $out $line
        }
```

```
    }
    puts $out "!!! Lines below here automatically added"
    puts $out "!!! [exec date]"
    puts $out "!!! Do not edit below here"
    foreach item $preferences {
        set varName [PrefVar $item]
        set resName [PrefRes $item]
        if [info exists pref(entry,$varName)] {
            PrefEntrySet $pref(entry,$varName) $varName
        }
        set value [PrefValue $varName $resName]
        puts $out [format "%s\t%s" *${resName}: $value]
    }
    close $out
    set new [glob $pref(userDefaults).new]
    set old [file root $new]
    if [catch {file rename -force $new $old} err] {
        Status "Cannot install $new: $err"
        return
    }
    PrefDismiss
}
```

There is one fine point in `PrefSave`. The value from the entry widget for general-purpose items is obtained explicitly in case the user has not already pressed `<Return>` to update the Tcl variable.

The interface is rounded out with the `PrefReset` and `PrefDismiss` procedures. A reset is achieved by clearing the option database and reloading it, and then temporarily clearing the preference items and their associated variables and then redefining them with `Pref_Add`.

Example 39–9 Read settings from the preferences file.

```
proc PrefReset {} {
    global pref
    # Re-read user defaults
    option clear
    PrefReadFile $pref(appDefaults) startup
    PrefReadFile $pref(userDefaults) user
    # Clear variables
    set items $pref(items)
    set pref(items) {}
    foreach item $items {
        uplevel #0 [list unset [PrefVar $item]]
    }
    # Restore values
    Pref_Add $items
}
proc PrefDismiss {} {
    destroy .pref
    catch {destroy .prefitemhelp}
}
```

Tracing Changes to Preference Variables

Suppose, for example, we want to repack the scrollbars when the user changes their `scrollside` setting from left to right. This is done by setting a trace on the `win(scrollside)` variable. When the user changes that via the user interface, the trace routine is called. The `trace` command and its associated procedure are shown in the next example. The variable must be declared global before setting up the trace, which is not otherwise required if `Pref_Add` is the only command using the variable.

Example 39–10 Tracing a Tcl variable in a preference item.

```
Pref_Add {
    {win(scrollside) scrollbarSide {CHOICE left right}
        "Scrollbar placement"
"Scrollbars can be positioned on either the left or
right side of the text and canvas widgets."}
}
global win
set win(lastscrollside) $win(scrollside)
trace variable win(scrollside) w ScrollFixup
# Assume win(scrollbar) identifies the scrollbar widget
proc ScrollFixup { name1 name2 op } {
    global win
    if {$win(scrollside) != $win(lastscrollside)} {
        set parent [lindex [pack info $win(scrollbar)] 1]
        pack forget $win(scrollbar)
        set firstchild [lindex [pack slaves $parent] 0]
        pack $win(scrollbar) -in $parent -before $firstchild \
            -side $win(scrollside) -fill y
        set win(lastscrollside) $win(scrollside)
    }
}
```

Improving the Package

One small improvement can be made to `Pref_Add`. If a user specifies a boolean resource manually, they might use "true" instead of one and "false" instead of zero. `Pref_Add` should check for those cases and set the boolean variable to one or zero to avoid errors when the variables are used in expressions.

The interface lets you dismiss it without saving your preference settings. This is either a feature that lets users try out settings without committing to them, or it is a bug. Fixing this requires introducing a parallel set of variables to shadow the real variables until the user hits `Save`, which is tedious to implement. You can also use a *grab* as described in Chapter 33 to prevent the user from doing anything but setting preferences.

This preference package is a slightly simplified version of one I developed for *exmh*, which has so many preference items that a two-level scheme is necessary. The first level is a menu of preference sections, and each section is created with a single call to `Pref_Add`. This requires additional arguments to `Pref_Add` to provide a title for the section and some overall information about the preference section. The display code changes a small amount. The code for the *exmh* is on the CD-ROM.

C H A P T E R 40

A User Interface to Bindings

This chapter presents a user interface to view and edit bindings.

A good way to learn about how a widget works is to examine the bindings that are defined for it. This chapter presents a user interface that lets you browse and change bindings for a widget or a class of widgets.

The interface uses a pair of listboxes to display the events and their associated commands. An entry widget is used to enter the name of a widget or a class. There are a few command buttons that let the user add a new binding, edit an existing binding, save the bindings to a file, and dismiss the dialog. Here is what the display looks like:

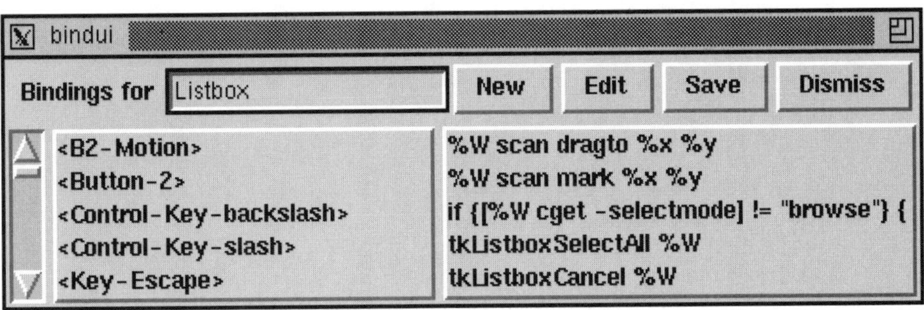

V. Tk Details

Example 40–1 A user interface to widget bindings.

```
proc Bind_Interface { w } {
   # Our state
   global bind
   set bind(class) $w

   # Set a class used for resource specifications
   set frame [toplevel .bindui -class Bindui]
   # Default relief
   option add *Bindui*Entry.relief sunken startup
   option add *Bindui*Listbox.relief raised startup
   # Default Listbox sizes
   option add *Bindui*key.width 18 startup
   option add *Bindui*cmd.width 25 startup
   option add *Bindui*Listbox.height 5 startup

   # A labeled entry at the top to hold the current
   # widget name or class.
   set t [frame $frame.top -bd 2]
   label $t.l -text "Bindings for" -width 11
   entry $t.e -textvariable bind(class)
   pack $t.l -side left
   pack $t.e -side left -fill x -expand true
   pack $t -side top -fill x
   bind $t.e <Return> [list Bind_Display $frame]

   # Command buttons
   button $t.quit -text Dismiss \
      -command [list destroy $frame]
   button $t.save -text Save \
      -command [list Bind_Save $frame]
   button $t.edit -text Edit \
      -command [list Bind_Edit $frame]
   button $t.new -text New \
      -command [list Bind_New $frame]
   pack $t.quit $t.save $t.edit $t.new -side right

   # A pair of listboxes and a scrollbar
   scrollbar $frame.s -orient vertical \
      -command [list BindYview \
         [list $frame.key $frame.cmd]]
   listbox $frame.key \
      -yscrollcommand [list $frame.s set] \
      -exportselection false
   listbox $frame.cmd \
      -yscrollcommand [list $frame.s set]
   pack $frame.s -side left -fill y
   pack $frame.key $frame.cmd -side left \
      -fill both -expand true

   foreach l [list $frame.key $frame.cmd] {
      bind $l <B2-Motion>\
         [list BindDragto %x %y $frame.key $frame.cmd]
      bind $l <Button-2> \
```

```
            [list BindMark %x %y $frame.key $frame.cmd]
        bind $l <Button-1> \
            [list BindSelect %y $frame.key $frame.cmd]
        bind $l <B1-Motion> \
            [list BindSelect %y $frame.key $frame.cmd]
        bind $l <Shift-B1-Motion> {}
        bind $l <Shift-Button-1> {}
    }
    # Initialize the display
    Bind_Display $frame
}
```

The `Bind_Interface` command takes a widget name or class as a parameter. It creates a toplevel and gives it the `Bindui` class so that resources can be set to control widget attributes. The `option add` command is used to set up the default listbox sizes. The lowest priority, `startup`, is given to these resources so that clients of the package can override the size with their own resource specifications.

At the top of the interface is a labeled entry widget. The entry holds the name of the class or widget for which the bindings are displayed. The `textvariable` option of the entry widget is used so that the entry's contents are available in a variable, `bind(class)`. Pressing `<Return>` in the entry invokes `Bind_Display` that fills in the display.

Example 40–2 `Bind_Display` presents the bindings for a widget or class.

```
proc Bind_Display { frame } {
    global bind
    $frame.key delete 0 end
    $frame.cmd delete 0 end
    foreach seq [bind $bind(class)] {
        $frame.key insert end $seq
        $frame.cmd insert end [bind $bind(class) $seq]
    }
}
```

The `Bind_Display` procedure fills in the display with the binding information. The `bind` command returns the events that have bindings, and what the command associated with each event is. `Bind_Display` loops through this information and fills in the listboxes.

A Pair of Listboxes Working Together

The two listboxes in the interface, `$frame.key` and `$frame.cmd`, are set up to work as a unit. A selection in one causes a parallel selection in the other. Only one listbox exports its selection as the `PRIMARY` selection. Otherwise, the last listbox to assert the selection steals the selection rights from the other widget. The following example shows the `bind` commands from `Bind_Interface` and the

BindSelect routine that selects an item in both listboxes:

Example 40–3 Related listboxes are configured to select items together.

```
foreach l [list $frame.key $frame.cmd] {
   bind $l <Button-1> \
      [list BindSelect %y $frame.key $frame.cmd]
   bind $l <B1-Motion> \
      [list BindSelect %y $frame.key $frame.cmd]
}
proc BindSelect { y args } {
   foreach w $args {
      $w select clear 0 end
      $w select anchor [$w nearest $y]
      $w select set anchor [$w nearest $y]
   }
}
```

A scrollbar for two listboxes.

A single scrollbar scrolls both listboxes. The next example shows the scrollbar command from Bind_Interface and the BindYview procedure that scrolls the listboxes:

Example 40–4 Controlling a pair of listboxes with one scrollbar.

```
scrollbar $frame.s -orient vertical \
   -command [list BindYview [list $frame.key $frame.cmd]]

proc BindYview { lists args } {
   foreach l $lists {
      eval {$l yview} $args
   }
}
```

The BindYview command is used to change the display of the listboxes associated with the scrollbar. The first argument to BindYview is a list of widgets to scroll, and the remaining arguments are added by the scrollbar to specify how to position the display. The details are essentially private between the scrollbar and the listbox. See page 347 for the details. The args keyword is used to represent these extra arguments, and eval is used to pass them through BindYview. The reasoning for using eval like this is explained in Chapter 10 on page 115.

The Listbox class bindings for <Button-2> and <B2-Motion> cause the listbox to scroll as the user drags the widget with the middle mouse button. These bindings are adjusted so that both listboxes move together. The following example shows the bind commands from the Bind_Interface procedure and the BindMark and BindDrag procedures that scroll the listboxes:

Example 40–5 Drag-scrolling a pair of listboxes together.

```
bind $l <B2-Motion>\
    [list BindDragto %x %y $frame.key $frame.cmd]
bind $l <Button-2> \
    [list BindMark %x %y $frame.key $frame.cmd]

proc BindDragto { x y args } {
    foreach w $args {
        $w scan dragto $x $y
    }
}
proc BindMark { x y args } {
    foreach w $args {
        $w scan mark $x $y
    }
}
```

The `BindMark` procedure does a `scan mark` that defines an origin, and `BindDragto` does a `scan dragto` that scrolls the widget based on the distance from that origin. All Tk widgets that scroll support `yview`, `scan mark`, and `scan dragto`. Thus the `BindYview`, `BindMark`, and `BindDragto` procedures are general enough to be used with any set of widgets that scroll together.

The Editing Interface

Editing and defining a new binding is done in a pair of entry widgets. These widgets are created and packed into the display dynamically when the user presses the `New` or `Edit` button:

Example 40–6 An interface to define bindings.

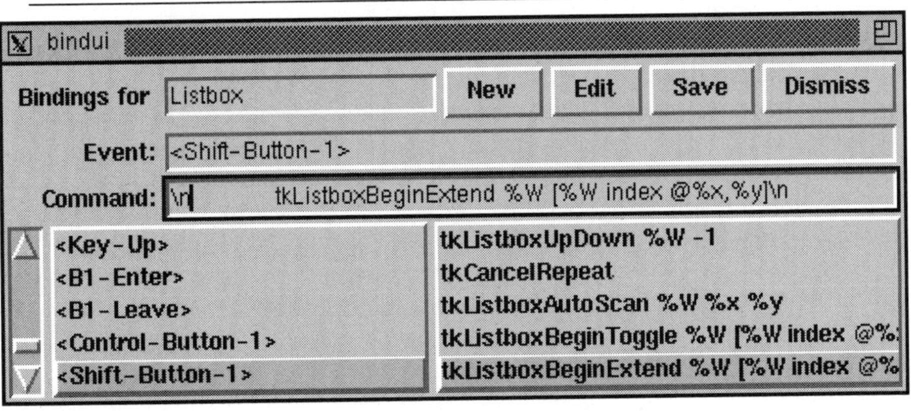


```
proc Bind_New { frame } {
    if [catch {frame $frame.edit} f] {
        # Frame already created
```

```
        set f $frame.edit
    } else {
        foreach x {key cmd} {
            set f2 [frame $f.$x]
            pack $f2 -fill x -padx 2
            label $f2.l -width 11 -anchor e
            pack $f2.l -side left
            entry $f2.e
            pack $f2.e -side left -fill x -expand true
            bind $f2.e <Return> [list BindDefine $f]
        }
        $f.key.l config -text Event:
        $f.cmd.l config -text Command:
    }
    pack $frame.edit -after $frame.top -fill x
}
proc Bind_Edit { frame } {
    Bind_New $frame
    set line [$frame.key curselection]
    if {$line == {}} {
        return
    }
    $frame.edit.key.e delete 0 end
    $frame.edit.key.e insert 0 [$frame.key get $line]
    $frame.edit.cmd.e delete 0 end
    $frame.edit.cmd.e insert 0 [$frame.cmd get $line]
}
```

The `-width 11` and `-anchor e` attributes for the label widgets are specified so the `Event:` and `Command:` labels will line up with the `Bindings for` label at the top.

Saving and Loading Bindings

All that remains is the actual change or definition of a binding, and some way to remember the bindings the next time the application is run. The `BindDefine` procedure attempts a `bind` command that uses the contents of the entries. If it succeeds, then the edit window is removed by unpacking it.

The bindings are saved by `Bind_Save` as a series of Tcl commands that define the bindings. It is crucial that the `list` command be used to construct the commands properly.

`Bind_Read` uses the `source` command to read the saved commands. The application must call `Bind_Read` as part of its initialization to get the customized bindings for the widget or class. It also must provide a way to invoke `Bind_Interface`, such as a button, menu entry, or key binding.

Example 40–7 Defining and saving bindings.

```
proc BindDefine { f } {
   if [catch {
      bind [$f.top.e get] [$f.edit.key.e get] \
         [$f.edit.cmd.e get]
   } err] {
      Status $err
   } else {
      # Remove the edit window
      pack forget $f.edit
   }
}
proc Bind_Save { dotfile args } {
   set out [open $dotfile.new w]
   foreach w $args {
      foreach seq [bind $w] {
         # Output a Tcl command
         puts $out [list bind $w $seq [bind $w $seq]]
      }
   }
   close $out
   file rename -force $dotfile.new $dotfile
}
proc Bind_Read { dotfile } {
   if [catch {
      if [file exists $dotfile] {
         # Read the saved Tcl commands
         source $dotfile
      }
   } err] {
      Status "Bind_Read $dotfile failed: $err"
   }
}
```

PART VI

C Programming

Part VI describes C programming and Tcl. The goal of this section is to get you started out in the right direction. For serious C programming you will need to consult the on-line reference material for detailed descriptions of the C APIs.

Chapter 41 provides an introduction to using Tcl at the C programming level. It gets you started with integrating Tcl and Tk into an existing application. Chapter 42 provides a survey of the facilities in the Tcl and Tk C libraries. Chapter 43 presents a sample digital clock Tk widget implementation in C.

C H A P T E R 41

C Programming and Tcl

This chapter explains how to extend a Tcl application with new built-in commands. Tcl 8.0 replaces the original string-based command interface with a more efficient dual-ported object interface. This chapter describes both interfaces.

Tcl is designed to be easily extensible by writing new command implementations in C. A command implemented in C is more efficient than an equivalent Tcl procedure. A more pressing reason to write C code is that it may not be possible to provide the same functionality purely in Tcl. Suppose you have a new device, perhaps a color scanner or a unique input device. The programming interface to that device is through a set of C procedures that initialize and manipulate the state of the device. Without some work on your part, that interface is not accessible to your Tcl scripts. You are in the same situation if you have a C library that implements some specialized function such as a database. Fortunately, it is rather straightforward to provide a Tcl interface that corresponds to the C interface. Unfortunately, it is not automatic. This chapter explains how to provide a Tcl interface as one or more new Tcl commands that you implement in C.

An alternative to writing new Tcl commands is to write stand-alone programs in C and use the Tcl `exec` command to run these programs. However, there is additional overhead in running an external program as compared to invoking a Tcl command that is part of the same application. There may be long-lived state associated with your application (e.g., the database), and it may make more sense for a collection of Tcl commands to provide an interface to this state than to run a program each time you want to access it. An external program is more suitable for one-shot operations like encrypting a file.

Another way to view Tcl is as a C library that is easy to integrate into your existing application. By adding the Tcl interpreter you can configure and control your application with Tcl scripts, and with Tk you can provide a nice graphical interface to it. This was the original model for Tcl. Applications would be largely application-specific C code and include a small amount of Tcl for configuration and the graphical interface. However, the basic Tcl shells proved so useful by themselves that relatively few Tcl programers need to worry about programming in C.

Using the Tcl C Library

Chapter 42 gives a high-level overview of all the procedures in the Tcl and Tk C library, but this book does not provide a complete reference. Refer to the on-line manual pages for the specific details about each procedure. This approach differs from the rest of the chapters on the Tcl scripting commands, but space and time preclude a detailed treatment of the Tcl C library. Besides, their manual pages are an excellent source of information.

This chapter provide a few working examples that explain how to initialize your application and create Tcl commands. It describes how to organize your code into packages. There are notes about compiling Tcl under UNIX, Windows, and Macintosh.

Application Structure

The relationship between the Tcl interpreter and the rest of your application can be set up in a variety of ways. Below is a general picture with a Tcl script layer on top of your application. C function calls are shown in thin arrows, and Tcl command calls are show in thick arrows:

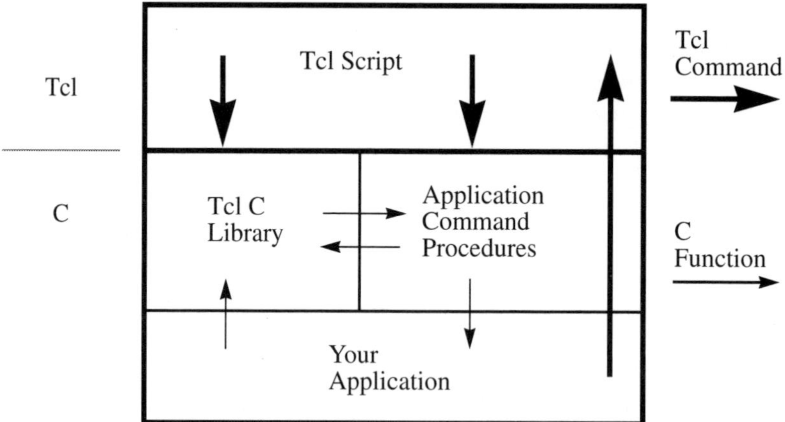

The Tcl C library implements the interpreter and the core Tcl commands such as `set`, `while`, `proc`, `open`, and `socket`. Application-specific Tcl commands are implemented in C or C++ and registered as commands in the interpreter. The interface to all Tcl commands is the same, and you can look at examples in the files tclCmdAH.c, tclCmdIL.c, and TclCmdMZ.c in the generic source directory. The interpreter calls these *command procedures* when the script uses a Tcl command. The application-specific command procedures are typically thin layers over existing functionality in your application. You can also load extensions that implement suites of Tcl commands in compiled code.

In the figure, the large arrow going up represents Tcl_Eval calls from your application back up to the script layer. The application can call out to the script layer at any point, even inside command procedures. You can also query and set Tcl variables from C using the Tcl_SetVar and Tcl_GetVar procedures. The Tcl_LinkVar procedure causes a Tcl variable to mirror a C variable. Modifications to the Tcl variable are reflected in the C variable, and reading the Tcl variable always returns the C variable's value.

The application creates an interpreter with Tcl_CreateInterp and registers new commands with Tcl_CreateCommand or Tcl_CreateObjCommand. Then it evaluates a script to initialize the application by calling Tcl_EvalFile. The script can be as simple as defining a few variables that are parameters of a computation, or it can be as ambitious as building a large user interface. This chapter provides several examples of C programming and Tcl, and the next chapter provides a broad overview of the C library facilities.

Creating a Loadable Package

You can organize your C code into a loadable package that can be dynamically linked into *tclsh*, *wish*, or your own Tcl application. The details about compiling the code are presented on page 543. When a package is loaded, Tcl calls a C procedure named *package*_Init, where *package* is the name of your package. Example 41–1 defines Random_Init:

Example 41–1 The initialization procedure for a loadable package.

```
/* random.c */
#include <tcl.h>
/*
 * Declarations for application-specific command procedures
 */
int RandomCmd(ClientData clientData,
             Tcl_Interp *interp,
             int argc, char *argv[]);
int RandomObjCmd(ClientData clientData,
             Tcl_Interp *interp,
             int objc, Tcl_Obj *CONST objv[]);
/*
 * The Initialization procedure that is called when
 * the package is loaded.
 */
int Random_Init(Tcl_Interp *interp) {
   /*
```

```
     * Register two variations of random.
     * The orandom command uses the object interface.
     */
    Tcl_CreateCommand(interp, "random", RandomCmd,
            (ClientData)NULL, (Tcl_CmdDeleteProc *)NULL);
    Tcl_CreateObjCommand(interp, "orandom", RandomObjCmd,
            (ClientData)NULL, (Tcl_CmdDeleteProc *)NULL);
    /*
     * Declare that we implement the random package
     * so scripts that do "package require random"
     * can load the library automatically. See page 137.
     */
    Tcl_PkgProvide(interp, "random", "1.1");
    return TCL_OK;
}
```

Example 41–1 registers a command procedure, `RandomCmd`, that implements a new Tcl command, `random`. When the Tcl script uses the `random` command, the `RandomCmd` procedure will be invoked by the Tcl interpreter. Two styles of command registrations are made for comparison: the original `Tcl_CreateCommand` and the new `Tcl_CreateObjCommand`. The command procedures are described in the next section. The call to `Tcl_PkgProvide` is discussed later.

The `load` Command

The Tcl `load` command is used to dynamically link in a compiled package:

```
load library package ?interp?
```

The *`library`* is the file name of the shared library file (i.e., the DLL), and *`package`* is the name of the package implemented by the library. The optional *`interp`* argument lets you load the library into a slave interpreter. If the library is in `/usr/local/lib/random.so`, then a Tcl script can `load` the package like this:

```
load /usr/local/lib/random.so Random
```

On most UNIX systems, you can set the `LD_LIBRARY_PATH` environment variable to a colon-separated list of directories that contain shared libraries. If you do that, then you can use relative names for the libraries:

```
load librandom.so Random
```

On Macintosh the `load` command looks for libraries in the same folder as the Tcl/Tk application (i.e., *Wish*) and in the `System:Extensions:Tool Command Language` folder:

```
load random.shlib Random
```

On Windows `load` looks in the same directory as the Tcl/Tk application, the current directory, the `C:\Windows\System` directory (or `C:\Windows\System32` on Windows NT), the `C:\Windows` directory, and then the directories listed in the `PATH` environment variable.

```
load random.dll Random
```

Using `Tcl_PkgProvide`

The package facility described in Chapter 12 hides the differences in `load` on different platforms. `Random_Init` uses `Tcl_PkgProvide` to declare what package is provided by the C code. This call helps the `pkg_mkIndex` procedure learn what libraries provide which packages. It saves this information in a package database, which is a file named `pkgIndex.tcl`. The `package require` command looks for the package database files along your `auto_path` and initializes the `auto_index` array to contain the proper `load` commands. The general process is:

- Create your shared library as described later. Put the library into a directory listed on your `auto_path` variable, or a subdirectory of one of the directories on your `auto_path`.
- Run the `pkg_mkIndex` procedure in that directory, giving it the names of all the script files and shared libraries it should index. Now your shared library is ready for use by other scripts.
- A script uses `package require` to request a package. The correct `load` command for your system will be used the first time a command from your package is used. The `package` command is the same on all platforms:

```
package require Random
```

A C Command Procedure

Tcl 8.0 introduced a new interface for Tcl commands that is designed to work efficiently with its internal on-the-fly byte code compiler. The original interface to commands was string oriented. This resulted in a lot of conversions between strings and internal formats such as integers, double-precision floating point numbers, and lists. The new interface is based on objects that can store different types of values. Conversions between strings and other types are done in a lazy fashion, and the saved conversions help your scripts run more efficiently.

The original command interface is still supported so you only need to update your code if you want the extra efficiency. The interfaces are very similar, so you should find updating your command procedures straightforward. If you are building a brand new command for Tcl 8.0, you should build an object-based command.

This chapter shows how to build a random number command using both the string and object interfaces. There are APIs to get values from command arguments and to set the command result value. The Tcl C library takes care of storage management quite well if you stick to the APIs.

The String Command Interface

The original interface to a C command procedure is much like the interface to the `main` program. The arguments from the Tcl command are available as an array of strings defined by an `argv` parameter and counted by an `argc` parameter. In addition, the handle on the interpreter is passed, along with the client data that is registered when the command was defined with `Tcl_CreateCommand`. The client data is useful if the same command procedure is implementing many different commands. Example 43–2 on page 569 shows a widget class command procedure that creates new Tcl commands that operate on instances of a widget. The client data for the instance commands holds a pointer to the data structure defining the particular instance of the widget.

The return value of a Tcl command is either a string or an error message. The `result` field in the `Tcl_Interp` data structure stores this value, and the command procedure returns either `TCL_OK` or `TCL_ERROR` to indicate success or failure. The procedure can also return `TCL_BREAK`, `TCL_CONTINUE`, or an application-specific code, which might be useful if you are implementing new kinds of built-in control structures. The examples in this book only use `TCL_OK` and `TCL_ERROR`. The use of the `result` field to return string values is described in the next section.

Example 41–2 The `RandomCmd` C command procedure.

```
/*
 * RandomCmd --
 * This implements the random Tcl command. With no arguments
 * the command returns a random integer.
 * With an integer valued argument "range",
 * it returns a random integer between 0 and range.
 */
int
RandomCmd(ClientData clientData, Tcl_Interp *interp,
		int argc, char *argv[])
{
	int rand, error;
	int limit = 0;
	if (argc > 2) {
		interp->result = "Usage: random ?range?";
		return TCL_ERROR;
	}
	if (argc == 2) {
		error = Tcl_GetInt(interp, argv[1], &limit);
		if (error != TCL_OK) {
			return error;
		}
	}
	rand = random();
	if (limit != 0) {
		rand = rand % limit;
	}
	sprintf(interp->result, "%d", rand);
	return TCL_OK;
}
```

The `random` implementation accepts an optional argument that is a range over which the random numbers should be returned. The `argc` parameter is tested to see if this argument has been given in the Tcl command. `argc` counts the command name as well as the arguments, so in our case `argc == 2` indicates that the command has been invoked something like:

```
random 25
```

The procedure `Tcl_GetInt` converts the string-valued argument to an integer. It does error checking and sets the interpreter's result field in the case of error, so we can just return if it fails to return `TCL_OK`.

Finally, the real work of calling `random` is done, and the result is formatted directly into the result buffer using sprintf. `TCL_OK` is returned to signal success.

Managing String Result

There is a simple protocol that manages the storage for a command procedure's result string. It involves `interp->result`, which holds the value, and `interp->freeProc`, which determines how the storage is cleaned up. When a command is called, the interpreter provides default storage of `TCL_RESULT_SIZE`, which is 200 bytes. The default cleanup action is to do nothing. These defaults support two simple ways to define the result of a command. One way is to use `sprintf` to format the result in place:

```
sprintf(interp->result, "%d", rand);
```

Using `sprintf` is suitable if you know your result string is short, which is often the case. The other way is to set `interp->result` to the address of a constant string. In this case the original result buffer is not used, and there is no cleanup required because the string is compiled into the program:

```
interp->result = "Usage: random ?random?";
```

In more general cases the following procedures should be used to manage the `result` and `freeProc` fields. Using these procedures has the benefit that the object command interface is very similar:

```
Tcl_SetResult(interp, string, freeProc)
Tcl_AppendResult(interp, str1, str2, str3, (char *)NULL)
Tcl_AppendElement(interp, string)
```

`Tcl_SetResult` sets the return value to be *string*. The *freeProc* argument describes how the result should be disposed of. `TCL_STATIC` is used in the case where the result is a constant string allocated by the compiler. `TCL_DYNAMIC` is used if the result is allocated with `Tcl_Alloc`, which is a platform- and compiler-independent version of `malloc`. `TCL_VOLATILE` is used if the result is in a stack variable. In this case the Tcl interpreter makes a copy of the result before calling any other command procedures. Finally, if you have your own memory allocator, pass in the address of the procedure that should free the result.

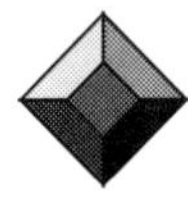

`Tcl_AppendResult` copies its arguments into the result buffer, reallocating the buffer if necessary. The arguments are concatenated onto the end of the existing result, if any. `Tcl_AppendResult` can be called several times to build a result. The result buffer is overallocated so several appends are efficient.

`Tcl_AppendElement` adds the string to the result as a proper Tcl list element. It might add braces or backslashes to get the proper structure.

The Object Command Interface

The Tcl 8.0 command interface replaces strings with *dual-ported objects*. The arguments to a command are an array of objects. The `objc` counts the objects in the Tcl command, including the command name, and `objv` is an array of pointers to them. The result of a command is also an object. Tcl variables have an object value, and so do Tcl scripts.

The dual-ported object structure stores a string representation and a second native object representation. The native representation depends on the type of the object. Integers are stored as 32-bit integers. Floating point values are stored in double-precision. Tcl lists are stored as an array of pointers to strings. Tcl scripts are stored as sequences of byte codes. Conversion between the native representation and a string are done upon demand. There are APIs for accessing object values so you do not have to worry about type conversions unless you implement a new type. Here is the `random` command procedure using the object interfaces:

Example 41–3 The `RandomCmd` C command procedure.

```
/*
 * RandomObjCmd --
 * This implements the random Tcl command from
 * Example 41-2 using the object interface.
 */
int
RandomObjCmd(ClientData clientData, Tcl_Interp *interp,
        int objc, Tcl_Obj *CONST objv[])
{
    Tcl_Obj *resultPtr;
    int rand, error;
    int limit = 0;
    if (objc > 2) {
        Tcl_WrongNumArgs(interp, 1, objv,
            "Usage: random ?range?");
        return TCL_ERROR;
    }
    if (objc == 2) {
        error = Tcl_GetIntFromObj(interp, objv[1], &limit);
        if (error != TCL_OK) {
            return error;
        }
    }
    rand = random();
    if (limit != 0) {
        rand = rand % limit;
    }
    resultPtr = Tcl_GetObjResult(interp);
    Tcl_SetIntObj(resultPtr, rand);
    return TCL_OK;
}
```

Compare Example 41–2 with Example 41–3. You can see that the two versions of the C command procedures are similar. The `Tcl_GetInt` call is replaced with `Tcl_GetIntFromObj` call. This gets an integer value from the command argument:

```
error = Tcl_GetIntFromObj(interp, objv[1], &limit);
```

The result is set by getting a handle on the result object and setting its value:

```
resultPtr = Tcl_GetObjResult(interp);
Tcl_SetIntObj(resultPtr, rand);
```

Example 41–3 does not do anything obvious about storage management. If you follow this simple example, then you do not have to worry about storage management for the Tcl objects. Tcl initializes the result object before calling your command procedure and takes care of cleaning it up later. It is sufficient to set a value and return `TCL_OK` or `TCL_ERROR`.

If your command procedure returns a string, then you will use `Tcl_SetStringObj`. This command makes a copy of the string you pass it. The new Tcl interfaces that take strings also take length arguments so you can pass binary data in strings. If the length is -1, then the string is terminated by a NULL byte. A command that always returned `boring` would do this:

```
resultPtr = Tcl_GetObjResult(interp);
Tcl_SetStringObj(resultPtr, "boring", -1);
```

Managing Object Reference Counts

In more complex situations you need to worry about the storage model for Tcl objects. The C type definition for `Tcl_Obj` is shown below. There are APIs to access all aspects of an object, so you should refrain from manipulating `Tcl_Obj` directly unless you are implementing a new type:

Example 41–4 The `Tcl_Obj` structure.

```
typedef struct Tcl_Obj {
    int refCount;
    char *bytes;          /* String representation */
    int length;           /* Number of bytes in the string */
    Tcl_ObjType *typePtr;/* Type implementation */
    union {
        long longValue;  /* Type data */
        double doubleValue;
        VOID *otherValuePtr;
        struct {
            VOID *ptr1;
            VOID *ptr2;
        } twoPtrValue;
    } internalRep;
} Tcl_Obj;
```

The Tcl objects are reference counted. Each type implementation provides a few procedures like this:

```
Tcl_GetTypeFromObj(interp, objPtr, valuePtr);
Tcl_SetTypeObj(resultPtr, value);
objPtr = Tcl_NewTypeObj(value);
```

The `Tcl_NewTypeObj` allocates storage for an object and sets its reference count to zero. `Tcl_IncrRefCount` and `Tcl_DecrRefCount` increment and decrement the reference count on an object. `Tcl_DecrRefCount` frees the storage for an object when it goes to zero. The initial reference count of zero was chosen because functions like `Tcl_SetObjResult` automatically increment the reference count on an object.

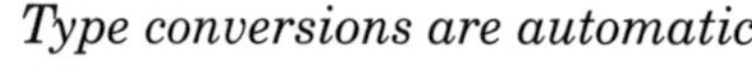
Type conversions are automatic.

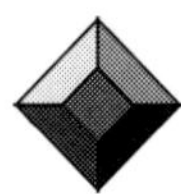

The `Tcl_GetTypeFromObj` and `Tcl_SetTypeObj` procedures just get and set the value; the reference count does not change. Type conversions are automatic. You can set an object to an integer and get back a string or double precision number later. The type implementations automatically take care of the storage for the object's value as it changes. Of course, if an object stays the same type, then accesses are more efficient.

Example 41–5 shows the `IdentityObjCmd` that just returns its argument. In this case the argument becomes shared. The original reference is from the command argument. Every object on `objv` has at least one reference when `RandomObjCmd` is called. When `IdentityObjCmd` takes one of these objects and uses it for the result, a new reference is added. The `Tcl_SetObjResult` does this for us. By manipulating reference counts instead of copying the object, the `IdentityObjCmd` runs efficiently:

Example 41–5 The `IdentityObjCmd` C command procedure.

```
/*
 * IdentityObjCmd --
 * This implements the identity function.
 */
int
IdentityObjCmd(ClientData clientData, Tcl_Interp *interp,
        int objc, Tcl_Obj *CONST objv[])
{
    if (objc != 2) {
        Tcl_WrongNumArgs(interp, 1, objv,
            "Usage: identity value");
        return TCL_ERROR;
    }
    /*
     * This increments the reference count on the argument,
     * which could have any type.
     */
    Tcl_SetObjResult(interp, objv[1]);
    return TCL_OK;
}
```

When a C command procedure is called, Tcl does not automatically increment the reference count on the arguments. However, extra references are created by Tcl procedure calls so that parameters can be passed without copying. Constants are also shared. This means an object referenced by `objv` may have one or more references. `Tcl_IsShared` returns 1 if there is more than one reference to an object. If a command procedure modifies a shared object, it must make a private copy with `Tcl_DuplicateObj`. Example 41–6 implements a `plus1` command that adds one to its argument. If the argument is not shared, then `plus1` can be implemented efficiently by modifying the native representation of the integer. Otherwise it has to make a copy of the object before modifying it:

Example 41–6 The `Plus1ObjCmd` procedure.

```
/*
 * Plus1ObjCmd --
 * This adds one to its input argument.
 */
int
Plus1ObjCmd(ClientData clientData, Tcl_Interp *interp,
      int objc, Tcl_Obj *CONST objv[])
{
   Tcl_Obj *objPtr;
   int i;
   if (objc != 2) {
      Tcl_WrongNumArgs(interp, 1, objv,
         "Usage: identity value");
      return TCL_ERROR;
   }
   objPtr = objv[1];
   if (Tcl_GetIntFromObj(interp, objPtr, &i) != TCL_OK) {
      return TCL_ERROR;
   }
   if (Tcl_IsShared(objPtr)) {
      objPtr = Tcl_DuplicateObj(objPtr);
   }
   /*
    * Assert objPtr ref count is 1.
    * OK to set the value to something new.
    * Tcl_SetIntObj overwrites the old value.
    */
   Tcl_SetIntObj(objPtr, i+1);
   /*
    * Setting the result object adds a new reference,
    * so we decrement because we no longer care about
    * the integer object we modified.
    */
   Tcl_SetObjResult(interp, objPtr);
   Tcl_DecrRefCount(objPtr);
   return TCL_OK;
}
```

Tcl_Main and Tcl_AppInit

This section describes how to make a custom main program that includes Tcl. However, the need for custom main programs has been reduced by the use of loadable modules. If you create your commands as a loadable package, you can just `load` them into *tclsh* or *wish*. Even if you do not need a custom main, this section will explain how all the pieces fit together.

The Tcl library supports the basic application structure through the `Tcl_Main` procedure that is designed to be called from your `main` program. `Tcl_Main` does three things:

- It calls `Tcl_CreateInterp` to create an interpreter that includes all the standard Tcl commands like `set` and `proc`. It also defines a few Tcl variables like `argc` and `argv`. These have the command-line arguments that were passed to your application.
- It calls `Tcl_AppInit`, which is not part of the Tcl library. Instead, your application provides this procedure. In `Tcl_AppInit` you can register additional application-specific Tcl commands.
- It reads a script or goes into an interactive loop.

You call `Tcl_Main` from your main program and provide an implementation of the `Tcl_AppInit` procedure:

Example 41–7 A canonical Tcl `main` program and `Tcl_AppInit`.

```
/* main.c */
#include <tcl.h>
int Tcl_AppInit(Tcl_Interp *interp);
/*
 * Declarations for application-specific command procedures
 */
int RandomCmd(ClientData clientData,
             Tcl_Interp *interp,
             int argc, char *argv[]);
int RandomObjCmd(ClientData clientData,
             Tcl_Interp *interp,
             int objc, Tcl_Obj *CONST objv[]);
int IdentityObjCmd(ClientData clientData,
             Tcl_Interp *interp,
             int objc, Tcl_Obj *CONST objv[]);
int Plus1ObjCmd(ClientData clientData,
             Tcl_Interp *interp,
             int objc, Tcl_Obj *CONST objv[]);

main(int argc, char *argv[]) {
   /*
    * Initialize your application here.
    *
    * Then initialize and run Tcl.
    */
   Tcl_Main(argc, argv, Tcl_AppInit);
```

```
        exit(0);
    }
    /*
     * Tcl_AppInit is called from Tcl_Main
     * after the Tcl interpreter has been created,
     * and before the script file
     * or interactive command loop is entered.
     */
    int
    Tcl_AppInit(Tcl_Interp *interp) {
        /*
         * Initialize packages
         * Tcl_Init sets up the Tcl library facility.
         */
        if (Tcl_Init(interp) == TCL_ERROR) {
            return TCL_ERROR;
        }
        /*
         * Register application-specific commands.
         */
        Tcl_CreateCommand(interp, "random", RandomCmd,
                (ClientData)NULL, (Tcl_CmdDeleteProc *)NULL);
        Tcl_CreateObjCommand(interp, "orandom", RandomObjCmd,
                (ClientData)NULL, (Tcl_CmdDeleteProc *)NULL);
        Tcl_CreateObjCommand(interp, "identity", IdentityObjCmd,
                (ClientData)NULL, (Tcl_CmdDeleteProc *)NULL);
        Tcl_CreateObjCommand(interp, "plus1", Plus1ObjCmd,
                (ClientData)NULL, (Tcl_CmdDeleteProc *)NULL);
        /*
         * Define start-up filename. This file is read in
         * case the program is run interactively.
         */
        Tcl_SetVar(interp, "tcl_rcFileName", "~/.mytcl",
            TCL_GLOBAL_ONLY);
        /*
         * Test of Tcl_Invoke, which is defined on page 538.
         */
        Tcl_Invoke(interp, "set", "foo", "$xyz [foo] {", NULL);
        return TCL_OK;
    }
```

The `main` program calls `Tcl_Main` with the `argc` and `argv` parameters passed into the program. These are the strings passed to the program on the command line, and `Tcl_Main` will store these values into Tcl variables by the same name. `Tcl_Main` is also given the address of the initialization procedure, which is `Tcl_AppInit` in our example. `Tcl_AppInit` is called by `Tcl_Main` with one argument, a handle on a newly created interpreter. There are three parts to the `Tcl_AppInit` procedure:

- The first part initializes the various packages the application uses. The example calls `Tcl_Init` to set up the script library facility. The core Tcl commands are defined by `Tcl_CreateInterp`, which is called by `Tcl_Main` before the call to Tcl_AppInit.

- The second part of Tcl_AppInit does application-specific initialization. The example registers a command procedure, RandomCmd, that implements a new Tcl command, random. When the Tcl script uses the random command, the RandomCmd procedure will be invoked by the Tcl library. The example also shows the object-based interface to command registration.
- The third part defines an application startup script, tcl_RcFileName, that executes if the program is used interactively.

Tk_Main

The structure of Tk applications is similar. The Tk_Main procedure creates a Tcl interpreter and the main Tk window. It calls out to a procedure you provide to complete initialization. After Tk_AppInit returns, Tk_Main goes into an event loop until all the windows in your application have been destroyed.

Example 41–8 shows a Tk_AppInit used with Tk_Main. The main program processes its own command-line arguments using Tk_ParseArgv, which requires a Tcl interpreter for error reporting. The example also sets up for the signal handler defined on page 542. The Tk_AppInit procedure initializes the Tcl debugger described on page 540, and it sets up for the clock widget example that is the topic of Chapter 43:

Example 41–8 A canonical Tk main program and Tk_AppInit.

```
/* main.c */
#include <tk.h>
#include <Dbg.h>
#include <signal.h>

int Tk_AppInit(Tcl_Interp *interp);

/*
 * Handler procedure for async event. See page 542.
 */
void Sig_Setup();
RETSIGTYPE Sig_HandleINT(int sig);
int Sig_HandleSafe(ClientData data,
        Tcl_Interp *interp, int code);
/*
 * Needed if entering the debugger from the idle loop.
 */
static Tcl_Interp *myInterp;

/*
 * A table for command line arguments.
 */
char *myoption1 = NULL;
static int debug = 0;
```

```
static Tk_ArgvInfo argTable[] = {
    {"-myoption1", TK_ARGV_STRING, (char *) NULL,
        (char *) &myoption1, "Explain myoption1"},
    {"-debug", TK_ARGV_CONSTANT, (char *) 1, (char *) &debug,
        "Enable the Tcl debugger"},
    {"", TK_ARGV_END, },
};

main(int argc, char *argv[]) {
    Tcl_Interp *interp;
    /*
     * Save a copy of the command line args for debugger.
     */
    argv = Dbg_ArgcArgv(argc, argv, 1);
    /*
     * Create an interpreter for the error message from
     * Tk_ParseArgv. Another one is created by Tk_Main.
     * Parse our arguments and leave the rest to Tk_Main.
     */
    interp = Tcl_CreateInterp();
    if (Tk_ParseArgv(interp, (Tk_Window) NULL, &argc, argv,
            argTable, 0) != TCL_OK) {
        fprintf(stderr, "%s\n", interp->result);
        exit(1);
    }
    Tcl_DeleteInterp(interp);
    /*
     * Set up a signal handler so we can enter the Tcl
     * debugger.
     */
    Sig_Setup();

    Tk_Main(argc, argv, Tk_AppInit);
    exit(0);
}

int ClockCmd(ClientData clientData,
             Tcl_Interp *interp,
             int argc, char *argv[]);

/*
 * Our pixmap image type.
 */
extern Tk_ImageType tkPixmapImageType;

int
Tk_AppInit(Tcl_Interp *interp) {
    /*
     * Initialize packages
     */
    if (Tcl_Init(interp) == TCL_ERROR) {
        return TCL_ERROR;
    }
    if (Tk_Init(interp) == TCL_ERROR) {
        return TCL_ERROR;
```

```
    }
    if (Dbg_Init(interp) == TCL_ERROR) {
        return TCL_ERROR;
    }
    if (debug) {
        /*
         * Enter the Tcl debugger before the first Tcl command.
         */
        Dbg_On(interp, 0);
    }
    myInterp = interp;
    /*
     * Define application-specific commands here.
     */
    Tcl_CreateCommand(interp, "clock", ClockCmd,
        (ClientData)Tk_MainWindow(interp),
        (Tcl_CmdDeleteProc *)NULL);

    Tk_CreateImageType(&tkPixmapImageType);

    /*
     * Define start-up filename. This file is read in
     * case the program is run interactively.
     */
    Tcl_SetVar(interp, "tcl_rcFileName", "~/.mytcl",
        TCL_GLOBAL_ONLY);
    return TCL_OK;
}
```

The Event Loop

An event loop is used to process window system events and other events like timers and network sockets. The different event types are described later. All Tk applications must have an event loop so they function properly in the window system environment. Tk provides a standard event loop with the `Tk_MainLoop` procedure, which is called at the end of `Tk_Main`. The *wish* shell provides an event loop automatically. The *tclsh* shell does not, although you can add an event loop using pure Tcl as shown in Example 15–2 on page 180.

You can provide your own event loop. In this case you must call `Tcl_DoOneEvent` to process any outstanding Tcl events. However, the best way to customize the event loop is to register handlers for different events and use `Tk_Main`. There are four event classes, and they are handled in the following order by `Tcl_DoOneEvent`:

- Window events. Use the `Tk_CreateEventHandler` procedure to register a handler for these events. Use the `TCL_WINDOW_EVENTS` flag to process these in `Tcl_DoOneEvent`.
- File events. Use these events to wait on slow devices and network connections. On UNIX you can register a handler for all files, sockets, and devices

with Tcl_CreateFileHandler. On Windows and Macintosh there are different APIs for registration because there are different system handles for files, sockets, and devices. On all platforms you use the TCL_FILE_EVENTS flag to process these handlers in Tcl_DoOneEvent.

- Timer events. You can set up events to occur after a specified time period. Use the Tcl_CreateTimerHandler procedure to register a handler for the event. Use the TCL_TIMER_EVENTS flag to process these in Tcl_DoOneEvent.
- Idle events. These events are processed when there is nothing else to do. Virtually all the Tk widgets use idle events to display themselves. Use the Tcl_DoWhenIdle procedure to register a procedure to call once at the next idle time. Use the TCL_IDLE_EVENTS flag to process these in Tcl_DoOneEvent.

Invoking Scripts from C

The main program is not the only place you can evaluate a Tcl script. You can use the Tcl_Eval procedure essentially at any time to evaluate a Tcl command:

```
Tcl_Eval(Tcl_Interp *interp, char *command);
```

This is how the command associated with a button is invoked, for example. The only caveat is that the script may destroy the widget or Tcl command that invoked it. To guard against this, the Tk_Preserve, Tk_Release, and Tk_EventuallyFree procedures can be used to manage any data structures associated with the widget or Tcl command. These are described on page 561.

Tcl_Eval modifies its argument.

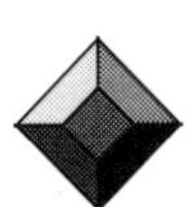

You should also be aware that Tcl_Eval may modify the string that is passed into it as a side effect of the way substitutions are performed. If you pass a constant string to Tcl_Eval, make sure your compiler has not put the string constant into read-only memory. If you use the *gcc* compiler, you may need to use the -fwritable-strings option. Later we show how to get the right compilation settings for your system.

There are a few variations on Tcl_Eval. The Tcl_GlobalEval procedure is like Tcl_Eval, but it evaluates at the global scope. Tcl_Eval uses the current scope so it has access to local variables if used in a command procedure called from a Tcl procedure. The Tcl_VarEval procedure takes a variable number of strings arguments and concatenates them before evaluation:

```
Tcl_VarEval(Tcl_Interp *interp, char *str, ..., NULL);
```

Tcl_EvalObj and Tcl_GlobalEvalObj take an object as an argument instead of a simple string. The string is compiled into byte codes the first time it is used. If you are going to execute the script many times, then the object caches the byte codes for you.

Bypassing Tcl_Eval

In a performance critical situation you may want to avoid some of the overhead associated with `Tcl_Eval`. David Nichols showed me how to call the implementation of a C command procedure directly. The trick is facilitated by the `Tcl_GetCommandInfo` procedure that returns the address of the C command procedure for a Tcl command, plus its client data pointer. The `Tcl_Invoke` procedure is shown in Example 41–9. It is used much like `Tcl_VarEval`, except that each of its arguments becomes an argument to the Tcl command without any substitutions being performed.

For example, you might want to insert a large chunk of text into a text widget without worrying about the parsing done by `Tcl_Eval`. You could use `Tcl_Invoke` like this:

```
Tcl_Invoke(interp, ".t", "insert", "insert", buf, NULL);
```

Or:

```
Tcl_Invoke(interp, "set", "foo", "$xyz [blah] {", NULL);
```

No substitutions are performed on any of the arguments because `Tcl_Eval` is out of the picture. The variable `foo` gets the following literal value:

```
$xyz [blah] {
```

Example 41–9 shows `Tcl_Invoke`. The procedure is complicated for two reasons. First, it has to handle a Tcl command that has either the object interface or the old string interface. Second, it has to build up an argument vector and may need to grow its storage in the middle of building it. It is a bit messy to deal with both at the same time, but it lets us compare the object and string interfaces. The string interfaces are simpler, but the object interfaces run more efficiently because they reduce copying and type conversions.

Example 41–9 Calling C command procedure directly.

```
#include <varargs.h>
#include <tcl.h>
/*
 * Tcl_Invoke --
 * Call this somewhat like Tcl_VarEval:
 * Tcl_Invoke(interp, cmdName, arg1, arg2, ..., NULL);
 * Each arg becomes one argument to the command,
 * with no substitutions or parsing.
 */
int
Tcl_Invoke(va_alist)
   va_dcl           /* Variable number of arguments */
{
   Tcl_Interp *interp;
   char *cmd;            /* Command name */
   char *arg;            /* Command argument */
   char **argv;          /* String vector for arguments */
   Tcl_Obj **objv;       /* Object vector for arguments */
   Tcl_Obj *resultPtr;   /* The result object */
   int argc, i, max;     /* Count of arguments */
   Tcl_CmdInfo info;     /* Info about command procedures */
   va_list pvar;         /* varargs stuff */
   int result;           /* TCL_OK or TCL_ERROR */
```

```
va_start(pvar);
interp = va_arg(pvar, Tcl_Interp *);
cmd = va_arg(pvar, char *);
/*
 * Map from the command name to a C procedure.
 */
if (! Tcl_GetCommandInfo(interp, cmd, &info)) {
   Tcl_AppendResult(interp, "Unknown command \"",
      cmd, "\"", NULL);
   va_end(pvar);
   return TCL_ERROR;
}
max = 10;
argc = 1;
if (info.isNativeObjectProc) {
   /*
    * The object interface is preferred for this command.
    */
   objv = (Tcl_Obj **)Tcl_Alloc(max * sizeof(Tcl_Obj *));
   objv[0] = Tcl_NewStringObj(cmd, strlen(cmd));
} else {
   argv = (char **)Tcl_Alloc(max * sizeof(char *));
   argv[0] = cmd;
}
Tcl_ResetResult(interp);

/*
 * Build a vector out of the rest of the arguments.
 */
while (1) {
   arg = va_arg(pvar, char *);
   if (info.isNativeObjectProc) {
      if (arg == (char *)NULL) {
         objv[argc] = (Tcl_Obj *)NULL;
      } else {
         objv[argc] = Tcl_NewStringObj(arg, strlen(arg));
         Tcl_IncrRefCount(objv[argc]);
         /* Ref count is one */
      }
   } else {
      argv[argc] = arg;
   }
   if (arg == (char *)NULL) {
      break;
   }
   argc++;
   if (argc >= max) {
      /*
       * Allocate a bigger vector and copy old values in.
       */
      if (info.isNativeObjectProc) {
         Tcl_Obj **old = objv;
         objv = (Tcl_Obj **)Tcl_Alloc(2*max *
                  sizeof(Tcl_Obj *));
```

```
                for (i=0 ; i<max ; i++) {
                    objv[i] = old[i];
                }
                free((char *)old);
            } else {
                char **old = argv;
                argv = (char **)Tcl_Alloc(2*max * sizeof(char *));
                for (i=0 ; i<max ; i++) {
                    argv[i] = old[i];
                }
                free((char *)old);
            }
            max = 2*max;
        }
    }
    va_end(pvar);
    /*
     * Invoke the C procedure.
     */
    if (info.isNativeObjectProc) {
        int len;
        result = (*info.objproc)(info.objClientData, interp,
                argc, objv);
        /*
         * Make sure the string value of the result is valid.
         */
        (void)Tcl_GetStringResult(interp);
    } else {
        result = (*info.proc)(info.clientData, interp,
                argc, argv);
    }
    /*
     * Release our references to the arguments.
     */
    if (info.isNativeObjectProc) {
        for (i=0 ; i<argc ; i++) {
            Tcl_DecrRefCount(objv[i]);
        }
        Tcl_Free((char *)objv);
    } else {
        Tcl_Free((char *)argv);
    }
    return result;
}
```

Expect's Tcl Debugger

This section describes how to add the debugger from the *expect* package to your application. *Expect* was designed and implemented by Don Libes. Historically it is the first extension package. It is used to script the use of interactive programs like *ftp*, *telnet*, and *passwd*. Libes wrote the initial version in about two weeks after he first heard about Tcl. He had long wanted to write something like *expect*, and Tcl provided just the infrastructure that he needed to get started. By now the *expect* package is quite sophisticated. Libes has an excellent book (*Exploring Expect*, Don Libes, O'Reilly & Associates, Inc., 1995).

As of this writing, the current version of *expect* is 5.13, and it is compatible with Tcl 7.4. A version 5.14 is expected, which will take advantage of some of the new features in Tcl and improve the debugger that comes with *expect*. You can always fetch the latest version of expect by FTP from the following site and file name:

```
ftp.cme.nist.gov:/pub/expect/expect.tar.Z
```

The *expect* C library includes a Tcl debugger. It lets you set breakpoints and look at the Tcl execution stack. This section explains what you need to add to your C program to make the debugger available to scripts. The interactive use of the debugger is described in Chapter 13 on page 158.

The Dbg C Interface

The debugger is implemented in one file, `Dbg.c`, that is part of the *expect* library. The `Dbg_cmd.c` file implements a debug command that causes your script to enter the debugger. You can make the debugger separate from *expect* as shown later, but it is easiest to link against the *expect* library. The core procedures are `Dbg_On` and `Dbg_Off`.[*]

```
void *Dbg_On(Tcl_Interp *interp, int immediate);
void *Dbg_Off(Tcl_Interp *interp);
```

If `immediate` is 1, then `Dbg_On` enters an interactive command loop right away. Otherwise the debugger waits until just before the next command is evaluated. It is reasonable to call `Dbg_On` with `immediate` set to zero from inside a `SIGINT` interrupt handler.

The `Dbg_ArgcArgv` call lets the debugger make a copy of the command-line arguments. It wants to print this information as part of its call stack display. If the *copy* argument is 1, a copy of the argument strings is made and a pointer to the allocated memory is returned. Otherwise it just retains a pointer and returns 0. The copy may be necessary because the `Tk_ParseArgv` procedure will modify the argument list. Call `Dbg_ArgcArgv` first.

```
char **Dbg_ArgcArgv(int argc, char *argv[], int copy);
```

The `Dbg_Active` procedure returns 1 if the debugger is currently on. It does no harm, by the way, to call `Dbg_On` if the debugger is already active.

```
int Dbg_Active(Tcl_Interp *interp);
```

The remaining procedures are only needed if you want to refine the behavior of the debugger. You can change the command interpreter, and you can filter

[*] I will give the C signatures for the procedures involved because I no longer see them in the standard *expect* documentation. You must read `Dbg.h`. Don Libes described the debugger in a nice little paper, "A Debugger for Tcl Applications," which appeared in the 1993 Tcl/Tk workshop.

out commands so the debugger ignores them.

The `Dbg_Interactor` procedure registers a command loop implementation and a client data pointer. It returns the previously registered procedure.

```
Dbg_InterProc
Dbg_Interactor(Tcl_Interp *interp,
     Dbg_InterProc *inter_proc, ClientData data);
```

The command loop procedure needs to have the following signature.

```
int myinteractor(Tcl_Interp *interp);
```

Look in the `Dbg.c` file at the `simple_interactor` procedure to see how the command loop works. In practice the default one is just fine.

The `Dbg_IgnoreFuncs` procedure registers a filtering function that decides what Tcl commands should be ignored. It returns the previously registered filter procedure. The filter should be relatively efficient because it is called before every command when the debugger is enabled.

```
Dbg_IgnoreFuncsProc
Dbg_IgnoreFuncs(Tcl_Interp *interp,
     Dbg_IgnoreFuncsProc *ignoreproc);
```

The `ignoreproc` procedure just takes a string as an argument, which is the name of the command about to be executed. It returns 1 if the command should be ignored.

```
int ignoreproc(char *s);
```

Handling SIGINT

A common way to enter the debugger is in response to a keyboard interrupt. The details of signal handling vary a little from system to system, so you may have to adjust Example 41–10 somewhat. The `Sig_Setup` procedure is meant to be called early in your main program. It does two things. It registers a signal handler, and it registers a Tcl asynchronous event. It isn't safe to do much more than set a variable value inside a signal handler, and it certainly is not safe to call `Tcl_Eval` in a signal handler. However, the Tcl interpreter lets you register procedures to be called at a safe point. The registration is done with `Tcl_AsyncCreate`, and the handler is enabled with `Tcl_AsyncMark`. Finally, within the async handler the debugger is entered by calling `Dbg_On`.

Example 41–10 A `SIGINT` handler.

```
#include <signal.h>
/*
 * Token and handler procedure for async event.
 */
static Tcl_AsyncHandler sig_Token;
int Sig_HandleSafe(ClientData data,
    Tcl_Interp *interp, int code);
/*
 * Set up a signal handler for interrupts.
```

```
 * This also registers a handler for a Tcl asynchronous
 * event, which is enabled in the interrupt handler.
 */
void
Sig_Setup(interp)
    Tcl_Interp *interp;
{
    RETSIGTYPE (*oldhandler)();
    oldhandler = signal(SIGINT, Sig_HandleINT);
    if ((int)oldhandler == -1) {
        perror("signal failed");
        exit(1);
    }
    sig_Token = Tcl_AsyncCreate(Sig_HandleSafe, NULL);
#ifdef HAVE_SIGINTERRUPT
    /*
     * Ensure that wait() kicks out on interrupt.
     */
    siginterrupt(SIGINT, 1);
#endif
}
/*
 * Invoked upon interrupt (control-C)
 */
RETSIGTYPE
Sig_HandleINT(sig)
    int sig;
{
    Tcl_AsyncMark(sig_Token);
}
/*
 * Invoked at a safe point sometime after Tcl_AsyncMark
 */
int
Sig_HandleSafe(data, interp, code)
    ClientData data;
    Tcl_Interp *interp;
    int code;
{
    if (interp == NULL) {
        /*
         * Called from the Tk idle loop.
         */
        interp = myInterp;
    }
    Dbg_On(interp, 1);  /* Enter the Tcl debugger */
}
```

Putting a Tcl Program Together

The CD-ROM contains the sources to the Tcl and Tk distributions, as well as sample Makefiles for UNIX, project files for Macintosh Code Warrior, Makefiles for Windows Visual C++, and Makefiles Borland compilation environments. The samples capture various platform-specific details about compiling programs that use Tcl.

A Simple UNIX Example

Example 41–11 shows a simple UNIX Makefile used to build *mytcl*, which has the `random` command and `Tcl_Invoke`. The details in this `Makefile` may not be correct for your system. In general, you need to know the locations of two things, the `tcl.h` include file and the Tcl C library. In some cases the math library (`-lm`) is included in the standard C library. We describe a way to figure out these details later:

Example 41–11 A Makefile for a simple Tcl C program.

```
INC = -I/tclcd/include
LIBS = -L/tclcd/lib -ltcl -lm
DEBUG = -g
CFLAGS =$(DEBUG) $(INC)

OBJS = tclMain.o random.o tclInvoke.o

mytcl: $(OBJS)
	$(CC) -o mytcl $(OBJS) $(LIBS)
```

Assuming you use `Tcl_Main`, which handles all the details about reading the script or prompting for interactive input, you can use *mytcl* like the other Tcl shells. You can specify your program in a script with the `#!` notation. If your program is stored in `/usr/joe/bin/mytcl`, start your script with:

```
#!/usr/joe/bin/mytcl
```

Autoconf

The best way to build Makefiles on UNIX is indirectly via the *autoconf* program. The *autoconf* program creates a script that figures out a wide variety of platform-specific details and generates a working Makefile. There are three steps in this process, and they are illustrated by the build process for Tcl and Tk:

- The developer of a source code package creates a `configure.in` template that expresses the system dependencies of the source code. They use the *autoconf* program to process this template into a `configure` script. For the Tcl and Tk sources the `configure` script has already been generated and can be found in the `unix` subdirectories of the Tcl and Tk source directories.
- A user of a source code package runs `configure` on each different platform they need to compile the sources. If you only have one platform, just run `configure` in the `/tclcd/tcl8.0/unix` directory:

```
% cd /tclcd/tcl8.0/unix
```

```
% /bin/sh configure
```

- If you build for multiple platforms, create subdirectories of `unix` and run `configure` from there. Using the complete pathname of `configure` helps Tcl find things during the configuration and build process:

```
% cd /tclcd/tcl8.0/unix/solaris
% /bin/sh /tclcd/tcl8.0/unix/configure
```

- The `configure` script uses the `Makefile.in` template to generate the `Makefile`. Once `configure` is complete, you build your program with *make*:

```
% make
```

Use `tclConfig.sh` from the Tcl sources.

An important side effect of the Tcl configuration process is the generation of a file named `tclConfig.sh`. This file is designed to be sourced by the `configure.in` templates of packages that use Tcl. Example 41–12 shows a `configure.in` we can use for the `random` package and the `clock` widget from Chapter 43. The `configure.in` is processed by *autoconf*, and it is a Bourne shell script that is preprocessed with the *m4* macro expander.

Example 41–12 A `configure.in` for your package.

```
# Name a file autoconf should find in the source directory
AC_INIT(randomPkg.c)

# See if there was a command-line option for where Tcl is; if
# not, assume that its top-level directory is a sibling of ours.
AC_ARG_WITH(tcl,
    [  --with-tcl=DIR       use Tcl 8.0 binaries from DIR],
    TCL_BIN_DIR=$withval, TCL_BIN_DIR=`cd ../tcl8.0/unix; pwd`)
if test ! -d $TCL_BIN_DIR; then
    AC_MSG_ERROR(Tcl directory $TCL_BIN_DIR doesn't exist)
fi
AC_ARG_WITH(tk,
    [  --with-tk=DIR        use Tk 8.0 binaries from DIR],
    TK_BIN_DIR=$withval, TK_BIN_DIR=`cd ../tk8.0/unix; pwd`)
if test ! -d $TK_BIN_DIR; then
    AC_MSG_ERROR(Tk directory $TK_BIN_DIR doesn't exist)
fi

# Determine signal handler return type
AC_TYPE_SIGNAL()
AC_CHECK_FUNC(siginterrupt, AC_DEFINE(HAVE_SIGINTERRUPT) ,)

# Use the information from the Tcl and Tk configuration

. $TCL_BIN_DIR/tclConfig.sh
. $TK_BIN_DIR/tkConfig.sh

CC=$TCL_CC
AC_SUBST(CC)

# Expand @references@ to autoconf variables in Makefile.in
```

```
# Expand @references@ to autoconf variables in Makefile.in

AC_SUBST(TCL_SHLIB_CFLAGS)
AC_SUBST(TCL_SHLIB_LD)
AC_SUBST(TCL_SHLIB_LD_LIBS)
AC_SUBST(TCL_SHLIB_SUFFIX)

AC_SUBST(TCL_LIB_SPEC)
AC_SUBST(TCL_DEFS)
AC_SUBST(TCL_LIBS)
AC_SUBST(TCL_PREFIX)

AC_SUBST(TK_LIB_SPEC)
AC_SUBST(TK_LIBS)
AC_SUBST(TK_DEFS)

# Extracted from the dbg configure.in
DBG_MAJOR_VERSION=5
DBG_MINOR_VERSION=21
DBG_MICRO_VERSION=0
DBG_VERSION=$DBG_MAJOR_VERSION.$DBG_MINOR_VERSION
DBG_VERSION_FULL=$DBG_VERSION.$DBG_MICRO_VERSION
DBG_INCLUDE_DIR=$TCL_SRC_DIR/generic

AC_SUBST(DBG_MAJOR_VERSION)
AC_SUBST(DBG_MINOR_VERSION)
AC_SUBST(DBG_MICRO_VERSION)
AC_SUBST(DBG_VERSION_FULL)
AC_SUBST(DBG_VERSION)
AC_SUBST(DBG_INCLUDE_DIR)

AC_OUTPUT(Makefile)
```

The various `AC_` constructs are *autoconf* macros, which I mostly take on faith. The `AC_ARG_WITH` allows for command-line arguments to `configure`. In this case the user can define where to find the directories that contain `tclConfig.sh` and `tkConfig.sh`. These are not necessary if your build directory is parallel to the Tcl/Tk build directories:

```
configure --with-tcl=/somewhere/tcl8.0/unix \
    --with-tk=/somewhere/tk8.0/unix
```

The `AC_DEFINE` macro adds to a variable named `DEFS`, which is designed to be used in the flags for the compiler. The example checks for a function and adds a definition if it exists. The `HAVE_SIGINTERUPT` flag is used in Example 41–10 on page 542. That example also uses `RETSIGTYPE`, which is defined by the `AC_TYPE_SIGNAL` macro.

The `configure.in` ultimately defines variables that will be expanded in the `Makefile.in` template. The `AC_SUBST` macro causes the variable expansion in the `Makefile.in`. If the `configure.in` script defines a variable named `TCL_SHLIB_LD`, then the `Makefile.in` can use that with `@TCL_SHLIB_LD@`. Example 41–13 shows the `Makefile.in` template:

Example 41–13 The Makefile.in template.

```
# The following definitions create Makefile variables
# that get values from autoconf variables.

CC = @CC@
TCL_LIB_SPEC =   @TCL_LIB_SPEC@
TK_LIB_SPEC =    @TK_LIB_SPEC@
LIBS =           $(TCL_LIB_SPEC) @TCL_LIBS@
TK_LIBS =        $(TK_LIB_SPEC) $(TCL_LIB_SPEC) @TK_LIBS@
DEFS =           @DEFS@ @TK_DEFS@ @TCL_DEFS@
SHLIB_CFLAGS =   @TCL_SHLIB_CFLAGS@
SHLIB_LD =       @TCL_SHLIB_LD@
SHLIB_LD_LIBS =  @TCL_SHLIB_LD_LIBS@
SHLIB_SUFFIX =   @TCL_SHLIB_SUFFIX@
SRC_DIR =        @srcdir@
TCL_INCLUDE_DIR= @TCL_PREFIX@/include

CC_SWITCHES = -g
CFLAGS = $(CC_SWITCHES) -I${SRC_DIR} -I${TCL_INCLUDE_DIR} \
    $(DEFS)
all: mytcl mywish simple random${SHLIB_SUFFIX}

random${SHLIB_SUFFIX}: $(SRC_DIR)/randomPkg.c
    $(CC) -c $(CFLAGS) ${SHLIB_CFLAGS} $(SRC_DIR)/randomPkg.c
    ${SHLIB_LD} -o random${SHLIB_SUFFIX} randomPkg.o \
        $(SHLIB_LD_LIBS)

DBG_OBJS = Dbg.o Dbg_cmd.o
DBG_INCLUDE_DIR = @DBG_INCLUDE_DIR@
Dbg.o : Dbg.c
    $(CC) -c Dbg.c $(CFLAGS) -I$(DBG_INCLUDE_DIR)
Dbg_cmd.o : Dbg_cmd.c
    $(CC) -c Dbg_cmd.c $(CFLAGS) -I$(DBG_INCLUDE_DIR) \
        -DDBG_VERSION=\"@DBG_VERSION@\"

MY_OBJS = tclMain.o randomPkg.o tclInvoke.o
mytcl: $(MY_OBJS)
    $(CC) -o mytcl $(MY_OBJS) $(LIBS)

simple: cprog1.o
    $(CC) -o simple cprog1.o $(LIBS)

TK_OBJS = tkMain.o tkWidget.o tkImgPixmap.o $(DBG_OBJS)
mywish: $(TK_OBJS)
    $(CC) -o mywish $(TK_OBJS) $(TK_LIBS)

clean:
    rm -f *.o *${SHLIB_SUFFIX} config.cache config.log \
        config.status mywish mytcl

distclean: clean
    rm -f Makefile
```

Windows

The easiest way to compile packages on Windows is to start with the binary distribution of Tcl and Tk. These have the Tcl and Tk DLLs. Your Makefiles will be different if you use Borland or Visual C++ compilers. The CD-ROM has two templates, `makefile.bc` and `makefile.vc`, for the two compilers. The `examples/build` directory has an example from the Tcl FTP site. The `examples/cprog` directory has the sources from this book.

- Install the binary release. The version on the CD-ROM can be installed by running `win80.exe`. You can always find an up-to-date release on the Internet at the FTP archive site listed in the Preface. Under Windows 95, avoid installing under `Program Files` because the space in that name may confuse the *make* and *nmake* programs.
- Copy the example source files from `examples/cprog` to a directory on your hard drive. You need all the `.c` files and either `makefile.bc` or `makefile.vc`. For the Borland compiler, copy `makefile.bc` and edit the definitions of `BORLAND` and `TCL` to be the directories where these are installed. For VC++, copy `makefile.vc` and edit the definitions of `TOOLS32` and `TCL` to be the directories where these are installed.
- Tcl and Tk are compiled with the Borland compiler, so if you use VC++ you need to get the `tcl80.lib` and `tk80.lib` import files needed link against the Tcl and Tk libraries. These can be found in `vclibs80.zip` on the CD-ROM, and up-to-date versions can also be found on the FTP site.
- Copy the `random.dll` file created by *make* (or *nmake*) into a directory on the Tcl `auto_path`, and then use `pkg_mkIndex` to update the `pkgIndex.tcl` file there.

Macintosh

The CD-ROM has a Code Warrior project file that builds the `random.shlib` file. The examples/build directory has an example from the Tcl FTP site. The examples/cprog directory has the sources from this book.You should put the sources into a folder that is a sibling of the Tcl/Tk source directory.

- Install the Macintosh source release. The installer for this is on the CD-ROM as `mactcltk8.0.sea`. Assume you install this into the `Hard Disk:Tcl/Tk 8.0` folder.
- Copy the sources for the random package from the CD-ROM into the `Hard Disk:Random 1.1` folder. Since this is at the same level as the Tcl/Tk sources, then the Code Warrior project file should work without modification.

CHAPTER 42

C Library Overview

This chapter provides a bird's eye view of the facilities in the Tcl and Tk C libraries. For details of the APIs, you will need to consult the on-line reference material.

C libraries provide comprehensive access to the Tcl and Tk implementation. You have complete control over the Tcl script environment, plus you can extend Tcl and Tk by writing new features in C. You can implement new commands, I/O channels, event sources, widgets, canvas items, image types, and geometry managers. The platform-independent I/O subsystem and the event loop are available for use from C. This chapter provides an overview of the Tcl and Tk C libraries.

For serious C programming you need to consult the on-line reference material. The manual pages describe groups of related C procedures. For example, `Tcl_CreateCommand` and `Tcl_DeleteCommand` are described in the `CrtCommand` man page. If you are looking directly at the file system, you will see files named `CrtCommand.3` or `CrtCommand.3.html`. The HTML versions are on the CD-ROM and the Web:

```
http://www.sunlabs.com/tcl/man/
```

The Tcl and Tk sources are also excellent reference material. Virtually all the exported APIs are used by Tcl and Tk themselves, so you can use these examples to see how the APIs are used. The Tcl and Tk sources are on the CD-ROM in `tcl8.0` and `tk8.0` directories. The sources are divided into `generic`, `unix`, `mac`, and `win` subdirectories.

An Overview of the Tcl C Library

Application Initialization

The Tcl_Main, and Tcl_AppInit procedures are described in the Tcl_Main and AppInit man pages, respectively. These procedures are illustrated by Example 41–7 on page 532.

Creating and Deleting Interpreters

A Tcl interpreter is created and deleted with the Tcl_CreateInterp and Tcl_DeleteInterp procedures, which are described in the CrtInterp man page. You can find out if a interpreter is in the process of being deleted with the Tcl_InterpDeleted call. You can register a callback to occur when the interpreter is deleted with Tcl_CallWhenDeleted. Unregister the callback with Tcl_DontCallWhenDeleted. These two procedures are described in the CallDel man page.

Slave interpreters are created and manipulated with Tcl_CreateSlave, Tcl_GetSlave, Tcl_GetSlaves, Tcl_CreateAlias, Tcl_GetAlias, Tcl_GetAliases, Tcl_IsSafe, Tcl_MakeSafe, Tcl_ExposeCommand, and Tcl_HideCommand. These are described in the CrtSlave man page.

Creating and Deleting Commands

Register a new Tcl command with Tcl_CreateCommand, and delete a command with Tcl_DeleteCommand. The Tcl_GetCommandInfo and Tcl_SetCommandInfo procedures query and modify the procedure that implements a Tcl command and the ClientData that is associated with the command. All of these are described in the CrtCommand man page.

The object interface Tcl_CreateObjCommand is described in the CrtObjCmd man page.

Dynamic Loading and Packages

Tcl_PkgRequire checks a dependency on another package. Tcl_PkgProvide declares that a package is provided by a library. These are equivalent to the package require and package provide Tcl commands. These are described in the PkgRequire man page.

The Tcl_StaticPackage call is used by statically linked packages so scripts can load them into slave interpreters. This is described on in the StaticPkg man page.

The Tcl_FindExecuatable procedure returns the absolute file name of the program being run. It is described in the FindExec man page.

Managing the Result String

The result string is managed through the Tcl_SetResult, Tcl_AppendResult, Tcl_AppendElement, and Tcl_ResetResult procedures. These are described in the SetResult man page.

The object interface is provided by Tcl_SetObjResult, Tcl_GetObjResult, and Tcl_ResetObjResult, which are described in the SetObjResult man page.

Error information is managed with the Tcl_AddErrorInfo, Tcl_AddObjErrorInfo, Tcl_SetErrorCode, and Tcl_PosixError procedures, which are described in the AddErrInfo man page. The Tcl_WrongNumArgs generates a common error message. The Tcl_SetErrno and Tcl_GetErrno provide platform-independent access to the errno global variable that stores POSIX error codes. It is described in the SetErrno man page.

Memory Allocation

The Tcl_Alloc, Tcl_Realloc, and Tcl_Free procedures provide platform and compiler independent functions to allocation and free heap storage. Use these instead of alloc, realloc, and free. These are described in the Alloc man page.

Lists and Command Parsing

If you are reading commands, you can test for a complete command with Tcl_CommandComplete, which is described in the CmdCmplt man page. Future versions of Tcl will include better support for parsing Tcl commands.

You can do backslash substitutions with Tcl_Backslash, which is described in the Backslash man page. The Tcl_Concat procedure, which is described in the Concat man page, concatenates its arguments with a space separator, just like the Tcl concat command.

You can chop a list up into its elements with Tcl_SplitList, which returns an array of strings. You can create a list out of an array of strings with Tcl_Merge. This behaves like the list command in that it will add syntax to the strings so that the list structure has one element for each of the strings. The Tcl_ScanElement and Tcl_ConvertElement procedures are used by Tcl_Merge. All of these are described in the SplitList man page.

The object interface to lists is provided by Tcl_NewListObj, Tcl_ListObjAppendList, Tcl_ListObjAppendElement, Tcl_ListObjGetElements, Tcl_ListObjLength, Tcl_ListObjIndex, and Tcl_ListObjReplace. These are described in the ListObj man page.

Command Pipelines

The Tcl_OpenCommandChannel procedure does all the work of setting up a pipeline between processes. It handles file redirection and implements all the syntax supported by the exec and open commands. It is described by the

OpenFileChnl man page.

If the command pipeline is run in the background, then a list of process identifiers is returned. You can detach these processes with Tcl_DetachPids, and you can clean up after them with Tcl_ReapDetachedProcs. These are described in the DetachPid man page.

Tracing the Actions of the Tcl Interpreter

There are several procedures that let you trace the execution of the Tcl interpreter and provide control over its behavior. The Tcl_CreateTrace registers a procedure that is called before the execution of each Tcl command. Remove the registration with Tcl_DeleteTrace. These are described in the CrtTrace man page.

You can trace modifications and accesses to Tcl variables with Tcl_TraceVar and Tcl_TraceVar2. The second form is used with array elements. Remove the traces with Tcl_UntraceVar and Tcl_UntraceVar2. You can query the traces on variables with Tcl_VarTraceInfo and Tcl_VarTraceInfo2. These are all described in the TraceVar man page.

Evaluating Tcl Commands

Tcl_Eval evaluates a string as a Tcl command. Tcl_VarEval takes a variable number of string arguments and concatenates them before evaluation. The Tcl_EvalFile command reads commands from a file. Tcl_GlobalEval evaluates a string at the global scope. These are all described in the Eval man page.

Tcl_EvalObj and Tcl_GlobalEvalObj provide an object interface. Their argument is a script object that gets compiled into byte codes and cached. Use these procedures if you plan to execute the same script several times. They are described in the EvalObj man page.

If you are implementing an interactive command interpreter and want to use the history facility, then call Tcl_RecordAndEval. This records the command on the history list and then behaves like Tcl_GlobalEval. This is described in the RecordEval man page.

You can set the recursion limit of the interpreter with Tcl_SetRecursionLimit, which is described in the SetRecLmt man page.

If you are implementing a new control structure, you may need to use the Tcl_AllowExceptions procedure. This makes it acceptable for Tcl_Eval and friends to return something other than TCL_OK and TCL_ERROR. This is described in the AllowExc man page.

Reporting Script Errors

If your widget makes a callback into the script level, what do you do when the callback returns an error? Use the Tcl_BackgroundError procedure that invokes the standard bgerror procedure to report the error to the user. This is described in the BackgdErr man page.

Manipulating Tcl Variables

You can set a Tcl variable with `Tcl_SetVar` and `Tcl_SetVar2`. The second form is used for array elements. You can retrieve the value of a Tcl variable with `Tcl_GetVar` and `Tcl_GetVar2`. You can delete variables with `Tcl_UnsetVar` and `Tcl_UnsetVar2`. These are all described in the `SetVar` man page.

The `Tcl_ObjSetVar2` and `Tcl_ObjGetVar2` command implement the object interface to variable values. They are described in the `ObjSetVar` man page.

You can link a Tcl variable and a C variable together with `Tcl_LinkVar` and break the relationship with `Tcl_UnlinkVar`. Setting the Tcl variable modifies the C variable, and reading the Tcl variable returns the value of the C variable. If you need to modify the Tcl variable directly, use `Tcl_UpdateLinkedVar`. These are described in the `LinkVar` man page.

Use the `Tcl_UpVar` and `Tcl_UpVar2` procedures to link Tcl variables from different scopes together. You may need to do this if your command takes the name of a variable as an argument as opposed to a value. These procedures are used in the implementation of the `upvar` Tcl command, and they are described in the `UpVar` man page.

Evaluating Expressions

The Tcl expression evaluator is available through the `Tcl_ExprLong`, `Tcl_ExprDouble`, `Tcl_ExprBool`, and `Tcl_ExprString` procedures. These all use the same evaluator, but they differ in how they return their result. They are described in the `ExprLong` man page.

The object interface to expressions is implemented with `Tcl_ExprLongObj`, `Tcl_ExprDoubleObj`, `Tcl_ExprBoolObj`, and `Tcl_ExprStringObj`, which are described in the `ExprLongObj` man page.

You can register the implementation of new math functions by using the `Tcl_CreateMathFunc` procedure, which is described in the `CrtMathFnc` man page.

Converting Numbers

You can convert strings into numbers with the `Tcl_GetInt`, `Tcl_GetDouble`, and `Tcl_GetBoolean` procedures, which are described in the `GetInt` man page. The `Tcl_PrintDouble` procedure converts a floating point number to a string. Tcl uses it anytime it must do this conversion. It is described in the `PrintDbl` man page.

Tcl Objects

Tcl 8.0 uses dual-ported objects instead of strings to improve execution efficiency. The basic interface to objects is provided by `Tcl_NewObj`, `Tl_DuplicateObj`, `Tcl_IncrRefCount`, `Tcl_DecrRefCount`, and `Tcl_IsShared`. These are described in the `Object` man page. Example 41–6 on page 531 and Example 41–9 on page 538 illustrate some of these procedures.

You can define new object types. The interface consists of Tcl_RegisterObjType, Tcl_GetObjType, Tcl_AppendAllObjTypes, and Tcl_ConvertToType, which are described in the ObjectType man page.

Primitive Object Types

The basic Tcl object types are boolean, integer, double precision real, and string. The types provide procedures for creating objects, setting values, and getting values: Tcl_NewBooleanObj, Tcl_SetBooleanObj, Tcl_GetBooleanFromObj, Tcl_NewDoubleObj, Tcl_SetDoubleObj, Tcl_GetDoubleFromObj, Tcl_NewIntObj, Tcl_GetIntFromObj, Tcl_SetIntObj, Tcl_NewLongObj, Tcl_GetLongFromObj, and Tcl_SetLongObj

Strings support Tcl_NewStringObj, Tcl_SetStringObj, Tcl_GetStringFromObj, Tcl_AppendToObj, Tcl_AppendStringsToObj, and Tcl_SetObjLength. Each type has its own man page: BoolObj, DoubleObj, IntObj, and StringObj.

String Keys for Data Structures

The Tcl_SetAssocData registers a string-valued key for a data structure. The Tcl_GetAssocData gets the data for a key, and Tcl_DeleteAssocData removes the key and pointer. The registration also includes a callback that is made when the interpreter is deleted. This is a layer on top of the hash table package described next. These routines are described in the AssocData man page.

Option Processing

The Tcl_GetIndexFromObj provides a way to look up keywords in a table. It returns the index of the table entry that matches a keyword. It is designed to work with options on a Tcl command. It is described in the GetIndex man page.

Hash Tables

Tcl has a nice hash table package that automatically grows the hash table data structures as more elements are added to the table. Because everything is a string, you may need to set up a hash table that maps from a string-valued key to an internal data structure. The procedures in the package are Tcl_InitHashTable, Tcl_DeleteHashTable, Tcl_CreateHashEntry, Tcl_DeleteHashEntry, Tcl_FindHashEntry, Tcl_GetHashValue, Tcl_SetHashValue, Tcl_GetHashKey, Tcl_FirstHashEntry, Tcl_NextHashEntry, and Tcl_HashStats. These are described in the Hash man page.

The next example uses a hash table to map from the first argument of a command procedure to the C procedure that handles the operation. The code is taken from *mxedit*, an editor built around a complex widget that supports many operations. The widget procedure looks up its first argument in a hash table instead of using many `if` statements to examine the argument:

Example 42–1 Using the `Hash` package.

```
static Tcl_HashTable mxInstanceCmdTable;

typedef struct {
    char *name;       /* Operation name. */
    int (*proc)();    /* Procedure to process operation. */
} CmdInfo;

static CmdInfo commands[] = {
    {"caret",     Mx_CaretCmd},
    {"clean",     Mx_CleanCmd},
    {"column",    Mx_ColumnCmd},
    {"configure", Mx_ConfigureCmd},
    /* Lines ommitted */
    {"write",     Mx_WriteCmd},
    {"written",   Mx_WrittenCmd},
    {(char *) NULL, (int (*)()) NULL}
};
/*
 * MxCmdInit creates a hash table of widget commands.
 * The hash table maps from argv[1] to C-procedures.
 */
void
MxCmdInit(mxwPtr)
  MxWidget *mxwPtr;
{
    CmdInfo *cmd;

    Tcl_InitHashTable(&mxInstanceCmdTable,
        TCL_STRING_KEYS);
    for (cmd = commands; cmd->name != NULL ; cmd++) {
        int newEntry;
        Tcl_HashEntry *entryPtr;
        entryPtr =
            Tcl_CreateHashEntry(&mxInstanceCmdTable,
            cmd->name, &newEntry);
        Tcl_SetHashValue(entryPtr, cmd->proc);
    }
    return;
}
/*
 * MxCmdFind uses the hash table to find the procedure
 * associated with an operation name.
 */
int (*
MxCmdFind(string))()
    char *string;
{
    Tcl_HashEntry *entryPtr;
    int (*handler)();
    entryPtr = Tcl_FindHashEntry(&mxInstanceCmdTable,
```

```
        string);
    if (entryPtr == NULL) {
        return NULL;
    }
    handler = (int(*)())Tcl_GetHashValue(entryPtr);
    return handler;
}
```

Dynamic Strings

The Tcl dynamic string package is designed for strings that get built up incrementally. You will need to use dynamic strings if you use the `Tcl_TranslateFileName` procedure. The procedures in the package are `Tcl_DStringInit`, `Tcl_DStringAppend`, `Tcl_DStringAppendElement`, `Tcl_DStringStartSublist`, `Tcl_DStringEndSublist`, `Tcl_DStringLength`, `Tcl_DStringValue`, `Tcl_DStringSetLength`, `Tcl_DStringFree`, `Tcl_DStringResult`, and `Tcl_DStringGetResult`. These are described in the `DString` man page.

Regular Expressions and String Matching

The regular expression library used by Tcl is exported through the `Tcl_RegExpMatch`, `Tcl_RegExpCompile`, `Tcl_RegExpExec`, and `Tcl_RegExpRange` procedures. These are described in the `RegExp` man page. The string match function is available through the `Tcl_StringMatch` procedure, which is described in the `StrMatch` man page.

Event Loop Interface

The standard event loop is implemented by `Tk_MainLoop`. If you write your own event loop you need to call `Tcl_DoOneEvent` so Tcl can handle its events. If you read window events directly, (e.g., through `Tk_CreateGenericHandler`), you can dispatch to the correct handler for the event with `Tcl_HandleEvent`. These are described in the `DoOneEvent` man page. Note that most of the event loop is implemented in the Tcl library, except for `Tk_MainLoop` and the window event handler interface that are part of the Tk library.

If you want to use the Tcl event loop mechanism without using the rest of the Tk toolkit, which requires a window system, then call `Tcl_EventInit` to set up the event registration mechanism. You can create handlers for file, timer, and idle events after this call.

Restrict or delay events with the `Tcl_RestrictEvent` procedure, which is described in the `RestrictEv` man page.

Handling Window Events

Use `Tk_CreateEventHandler` to set up a handler for specific window events.

Widget implementations need a handler for expose and resize events, for example. Remove the registration with `Tk_DeleteEventHandler`. These are described in the `EventHndlr` man page.

You can set up a handler for all window events with `Tk_CreateGenericHandler`. This is useful in some modal interactions where you have to poll for a certain event. Delete the handler with `Tk_DeleteGenericHandler`. These are described in the `CrtGenHdlr` man page.

File Handlers

Use `Tcl_CreateFileHandler` to register handlers for I/O streams. You set up the handlers to be called when the I/O stream is ready for reading or writing, or both. File handlers are called after window event handlers. These are described in the `CrtFileHdlr` man page.

`Tcl_CreateFileHandler` is UNIX specific because UNIX has a unified handle for files, sockets, pipes, and devices. On Windows and the Macintosh there are different system APIs to wait for events from these different classes of I/O objects. These differences are hidden by the channel drivers for sockets and pipes. For non-standard devices, the best thing to do is use the channel driver interfaces. Otherwise you can write a custom event loop and call the system-dependent APIs to check your other devices.

Timer Events

Register a callback to occur at some time in the future with `Tcl_CreateTimerHandler`. The handler is called only once. If you need to delete the handler before it gets called, use `Tcl_DeleteTimerHandler`. These are described in the `TimerHndlr` man page.

Idle Callbacks

If there are no outstanding events, the Tk makes idle callbacks before waiting for new events to arrive. In general, Tk widgets queue their display routines to be called at idle time. Use `Tcl_DoWhenIdle` to queue an idle callback, and use `Tcl_CancelIdleCall` to remove the callback from the queue. These are described in the `DoWhenIdle` man page.

Sleeping

The `Tcl_Sleep` procedure delays execution for a specified number of milliseconds. It is described in the `Sleep` man page.

Event Loop Implementation

The event loop implementation is described in the `Notifier` man page. As of this writing the event loop is being reimplemented so you will have to consult that man page for an overview of the interface. The general idea is that channel drivers can add events to a queue that is serviced by the event loop.

Input/Output

The Tcl I/O subsystem provides buffering and works with the event loop to provide event-driven I/O. The interface consists of `Tcl_OpenFileChannel`, `Tcl_OpenCommandChannel`, `Tcl_Close`, `Tcl_Read`, `Tcl_Gets`, `Tcl_Write`, `Tcl_Flush`, `Tcl_Seek`, `Tcl_Tell`, `Tcl_Eof`, `Tcl_InputBlocked`, `Tcl_GetChannelOption`, and `Tcl_SetChannelOption`.

I/O Channel Drivers

Tcl provides an extensible I/O subsystem. You can implement a new channel (i.e., for a UDP network socket) by providing a Tcl command to create the channel and registering a set of callbacks that are used by the standard Tcl I/O commands like `puts`, `gets`, and `close`. The interface to channels consists of these procedures, which are described in the `CrtChannel` man page: `Tcl_CreateChannel`, `Tcl_GetChannelInstanceData`, `Tcl_GetChannelType`, `Tcl_GetChannelName`, `Tcl_GetChannelFile`, `Tcl_GetChannelMode`, `Tcl_GetChannelBufferSize`, `Tcl_SetDefaultTranslation`, and `Tcl_SetChannelBufferSize`.

The `Tcl_CreateChannelHandler` and `Tcl_DeleteChannelHandler` are used in the interface to the main event loop. These are described in the `CrtChnlHdlr` man page. The `Tcl_CreateCloseHandler` and `Tcl_DeleteCloseHandler` set and delete a callback that occurs when a channel is closed. These are described in the `CrtCloseHdlr` man page.

The `Tcl_GetFile`, `Tcl_FreeFile` and `Tcl_GetFileInfo` manipulate the operating system handles corresponding to files and sockets. The `Tcl_GetOpenFile` procedure returns a pointer to a standard `FILE` structure for a channel. The `Tcl_GetNotifierData` and `Tcl_SetNotifierData` are used if you implement a new event source for Tcl. These are described in the `GetFile` man page.

The `Tcl_GetStdChannel` and `Tcl_SetStdChannel` are used to manipulate the standard input and standard output channels of your application. These are described in the `GetStdChnl` man page.

Network sockets are created with `Tcl_OpenTcpClient`, and `Tcl_OpenTcpServer`. The `Tcl_MakeTcpClientChannel` provides a platform-independent way to create a Tcl channel structure.

Manipulating File Names

The `Tcl_SplitPath`, `Tcl_JoinPath`, and `Tcl_GetPathType` procedures provide the implementation for the `file split`, `file join`, and `file pathtype` Tcl commands that are used to manipulate file names in a platform-independent manner. They are described in the `SplitPath` man page.

The Tcl_TranslateFileName procedure converts a file name to native syntax. It also expands ~ in file names into user home directories.

Working with Signals

Tcl provides a simple package for safely dealing with signals and other asynchronous events. You register a handler for an event with Tcl_AsyncCreate. When the event occurs, you mark the handler as ready with Tcl_AsyncMark. When the Tcl interpreter is at a safe point, it uses Tcl_AsyncInvoke to call all the ready handlers. Your application can call Tcl_AsyncInvoke, too. Use Tcl_AsyncDelete to unregister a handler. These are described in the Async man page.

Exit Handlers

The Tcl_Exit procedure terminates the application. The Tcl_Finalize procedure cleans up Tcl's memory usage and calls exit handlers, but it does not exit. This is necessary when unloading the Tcl DLL. The Tcl_CreateExitHandler and Tcl_DeleteExitHandler set up callbacks that occur when Tcl_Exit is called. These are described in the Exit man page.

An Overview of the Tk C Library

Parsing Command-Line Arguments

The Tk_ParseArgv procedure parses command-line arguments. This procedure is designed for use by main programs, and it is described by the ParseArgv man page.

The Standard Application Setup

The Tk_Main procedure does the standard setup for your application's main window and event loop. It is described by the TkMain man page. Example 41–8 on page 534 uses Tk_Main.

Creating Windows

The Tk_Init procedure creates the main window for your application. It is described in the TkInit man page. The Tk_CreateWindow and Tk_CreateWindowFromPath are used to create windows for widgets. The actual creation of the window in the X server is delayed until an idle point. You can force the window to be created with Tk_MakeWindowExist or destroy a window with Tk_DestroyWindow. These are described in the CrtMainWin man page.

The Tk_MainWindow procedure returns the handle on the application's main window. It is described in the MainWin man page. The Tk_MapWindow and Tk_UnmapWindow are used to display and withdraw a window, respectively. They are described in the MapWindow man page. The Tk_MoveToplevelWindow call is used to position a top-level window. It is described in the MoveToplev man page.

Translate between window names and the Tk_Window type with Tk_Name, Tk_PathName, and Tk_NameToWindow. These are described in the Name man page. You can convert from an operating system window ID to the corresponding Tk_Window with Tk_IdToWindow procedure, which is described in the IdToWindow man page.

Application Name for Send

The name of the application is defined or changed with Tk_SetAppName. This name is used when other applications send it Tcl commands using the send command. This procedure is described in the SetAppName man page.

Configuring Windows

The configuration of a window includes its width, height, cursor, and so on. Tk provides a set of routines that use Xlib routines to configure a window and also cache the results. This makes it efficient to query these settings because the X server does not need to be contacted. The window configuration routines are Tk_ConfigureWindow, Tk_MoveWindow, Tk_ResizeWindow, Tk_MoveResizeWindow, Tk_SetWindowBorderWidth, Tk_ChangeWindowAttributes, Tk_SetWindowBackground, Tk_SetWindowBackgroundPixmap, Tk_SetWindowBorder, Tk_SetWindowBorderPixmap, Tk_SetWindowColormap, Tk_DefineCursor, and Tk_UndefineCursor. These are described in the ConfigWind man page.

Window Coordinates

The coordinates of a widget relative to the root window (the main screen) are returned by Tk_GetRootCoords. This is described in the GetRootCrd man page. The Tk_GetVRootGeometry procedure returns the size and position of a window relative to the virtual root window. This is described by the GetVRoot man page. The Tk_CoordsToWindow procedure locates the window under a given coordinate. It is described in the CoordToWin man page.

Window Stacking Order

Control the stacking order of windows in the window hierarchy with Tk_RestackWindow. This is described in the Restack man page.

Window Information

Tk keeps lots of information associated with each window, or widget. The following calls are fast macros that return the information without calling the X server: Tk_WindowId, Tk_Parent, Tk_Display, Tk_DisplayName, Tk_ScreenNumber, Tk_Screen, Tk_X, Tk_Y, Tk_Width, Tk_Height, Tk_Changes, Tk_Attributes, Tk_IsMapped, Tk_IsTopLevel, Tk_ReqWidth, Tk_ReqHeight, Tk_InternalBorderWidth, Tk_Visual, Tk_Depth, and Tk_Colormap. These are described in the WindowId man page.

Configuring Widget Attributes

The Tk_ConfigureWidget procedure parses command-line specification of attributes and allocates resources like colors and fonts. Related procedures include Tk_Offset, Tk_ConfigureInfo, Tk_ConfigureValue, Tk_FreeOptions, and these are described in the ConfigWidg man page.

The Tk_GetScrollInfo parses arguments to scrolling commands like the xview and yview widget operations. It is described in GetScroll man page.

Safe Handling of the Widget Data Structure

If your widget makes callbacks to the script level, it might invoke a Tcl command that deletes the widget. To avoid havoc in such situations, a simple reference counting scheme can be implemented for data structures. Call Tk_Preserve to increment the use count, and call Tk_Release to decrement the count. Then, when your widget is destroyed, use the Tk_EventuallyFree procedure to indirectly call the procedure that cleans up your widget data structure. If the data structure is in use, then the cleanup call is delayed until after the last reference to the data structure is released with Tk_Release. These procedures are described in the Preserve man page.

The Selection and Clipboard

Retrieve the current selection with Tk_GetSelection. This is described in the GetSelect man page. Clear the selection with Tk_ClearSelection, which is described in the ClrSelect man page. Register a handler for selection requests with Tk_CreateSelHandler. Unregister the handler with Tk_DeleteSelHandler. These are described in the CrtSelHdlr man page. Claim ownership of the selection with Tk_OwnSelection. This is described in the OwnSelect man page.

Manipulate the clipboard with Tk_ClipboardClear and Tk_ClipboardAppend, which are described in the Clipboard man page.

Event Bindings

The routines that manage bindings are exported by the Tk library so you can manage bindings yourself. For example, the canvas widget does this to implement bindings on canvas items. The procedures are Tk_CreateBindingTable, Tk_DeleteBindingTable, Tk_CreateBinding, Tk_DeleteBinding, Tk_GetBinding, Tk_GetAllBindings,

Tk_DeleteAllBindings, and Tk_BindEvent. These are described in the Bind-Table man page.

Handling Graphic Protocol Errors

You can handle graphic protocol errors by registering a handler with Tk_CreateErrorHandler. Unregister it with Tk_DeleteErrorHandler. These are described in the CrtErrHdlr man page. UNIX has an asynchronous interface so the error will be reported sometime after the offending call was made. You can call the Xlib XSynchronize routine to turn off the asynchronous behavior in order to help you debug.

Using the Resource Database

The Tk_GetOption procedure looks up items in the resource database. This is described in the GetOption man page.

The resource class of a window is set with Tk_SetClass, and the current class setting is retrieved with Tk_Class. These are described in the SetClass man page.

Managing Bitmaps

Tk maintains a registry of bitmaps by name, (e.g., gray50 and questhead). You can define new bitmaps with Tk_DefineBitmap, and you can get a handle on the bitmap from its name with Tk_GetBitmap. Related procedures include Tk_NameOfBitmap, Tk_SizeOfBitmap, Tk_FreeBitmap, and Tk_GetBitmapFromData. These are described in the GetBitmap man page.

Creating New Image Types

The Tk_CreateImageType procedure is used to register the implementation of a new image type. The registration includes several procedures that call back into the implementation to support creation, display, and deletion of images. The interface to an image implementation is described in the CrtImgType man page.

When an image changes, the widgets that display it are notified by calling Tk_ImageChanged. This is described in the ImgChanged man page. The Tk_NameOfImage procedure returns the Tcl name of an image.

Using an Image in a Widget

The following routines support widgets that display images. Tk_GetImage maps from the name to a Tk_Image data structure. Tk_RedrawImage causes the image to update its display. Tk_SizeOfImage tells you how big it is. When the image is no longer in use, call Tk_FreeImage. These are described in the GetImage man page. The Tk_DeleteImage deletes an image. This is described in the DeleteImg man page.

Photo Image Types

One of the image types is photo, which has its own C interface for defining new formats. The job of a format handler is to read and write different image formats such as GIF or JPEG so that the photo image can display them. The Tk_CreatePhotoImageFormat procedure sets up the interface, and it is described in the CrtPhImgFmt man page.

There are several support routines for photo format handlers. The Tk_FindPhoto procedure maps from a photo name to its associated Tk_PhotoHandle data structure. The image is updated with Tk_PhotoBlank, Tk_PhotoPutBlock, and Tk_PhotoPutZoomedBlock. The image values can be obtained with Tk_PhotoGetImage. The size of the image can be manipulated with Tk_PhotoExpand, Tk_PhotoGetSize, and Tk_PhotoSetSize. These support routines are described in the FindPhoto man page.

Canvas Object Support

The C interface for defining new canvas items is exported via the Tk_CreateItemType procedure. The description for a canvas item includes a set of procedures that the canvas widget uses to call the implementation of the canvas item type. The Tk_GetItemTypes returns information about all types of canvas objects. This interface is described in detail in the CrtItemType man page.

There are support routines for the managers of new item types. The CanvTkwin man page describes Tk_CanvasTkwin, Tk_CanvasGetCoord, Tk_CanvasDrawableCoords, Tk_CanvasSetStippleOrigin, Tk_CanvasWindowCoords, and Tk_CanvasEventuallyRedraw. The following procedures help with the generation of postscript: Tk_CanvasPsY, Tk_CanvasPsBitmap, Tk_CanvasPsColor, Tk_CanvasPsFont, Tk_CanvasPsPath, and Tk_CanvasPsStipple. These are described by the CanvPsY man page. If you are manipulating text items directly, then you can use the Tk_CanvasGetTextInfo procedure to get a description of the selection state and other details about the text item. This procedure is described in the CanvTxtInfo man page.

Geometry Management

A widget requests a certain size with the Tk_GeometryRequest procedure. If it draws a border inside that area, it calls Tk_SetInternalBorder. The geometry manager responds to these requests, although the widget may get a different size. These are described in the GeomReq man page.

The Tk_ManageGeometry procedure sets up the relationship between the geometry manager and a widget. This is described in the ManageGeom man page.

The Tk_MaintainGeometry procedure arranges for one window to stay at a fixed position relative to another widget. This is used by the place geometry manager. The relationship is broken with the Tk_UnmaintainGeometry call. These are described in the MaintGeom man page.

The Tk_SetGrid call enables gridded geometry management. The grid is turned off with Tk_UnsetGrid. These are described in the SetGrid man page.

String Identifiers (UIDS)

Tk maintains a database of string values such that a string only appears in it once. The Tk_Uid type refers to such a string. You can test for equality by using the value of Tk_Uid, which is the string's address, as an identifier. A Tk_Uid is used as a name in the various GetByName calls introduced below. The Tk_GetUid procedure installs a string into the registry. It is described in the GetUid man page.

Colors, Colormaps, and Visuals

Use Tk_GetColor and Tk_GetColorByValue to allocate a color. You can retrieve the string name of a color with Tk_NameOfColor. When you are done using a color, you need to call Tk_FreeColor. You can get a graphics context for drawing a particular color with Tk_GCForColor. Colors are shared among widgets, so it is important to free them when you are done using them. These are described in the GetColor man page.

Use Tk_GetColormap and Tk_FreeColormap to allocate and free a colormap. Colormaps are shared, if possible, so you should use these routines instead of the lower-level X routines to allocate colormaps. These are described in the GetClrmap man page.

The window's visual type is set with Tk_SetWindowVisual. This is described in the SetVisual man page. You can get a visual context with Tk_GetVisual.

3D Borders

The three-dimensional relief used for widget borders is supported by a collection of routines described by the 3DBorder man page. The routines are Tk_Get3DBorder, Tk_Draw3DRectangle, Tk_Fill3DRectangle, Tk_Draw3DPolygon, Tk_Fill3DPolygon, Tk_3DVerticalBevel, Tk_3DHorizontalBevel, Tk_SetBackgroundFromBorder, Tk_NameOf3DBorder, Tk_3DBorderColor, Tk_3DBorderGC, and Tk_Free3DBorder.

Widgets use Tk_DrawFocusHighlight to draw their focus highlight. This is described in the DrawFocHlt man page.

Mouse Cursors

Allocate a cursor with Tk_GetCursor and Tk_GetCursorFromData. Map back to the name of the cursor with Tk_NameOfCursor. Release the cursor resource with Tk_FreeCursor. These are described in the GetCursor man page.

Fonts and Text Display

Allocate a font with Tk_GetFont. Get the name of a font with

Tk_NameOfFont. Release the font with Tk_FreeFont. These are described in the GetFont man page.

Once you have a font you can get information about it with Tk_FontId, Tk_GetFontMetrics, and Tk_PostscriptFontName. These are described in the FontId man page.

Tk_MeasureChars, Tk_TextWidth, Tk_DrawChars, and Tk_UnderlineChars measure and display simple strings. They are described in the MeasureChar man page.

Tk_ComputeTextLayout, Tk_FreeTextLayout, Tk_DrawTextLayout, Tk_UnderlineTextLayout, Tk_PointToChar, Tk_CharBbox, Tk_DistanceToTextLayout, Tk_IntersectTextLayout, and Tk_TextLayoutToPostscript measure and display multiline, justified text. They are described in the TextLayout man page.

Graphics Contexts

Allocate a graphics context with Tk_GetGC and free it with Tk_FreeGC. These are described in the GetGC man page.

Allocate a Pixmap

Allocate and free pixmaps with Tk_GetPixmap and Tk_FreePixmap. These are described in the GetPixmap man page.

Screen Measurements

Translate between strings like 4c or 72p and screen distances with Tk_GetPixels and Tk_GetScreenMM. The first call returns pixels (integers), the second returns millimeters as a floating point number. These are described in the GetPixels man page.

Relief Style

Translate between relief styles and names with Tk_GetRelief and Tk_NameOfRelief. These are described in the GetRelief man page.

Text Anchor Positions

Translate between strings and anchor positions with Tk_GetAnchor and Tk_NameOfAnchor. These are described in the GetAnchor man page.

Line Cap Styles

Translate between line cap styles and names with Tk_GetCapStyle and Tk_NameOfCapStyle. These are described in the GetCapStyl man page.

Line Join Styles

Translate between line join styles and names with `Tk_GetJoinStyle` and `Tk_NameOfJoinStyle`. These are described in the `GetJoinStl` man page.

Text Justification Styles

Translate between line justification styles and names with `Tk_GetJustify` and `Tk_NameOfJustify`. These are described in the `GetJustify` man page.

Atoms

An atom is an integer that references a string that has been registered with the X server. Tk maintains a cache of the atom registry to avoid contacting the X server when atoms are used. Use `Tk_InternAtom` to install an atom in the registry, and `Tk_GetAtomName` to return the name given an atom. These are described by the `InternAtom` man page.

X Resource ID Management

Each X resource like a color or pixmap has a resource ID associated with it. The `Tk_FreeXId` call releases an ID so it can be reused. This is used, for example, by routines like `Tk_FreeColor` and `Tk_FreePixmap`. It is described in the `FreeXId` man page.

CHAPTER 43

Writing a Tk Widget in C

This chapter describes in the implementation of a simple clock widget.

A custom widget implemented in C has the advantage of being efficient and flexible. However, it is more work, too. This chapter illustrates the effort by explaining the implementation of a clock widget. It is a digital clock that displays the current time according to a format string. The formatting is done by the `strftime` library procedure, so you can use any format supported by that routine.

This is something you could implement in several lines of Tcl using a label widget, the `clock` command, and `after` for periodic updates. However, the point of the example is to show the basic structure for a Tk widget implemented in C, not how much easier Tcl programming is :-). The implementation of a widget includes:

- A data structure to describe one instance of the widget.
- A class procedure to create a new instance of the widget.
- An instance procedure to operate on an instance of the widget.
- A set of configuration options for the widget.
- A configuration procedure used when creating and reconfiguring the widget.
- An event handling procedure.
- A display procedure.
- Other widget-specific procedures.

The Widget Data Structure

Each widget is associated with a data structure that describes it. Any widget structure will need a pointer to the Tcl interpreter, the Tk window, and the display. The interpreter is used in most of the Tcl and Tk library calls, and it provides a way to call out to the script or query and set Tcl variables. The Tk window is needed for various Tk operations, and the display is used when doing low-level graphic operations. The rest of the information in the data structure depends on the widget. The different types will be explained as they are used in the rest of the code. The structure for the clock widget follows:

Example 43–1 The `Clock` widget data structure.

```
#include "tk.h"

typedef struct {
    Tk_Window tkwin;          /* The window for the widget */
    Display *display;         /* Tk's handle on the display */
    Tcl_Interp *interp;       /* Interpreter of the widget */
    Tcl_Command widgetCmd;    /* clock instance command. */
    /*
     * Clock-specific attributes.
     */
    int borderWidth;          /* Size of 3-D border */
    int relief;               /* Style of 3-D border */
    Tk_3DBorder background;   /* Color for border & background */
    XColor *foreground;       /* Color for the text */
    XColor *highlight;        /* Color for active highlight */
    XColor *highlightBg;      /* Color for neutral highlight */
    int highlightWidth;       /* Thickness of highlight rim */
    Tk_Font tkfont;           /* Font info for the text */
    char *format;             /* Format for time string */
    /*
     * Graphic contexts and other support.
     */
    GC textGC;                /* Text graphics context */
    Tk_TimerToken token;      /* Periodic callback handle*/
    char *clock;              /* Pointer to the clock string */
    int numChars;             /* length of the text */
    int textWidth;            /* in pixels */
    int textHeight;           /* in pixels */
    int padX;                 /* Horizontal padding */
    int padY;                 /* Vertical padding */
    int flags;                /* Flags defined below */
} Clock;
/*
 * Flag bit definitions.
 */
#define REDRAW_PENDING  0x1
#define GOT_FOCUS       0x2
#define TICKING         0x4
```

The Widget Class Command

The Tcl command that creates an instance of a widget is known as the *class command*. In our example, the `clock` command creates a clock widget. The command procedure for `clock` follows. The procedure allocates the `Clock` data structure. It registers an event handler that gets called when the widget is exposed, resized, or gets focus. It creates a new Tcl command that operates on the widget. Finally, it calls `ClockConfigure` to set up the widget according to the attributes specified on the command line and the default configuration specifications.

Example 43–2 The `ClockCmd` command procedure.

```
int
ClockCmd(clientData, interp, argc, argv)
    ClientData clientData;/* Main window of the app */
    Tcl_Interp *interp; /* Current interpreter. */
    int argc;           /* Number of arguments. */
    char **argv;        /* Argument strings. */
{
    Tk_Window main = (Tk_Window) clientData;
    Clock *clockPtr;
    Tk_Window tkwin;

    if (argc < 2) {
        Tcl_AppendResult(interp, "wrong # args: should be \"",
            argv[0], " pathName ?options?\"", (char *) NULL);
        return TCL_ERROR;
    }
    tkwin = Tk_CreateWindowFromPath(interp, main,
            argv[1], (char *) NULL);
    if (tkwin == NULL) {
        return TCL_ERROR;
    }
    /*
     * Set resource class.
     */
    Tk_SetClass(tkwin, "Clock");
    /*
     * Allocate and initialize the widget record.
     */
    clockPtr = (Clock *) ckalloc(sizeof(Clock));
    clockPtr->tkwin = tkwin;
    clockPtr->display = Tk_Display(tkwin);
    clockPtr->interp = interp;
    clockPtr->borderWidth = 0;
    clockPtr->highlightWidth = 0;
    clockPtr->relief = TK_RELIEF_FLAT;
    clockPtr->background = NULL;
    clockPtr->foreground = NULL;
    clockPtr->highlight = NULL;
    clockPtr->highlightBg = NULL;
    clockPtr->tkfont = NULL;
    clockPtr->textGC = None;
```

```
    clockPtr->token = NULL;
    clockPtr->clock = NULL;
    clockPtr->format = NULL;
    clockPtr->numChars = 0;
    clockPtr->textWidth = 0;
    clockPtr->textHeight = 0;
    clockPtr->padX = 0;
    clockPtr->padY = 0;
    clockPtr->flags = 0;
    /*
     * Register a handler for when the window is
     * exposed or resized.
     */
    Tk_CreateEventHandler(clockPtr->tkwin,
       ExposureMask|StructureNotifyMask|FocusChangeMask,
       ClockEventProc, (ClientData) clockPtr);
    /*
     * Create a Tcl command that operates on the widget.
     */
    clockPtr->widgetCmd = Tcl_CreateCommand(interp,
       Tk_PathName(clockPtr->tkwin),
       ClockInstanceCmd,
       (ClientData) clockPtr, (void (*)()) NULL);
    /*
     * Parse the command line arguments.
     */
    if (ClockConfigure(interp, clockPtr,
            argc-2, argv+2, 0) != TCL_OK) {
       Tk_DestroyWindow(clockPtr->tkwin);
       return TCL_ERROR;
    }
    interp->result = Tk_PathName(clockPtr->tkwin);
    return TCL_OK;
}
```

The Widget Instance Command

For each instance of a widget a new command is created that operates on that widget. This is called the *widget instance command*. Its name is the same as the Tk pathname of the widget. In the clock example, all that is done on instances is to query and change their attributes. Most of the work is done by `Tk_ConfigureWidget` and `ClockConfigure`, which are shown in the next section. The `ClockInstanceCmd` command procedure is shown in the next example:

Example 43–3 The `ClockInstanceCmd` command procedure.

```
static int
ClockInstanceCmd(clientData, interp, argc, argv)
   ClientData clientData;/* A pointer to a Clock struct */
   Tcl_Interp *interp; /* The interpreter */
   int argc;           /* The number of arguments */
```

```
    char *argv[];           /* The command line arguments */
{
    Clock *clockPtr = (Clock *)clientData;
    int result = TCL_OK;
    char c;
    int len;

    if (argc < 2) {
        Tcl_AppendResult(interp, "wrong # args: should be \"",
            argv[0], " option ?arg arg ...?\"", (char *) NULL);
        return TCL_ERROR;
    }
    c = argv[1][0];
    len = strlen(argv[1]);
    if ((c == 'c') && (strncmp(argv[1], "cget", len) == 0)
            && (len >= 2)) {
        if (argc != 3) {
            Tcl_AppendResult(interp,
                    "wrong # args: should be \"",
                argv[0], " cget option\"",
                (char *) NULL);
            return TCL_ERROR;
        }
        result = Tk_ConfigureValue(interp, clockPtr->tkwin,
             configSpecs, (char *) clockPtr, argv[2], 0);
    } else if ((c == 'c') && (strncmp(argv[1], "configure", len)
                == 0) && (len >= 2)) {
        if (argc == 2) {
            /*
             * Return all configuration information.
             */
            result = Tk_ConfigureInfo(interp, clockPtr->tkwin,
                configSpecs, (char *) clockPtr,
                (char *) NULL,0);
        } else if (argc == 3) {
            /*
             * Return info about one attribute, like cget.
             */
            result = Tk_ConfigureInfo(interp, clockPtr->tkwin,
                configSpecs, (char *) clockPtr, argv[2], 0);
        } else {
            /*
             * Change one or more attributes.
             */
            result = ClockConfigure(interp, clockPtr, argc-2,
                argv+2,TK_CONFIG_ARGV_ONLY);
        }
    } else {
        Tcl_AppendResult(interp, "bad option \"", argv[1],
            "\": must be cget, configure, position, or size",
            (char *) NULL);
        return TCL_ERROR;
    }
    return result;
}
```

Configuring and Reconfiguring Attributes

When the widget is created or reconfigured, then the implementation needs to allocate the resources implied by the attribute settings. Each clock widget uses some colors and a font. These are described by graphics contexts that parameterize operations. Instead of specifying every possible attribute in graphics calls, a graphics context is initialized with a subset of the parameters and this is passed into the graphic commands. The context can specify the foreground and background colors, clip masks, line styles, and so on. The clock widget allocates a graphics context once and reuses it each time the widget is displayed.

There are two kinds of color resources used by the widget. The focus highlight and the text foreground are simple colors. The background is a `Tk_3DBorder`, which is a set of colors used to render 3D borders. The background color is specified in the attribute, and the other colors are computed based on that color. The code uses `Tk_3DBorderColor` to map back to the original color for use in the background of the widget.

After the resources are set up, a call to redisplay the widget is scheduled for the next idle period. This is a standard idiom for Tk widgets. It means that you can create and reconfigure a widget in the middle of a script, and all the changes only result in one redisplay. The `REDRAW_PENDING` flag is used to ensure that only one redisplay is queued up at any time. The `ClockConfigure` procedure is shown in the next example:

Example 43–4 `ClockConfigure` allocates resources for the widget.

```
static int
ClockConfigure(interp, clockPtr, argc, argv, flags)
    Tcl_Interp *interp;/* For return values and errors */
    Clock *clockPtr; /* The per-instance data structure */
    int argc;        /* Number of valid entries in argv */
    char *argv[];    /* The command line arguments */
    int flags;       /* Tk_ConfigureWidget flags */
{
    XGCValues gcValues;
    GC newGC;

    /*
     * Tk_ConfigureWidget parses the command line arguments
     * and looks for defaults in the resource database.
     */
    if (Tk_ConfigureWidget(interp, clockPtr->tkwin,
            configSpecs, argc, argv, (char *) clockPtr, flags)
                != TCL_OK) {
        return TCL_ERROR;
    }
    /*
     * Give the widget a default background so it doesn't get
     * a random background between the time it is initially
     * displayed by the X server and we paint it
     */
```

```
    Tk_SetWindowBackground(clockPtr->tkwin,
       Tk_3DBorderColor(clockPtr->background)->pixel);
    /*
     * Set up the graphics contexts to display the widget.
     * The context is used to draw off-screen pixmaps,
     * so turn off exposure notifications.
     */
    gcValues.background =
       Tk_3DBorderColor(clockPtr->background)->pixel;
    gcValues.foreground = clockPtr->foreground->pixel;
    gcValues.font = Tk_FontId(clockPtr->tkfont);
    gcValues.graphics_exposures = False;
    newGC = Tk_GetGC(clockPtr->tkwin,
       GCBackground|GCForeground|GCFont|GCGraphicsExposures,
       &gcValues);
    if (clockPtr->textGC != None) {
        Tk_FreeGC(clockPtr->display, clockPtr->textGC);
    }
    clockPtr->textGC = newGC;

    /*
     * Determine how big the widget wants to be.
     */
    ComputeGeometry(clockPtr);

    /*
     * Set up a call to display ourself.
     */
    if ((clockPtr->tkwin != NULL) &&
            Tk_IsMapped(clockPtr->tkwin)
          && !(clockPtr->flags & REDRAW_PENDING)) {
       Tk_DoWhenIdle(ClockDisplay, (ClientData) clockPtr);
       clockPtr->flags |= REDRAW_PENDING;
    }
    return TCL_OK;
}
```

Specifying Widget Attributes

Several of the fields in the `Clock` structure are attributes that can be set when the widget is created or reconfigured with the `configure` operation. The default values, their resource names, and their class names are specified with an array of `Tk_ConfigSpec` records, and this array is processed by the `Tk_ConfigureWidget` operation. The specifications for the `Clock` structure are given in the next example.

Example 43–5 Configuration specs for the clock widget.

```
static Tk_ConfigSpec configSpecs[] = {
   {TK_CONFIG_BORDER, "-background", "background",
      "Background", "light blue",
```

```
        Tk_Offset(Clock, background), TK_CONFIG_COLOR_ONLY},
    {TK_CONFIG_BORDER, "-background", "background",
        "Background", "white", Tk_Offset(Clock, background),
        TK_CONFIG_MONO_ONLY},
    {TK_CONFIG_SYNONYM, "-bg", "background", (char *) NULL,
        (char *) NULL, 0, 0},

    {TK_CONFIG_SYNONYM, "-bd", "borderWidth", (char *) NULL,
        (char *) NULL, 0, 0},
    {TK_CONFIG_PIXELS, "-borderwidth", "borderWidth",
        "BorderWidth","2", Tk_Offset(Clock, borderWidth), 0},
    {TK_CONFIG_RELIEF, "-relief", "relief", "Relief",
        "ridge", Tk_Offset(Clock, relief), 0},

    {TK_CONFIG_COLOR, "-foreground", "foreground",
        "Foreground", "black", Tk_Offset(Clock, foreground),
        0},
    {TK_CONFIG_SYNONYM, "-fg", "foreground", (char *) NULL,
        (char *) NULL, 0, 0},

    {TK_CONFIG_COLOR, "-highlightcolor", "highlightColor",
        "HighlightColor", "red", Tk_Offset(Clock, highlight),
        TK_CONFIG_COLOR_ONLY},
    {TK_CONFIG_COLOR, "-highlightcolor", "highlightColor",
         "HighlightColor", "black",
        Tk_Offset(Clock, highlight),TK_CONFIG_MONO_ONLY},
    {TK_CONFIG_COLOR, "-highlightbackground",
        "highlightBackground", "HighlightBackground",
        "light blue", Tk_Offset(Clock, highlightBg),
        TK_CONFIG_COLOR_ONLY},
    {TK_CONFIG_COLOR, "-highlightbackground",
        "highlightBackground", "HighlightBackground",
        "black", Tk_Offset(Clock, highlightBg),
        TK_CONFIG_MONO_ONLY},
    {TK_CONFIG_PIXELS, "-highlightthickness",
        "highlightThickness","HighlightThickness",
        "2", Tk_Offset(Clock, highlightWidth), 0},

    {TK_CONFIG_PIXELS, "-padx", "padX", "Pad",
        "2", Tk_Offset(Clock, padX), 0},
    {TK_CONFIG_PIXELS, "-pady", "padY", "Pad",
        "2", Tk_Offset(Clock, padY), 0},

    {TK_CONFIG_STRING, "-format", "format", "Format",
        "%H:%M:%S", Tk_Offset(Clock, format), 0},
    {TK_CONFIG_FONT, "-font", "font", "Font",
        "Courier 18",
         Tk_Offset(Clock, tkfont), 0},

    {TK_CONFIG_END, (char *) NULL, (char *) NULL,
         (char *) NULL, (char *) NULL, 0, 0}
};
```

The initial field is a type, such as TK_CONFIG_BORDER. Colors and borders will be explained shortly. The next field is the command-line flag for the attribute, (e.g., -background). Then comes the resource name and the class name. The default value is next, (e.g., light blue). The offset of a structure member is next, and the Tk_Offset macro is used to compute this offset. The last field is a bitmask of flags. The two used in this example are TK_CONFIG_COLOR_ONLY and TK_CONFIG_MONO_ONLY, which restrict the application of the configuration setting to color and monochrome displays, respectively. You can define additional flags and pass them into Tk_ConfigureWidget if you have a family of widgets that share most, but not all, of their attributes. The tkButton.c file in the Tk sources has an example of this.

Table 43–1 lists the correspondence between the configuration type passed Tk_ConfigureWidget and the type of the associated field in the widget data structure. The complete details are given in the ConfigWidg man page. Some of the table entries reference a Tk procedure like Tk_GetCapStyle. In those cases an integer-valued field takes on a few limited values that are described in the man page for that procedure.

Table 43–1 Configuration flags and corresponding C types.

TK_CONFIG_ACTIVE_CURSOR	Cursor
TK_CONFIG_ANCHOR	Tk_Anchor
TK_CONFIG_BITMAP	Pixmap
TK_CONFIG_BOOLEAN	int (0 or 1)
TK_CONFIG_BORDER	Tk_3DBorder *
TK_CONFIG_CAP_STYLE	int (see Tk_GetCapStyle)
TK_CONFIG_COLOR	XColor *
TK_CONFIG_CURSOR	Cursor
TK_CONFIG_CUSTOM	
TK_CONFIG_DOUBLE	double
TK_CONFIG_END	(signals end of options)
TK_CONFIG_FONT	Tk_Font
TK_CONFIG_INT	int
TK_CONFIG_JOIN_STYLE	int (see Tk_GetJoinStyle)
TK_CONFIG_JUSTIFY	Tk_Justify
TK_CONFIG_MM	double
TK_CONFIG_PIXELS	int
TK_CONFIG_RELIEF	int (see Tk_GetRelief)

Table 43–1 Configuration flags and corresponding C types. (Continued)

TK_CONFIG_STRING	char *
TK_CONFIG_SYNONYM	(alias for other option)
TK_CONFIG_UID	Tk_Uid
TK_CONFIG_WINDOW	Tk_Window

Displaying the Clock

There are two parts to a widget's display. First the size must be determined. This is done at configuration time, and then that space is requested from the geometry manager. When the widget is later displayed, it should use the `Tk_Width` and `Tk_Height` calls to find out how much space it was actually allocated by the geometry manager. The next example shows `ComputeGeometry`.

Example 43–6 `ComputeGeometry` computes the widget's size.

```
static void
ComputeGeometry(Clock *clockPtr)
{
    int width, height;
    Tk_FontMetrics fm;          /* Font size information */
    struct tm *tmPtr;           /* Time info split into fields */
    struct timeval tv;          /* BSD-style time value */
    int bd;                     /* Padding from borders */
    char clock[1000];           /* Displayed time */

    /*
     * Get the time and format it to see how big it will be.
     */
    gettimeofday(&tv, NULL);
    tmPtr = localtime(&tv.tv_sec);
    strftime(clock, 1000, clockPtr->format, tmPtr);
    if (clockPtr->clock != NULL) {
        ckfree(clockPtr->clock);
    }
    clockPtr->clock = ckalloc(1+strlen(clock));
    clockPtr->numChars = strlen(clock);

    bd = clockPtr->highlightWidth + clockPtr->borderWidth;
    Tk_GetFontMetrics(clockPtr->tkfont, &fm);
    height = fm.linespace + 2*(bd + clockPtr->padY);
    Tk_MeasureChars(clockPtr->tkfont, clock,
        clockPtr->numChars, 0, 0, &clockPtr->textWidth);
    width = clockPtr->textWidth + 2*(bd + clockPtr->padX);

    Tk_GeometryRequest(clockPtr->tkwin, width, height);
    Tk_SetInternalBorder(clockPtr->tkwin, bd);
}
```

Finally we get to the actual display of the widget! The routine is careful to check that the widget still exists and is mapped. This is important because the redisplay is scheduled asynchronously. The current time is converted to a string. This uses the POSIX library procedures `gettimeofday`, `localtime`, and `strftime`. There might be different routines on your system. The string is painted into a pixmap, which is a drawable region of memory that is off-screen. After the whole display has been painted, the pixmap is copied into on-screen memory to avoid flickering as the image is cleared and repainted. The text is painted first, then the borders. This ensures that the borders overwrite the text if the widget has not been allocated enough room by the geometry manager.

This example allocates and frees the off-screen pixmap for each redisplay. This is the standard idiom for Tk widgets. They temporarily allocate the off-screen pixmap each time they redisplay. In the case of a clock that updates every second, it might be reasonable to permanently allocate the pixmap and store its pointer in the `Clock` data structure. Make sure to reallocate the pixmap if the size changes.

After the display is finished, another call to the display routine is scheduled to happen in one second. If you were to embellish this widget, you might want to make the uptime period a parameter. The `TICKING` flag is used to note that the timer callback is scheduled. It is checked when the widget is destroyed so that the callback can be canceled. The next example shows `ClockDisplay`.

Example 43–7 The `ClockDisplay` procedure.

```
static void
ClockDisplay(ClientData clientData)
{
   Clock *clockPtr = (Clock *)clientData;
   Tk_Window tkwin = clockPtr->tkwin;
   GC gc;                  /* Graphics Context for highlight
*/
   Tk_TextLayout layout;   /* Text measurement state */
   Pixmap pixmap;          /* Temporary drawing area */
   int offset, x, y;       /* Coordinates */
   int width, height;      /* Size */
   struct tm *tmPtr;       /* Time info split into fields */
   struct timeval tv;      /* BSD-style time value */

   /*
    * Make sure the clock still exists
    * and is mapped onto the display before painting.
    */
   clockPtr->flags &= ~(REDRAW_PENDING|TICKING);
   if ((clockPtr->tkwin == NULL) || !Tk_IsMapped(tkwin)) {
      return;
   }
   /*
    * Format the time into a string.
    * localtime chops up the time into fields.
    * strftime formats the fields into a string.
```

```
 */
gettimeofday(&tv, NULL);
tmPtr = localtime(&tv.tv_sec);
strftime(clockPtr->clock, clockPtr->numChars+1,
   clockPtr->format, tmPtr);
/*
 * To avoid flicker when the display is updated, the new
 * image is painted in an offscreen pixmap and then
 * copied onto the display in one operation. Allocate the
 * pixmap and paint its background.
 */
pixmap = Tk_GetPixmap(clockPtr->display,
   Tk_WindowId(tkwin), Tk_Width(tkwin),
   Tk_Height(tkwin), Tk_Depth(tkwin));
Tk_Fill3DRectangle(tkwin, pixmap,
   clockPtr->background, 0, 0, Tk_Width(tkwin),
   Tk_Height(tkwin), 0, TK_RELIEF_FLAT);

/*
 * Paint the text first.
 */
layout = Tk_ComputeTextLayout(clockPtr->tkfont,
   clockPtr->clock, clockPtr->numChars, 0,
   TK_JUSTIFY_CENTER, 0, &width, &height);
x = (Tk_Width(tkwin) - width)/2;
y = (Tk_Height(tkwin) - height)/2;
Tk_DrawTextLayout(clockPtr->display, pixmap,
   clockPtr->textGC, layout, x, y, 0, -1);

/*
 * Display the borders, so they overwrite any of the
 * text that extends to the edge of the display.
 */
if (clockPtr->relief != TK_RELIEF_FLAT) {
   Tk_Draw3DRectangle(tkwin, pixmap,
      clockPtr->background,
      clockPtr->highlightWidth,
      clockPtr->highlightWidth,
      Tk_Width(tkwin) - 2*clockPtr->highlightWidth,
      Tk_Height(tkwin) - 2*clockPtr->highlightWidth,
      clockPtr->borderWidth, clockPtr->relief);
}
if (clockPtr->highlightWidth != 0) {
   GC gc;

   /*
    * This GC is associated with the color, and Tk caches
    * the GC until the color is freed. Hence no freeGC.
    */

   if (clockPtr->flags & GOT_FOCUS) {
      gc = Tk_GCForColor(clockPtr->highlight, pixmap);
   } else {
      gc = Tk_GCForColor(clockPtr->highlightBg, pixmap);
   }
```

```
        Tk_DrawFocusHighlight(tkwin, gc,
            clockPtr->highlightWidth, pixmap);
    }
    /*
     * Copy the information from the off-screen pixmap onto
     * the screen, then delete the pixmap.
     */

    XCopyArea(clockPtr->display, pixmap, Tk_WindowId(tkwin),
        clockPtr->textGC, 0, 0, Tk_Width(tkwin),
        Tk_Height(tkwin), 0, 0);
    Tk_FreePixmap(clockPtr->display, pixmap);

    /*
     * Queue another call to ourselves. The rate at which
     * this is done could be optimized.
     */
    clockPtr->token = Tk_CreateTimerHandler(1000,
        ClockDisplay, (ClientData)clockPtr);
    clockPtr->flags |= TICKING;
}
```

The Window Event Procedure

Each widget registers an event handler for expose and resize events. If it implements a focus highlight, it also needs to be notified of focus events. If you have used other toolkits, you may expect to register callbacks for mouse and keystroke events too. You should not need to do that. Instead, use the regular Tk bind facility and define your bindings in Tcl. That way they can be customized by applications.

Example 43–8 The `ClockEventProc` handles window events.

```
static void
ClockEventProc(ClientData clientData, XEvent *eventPtr)
{
    Clock *clockPtr = (Clock *) clientData;
    if ((eventPtr->type == Expose) &&
        (eventPtr->xexpose.count == 0)) {
            goto redraw;
    } else if (eventPtr->type == DestroyNotify) {
        Tcl_DeleteCommandFromToken(clockPtr->interp,
                clockPtr->widgetCmd);
        /*
         * Zapping the tkwin lets the other procedures
         * know we are being destroyed.
         */
        clockPtr->tkwin = NULL;

        if (clockPtr->flags & REDRAW_PENDING) {
            Tk_CancelIdleCall(ClockDisplay,
```

```
                (ClientData) clockPtr);
            clockPtr->flags &= ~REDRAW_PENDING;
        }
        if (clockPtr->flags & TICKING) {
            Tk_DeleteTimerHandler(clockPtr->token);
            clockPtr->flags &= ~TICKING;
        }
        /*
         * This results in a call to ClockDestroy.
         */
        Tk_EventuallyFree((ClientData) clockPtr,
            ClockDestroy);
    } else if (eventPtr->type == FocusIn) {
        if (eventPtr->xfocus.detail != NotifyPointer) {
            clockPtr->flags |= GOT_FOCUS;
            if (clockPtr->highlightWidth > 0) {
                goto redraw;
            }
        }
    } else if (eventPtr->type == FocusOut) {
        if (eventPtr->xfocus.detail != NotifyPointer) {
            clockPtr->flags &= ~GOT_FOCUS;
            if (clockPtr->highlightWidth > 0) {
                goto redraw;
            }
        }
    }
    return;
redraw:
    if ((clockPtr->tkwin != NULL) &&
            !(clockPtr->flags & REDRAW_PENDING)) {
        Tk_DoWhenIdle(ClockDisplay, (ClientData) clockPtr);
        clockPtr->flags |= REDRAW_PENDING;
    }
}
```

Final Cleanup

When a widget is destroyed you need to free up any resources it has allocated. The resources associated with attributes are cleaned up by `Tk_FreeOptions`. The others you must take care of yourself. The `ClockDestroy` procedure is called as a result of the `Tk_EventuallyFree` call in the `ClockEventProc`. The `Tk_EventuallyFree` procedure is part of a protocol that is needed for widgets that might get deleted when in the middle of processing. Typically the `Tk_Preserve` and `Tk_Release` procedures are called at the beginning and end of the widget instance command to mark the widget as being in use. `Tk_EventuallyFree` will wait until `Tk_Release` is called before calling the cleanup procedure. The next example shows `ClockDestroy`:

Example 43–9 The `ClockDestroy` cleanup procedure.

```
static void
ClockDestroy(clientData)
 ClientData clientData;/* Info about entry widget. */
{
   register Clock *clockPtr = (Clock *) clientData;

   /*
    * Free up all the stuff that requires special handling,
    * then let Tk_FreeOptions handle resources associated
    * with the widget attributes.
    */
   if (clockPtr->textGC != None) {
      Tk_FreeGC(clockPtr->display, clockPtr->textGC);
   }
   if (clockPtr->clock != NULL) {
      ckfree(clockPtr->clock);
   }
   if (clockPtr->flags & TICKING) {
      Tk_DeleteTimerHandler(clockPtr->token);
   }
   if (clockPtr->flags & REDRAW_PENDING) {
      Tk_CancelIdleCall(ClockDisplay,
         (ClientData) clockPtr);
   }
   /*
    * This frees up colors and fonts and any allocated
    * storage associated with the widget attributes.
    */
   Tk_FreeOptions(configSpecs, (char *) clockPtr,
      clockPtr->display, 0);
   ckfree((char *) clockPtr);
}
```

PART VII

Changes

Part VII describes the changes between versions of Tcl and Tk.

Chapter 44 has notes about porting your scripts to Tcl 7.4 and Tk 4.0. Chapter 45 describes changes in Tcl 7.5 and Tk 4.1. Chapter 46 describes changes in Tcl 7.6 and Tk 4.2. The Tcl and Tk version numbers were unified in the next release, Tcl/Tk 8.0, which is described in Chapter 47.

Chapter 48 describes the Tcl/Tk Plug-in for Web browsers. The first version of the plug-in used Tcl 7.7 and Tk 4.3, but no release of these versions was made outside the plug-in. The second version of the plug-in is based on Tcl/Tk 8.0.

CHAPTER 44

Tcl 7.4/Tk 4.0

This chapter has notes about upgrading your application to Tcl 7.4 and Tk 4.0 from earlier versions of Tk such as Tk 3.6. This includes notable new features that you may want to take advantage of as well as things that need to be fixed because of incompatible changes.

Porting your scripts from any of the Tk version 3 releases is easy. Not that many things have changed. The sections in this chapter summarize what has changed in Tk 4.0 and what some of the new commands are.

wish

The *wish* shell no longer requires a `-file` (or `-f`) argument, so you can drop this from your script header lines. This flag is still valid, but no longer necessary.

The class name of the application is set from the name of the script file instead of always being `Tk`. If the script is `/usr/local/bin/foobar`, then the class is set to `Foobar`, for example.

Obsolete Features

Several features that were replaced in previous versions are now completely unsupported.

The variable that contains the version number is `tk_version`. The ancient (version 1) `tkVersion` is no longer supported.

Button widgets no longer have `activate` and `deactivate` operations. Instead, configure their `state` attribute.

Menus no longer have enable and disable operations. Instead, configure their state attribute.

The cget Operation

All widgets support a cget operation that returns the current value of the specified configuration option. The following two commands are equivalent:

```
lindex [$w config option] 4
$w cget option
```

Nothing breaks with this change, but you should enjoy this feature.

Input Focus Highlight

Each widget can have an input focus highlight, which is a border that is drawn in color when the widget has the input focus. This border is outside the border used to draw the 3D relief for widgets. It has the pleasant visual effect of providing a little bit of space around widgets, even when they do not have the input focus. The addition of the input focus highlight does not break anything, but it changes the appearance of your interfaces a little. In particular, the highlight on a canvas obscures objects that are at its edge. See page 447 for a description of the generic widget attributes related to the input focus highlight.

Bindings

The hierarchy of bindings has been fixed so that it is actually useful to define bindings at each of the global (i.e., all), class, and instance levels. The new bindtags command defines the order among these sources of binding information. You can also introduce new binding classes, (e.g., InsertMode) and bind things to that class. Use the bindtags command to insert this class into the binding hierarchy. The order of binding classes in the bindtags command determines the order in which bindings are triggered. Use break in a binding command to stop the progression, or use continue to go on to the next level.

```
bindtags $w [list all Text InsertMode $w]
```

The various Request events have gone away: CirculateRequest, ConfigureRequest, MapRequest, and ResizeRequest. The Keymap event is gone, too.

Extra modifier keys are ignored when matching events. While you can still use the Any wild card modifier, it is no longer necessary. The Alt and Meta modifiers are set up in a general way so they are associated with the Alt_L, Alt_R, Meta_L, and Meta_R keysyms.

Chapter 23 describes bindings starting at page 285.

Scrollbar Interface

The interface between scrollbars and the scrollable widgets has changed. Happily, the change is transparent to most scripts. If you hook your scrollbars to widgets in the straightforward way, the new interface is compatible. If you use the `xview` and `yview` widget commands directly, however, you might need to modify your code. The old interface still works, but there are new features of these operations that give you even better control. You can also query the view state so you do not need to watch the scroll `set` commands to keep track of what is going on. Finally, scrollable widgets are constrained so that the end of their data remains stuck at the bottom (right) of their display. In most cases, nothing is broken by this change. Chapter 27 describes the scrollbar protocol starting at page 347.

`pack info`

Version 3 of Tk introduced a new syntax for the `pack` command, but the old syntax was still supported. This continues to be true in nearly all cases except the `pack info` command. If you are still using the old packer format, you should probably take this opportunity to convert to the new packer syntax.

The problem with `pack info` is that its semantics changed. The new operation used to be known as `pack newinfo`. In the old packer, `pack info` returned a list of all the slaves of a window and their packing configuration. Now `pack info` returns the packing configuration for a particular slave. You must first use the `pack slaves` command to get the list of all the slaves and then use the (new) `pack info` to get their configuration information. Chapter 20 describes the pack geometery manager starting at page 252.

Focus

The focus mechanism has been cleaned up to support different focus windows on different screens. The `focus` command takes a `-displayof` argument. Tk remembers which widget inside each toplevel has the focus. When the focus is given to a toplevel by the window manager, Tk automatically assigns focus to the right widget. The `-lastfor` argument queries which widget in a toplevel will get the focus by this means. Chapter 33 describes focus starting at page 434.

The `focus default` and `focus none` commands are no longer supported. There is no real need for `focus default` anymore, and `focus none` can be achieved by passing an empty string to the regular `focus` command.

The `tk_focusFollowsMouse` procedure changes from the default explicit focus model where a widget must claim the focus to one in which moving the mouse into a widget automatically gives it the focus.

The `tk_focusNext` and `tk_focusPrev` procedures implement keyboard traversal of the focus among widgets. Most widgets have bindings for `<Tab>` and `<Shift-Tab>` that cycle the focus among widgets.

The `send` Command

The `send` command has been changed so that it does not time out after 5 seconds, but instead waits indefinitely for a response. Specify the `-async` option if you do not want to wait for a result. You can also specify an alternate display with the `-displayof` option. Chapter 37 describes `send` starting on page 478.

The name of an application can be set and queried with the new `tk appname` command. Use this instead of `winfo name "."`.

Because of the changes in the `send` implementation, it is not possible to use `send` between Tk 4.0 applications and earlier versions.

Internal Button Padding

Buttons and labels have new defaults for the amount of padding around their text. There is more padding now, so your buttons get bigger if you use the default `padX` and `padY` attributes. The old defaults were one pixel for both attributes. The new defaults are `3m` for `padX` and `1m` for `padY`, which map into three pixels and ten pixels on my display.

There is a difference between buttons and the other button-like widgets. An extra two pixels of padding is added, in spite of all `padX` and `padY` settings in the case of simple buttons. If you want your checkbuttons, radiobuttons, menubuttons, and buttons all the same dimensions, you'll need two extra pixels of padding for everything but simple buttons.

Radiobutton Value

The default value for a radiobutton is no longer the name of the widget. Instead, it is an empty string. Make sure you specify a `-value` option when setting up your radiobuttons.

Entry Widget

The `scrollCommand` attribute changed to `xScrollCommand` to be consistent with other widgets that scroll horizontally. The `view` operation changed to the `xview` operation for the same reason. Chapter 28 describes the entry widget starting on page 353.

The `delete` operation has changed the meaning of the second index so that the second index refers to the character just after the affected text. The selection operations have changed in a similar fashion. The `sel.last` index refers to the character just after the end of the selection, so deleting from `sel.first` to `sel.last` still works. The default bindings have been updated, of course, but if you have custom bindings you must fix them.

Menus

The menu associated with a menubutton must be a child widget of the menubutton. Similarly, the menu for a cascade menu entry must be a child of the menu.

The `@y` index for a menu always returns a valid index, even if the mouse cursor is outside any entry. In this case, it simply returns the index of the closest entry, instead of `none`.

The `selector` attribute is now `selectColor`.

The `postcascade` operation posts the menu of a `cascade` entry:

```
$menu postcascade index
```

The insert operation adds a menu entry before a specified entry:

```
$menu insert index type options...
```

Chapter 24 describes menus starting at page 312.

Listboxes

Listboxes changed quite a bit in Tk 4.0. See Chapter 29 for all the details. There are now four Motif-like selection styles, and two of these support disjoint selections. The `tk_listboxSingleSelect` procedure no longer exists. Instead, configure the `selectMode` attribute of the listbox. A listbox has an active element, which is drawn with an underline. It is referenced with the `active` index keyword.

The selection commands for listboxes have changed. Change:

```
$listbox select from index1
$listbox select to index2
```

To:

```
$listbox select anchor index1
$listbox select set anchor index2
```

The `set` operation takes two indices, and `anchor` is a valid index, which typically corresponds to the start of a selection.

You can selectively clear the selection, and query if there is a selection in the listbox. The command to clear the selection has changed. It requires one or two indices. Change:

```
$listbox select clear
```

To:

```
$listbox select clear 0 end
```

No `geometry` Attribute

The frame, toplevel, and listbox widgets no longer have a `geometry` attribute. Use the `width` and `height` attributes instead. The `geometry` attribute got confused with geometry specifications for top-level windows. The use of `width` and `height` is more consistent. Note that for listboxes the `width` and `height` are in terms of lines and characters, while for frames and toplevels it is in screen units.

Text Widget

The tags and marks of the text widgets have been cleaned up a bit, justification and spacing are supported, variable tab stops can be defined, and you can embed widgets in the text display.

A mark now has a gravity, either left or right, that determines what happens when characters are inserted at the mark. With right gravity you get the old behavior: the mark gets pushed along by the inserted text by sticking to the right-hand character. With left gravity it remains stuck. The default is right gravity. The `mark gravity` operation changes it.

When text is inserted, it only picks up tags that are present on both sides of the insert point. Previously it would inherit the tags from the character to the left of the insert mark. You can also override this default behavior by supplying tags to the insert operation.

The widget scan operation supports horizontal scrolling. Instead of using marks like `@y`, you need a mark like `@x,y`.

For a description of the new features, see Chapter 30.

Color Attributes

Table 44–1 lists the names of the color attributes that changed. These attributes are described in more detail in Chapter 35 starting at page 452.

Table 44–1 Changes in color attribute names.

Tk 3.6	Tk4.0
`selector`	`selectColor`
`Scrollbar.activeForeground`	`Scrollbar.activeBackground`
`Scrollbar.background`	`troughColor`
`Scrollbar.foreground`	`Scrollbar.background`
`Scale.activeForeground`	`Scale.activeBackground`
`Scale.background`	`troughColor`
`Scale.sliderForeground`	`Scale.background`
`(did not exist)`	`highlightBackground`
`(did not exist)`	`highlightColor`

Color Allocation and `tk colormodel`

In Tk 3.6 color allocations could fail if the colormap was full. In this case Tk would revert its colormodel to monochrome and only use black and white. The `tk colormodel` command was used to query or set the colormodel. In Tk 4.0 color allocations do not fail. Instead, the closest possible color is allocated. Because of this, the `tk colormodel` operation is no longer supported. Use the `winfo visual` command to find out the characteristics of your display, which is described on page 456.

Canvas `scrollincrement`

The canvas widget changed the `scrollIncrement` attribute to a pair of attributes: `xScrollIncrement` and `yScrollIncrement`. The default for these is now one-tenth the width (height) of the canvas instead of one pixel. Scrolling by one page scrolls by nine-tenths of the canvas display.

The Selection

The selection support has been generalized in Tk 4.0 to allow use of other selections such as the `CLIPBOARD` and `SECONDARY` selections. The changes do not break anything, but you should check out the new `clipboard` command. Some other toolkits, notably OpenLook, can only paste data from the clipboard. Chapter 32 describes the selection starting at page 423.

The `bell` Command

The `bell` command rings the bell associated with the terminal. You need to use the *xset* program to modify the parameters of the bell such as volume and duration. This command is described on page 344.

CHAPTER 45

Tcl 7.5/Tk 4.1

Tk 4.1 is notable for its cross-platform support. Your Tk scripts can run on Windows, Macintosh, as well as UNIX. The associated Tcl release, 7.5, saw significant changes in event-driven I/O, network sockets, and multiple interpreters.

Cross-platform support, network sockets, multiple Tcl interpreters, and an enhanced `foreach` command are the highlights of Tcl 7.5 and Tk 4.1.

Cross-Platform Scripts

Cross-platform support lets a Tcl/Tk script run unchanged on UNIX, Windows, and Macintosh. However, you could still have platform dependencies in your program. The most obvious is if your script executes other programs or uses C-level extensions. These need to be ported for your script to continue to work.

File Name Manipulation

File naming conventions vary across platforms. New file operations were added to help you manipulate file names in a platform-independent manner. These are the `file join`, `file split`, and `file pathtype` operations, which are described on page 95. Additional commands to copy, delete, and rename files were added in Tcl 7.6

Newline Translations

Windows and Macintosh have different conventions for representing the end of line in files. These differences are handled automatically by the new I/O subsystem. However, you can use the new `fconfigure` command described on page 181 to control the translations.

The `tcl_platform` Variable

In practice you may need a small amount of platform-specific code. The `tcl_platform` array holds information about the computer and operating system that your script is running on. This array is described on page 153. You can use a script file with the name of the platform to isolate all your platform-specific code. The following command sources either `unix.tcl`, `windows.tcl`, or `macintosh.tcl` from your script library:

```
source [file join $lib $tcl_platform(platform).tcl]
```

The `console` Command

The Windows and Macintosh versions of *wish* have a built-in console. The commands you enter in the console are evaluated in the main Tcl interpreter, but the console is really implemented in another Tcl interpreter to avoid conflicts. You can show and hide the console with the `console` command, which is described on page 26.

The `clock` Command

The `clock` command eliminates the need to `exec date` to get the time of day in Tcl. The equivalent is:

```
clock format [clock seconds]
```

The `format` operation takes an optional format string that lets you control the date and time string. There is also `clock scan` to parse clock values, and `clock clicks` to get high resolution clock values. The `clock` command is described on page 145.

The `load` Command

The `load` command supports shared libraries (i.e., DLLs) that implement new Tcl commands in compiled code. With this feature the preferred way to package extensions is as a shared library. This eliminates the need to compile custom versions of *wish* if you use extensions. The details about creating shared libraries are described on page 523. For example, you could load the `Tix` library with:

```
load libtix.so Tix
```

The `info` command added two related operations, `sharedlibextention` and `nameofexecutable`, which are described on page 152.

The package Command

The package command provides an alternate way to organize script libraries. It also supports extensions that are added with the load command. The package command supports a provide/require model where packages are provided by scripts in a library, and your application specifies what it needs with package require commands. The package facility supports multiple versions of a package, if necessary. Packages are described on page 136.

Multiple foreach loop variables

This is one of my favorite features. The foreach command supports multiple loop variables and multiple value lists. This means you can assign values to multiple variables during each loop iteration. The values can come from the same list, or from lists that are processed in parallel. This is described on page 69. For example, you can iterate through the contents of an array with:

```
foreach {name value} [array get arrName] {
    # arrName($name) is $value
}
```

Event Loop Moves from Tk to Tcl

To support network sockets, the event loop was moved from Tk to Tcl. This means that the after and update commands are now part of Tcl. The fileevent command was added to support non-blocking I/O. The vwait command was added to Tcl, and this is equivalent to the tkwait variable command. Event-driven I/O is described in Chapter 15 starting on page 177.

The tkerror command has been replaced by bgerror. This is the procedure that is called when an error occurs while processing an event. Backwards compatibility is provided if you already define tkerror. These procedures are described on page 162.

Network Sockets

The socket command provides access to TCP/IP sockets. There are C APIs to define new *channels*, and there are extensions that provide UDP and other protocols. Chapter 16 describes sockets starting on page 186. Example 37–4 on page 483 uses sockets as a replacement for the Tk send command.

info hostname

The info hostname command was added to find out your host identifier.

The `fconfigure` Command

The best way to use sockets is with event-driven I/O. The `fileevent` command provides part of the solution. You also need to be able to control the blocking behavior and buffering modes of sockets. The `fconfigure` command lets you do this, and more. You can also control the newline translation modes and query socket-specific settings. The `fconfigure` command is described on page 181.

Multiple Interpreters and Safe-Tcl

Chapter 17 describes the new `interp` command and the Safe-Tcl security mechanism. You can create multiple Tcl interpreters in your application and control them with the `interp` command. You create command aliases so that the interpreters can exchange Tcl commands. If an interpreter is created in a safe mode, then its set of Tcl commands is restricted so that its scripts cannot harm your computer or application. However, with aliases you can give the untrusted scripts limited access to resources.

The `grid` Geometry Manager

Chapter 21 describes the new `grid` geometry manager that provides a table-like metaphor for arranging widgets. Like `pack`, `grid` is constraint-based so the grid automatically adjusts if widgets change size or if widgets are added and deleted. The `grid` command was influenced by the `blt_table` geometry manager, but it is a whole new implementation.

The Text Widget

A handful of new operations were added to the text widget. The `dump` operation provides a way to get all the information out of the widget, including information about tags, marks, and embedded windows. The `mark next` and `mark previous` operations let you search for marks. The `tag prevrange` is the complement of the existing `tag nextrange` operation.

The Entry Widget

The `bbox` operation was added to the entry widget. This is used to refine the bindings that do character selection and set the input cursor.

CHAPTER 46

Tcl 7.6/Tk 4.2

Tk 4.2 saw improvements in its cross-platform support., including virtual events, additions to the file command, improvements to the exec command on Windows, and the addition of common dialogs for choosing colors and selecting files. The grid geometry manager was rebuilt to improve its layout algorithm.

Grid saw a major rewrite for Tk 4.2 to improve its layout algorithm. Cross-platform scripts were enhanced by the addition of standard dialogs and virtual events. Tcl 7.6 saw improvements in exec and pipelines on Windows. The Macintosh version got a significant performance boost from a new memory allocator.

More file Operations

The file command was rounded out with copy, rename, delete, and mkdir operations. These operations are described on page 97.

Virtual Events

The new event command defines virtual events like <<Cut>> <<Copy>> and <<Paste>>. These virtual events map to different physical events on different platforms. For example, <<Copy>> is <Control-c> on Windows and <Command-c> on Macintosh. You can write your scripts in terms of virtual events, and you can define new virtual events for your application. You can also use the event command to generate events for testing purposes. Virtual events and the event command are described starting at page 297.

Standard Dialogs

Several standard dialogs were added to Tk. These let you display alerts, prompt the user, choose colors, and select files using dialogs that are implemented in native look for each platform. For example, to ask the user a yes/no question:

```
tk_messageBox -type yesno \
     -message "Ok to proceed?" \
     -icon question
=> yes
```

To open an existing file:

```
set file [tk_getOpenFile]
```

The standard dialogs are described in Chapter 33 starting at page 431.

New `grid` Geometry Manager

The `grid` geometry manager was overhauled to improve its layout algorithm, and there were several user-visible changes. The weights on rows and columns that affect resize behavior were changed from floating point values to integers. A `-pad` row and column attribute was added to provide padding for a whole row or column. The `columnconfigure` and `rowconfigure` operations now return the current settings if given no arguments. There are two new `grid` operations. The `update` operation forces an update of the grid layout. The `remove` operation removes a widget from the grid but remembers all its grid settings so it is easy to put it back into the grid later.

Macintosh `unsupported1` Command

The `unsupported1` command provides access to different window styles on the Macintosh. If supported it might be a `style` operation in the `wm` command, but it is Macintosh specific so it is not fully supported. However, you can use it to get several different styles of Macintosh windows. This command is described on page 335.

CHAPTER 47

Tcl/Tk 8.0

Tcl 8.0 includes an on-the-fly byte code compiler that improves performance of scripts from 2 to 20 times depending on what commands they use. The Tk version number was set to match Tcl. Tk 8.0 uses native buttons, menus, menubars, and scrollbars. Font objects allow flexible font handling in a platform-independent way.

Tcl 8.0 added a byte-code compiler that improves performance dramatically. The compiler is transparent to Tcl scripts so you do not have to do anything special to take advantage of it. The other main addition to Tcl is support of binary data. It is now safe to read binary data into Tcl variables, and new commands convert between strings and binary representations.

Tk 8.0 has native look and feel on UNIX, Windows, and Macintosh. This is due to native buttons, native menus, native scrollbars, and a new cross-platform menu bar facility. A new cross-platform font facility improves the font support. Tk also has support for application embedding, which is used in the Web browser plug-in described in Chapter 48.

The Tcl Compiler

The Tcl Compiler is an *on-the-fly* compiler that is virtually transparent to Tcl scripts. The compiler translates a script to byte codes the first time it evaluates it. If the script is evaluated again, such as in a loop or in a procedure body, then the byte codes are executed and the translation step is saved. If a procedure is redefined, then the compiler discards any translated byte codes for it.

The compiler uses a dual-ported object model instead of the simple string-based model used in earlier versions of Tcl. The dual-ported objects hold a string value and a native representation of that string such as an integer, double-precision floating point value, or compiler byte codes. This makes it possible to save translations between strings and the native representations. The object model is described in Chapter 41 starting at page 528.

The performance improvement for your application will depend on what features you use. Math expressions and list accesses have improved a lot. Overall you should expect a factor of 2 speedup, and I have heard reports of 10 and 20 times improvement in parts of some applications.

Compile-Time Errors

The compiler catches some sorts of errors earlier than the pure interpreted version. The first time a compiler runs a procedure, it translates the whole thing to byte codes first. If there are syntax errors at the end of the procedure it prevents any code in the procedure from running.

A similar problem occurs with list data. If a string is not a perfect list, then the list commands will fail when parsing it, even if they do not use the damaged part of the list. For example, `lindex` used to process only enough of a list to find the requested element. In Tcl 8.0 the whole list is converted into a native representation. Errors at the end of a list will prevent you from getting elements at the beginning. This is mainly an issue when you use list operations on arbitrary input data.

Binary String Support

Tcl now supports binary data. This means that an embedded NULL byte no longer terminates a value. Instead, Tcl keeps a byte count for its string objects. This is facilitated by the switch from simple strings to dual-ported objects.

As of this writing the binary data support is not complete. There are some commands that still treat strings as null terminated. By the time 8.0 goes final, the support should be in place everywhere.

The `binary format` and `binary scan` commands support conversions between binary data and strings. These are described on page 49. The `unsupported0` command was improved and became the `fcopy` command, which is described on page 197.

Namespaces

Chapter 14 describes the Tcl namespace facility that partitions the global scope for variables and procedures. Namespaces are optional. Simple scripts can avoid them, but larger applications can use them for structuring.

Safe-Tcl

Hidden commands were added to the Safe-Tcl security model. Instead of removing unsafe commands from an interpreter, they are hidden. The master can invoke hidden commands inside a slave. This is necessary so that the command sees the correct context. This adds new operations to the `interp` command: `invokehidden`, `hide`, `expose`, and `hidden`. Hidden commands are described on page 209.

Initialization of a safe interpreter with a *safe base* that supports auto loading and a standard `exit` alias has been abstracted into a Tcl interface. The `safe::interpCreate` and `safe::interpInit` procedures create or initialize a slave with the safe base. The `safe::interpDelete` procedure cleans up. The safe base is described on page 212.

To support the `Trusted` security policy, the `interp marktrusted` command was added. This promotes an unsafe interpreter back into a trusted one. Of course, only the master can do this.

New `lsort`

The `lsort` command was reimplemented. The new implementation is reentrant, which means you can use `lsort` inside a sorting function called by `lsort`. New options have lessened the need for custom sorting procedures, too. The `-dictionary` option sorts cases together and it handles numbers better. The `-index` option sorts lists on a key field. These are described on page 58.

No `tcl_precision` Variable

The `tcl_precision` variable is no longer used when formatting the results of expressions. Full precision is now used all the time.

Year 2000 Convention

The `clock` command now implements the following standard convention for two-digit year names:

70-99 map to 1970 - 1999.
00-38 map to 2000 - 2038.
The remaining two-digit years are undefined.

Http Package

A Tcl implementation of the HTTP/1.0 protocol was added to the Tcl script library. The `http::geturl` command is described on page 201.

Serial Line I/O

Support for serial line devices was added to `fconfigure`. The `-mode` argument specifies the baud rate, parity setting, and the number of data and stop bits. The `-mode` option to `fconfigure` is described on page 183.

Windows has some special device names that always connect you to the serial line devices when you use `open`. They are `com1` and `com2`. UNIX has names for serial devices in `/dev`. Interactive applications can open the current terminal with `/dev/tty`.

As of this writing there is no way to open serial devices on the Macintosh. I expect a new `serial` command for this purpose, or possibly a flag to `open`.

Platform-Independent Fonts

A platform-independent font naming system was added in Tk 8.0. Names like `times 10 bold` are interpreted on all platforms. The `font` command lets you create font objects that can be associated with widgets. The `font metrics` command returns detailed size information. The `font` command is described on page 471.

The `tk scaling` Command

The `tk scaling` command queries or sets the mapping from pixels to points. Points are used with fonts, and points and other screen measures are used in the canvas. The `tk scaling` command is described on page 498.

Application Embedding

Tk supports application embedding. Frames and toplevels have a `-container` attribute that indicates they embed another application. This is necessary for geometry management and focus protocols. Frames and toplevels have a `-use` parameter that embeds them into an existing window. *Wish* also takes a `-use` command-line argument. Embedding is described on page 335 and 606.

Native Menus and Menubars

Tk 8.0 has a native menubar mechanism. You define a menu and associate it with a toplevel. On the Macintosh this menu appears along the top of the screen when the window is activated. On Windows and UNIX the menubar appears along the top of the window. This facility is described on page 313.

Tear-off menus now track any changes to the menu they were created from. As part of this, the `-transient` attribute was replaced with a `-type` attribute.

You can create multicolumn menus with the `-columnbreak` attribute.

CDE Border Width

On UNIX, the default border width changed from 2 to 1 to match the CDE look and feel.

Native Buttons and Scrollbars

Buttons, menus, and scrollbars are native widgets on Windows and Macintosh. This goes a long way to providing your applications with a native look. The bindings on the text and entry widgets were also tuned to match platform standard bindings. See page 248 for an example of the same Tk program on all platforms.

Buttons on all platforms support a `-default` attribute, which has three values: `active`, `normal`, and `disabled`. The `active` state displays as a default button. The `normal` state displays like a regular button, but leaves room for the highlight used in the `active` state. The `disabled` state, which is the default, may be smaller. You still need to program a key binding that invokes the button.

Images in Text Widgets

The text widget supports embedded images. They work much like the embedded windows but provide a more efficient way to embed images. These are described on page 382.

No Errors from `destroy`

The `destroy` command used to raise an error if the window did not exist. Now it does not.

`grid rowconfigure`

The `grid columnconfigure` and `rowconfigure` commands take an argument that specifies a row or column. This value can be a list:

```
grid columnconfigure {0 3} -weight 1
```

Late Breaking News

This book first went to press after Tcl/Tk 8.0a2, the 2nd alpha release, and just before the first beta release. I tried to document the last major changes to Tcl/Tk 8.0 such as namespaces, binary I/O, and menu enhancements that appeared in the beta and final versions. However, I could not anticipate every change made before Tcl/Tk 8.0 went final. The rest of this section summarizes updates made in the 2nd and later reprints. Please consult http://www.beedub.com/book/ for errata and news about Tcl/Tk updates.

`namespace eval`

The `eval` keyword is required when putting code inside namespaces. Otherwise there is ambiguity between the other namespace operations (e.g., `import`) and namespaces with the same name. This affects several of the examples in Chapter 14.

`http` Package

A 2nd version of the http package was created that uses the ::http namespace. The functionality is the same, but the names of the procedures changed. See page 201.

Safe-Tcl Safe Base

The safe base was completely redone. It uses the ::safe namespace and no longer supports the use of package require to request security policies. See page 212.

Object Reference Counts

The initial reference count of an object is now zero, not one. This affected the implementation of `Tcl_Invoke` shown in Example 41–9 on page 538

The Web Browser Plug-in

The plug-in changed a lot. The mechanism to load security policies was shifted from the safe base into the plug-in. Instead of using `package require`, a new `policy` command is used by slaves. The set of security policies also changed. As of this printing the plug-in is just going into is 2.0beta2 release. The best documentation will probably be on the web at `http://sunscript.sun.com/plugin/`.

CHAPTER 48

Safe-Tk and the Browser Plug-In

This chapter describes Safe-Tk that lets untrusted scripts display and manipulate graphical user interfaces. The main application of Safe-Tk is the Tcl/Tk plug-in for Web browsers like Netscape Navigator and Internet Explorer.

Safe-Tk supports network applets that display user interfaces. The main vehicle for Safe-Tk is a plug-in for Netscape Navigator and Internet Explorer. The plug-in supports Tcl applets, or *Tclets*, that are downloaded from the Web server and execute inside a window in a Web browser. For the most part Tcl/Tk applications can run unchanged in the plug-in. However, security policies place some restrictions on Tclets. The plug-in supports multiple security policies, so Tclets can do a variety of interesting things in a safe manner.

There are two versions of the browser plug-in. Version 1 uses Tcl 7.7 and Tk 4.3, which were not released by themselves. Instead of providing *wish* and *tclsh*, only the shared libraries needed by the plug-in were distributed. These versions of Tcl and Tk had support for application embedding and some improvements in Safe-Tcl that later appeared in Tcl/Tk 8.0.

Version 2 of the plug-in uses Tcl/Tk 8.0. You can configure the plug-in to use an existing *wish* application to host the Tcl applets, or the plug-in can load the Tcl/Tk shared libraries and everything runs in the browser process. You can use a custom *wish* that has extensions built in or dynamically loaded. This gives intranet applications of the plug-in the ability to access databases and other services that are not provided by the Tcl/Tk core. With the security policy mechanism you can still provide mediated access to these resources. This chapter describes how to set up the plug-in.

Tk in Child Interpreters

A child interpreter starts out with the core Tcl commands. It does not include Tk or any other extensions that might be available to the parent interpreter. This is true whether or not the child interpreter is declared safe. You add extensions to child interpreters by using a form of the `load` command that specifies an interpreter:

```
load {} Tk child
```

Normally, `load` takes the name of the library file that contains the extension. In this case, the Tk package is a *static package* that is already linked into the program (e.g., *wish* or the plug-in), so the file name is the empty string. The `load` command calls the Tk initialization procedure to register all the Tcl commands provided by Tk.

Embedding Tk Windows

By default, a slave interpreter that loads Tk gets a new top-level window. Tk 8.0 supports a `-use` command line option that directs Tk to use an existing window as dot. You can use this to embed an application within another, but typically it is used with child interpreters. To pass `-use` to a child interpreter, you need to define the `argv` variable inside that interpreter before you load Tk:

```
interp eval child [list set argv [list -use [winfo id win]]
interp eval child [list set argc 2]
```

Passing `-use` to a safe interpreter is handled automatically by the `safe::loadTk` procedure. If `safe::loadTk` is not given `-use`, it adds a wrapper around the slave that is very similar to the one in Example 48–1.

Example 48–1 Embedding a Tk window.

```
# Create a toplevel that indicates it contains an applet
toplevel .embed
frame .embed.but ; pack .embed.but -side top -fill x
label .embed.but.l -text "Untrusted Applet" -anchor w \
	-bg red -fg white
button .embed.but.quit -text Quit \
	-command {::safe::interpDelete safetk}
pack .embed.but.quit -side right
pack .embed.but.l -side top -fill x

# Create the frame in which to embed the applet
set rim [frame .embed.rim -bd 4 -bg red]
pack $rim -fill both -expand true
set embed [frame $rim.child -container true]
pack $embed -fill both -expand true

# Create a safe interpreter and load Tk into it
::safe::interpCreate safetk
::safe::loadTk safetk -use [winfo id $embed]
```

Safe-Tk Restrictions

When you load an extension into a safe interpreter the extension is initialized with its `SafeInit` procedure. If there is no `SafeInit`, then the `load` fails. The `Tk_SafeInit` procedure hides several Tk commands. Primarily these are hidden to prevent *denial of service* attacks against the main process. For example, if a child interpreter did a global `grab` and never released it, all input would be forever directed to the child. Table 48–1 lists the Tk commands hidden by default from a safe interpreter. The Tcl commands that are hidden are listed on page 207.

Table 48–1 Tk commands omitted from safe interpreters.

`bell`	Ring the terminal bell.
`clipboard`	Access the `CLIPBOARD` selection.
`grab`	Direct input to a specified widget.
`menu`	Create and manipulate menus, because menus need `grab`.
`selection`	Manipulate the selection.
`send`	Execute a command in another Tk application.
`tk`	Set the application name.
`tk_chooseolor`	Color choice dialog.
`tk_getOpenFile`	File open dialog.
`tk_getSaveFile`	File save dialog.
`tk_messageBox`	Simple dialog boxes.
`toplevel`	Creates a detached window.
`wm`	Control the window manager.

The Browser Plug-In

The HTML `<EMBED>` tag is used to put various objects into a Web page, including a Tcl program. For example:

```
<EMBED src=eval.tcl width=400 height=300>
```

The `width` and `height` are interpreted by the plug-in as the size of the embedded window. The `src` specifies the URL of the program. These parameter names (e.g., `width`) are case sensitive and should be lowercase. In the above example, `eval.tcl` is a relative URL, so it should be in the same directory as the HTML file that has the `EMBED` tag. The window size is fixed in the browser, which is different than normal toplevels in Tk. The plug-in turns off geometry propagation on your main window so your Tclet stays the size allocated.

The parameters in the `<EMBED>` tag are available to the Tcl program in the `embed_args` variable, which is an array with the parameter names as the index values. For example, the string for a ticker-tape Tclet can be passed in the `<EMBED>` tag as the `string` parameter, and the Tclet will use `$embed_args(string)` as the value to display:

```
<EMBED src=ticker.tcl width=400 height=50
   string="Hello World">
```

Note that HTML tag parameters are case sensitive. Your Tclet may want to map all the parameter names to lowercase for convenience:

```
foreach {name value} [array get embed_args] {
   set embed_args([string tolower $name]) $value
}
```

The `plugin` array has `version`, `patchLevel`, and `release` elements that identify the version and release date of the plugin implementation. Note that version 1.0 of the plug-in does not support security policy mechanism described later, and that the 2.0 version changed substantially between the alpha2 and beta1 releases.

Plug-in example home page.

The plug-in home page is a great place to find Tclet examples. There are several plug-ins done by the Tcl/Tk team at Sunlabs, plus links to a wide variety of Tclets done on the Net. There is also a tutorial page about writing Tclets.

```
http://sunscript.sun.com/tcl/plugin/
http://sunscript.sun.com/tcl/plugintut/
```

I wrote a cute little plug-in that calculates the effective wheel diameter of multigear bicycles. Brian Lewis explained to me the concept and how important this information is to bicycle enthusiasts. I put together a Tclet that displays the gear combinations on a Tk canvas and lets you change the number of gears and their size. You can find the result at:

```
http://www.beedub.com/plugin/bike.html
```

Setting Up the Plug-In

There are plug-in versions for UNIX, Windows, and Macintosh. The installation scripts take care of installing the plug-in in the correct locations, which are described in the next sections about each platform. The plug-in and the security policies that are distributed with it will continue to be updated. You should get the latest version from the Tcl/Tk Web site, `http://sunscript.sun.com/tcl/plugin/`. If that URL changes, you can find an up-to-date pointer under `http://www.beedub.com/book/`. The plug-in may already be installed at your site. Bring up the `About Plug-ins` dialog under `Help` in your browser to see if the Tcl/Tk plug-in is listed.

The plug-in is composed of the following parts, although the location of these files varies somewhat among platforms:

- The plug-in shared libraries (i.e., DLLs). The Web browser dynamically loads the plug-in implementation when it needs to execute a Tclet embedded in a Web page. There is a standard directory that the browser scans for the libraries that implement plug-ins.
- The Tcl/Tk script libraries. The plug-in needs the standard script libraries that come with Tcl and Tk, plus it has its own scripts that complete its implementation. Each platform has a plug-in script directory with these subdirectories: `tcl8.0`, `tk8.0`, `plugin`, `policies`, and `trust`. The plug-in implementation is in the `plugin` directory.
- The security policies. These are kept in a `policies` directory that is a peer of the Tcl script library.
- The trust map. This defines what Tclets can use which security policies. This is in a `trust` directory that is a peer of the Tcl script library.
- Local hooks. Local customization is supported by two hooks, `siteInit` and `siteSafeInit`. The `siteInit` procedure is called from the plug-in when it first loads, and `siteSafeInit` is called when each applet is initialized. It is called with the name of the slave interpreter and the list of arguments from the `<EMBED>` tag. You can provide these as scripts that get loaded from the `auto_path` of the master interpreter. Chapter 12 describes how to manage script libraries found in the `auto_path`. The plug-in also sources a personal start up script in which you can define `siteInit` and `siteSafeInit`. This script is `~/.pluginrc` on UNIX and `plugin/tclplugin.rc` on Windows and Macintosh.

The plug-in is configured to use *wish* instead of linking Tk into the Web browser. This only works on UNIX and Windows. You can define the `TCL_PLUGIN_WISH` environment variable to be the pathname of the executable *wish*. It must be a Tk 8.0 or greater version of *wish*, which supports embedding. There are two advantages to using *wish*. First, it means the embedded Tcl application runs in a separate process from the Web browser, which can be more efficient. Second, it allows for custom *wish* applications that have extensions built in or dynamically loaded. If you want to run Tk directly in the browser process, define the `TCL_PLUGIN_INPROCESS` variable to 1.

If you set the `TCL_PLUGIN_CONSOLE` environment variable to 1, then a console window is opened when a Tclet starts. This console lets you evaluate Tcl commands in the master interpreter. In particular, if you do `interp slaves` you can find out the names of the safe interpreters used for Tclets. You can use other facilities of the `interp` command to examine and manipulate the Tclets. The `interp` command is described on page 204. If the value of `TCL_PLUGIN_CONSOLE` is something else, it is treated as a file name and that file is sourced in order to define the console.

UNIX Configuration

Netscape looks in each user's `~/.netscape/plugins` for the shared libraries that implement plug-ins. It also looks in a `plugins` directory under its main directory, which will vary from site to site. You can define a search path for plug-ins with the `NXP_PLUGIN_PATH` environment variable. The plug-in script library is in `~/.tclplug/2.0/plugin`. You can change this default location by setting the `TCL_PLUGIN_DIR` environment variable. Once the plug-in finds its script library, it assumes the Tcl and Tk script directories, the security policies, and the trust map are in peer directories.

Windows Configuration

The default location for plug-ins is in the `PLUGINS` directory of the Netscape installation. The Tcl/Tk plug-in also works in Internet Explorer from the same location. The script libraries are found under `C:\TCLPLUG\2.0`. You can change this location by setting the registry variable `Software\Sun\Tcl Plugin\2.0\Directory`.

Macintosh Configuration

As of this writing the Macintosh plug-in is only available in the 1.0 version. The 2.0 version is expected in the next few months.

Security Policies and Browser Plug-in

Version 2 of the plug-in uses the safe base described on page 212. If a Tclet wants a non-default security policy, it requests one with the `policy` command:

```
policy name
```

The policies that are part of the standard plug-in distribution are described below. The `home`, `inside`, and `outside` policies all provide network access. They differ in what set of hosts are accessible.

- `home`. This provides a `socket` and `fconfigure` command that are limited to connecting to the host from which the Tclet was downloaded. You can specify an empty string for the host argument to `socket` to connect back to the home host. This policy also supports `open` and `file delete` that are similar to the `Tempfile` policy shown in Example 17–9 on page 216. This provides limited local storage that is inside a directory that is, by default, private to the Tclet. Files in the private directory persist after the Tclet exits, so it can maintain long term state. Tclets from the same server can share the directory by putting the same `prefix=`*`partialurl`* argument in their `<EMBED>` tag. The *`partialurl`* must be a prefix of the Tclet's URL. Finally, the `home` policy automatically provides a `browser` package that is described later.
- `inside`. This is just like the `home` policy, except the site administrator controls a table of hosts and ports to which untrusted slaves can connect with `socket`. A similar set of tables control what URLs can be accessed with the `browser` package. This is similar to the `Safesock` policy is shown in Example 17–8 on page 214. The set of hosts is supposed to be inside the firewall.

The files used by this policy are distinct from those used by the home and outside policies. This is true even if Tclets try to share by using the `prefix=`*`partialurl`* parameter.

- `outside`. This is just like the `home` and `inside` policies, except that the set of hosts is configured to be outside the firewall. The files used by this policy are distinct from those used by the `home` and `inside` policies.
- `trusted`. This policy restores all features of Tcl and Tk. This policy lets you launch all your Tcl and Tk applications from the Web browser. The default trust map settings do not allow this for any Tclet. The trust map is described briefly on page 612.
- `javascript`. This policy provides a superset of the browser package that lets you invoke arbitrary Javascript and to write HTML directly to frames. This does not have the limited socket or temporary file access that the `home`, `inside`, and `outside` policies have. However, the `javascript` policy places no restrictions on the URLs you can fetch, plus it lets Tclets execute Javascript, which may have its own security risks. The default trust map settings do not allow this for any Tclet.

The Browser Package

The `browser` package is bundled with several of the security policies. It makes many features of the Web browser accessible to Tclets. They can fetch URLs and display HTML in frames. However, the `browser` package has some risks associated with it. HTTP requests can be used to transmit information, so a Tclet using the policy could leak sensitive information if it can fetch a URL outside the firewall. To avoid information leakage, the `inside`, `outside`, and `home` policies restrict the URL that can be fetched with `browser::geturl`. Table 48–2 lists the aliases defined by the `browser` package.

Table 48–2 Aliases defined by the `browser` package.

`browser::status` *`string`*	Display *`string`* in the browser status window.
`browser::geturl` *`url`* `?`*`options`*`?`	Fetch *`url`*, if allowed by the security policy. The *`options`* are described in Table 48–3.
	The remaining functions are only available in the `javascript` security policy.
`browser::openFrame` *`name`*	Open a new or existing HTML frame.
`browser::closeFrame` *`name`*	Close the channel to an HTML frame.
`browser::writeFrame` *`name`* *`html`*	Write HTML to a frame. Writing <p> or causes a flush of data to the page.
`browser::javascript` *`script`* `?`*`callback`*`?`	Invoke the Javascript *`script`* and return the result as a string. The *`callback`* is called with two parameters: the *`script`* and the results of the script.

The `browser::geturl` function is compatible with the `http::geturl` function described on page 198. It returns a token that represents the transaction, and you use that token as the name of a state array as described on page 199. However, `browser::geturl` uses the browser's built-in functions, so it understands proxies and supports `ftp:`, `http:`, and `file:` urls. In addition, `browser::geturl` can display the results in a browser frame if you give it a `-frame` argument. Some options to `http::geturl` may not be fully supported and `browser::geturl` will just ignore them. The full set of options are not defined as of this writing. The known options to `browser::geturl` are described in Table 48–3

Table 48–3 Options to the `browser::geturl` procedure.

`-command` *`callback`*	Call *`callback`* when the transaction completes. The callback gets the token returned by `browser::geturl`.
`-frame` *`frame`*	Display the url data in the named frame. If *`frame`* does not exist, a new top-level browser window is created.
`-progress` *`command`*	Call *`command`* after each block is copied from *`url`*. It gets called with three parameters: the *`url totalsize currentsize`*
`-query` *`codedstring`*	Issue a POST request with the *`codedstring`* form data.

Configuring Security Policies

Each security policy has a configuration file associated with it. For example, the `outside` policy uses the file `outside.cfg` file in the `policies` directory to specify what hosts and ports are accessible to Tclets using the outside policy. For the `inside` and `outside` policies, the configuration files are similar in spirit to the `safesock` array used to configure the `Safesock` security policy shown on page 214. There are a set of allowed hosts and ports, and a set of excluded hosts. The excluded hosts are an exception list. If a host matches the include set but also matches the exclude set, it is not accessible. There is an include and exclude set for URLs that affect `browser::geturl`. The settings from the `Tempfile` policy shown on page 216 are also part of the `home`, `inside`, and `outside` configuration files. The configuration files are well commented, and you should read through them to learn about the configuration options for each security policy.

In addition, there is a permission list, or *trust map*, that controls what Tclets are allowed to use which security policies. Currently there are just three ways to specify access: no Tclets can use a policy, all Tclets can use a policy, or Tclets whose URL matches an allowed set can use a policy. This map is defined in the `trust/trust.cfg` file. The URL matching is defined in `trust/trusteDurl.cfg`. Eventually the plug-in will allow certificate based authentication of Tclets so you can restrict security policies based their certificates.

Notes

The Web browser plug-in is going to continue to develop and improve, especially in the area of security policies. This chapter reflects the features of the 2.0 beta 1 release, and there will surely be some changes as the plug-in stabilizes. Consult these web pages for news about new releases of the plug-in:

```
http://sunscript.sun.com/tcl/plugin/
http://www.beedub.com/plugin/
```

Index

A

D

E

F

G

H

I

J

K

Q

R

T

U

V

W

X

Z

LICENSE AGREEMENT AND LIMITED WARRANTY

READ THE FOLLOWING TERMS AND CONDITIONS CAREFULLY BEFORE OPENING THIS CD PACKAGE, *PRACTICAL PROGRAMMING IN TCL AND TK, 2ND EDITION.* THIS LEGAL DOCUMENT IS AN AGREEMENT BETWEEN YOU AND PRENTICE-HALL, INC. (THE "COMPANY"). BY OPENING THIS SEALED CD PACKAGE, YOU ARE AGREEING TO BE BOUND BY THESE TERMS AND CONDITIONS. IF YOU DO NOT AGREE WITH THESE TERMS AND CONDITIONS, DO NOT OPEN THE CD PACKAGE. PROMPTLY RETURN THE UNOPENED CD PACKAGE AND ALL ACCOMPANYING ITEMS TO THE PLACE YOU OBTAINED THEM FOR A FULL REFUND OF ANY SUMS YOU HAVE PAID.

1. **GRANT OF LICENSE:** In consideration of your purchase of this book, and your agreement to abide by the terms and conditions of this Agreement, the Company grants to you a nonexclusive right to use and display the copy of the enclosed software program (hereinafter the "SOFTWARE") on a single computer (i.e., with a single CPU) at a single location so long as you comply with the terms of this Agreement. The Company reserves all rights not expressly granted to you under this Agreement.

2. **OWNERSHIP OF SOFTWARE:** You own only the magnetic or physical media (the enclosed CD) on which the SOFTWARE is recorded or fixed, but the Company and the software developers retain all the rights, title, and ownership to the SOFTWARE recorded on the original CD copy(ies) and all subsequent copies of the SOFTWARE, regardless of the form or media on which the original or other copies may exist. This license is not a sale of the original SOFTWARE or any copy to you.

3. **COPY RESTRICTIONS:** This SOFTWARE and the accompanying printed materials and user manual (the "Documentation") are the subject of copyright. The individual programs on the CD are copyrighted by the authors of each program. Some of the programs on the CD include separate licensing agreements. If you intend to use one of these programs, you must read and follow its accompanying license agreement. You may not copy the Documentation or the SOFTWARE, except that you may make a single copy of the SOFTWARE for backup or archival purposes only. You may be held legally responsible for any copying or copyright infringement which is caused or encouraged by your failure to abide by the terms of this restriction.

4. **USE RESTRICTIONS:** You may not network the SOFTWARE or otherwise use it on more than one computer or computer terminal at the same time. You may physically transfer the SOFTWARE from one computer to another provided that the SOFTWARE is used on only one computer at a time. You may not distribute copies of the SOFTWARE or Documentation to others. You may not reverse engineer, disassemble, decompile, modify, adapt, translate, or create derivative works based on the SOFTWARE or the Documentation without the prior written consent of the Company.

5. **TRANSFER RESTRICTIONS:** The enclosed SOFTWARE is licensed only to you and may not be transferred to any one else without the prior written consent of the Company. Any unauthorized transfer of the SOFTWARE shall result in the immediate termination of this Agreement.

6. **TERMINATION:** This license is effective until terminated. This license will terminate automatically without notice from the Company and become null and void if you fail to comply with any provisions or limitations of this license. Upon termination, you shall destroy the Documentation and all copies of the SOFTWARE. All provisions of this Agreement as to warranties, limitation of liability, remedies or damages, and our ownership rights shall survive termination.

7. **MISCELLANEOUS:** This Agreement shall be construed in accordance with the laws of the United States of America and the State of New York and shall benefit the Company, its affiliates, and assignees.

8. **LIMITED WARRANTY AND DISCLAIMER OF WARRANTY:** The Company warrants that the SOFTWARE, when properly used in accordance with the Documentation, will operate in substantial conformity with the description of the SOFTWARE set forth in the Documentation. The